"In this updated and expanded edition of her excellent telecommunications primer, Lili explains in just the right detail everything you need to know to become fluent in this most important and fascinating industry. Besides including a satisfying amount of expert technical detail, the book also discusses equally crucial aspects of how communications technology affects society, culture, and politics. Electronic communications is changing the world for the better; learn from Lili's expertise how you, too, can participate in the revolution."

—STEVE RILEY, SENIOR SECURITY STRATEGIST, MICROSOFT CORPORATION

"The book you hold in your hand is a rarity. In more than thirty years of teaching, administration, and research in telecommunications, I have never found a single book that could serve these diverse areas. The search is over. *Telecommunications Essentials* is best-of-breed in telecommunications publishing and represents the most thorough, comprehensive, and forward-looking resource to date. Both student and practitioner alike will find the unique blend of introductory and advanced material a 'one-stop-shop.' If it was a movie, this book would receive two thumbs up!"

—DR. ART ST. GEORGE, MANAGER OF ADVANCED TECHNOLOGIES, UNIVERSITY OF NEW MEXICO

"*Telecommunications Essentials* should be on the shelf of every professional working in voice and data networking. It is the first place I go when I need to look up something that I am unsure of or when I encounter a new or unfamiliar term. I have been using *Telecommunications Essentials* now for two years as the course text for business technology students taking Introduction to Telecommunications. My course covers the entire book and the students end up with a practical knowledge base of the components, technologies, and connectivity that make today's networks work. This new edition is most welcome since it includes new advances in the areas of fiber optics, wireless, Voice over IP, and broadband technologies that have emerged since the publication of the first edition. This new edition will replace my well-worn copy of my first edition of *Telecommunications Essentials*, which has served me well so far."

—ROBERT HUDYMA, PROFESSOR OF BUSINESS, RYERSON UNIVERSITY

"This is an excellent reference book on telecommunications. It's up-to-date on the latest technology, it's comprehensive, and most of all, it's easy to read and understand. Lili has the rare ability to explain very complex subjects well. If you need a good reference book on telecommunications, I would start with this."

—TO CHEE ENG, RESEARCH DIRECTOR, COMMUNICATIONS, GARTNER

"Lillian makes telecoms fun."

—NI QUIAQUE LAI, CFO, HONG KONG BROADBAND NETWORK LTD.

"Goleniewski's *Telecommunications Essentials* sets the stage by discussing forward-looking applications that are made possible by advances in telecommunications technology, including embedded devices, intelligent wearables, intelligent robot squads, and many others. This initial discussion is quite motivating for students and makes them eager to learn about various networking technologies, which are covered quite well in the rest of the book. The first edition (published in 2003) was already a great book for teaching telecommunications essentials, and it is clear that the second edition brings us up to the present and is a remarkable treatment of the topic."

—DR. LUNDY LEWIS, CHAIR OF THE DEPARTMENT OF INFORMATION TECHNOLOGY, SOUTHERN NEW HAMPSHIRE UNIVERSITY

"The book covers not just the fundamentals of telecommunications, but it easily guides the readers through the wide variety of technical details of next-generation network services, converged network architectures, and technologies. Lillian's elegant and clear style of presentation makes the book an excellent reference for system developers as well as telecommunications system designers to understand the current and emerging technologies that support business applications."

—DR. TIBRO GYIRES, PROFESSOR, ILLINOIS STATE UNIVERSITY,
SCHOOL OF INFORMATION TECHNOLOGY

"When Lili published her first edition of *Telecommunications Essentials*, I was a consultant in the communications field. Her guide was the only one I used to keep current. Now I'm in different field altogether but I need to understand this highly extensive field. *Telecommunications Essentials* is comprehensive, user-friendly, insightful, and fun. It's the only resource to have if you want to know telecom."

—DAVE FELDMAN, CONSUL, TRADE AND INVESTMENT, BRITISH EMBASSY

"After four decades of working in the computer and telecommunications fields, and more than twenty years of teaching graduate-level courses in telecommunications and network management at four universities, I finally have a book that meets the needs of students who are working to gain an in-depth and comprehensive grasp of an ever-changing field. Lili Goleniewski wrote that book. Her second edition is an outstanding contribution to the field and will be the best teaching aid I have ever had. If you teach you should use this book. If you want to really learn about telecommunications and data networks you should insist that your school adopt the book as a text."

—MICHAEL ERBSCHLOE, CONSULTANT, AUTHOR, AND EDUCATOR

"Telecommunications is not just about the legacy telephone network or the evolving wireless networks or the rapidly expanding Internet. It is about all of these and much more. It requires years of expertise in this fascinating field, combined with skillful writing ability, to develop a book that presents in an interesting and insightful manner the multifaceted disciplines of telecommunications. Lillian Goleniewski has accomplished this immense task with great skill in her book *Telecommunications Essentials*. Beginning students and professionals alike will benefit from this book. It can serve as an excellent reference book for telecommunications executives and business professionals who need to understand the basics of telecommunications and the workings of next-generation networks. Congratulations to the author on a task well done!"

—DR. SESHADRI MOHAN, CHAIR AND PROFESSOR, SYSTEMS ENGINEERING DEPARTMENT,
UNIVERSITY OF ARKANSAS AT LITTLE ROCK

"*Telecommunications Essentials* is a brilliant book for a broad and in-depth picture of the nitty-gritty aspects of telecommunications. Lili has a way of explaining complicated topics very well. It is a must-have book for any person who works in the IT world."

—LINO ALBERTS, DEPARTMENT MANAGER TECHNOLOGY OPERATIONS, RBTT BANK ARUBA N.V.

"A truly amazing book. A 'must-have' for anyone who wants to know the basics of telecommunication, how it works, and where the industry is heading. This book is excellent for all audiences—from novice to expert. Lili has successfully broken down the complexity of telecommunication so it can be easily understood."

—MOHD RADZI B. MOHD YUSOFF, SENIOR MANAGER,
MSC TECHNOLOGY CENTRE, SDN BHD, MALAYSIA

"*Telecommication Essentials* describes the most technical elements of the subject in layperson's terms, while remaining engaging for those with greater understanding. In providing the link between the most complex of telecommunications technology and its most simple applications, both now and in the future, *Telecommunication Essentials* is the most readable book on the subject both for newcomers and for 'old hands.' Lili exudes enthusiasm throughout, providing a vision for the future that draws the reader in."

—NEIL JUGGINS, HEAD OF RESEARCH, EVOLUTION SECURITIES CHINA

"One of the great challenges facing those responsible for setting public policy or regulation associated with the converging technologies of telecommunications, IT, and media is that before the 'ink is dry' on their pronouncements, advancements in the underlying science and technology has often made the 'new' policy, laws, and regulation out-of-date or irrelevant. While Lili does not claim to predict the future in her second edition of *Telecommunications Essentials*, she takes what is to many 'Rocket Science' and delivers it up in ways that those responsible for protecting the 'public good' and maintaining more competitive communications marketplaces can easily understand. Lili is one of the few telecommunications educators out there, catering to a diverse reader base, who has been keeping up with Moore's Law and what it really means in the real world of telecommunications. She continues to maintain her technological neutrality, never attempting to 'sell' a particular flavor-of-the-year with regard to who is the 'best' at delivering 'what' to 'whom,' nor falling into a mumbo-jumbo mantra of which national regulatory authority has invented the best-of-the-best new legal regime, something sorely needed by those needing a bias free technology primer."

—THOM RAMSEY, PARTNER, SQUIRE, SANDERS & DEMPSEY (BRUSSELS & WASHINGTON, D.C) AND FORMER DEPUTY UNITED STATES COORDINATOR FOR INTERNATIONAL COMMUNICATIONS AND INFORMATION POLICY, U.S. DEPARTMENT OF STATE

"As a journalist who writes about the Defense Department's most complicated space programs, I need to have a very clear and current handle on the technology and the operational aspects of the equipment and platforms. I am always on the prowl for materials that provide me that kind of background, concisely and accurately. The best single source for such an understanding was *Telecommunications Essentials*. That was, until author Lillian Goleniewski put together *Telecommunications Essentials, Second Edition*. Since the publication of the first *Telecommunications Essentials*, technology has grown enormously and an understanding of those changes is an absolute must for a reporter who writes stories about the U.S. Air Force's latest satellite success or folly. In her second edition, Lillian Goleniewski does just that. And, in the same manner of the first, she explains the technology without talking down to or over the head of less-than-savvy readers. Yet, even those knowledgeable in these technology areas will find plenty of gold to mine in the text. With updates on technology and operations, the book is not only a must-have, but will remain a sought-after reference and companion for those who need to understand the industry for years to come."

—MIKE FABEY, AIR AND SPACE WARFARE REPORTER, DEFENSE NEWS

Telecommunications Essentials

Second Edition

Telecommunications Essentials

The Complete Global Source

Second Edition

Lillian Goleniewski
Edited by Kitty Wilson Jarrett

✦✦Addison-Wesley

Upper Saddle River, NJ • Boston • Indianapolis • San Francisco
New York • Toronto • Montreal • London • Munich • Paris • Madrid
Capetown • Sydney • Tokyo • Singapore • Mexico City

The publisher offers excellent discounts on this book when ordered in quantity for bulk purchases or special sales, which may include electronic versions and/or custom covers and content particular to your business, training goals, marketing focus, and branding interests. For more information, please contact:

U.S. Corporate and Government Sales
(800) 382-3419
corpsales@pearsontechgroup.com

For sales outside the United States please contact:

International Sales
international@pearsoned.com

Visit us on the Web: www.awprofessional.com

This Book Is Safari Enabled

The Safari® Enabled icon on the cover of your favorite technology book means the book is available through Safari Bookshelf. When you buy this book, you get free access to the online edition for 45 days.

Safari Bookshelf is an electronic reference library that lets you easily search thousands of technical books, find code samples, download chapters, and access technical information whenever and wherever you need it.

To gain 45-day Safari Enabled access to this book:

• Go to http://www.awprofessional.com/safarienabled
• Complete the brief registration form
• Enter the coupon code 58BT-V14B-3A2G-XBBW-Z24T

If you have difficulty registering on Safari Bookshelf or accessing the online edition, please e-mail customer-service@safaribooksonline.com.

Library of Congress Cataloging-in-Publication Data

Goleniewski, Lillian.
    Telecommunications essentials : the complete global source / Lillian
Goleniewski ; edited by Kitty Wilson Jarrett. — 2nd ed.
        p. cm.
    Includes index.
    ISBN 0-321-42761-0 (pbk. : alk. paper)
    1. Telecommunication.   I. Jarrett, Kitty Wilson.   II. Title.

    TK5101.G598   2006
    621.382—dc22   2006022505

ISBN 0-321-42761-0
Text printed in the United States on recycled paper at Courier in Stoughton, Massachusetts.
First printing, October 2006

This book is dedicated to those eager to master the arts and sciences of telecommunications and to those seeking to gain a deeper understanding and appreciation of the vital role of information and communications technologies. I welcome you to the study of one of the most critical infrastructures of the twenty-first century and applaud your undertaking. I know you will find the universe of ICT to be as vast and full of potential as I do, and I hope this stimulates you to continue learning all you can about the wonderful world of telecommunications!

Contents

About the Author

Lillian Goleniewski is founder and president of the **LIDO Organization, Inc.**, an internationally acclaimed provider of education, information, and advisory services in the area of telecommunications technologies, services, and networks.

Ms. Goleniewski lectures extensively on telecommunications technology and management topics throughout the world. She is the author and creator of **LIDO Telecommunications Essentials** (www.telecomessentials.com). Ms. Goleniewski's seminars and e-learning series have been conducted on an international basis since 1984 and are offered throughout Asia, Australia/New Zealand, Africa, Europe, the Middle East, North America, and South America. Ms. Goleniewski is also the author of *Telecommunications Essentials: The Complete Global Source for Communications Fundamentals, Data Networking and the Internet, and Next-Generation Networks* (Addison-Wesley, 2002).

Ms. Goleniewski continues to be active in designing, developing, and participating in major industry conferences, having served as Industry Advisory Board Member for numerous conferences since 1991, including COMDEX, ComNet, E.J. Krause's EXPO COMM, and IIR conferences worldwide.

Ms. Goleniewski's diverse industry participation has included serving as a judge for the Global Information Infrastructure Awards (GII Awards), as well as being a founding member for the Standard for Internet Commerce. Ms. Goleniewski has served as a member of the Michigan Information Network (MIN) technical committee and a reviewer for the CommerceNet/State of California Next Generation Internet grant program. She has also served as an instructor for the San Francisco State University College of Extended Learning. She is a member of the Technology Empowerment Network (TEN), the IEEE, and the IEEE Computer Society. She is currently serving as a judge for the Baltic Challenge Awards program.

Prior to forming the LIDO Organization, Ms. Goleniewski held the position of telecommunications operations manager at the Electric Power Research Institute (EPRI), the research and development arm of the U.S. utility industry. Before joining EPRI, Ms. Goleniewski was vice-president of operations of a San Francisco–based telecommunications consulting firm.

Ms. Goleniewski graduated Phi Beta Kappa and summa cum laude from Wayne State University in Detroit, Michigan. She holds a B.A. in psychology and has completed numerous postgraduate studies in information technologies as well as psychology. Ms. Goleniewski was the recipient of an NSF Award to conduct research in the area of human perception and information processing.

Ms. Goleniewski is fluent in Polish and has conversational skills in both Russian and French.

About LIDO

As founder and president of the LIDO Organization (www.telecomessentials.com), I have been involved in providing educational and advisory services to developers, suppliers, regulators, investors, consultants, and users of telecommunications technologies and networks since 1984. I want to share my knowledge of telecommunications with people in the format that best fits their learning styles. Some learn best in a classroom situation, where they can make eye contact with the instructor, view graphics while the instructor is explaining concepts, and ask questions in person. LIDO has been providing seminars for these learners for 23 years. Some people prefer to learn at their own pace, and they like the convenience and ability to track down further information that online learning affords. For these people, LIDO has provided e-learning programs (via software license) since 1999. Today the LIDO Telecommunications Essentials e-learning series includes over 30 hours of rich multimedia content. Yet other people learn best from books—when they can carry their learning tool with them anywhere and read and reread as time and circumstances allow. Therefore, I decided to write this book, to provide a comprehensive source on telecommunications essentials.

Because telecommunications technologies continue to develop at an impressive pace, this second edition provides extensive coverage of the most recent developments in next-generation networks, IP networks and services, optical networking, and broadband access. And because wireless communications has experienced such dramatic growth, this book now includes four chapters devoted entirely to wireless principles, technologies, and applications. With these latest updates, I think you will find that *Telecommunications Essentials* is truly a complete global reference to communications fundamentals, data networking and the Internet, next-generation networks, and wireless communications.

A 1775 quote from Samuel Johnson summarizes LIDO's approach to knowledge solutions in telecommunications: "Knowledge is of two kinds: We know a subject or we know where we can find information upon it." LIDO presents this book to help you learn, and it offers the Telecom Essentials Learning Center (www. telecomessentials.com/learningcenter) to help you keep learning. The Telecom Essentials Learning Center offers a number of helpful resources to reinforce your telecommunications knowledge:

- **Online quizzes**—The online quizzes allow you to test your knowledge after reading each chapter. The quizzes are designed to reinforce what you have learned and assess those areas where you might wish to review the chapter.

- **Online telecommunications glossary**—The telecommunications vocabulary seems to grow daily. You can use the online glossary to search thousands of terms to find definitions quickly.

- **Links to thousands of related Web sites**—Each chapter is supported with links to recommended books, recommended magazines, and a comprehensive list of key sites to visit. This portal includes thousands of links to important destinations in the world of telecom.

The Telecom Essentials Learning Center will help you to keep learning long after you have mastered the essentials of telecommunications.

As a LIDO student, you can also enjoy full access to Telecom WebCentral (www.telecomwebcentral.com). At Telecom WebCentral, you will have at your fingertips up-to-the-moment information on the latest applications and financial and legal news, as well as connections to telecom career groups and newsgroups.

Whether in seminar, book, or e-learning format, LIDO explains telecommunications technologies very clearly and in an entertaining and interesting fashion to a very diverse professional and academic audience. LIDO seminars are offered worldwide, and the perspectives you gain by reading this book, attending LIDO seminars, or participating in e-learning programs are not U.S.-centric. They provide knowledge and understanding of telecommunications environments on a global basis.

Acknowledgments

There are many gratifying moments in the writing and publishing of a book, but one of my favorites is the opportunity to acknowledge the colleagues and friends whose contributions have helped to inspire and create the final masterpiece.

I'm sure you have heard the expression that "it takes a village to raise a child." Well, believe me, it takes a village to publish a book as well, and I had the ultimate delight of the cooperation of a most talented, focused, hard-working, yet easygoing village! To start, the first acknowledgment must go to the woman who recognized the need for and value of publishing the second edition of *Telecommunications Essentials*: my acquisitions editor at Addison-Wesley, Catherine Nolan. Thank you, Catherine, for your recognition of the fact that our readers worldwide were ready and waiting for an update to the expanding realm of telecommunications technologies, infrastructures, and applications.

The next hugely important recognition goes to Kitty Wilson Jarrett, my superb editor, who knows her craft better than any other editor I've ever worked with. Our close working relationship on both editions has resulted in work of high integrity and has also led us to a great friendship, one that will bring rewards beyond those we gain from having created a book that will serve many a mind yearning to learn all about the wonders of telecommunications—and that means you benefit from a collaboration intent on providing the highest quality possible!

Of course, the contributions of my reviewers are all important, and I consider myself very fortunate to have had their attention and commentary; after all, they had over 800 pages of new content to review! With their busy schedules, I am astounded at the level of commitment they made to reviewing the new edition and their attention to detail. I very much took to heart their different perspectives, which added great value to this book. It is with great pleasure that I individually thank them:

- Steve Riley, senior security strategist in Microsoft's Security Technology Unit, was also a reviewer for the first edition. Along with being a super-smart technology guru, particularly in all things to do with the Internet, IP, and security, he has the distinct talent of providing me with a heap of witty and humorous comments throughout his reviews—and that is priceless!

- Dr. Art St. George, manager of Advanced Technologies and professor at the University of New Mexico, is a most impressive technologist. He has far-reaching experience, from academia to research to administration, and leadership roles in the most pertinent of standards organizations and forums. As a tenured professor, he ensures that the materials are appropriate for all audiences, from undergrad to graduate, from technical to business, from academic to practitioner. How wonderful to have one person represent so many interests!

- Robert Hudyma, professor at Ryerson University in Toronto, not only provided substantial feedback to ensure technical clarity but also provided the insight needed to ensure that the book will be highly successful in building a new generation of telecom thinkers. He went the extra mile to help develop appropriate testing, lab, and homework supplements for the book.

- Dr. Chigurupati S. Rani, assistant professor, Department of Computer Information Systems at the Borough of Manhattan Community College, shares with me not just the practice of telecom education but also a particular view of the spirit. Rani spends a lot of time ensuring that her students are provided with the knowledge they will need to succeed, including creating additional testing and lab exercises to supplement the quizzes in the book. She provides me with additional insight into what is needed to conduct a successful telecom program.

- Brent D. Stewart, course director at Global Knowledge, is a fellow instructor who provided me with yet another way to look at the phrasing of technical details.

These esteemed colleagues brought their own unique knowledge, background, talents, and even some humor (thank God!) to their reviews. Readers will benefit from this book's thorough review by some of the best minds in the industry, professionals charged with developing and delivering telecommunications education in all contexts—academic, professional, government, financial, consulting, education, entertainment, and health care. I couldn't have hoped for a better set of reviewers!

In addition, my sincere and heartfelt thanks go to all those behind the scenes at Addison-Wesley. From the editors and production staff to the marketing team and artists: You've all been an absolute pleasure to work with again on this second edition of *Telecommunications Essentials*! In particular, I'd like to thank Chrysta Meadowbrooke, our copyeditor; both Kitty and I are extremely impressed with her thoroughness and commitment, and she definitely made a difference in ensuring that there were no loose ends! I would also like to thank Alan Clements, the designer for the book cover. He made sure my vision came to life, and as a result, we have a cover that is exciting visually and conveys all the key concepts the book represents. Thanks to Julie Nahil, Kim Arney, and all the rest of the talented people who worked on this project.

Aside from those intimately involved with the production of this second edition, there are my faithful colleagues and friends whose support and informal contributions were also of tremendous value to me. You all know who you are, and you know I thank you from the bottom of my heart for your continued support and inspiration. It is my grand fortune to have so many treasured friends and colleagues that I am not able to name you all without making a chapter out of it!

Finally, I'd like to thank my patient and loving mother, who understands the massive amount of work required to write such a book, supports my efforts by taking care of my homes and 11 birds, listens to my occasional grumblings, offers commentary and feedback, when asked, and praises and motivates when and as needed. I love you, Mom, and thank you for always being there!

Introduction: Understanding the Broadband Evolution

I love telecommunications. It is powerful and it empowers, with far-reaching consequences. It has demonstrated the potential to transform society and business, and the revolution has only just begun. With the invention of the telephone, human communications and commerce were forever changed: Time and distance began to melt away as barriers to doing business, keeping in touch with loved ones, and immediately responding to major world events. Through the use of computers and telecommunications networks, humans have been able to extend their powers of thinking, influence, and productivity, just as those in the Industrial Age were able to extend the power of their muscles, or physical self, through the use of heavy machinery. Today, new inventions and developments are again poising telecommunications as a force to be reckoned with, changing human communications and commerce, and introducing machines as members of the networked society. This is an exciting era, and we face a host of new telecommunications technologies and applications that bring breathtaking new opportunities, particularly in the industries of entertainment, education, health care, government, advertising, lifestyle, and, sadly, warfare.

Although the information and communications technologies (ICT) industry has suffered greatly in recent years, exciting developments continue unabated in many areas that are key to the ongoing evolution of broadband devices, applications, and network infrastructures. These remarkable developments are propelling the broadband evolution, creating good reasons to pursue next-generation networks.

■ Measurements of the Digital World

There are three main measurements of the digital world:

- ■ Processing power, measured in the number of transistors and operations per second
- ■ Storage, measured in the number of bytes
- ■ Bandwidth, or digital data transmission, measured in bits per second

The following sections discuss these three measures.

Processing Power

Moore's Law says that the number of gates on a chip—hence the power of the microprocessor—doubles every 18 months. Intel's original microprocessor, introduced in 1971, had 2,300 transistors. Top-of-the-line computers in 2001 contained some 42 million transistors that performed 100 billion operations per second. Today, Intel's high-end chip contains more than 1.7 billion transistors, and that number is expected to exceed 10 billion by 2010.

Unfortunately, there's also an awful truth about Moore's Law. Today's transistors are about a micrometer in overall length, which means dozens of them could sit on top of a human red blood cell. This very success is bringing chipmakers to the brink of a new, steep obstacle to further gains in performance. The problem lies in the tiny metal wires that weave the transistors into integrated circuits. For the sake of illustration, consider that the Intel 130-nm Pentium IV processor chip contains 55 million transistors and uses roughly 3 *miles* (4.8 km) of interconnects to support each square *centimeter* of its circuitry. With the introduction of 90-nm microprocessors, the chips house 110 million transistors and nearly 4.25 miles (6.9 km) of interconnects per square centimeter. Today's most advanced integrated circuits switch up to 10 billion times per second, and their metal interconnects can barely keep up.

Each new generation of chips makes the situation worse. While interconnect delay times are stretching out, transistor switching is getting faster, sending more signals down slow lines. Additional trouble areas include heat buildup, electrical currents leaking out of circuits, and electrical crosstalk between neighboring wires. Copper, the traditional interconnect technology, is running out of speed. The good news is that the industry is working on several solutions. Two main approaches are emerging: one designed to change the propagation characteristics of those tiny on-chip transmission lines and the other involving the development of silicon photonics.

Researchers are developing thin films that have a lower dielectric constant (k) than the silicon dioxide insulating layer used most commonly until now. This approach lowers the line's capacitance by changing the material that insulates it from the surrounding silicon chip, as well as from its neighboring wire. The bad news is that the low-k films are extremely difficult to integrate into the manufacturing. They are soft and weak, they adhere poorly to both the silicon and the metal wire, and they crack and delaminate easily. The next generation of chips will require even lower-k films that are even more challenging to process.

The more significant development comes from Intel's recent reports of the successful demonstration of the first continuous all-silicon laser. Silicon photonics have the potential to greatly extend the lifetime of Moore's Law. Optical connections can carry thousands of times more data per second than copper wires can. Unfortunately, existing optical components are far too expensive for use in individual computers or even local networks. If we could make optical devices out of silicon, which is cheap and easy to manufacture, that would change everything. Eventually, silicon photonics might also replace copper wires between processors within a single chip and be used in the internal clocks that microprocessors use to execute instructions, dramatically increasing clock speeds and thus computing speeds.

On the positive side, however, thanks to Moore's Law, network endpoints today are small, powerful, inexpensive devices. With such power in the endpoints, the need to embed the functions of a network in the network's core shrinks. In addition, smart end devices can set up and manage calls far better than a centralized network can. In fact, implementing voice in end devices makes it possible to mix it into other kinds of interactions as well, such as online game play, collaboration, and shared Web surfing.

The latest processors also support fast visualization of large data sets and intensive math for real-time simulations, such as digital entertainment, three-dimensional games, graphics, astronomy, biosciences, and predictive modeling. Examples of applications include simulation of blood flow in the human body, space weather modeling, virtual tests for therapeutic cancer drugs, global modeling of the earth's magnetosphere, simulations of shock waves and eddies in turbulent fluids, large-scale structures of galaxies and galaxy clusters, modeling of the interaction of proteins within individual cells, and testing models of the formation of cosmological structures. A number of these applications apply specifically to the science and engineering communities, but there will be applications designed for education and entertainment products as well.

Storage

Fast processors that support today's visualization and multimedia applications are just one piece of the puzzle. The second element is storage. Currently, storage density doubles every 12 months. Emerging solutions promise incredible improvements in storage density and size.

Before we get into some of the developments in storage, let's quickly review some examples of storage requirements:

- 1.5KB (i.e., about 12,000 bits) can basically store one double-spaced type-written page.
- 1MB can store one long novel as text, one full-page black-and-white image, a 3-by-5-inch color picture, 2 minutes of telephone-quality sound, 7 seconds of CD-quality sound, or 0.04 seconds of broadcast-quality video.
- 4GB can store an average feature-length film.

New storage devices will enable up to 1TB (terabyte) of storage; such a storage device would be able to contain 250 full-length films!

The storage media available today are a huge improvement over the storage media of the past, but they're nothing compared to what we'll see in the future. Today, CD-ROMs offer a capacity of some 650MB, and DVDs offer a range of 4.6GB to 17GB, supporting a transfer rate of 600Kbps to 1.3Mbps. Some exciting new storage devices are being developed, including bacterial protein memory, holographic storage systems, and magnetic sensors.

Bacterial Protein Memory

Bacteriorhodopson (BR) was one of the first building blocks of life on our planet—a protein grown by salt marsh bacteria at least 2.3 billion years ago—and it is likely to become the wave of the future in computer data storage and manipulation. BR is a tiny, rugged protein that, through billions of years of evolution, has become extremely efficient at converting light into energy. As a biological substance, the protein also enables data to be stored in three dimensions, just as it is in the human brain.

A BR memory stick, called a *cuvette*, is a transparent vehicle that is about 1 cm × 1 cm × 3 cm. Each BR stick has the capacity to store the entire Library of Congress, which is about 10TB of information. For the average consumer, BR memory would reduce the cost and increase the portability of offline data storage. Scientists estimate that a 10GB cuvette would cost about US$10. For maybe US$100, you could have all the storage you might ever need. And you could stick the cuvette in your pocket, take it home, and pop it into your computer. Scientists are also anticipating the protein's use in satellite imaging, where high above the earth, its natural imperviousness to gamma ray emission would safeguard the data it holds from sun storms and other high-energy radiation.

Holographic Storage Systems

To achieve a full-scale optical computing environment with great computing power, it's necessary to have memories with rapid access time and large storage capacity. A volume holographic storage device, also referred to as a *holostore*, is a page-oriented device that writes and reads data in an optical form. The holography technology achieves the necessary high storage densities as well as fast access times. Holography records the information from a three-dimensional object in such a way that a three-dimensional image can subsequently be constructed. Holographic data storage enables discs the same size as today's DVDs to store more than 1TB of data. Because such a system has no moving parts, and its pages are accessed in parallel, it is estimated that data throughput will reach 1Gbps or more.

Magnetic Sensors

Tiny magnetic sensors could help break a technical barrier to ushering in the next generation of computer disc storage capacity. The sensors, microscopic whiskers of nickel only a few atoms wide (thinner than a wavelength of visible light), are capable of detecting extremely weak magnetic fields. Normal magnetic sensors can read a signal that begins with a strength of 1 and swings between an off reading of 0.8 and an on reading of 1.2. The new sensors can read a range that swings between −1000 and +1000. That degree of sensitivity means terabits (i.e., trillions of bits) of data could be stored in a square inch of disc space.

Bandwidth

Along with processing power and storage, the third of the three key measurements of the digital world is bandwidth. The term *bandwidth* comes from the visualization of the electromagnetic spectrum, where the spectrum is divided into bands. Each band and the channel within it has a width, expressed in Hertz (Hz), or cycles per second. The wider the band, the more information it can carry. The information transfer rate is expressed in the number of bits per second. Table I.1 lists the units commonly used in describing the data rates of various bandwidths.

Particularly over the past decade, networks have begun carrying greater and greater data rates. Gbps networks are now common, Pbps networks are beginning to emerge, and Ebps networks are expected to make an appearance within about five years.

What relevance do bandwidth and transfer rate have to you? Well, wider can be faster, which means shorter download times. Consider these examples:

Type and Size of File	Download Time 56Kbps (Narrowband)	768Kbps (Broadband [e.g., DSL])
Photo from ski trip (1MB)	4 minutes	25 seconds
MP3 of favorite song (1.5MB)	6 minutes	40 seconds
Gaming demo (2.5MB)	10 minutes	60 seconds
PowerPoint presentation for sales meeting (6MB)	25 minutes	2 minutes

Table I.1 Common Bandwidth Units

Unit	Prefix Meaning	Transfer Rate
Kilobits per second (Kbps)	Kilo = 1 thousand	1,000bps
Megabits per second (Mbps)	Mega = 1 million	1,000,000bps
Gigabits per second (Gbps)	Giga = 1 billion	1,000,000,000bps
Terabits per second (Tbps)	Tera = 1 trillion	1,000,000,000,000bps
Petabits per second (Pbps)	Peta = 1,000 trillion	1,000,000,000,000,000bps
Exabits per second (Ebps)	Exa = 1 billion billion	1,000,000,000,000,000,000bps

Shorter download times mean greater productivity. Much of the economic growth of the late 1990s has been attributed to productivity gains realized as a result of new communications and IT products: Workers with broadband are more productive than workers using dialup, and the greater the productivity of a country, the stronger the economy.

To get an idea of how bandwidth affects transfer time, think about downloading the entire Library of Congress, which is often used as the yardstick for the measure of all human knowledge. Table I.2 shows how long it would take to download the Library of Congress at various data rates.

Table I.2 Transfer Times for Downloading the Library of Congress

Data Rate	Transfer Time
2400bps	1,900.0 years
56Kbps	81.5 years
1.5Mbps	3.0 years
1.7Gbps	23.5 hours
10Gbps	2.35 hours
100Gbps	14.1 minutes
1Tbps	1.41 minutes
1Pbps	8.26 seconds
1Ebps	0.826 seconds

Table I.3 Backbone Bandwidth Requirements of Various Applications

Application	Backbone Bandwidth Required
Online virtual reality	1,000Tbps to 10,000Tbps
3D holography	30,000Tbps to 70,000Tbps
Grid computing	50,000Tbps to 200,000Tbps
Web agents	50,000Tbps to 200,000Tbps

You aren't likely to need to download the Library of Congress many times, if ever, in your lifetime, but you will need to transfer huge amounts of other sorts of data. We're entering an era of bandwidth-hungry applications, such as those listed in Table I.3, that will require Pbps networks and, ultimately, Ebps networks.

What technology is going to provide us with the bandwidth abundance needed to facilitate these emerging applications? Certainly one of the greatest contributions is coming out of the optical arena. Developments in microfluidic optical fibers and integrated optical chips will usher in a new era of bandwidth abundance. As the capacity of broadband access lines approaches 100Mbps and beyond, core network capacity will demand expansion. As we talk about next-generation network infrastructures in Part III, "The New Generation of Networks," we'll spend quite a bit of time on new optical core and optical edge technologies. For now, let's look at the equivalent of Moore's Law in the optical bandwidth realm: The number of bits per second being carried per lambda (or wavelength) is doubling every 12 months, and the number of lambdas per fiber is also doubling every 12 months, resulting in a 50% drop every 9 months in the cost of transmitting a bit of information. As with CPUs (cost per MIPS) and storage (cost per KB), the cost per Kbps of bandwidth is rapidly approaching $0.

Numerous developments made in the wireless arena are bringing us capacity that will be beneficial and instrumental to ensuring mobility. We'll explore the wireless trends in Part IV, "Wireless Communications."

■ Adapting to New Traffic Patterns

Sharing of information can occur in a number of ways—via smoke signals, by letters sent through the postal service, or as transmissions through electrical or optical media, for example. Before we get into the technical details of the technologies in the industry, it's important to understand the driving forces behind computing and communications. You need to understand the impact these forces have on network traffic and therefore on network infrastructure.

The telecommunications revolution has spawned great growth in the amount and types of traffic, and we'll see even more types of traffic as we begin to incorporate human senses as part of the network. The coming chapters talk in detail about what a network needs in order to handle the various traffic types.

Traffic Types

Given today's digital scenario, the traditional distinctions between traffic types are no longer relevant; in the end, everything is a series of ones and zeros. Nonetheless, there are still specific requirements in terms of bandwidth needed, latency considerations, and loss tolerance, and it therefore still makes sense to differentiate between the traffic types. In today's environment, telecommunications embodies four main traffic types, each of which has different requirements in terms of network capacity, tolerance for delays—and particularly variations in the delay—in the network, and tolerance for potential congestion and therefore losses in the network: voice, data, image, and video. The following sections describe these traffic types.

Voice Traffic

Voice traffic has been strong in the developed world for years, and more subscriber lines are being deployed all the time. However, some 3 billion people in the world have never used even a basic telephone, so there is yet a huge market to serve. Voice communications are typically referred to as being *narrowband*, meaning that they don't require a large amount of network capacity. But it is important to note that the days of voice as a distinct category are numbered. In the digital era, voice bits are no different from data or video bits: They are all ones and zeros being exchanged over a network. However, for voice services to be intelligible and easy to use, delays must be kept to a minimum, so the delay factors in moving information from Point A to Point B have to be tightly controlled in order to support real-time voice streams. Losses must also be controlled; while a few lost packets results in pops and clicks, a substantial loss renders a conversation unintelligible. (Concepts such as delay, latency, and error control are discussed in Chapter 5, "Data Communications Basics.")

Data Traffic

The term *data communications* refers to the exchange of digitized text or document information between two machines (see Chapter 5). Data encompasses many different information types. In the past, we saw these different types as separate entities (e.g., video and voice in a videoconference), but in the future, we must be careful not to separate things this way because, after all, in the digital age, all data is represented as ones and zeros. Perhaps it is best to think of traditional data as involving text and document exchange. Depending on the application supported, the bandwidth or capacity requirements can range from medium to high. As more objects that are visual in nature (such as images and video) are included with the data, that capacity demand increases. Different types of data applications have varying levels of tolerance for delay. Text-based exchanges are generally quite tolerant of delays. The more real-time nature there is to the information type, as in video, the tighter the control you need over the latencies.

Data traffic is growing much faster than voice traffic; it has grown at an average rate of about 30% to 40% per year for the past decade. To accommodate data communication, network services have been developed to address the need for greater capacity, cleaner transmission facilities, and smarter network management tools.

Image Traffic

Image communications require medium to high bandwidth: The greater the resolution required, the greater the bandwidth required. For example, many of the images taken in medical diagnostics require very high resolution. Image traffic tolerates some delay because it includes no motion artifacts that would be affected by any distortions in the network.

Video Traffic

Video communications, which are becoming increasingly popular and are requiring ever-greater bandwidth, are extremely sensitive to delay. The future is about visual communications. We need to figure out how to make video available over a network infrastructure that can support it and at a price that consumers are willing to pay. When our infrastructures are capable of supporting the capacities and the delay limitations required by real-time applications, video will grow by leaps and bounds.

An example of a valuable video application comes from the United Kingdom: If a subscriber to Vodaphone in the United Kingdom hears a song she likes at a dance club, she can hold up her phone in the air for a few seconds, and the phone will then receive an SMS providing the name of the song and artist, along with a "click-here" link to buy the CD, charge it to her phone bill, and ship it to her address on file. Not only is this a major convenience for the customer, it is also a substantial revenue generator for the service provider.

Increasing Backbone and Access Bandwidth

All the new voice, data, and video traffic means that backbone traffic levels are growing as well. Many of the changes discussed so far—primarily the changes in traffic patterns and applications—will require immense amounts of backbone bandwidth. In addition, advances in broadband access technologies will drive demand for additional capacity in network backbones. When 100Gbps broadband residential access becomes available (and there are developments on the horizon), the core networks will require capacities measured in exabits per second (i.e., 1 billion billion bps). These backbone bandwidth demands make the revolutionary forces of optical networking and wireless broadband critical to our future. (Optical networking is discussed in detail in Chapter 11, "Optical Networking.")

Handling New Types of Applications

The new traffic patterns imply that the next-generation network will be host to a new set of applications—not just to simple voice or text-based data but also to new genres of applications that combine the various media types.

The ability to handle digital entertainment applications in a network is crucial. In some parts of the world, such as Asia, education may have the primary focus, and that should tell us where we can expect greater success going forward. But throughout much of the world, entertainment is where people are willing to spend the limited amount of money they have for electronic goods and services. The digital entertainment realm increasingly includes video editing, digital content creation, digital imaging, three-dimensional gaming, and virtual reality applications, and all these will drive the evolution of the network. It's the chicken-and-the-egg story: What comes first, the network or the applications? Why would you want a fiber-optic broadband connection if there's nothing good to draw over that connection? Why would you want to create a three-dimensional virtual reality application when there's no way to distribute it? The bottom line is that the applications and the infrastructures have to evolve hand in hand to manifest the benefits and the money we associate with their future.

Another form of application that will be increasingly important is in the realm of streaming media. A great focus is put on the real-time delivery of information, as in entertainment, education, training, customer presentations, IPO trade shows, and telemedicine consultations. (Streaming media is discussed in detail in Chapter 9, "IP Services.")

E-commerce (electronic commerce) and m-commerce (mobile commerce) introduce several new requirements for content management, transaction platforms, and privacy and security tools, so they affect the types of information that have to be encoded into the basic data stream and how the network deals with knowledge of what's contained within those packets. (Security is discussed in detail in Chapter 9.)

ICT Trends Driving the Broadband Evolution

The age of intelligence and the new generation of networks have the potential to reshape the ICT industry and forever change the telecommunications landscape. A number of key ICT trends are driving the broadband evolution, including embedded devices, intelligent wearables, human–machine interactions, grid computing, and real-time communications.

Embedded Devices

The devices used to communicate with the Internet today—including PCs, organizers, telephones, and mobile devices—present two problems: They are at odds with human behavior, and they are often the bottlenecks impeding the process and progress of information exchange.

Recognizing the need to address this reality, research efforts worldwide are pursuing the vision of *ubiquitous computing*, also known as *ambient*, *calm*, or *pervasive computing*. This vision takes computers out of boxes and puts them into ordinary, everyday things. Embedded devices will be integrated into larger systems, where they will perform control functions and communicate with one another over the Internet. Billions of these microprocessors, many of them invisible, will be used for countless applications.

Embedded devices will affect ubiquitous computing in three main areas:

- **Smart tags, specifically radio frequency identification (RFID)**—RFID can be used for identification of objects and people at distances from a few centimeters to tens of kilometers, depending on the frequency, the size of the tags, and the reader being used. There's a growing list of RFID applications, including transportation, consumer product identifiers, drug and food ID and shelf life information, patient identification, smart houses, and a new era of textiles. (RFID is discussed in detail in Chapter 15, "WMANs, WLANs, and WPANs.")

- **Smart devices**—These include appliances, furniture, automobiles, industrial and medical equipment, clothing, accessories, and structures.

- **Smart offices**—Roomware in the workplace will ensure greater efficiency and better working conditions. Sensor technology will support the automatic configuration of specific environments or the provision of content. (Sensor-based networks are discussed in Chapter 15.)

The following sections describe some of the exciting new emerging embedded devices. These devices have the potential for both good and bad uses; it is up to all of us to make sure these emerging technologies improve our lives, not invade our privacy. In this brave new age of technology and embedded intelligence, we all bear a great responsibility in ensuring that these new tools are in fact used to promote cooperation, collaboration, and communication among people.

Embedded Devices for the Home

Some examples of embedded devices that exist today are a smart refrigerator with an LCD panel that allows you to browse e-mails or perhaps engage in a videoconference. If the fridge interacts with smart-tagged food containers, it can report on the status and shelf life of your food and place orders. (Of course, looking at it another way, this information could be transmitted to your insurance company to keep track of your behavior and consumption patterns.)

Another example is a smart washing machine capable of reading RFID tags embedded in clothing or in fabrics and making decisions about what sort of wash cycle to use, based on the construction and age of the fabric. (However, one could imagine that, in the name of ensuring revenues, the tumbler might run a bit faster, and the temperature be a bit hotter, causing an earlier demise of the fabric—certainly not the intent of responsible technologists, but a possibility in the hands of the wrong individual.)

A smart picture frame allows friends and family to send photos to you, providing a constant source of entertainment from those you love. A smart surfboard allows a surfer to do some instant messaging with fellow surfers while waiting for the perfect wave. And then there are smart coffeepots, no-burn toasters, smart tablecloths, smart nametags, smart screwdrivers that automatically adjust, and smart dustbins that can pull the dust off your floor without the need for a dustpan.

One of my favorite new embedded devices is a smart bed equipped with wireless sensors that measure pulse rate, breathing, and restlessness (based on the movements of a patient in bed); a patient need only lie down to check and transmit medical information. Such information can also be used to track caregiver activities or be sent to a central nursing station. The goal of this research is to improve patient care in nursing home environments and to automatically document the level of care being provided. This is just one of many projects and prototypes. You can easily see the commercial applications of this research: As you sleep throughout the night, the bed takes all sorts of measurements, including your temperature, your heart rate, and your respiratory rate. When you awaken, it gives you a readout of the findings. It might report that you were tossing and turning 10 times last night and recommend that you do some yoga stretches, providing a Web agent that helps you through some of those stretches.

What today is a dumb bathroom will become a smart one. When you brush your teeth, your toothbrush will take your blood pressure and look for cavities. When you look in the mirror, a little camera will look at your eyes to check your diabetes or hardening of the arteries or any of the thousands of other diseases that can be seen in a person's eyes. When you go to the toilet, it will check what's in there. If you forget to take your medication, the toilet will know and remind you. In the near future, the smart room will become a medical aid.

Mobile Embedded Devices

A number of mobile smart devices have been developed, such as the smart pillbox. If you forget to take your medication, the pillbox sends an SMS message to your mobile device or calls you, and if you don't open the pillbox to take the pill, the smart pillbox contacts your caregiver.

Another smart accessory—interactive nametags—is particularly useful at large conferences. You program into the nametag various information, such as your name, title, company address, and access numbers, as well as your particular likes and dislikes. As you and another person wearing such a nametag approach each other during the conference, you automatically get a sense of whether you have anything in common to talk about or whether you should simply move on. (Again, such products could result in negative social implications, serving to further divide people rather than providing social interaction among diverse groups.)

A new shirt mobile phone is a flexible display screen that ushers in a new type of expression: The image a person wears personalizes his or her clothes to reflect the wearer's surroundings, interests, moods, and so on. Users choose the type of information they want to highlight on themselves, including drawings, logos, animations, or short messages they either generate themselves or receive from others.

The transportation industry is another forum for embedded intelligence. Today's automobiles are increasingly equipped with a host of communications options, including video monitors, navigational systems, Internet connections, mobile telephony and Bluetooth communications built into steering wheels, and, of course, entertainment panels for passengers. No longer is your car simply a leisure vehicle. Now it's an office and an entertainment center.

One of the interesting things about the notion of smart cars and intelligent highways is that the choice of networking architecture has changed substantially. A few years ago, we were looking toward an intelligent highway system composed of bay stations along roadways that would communicate with the vehicles regarding traffic management information and routing. Given the progress we've made in wireless LANs, the infrastructure that's now associated with smart vehicles and roadways involves making each car essentially a node on a network; this is an intriguing application of 802.11x wireless LANs or one of the myriad emerging WMAN (wireless metropolitan area network) technologies. The vision is that as automobiles cruise through the city or the country, they will be able to relay information to one another regarding road conditions, accidents, or potential rerouting that needs to be observed for maximum efficiency in travel time. So every automobile becomes a network on its own as well as a subnetwork in a large virtual internetwork of automobiles; "autonet" will no doubt emerge as a key term in the transportation lexicon.

Intelligent Implants Using RFID

The ultimate in embedded intelligence is intelligence that is actually implanted in the person versus being embedded in a device. Today there are tens of thousands of people who can hear the song of a bird or the whisper of romance due to cochlear implants. We now have a number of other exciting developments. For example, there's a bio-implant that can be used for many purposes, from personal location (for people wanting to protect their children or be assured of where they are) to health care (where the individual's entire medical history is contained on the chip) to financial information (so that you no longer need credit cards or wallets—you simply run your arm by a scanner).

Subdermal personal verification technology is being used for security, medical, and emergency applications in many countries. In October 2004, the U.S. FDA approved an implantable microchip for use in humans, a tiny subcutaneous RFID tag. Now several U.S. companies are mass-producing RFID chips and stocking chip warehouses and implantation centers. Upper-level government officials are getting "chipped" to encourage public acceptance of the technology, and they are very quick to highlight the humanitarian uses of tracking devices in humans. Children and pets can be chipped in case they get lost. Chipping children can help locate kidnapped kids. (On the other hand, overwhelming evidence indicates that most child kidnappings are conducted by family members or people the parents trust, and chances are that the children would be too far away from the range of any RFID reader for this technology to be truly lifesaving. Therefore, it is not unrealistic to state that, in some cases, the business plans of companies offering such technologies are many times largely based on promoting fear. Still, as in the case of lost pets, there can be great value in embedded identification for recovery of loved ones.) Chipping senior citizens can give hospitals immediate access to their medical records. Many wealthy individuals are getting themselves and their children chipped for security reasons. Large herds of cattle and sheep are implanted with chips to assist ranchers and farmers with efficient tracking.

Yet another implant is an RFID biosensor that is being developed for diabetics. An incredible implant called a diabetes infusion pump is expected on the market within 2006. An even more dramatic breakthrough is being developed: an implantable pump with a biosensor that monitors blood glucose and continuously provides the right amount of insulin.

RFID and chipping are used for banks, gas stations, hospitals, drivers' license branches, schools, the military, automobiles, telephones and mobile phones, televisions, computer systems, prisons, governments, workplaces, corporations, bars, restaurants, and private clubs—in other words, they are everywhere.

Intelligent Wearables

The evolution of wearables is truly an exciting frontier. Steve Mann, a professor at the University of Toronto, is an advocate, and arguably the founder, of the field of wearable computing. Beginning with his early work in personal imaging, Mann has been involved intimately with the study of wearables for over two decades. From the early 1980s to the mid-1990s, his devices were functional but bulky and awkward. By the late 1990s, his intelligent wearables could pass for a pair of sunglasses and a mobile phone. (For more information on Mann's research, see www.eecg.toronto.edu/~mann.)

From molecular manufacturing to processes inspired by archeological digs, researchers are finding new ways to custom-fit clothing, create clean clothing, and dye clothing. Clothes may soon shield us from pollution, find our keys, read our e-mail aloud, and release pheromones to attract the perfect mate. Or they may help safeguard our privacy, preventing access to all the RFID chips implanted in our bodies and stuffed into our personal electronic devices.

Business professionals, general consumers, and youths worldwide are carrying an increasing number of portable electronic ICT gadgets: mobile phones, PDAs, digital cameras, MP3 players, gaming platforms, and so forth. E-textiles are emerging as a more versatile and elegant alternative. Shirts, sweaters, shoes, carpeting, or even wallpaper may have devices embedded in them.

A smart shirt has been developed to detect bullet wounds in combat. Standard textile techniques are used to weave conductive polymer and metallic fibers into the fabric. The fibers serve as data buses and power lines between the microcontrollers, actuators, and sensors embedded in the cloth. Manufacturers can mix and match sensors, processors, and communications devices that plug into knitted or woven garments made from cotton, polyester, and blends. Dime-size sensors plug into tiny connectors, 5 mm in diameter, called t-connectors, that look like snaps. The sensors are placed over appropriate spots, such as the heart or diaphragm. Depending on the application, the garment could have dozens or hundreds of connectors. A flexible data bus integrated into the fabric writes data from the sensors to the smart shirt controller, which uses a proprietary chipset in a plastic package the size of a pager. Powered by a watch battery, the controller presses into the fabric like a fastener to contact the conductive fibers. It processes the signals from the sensors to compute vital signs and wirelessly transmits the data directly to a PDA or PC, using Bluetooth or IEEE 802.11 standards. Smart garments have the look and feel of traditional clothes, and after you unplug the attachments, you can simply toss them into the washing machine.

The following are some examples of the usefulness of smart garments:

- An army commander could monitor a platoon of soldiers dressed in smart shirt gear. The smart shirts could communicate vital signs in real-time, allowing the commander to see the entire battlefield at a glance and determine who has been hit and who is critically injured and requires immediate attention. On the other hand, it's not difficult to imagine why and how an enemy might want to intercept and alter the communications between the garments and the field commander. Again, we need to view these developments from all angles and ensure that we understand all the possible ramifications so that proper measures can be taken to prevent the "evil" scenarios.

- A fire chief could monitor firefighters as they enter a burning building and order them out when the sensors they're wearing transmit data back to the command center indicating that the firefighters are inhaling hazardous fumes or too much smoke, or that the fire is too hot to handle.

- Those interested in fashion applications will be glad to meet the firefly dress and its associated jewelry. This dress and necklace will actually change luminance and colors, responding to changes in the wearer's physiology as he or she changes moods, so those approaching know whether to proceed with glee or look for another firefly. (Of course, such garments also mean that you don't have to be a professional psychological profiler to determine someone's state of mind.) Or a skirt may change colors and patterns in response to the presence of pollution, rising temperatures, or precipitation.

- Athletes will benefit greatly from smart garments. A cyclist, for instance, could be attired in a smart racing suit, dotted with moisture, temperature, and pulse sensors. Such a suit would have warned his team manager that Lance Armstrong was becoming dehydrated while warming up during the first individual time trial of the 2003 Tour de France, when Armstrong lost 6.5 kilos. With the data available from a smart racing suit, the manager would have ordered Armstrong to drink replacement fluids before he launched from the starting line.

- Another example of performance- and safety-enhancing clothing involves outerwear for snowmobilers. The ensemble includes a machine-washable jacket, vest, trousers, and two-piece underwear. The jacket is embedded with a GSM chip; sensors that monitor position, motion, and temperature; an electric conductivity sensor; and two accelerometers to sense impact. If a crash occurs, the jacket automatically detects it and sends a distress message to emergency medical officials via SMS. The message includes the rider's coordinates, local environmental conditions, and data taken from a heart monitor embedded in the undershirt.

Progress in nanotechnology is also now finding its way into the fashion world. The discovery of carbon nanotubes, along with recent progress in manipulating their conductive properties, has enticed a number of companies into a development race for a new generation of wearable intelligence. Whatever technology is available will be applied to making fabrics considerably more sophisticated, to the point where you won't be able to define whether someone is wearing a textile or a machine.

Future plans for clothing are vast and wide, including flexible electronic computer displays that will result in outfits that change images, projections, and patterns. Temperature-sensitive fibers could be woven into mood fabrics. The military is financing research into the ultimate camouflage: chameleon fabrics with colors and patterns that would change in response to electrical commands. Smart clothes will likely be powered by photovoltaic fibers, converting light or heat into various functions.

If you have seen or read about Harry Potter, do you remember his invisible cloak? I bet there are times you wish you had one, maybe just to attend that special board meeting. Well, you may be able to acquire one in the near future. Researchers in Japan have recently unveiled their first generation of optical camouflage. Tiny cameras positioned on the back of a garment allow the image behind the wearer to be projected onto the front of the garment, and as a result, the wearer appears transparent.

Bacteria may also affect tomorrow's clothing; some fabrics may be engineered to eat odor-causing chemicals in human sweat or to secrete protective coatings. Eventually, we may see pollution-resistant, self-cleaning, color-shifting unitards created by molecule-sized machines that can build fabrics and garments from the bottom up, molecule by molecule.

Are you wondering what all this has to do with next-generation networks? It has to do with changing traffic patterns. Researchers project that by 2010, 95% of the traffic on networks will come from machine-to-machine communications (i.e., with no human involvement). Embedded devices and intelligent wearables will require access to communications networks in order to be of value and must therefore be considered as vital users in the development of next-generation networks.

Human–Machine Interactions

The realm of human–machine interactions covers a wide range of activities, including affective computing, brain–computer interfaces, software agents, augmented reality, virtual reality, teleimmersion, and the growing presence of robots. Today's computers generally respond only to keyboard inputs and mouse movements. Users have to learn special operating procedures to control their machines rather than rely on their natural communication abilities.

ICT development is increasingly focusing on the creation of powerful human–machine interfaces. These emerging physical interfaces can be used for control purposes, including not just voice but also gestures, touch, and mime. It is even possible that the flows of electrical waves through the human brain will be used. Humans have five direct input channels—sight, hearing, smell, feel, and taste—and two output communications channels—speech and limb movement. Machines, on the other hand, can have a large number of input and output channels, but today they are limited by the range of human capabilities. The future promises to allow the use of indirect human communications channels, including thoughts, emotions, brain waves, and gaze tracking.

Affective Computing

Affective computing, in essence, involves building emotions into computers. It gives computers the capability of recording human responses and identifying behavior patterns. Wearable computers are sensors embedded in clothing that register biological and physiological parameters and communicate them, if appropriate. Such biometrics opens the door to security applications based on the unique properties of the physical attributes of a human, including voice, fingerprints, hand geometry, the shape of the face, or the structure of the iris.

One goal of affective computing is to build computer systems that can sense users' emotional states. Imagine a computer that can detect that you are frustrated and pause to help you overcome your problem. One approach to achieving this goal would be through affective wearable computing—wearing small but powerful computers in your clothing that use noninvasive biosensors to sense biophysiological changes that reflect changes in emotional state.

An affective jewelry project is an attempt to create low-cost biosensors that are comfortable and aesthetically acceptable and that fit into the existing kinds of clothing that people wear. Skin conductivity sensors have been integrated into rings and shoes, and an earring has even been made out of a blood volume pressure sensor. A pair of galvanic skin response shoes may not be the height of fashion yet, but they could help you monitor your heart rate or reduce your blood pressure.

Another possibility in the realm of affective computing is expression glasses, helpful to anyone addressing an audience. People in the audience would don a pair of these expression glasses, which could monitor the individual's physical state. The speaker would have, at the podium, a display showing whether the audience members are feeling confused, whether they are bored, whether they are understanding the presentation, or whether they are interested and excited. A speaker could adjust his or her presentation in real-time to meet the needs of the audience.

Brain–Computer Interfaces

Another exciting new frontier is in the area of brain–computer interfaces, which allow computers to be controlled by the power of thought. A user wears a hood that contains more than 100 electrodes that measure the flow of electrical waves through the brain. The EEG signals are amplified, and noise pulses are filtered out. The signals are then transmitted to a computer, which converts them online into control commands, with the assistance of specially developed learning and signal-processing algorithms. Such devices are currently undergoing trials.

Much of this research started in the health care arena, with people injured or paralyzed through stroke or spinal cord damage from accidents. There is, in fact, a microelectrode array that can be implanted into the motion cortex of the brain to allow a paralyzed person to think a cursor into motion. This device was designed to allow those who have lost their mobility to interact with computers.

Such developments or inventions are quickly captured for commercial use. A company is preparing to release the first brain-controlled videogame. As a game player, you wear special headgear and, through the power of thought, move the character in the game. If you want the character to go to the left, you simply think about it, and he does.

Software Agents

Software agents will perform routine tasks and act proactively. These advanced agents will be configured with a profile made of the user's wishes. They will be automatically activated and able to make decisions independently. These agents will support users by performing routine tasks or submitting proposals when a decision needs to be made. They will also attend to any changes and respond to external events. Various digital assistants operate in a personalized agent system:

- **Intelligent agents**—Intelligent agents can draw their own conclusions and make decisions independently.

- **User agents**—User agents can execute orders, conduct negotiations, and communicate independently with other agents, acting as a substitute for the user.

- **Cooperative agents**—Cooperative agents perform a liaison function, analyzing and interpreting the user's tasks and then deciding which functional agent would be appropriate.

- **Functional agents**—Functional agents contain the specific knowledge required to carry out a particular function.

The Semantic Web

A new, more intelligent Internet is a key requirement for communications between the various software agents. This new network will not only transport the signals, it will also understand their meanings. The semantic network, or the Semantic Web, is a current project of Tim Berners-Lee. The objectives of the Semantic Web include refined indexing and searching, as well as enhanced processing of structured information, where, for example, you can search by business documents versus scientific data, or where you can recognize the difference between an author and an entertainer. Also, the Semantic Web will be critical in the command and control of scientific instruments and the labeling of data. This is very important to data collection and archiving of all the data coming from the exploding population of sensors.

The Semantic Web is a fascinating area of development, and I encourage you to learn more about it. The best starting point is the W3C Technology and Society domain website focusing on Semantic Web activity, at www.w3.org/2001/sw.

Software agents must be capable of interworking as well as delegating subfunctions. As an example of the use of software agents, an electronic travel support service is being developed. The project mission is to optimize travel by interlinking transportation media and travel information. Using an Internet PC, mobile phone, or other mobile device, travelers establish contact with personal travel assistant (PTA) servers. The agent can perform various services, such as obtaining information about air and rail connections, booking hotels and restaurants, and providing a continuous supply of traffic information. For instance, if the user does not have a driver's license, the PTA will automatically offer a rail trip in place of a rental car. For drivers, it can provide the latest traffic information from control centers or identify special parking systems.

Software agents are due to become a key link to our interactions over the Internet. In one of my favorite books, *The Age of Spiritual Machines: When Computers Exceed Human Intelligence*, author Ray Kurzweil forecasts that by 2009, most routine business transactions will take place between a human and a virtual personality or Web agent. Web agents are destined to be one of the main consumers of bandwidth in next-generation networks.

Augmented Reality

Augmented reality is a form of human–machine interaction that involves superimposing computer data on real images. With this approach, hidden information about all types of objects can be made visible. This can be accomplished through several techniques, such as using holographic projections or data eyeglasses. Augmented reality has applications in numerous areas, including architecture, building engineering, maintenance operations, surgical procedures, and warfare.

Several product lines of data eyeglasses exist for physicians, construction workers, and design engineers. In each of these cases, virtual information is overlaid on the real documents, patients, or blueprints that the professional is working with. This is such a popular tool that it has entered the consumer realm. One company is making heads-up displays for athletes. A scuba mask, a motorcycle helmet, and a biker's helmet have all been designed to provide critical information that assists athletes in their performance. In the case of the diver, the glasses may show the water temperature or the depth of the dive. The biker's helmet might show the biker's speed or heart rate.

One of the early innovators in augmented reality is the military. For example, battle gear being imagined for 2025 includes a helmet that allows the soldier to get a full 360° view and thermal sensors that allow him or her to detect whether any people or armaments are hidden behind doors, walls, or other structures.

Virtual Reality

Virtual reality is the most intensive form of human–machine interaction, involving a total immersion into a computer-generated three-dimensional environment. Virtual reality allows holographic projections to be processed in the same manner as real objects. It increases productivity by substantially decreasing the time span between a basic idea and the finished product.

For design purposes, developers can use virtual reality to work with a three-dimensional object in a virtual domain. They can view the object from any angle and modify and test it at will. Project members can be geographically dispersed if needed, greatly simplifying collaboration between design teams. Virtual reality opens the door to a new generation of services, with applications ranging from surgical procedures to building simulations to virtual product development to the training of athletes.

Haptic interfaces, or sensual technologies, are adding further value to virtual reality:

- With the use of a special data glove when testing an automobile, the user can sense the drag being experienced on mud versus traveling on a dry surface.
- An emerging product allows a distributed team to mold objects in three dimensions and share that information with one another over a network, inducing changes in the remote lump of smart clay.
- In the health care arena, a haptic interface enables a physician's assistant or a nurse to conduct a diagnostic examination remotely and transmit that information to an expert physician at a distant location.

Teleimmersion

Virtual reality involves teleimmersion, which is the combination of real and virtual environments for purposes of display or interaction. The main applications of teleimmersion include telemeetings, teletraining, collaborative engineering and design, medical applications, and entertainment services.

With teleimmersion, a sea of hidden cameras provides many points of view that are compared to create a three-dimensional model of users and their surroundings. The cameras can be hidden behind tiny perforations in a screen or placed on the ceiling, in which case the display screen must also serve as a selectively reflective surface. Teleimmersion also involves shared simulation objects. These objects appear in the space between users and can be manipulated as if they were working models. Teleimmersion is being used to find better techniques to combine models developed by people on different ends of a dialogue, using incompatible local software design tools.

Another factor in teleimmersion is imperceptible structured light. To the naked eye, it looks like standard white illumination, but it projects unnoticeably brief flickerings of patterns that help computers make sense of otherwise featureless visual expanses. Current prototypes of the necessary screen use two overlapping projections of polarized images and require users to wear polarized glasses so that each image is seen by only one eye. This technique will be replaced in the future by autostereoscopic displays that channel images to each eye differently, without the need for glasses.

Finally, there are plans for interface design features, such as a virtual mirror, which would allow users to check how they and their environment appear to others. As an example, a user may choose to appear in more formal clothing than he or she is wearing in reality. Software to achieve this transformation does not yet exist, but early examples of related visual filtering have already appeared.

One exciting teleimmersion project is designed specifically for surgical training. Say a physician is engaged in a surgical procedure, and the entire process is videotaped. That video is then encoded into an e-book, where additional data is overlaid. By donning the appropriate data gloves and eyeglasses, another physician or student can then participate in that surgery virtually, performing it at his or her own pace and getting cues from the e-book when he or she is about to take a dangerous turn with the instruments. This will add incredible value to the medical education process. With a surgical e-book, a student gets all the feedback necessary to experience with a living patient.

To really see the possibilities of teleimmersion, I recommend that you take a moment to view a short video that demonstrates the use of teleimmersion in military training today: Go to Atlantis Cyberspace, at www.atlantiscyberspace.com, and select to view the Immersive Group Simulation (IGS) demonstration video.

Intelligent Robot Squads
Another part of human–machine interactions involves a whole new genre of being: robots. Intelligent robot squads—self-organizing groups of robots, under the control of neural networks—will eliminate the need for humans to perform hazardous tasks. The performance of an overall robot squad is enhanced by the interaction of

numerous individual thought processes, much like the behavior observed in flocks of birds or armies of ants. At the moment, it is a distant prospect, but it is coming.

Today, a large variety of both single- and multipurpose robots perform a number of functions:

- A six-wheeled, one-armed robotic vehicle is capable of explosives handling and defusing, nuclear surveillance and maintenance, hazmat response, SWAT operations, and airport security.
- Robot farmers can plow fields while taking measurements of soil composition.
- Hospital courier robots deliver mail as well as medical records throughout hospitals.
- Factory robots do a wide variety of tasks, from assembly to welding to moving parts.
- NASA has designed Robonauts to take space walks and fix space platforms and satellites when they go awry.

A fascinating new development is the micromechanical flying insect. Say a country is at war in an unfamiliar territory, and a battle is about to begin. The enemy doesn't know that its every move is being monitored by dime-sized flying robotic insects equipped with tiny cameras. It is likely that the first use of these robotic bugs will be as spy flies; they'll be used for reconnaissance missions, controlled by soldiers on the ground to relay images of troop movements and to detect biological, chemical, and nuclear weapons. The robotic insects would also be able to land on an enemy vehicle and place an electronic tag on it. These tiny flying robots would also be valuable in the aftermath of disasters. Their small size and ability to fly and hover would make them useful for searching for people buried in rubble. They could fly between crevices that humans and larger machines cannot navigate. Other uses include traffic monitoring and border surveillance. These "spy flies" are yet another example of how technology can help us perform dangerous tasks, allowing humans to stay out of harm's way.

Evil Uses of Technology

At this point, you may be wondering about the possibility of the malicious use of all these technologies. I like the way one of my colleagues, Steve Riley of Microsoft, has commented on this observation: "Some readers may very well envision how malicious people might abuse many of these wonderful technologies, subverting their purposes into mechanisms of possibly great harm, and say that, therefore, such technology shouldn't be developed." It is worth noting this possibility, but as Steve also comments, "Technology is neutral; innovation knows no political allegiance. It's the decisions that humans make to put the service of technology to good or evil." From my point of view, the fact that you are taking the initiative to learn about telecom technologies means you are aware of the potential uses, and you must exercise your voice in ensuring that these technologies are put to proper and humanitarian use.

Robots are also entering the consumer realm, helping individuals with everyday living:

- Roomba, the vacuum-cleaning robot, is now the number-one item requested on bridal registries.
- Robo Mower allows you to relax on Sunday rather than having to mow the lawn.
- A dinosaur-looking device is a security robot that functions as a fire alarm as well as an intruder detection device that can emit noxious aromas to detract the intruder from entering.
- A companion robot monitors the user's physiological status throughout the day and also gives the user companionship.

My favorite currently available robot is Valerie, the domestic android, who costs US$59,000 and comes with a one-year warranty (www.androidworld.com). You can configure her to meet your particular aesthetic preferences—order her as an African, an Asian, or a Caucasian; choose her hair and eye color; and so on. Valerie can mimic all human muscle movements. She can understand spoken commands in several languages. She can speak to you in English or several other languages. She can remember conversations she's had with you. She can remember a daily list of household chores and perform a wide array of them, including cleaning, clearing the table, changing light bulbs, doing laundry, dusting, lifting and carrying things up to 50 pounds, putting things away, painting, setting the table, sweeping, washing dishes, and vacuuming. She can access the Internet to do such things as check stock prices or sports scores, find information for you, book plane tickets, and find addresses, phone numbers, or directions. She can call the police in an emergency or the fire department in case of a fire. She can dress and undress herself, and she has a sense of touch all over, just like people do. But Valerie can't do everything a person can do. She can't eat or drink, breathe, perform other bodily functions, hurt people, have sex, put her head under water, or take any water or other liquids into her head or mouth. She can't drive a car or run a lawn mower because she's not allowed to go outside. She can't do physical actions that people can't do, and she doesn't sleep.

Grid Computing

Grid computing is the key to the future of e-business, and it represents the next step in the development of the Internet as a real-time computing platform. Today, some 80% to 90% of processing capacity—whether PC workstation or mainframe—is unused. Grid computing aims to remedy this situation.

The vision of grid computing is to bundle computing resources into a network and, similarly to electricity, allow processing power to flow from the socket wherever and whenever it is needed. Grid computing is emerging as the next-generation concept of the World Wide Web, something that's being called the World Wide Grid. Rather than simply engaging in information interchange, the future Internet will enable access to high-performance computers anytime and everywhere in the world. Grid-computing technology will be of particular use in performing resource-intensive tasks and solving complex calculations. As you can well imagine, security will be a critical issue with grid computing.

Grid computing has three main applications areas:

- **On-demand computing grids**—On-demand computing grids connect the computing resources owned by different groups and execute processing-intensive applications much faster. A growing range of industries require the intensive processing power of grid computing, including the research and scientific communities, automobile manufacturing, electronic design companies, life sciences, energy, and financial services.

- **Data storage grids**—For commercial and industrial use, computers must be able to automatically and transparently locate computers with the required programs and data. The use of idle storage resources is the major advantage of a data grid, and the focus is on the intelligent distribution and broadband interconnection of data pools.

- **Collaboration grids**—Research and knowledge workers will increasingly depend on collaborating with different distributed work groups, each with different competencies. Collaboration grids will contribute to better cooperation by connecting the systems of various owners. Such collaboration grids will simplify access to an exchange of data between these partners, accelerating processes and providing capacity on demand. This will lead to a reduction in development time and cost.

Europe's CERN (www.cern.ch) is undertaking an exciting project involving grid computing. CERN is planning to start testing the Large Hadron Collider (the world's largest particle accelerator) in 2007, and it is building a data grid to accomplish that. This experiment involves 40TBps, equivalent to the data generated if each person on the planet were speaking simultaneously into 20 phones. Even with a reduction of data via compression and such, it will still generate 8PB of data per year. In addition to CERN, 8 to 10 other large research centers, some 100 university research centers, and more than 1,000 other research institutions around the world plan to provide storage capacity.

In the 1990s, the popular vision was that the network was the *computer*. In this decade, the network is *computing*.

Real-Time Communications

Industry analysts believe that within the next decade, the majority of business processes will be transacted in real-time, or at least near real-time. Real-time communications will generate added value by reengineering and differentiating business processes. Real-time communications will substantially increase the speed, efficiency, and security of business processes. The core element of real-time communications is the convergence of voice and data, based on Internet Protocol (IP). This technology allows enterprises to achieve a unified communications environment.

The first IP communication generation is focused on using existing network infrastructure for converged applications in order to cut costs. The second IP communication generation will primarily focus on reengineering and differentiating business processes. By integrating real-time communications into IT, enterprises will enable their business processes, creating the possibility of real-time business. New productivity gains are expected from two key applications:

- **Process-supporting communications**—Process-supporting communications involves all semi-automated activities in which human operators have to intervene at certain points and communicate with users. They are largely based on integrated IT and telecom processes.
- **Ad hoc communications**—In these activities, several persons interchange information spontaneously with one another. This is based on suitable infrastructure and technology.

An international telecom carrier recently implemented real-time communications to manage invoice complaints. It reduced the time for processing complaints by 30% and achieved cost reductions of 25% as a result of improved transparency in processes and access to personnel resources. The proportion of transactions settled satisfactorily on the first attempt rose to 80%, and overall service quality improved by 5%. Productivity gains of these magnitudes translate into substantial top-line revenue enhancements by accelerating sales cycles; they translate into bottom-line cost reductions through new efficiencies. At the same time, gains in responsiveness can help raise brand awareness and loyalty and reduce customer churn while extending market reach.

■ The New Generation of Networks

Given the revolutionary changes in telecommunications, it is clear that we are moving toward a new public network. The new public network needs to have end-to-end digitalization. We began implementing digital technology in the early 1960s, and we have done quite well at deploying it throughout the various backbone networks. Worldwide, probably some 80% of backbones are now digitalized. However, the local loop—that is, the last mile between the subscriber and the network—is still largely analog. Only around 10% of the subscriber lines today are digital, so the vast majority of users are functionally limited to analog usage.

We face an incredible modernization task to digitalize the local loop and to truly make the network digital from end to end. However, the even greater challenge rests in the "last mile" economics and politics. The regulatory and political issues are critical as well as burdensome. Without broadband access, the Internet can't grow, advanced applications can't take off, revenues can't be realized, and we can't progress. The local loop is largely under the control of the incumbent telephone companies worldwide, and they do not seem to have the political and economic incentive to make end-to-end digitalization happen. There's lots of discussion on how to resolve this, particularly at the government level—by regulation, by enforcement, or by market forces. When we find some resolution, the telecommunications industry will blossom like never before. (See Chapter 1, "Telecommunications Technology Fundamentals," and Chapter 12, "Broadband Access Alternatives.")

Another factor that affects the new public network is that we are now in the last years of the electronic era and in the first years of a new generation of optical networking. Conversions between electrical and optical signals reduce the data rates and introduce the potential for distortion; hence, they affect the data stream. To eliminate these conversions, we need to work toward achieving an end-to-end optical networking scenario. (See Chapter 11.)

The new public network must also be an intelligent programmable network. That is, we want to distribute service logic via databases on a networkwide basis so that anywhere in the world, you can access any service or feature you want, regardless of the network provider or network platform that you are connected to. This intelligent programmable network requires some form of communication between the network elements. In the public switched telephone network (PSTN), this communication occurs through the use of high-speed common-channel signaling systems that allow real-time communications between the network elements. In essence, it's like a private subnetwork. No voice, data, or image traffic is carried on these channels—only the signaling information that dictates who is calling, what rights they have, what features and services they want to use, and so on. Because there are many manufacturers and providers of network platforms, it is important that the programmable platforms use open application programming interfaces. In today's converged network infrastructures, the IP Multimedia Subsystem (IMS) creates a telephony-oriented signaling network that overlays an underlying IP network, replacing traditional telco SS7 signaling and acting as a control plane for both wireless and wireline networks. (See Chapter 4, "The PSTN," and Chapter 10, "Next-Generation Networks.")

The new public network requires a new broadband infrastructure that has very high capacities and offers multichannel service (i.e., one physical medium can carry multiple conversations). The two dominant media types in the broadband arena are high-speed fiber (run as close as possible to the customer) and broadband wireless (over the last few meters to the customer, if needed). (See Chapters 11 and 15.)

It is important that the new public network be a low-latency network. Humans cannot suffer much delay—only on the order of 650 milliseconds—in receiving information before it becomes unintelligible. To give you some perspective on this, on a satellite call, the delay between the time you say "Hi" to the time you hear the response is annoying, but it lasts only 500 milliseconds. Current infrastructures, such as the Internet, may impart as much as 1,000 or 2,000 milliseconds of delay. They therefore play havoc with any type of traffic that is delay sensitive, such as voice, video, and multimedia. So when we say we want to build low-latency networks for the future, we mean networks that impose no delays that result from congestion points. (See Chapter 10.)

Another characteristic of the new public network is that, in contrast to today's world, where we have separate platforms for each of the traffic types, the platforms need to be multiservice—they have to accommodate voice, data, and video streams, as well as any streams invented in the future. (See Chapter 10.)

The new public network should also be agnostic. That is, it should not follow only one protocol, but it should understand that the universe truly is multiprotocol. The best way to create an agnostic network is to have a box that enables interfaces for the most prevalent of the data protocols. However, the reality is that while such a box may be highly desirable, it is an expensive proposition to create such a utopian device. Given the popularity and pervasiveness of IP, it is difficult to make a business case for addressing a smaller population of older protocols. (See Chapter 10.)

The new public network also needs to include a new generation of telephony services, one that makes use of packet-switching technologies to derive transmission efficiencies, while also allowing voice to be bundled with more standard data applications, to provide for more robust environments. (See Chapter 9.)

Quality of service (QoS) guarantees are an absolute prerequisite for the new public network. The network must be able to distinguish between the various traffic types so that it can apply the appropriate network resources and ensure that the latency requirements are being met, that the loss requirements are being met, and that the bandwidth required is being allocated. (See Chapter 10.)

Finally, encryption and security services are necessary in telecommunications devices and networks. Once upon a time, this was a separate function within the company, but now it is an essential element of telecom service. (See Chapter 9.)

■ What This Book Covers

The rapid progress in embedded devices, intelligent wearables, virtual reality, robotics, grid computing, and real-time communications is ushering in a new era of applications—applications that require enormous bandwidth, low latencies, minimal loss, guaranteed performance, wireless broadband, and converged infrastructures.

This book provides a thorough foundation for understanding a wide range of telecommunications principles and technologies. It provides a concentrated, high-level overview of the terminology and issues that comprise telecommunications, and it discusses the major telecommunications infrastructures, including the PSTN, the Internet, cable TV, and wireless. It also examines the latest perspectives and developments governing next-generation networks, including next-generation architectures, infrastructures, IP telephony, VPNs, broadband access alternatives, and broadband wireless applications. Even though the ICT industry has gone through some hard times lately, logic dictates that we can only look forward to greater emphasis on the use of ICT.

The book is divided into four parts:

- Part I, "Communications Fundamentals," discusses the basics, the arts and sciences of telecommunications. It begins by explaining the factors contributing to the telecommunications revolution and talks about some of the exciting new technologies on the horizon. Part I gives you a good grounding in the basics of telecommunications technology and terminology, covering communications fundamentals and including the characteristics and uses of the various transmission media. Part I also discusses the processes involved in establishing communications channels, examines the differences between circuit-switched and packet-switched networks, and explores the nature of the traditional PSTN.

- Part II, "Data Networking and the Internet," introduces the basics of data communications and networking. It discusses today's local area and wide area networking alternatives, as well as how the public Internet is structured. It also explores next-generation network services, such as VPNs, VoIP, and IPTV.

- Part III, "The New Generation of Networks," explores the realm of broadband networking, next-generation network architectures, optical networking, broadband access alternatives, and home area networking.

■ Part IV, "Wireless Communications," discusses the world of wireless networking—including wireless WANs, MANs, LANs, and PANs—and it also
explores emerging technologies, including the near and distant future of
communications and its convergence with related IT industries.

The book also includes a very comprehensive glossary of ICT-related terms.

Prevailing Conditions

In almost every aspect of life, it's important to put and keep things in context. A good
idea in one situation might be a terrible idea in another situation. This is often the case
with telecommunications; there is no one-size-fits-all, be-all and end-all telecommunications solution. In assessing telecommunications needs, it is important to think about the
prevailing conditions so that you can choose the best transmission media, the best network architecture, and so on for the situation. It's also important to remember that prevailing conditions change. So what's right for you today may change six months down
the road. As you plan a telecommunications strategy, it is important to look as far into the
future as you can, to make your network as adaptable to future innovations as possible.

If you are new to the communications and information industry, or if you simply want an understandable yet comprehensive overview of telecommunications,
this book is for you. *Telecommunications Essentials* will equip you with a blueprint
on which you can build. The telecommunications landscape is vast; for a new-
comer, it is treacherous terrain to navigate. This book provides a logical progression in gluing together all the pieces of the telecommunications puzzle. It helps
you master the basic building blocks of key technologies, from the principles of
telecommunications transmission and networking to the current and evolving
nature of the Internet, broadband architecture, and optical networking, addressing
both wired and wireless alternatives.

Part I

Communications Fundamentals

Chapter 1

Telecommunications Technology Fundamentals

This chapter talks about the types of transmission lines and network connections, the electromagnetic spectrum, and what bandwidth is all about in the emerging broadband era. It looks at the differences between analog and digital signals, and it discusses multiplexing. Finally, this chapter describes the various standards bodies and their roles in shaping aspects of telecommunications.

▪ Transmission Lines

Two prerequisites must be satisfied to have successful communication. The first prerequisite is understandability. The transmitter and receiver must speak the same language. It doesn't matter how big or how clean the pipe between the two endpoints. If they're not speaking the same language, they will not be able to understand the message. In the case of data communications, we've resolved these issues quite elegantly: We have software and hardware translation devices that can convert between the different languages that individual computing systems speak. In the realm of human communications, we're about to embark on that exciting journey as well. Through the use of advanced voice-processing systems, in the next five to seven years we should have the ability to do real-time foreign language translation as part of the network service. And of course, some search engines, such as Google, already provide Web page translation—and do a pretty good job at it.

The second prerequisite is the capability to detect errors as they occur and to have some procedure for resolving those errors. In the case of human communications, intelligent terminals at either end—human beings—can detect noise that may have affected a transmission and request a retransmission, thereby correcting for that error. In the case of data devices, similar logic must be built in to end devices so that they can detect errors and request a retransmission in order to correct for the errors.

If these two prerequisites—understandability and error control—are met, then communication can occur. We communicate by using data devices over what is generically termed a *transmission line*. There are five main types of transmission lines—circuits, channels, lines, trunks, and virtual circuits—each of which has a specific meaning. (Keep in mind that these transmission lines can be composed of either wired or wireless media, and in fact, these days, we're seeing more and more use of wireless facilities to accomplish networking, from simple mobile phones to the Interplanetary Internet.) The following sections describe each of these types of transmission lines in detail.

Circuits

A *circuit* is the physical path that runs between two or more points. It terminates on a *port* (i.e., a point of electrical or optical interface), and that port can be in a host computer, on a multiplexer, on a switch, or in another device, as discussed later in this chapter.

In and of itself, a circuit does not define the number of simultaneous conversations that can be carried; that is a function of the type of circuit it is. For example, a simple, traditional telephone circuit is designed to carry just one conversation over one physical pathway. (But note that I specifically reference "traditional telephone circuit"; digital broadband facilities, such as DSL, permit multiple channels, such as separate voice and data channels, over the one physical pathway.) However, converting to a digital circuit makes it possible to extract or derive multiple channels over that circuit, subsequently facilitating multiple simultaneous conversations. The circuit is therefore the measure of the connectivity between two endpoints.

There are two types of circuits: two-wire circuits and four-wire circuits.

Two-Wire Circuits

A two-wire circuit has two insulated electrical conductors: One wire is used for transmission of the information, and the other wire acts as the return path to complete the electrical circuit. Two-wire circuits are generally deployed in the analog local loop, which is the last mile between the subscriber and the subscriber's first point of access into the network. Figure 1.1 shows an example of a two-wire circuit.

Figure 1.1 A two-wire circuit

Two-Wire and Four-Wire Versus Two-Pair and Four-Pair

Don't confuse the terms *two-wire circuit* and *four-wire circuit* with the terms *two-pair* and *four-pair*. *Two-pair* and *four-pair* refer to the number of wires in the internal cabling plan. *Two-wire* and *four-wire* have to do with the number of electrical conductors associated with a transmission line.

Four-Wire Circuits

A four-wire circuit has two pairs of conductors. That is, it has two sets of one-way transmission paths: one path for each direction and a complementary path to complete the electrical circuit (see Figure 1.2). Four-wire circuits are used where the distance between the termination points requires that the signal be strengthened (amplified) periodically. So, for example, four-wire circuits connect the various switches that make up the public switched telephone network (PSTN). Four-wire circuits are also used with leased lines, where a customer may be connecting locations of its own that are separated by distance. Also, all digital circuits are provisioned on a four-wire basis.

There are two types of four-wire circuits: physical four-wire and logical four-wire. In physical four-wire, you can actually count four wires. In logical four-wire, physically there are only two wires, but you derive the four individual paths by splitting the frequency. Half of the frequency band carries the transmit signal, and the other half carries the receive signal. So you can't always tell just by looking what kind of circuit you're dealing with; the application dictates the type of circuit it is.

Figure 1.2 A four-wire circuit

Using Two-Wire and Four-Wire Circuits

When you release energy into space, it loses power as it travels. Because networks were designed to carry communications over a distance, they need tools to regenerate *attenuated signals*—that is, signals that lose power as they travel across the network. These tools are called *amplifiers* and *repeaters*. An amplifier boosts an attenuated signal back up to its original power level so it can continue to make its way across the network. The PSTN traditionally used copper wires. Based on how quickly the signals attenuate over the copper wires, there's a certain distance limitation between amplifiers. The distance limitation between amplifiers is relatively short on copper wires—generally about 6,000 feet (1,800 m). As networks were built, these distance considerations were kept in mind. (Repeaters are discussed later in this chapter, in the section "Digital Transmission.")

Network builders had to give some thought to another aspect of amplifiers: First-generation amplifiers were unidirectional. They could only amplify a signal moving in one direction, so to provision a circuit that was going to be crossing a distance, it was necessary to literally provision two circuits—one to amplify the information in the transmit direction and a second to amplify the information in the receive direction. Therefore, whenever a network was crossing a distance, it needed to use a four-wire circuit. But in building the millions of local loops for subscribers, it was seen as being cost-effective to pull only two wires into every home rather than four. Therefore, the local loops were intentionally engineered to be very short; some 70% to 80% of the local loops worldwide are less than 2 miles (3.2 km) long. Because the local loops are short, they don't need amplifiers, and therefore the subscriber access service can be provisioned over a two-wire circuit. However, the local loop is increasingly being digitalized, so as we migrate to an end-to-end digital environment, everything becomes four-wire. Figure 1.3 shows an example of a segment of a network in which two- and four-wire circuits are traditionally used.

Channels

A *channel* defines a logical conversation path. It is the frequency band, time slot, or wavelength (also referred to as *lambda*, λ) allocated to a single conversation. In the context of telecommunications, a channel is a child of the digital age because digital facilities enable multiple channels, greatly increasing the carrying capacity of an individual circuit. Because we are becoming more digitalized all the time, people often refer to the number of channels rather than the number of circuits.

Lines and Trunks

Lines and trunks are basically the same thing, but they're used in different situations. A *line* is a connection configured to support a normal calling load generated

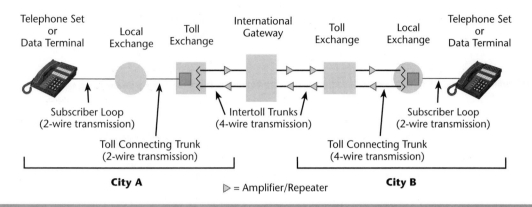

Figure 1.3 Using two-wire and four-wire circuits

by one individual. A *trunk* is a circuit configured to support the calling loads generated by a group of users; it is the transmission facility that ties together switching systems. A *switching system* is a device that connects two transmission lines. There are two major categories of switching systems:

- **CPE switches**—The most prevalent form of switch in the customer premises equipment (CPE) environment is the private branch exchange (PBX), which is called a private automatic branch exchange (PABX) in some parts of the world. A PBX is used to establish a connection between two points. It establishes connections between telephones that are internal to the organization, and it establishes connections between internal extensions and the outside world (i.e., the PSTN).

- **Network switches**—A hierarchy of network switches has evolved over time, and the appropriate switch is called into action, depending on which two points the switches connect. For example, in Figure 1.4 the CPE is on the left-hand side. Each individual single-line instrument represents a subscriber line. (Again, the fact that it's called a *line* means that it's a circuit configured to carry the calling load of just one user.) Above the single-line instrument is a business enterprise with a PBX. The connection from this PBX to the PSTN occurs over a trunk specifically configured to carry the calling load of multiple users. Beyond the PBX are multiple end users that are attached to that PBX. Each end user's connection is referred to as a *station line*, again emphasizing that the line is carrying the calling load of one user.

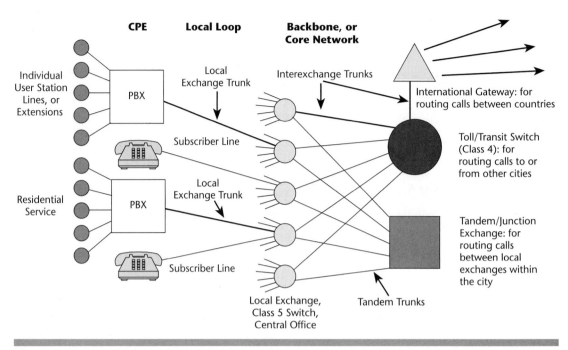

Figure 1.4 Lines, trunks, and switches

The customer environment attaches to the PSTN, and the first point of access is the *local exchange*, which is also referred to as a *Class 5 office* or a *central office*. The traditional (electromechanical and crossbar) local exchange switch can handle one or more exchanges, with each exchange capable of handling up to 10,000 subscriber lines, numbered 0000 to 9999. Electronic switches, available since 1980, can handle up to 50,000 subscribers. The only kind of call that a local exchange can complete on its own, without touching any of the other switches in the network, is to another number in that same local exchange. (Local exchanges are discussed in detail in Chapter 4, "The PSTN.")

PSTN local exchanges are interconnected into a hierarchy. For a local exchange to call a neighbor who resides 10 miles (16 km) away and who draws a dial tone from a different local exchange, the connection between those two different exchanges is accomplished through the second part of the hierarchy—a *tandem switch* (also called a *junction exchange*). The tandem switch is used to connect local exchanges throughout the metropolitan area. When it's time to make a long-distance toll call, another switching center is called into action—the *toll center* (also called the *Class 4 office*, *transit switch*, or *trunk exchange*). The toll center is responsible for establishing and completing national long-distance communications.

The top of the hierarchy is the *international gateway*, whose exchanges are specifically designed to connect calls between different countries.

A trunk supplies the connections between the numerous switches within the PSTN, between customer-owned switches such as the PBX, and between the PBXs and the PSTN. On the other hand, a line supports a single user in the form of a subscriber line in the PSTN or an extension provisioned from the PBX. (Chapter 4 describes in detail the entities involved in managing local, tandem, and toll exchanges.)

Virtual Circuits

Today, because of the great interest in and increased use of packet switching, most networks use virtual circuits. Unlike a physical circuit, which terminates on specific physical ports, a *virtual circuit* is a series of logical connections between sending and receiving devices (see Figure 1.5). A virtual circuit is a connection between two devices that acts as though it's a direct connection, but it may, in fact, be composed of a variety of different routes. The routes might change at any time, and the incoming return route doesn't have to mirror the outgoing route. These connections are defined by table entries inside the packet-switching device. A connection is established after the two devices agree on (1) communications parameters that are important to establishing and maintaining the connection and (2) how to provide

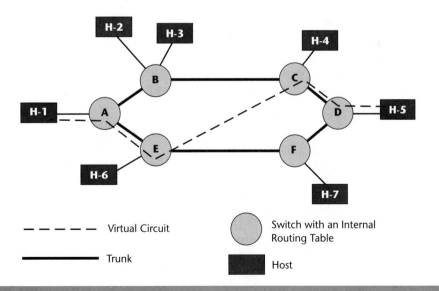

Figure 1.5 A virtual curcuit

the proper performance for the application they are supporting. The types of communication parameters that could be included are message size, the path to be taken, how to deal with acknowledgments in the event of errors, flow control procedures, error control procedures, and policies or agreements negotiated between carriers. The term *virtual circuit* is largely used to describe connections between two hosts in a packet-switching network, where the two hosts can communicate as though they have a dedicated connection, although the packets may be taking very different routes to arrive at their destination.

Interplanetary Networking Protocols

With the imminent onset of space colonization, Vinton Cerf, Adrian Hooke, and others are looking at ways to make interplanetary communications faster. An interesting article in *Wired News* ("Pushing the Internet into Space," at www.wired.com/news/technology/ 0,70377-0.html) talks about their new form of delay-tolerant networking, which involves "bundling," a sort of store-and-forward protocol that is really the opposite of packet switching. Rather than cutting up data into little bits, bundling builds large data collections that hold themselves together and are not affected by the lengthy latencies (sometimes hours) introduced by enormous distances (millions of miles).

There are two types of virtual circuits: permanent virtual circuits (PVCs) and switched virtual circuits (SVCs). The vast majority of implementations today involve PVCs. PVCs and SVCs are commonly used in packet-switching networks (e.g., X.25, Frame Relay, ATM).

PVCs

A *PVC* is a virtual circuit that is permanently available; that is, the connection always exists between the two locations or two devices in question. A PVC is manually configured by a network management system, and it remains in place until the user reconfigures the network. Its use is analogous to the use of a dedicated private line because it provides an always-on condition between two locations or two devices.

SVCs

In contrast to PVCs, *SVCs* are set up on demand. They are provisioned dynamically by using signaling techniques. An SVC must be reestablished each time data is to be sent; after the data has been sent, the SVC disappears. An SVC is therefore analogous to a dialup connection in the PSTN. The main benefit of an SVC is that you can use it to access the network from anyplace. The predominant application for SVCs is to accommodate people who are working at home, in a hotel, at an airport, or otherwise outside the physical location of the enterprise network.

■ Types of Network Connections

Three major types of networks connections can be made:

- ■ **Switched network connections**—A switched connection is referred to as a *dialup* connection. This implies that it uses a series of network switches to establish the connection between the parties.

- ■ **Leased-line network connections**—A leased line is also referred to as a private line. With a leased line, the same locations or the same devices are always connected, and transmission between those locations or devices always occurs on the same path.

- ■ **Dedicated network connections**—In essence, a dedicated line works exactly like a leased line. It is always connected, and it always uses the same path for transmission. However, the end user may own the transmission facility (rather than lease it) such that it is exclusive to that user.

■ The Electromagnetic Spectrum and Bandwidth

The following sections talk about bandwidth and about where the various transmission media lie within the electromagnetic spectrum.

The Electromagnetic Spectrum

When electrons move, they create electromagnetic waves that can propagate through free space. James Maxwell first predicted the existence of this phenomenon in 1865, and Heinrich Hertz first produced and observed it in 1887. All modern communication depends on manipulating and controlling signals within the electromagnetic spectrum.

The electromagnetic spectrum ranges from extremely low-frequency radio waves of 30Hz, with wavelengths nearly double the earth's diameter, to high-frequency cosmic rays of more than 10 million trillion Hz, with wavelengths smaller than the nucleus of an atom. The electromagnetic spectrum is depicted as a logarithmic progression: The scale increases by multiples of 10, so the higher regions encompass a greater span of frequencies than do the lower regions.

Although the electromagnetic spectrum represents an enormous range of frequencies, not all the frequencies are suitable for human communications. At the very low end of the spectrum are signals that are transmitted over 30Hz (i.e., at 30 cycles per second). One of the most important benefits of a very low frequency is that it travels much farther than a high frequency before it loses power (i.e., before it attenuates). So a 30Hz signal can travel halfway around the world before it requires some form of amplification. For example, one defense agency uses 30Hz to communicate with its submarines by using telemetry (e.g., a message that says "We're still here. We're still here" is sent, and the subs know that if they don't get that message, they'd better see what's going on).

At the high end of the electromagnetic spectrum, signals travel over a band of 10 million trillion Hz (i.e., 10^{22}Hz). This end of the spectrum has phenomenal bandwidth, but it has its own set of problems. The waveforms are so miniscule that they're highly distorted by any type of interference, particularly from environmental sources such as precipitation. In addition, the faster the bit rate, the more power consumed. For example, submarine fiber-optic cables require approximately 20,000 watts of power on each end to work. Furthermore, higher-frequency waveforms such as x-rays, gamma rays, and cosmic rays are not very good to human physiology and therefore aren't available for us to use for communication at this point.

Because of the problems with very low and very high frequencies, we primarily use the middle of the electromagnetic spectrum for communication—the radio, microwave, infrared, and visible light portions of the spectrum. We do this by modulating the amplitudes, frequencies, and phases of the electromagnetic waves. Bandwidth is actually a measure of the difference between the lowest and highest frequencies being carried. Each of the communications bands offers differing amounts of bandwidth, based on the range of frequencies they cover. The higher up in the spectrum, the greater the range of frequencies involved. However, this is largely a licensing issue; the spectrum is controlled and allocated by government agencies, such as the Federal Communications Commission (FCC; www.fcc.gov), Canadian Radio-television and Telecommunications Commission (CRTC; www.crtc.gc.ca), and International Telecommunication Union (ITU; www.itu.int).

Infrasound and the Animal World

The universe is full of *infrasound*, the frequencies below the range of human hearing. Earthquakes, wind, thunder, volcanoes, and ocean storms—massive movements of earth, air, fire, and water—generate infrasound. In the past, very-low-frequency sound was not thought to play much of a role in animals' lives. However, we know now that sound at the lowest frequencies of elephant rumbles (14Hz to 35Hz) has remarkable properties. It is little affected by passage through forests and grasslands, and male and female elephants use it to find one another for reproduction. It seems that elephants communicate with one another by using calls that are too low-pitched for human beings to hear, and because of the properties of the infrasound range, these communications can take place over very long distances. Intense infrasonic calls have also been recorded from finback whales.

Figure 1.6 shows the electromagnetic spectrum and where some of the various transmission media operate. Along the right-hand side is the terminology that the ITU applies to the various bands: Extremely low, very low, low, medium, high, very

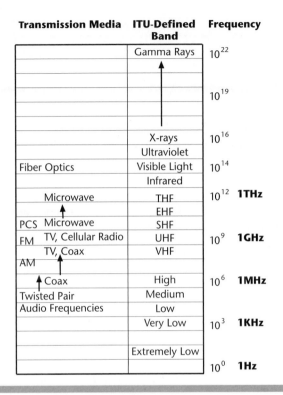

Transmission Media	ITU-Defined Band	Frequency	
	Gamma Rays	10^{22}	
		10^{19}	
	X-rays	10^{16}	
	Ultraviolet		
Fiber Optics	Visible Light	10^{14}	
	Infrared		
Microwave	THF	10^{12}	**1THz**
	EHF		
PCS Microwave	SHF		
FM TV, Cellular Radio	UHF	10^{9}	**1GHz**
TV, Coax	VHF		
AM			
Coax	High	10^{6}	**1MHz**
Twisted Pair	Medium		
Audio Frequencies	Low		
	Very Low	10^{3}	**1KHz**
	Extremely Low		
		10^{0}	**1Hz**

Figure 1.6   The electromagnetic spectrum

high (VHF), ultrahigh (UHF), superhigh (SHF), extremely high (EHF), and tremendously high (THF) frequencies are all various forms of radio bands. And then we move into the light range, with infrared and visible light. You can see just by the placement of the various transmission media that not all are prepared to face the high-bandwidth future that demanding advanced applications (such as streaming media, e-learning, networked interactive games, interactive TV, telemedicine, metacomputing, and Web agents) require.

The radio, microwave, infrared, and visible light portions of the spectrum can all be used to generate electromagnetic waves that carry information. It is possible to modulate various measurements related to electromagnetic waves (see Figure 1.7):

- **Frequency**—The number of oscillations per second of an electromagnetic wave is called its *frequency*.

- **Hertz**—Frequency is measured in *Hertz (Hz)*, in honor of Heinrich Hertz, a German physicist who, in 1887, invented the oscillator (an alternating-current generator) and was credited with the discovery of radio waves.

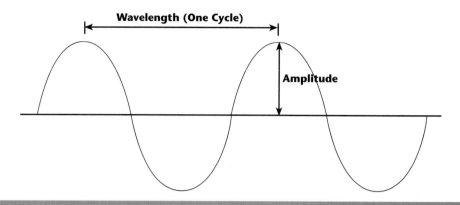

Figure 1.7 An electromagnetic wave

- **Wavelength**—The *wavelength* is the distance between two consecutive maxima or minima of the waveform.

- **Amplitude**—*Amplitude* is a measure of the height of the wave, which indicates the strength, or power, of the signal.

- **Phase**—*Phase* describes the current state of something that changes cyclically (i.e., oscillates). The phase of a wave refers to the angle of the waveform at any given moment; more specifically, it defines the offset of the wave from a reference point.

- **Bandwidth**—The range of frequencies (i.e., the difference between the lowest and highest frequencies carried) that make up a signal is called *bandwidth*.

You can manipulate frequency, amplitude, and phase in order to generate a one and a zero. Hence, you can represent digital information over the electromagnetic spectrum, for example, by sending ones at a high frequency and zeros at a low frequency. Devices that change the frequency in order to carry information are called *frequency-modulated devices*. You can also modulate amplitude by sending ones at a high amplitude or voltage and zeros at a low amplitude. A complementary receiving device could then determine whether a one or a zero is being sent. As yet another example, because the phase of the waveform refers to shifting where the signal begins, you could have ones begin at 90 degrees and zeros begin at 270 degrees. The receiving device could discriminate between these two bit states (zero versus one) based on the phase of the wave as compared to a reference wave.

Twisted-pair cable, which was the original foundation of the PSTN (telephony) network, has a maximum usable bandwidth of about 1MHz. Coax, on the other hand, has greater capacity because it can carry up to a total of 1GHz of frequency spectrum. Within the radio range, microwave is the workhorse of the radio spectrum. It provides 100GHz to operate with. In comparison, fiber optics operates over a band of more than 200THz (terahertz). As we see increasingly more bandwidth-hungry applications, we'll need to use fiber optics to carry the amount of traffic those applications generate.

Of course, it is vital to note that the physical territory ultimately dictates which medium makes the most sense; for example, in a nation like Indonesia, composed of more than 10,000 islands, pulling fiber cable is not practical, so wireless presents a much more cost-effective solution, despite performance problems due to weather issues. Twisted-pair will see little use with the future application set. Although there have been some vast improvements in carrying high bit rates over very-short-distance twisted-pair, such as VDSL (covered in Chapter 12, "Broadband Access Alternatives"), this is not a long-term solution; it is simply a way to extend the useful life of an embedded base of copper. This is why you don't see any new housing developments being wired with copper; instead, telcos and even developers are engaged in bringing fiber to and into the home. And of course, wireless will also figure prominently in enabling mobility. Figure 1.8 plots various telecommunications devices on the electromagnetic spectrum.

Bandwidth

As mentioned earlier, *bandwidth* is the range of frequencies that make up a signal. (Note that the term is today commonly used to refer to data rate, even though that is not the technically correct definition.) There are three major classes of bandwidth in telecommunications networks: narrowband, wideband, and broadband.

Narrowband

Narrowband can accommodate up to 64Kbps, which is also known as the DS-0 (Digital Signal level 0) channel. This is the fundamental increment on which digital networks were built. Initially, this metric of 64Kbps was derived based on our understanding of what it would take to carry voice in a digital manner through the network. If we combine these 64Kbps channels, we can achieve wideband transmission rates.

Wideband

Wideband is defined as accommodating $n \times 64$Kbps, up to approximately 45Mbps. A range of services are provisioned to support wideband capabilities, including T-carrier, E-carrier, and J-carrier services. These are the services on which the first generation of digital hierarchy was built.

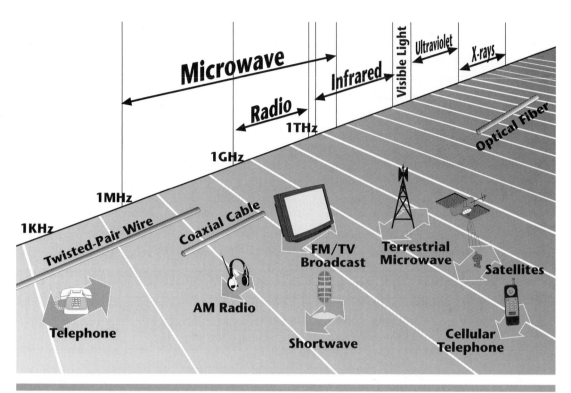

Figure 1.8 Telecommunications devices and the electromagnetic spectrum

T-1, which offers 1.544Mbps, is a North American standard. T-1 is used in the United States and in some overseas territories, such as South Korea and Hong Kong. E-1, which provides a total of 2.048Mbps, is specified by the ITU. It is the international standard used throughout Europe, Africa, most of Asia-Pacific, the Middle East, and Latin America. J-carrier is the Japanese standard, and J-1 offers 1.544Mbps.

Not every office or application requires the total capacity of T-1, E-1, or J-1. In some places, it is possible to subscribe to *fractional services*, which means you subscribe to bundles of channels that offer less than the full rate. Fractional services are normally provided in bundles of 4, so you can subscribe to 4 channels, 8 channels, 12 channels, and so on. Fractional services are also referred to as $n \times 56$Kbps/64Kbps in the T-carrier system and $n \times 64$Kbps under E-carrier. Fractional services are by no means offered ubiquitously. Much depends on the regulations; also, DSL, where available, has replaced the need for fractional services.

High-bandwidth facilities include T-3, E-3, and J-3. T-3 offers 45Mbps, E-3 offers 34Mbps, and J-3 supports 32Mbps. (T-, E-, and J-carrier services are discussed in more detail in Chapter 4.)

Broadband

The future hierarchy rests on broadband capacities, and *broadband* can be defined in different ways, depending on what part of the industry you're talking about. Technically speaking, the ITU has defined broadband as accommodating anything over 2Mbps. But this definition was created in the 1970s, when 2Mbps seemed like a remarkable capacity.

The Impact of Fiber Optics on Bandwidth

So far this chapter has used a lot of bits-per-second measurements. It can be difficult to grasp what these measurements really mean. So, here's a real-world example. Today, fiber optics very easily accommodates 10Gbps (i.e., 10 billion bits per second). But what does that really mean? At 10Gbps you'd be able to transmit all 32 volumes of the *Encyclopedia Britannica* in 1/10 second—the blink of an eye. That is an incredible speed. Not many people have a computer capable of capturing 10Gbps.

Keep in mind that underlying all the various changes in telecommunications technologies and infrastructures, a larger shift is also occurring—the shift from the electronic to the optical, or photonic, era. To extract and make use of the inherent capacity that fiber optics affords, we need an entirely new generation of devices that are optical at heart. Otherwise, we need to stop a signal, convert it back into an electrical form to process it through the network node, and then convert it back into optics to pass it along. (Conversion is discussed later in this chapter.) Consider a fax between Steve in the United States and his friend in Singapore. It begins as a piece of paper (analog). Steve's fax machine scans it (to digital). The modem in Steve's machine converts it (to analog). The Class 5 switch at Steve's local exchange converts it (to digital). The Class 4 switch in the United States converts it (to analog). The receiving Class 4 switch in Singapore converts it (to digital). The Class 5 switch at Steve's friend's local exchange converts it (to analog). The modem in the friend's fax machine converts it (to digital), and his fax machine prints it on paper (analog). That's *eight* conversions! Needing to make so many conversions will not allow us to exercise the high data rates we're beginning to envision.

Given today's environment, for wireline facilities, it may be more appropriate to think of broadband as starting where the optical network infrastructure starts. Synchronous Digital Hierarchy (SDH) and Synchronous Optical Network (SONET) are part of the second generation of digital hierarchy, which is based on fiber optics as the physical infrastructure. (SDH and SONET are discussed in detail in Chapter 4.) The starting rate (i.e., the lowest data rate supported) on SDH/SONET is roughly 51Mbps. For the wireline technologies—those used in the core, or backbone, network—51Mbps is considered the starting point for broadband. In the wireless realm, though, if we could get 2Mbps to a handheld today, we'd be extremely happy and would be willing to call it broadband. So remember that the definition of broadband really depends on the situation. But we can pretty easily say that broadband is always a multichannel facility that affords higher capacities than the traditional voice channel, and in the local loop, 2Mbps is a major improvement.

■ Analog and Digital Transmission

There are a number of differences between analog and digital transmission, and it is important to understand how conversions between analog and digital occur. Let's look first at the older form of transmission, analog.

Analog Transmission

An analog waveform (or signal) is characterized by being continuously variable along amplitude and frequency. In the case of telephony, for instance, when you speak into a handset, the air pressure changes around your mouth. Those changes in air pressure fall onto the handset, where they are amplified and then converted into current, or voltage fluctuations. Those fluctuations in current are an analog of the actual voice pattern—hence the use of the term *analog* to describe these signals (see Figure 1.9).

When it comes to an analog circuit—what we also refer to as a *voice-grade line*—we need to define the frequency band in which it operates. The human voice, for example, can typically generate frequencies from 100Hz to 10,000Hz, for a bandwidth of 9,900Hz. But the ear does not require a vast range of frequencies to elicit meaning from ordinary speech; the majority of sounds we make that constitute intelligible speech fall between 250Hz and 3,400Hz. Therefore, the phone company typically allotted a total bandwidth of 4,000Hz for voice transmission. Remember that the total frequency spectrum of twisted-pair is 1MHz. To provision

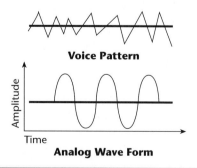

Figure 1.9 Analog transmission

a voice-grade analog circuit, bandwidth-limiting filters are put on that circuit to filter out all frequencies above 4,000Hz. That's why analog circuits can conduct only fairly low-speed data communications. The maximum data rate over an analog facility is 33.6Kbps when there are analog loops at either end.

How 56Kbps Modems Break the 33.6Kbps Barrier

With 56Kbps modems, only one end of the loop can be analog. The other end of the connection has to be digital. So, in other words, if you're using a 56Kbps modem to access your ISP, you have an analog connection from your home to the local exchange. But the ISP has a DSL or a digital termination facility from its location to its exchange.

Analog facilities have limited bandwidth, which means they cannot support high-speed data. Another characteristic of analog is that noise is accumulated as the signal traverses the network. As the signal moves across the distance, it loses power and becomes impaired by factors such as moisture in the cable, dirt on a contact, and critters chewing on the cable somewhere in the network. By the time the signal arrives at the amplifier, it is not only attenuated, it is also impaired and noisy. One of the problems with a basic amplifier is that it is a dumb device. It knows only how to add power, so it takes a weak and impaired signal, adds power to it, and brings it back up to its original power level. But along with an increased signal, the amplifier passes along an increased noise level and adds its own internal noise. So in an analog network, each time a signal goes through an amplifier, it accumulates noise. After you mix together coffee and cream, you can no longer separate them. The same concept applies in analog networks: After you mix the signal and the noise, you can no longer separate the two, and, as a result, you end up with a lot of noise and very high error rates.

Digital Transmission

Digital transmission is quite different from analog transmission. For one thing, the signal is much simpler. Rather than being a continuously variable waveform, it is a series of discrete pulses, representing one bits and zero bits (see Figure 1.10). Each computer uses a coding scheme (called a *collating sequence*) that defines what combinations of ones and zeros constitute all the characters in a character set (e.g., lowercase letters, uppercase letters, punctuation marks, digits, keyboard control functions).

How the ones and zeros are physically carried through the network depends on whether the network is electrical or optical. In electrical networks, one bits are represented as high voltage, and zero bits are represented as null, or low voltage. In

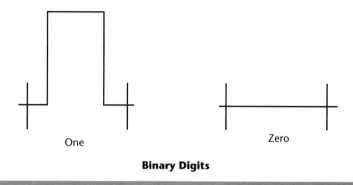

One   Zero

Binary Digits

Figure 1.10 Digital transmission

optical networks, one bits are represented by the presence of light, and zero bits are represented by the absence of light. The ones and zeros—the on/off conditions— are carried through the network, and the receiving device repackages the ones and zeros to determine what character is being represented.

Because a digital signal is easier to reproduce than an analog signal, we can treat it with a little less care in the network. Rather than use dumb amplifiers, digital networks use *regenerative repeaters*, also referred to as *signal regenerators*. As a strong, clean, digital pulse travels over a distance, it loses power, similar to an analog signal. The digital pulse, like an analog signal, is eroded by impairments in the network. But the weakened and impaired signal enters the regenerative repeater, where the repeater examines the signal to determine what was supposed to be a one and what was supposed to be a zero. The repeater regenerates a new signal to pass on to the next point in the network, in essence eliminating noise and thus vastly improving the error rate.

Analog Versus Digital Transmission

Table 1.1 summarizes the characteristics of analog and digital networks.

Conversion: Codecs and Modems

Today we don't have all-digital or all-analog networks; we have a mix of the two. Therefore, at various points in a network, it is necessary to convert between the two signal types. The devices that handle these conversions are codecs and modems (see Figure 1.11).

Table 1.1 Characteristics of Analog and Digital Networks

Feature	Analog Characteristics	Digital Characteristics
Signal	Continuously variable, in both amplitude and frequency	Discrete signal, represented as either changes in voltage or changes in light levels
Capacity measurement	Hz (e.g., a telephone channel is 4KHz)	Bits per second (e.g., a T-1 line carries 1.544Mbps, and an E-1 line transports 2.048Mbps)
Bandwidth	Low bandwidth (4KHz), which means low data transmission rates (up to 33.6Kbps) because of limited channel bandwidth	High bandwidth that can support high-speed data applications that involve video and multimedia
Network capacity	Low; one conversation per telephone channel	High; multiplexers enable multiple conversations to share a communications channel and hence to achieve greater transmission efficiencies
Network manageability	Poor; a lot of labor is needed for network maintenance and control because dumb analog devices do not provide management information streams that allow the device to be remotely managed	Good; smart devices produce alerts, alarms, traffic statistics, and performance measurements, and technicians at a network control center (NCC) or network operations center (NOC) can remotely monitor and manage the various network elements
Signal structure	High; the signal contains a wide range of frequencies and amplitudes	Low; only two discrete signals—the one and the zero—need to be transmitted
Security	Poor; when you tap into an analog circuit, you hear the voice stream in its native form, and it is difficult to detect an intrusion	Good; encryption can be used
Error rates	High; 10^{-5} bits (i.e., 1 in 100,000 bits) is guaranteed to have an error	Low; with twisted-pair, 10^{-7} bits (i.e., 1 in 10 million bits) has an error; with satellite, 10^{-9} bits (i.e., 1 in 1 billion bits) has an error; and with fiber, 10^{-11} bits (i.e., 1 in 100 billion bits) to 10^{-13} bits (i.e., 1 in 10 trillion bits) has an error

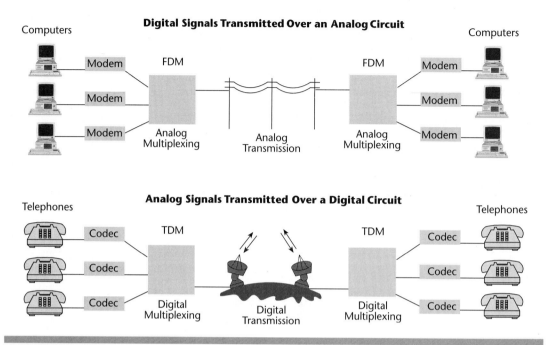

Figure 1.11 Codecs and modems

A *codec* (which is a contraction of *coder–decoder*) converts analog signals into digital signals. There are different codecs for different purposes. For the PSTN, for example, there are codecs that minimize the number of bits per second required to carry voice digitally through the PSTN. In cellular networks, because of the constraints and available spectrum, a codec needs to compress the voice further to get the most efficient use of the spectrum. Codecs applied to video communication also require very specific compression techniques to move those high-bandwidth signals over what may be somewhat limited channels today.

A *modem* (which is a contraction of the terms *modulate* and *demodulate*) is used to infuse digital data onto transmission facilities and vice versa. Some modems are designed specifically to work with analog voice-grade lines. There are also modems designed to work specifically with digital facilities (e.g., ISDN modems, ADSL modems). A modem manipulates the variables of the electromagnetic wave to differentiate between the ones and zeros.

Although it is possible to convert between analog and digital networks, in general, conversions are a weak link in a network. A conversion is a point at which network troubles can occur, an opportunity for errors and distortions to be introduced. Therefore, ideally, we want to move toward an end-to-end digital and end-to-end optical environment. This means that nowhere between the transmitter and the receiver do signal conversions need to be done.

■ Multiplexing

Multiplexers, often called *muxes*, are extremely important to telecommunications. Their main reason for being is to reduce network costs by minimizing the number of communications links needed between two points. Like all other computing systems, multiplexers have evolved. Each new generation has additional intelligence, and additional intelligence brings more benefits. The types of benefits that have accrued, for example, include the following:

- The capability to compress data in order to encode certain characters with fewer bits than normally required and free up additional capacity for the movement of other information.
- The capability to detect and correct errors between the two points being connected to ensure that data integrity and accuracy are maintained.
- The capability to manage transmission resources on a dynamic basis, with such things as priority levels. If you have only one 64Kbps channel left, who gets it? Or what happens when the link between San Francisco and Hong Kong goes down? How else can you reroute traffic to get the high-priority information where it needs to go? Multiplexers help solve such problems.

The more intelligent the multiplexer, the more actively and intelligently it can work to dynamically make use of the available transmission resources.

When you're working with network design and telecommunications, you need to consider line cost versus device cost. You can provide extremely high levels of service by ensuring that everybody always has a live and available communications link. But you must pay for those services on an ongoing basis, and their costs become extremely high. You can offset the costs associated with providing large numbers of lines by instead using devices such as multiplexers that help make more intelligent use of a smaller number of lines.

Figure 1.12 illustrates a network that has no multiplexers. Let's say this network is for Bob's department stores. The CPU is at Location A, a data center that's in New York that manages all the credit authorization functions for all the Bob's stores. Location B, the San Francisco area, has five different Bob's stores in different locations. Many customers will want to make purchases using their Bob's credit cards, so we need to have a communications link back to the New York credit

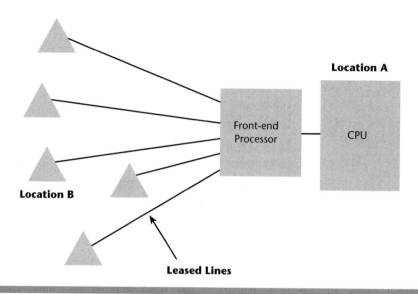

Figure 1.12 A network without multiplexers

authorization center so that the proper approvals and validations can be made. Given that it's a sales transaction, the most likely choice of communications link is the use of a leased line from each of the locations in San Francisco back to the main headquarters in New York.

Remember that using leased lines is a very expensive type of network connection. Because this network resource is reserved for one company's usage only, nobody else has access to that bandwidth, and providers can't make use of it in the evenings or on the weekends to carry residential traffic, so the company pays a premium. Even though it is the most expensive approach to networking, the vast majority of data networking today still takes place using leased lines because they make the network manager feel very much in control of the network's destiny (but don't forget the added incentive for telco salespeople to push these highly profitable lines). With leased lines, the bandwidth is not affected by sudden shifts of traffic elsewhere in the network, the company can apply its own sophisticated network management tools, and the network manager feels a sense of security in knowing who the user communities are at each end of that link. But leased lines have another negative attribute: They are mileage sensitive, so the longer the communications link, the higher the cost. And in a network that doesn't efficiently use that communications link all day long, leased lines can be overkill—and expensive. Plus, beyond the local loop, even leased lines are often bundled together onto a provider's backbone, thus intermixing everyone's presumed-to-be-private data into one seething, heaving mass.

Because of the problems with leased lines, the astute network manager at Bob's thinks about ways to make the network less expensive. One solution, shown in Figure 1.13, is to use multiplexers. Multiplexers always come in pairs, so if you have one at one end, you must have one at the other end. They are also symmetrical, so if there are five outputs available in San Francisco, there must also be five inputs in the New York location. The key savings in this scenario comes from using only one leased line between New York and California. In San Francisco, short leased lines, referred to as *tail circuits*, run from the centrally placed multiplexer to each of the individual locations. Thus, five locations are sharing one high-cost leased line, rather than each having its own leased line. Intelligence embedded in the multiplexers allows the network manager to manage access to that bandwidth and to allocate network services to the endpoints.

Various techniques—including Frequency Division Multiplexing (FDM), Time Division Multiplexing (TDM), Statistical Time Division Multiplexing (STDM), Code Division Multiple Access (CDMA), intelligent multiplexing, inverse multiplexing, Wavelength Division Multiplexing (WDM), Dense Wavelength Division Multiplexing (DWDM), and Coarse Wavelength Division Multiplexing (CWDM)—enable multiple channels to coexist on one link. The following sections examine

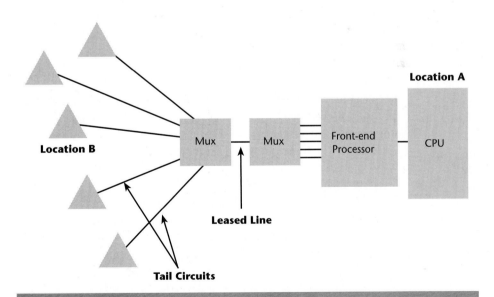

Figure 1.13 A network with multiplexers

these techniques (except CDMA, which is covered in Chapter 13, "Wireless Communications Basics").

FDM

With FDM, the entire frequency band available on the communications link is divided into smaller individual bands or channels (see Figure 1.14). Each user is assigned to a different frequency. The signals all travel in parallel over the same communications link, but they are divided by frequency—that is, each signal rides on a different portion of the frequency spectrum. Frequency, which is an analog parameter, implies that the type of link used with FDM is usually an analog facility. A disadvantage of frequency division muxes is that they can be difficult to reconfigure in an environment in which there's a great deal of dynamic change. For instance, to increase the capacity of channel 1 in Figure 1.14, you would also have to tweak channels 2, 3, and 4 to accommodate that change.

In an enterprise that has a high degree of moves, additions, and changes, an FDM system would be expensive to maintain because it would require the additional expertise of frequency engineering and reconfiguration. Today's environment doesn't make great use of FDM, but it is still used extensively in cable TV and radio. In cable TV, multiple channels of programming all coexist on the coax coming into a home, and they are separated based on the frequency band in which they travel. When you enter a channel number on your set-top box or cable-ready TV, you're essentially selecting the channel (set of frequencies) that you want your television to decode into a picture and sound stream to watch.

TDM

The second muxing technique to be delivered to the marketplace was TDM. There are various levels of TDM. In the plain-vanilla TDM model, as shown in Figure 1.15, a dedicated time slot is provided for each port, or point of interface, on the system. Each device in a predetermined sequence is allotted a time slot during which it can

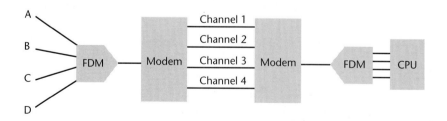

Figure 1.14 FDM

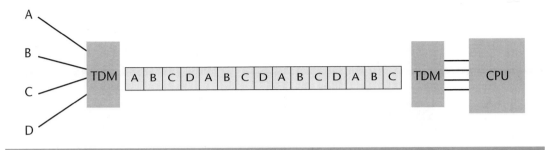

Figure 1.15 TDM

transmit. That time slot enables one character of data, or 8 bits of digitized voice, to be placed on the communications link. The allocated time slots have to be framed in order for the individual channels to be separated out.

A problem with a standard time division mux is that there is a one-to-one correlation between each port and time slot, so if the device attached to port 2 is out for the day, nobody else can make use of time slot 2. Hence, there is a tendency to waste bandwidth when vacant slots occur because of idle stations. However, this type of TDM is more efficient than standard FDM because more subchannels can be derived. Time division muxes are used a great deal in the PSTN, with two generations currently in place: those used in the Plesiochronous Digital Hierarchy (PDH) infrastructure, better known as T-/E-/J-carrier muxes, and those used in the SDH/SONET optical networks (described in Chapter 4).

FDM and TDM can be combined. For example, you could use FDM to carve out individual channels and then within each of those channels apply TDM to carry multiple conversations on each channel. This is how some digital cellular systems work (e.g., Global System for Mobile Communications [GSM]). Digital cellular systems are discussed in Chapter 14, "Wireless WANs."

STDM

STDM was introduced to overcome the limitation of standard TDM, in which stations cannot use each other's time slots. Statistical time division multiplexers, sometimes called *statistical muxes* or *stat muxes*, dynamically allocate the time slots among the active terminals, which means you can actually have more terminals than you have time slots (see Figure 1.16).

A stat mux is a smarter mux, and it has more memory than other muxes, so if all the time slots are busy, excess data goes into a buffer. If the buffer fills up, the additional access data gets lost, so it is important to think about how much traffic to put through a stat mux in order to maintain performance variables. Dynamically

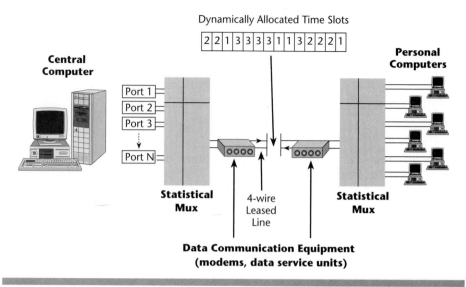

Figure 1.16 STDM

allocating the time slots enables you to make the most efficient use of bandwidth. Furthermore, because these are smarter muxes, they have the additional intelligence mentioned earlier in terms of compression and error control features. Because of the dynamic allocation of time slots, a stat mux can carry two to five times more traffic than a traditional time division mux. But, again, as you load the stat mux with traffic, you run the risk of delays and data loss.

Stat muxes are extremely important because they are the basis on which packet-switching technologies (e.g., X.25, IP, Frame Relay, ATM) are built. The main benefit of a stat mux is the efficient use of bandwidth, which leads to transmission efficiencies.

Intelligent Multiplexing

An intelligent multiplexer is often referred to as a *concentrator*, particularly in the telecom world. Intelligent muxes are not used in pairs; they are used alone. An intelligent mux is a line-sharing device whose purpose is to concentrate large numbers of low-speed lines to be carried over a high-speed line to a further point in the network.

A good example of a concentrator is in a device called the *digital loop carrier* (DLC), which is also referred to as a *remote concentrator* or *remote terminal*. In Figure 1.17, twisted-pairs go from the local exchange to the neighborhood. Before the

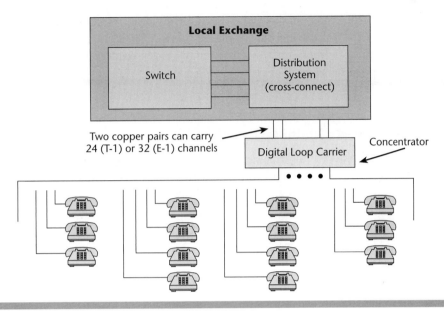

Figure 1.17   Intelligent multiplexing: concentrators

advent of DLCs, each household needed a twisted-pair. If the demand increased beyond the number of pairs available for that local exchange, the users were out of luck until a new local exchange was added.

Digital technology makes better use of the existing pairs than does analog. Instead of using each pair individually per subscriber from the local exchange to the subscriber, you can put a DLC in the center. A series of either fiber-optic pairs or microwave beams connects the local exchange to this intermediate DLC, and those facilities then carry multiplexed traffic. When you get to the DLC, you break out the individual twisted-pairs to the households. This allows you to eliminate much of what used to be an analog plant leading up to the local exchange. It also allows you to provide service to customers who are outside the distance specifications between a subscriber and the local exchange. So, in effect, that DLC can be used to reduce the loop length.

Traditional DLCs are not interoperable with some DSL offerings, including ADSL and SDSL. For example, about 30% to 40% of the U.S. population is serviced through DLCs. And in general, globally, the more rural or remote a city or neighborhood, the more likely that it is serviced via a DLC. For those people to be able to subscribe to high-bandwidth DSL services, the carrier has to replace the DLC with a newer generation of device. Lucent's xDSL Access Gateway, for example, is such a device; it offers a multiservice access system that provides Lite and full-rate

ADSL, Integrated Services Digital Network (ISDN), Asynchronous Transfer Mode (ATM), and plain old telephone service (POTS), which is analog over twisted-pair lines or fiber. Or the carrier may simply determine that the market area doesn't promise enough revenue and leave cable modems or broadband wireless as the only available broadband access technique.

Inverse Multiplexing

The inverse multiplexer, which arrived on the scene in the 1990s, does the opposite of what the multiplexers described so far do: Rather than combine lots of low-bit-rate streams to ride over a high-bit-rate pipe, an inverse multiplexer breaks down a high-bandwidth signal into a group of smaller-data-rate signals that can be dispersed over a range of channels to be carried over the network. A primary application for inverse multiplexers is to support high-bandwidth applications such as videoconferencing.

In Figure 1.18, a videoconference is to occur at 1.5Mbps. A good-quality, full-motion, long-session video requires substantial bandwidth. It's one thing to tolerate pixilation or artifacts in motion for a 15-minute meeting that saves you the time of driving or flying to meet colleagues. However, for a two-hour meeting to evaluate a new advertising campaign, the quality needs to parallel what most of us use as a reference point: television. Say that company policy is to hold a two-hour videoconferenced meeting twice each month. Very few customers are willing to pay for a 1.5Mbps to 2Mbps connection for an application that they're using just four hours each month. Instead, they want their existing digital facilities to carry that traffic. An inverse mux allows them to do so. In Figure 1.18, the 1.5Mbps video stream is introduced into the inverse multiplexer, the inverse mux splits that up into 24 64Kbps channels, and each of these 24 channels occupies a separate channel on an existing T-1/E-1 facility or PRI ISDN. (PRI ISDN is discussed in Chapter 2, "Traditional Transmission Media.") The channels are carried across the network separately. At the destination point, a complementary inverse mux reaggregates, resynchronizes, and reproduces that high-bandwidth signal so that it can be projected on the destination video monitor.

Inverse multiplexing therefore allows you to experience a bit of elastic bandwidth. You can allocate existing capacity to a high-bandwidth application without having to subscribe to a separate link just for that purpose.

WDM, DWDM, and CWDM

WDM was specifically developed for use with fiber optics. In the past, we could use only a fraction of the available bandwidth of a fiber-optic system. This was mainly because we had to convert the optical pulses into electrical signals to regenerate

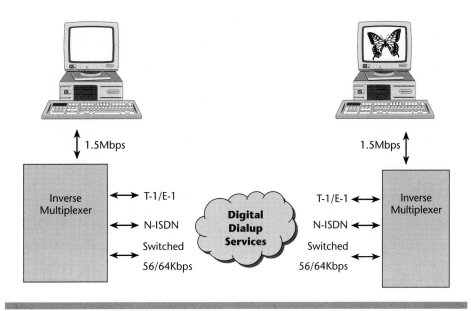

Figure 1.18   Inverse multiplexing

them as they moved through the fiber network. As optical signals travel through fiber, the impurities in the fiber absorb the signal's strength. Because of this, somewhere before the original signal becomes unintelligible, the optical signal must be regenerated (i.e., given new strength) so that it will retain its information until it reaches its destination or at least until it is amplified again. And because repeaters were originally electronic, data rates were limited to about 2.5Gbps. In 1994, something very important happened: Optical amplifiers called *erbium-doped fiber amplifiers* (EDFAs) were introduced. Erbium is a chemical that's injected into the fiber. As a light pulse passes through the erbium, the light is amplified and continues on its merry way, without having to be stopped and processed as an electrical signal. The introduction of EDFAs immediately opened up the opportunity to make use of fiber-optic systems operating at 10Gbps.

EDFAs also paved the way to developing wavelength division multiplexers. Before the advent of WDM, we were using only one wavelength of light within each fiber, although the visible light spectrum engages a large number of different wavelengths. WDM takes advantage of the fact that multiple colors, or frequencies, of light can be transmitted simultaneously down a single optical fiber. The data rate that each of the wavelengths supports depends on the type of light source. Today, the most common data rates supported are OC-48, which is shorthand for 2.5Gbps, and OC-192, which is equivalent to 10Gbps. 40Gbps systems are also now commercially available. In the future, we'll go beyond that. Part of the evolution of

WDM is that every year, we double the number of bits per second that can be carried on a wavelength, and every year we double the number of wavelengths that can be carried over a single fiber. But we have just begun. Soon light sources should be able to pulse in the terabits-per-second range, and within a few years, light sources that produce petabits per second (1,000Tbps) will emerge.

One thing to clarify about the first use of WDM is that unlike the other types of multiplexing, where the goal is to aggregate smaller channels into one larger channel, WDM is meant to furnish separate channels for each service, at the full data rate. Increasingly, enterprises are making use of high-capacity switches and routers equipped with 2.5Gbps interfaces, so there's a great deal of desire within the user community to plug in to a channel of sufficient size to carry a high-bandwidth signal end to end, without having to break it down into smaller increments only to build them back out at the destination. WDM addresses this need by furnishing a separate channel for each service at the full rate.

Systems that support more than 8 wavelengths are referred to as DWDM (see Figure 1.19). Systems at both the OC-48 (2.5Gbps) and OC-192 (10Gbps) levels can today support upward of 128 channels, or wavelengths. New systems that operate at 40Gbps (OC-768) are also now available, and Bell Labs is working on a technique that might enable us to extract up to 15,000 channels or wavelengths on a single fiber. Meanwhile, CWDM has been introduced to address metro area and campus environments, where long distance is not an issue, but cost is. These systems rely on lower-cost light sources that reduce costs, but at the same time, they require increased spacing between the channels and therefore limit CWDM sys-

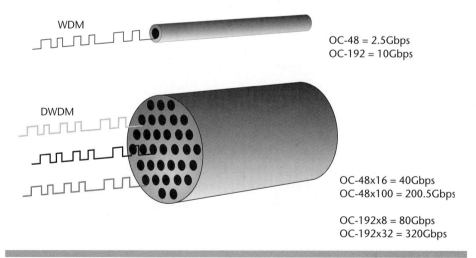

Figure 1.19 WDM and DWDM

tems to 32 or 64 channels, at most. An important point to note is that at this time, DWDM and CWDM systems do not always interoperate; of course, this will be resolved in the near future, but for the time being, it is a limitation that needs to be acknowledged.

The revolution truly has just begun. The progress in this area is so great that each year we're approximately doubling performance while halving costs. Again, great emphasis is being placed on the optical sector, so many companies—traditional telecom providers, data networking providers, and new startups—are focusing attention on the optical revolution. (WDM, DWDM, CWDM, and EDFAs are discussed in more detail in Chapter 11, "Optical Networking.")

■ Political and Regulatory Forces in Telecommunications

New developments always bring politics with them. Different groups vie for money, power, the ability to bring new products to market first and alone, and the right to squash others' new ideas. A prominent characteristic of the telecommunications sector is the extent to which it is influenced by government policy and regulation. The forces these exert on the sector are inextricably tied to technological and market forces.

Because of the pervasive nature of information and communications technologies and the services that derive from them, coupled with the large prizes to be won, the telecommunications sector is subject to a lot of attention from policymakers. Regulation has been a government priority since the early twentieth century. But particularly over the past 22 years or so, telecommunications policy and regulation have been prominent on the agendas of governments around the world, focusing on deregulation (Telecommunications Act of 1997) and intellectual property protection (Digital Millennium Copyright Act), which are both very important for the industry. This reflects the global trend toward liberalization, including, in many countries, privatization of the former monopoly telcos. However, interest from policymakers in telecommunications goes much deeper than this. A great deal of this interest stems from the extended reach and wide impact that information and communications technologies have. Here are some examples:

- Telephony, e-mail, and information services permit contact between friends and families and offer convenience to people in running their day-to-day lives. Thus, these services have major economic and social implications.
- In the business arena, information and communications technologies offer business efficiency and enable the creation of new business activities. Thus, they have major employment and economic implications.

- Multimedia and the Internet offer new audio, video, and data services that affect entertainment and education, among other areas. These new services overlap with traditional radio and television broadcasting, and major cultural implications are appearing.

- News delivery influences peoples' perceptions of governments and their own well-being, thereby influencing voter attitudes. Telecommunications brings attention to cultural trends, with major political as well as cultural implications.

- Government applications of information and communications technologies affect the efficiency of government. Defense, national security, and crime-fighting applications bring with them major political implications.

Given this background of the pervasive impact that information and communications technologies have, it is hardly surprising that they get heavy policy attention.

Regulatory Background

Although many national regulatory authorities today are separate from central government, they are built on foundations of government policy. Indeed, the very act of creating an independent regulatory body is a key policy decision. Historically, before telecommunications privatization and liberalization came to the fore, regulation was often carried out within central government, which also controlled the state-run telcos. That has changed in recent years in many, but not all, countries.

Given their policy foundation, and the fact that government policies vary from country to country and from time to time, it is not surprising that regulatory environments evolve and differ. These evolutions and international variations sometimes pose planning problems for the industry, and these problems can lead to frustrations and tensions between companies and regulatory agencies. They can also lead to disagreements between countries (e.g., over trade issues). Although moves to encourage international harmonization of regulatory regimes (e.g., by the ITU and by the European Commission) have been partially successful, differences remain in the ways in which countries interpret laws and recommendations. Moreover, given that regulations need to reflect changing market conditions and technological capabilities, it is inevitable that over time regulatory environments will change, too. So regulation is best viewed as another of the variables, such as technological change, that the telecommunications industry needs to take into account.

The Policy and Regulatory Players

At the global level, a number of international bodies govern or make recommendations about telecommunications policy and regulation. In addition to the ITU and the European Commission, there are various standards bodies (discussed later in this chapter, in the section "Standards Organizations") and industry associations (e.g., the European Competitive Telecommunications Association [ECTA; www.ectaportal. com/en/], the Telecommunications Industry Association [TIA; www.tiaonline.org]). Representatives of national governments and regulatory authorities meet formally (e.g., ITU World Radio Conferences, where many countries are represented) and informally (e.g., Europe's National Regulatory Authorities [NRAs] exchange views at Independent Regulators Group [IRG] meetings). Other organizations, such as the World Trade Organization (WTO; www.wto.org) and regional bodies, also influence telecommunications policy and regulation at the international level.

At the national level, several parts of central government are generally involved, and there can sometimes be more than one regulatory body for a nation. Some of these organizations are major players; others play less prominent but nevertheless influential roles. In the United States, for example, the FCC is the national regulatory body, and public utility commissions regulate at the state level. The U.S. State Department coordinates policy regarding international bodies such as the ITU. The White House, the Department of Commerce (largely through the National Telecommunications and Information Administration [NTIA; www.ntia. doc.gov]), the Justice Department, the Trade Representative, and the Department of Defense are among the various parts of the administration that set or contribute to telecommunications policy. The U.S. Congress and the U.S. government's legislative branch also play important roles. In addition, industry associations, policy "think tanks," regulatory affairs departments within companies, telecommunications lawyers, and lobbyists all contribute to policy debates and influence the shape of the regulatory environment.

Other countries organize their policy and regulatory activities differently from the United States. For example, in the United Kingdom, the Office of Telecommunications (OFTEL) mainly regulated what in the United States would be known as "common carrier" matters, whereas the Radiocommunications Agency (RA) dealt with radio and spectrum matters. However, in 2003, OFTEL and RA were combined into a new Office of Communications (OFCOM; www.ofcom.org.uk). In Hong Kong, telecommunications regulation was previously dealt with by the post office, but now the Office of the Telecommunications Authority (OFTA; www.ofta. gov.hk) is the regulatory body. As you can see, not only do regulatory environments change, but so do the regulatory players.

The Main Regulatory Issues

Let's look briefly at what regulators do. Again, this varies somewhat from country to country and over time. In the early years of liberalization, much time would typically be spent in licensing new entrants and putting in place regulations designed to keep a former monopoly telco from abusing its position by, for example, stifling its new competitors or by charging inappropriately high prices to its customers. Here the regulator is acting as a proxy for market forces. As effective competition takes root, the role of the regulator changes somewhat. Much of the work then typically involves ensuring that all licensed operators or service providers meet their license obligations and taking steps to encourage the development of the market such that consumers benefit.

The focus of most regulatory bodies is, or should be, primarily on looking after the interests of the various end users of telecommunications. However, most regulators would recognize that this can be achieved only if there is a healthy and vibrant industry to deliver the products and services. So while there are often natural tensions between a regulator and the companies being regulated, it is at the same time important for cooperation between the regulator and the industry to take place. In Ireland, for example, the role of the regulator is encapsulated by the following mission statement: "The purpose of the Office of the Director of Telecommunications Regulation is to regulate with integrity, impartiality, and expertise to facilitate rapid development of a competitive leading-edge telecommunications sector that provides the best in price, choice, and quality to the end user, attracts business investment, and supports ongoing social and economic growth."

Flowing from regulators' high-level objectives are a range of activities such as licensing, price control, service-level agreements, interconnection, radio spectrum management, and access to infrastructure. Often, regulatory bodies consult formally with the industry, consumers, and other interested parties on major issues before introducing regulatory changes. You can obtain a more detailed appreciation of what telecommunications regulators do and what their priorities are by looking at the various reports, consultation papers, and speeches at regulatory bodies' Web sites.

Internet Governance

The subject of Internet governance has become increasingly important in recent years. There are many different Internet stakeholders, many of whom have entirely different visions of how the Internet should work and how it should (or should not) be governed. Needless to say, the policies and mechanisms for Internet governance have been the subject of heated debate.

At the December 2003 World Summit on the Information Society (WSIS; www.itu.int/wsis) in Geneva, governments adopted a plan of action that called on the secretary-general of the United Nations to set up the Working Group on Internet Governance (WGIG; www.wgig.org). The WGIG's mandate was to analyze the governance of the Internet and make proposals for action, as appropriate; develop a working definition of *Internet governance*; identify the public policy issues involved; and advance a common understanding of the respective roles and responsibilities of the various stakeholders. The WGIG is composed of 40 individuals from government, the private sector, and civil society, appointed by U.N. Secretary-General Kofi Annan in November 2004. The WGIG report, published in June 2005, provides a working definition of *Internet governance*: "Internet governance is the development and application by Governments, the private sector and civil society, in their respective roles, of shared principles, norms, rules, decision-making procedures, and programmes that shape the evolution and use of the Internet" (*Report of the Working Group on Internet Governance*, June 2005, www.wgig.org/docs/WGIGREPORT.pdf).

Not everyone agrees with the WGIG's definition, and the heated debate continues. Regardless, the WGIG was asked to present the result of its work for the second phase of the WSIS conference held in Tunis in November 2005. A dispute over control of the Internet threatened to derail the conference. However, a last-minute decision to leave control in the hands of the U.S.-based Internet Corporation for Assigned Names and Numbers (ICANN; www.icann.org) for the time being avoided a major blowup. The participants of the November 2005 WSIS conference agreed on a compromise to allow for wider international debate on the policy principles and agreed to set up an international Internet Governance Forum (www.intgovforum.org), with a purely consultative role, to be convened by the U.N. secretary-general.

Internet governance is an area of critical concern, and you should monitor the ongoing activities of the associated groups. To understand the issues under consideration, read the complete WGIG June 2005 report (www.wgig.org/docs/WGIGREPORT.pdf). In addition, the Center for Democracy and Technology Web site (www.cdt.org/dns) explores many of the controversial issues in this area.

Standards Organizations

Networking is an international phenomenon, and recommendations must be made on how systems and networks should interoperate. Standardization within the industry is intended to perform three basic functions:

- Facilitate interconnection between different users
- Facilitate the portability of equipment within different regions and applications, with the intent of increasing market size, resulting in reduced costs for all
- Ensure equipment interoperability so that different vendors' products work with each other

Standards bodies that make such recommendations have traditionally been active in Europe, North America, Japan, and, more and more, China. In recent years, the

Internet Society (ISOC; www.isoc.org) has also become an increasingly important organization.

The ITU is a body of the United Nations that includes members from around the world. Three specific groups within the ITU are relevant to telecommunications. The ITU-T (www.itu.int/ITU-T), the telecommunications standardization sector, develops recommendations for wireline networks. The ITU-R (www.itu.int/ITU-R), the radio communications standardization sector, deals with the wireless arena. The ITU-D (www.itu.int/ITU-D) works on standards for developing nations. The ITU standards are followed throughout most of the world, including Africa, most of Asia-Pacific, Europe, Latin America, and the Middle East.

Standards Organization Time Line

The following time line shows some of the important dates in the history of standards organizations:

1865   The ITU was established by 20 European states at the first International Telegraph Convention.

1923   The CCIF was established in Paris, for the study of long-distance telephony.

1925   The CCITT (now the ITU-T) was established for the technical study of telephony problems. The CCIF and CCITT both became part of the ITU.

1927   The CCIR was formed in Washington, with the objective of concentrating on technical issues surrounding radio communications.

1947   The ITU was recognized as an agency of the United Nations, specializing in telecommunications.

1959   The CCIF and the CCITT were combined and became known simply as the CCITT, now called the ITU-T.

The second major standards body is the America National Standards Institute (ANSI; www.ansi.org), whose recommendations are followed throughout North America and in some Asian countries.

The third major body is the Telecommunications Technology Committee (TTC; http://inetserv.ttc.or.jp/e/), whose recommendations are followed in Japan.

ISOC has an agreement to work with the ITU to ensure that developments do not take place separately in evolving the PSTN versus the Internet. These organizations are working toward converging networks on the same sets of requirements and functions.

In order to make room for the many—often conflicting—interests, the international standards-making organizations concentrate on producing *base standards*. These base standards contain allowable variants or options, which are defined by the implementer. By adopting any of the variants or options, the implementer complies with the standard, but there is no guarantee that the equipment will interoperate with the equipment of other vendors. This problem of interoperability and internetworking is addressed by regional and national standards bodies, often involving trade organizations and user groups. These groups adapt the international base standards as functional standards, which contain a limited number of agreed-upon allowable options. These groups also develop test specifications and methods, and independent test houses then perform the necessary conformance testing and certify products that meet the requirements. (See Figures 1.20 and 1.21.)

Table 1.2 lists some of the key standards organizations throughout the world.

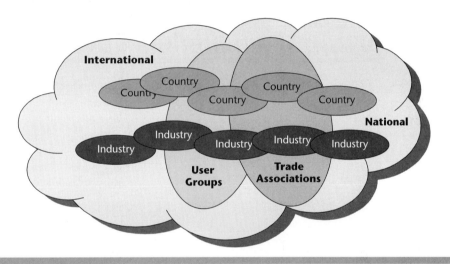

Figure 1.20 Standards-making groups

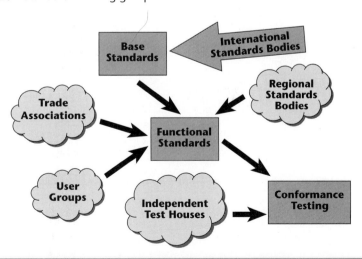

Figure 1.21 The standards-making process

Table 1.2 Standards Organizations

Region	Standards Organizations
International	ITU, ITU-T, ITU-R, ITU-D, IEC, ISO
Australia	ACA, ACC, AIIA, ATUG
Europe	AFNOR (France), CEN and CENLEC, CEPT, DIN (Germany), DTI (UK), ETSI, European Community (EU)
Japan	JISC, TTC
New Zealand	ITANZ
North America	ANSI (USA), EIA, FCC (USA), IEEE, NIST, SCC (Canada)

Chapter 2

Traditional Transmission Media

Transmission media are the physical pathways that connect computers, other devices, and people on a network—the highways and byways that comprise the information superhighway. Each transmission medium requires specialized network hardware that has to be compatible with that medium. You have probably heard terms such as Layer 1, Layer 2, and so on. These refer to the OSI reference model, which defines network hardware and services in terms of the functions they perform. (The OSI reference model is discussed in detail in Chapter 5, "Data Communications Basics.") Transmission media operate at Layer 1 of the OSI model: They encompass the physical entity and describe the types of highways on which voice and data can travel.

It would be convenient to construct a network of only one medium. But that is impractical for anything but an extremely small network. In general, networks use combinations of media types. There are three main categories of media types:

- **Copper cable**—Types of cable include unshielded twisted-pair (UTP), shielded twisted-pair (STP), and coaxial cable. Copper-based cables are inexpensive and easy to work with compared to fiber-optic cables, but as you'll learn when we get into the specifics, a major disadvantage of cable is that it offers a rather limited spectrum that cannot handle the advanced applications of the future, such as teleimmersion and virtual reality.

- **Wireless**—Wireless media include radio frequencies, microwave, satellite, and infrared. Deployment of wireless media is faster and less costly than deployment of cable, particularly where there is little or no existing infra-structure (e.g., Africa, Asia-Pacific, Latin America, eastern and central Europe). Wireless is also useful where environmental circumstances make it impossible or cost-prohibitive to use cable (e.g., in the Amazon, in the Empty Quarter in Saudi Arabia, on oil rigs).

■ There are a few disadvantages associated with wireless, however. Histori-cally, wireless solutions support much lower data rates than do wired solu-tions, although with new developments in wireless broadband, that is becoming less of an issue (see Part IV, "Wireless Communications"). Wire-less is also greatly affected by external impairments, such as the impact of adverse weather, so reliability can be difficult to guarantee. However, new developments in laser-based communications—such as virtual fiber—can improve this situation. (Virtual fiber is discussed in Chapter 15, "WMANs, WLANs, and WPANs.") Of course, one of the biggest concerns with wire-less is security: Data must be secured in order to ensure privacy.

■ **Fiber optics**—Fiber offers enormous bandwidth, immunity to many types of interference and noise, and improved security. Therefore, fiber provides very clear communications and a relatively noise-free environment. The downside of fiber is that it is costly to purchase and deploy because it requires specialized equipment and techniques.

Prevailing Conditions and Network Diversity

No one of the three categories of media types can be considered best. Each is useful in different situations, and most networks need to take advantage of a number of media types. When building a new network or upgrading an old one, the choice of media type should be based on the prevailing conditions.

The saying "Don't put all your eggs in one basket" can be applied to networking. Having multiple pathways of fibers in and out of a building is not always enough. Diver-sity—terrestrial and nonterrestrial facilities combined—is important because in disastrous events such as earthquakes, floods, and fires, if one alternative is completely disabled, another medium might still work. As discussed in this chapter, you can assess various parameters to determine which media type is most appropriate for a given application.

This chapter focuses on the five traditional transmission media formats: twisted-pair copper used for analog voice telephony, coaxial cable, microwave and satellite in the context of traditional carrier and enterprise applications, and fiber optics. (Contemporary transmission solutions are discussed in subsequent chap-ters, including Chapter 11, "Optical Networking," and Chapter 16, "Emerging Wireless Applications.") Table 2.1 provides a quick comparison of some of the

Table 2.1 Traditional Transmission Media Characteristics

Media Type	Bandwidth	Performance: Typical Error Rate
Twisted-pair for analog voice applications	1MHz	Poor to fair (10^{-5})
Coaxial cable	1GHz	Good (10^{-7} to 10^{-9})
Microwave	100GHz	Good (10^{-9})
Satellite	100GHz	Good (10^{-9})
Fiber	75THz	Great (10^{-11} to 10^{-13})

important characteristics of these five media types. Note that recent developments in broadband alternatives, including twisted-pair options such as DSL and wireless broadband, constitute a new categorization of media.

The frequency spectrum in which a medium operates directly relates to the bit rate that can be obtained with that medium. You can see in Table 2.1 that traditional twisted-pair affords the lowest bandwidth (i.e., the difference between the highest and lowest frequencies supported), a maximum of 1MHz, whereas fiber optics affords the greatest bandwidth, some 75THz.

Another important characteristic is a medium's susceptibility to noise and the subsequent error rate. Again, twisted-pair suffers from many impairments. Coax and fiber have fewer impairments than twisted-pair because of how the cable is constructed, and fiber suffers the least because it is not affected by electrical interference. The error rate of wireless depends on the prevailing conditions, especially weather and the presence of obstacles, such as foliage and buildings.

Yet another characteristic you need to evaluate is the distance required between repeaters. This is a major cost issue for those constructing and operating networks. In the case of twisted-pair deployed as an analog telephone channel, the distance between amplifiers is roughly 1.1 miles (1.8 km). When twisted-pair is used in digital mode, the repeater spacing drops to about 1,800 feet (550 m). With twisted-pair, a great many network elements must be installed and subsequently maintained over their lifetime, and they can be potential sources of trouble in the network. Coax offers about a 25% increase in the distance between repeaters over twisted-pair. With microwave and satellite, the distance between repeaters depends on the frequency bands in which you're operating and the orbits in which the satellites travel. In the area of fiber, new innovations appear every three to four months, and, as discussed later in this chapter, some new developments promise distances as great as 4,000 miles (6,400 km) between repeaters or amplifiers in the network.

Security is another important characteristic. There is no such thing as complete security, and no transmission medium in and of itself can provide security. But using encryption and authentication helps ensure security. (Chapter 9, "IP Services," discusses security in more detail.) Also, different media types have different characteristics that enable rapid intrusion as well as characteristics that enable better detection of intrusion. For example, with fiber, an optical time domain reflectometer (OTDR) can be used to detect the position of splices that could be the result of unwanted intrusion. (Some techniques allow you to tap into a fiber cable without splices, but they are extremely costly and largely available only to government security agencies.)

Finally, you need to consider three types of costs associated with the media types: acquisition cost (e.g., the costs of the cable per foot [meter], of the transceiver and laser diode, and of the microwave tower), installation and maintenance costs (e.g., the costs of parts as a result of wear and tear and environmental conditions), and internal premises costs for enterprises (e.g., the costs of moves, adds, and changes, and of relocating workers as they change office spaces).

The following sections examine these five media types—twisted-pair, coaxial cable, microwave, satellite, and fiber optics—in detail.

■ Twisted-Pair

The historical foundation of the public switched telephone network (PSTN) lies in twisted-pair, and even today, most people who have access to networks access them through a local loop built on twisted-pair. Although twisted-pair has contributed a great deal to the evolution of communications, advanced applications on the horizon require larger amounts of bandwidth than twisted-pair can deliver, so the future of twisted-pair is diminishing. Figure 2.1 shows an example of four-pair UTP.

Characteristics of Twisted-Pair

The total usable frequency spectrum of telephony twisted-pair copper cable is about 1MHz (i.e., 1 million cycles per second). Newer standards for broadband DSL, also based on twisted-pair, use up to 2.2MHz of spectrum. Loosely translated into bits per second (bps)—a measurement of the amount of data being transported, or capacity of the channel—twisted-pair cable offers about 2Mbps to 3Mbps over 1MHz of spectrum. But there's an inverse relationship between distance and the data rate that can be realized. The longer the distance, the greater the impact of errors and impairments, which diminish the data rate. In order to achieve higher data rates, two techniques are commonly used: The distance of the loop can be shortened, and advanced modulation schemes can be applied, which

Figure 2.1   Twisted-pair

means we can encode more bits per cycle. A good example of this is Short Reach VDSL2 (discussed in Chapter 12, "Broadband Access Alternatives"), which is based on twisted copper pair but can support up to 100Mbps, but over a maximum loop length of only 330 feet (100 m). New developments continue to allow more efficient use of twisted-pair and enable the higher data rates that are needed for Internet access and Web surfing, but each of these new solutions specifies a shorter distance over which the twisted-pair is used, and more sophisticated modulation and error control techniques are used as well.

Another characteristic of twisted-pair is that it requires short distances between repeaters. Again, this means that more components need to be maintained and there are more points where trouble can arise, which leads to higher costs in terms of long-term operation.

Twisted-pair is also highly susceptible to interference and distortion, including electromagnetic interference (EMI), radio frequency interference (RFI), and the effects of moisture and corrosion. Therefore, the age and health of twisted-pair cable are important factors.

The greatest use of twisted-pair in the future is likely to be in enterprise premises, for desktop wiring. Eventually, enterprise premises will migrate to fiber and forms of wireless, but in the near future, they will continue to use twisted-pair internally.

Categories of Twisted-Pair

There are two types of twisted-pair: UTP and STP. In STP, a metallic shield around the wire pairs minimizes the impact of outside interference. Most implementations today use UTP.

Twisted-pair is divided into categories that specify the maximum data rate possible. In general, the cable category term refers to ANSI/TIA/EIA 568-A: Commercial Building Telecommunications Cabling Standards. The purpose of EIA/TIA 568-A was to create a multiproduct, multivendor standard for connectivity. Other standards bodies—including the ISO/IEC, NEMA, and ICEA—are also working on specifying Category 6 and above cable.

The following are the cable types specified in ANSI/TIA/EIA 568-A:

- **Category 1**—Cat 1 cable was originally designed for voice telephony only, but thanks to some new techniques, long-range Ethernet and DSL, operating at 10Mbps and even faster, can be deployed over Cat 1.

- **Category 2**—Cat 2 cable can accommodate up to 4Mbps and is associated with token-ring LANs.

- **Category 3**—Cat 3 cable operates over a bandwidth of 16MHz on UTP and supports up to 10Mbps over a range of 330 feet (100 m). Key LAN applications include 10Mbps Ethernet and 4Mbps token-ring LANs.

- **Category 4**—Cat 4 cable operates over a bandwidth of 20MHz on UTP and can carry up to 16Mbps over a range of 330 feet (100 m). The key LAN application is 16Mbps token ring.

- **Category 5**—Cat 5 cable operates over a bandwidth of 100MHz on UTP and can handle up to 100Mbps over a range of 330 feet (100m). Cat 5 cable is typically used for Ethernet networks running at 10Mbps or 100Mbps. Key LAN applications include 100BASE-TX, ATM, CDDI, and 1000BASE-T. It is no longer supported, having been replaced by Cat 5e.

- **Category 5e**—Cat 5e (enhanced) operates over a bandwidth of 100MHz on UTP, with a range of 330 feet (100 m). The key LAN application is 1000BASE-T. The Cat 5e standard is largely the same as Category 5, except that it is made to somewhat more stringent standards. Category 5e is recommended for all new installations and was designed for transmission speeds of up to 1Gbps (Gigabit Ethernet). Although Cat 5e can support Gigabit Ethernet, it is not currently certified to do so.

- **Category 6**—Cat 6, specified under ANSI/TIA/EIA-568-B.2-1, operates over a bandwidth of up to 400MHz and supports up to 1Gbps over a range of 330 feet (100 m). It is a cable standard for Gigabit Ethernet and other network protocols that is backward compatible with the Cat 5/5e and Cat 3 cable standards. Cat 6 features more stringent specifications for crosstalk and system noise. Cat 6 is suitable for 10BASE-T/100BASE-TX and 1000BASE-T (Gigabit Ethernet) connections.

- **Category 7**—Cat 7 is specified in the frequency range of 1MHz to 600MHz. ISO/IEC11801:2002 Category 7/Class F is a cable standard for Ultra Fast Ethernet and other interconnect technologies that can be made backward compatible with traditional Cat 5 and Cat 6 Ethernet cable. Cat 7, which is based on four twisted copper pairs, features even more stringent specifications for crosstalk and system noise than Cat 6. To achieve this, shielding has been added for individual wire pairs and the cable as a whole.

The predominant cable categories in use today are Cat 3 (due to widespread deployment in support of 10Mbps Ethernet—although it is no longer being deployed) and Cat 5e. Cat 4 and Cat 5 are largely defunct.

Applications of Twisted-Pair

The primary applications of twisted-pair are in premises distribution systems, telephony, private branch exchanges (PBXs) between telephone sets and switching cabinets, LANs, and local loops, including both analog telephone lines and broadband DSL.

Analog and Digital Twisted-Pair

Twisted-pair is used in traditional analog subscriber lines, also known as the telephony channel or 4KHz channel. Digital twisted-pair takes the form of Integrated Services Digital Network (ISDN) and the new-generation family of DSL standards, collectively referred to as xDSL (see Chapter 12).

ISDN

Narrowband ISDN (N-ISDN) was introduced in 1983 as a network architecture and set of standards for an all-digital network. It was intended to provide end-to-end digital service using public telephone networks worldwide and to provide high-quality, error-free transmission. N-ISDN entails two different specifications:

- **Basic Rate Interface (BRI)**—Also referred to as Basic Rate Access (BRA), BRI includes two B-channels and one D-channel (often called 2B+D). The B-channels are the bearer channels, which, for example, carry voice, data, or fax transmissions. The D-channel is the delta channel, where signaling takes place. Because signaling doesn't occur over long periods of time, where allowed by the service provider, the D-channel can also be used to carry low-speed packet-switched data. Each B-channel offers 64Kbps, and the D-channel provides 16Kbps. So, in total, 2B+D offers 144Kbps, delivered over a single twisted-pair with a maximum loop length of about 3.5 miles (5.5 km). BRI is used in residences, in small businesses that need only a couple lines, and for centrex customers. (A *centrex customer* leases extensions from the local exchange rather than acquiring its own PBX for the customer premise. Thus, the local exchange pretends to be a private PBX that performs connections among the internal extensions and between the internal extensions and the outside network.)

■ **Primary Rate Interface (PRI)**—Also referred to as Primary Rate Access (PRA), PRI is used for business systems. It terminates on an intelligent system (e.g., a PBX, a multiplexer, an automatic call distribution system such as those with menus). There are two different PRI standards, each deployed over two twisted-pair: The North American and Japanese infrastructure uses 23B+D (T-1), and other countries use 30B+D (E-1). As with BRI, in PRI each of the B-channels is 64Kbps. With PRI, the D-channel is 64Kbps. So, 23B+D provides 23 64Kbps B-channels for information and 1 64Kbps D-channel for signaling and additional packet data. And 30B+D provides 30 64Kbps channels and 1 64Kbps D-channel.

Given today's interest in Internet access and Web surfing, as well as the availability of other high-speed options, BRI is no longer the most appropriate specification. We all want quicker download times. Most people are willing to tolerate a 5-second download of a Web page, and just 1 second can make a difference in customer loyalty. As we experience more rapid information access, our brains become somewhat synchronized to that, and we want it faster and faster and faster. Therefore, N-ISDN has seen better days, and other broadband access solutions are gaining ground. (ISDN is discussed further in Chapter 7, "Wide Area Networking.")

xDSL
The DSL family includes the following:

■ High-Bit-Rate DSL (HDSL)

■ Asymmetrical DSL (ADSL, ADSL2, ADSL2+)

■ Symmetrical (or Single-Line) DSL (SDSL)

■ Symmetric High-Bit-Rate DSL (SHDSL)

■ Rate-Adaptive DSL (RADSL)

■ Very-High-Bit-Rate DSL (VDSL, VDSL2)

Some of the members of the DSL family are symmetrical and some are asymmetrical, and each member has other unique characteristics.

As in many other areas of telecommunications, with xDSL there is not one perfect solution. One of the main considerations with xDSL is that not every form of xDSL is available in every location from all carriers. The solution also depends on the environment and the prevailing conditions. For example, the amount of bandwidth needed at the endpoint of a network—and therefore the appropriate DSL family member—is determined by the applications in use. If the goal is to surf the Web, you want to be able to download quickly in one direction, but you need only a small channel on the return path to handle mouse clicks. In this case, you can get by with an asymmetrical service. On the other hand, if you're working from home, and you want to transfer images or other files, or if you want to engage in videoconferencing, you need substantial bandwidth in the upstream direction as well as the downstream direction; in this case, you need a symmetrical service.

The following sections briefly describe each of these DSL family members, and Chapter 12 covers xDSL in more detail.

HDSL Carriers use HDSL to provision T-1 or E-1 capacities because HDSL deployment costs less than other alternatives when you need to think about customers who are otherwise outside the permitted loop lengths. HDSL can be deployed over a distance of about 2.2 miles (3.6 km). HDSL is deployed over two twisted-pairs, and it affords equal bandwidth in both directions (i.e., it is symmetrical).

HDSL is deployed as two twisted-pairs, but some homes have only a single pair of wires running through the walls. Therefore, a form of HDSL called HDSL2 (for two-pair) has been standardized for consumer/residential action. HDSL2 provides symmetrical capacities of up to 1.5Mbps or 2Mbps over a single twisted-pair.

ADSL ADSL is an asymmetrical service deployed over one twisted-pair. With ADSL, the majority of bandwidth is devoted to the downstream direction, from the network to the user, with a small return path that is generally sufficient to enable telephony or simple commands. ADSL is limited to a distance of about 3.5 miles (5.5 km) from the exchange point. With ADSL, the greater the distance, the lower the data rate; the shorter the distance, the better the throughput. New developments allow the distance to be extended because remote terminals can be placed closer to the customer.

There are two main ADSL standards: ADSL and ADSL2. The vast majority of the ADSL that is currently deployed and available is ADSL. ADSL supports up to 7Mbps downstream and up to 800Kbps upstream. This type of bandwidth is sufficient to provide good Web surfing, to carry a low grade of entertainment video, and to conduct upstream activities that don't command a great deal of bandwidth. However, ADSL is not sufficient for things such as digital TV or interactive services. For these activities, ADSL2, which was ratified in 2002, is preferred. ADSL2 supports up to 8Mbps downstream and up to 1Mbps upstream. An additional enhancement, known as ADSL2+, can support up to 24Mbps downstream and up to 1Mbps upstream.

SDSL   SDSL is a symmetrical service that has a maximum loop length of 3.5 miles (5.5 km) and is deployed as a single twisted-pair. It is a good solution in businesses, residences, small offices, and home offices, and for remote access into corporate facilities. You can deploy variable capacities for SDSL, in multiples of 64Kbps, up to a maximum of 2Mbps in each direction.

SHDSL   SHDSL, the standardized version of SDSL, is a symmetric service that supports up to 5.6Mbps in both the downstream and upstream directions.

RADSL   RADSL has a maximum loop length of 3.5 miles (5.5 km) and is deployed as a single twisted-pair. It adapts the data rate dynamically, based on any changes occurring in the line conditions and on the loop length. With RADSL, the rates can vary widely, from 600Kbps to 7Mbps downstream and from 128Kbps to 1Mbps upstream. RADSL can be configured to be a symmetrical or an asymmetrical service.

VDSL   VDSL provides a maximum span of about 1 mile (1.5 km) over a single twisted-pair. Over this distance, you can get a rate of up to 13Mbps downstream. But if you shorten the distance to 1,000 feet (300 m), you can get up to 55Mbps downstream and up to 15Mbps upstream, which is enough capacity to facilitate delivery of several HDTV channels as well as Internet access and VoIP. With VDSL2 you can get up to 100Mbps both downstream and upstream, albeit over very short distances.

Advantages and Disadvantages of Twisted-Pair

Twisted-pair has several key advantages:

- ■ **High availability**—More than 1 billion telephone subscriber lines based on twisted-pair have been deployed, and because it's already in the ground, the telcos will use it. Some say that the telcos are trapped in their copper cages; rather than build an infrastructure truly designed for tomorrow's applications, they hang on to protecting their existing investment. It is a huge investment: More than US$250 billion in terms of book value is associated with the twisted-pair deployed worldwide. This can be construed as both an advantage and a disadvantage.

- **Low cost of installation on premises**—The cost of installing twisted-pair on premises is very low.
- **Low cost for local moves, adds, and changes in places**—An individual can simply pull out the twisted-pair terminating on a modular plug and replace it in another jack in the enterprise, without requiring the intervention of a technician. Of course, this assumes that the wiring is already in place; otherwise, there is the additional cost of a new installation.

Twisted-pair has the following disadvantages:

- **Limited frequency spectrum**—The total usable frequency spectrum of twisted-pair copper cable is about 1MHz.
- **Limited data rates**—The longer a signal has to travel over twisted-pair, the lower the data rate. At 30 feet (100 m), twisted-pair can carry 100Mbps, but at 3.5 miles (5.5 km), the data rate drops to 2Mbps or less.
- **Short distances required between repeaters**—More components need to be maintained, and those components are places where trouble can arise, which leads to higher long-term operational costs.
- **High error rate**—Twisted-pair is highly susceptibility to signal interference such as EMI and RFI.

Although twisted-pair has been deployed widely and adapted to some new applications, better media are available to meet the demands of the broadband world.

Coaxial Cable

The second transmission medium to be introduced was coaxial cable (often called *coax*), which began being deployed in telephony networks around the mid-1920s. Figure 2.2 shows the components of coax. In the center of a coaxial cable is a copper wire that acts as the conductor, where the information travels. The copper wire in coax is thicker than that in twisted-pair, and it is also unaffected by surrounding wires that contribute to EMI, so it can provide a higher transmission rate than twisted-pair. The center conductor is surrounded by plastic insulation, which helps filter out extraneous interference. The insulation is covered by the return path, which is usually braided-copper shielding or aluminum foil–type covering. Outer jackets form a protective covering for coax; the number and type of outer jackets depend on the intended use of the cable (e.g., whether the cable is meant to be strung in the air or underground, whether rodent protection is required).

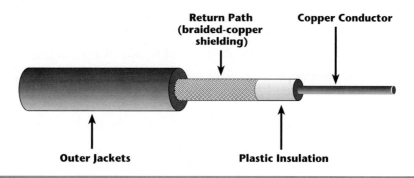

Figure 2.2 Coaxial cable

Characteristics of Coaxial Cable

Coax affords a great deal more frequency spectrum than does twisted-pair. Traditional coaxial cable television networks generally support 370MHz. Newer deployments, such as hybrid fiber coax (HFC) architectures, support 750MHz or 1,000MHz systems. (HFC is discussed in detail in Chapter 12.) Therefore, coax provides from 370 to 1,000 times more capacity than single twisted-pair. With this additional capacity, you can carve out individual channels, which makes coax a broadband facility. Multiplexing techniques can be applied to coax to derive multiple channels. Coax offers slightly better performance than twisted-pair because the metallic shielding protects the center conductor from outside interferences; hence the performance of coax is on the order of 10^{-9} (i.e., 1 in 1 billion) bps received in error. Amplifiers need to be spaced every 1.5 miles (2.5 km), which is another improvement over twisted-pair, but it still means a substantial number of amplifiers must be deployed throughout the network.

Cable TV operators, like the telephony network providers, have been prevalent users of coax, but in the past decade, they have been reengineering their backbone networks so that they are fiber based, thereby eliminating many amplifiers and subsequently improving performance. Remember from Chapter 1, "Telecommunications Technology Fundamentals," that amplifiers accumulate noise over a distance. In a large franchise area for a cable TV operator, toward the outer fringes, greater noise accumulates and a lower service level is provided there than to some of the users upstream. By reengineering their backbones to be fiber based, cable providers can also limit how many amplifiers have to be deployed, along with reaping other advantages, such as high bandwidth, immunity to electrical interference, and improved security.

One problem with coax has to do with the deployment architecture. Coaxial cable and HFC architectures are deployed in bus topologies. In a bus topology, the

bandwidth is shared, which means congestion levels increase as more users in the neighborhood avail themselves of these features and services. A bus topology also presents security risks. It's sort of like going back to the party line in telephony. You do not have your own dedicated twisted-pair that's yours and only yours. Instead, several channels devoted to voice telephony are shared by everyone in the neighborhood, which makes encryption important. Also, there are some problems with noise in bus topologies. The points where the coax connects into set-top boxes or cable-ready TV sets tend to collect noise, so the cable tends to pick up extraneous noise from vacuum cleaners or hair dryers or passing motorcycles. Thus, if every household on the network is running a hair dryer at 6:30 AM, the upstream paths are subjected to this noise, resulting in some performance degradation. (Bus topologies are discussed in more detail in Chapter 6, "Local Area Networking.")

Applications of Coaxial Cable

In the mid-1920s, coax was applied to telephony networks as interoffice trunks. Rather than having to add more copper cable bundles with 1,500 or 3,000 pairs of copper wires in them, it was possible to replace those big cables (which are very difficult to install cost-effectively) with a much smaller coaxial cable.

The next major use of coax in telecommunications occurred in the 1950s, when it was deployed as submarine cable to carry international traffic. It was then introduced into the data-processing realm in the mid- to late 1960s. Early computer architectures required coax as the media type from the terminal to the host. LANs were predominantly based on coax from 1980 to about 1987.

Coax has been used in cable TV and in the local loop, in the form of HFC architectures. HFC brings fiber as close as possible to the neighborhood; then on a neighborhood node, it terminates that fiber, and from that node it fans the coax out to the home service by that particular node. (This is described in detail in Chapter 12.)

Advantages and Disadvantages of Coaxial Cable

The advantages of coax include the following:

- **Broadband system**—Coax has a sufficient frequency range to support multiple channels, which allows for much greater throughput.
- **Greater channel capacity**—Each of the multiple channels offers substantial capacity. The capacity depends on where you are in the world. In the North American system, each channel in the cable TV system is 6MHz wide, according to the National Television Systems Committee (NTSC) standard. In Europe, with the Phase Alternate Line (PAL) standard, the channels are 8MHz wide. Within one of these channels, you can provision high-speed

Internet access—that's how cable modems operate. But that one channel is now being shared by everyone using that coax from that neighborhood node, which can range from 200 to 2,000 homes.

■ **Greater bandwidth**—Compared to twisted-pair, coax provides greater bandwidth systemwide, and it also offers greater bandwidth for each channel. Because it has greater bandwidth per channel, it supports a mixed range of services. Voice, data, and even video and multimedia can benefit from the enhanced capacity.

■ **Lower error rates**—Because the inner conductor is in a Faraday shield, noise immunity is improved, and coax has lower error rates and therefore slightly better performance than twisted-pair. The error rate is generally 10^{-9} (i.e., 1 in 1 billion) bps.

■ **Greater spacing between amplifiers**—Coax's cable shielding reduces noise and crosstalk, which means amplifiers can be spaced farther apart than with twisted-pair.

The main disadvantages of coax are as follows:

■ **Problems with the deployment architecture**—The bus topology in which coax is deployed is susceptible to congestion, noise, and security risks.

■ **Bidirectional upgrade required**—In countries that have a history of cable TV, the cable systems were designed for broadcasting, not for interactive communications. Before they can offer to the subscriber any form of two-way services, those networks have to be upgraded to bidirectional systems.

■ **Great noise**—The return path has some noise problems, and the end equipment requires added intelligence to take care of error control.

■ **High installation costs**—Installation costs in the local environment are high.

■ **Susceptible to damage from lightning strikes**—Coax may be damaged by lightning strikes. People who live in an area with a lot of lightning strikes must be wary because if that lightning is conducted by a coax, it could very well fry the equipment at the end of it.

■ Microwave

Microwave was used during World War II in military applications, and when it was successful in that environment, it was introduced into commercial communications. Microwave was deployed in the PSTN as a replacement for coaxial cable in the late 1940s.

As mentioned earlier, twisted-pair and coax both face limitations because of the frequency spectrum and the manner in which they are deployed. But microwave promises to have a much brighter future than twisted-pair or coax. Many locations cannot be cost-effectively cabled by using wires (e.g., the Sahara, the Amazon, places where buildings are on mountaintops, villages separated by valleys), and this is where microwave can shine. In addition, the microwave spectrum is the workhorse of the wireless world: The vast majority of wireless broadband solutions operate in the microwave spectrum.

Note that the discussion of microwave in this chapter focuses on its traditional application in carrier and enterprise private networks, but there are indeed many more systems and applications to discuss, and those are covered at length in Chapter 13, "Wireless Communications Basics," and Chapter 16, "Emerging Wireless Applications." This chapter focuses on the general characteristics of microwave and its use in traditional carrier backbones and enterprise private networks.

Characteristics of Microwave

Microwave is defined as falling in the 1GHz to 100GHz frequency band. But systems today do not operate across this full range of frequencies. In fact, current microwave systems largely operate up to the 50GHz range. At the 60GHz level, we encounter the *oxygen layer*, where the microwave is absorbed by the surrounding oxygen, and the higher frequencies are severely affected by fog. However, we are now producing systems called *virtual fiber* that operate in the 70GHz to 95GHz range at very short distances. Given the growing demand for wireless access to all forms of media, we can expect to see many developments in coming years that take advantage of the high-bandwidth properties of the higher frequency bands.

The amount of bandwidth that you can realize out of the very large microwave spectrum is often limited by regulations as much as by technology. Before you can deploy a microwave system outside your own private campus, you have to be licensed to operate that system in all environments. In your own private territory, you can use unlicensed bands, but if you want to cross the public domain using licensed spectrum, you must first be granted approval by your spectrum management agency to operate within a given frequency allocation.

Some communities are very concerned about the potential health hazards of microwave and create legislation or council laws that prohibit placement of such systems. In addition, some communities are very sensitive to the unsightliness of towers and argue that the value of real estate will drop if they are constructed. Therefore, several companies specialize in building camouflaged towers. When you see a tall tree, a church steeple, a light post, or a chimney, it could be a wireless tower disguised to protect your aesthetic balance.

Microwave is generally allocated in chunks of 30MHz to 45MHz channels, so it makes available a substantial amount of bandwidth to end users and operators of telecommunications networks.

Microwave is subject to the uncertainties of the physical environment. Metals in the area, precipitation, fog, rainfall, and a number of other factors can cause reflections and therefore degradations and echoes. The higher (in elevation) we move away from land-based systems, the better the performance because there is less intrusion from other land-based systems, such as television, radio, and police and military systems.

Repeater spacing with microwave varies depending on the frequency of transmission. Remember from Chapter 1 that lower frequencies can travel farther than higher frequencies before they attenuate. Higher frequencies lose power more rapidly. In microwave systems that operate in the 2GHz, 4GHz, and 6GHz bands, towers can be separated by 45 miles (72 km). In the higher-frequency allocations, such as 18GHz, 23GHz, and 45GHz, the spacing needs to be much shorter, in the range of 1 to 5 miles (1.6 to 8 km). This is an important issue in network design and, depending on the scope over which you want to deploy these facilities, it can have a significant impact on the investment required.

Another important design criterion is that microwave requires line of sight and is a highly directional beam. Microwave requires a clear, unobstructed view, and it can't move through any obstacles, even things you wouldn't think would be obstacles, such as leaves on a tree. Technologies that depend on line of sight may work brilliantly in areas that have the appropriate terrain and climate, and they may not perform very well where there are many obstacles or where there is a lot of precipitation. Furthermore, line of sight is restricted by the curvature of the earth, which interrupts the line of sight at about 90 miles (144 km). However, new spectrum utilization techniques such as Orthogonal Frequency Division Multiplexing (OFDM) permit non-line-of-sight operation, greatly expanding the use of microwave. (Chapter 15 discusses OFDM in detail.)

The impact of precipitation on microwave can be great. Microwave beams are small, and as you go up into the higher bands, the waveforms get smaller and smaller. Pretty soon, they're smaller than a raindrop, and they can be absorbed by a raindrop and then scattered in a million directions. Therefore, in wet atmospheric conditions, there is a great potential for problems with microwave. As a result, practicing network diversity—using both terrestrial and nonterrestrial alternatives—is critical.

Traditional Applications of Microwave

One application associated with microwave is to replace the use of leased lines in a private network. Figure 2.3 shows a simple voice environment that initially made

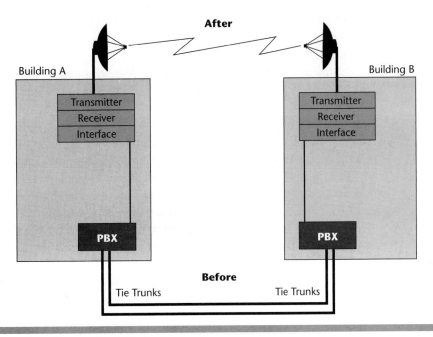

Figure 2.3 Connecting PBXs by using microwave

use of dedicated leased lines, also known as tie trunks, to link two PBXs in two different buildings across town from one another. Because these tie trunks were billed on a monthly basis and were mileage sensitive, they were going to be a cost factor forever. Therefore, a digital microwave system was purchased to replace the tie trunks. This system provides capacity between the buildings and does away with the monthly cost of the leased lines. This setup is commonly used by multinode or multilocation customers (e.g., a health care facility with clinics and hospitals scattered throughout a state or territory, a university with multiple campuses, a retail location with multiple branches, a bank with multiple branches).

Another key application of microwave is *bypassing*, which can be interpreted in multiple ways. Initially, this technique was used to bypass the local telecommunications company. With the introduction of competition in the long-distance marketplace, end users in the United States initially had choices about who would be their primary long-distance carrier (i.e., interexchange carrier). But to get to that carrier to transport the long-distance portion of the call, we still needed to get special local access trunks that led through the local operator to the competing interexchange provider. That meant paying an additional monthly fee for these local access trunks. In an attempt to avoid those additional costs, businesses began to bypass the local telephone company by simply putting up a digital microwave system—a microwave tower with a shot directly to the interexchange carrier's point of presence.

Bypassing can also be used to circumvent construction. Say that a pharmaceutical company on a large campus has a public thoroughfare, and across the street there's a lovely park where the employees take their lunch and otherwise relax during the day. No one foresaw the fame and fortune the company would achieve with its latest migraine medicine, so it had not planned to build another facility to house the 300 people it now needed to add. Nobody ever provisioned conduit leading to that park across the street. The cost and time to get permission to break ground, lay conduit, pull cable, repave, and relandscape would be cost- and time-prohibitive. To bypass that entire operation, microwave could be used between the main campus and the remote park (see Figure 2.4). This is essentially the same strategy that wireless local loop is pursuing. Rather than take the time and money to build a wireline facility, you can do it much more rapidly and much more cost-effectively on a wireless basis.

Whereas provisioning twisted-pair or coaxial cable costs roughly US$1,000 to US$1,500 per subscriber and requires a 12- to 18-month deployment time, wireless costs US$300 to US$800 per subscriber and requires 3 to 6 months of deployment time. Something could always delay the process (e.g., contractual problems with

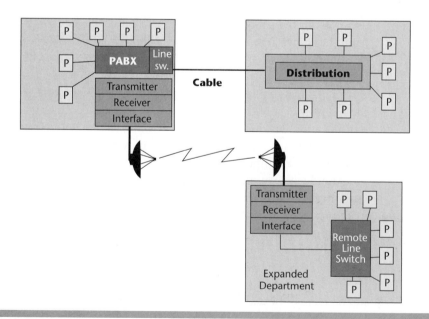

Figure 2.4 A bypassing construction that uses microwave

the building developer), but, generally, you can deploy a microwave system much more rapidly and at a much lower price point. Therefore, these systems are especially popular in parts of the world where there is not already a local loop infrastructure. In addition, there are several unlicensed bands in the microwave spectrum, which means anyone can use them without needing to apply for and receive a license from the spectrum management agency. This includes the popular 2.4GHz and 5GHz bands used for Wi-Fi, the popular wireless LAN (WLAN) technology used in thousands of "hot spots" around the globe. This makes it even easier for a service provider or an entrepreneur to quickly deploy a wireless network to serve constituents.

Another application for microwave is in the data realm. Say that in your company, the buildings that have telephone systems today are going to have LANs as well, and you want to unite the disparate LANs to create a virtual whole. You can use microwave technology as a bridge between two different LANs, to give the combined network the appearance of being one LAN (see Figure 2.5).

The main factor that inhibits or potentially slows the growth of microwave is that only so many people can be operating on the same frequencies in the same area. Therefore, a big limitation of microwave is potential congestion in key metropolitan areas.

Microwave has a disaster-recovery application as well. Because microwave is relatively inexpensive and quick to deploy, it is a good candidate for use after a disaster damages wireline media, systems, or structures.

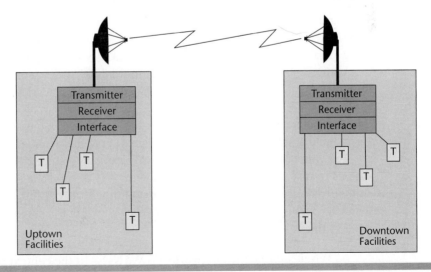

Figure 2.5 A LAN interconnect using microwave

Advantages and Disadvantages of Microwave

The advantages of microwave are as follows:

■ **Cost savings**—Using microwave is less expensive than using leased lines.

■ **Portability and reconfiguration flexibility**—You can pick up a microwave transceiver and carry it to a new building. You can't do that with cables.

■ **Substantial bandwidth**—A substantial amount of microwave bandwidth is allocated, so high-speed data, video, and multimedia can be supported.

The main disadvantages of microwave are as follows:

■ **Line-of-sight requirement**—You need to ensure that there are no obstacles between towers.

■ **Susceptibility to environmentally caused distortions**—Because the environment (e.g., heavy rainstorms) can cause distortion, you need to have backups.

■ **Regulatory licensing requirement**—The requirement for regulatory licensing means that you must have time and flexibility to deal with the spectrum agency.

■ **Potential environmental restrictions**—Some communities do not allow microwave towers or require that they be camouflaged.

The New Era of Microwave: Wireless Broadband

As mentioned earlier, the initial application of microwave was focused on the replacement of twisted-pair and coaxial cables used in the PSTN. In fact, MCI first utilized microwave to provide voice and data service, introducing the first major competitive action against AT&T, which until 1984 had a monopoly on local and long-distance telephone service in the United States. The 1984 divestiture ruling formally sanctioned competition in the long-distance arena. Microwave offered great cost efficiencies because no cables had to be laid, allowing a new entrant to easily build a network of long-haul trunks to serve busy routes.

The role of microwave has been greatly expanded since the 1980s, with applications in just about every network domain. It is beyond the scope of this discussion of basic characteristics to go into detail on all the options available today, but detailed coverage is provided in Part IV. The following is a summary of the wireless systems that rely on microwave:

■ **Wireless wide area networks (WWANs)**—In the context of WWANs, microwave is used to support 2G cellular PCS services (TDMA, GSM, CDMA), 2.5G enhanced data services (GPRS, HSCSD, EDGE), 3G high-speed data and multimedia services (W-CDMA, UMTS, CDMA2000, TD-SCDMA), 3.5G IP backbones (HSDPA, HSUPA, HSOPA), and 4G mobile broadband systems (using OFDM and MIMO technologies). WWANs are discussed further in Chapter 14, "Wireless WANs."

- **Wireless metropolitan area networks (WMANs)**—When it comes to WMANs, the microwave spectrum is used in support of broadband fixed wireless access (BFWA) systems, IEEE 802.16 WiMax standards, the Korean WiBro specification, ETSI's broadband radio access network (BRAN), HiperMAN and HiperAccess, Flash-OFDM, IEEE 802.20 Mobile-Fi, iBurst Personal Broadband System, IEEE 802.22 Wi-TV standards, and virtual fiber or millimeter wave technology. WMANs are discussed further in Chapter 15.

- **Wireless local area networks (WLANs)**—The ever-so-popular WLANs, including the IEEE 802.11 family of protocols and ETSI HiperLAN and HiperLan2, operate in the microwave band, relying on the unlicensed bands of 2.4GHz and 5GHz. WLANs are discussed further in Chapter 15.

- **Wireless personal area networks (WPANs)**—WPAN standards make use of unlicensed portions of the microwave spectrum, including IEEE 802.15.1 Bluetooth, IEEE 802.15.3 WiMedia, Ultra-Wideband (UWB), IEEE 802.15.4 ZigBee, and some applications of RFID. WPANs are discussed further in Chapter 15.

As you can see, microwave is truly the workhorse of the wireless world. Part IV of this book therefore dedicates much attention to its variations.

Satellite

In May 1946, Project RAND released *Preliminary Design of an Experimental World-Circling Spaceship*, which stated, "A satellite vehicle with appropriate instrumentation can be expected to be one of the most potent scientific tools of the Twentieth Century. The achievement of a satellite craft would produce repercussions comparable to the explosion of the atomic bomb." In 1947, Arthur C. Clarke (well known for his science fiction, particularly *2001: A Space Odyssey*) presented a paper to the scientific community in which he suggested that if we explored orbits in higher elevations above the earth, we might achieve an orbit at which a satellite would be able to serve as a communications broadcast tool. Until that point, we were beginning early explorations of satellites, but they were what we today would call low-earth-orbit satellites, which means they were at relatively low altitudes over the earth and revolved around the earth much faster than the earth rotates on its own axis. Clarke theorized that if we sent a satellite into a higher orbit, it would encounter a geosynchronous orbit, meaning that the satellite would rotate around the earth at exactly the same rate at which the earth rotates on its axis; the orbiting device would appear to hang stationary over a given point on earth. Clarke's hypotheses were supported and thus began the development of the communications sector for the space industry.

The first artificial satellite was Sputnik 1, launched by the Soviet Union on October 4, 1957. In the United States, NASA launched the first experimental communications satellite in 1963. The first commercial communications satellite was launched two years later, so 1965 marked the beginning of the use of satellite communications to support public telephony as well as television, particularly international television. Since then, large numbers of satellites have been launched. At this point, there are more than 250 communications-based satellites in space, as well as hundreds of other specialized satellites used for meteorological purposes, defense, remote sensing, geological exploration, and so on, for a total of more than 700 satellites orbiting the earth. And it seems that many more satellites will be launched in the future.

There are still approximately 3 billion people on the planet who are not served by even basic communications services, and we can't possibly deploy enough wireline facilities in a short enough time frame to equalize the situation worldwide. Therefore, satellites are very important in bringing infrastructure into areas of the world that have previously not enjoyed that luxury.

In descriptions of satellite services, three abbreviations relate to the applications that are supported:

- **FSS**—*Fixed satellite services*, the conventional fixed services, are offered in both the C-band and the Ku-band allocations.

- **BSS**—*Broadcast satellite services* include standard television and direct broadcast. These largely operate in the Ku-band, at 18GHz. Because the general application of television so far has been one way, 18GHz shows just the downlink frequency allocation. As we begin to move toward interactive TV, we'll start to see the use of two different bands in BSS.

- **MSS**—*Mobile satellite services* accommodate mobility (i.e., mobile users). They make use of either Ka-band or L-band satellites.

A satellite's *footprint* refers to the area of earth that the satellite's beams cover. Much of the progress in satellite developments has been in new generations of antennas that can provide more spot beams that can deliver higher-quality service to targeted areas rather than simply one big beam, with which users at the fringes of the footprint begin to see a degradation in service.

Another thing that's very important about and unique to satellites is the broadcast property. After you send data uplink to a satellite, it comes back downlink over the entire footprint. So a satellite can achieve point-to-multipoint communications very cost-effectively. This had a dramatic impact on the media business. Consider a big newspaper that has seven regional printing presses within the United States. Before satellites, the paper would have had to send a separate transmission to each of those printing locations so local ads could be inserted and such, but with a satellite, you beam it up once, and when it comes down, it rains over the entire footprint of the United States. If each of the printing presses has a satellite station properly focused on the satellite and knows what frequency to receive on, it will get the information instantaneously.

An interesting design parameter associated with satellites is that as the number of locations increases, the economic benefit of using satellites increases. With leased lines, the more locations and the greater the distances between them, the more expensive the network. But when using satellite technology, the more locations that are sharing the hub station and transponder, the less expensive the network becomes for all concerned. Thus, satellite technology presents a very attractive networking solution for many customers.

Remember that there are 700 or so satellites in space. On top of those 700 satellites, there are about 250,000 pieces of debris that have been cataloged by the space agencies. Furthermore, we are seeing an increase in comet and solar flare activity. A solar flare can decommission a satellite in one pulse, and a little speck of comet dust can put a baseball-sized crater into a solar panel. Because of these types of hazards, strategies must be put in place to protect existing satellites.

We often don't recognize what great capabilities satellite can provide. But if we set our sights on more than just the planet earth and realize that there is a great frontier to explore, we realize that although fiber may be the best solution on the planet, when we want to advance in space, satellite communication is extremely important.

Frequency Allocations of Satellite

The frequency spectrum in which most satellites operate is the microwave frequency spectrum. (GPS runs at VHF frequencies and is a very important application.) Therefore, microwave and satellite signals are really the same thing. The difference is that with satellite, the repeaters for augmenting the signals are placed on platforms that reside in high orbit rather than on terrestrial towers. Of course, this means that the power levels associated with satellite communications are greater than those of terrestrial microwave networks. The actual power required depends on the orbit the satellite operates in (geosynchronous-orbit satellites require the most power, and low-earth-orbit satellites require the least), as well as the size of the dish on the ground. If the satellite has a lot of power, you don't need as big a dish on the ground. This is particularly important for satellite TV, where the dish size should be 2 feet (0.6 m) or smaller. A number of factors are involved in the bandwidth availability of satellite: what spectrum the regulatory agencies have allocated for use within the nation, the portion of the frequency spectrum in which you're actually operating, and the number of transponders you have on the satellite. The *transponder* is the key communications component in satellite. It accepts the signal coming from the earth station and then shifts that signal to another frequency. When the signal is on the new frequency, it is amplified and rebroadcast downlink.

In satellite communications, the frequency allocations always specify two different bands: One is used for the uplink from earth station to satellite and one for the downlink from satellite to earth station. Many different bands are specified in the various satellite standards, but the most dominant frequency bands used for communications are C-band, Ku-band, Ka-band, and L-band.

C-Band

C-band transmits uplink around the 6GHz range and downlink around the 4GHz range. The advantage of C-band, as compared to other bands, is that because it operates in the lower frequency bands, it is fairly tolerant of adverse weather conditions. It has larger waveforms, so it doesn't suffer as much disturbance as do smaller waveforms in the presence of precipitation, for instance.

The disadvantage of C-band is that its allocation of frequencies is also shared by terrestrial systems. So selecting sites can take time because you have to contend with what your neighbors have installed and are operating. Licensing can take time, as well.

Ku-Band

Ku-band was introduced in the early 1980s, and it revolutionized how we use satellite communications. First, it operates on the uplink at around 14GHz and on the downlink at around 11GHz. The key advantage of Ku-band is that this frequency band allocation is usually reserved specifically for satellite use, so there are no conflicts from terrestrial systems. Therefore, site selection and licensing can take place much more rapidly. Second, because it doesn't interfere with terrestrial systems, it offers portability. Therefore, a Ku-band dish can be placed on top of a news van or inside a briefcase, and a news reporter can go to a story as it is breaking to broadcast it live and without conflict from surrounding systems.

The disadvantage of Ku-band is that it is a slightly higher frequency allocation than C-band, so it can experience distortions under bad climactic conditions (e.g., humidity, fog, rain).

Ka-Band

The new generation of satellite—the broadband satellites—operates in the Ka-band. The key advantage of Ka-band is that it offers a wide frequency band: about 30GHz uplink and about 20GHz downlink. The difference between 20GHz and 30GHz for Ka-band is much greater than the difference between 4GHz and 6GHz for C-band. This expanded bandwidth means that Ka-band satellites are better prepared than satellites operating at other bands to accommodate telemedicine, tele-education, telesurveillance, and networked interactive games.

A disadvantage of Ka-band is that it's even higher in the frequency band than the other bands, so rain fade (i.e., degradation of signal because of rain) can be a more severe issue. Thus, more intelligent technologies have to be embedded at the terminal points to cost-effectively deal with error detection and correction.

L-Band

L-band operates in the 390MHz to 1,550MHz range, supporting various mobile and fixed applications. Because L-band operates in the lower frequencies, L-band systems are more tolerant of adverse weather conditions than are other systems. It is largely used to support very-small-aperture terminal (VSAT) networks and mobile communications, including handheld terminals (such as PDAs), vehicular devices, and maritime applications.

> ### Shrinking Earth Stations
>
> We've progressed very quickly in satellite history. The first earth station that accompanied the Early Bird satellite in 1965 had a massive facility. The dome on the building was 18 stories high, the antenna weighed 380 tons, and the entire building had liquid helium running through it to keep it cool. This was not something an end user could wheel into a parking lot or place on top of a building. But we have continued to shrink the sizes of earth stations, and today many businesses use VSATs, in which the dish diameter is 2 feet (0.6 m) or less. You can literally hang a VSAT outside your window and have a network up and running within several hours (assuming that you have your frequency bands allocated and licensed).

Satellite Network Segments

Satellite networks have three major segments:

- **Space segment**—The space segment is the actual design of the satellite and the orbit in which it operates. Most satellites have one of two designs: a barrel-shaped satellite, normally used to accommodate standard communications, or a satellite with a very wide wingspan, generally used for television.

Satellites are launched into specific orbits to cover the parts of the earth for which coverage is desired.

■ **Control segment**—The control segment defines the frequency spectrum over which satellites operate and the types of signaling techniques used between the ground station and the satellite to control those communications.

■ **Ground segment**—The ground segment is the earth station—the antenna designs and the access techniques used to enable multiple conversations to share the links up to the satellite. The ground segment of satellites continues to change as new technologies are introduced.

Satellite Orbits

Another important factor that affects the use and application of satellites is the orbits in which they operate. As shown in Figure 2.6, there are three major orbits: geosynchronous orbit (GEO), middle earth orbit (MEO), and low earth orbit (LEO). The majority of communications satellites in use are GEOs.

GEO Satellites

A GEO satellite is launched to 22,300 miles (36,000 km) above the equator. A signal from such a satellite must travel quite a distance; as a result, there is a delay of 0.25 seconds in each direction, so from the time you say, "Hello, how are you?" to the time that you hear the person's response, "Fine," there is a 0.5-second delay, which results in somewhat of a stilted conversation. Many data applications, espe-

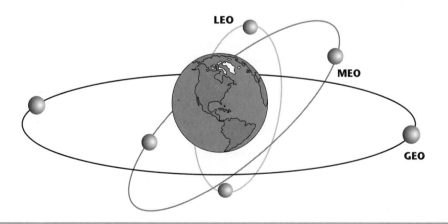

Figure 2.6 Satellite orbits

cially those that involve entertainment, such as games, cannot perform with a delay this great.

GEO satellites have the benefit of providing the largest footprint of the satellite types. Just three GEO satellites can cover the entire world, but the delay factor in getting to that orbit inhibits its use with the continuously growing range of real-time applications that are very sensitive to delay.

The fact that it is launched at such a high orbit also means that a GEO satellite requires the most power of all the satellite systems. And because the trend in satellites has been to deliver more data as well as interactive services (which are very delay sensitive) directly to the user, more satellites are now being launched at the lower orbits.

We are beginning to see data rates of up to 155Mbps with GEO systems, particularly in the Ka-band. That data rate is not commonly available today, but it is feasible with the new generation of broadband satellites. Going to higher data rates, however, necessitates larger antennas, more so for GEO systems than for satellites in other orbits. Parabolic satellite antennas 33 feet (10 m) in diameter can now be built, and it should soon be possible to extend them to 66 feet (20 m) or 100 feet (30 m).

The main applications of GEO systems are one-way broadcast, VSAT systems, and point-to-multipoint links. There are no delay factors to worry about with one-way broadcasts from GEO systems. As a result, international television is largely distributed over these satellite networks today.

VSATs   Business enterprises use VSAT networks as a means of private networking, essentially setting up point-to-point links or connections between two locales. A VSAT station is so compact that it can be put outside a window in an office environment. VSATs are commonly deployed to reduce the costs associated with leased lines, and depending on how large the network is, they can reduce those costs by as much as 50%. Most users of VSATs are enterprises that have 100 or more nodes or locations (e.g., banks that have many branches, gas stations that have many locations, convenience stores). VSATs elegantly and economically help these types of enterprises do things such as transport information relevant to a sale made from a remote location to a central point, remotely process information, and process reservations and transactions. (See Figure 2.7.)

Another use for VSATs is business video. Before about 1994, the only way to do point-to-multipoint video was by satellite. No terrestrial conference bridges would allow it. So, if you wanted to have a CEO provide a state-of-the-company address to all employees at different locations, the easiest way to get that footprint was by satellite.

Because you can set up a VSAT system very quickly, VSATs offer valuable help in the event of a major disaster, when land-based facilities are disabled.

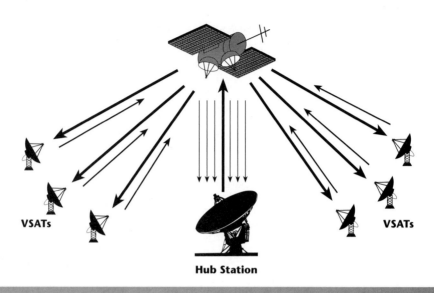

VSATs

VSATs

Hub Station

Figure 2.7 A VSAT system

VSATs are also useful in vehicle-tracking systems, to communicate with drivers, arrange for payload drop-offs and pickups, and handle standard messaging without disrupting drivers' transportation schedules.

An emerging application for VSAT is broadband Internet access. Products such as Hughes DIRECWAY (www.hns.com) provide Internet downloads at up to 1Mbps. Similarly, intranets (i.e., site-to-site connections between company locations) can be based on VSATs.

The following are the key advantages of VSATs:

■ **Easy access to remote locations**—Where it would be difficult to facilitate a wireline arrangement, such as on an oil rig, a VSAT can easily be set up.

■ **Rapid deployment**—A VSAT system can be installed in two to four hours (as long as you have already secured the license to operate within an allocated spectrum).

■ **Scalable**—A VSAT system can grow to facilitate more bandwidth with the addition of more interfaces.

■ **Platform agnostic**—A VSAT can support a variety of data networking protocols.

■ **Insensitive to distance-related transmission costs**—The transmission cost is the same whether your locations are 100 miles (150 km) apart or 3,000 miles (5,000 km) apart. As long as the locations are within the footprint of the satellite, the costs are distance insensitive. (This does not necessarily translate to distance-insensitive pricing.)

- **Cost reductions via shared-hub facilities**—The more you share the system, the more your costs are reduced.

- **Flexible network configuration**—You can be flexible with your network configurations. As with a microwave system, you can pick it up and move it.

Disadvantages of VSATs include the following:

- **Transmission quality subject to weather conditions**—Stormy weather can cause disruptions. Most large users of VSAT networks have some leased lines available to use as backup when disruptions occur.

- **Potentially high startup costs for small installations**—A small company may face a high startup cost if it does not have many nodes. (If VSAT is the only available recourse—if there is no way to communicate without it—then the installation cost is a moot point.)

MEO Satellites

MEO satellites orbit at an elevation of about 6,200 to 9,400 miles (10,000 to 15,000 km). MEO satellites are closer to the earth than GEO satellites, so they move across the sky much more rapidly—in about one to two hours. As a result, to get global coverage, you need more satellites (about five times more) than with GEO systems. But because the altitude is lower, the delay is also reduced, so instead of a 0.5-second delay, you see a 0.1-second delay.

The main applications for MEOs are in regional networks, to support mobile voice and low-speed data, in the range of 9.6Kbps to 38Kbps. The companies that use MEOs tend to have their movement within a region rather than over the entire globe, so they want a larger footprint over, for example, the Asia-Pacific region, to support mobility of mainly voice communications.

Unusable Satellite Orbiting Altitudes

The orbiting altitudes between about 1,000 miles and 6,200 miles (about 1,600 km and 10,000 km) cannot be used for satellites because the Van Allen radiation belts act negatively on satellites. The Van Allen belts are an area of charged particles (resulting from cosmic rays) above the earth trapped by the earth's magnetic field.

LEO Satellites

LEOs are a lot like cellular networks, except that in the case of LEOs, the cells as well as the users are moving. Because LEOs are in such low orbits, they greatly reduce the transit times, so the delays are comparable to what you'd experience on the PSTN, and therefore delay-sensitive applications can survive. Their low orbits also mean that power consumption is much lower than with a higher-orbiting satellite, so you can direct their transmissions into a user's handheld. Also, LEOs offer greatly increased network capacity overall on a global basis.

LEOs orbit at about 400 to 1,000 miles (640 to 1,600 km). LEOs can be used with smaller terminals than can the other satellites because they are much closer to the earth (40 times closer). But, again, because they are closer, you need many more LEOs than other satellites to get the same coverage (about 20 times more LEOs than GEOs and 5 times more LEOs than MEOs). A user must always be able to see at least one LEO satellite that is well clear of the horizon.

As mentioned earlier, the very first satellites rotated around the earth so fast that we couldn't use them for communications. But LEO satellite platforms include switching, so as a LEO satellite begins to go out of view, a call is switched—that is, handed over—to the next satellite coming in. This works very much like the cellular system, where a caller is handed off to different frequencies during a conversation while transiting between cells. Of course, a benefit of being lower in the sky means that the delay with LEOs is reduced—to only about 0.05 seconds—and this makes LEOs very appealing for interactive services.

The key applications for LEOs are support for mobile voice, low-speed data, and high-speed data. There are three categories of LEOs, and each category is optimized for certain applications:

■ **Little LEOs**—Little LEOs offer 2.4Kbps to 300Kbps and operate in the 800MHz range. They are ideal for delivering messaging, paging, and vehicle location services.

■ **Big LEOs**—Big LEOs offer 2.4Kbps to 9.6Kbps and operate in the 2GHz range. They have rather low data rates and are largely designed to provide voice services to areas that aren't currently served by any form of terrestrial or cellular architecture.

■ **Broadband LEOs**—Broadband LEOs offer 16Kbps to 155Mbps. They operate in the Ka-band, at 20GHz to 30GHz, and they support data and multimedia files at up to 155Mbps.

Applications of Satellite

The traditional applications for satellites have been to serve remote areas where terrestrial facilities were not available; to provide the capability for point-to-multipoint communications for cost-efficiencies; to provide disaster-recovery support; to provide remote monitoring and control; to facilitate two-way data messaging, vehicle tracking, mobile communications, and maritime and air navigation; to distribute TV, video, and multimedia; and to provide for defense communications.

Two recent applications of new consumer satellite services are automotive navigation and digital audio radio, such as the SIRIUS system, with which you can receive more than 100 radio stations throughout the footprint of the satellite. Not only do you receive the music or programming you want, but you can immediately determine who the artist is and what CD it is from, and you can even compile a customized version for yourself. By now everyone is at least aware of the benefits of automotive systems like GM's OnStar, which not only provide navigational assistance but also support vital emergency services, with the potential to make the difference between life and death.

Satellite is being used in a number of other applications. Use of satellite in Internet backbones is another emerging application because of the huge growth in traffic levels. Terrestrial facilities can't handle all this traffic alone, so we have to rely on some satellite backbones, especially to reach into places such as Africa, Antarctica, and Latin America. Additional emerging applications include Internet access, data caching, and multimedia. The farther you are from the point at which an application resides, the worse the experience you have. If we put applications on a satellite, everybody within the footprint is always only one hop away, thereby greatly reducing the latencies, or delays, encountered in ultimately drawing on the content. Again, what may make a difference here is whether it's an interactive application and what orbit that satellite is in, but this is one application that merges the ISP and satellite industries. Other emerging applications of satellites include telemedicine, distance learning, remote imaging, and weather information.

Satellites have seen a number of innovations and are facing yet more in the future. The most significant change in the coming years is that satellites will increasingly deliver information directly to the consumer rather than to a commercial data hub. This might mean that aerospace corporations become major competitors of traditional telecom carriers.

Another key innovation is phased-array antennas. A phased-array antenna consists of multiple transmitting elements, arranged in a fixed geometric array. These small, flat antennas are steered electronically, and they provide great agility and fast tracking. Phased-array antennas, as well as other new designs in antennas, are discussed in Chapter 13.

Key challenges for satellites today are related to power and mobile services. Because the small antennas now used in portable transceivers intercept only a tiny fraction of the satellite signal, satellites must have a lot of power and sensitivity; a typical solar array on a GEO satellite increased in power from 2kW to more than 10kW in just several years. Another innovation involves moving further up the frequency spectrum, to make use of extremely high frequencies (EHF). The highest-frequency satellite systems today use wavelengths comparable to the size of a raindrop. Consequently, a raindrop can act as a lens, bending the waves and distorting the signals. But these ill effects can be mitigated by using error correction techniques, by applying more power when necessary, or by using more ground terminals so data can follow diverse paths. When wavelengths are smaller than a millimeter, there are yet more obstacles. Infrared and optical beams are easily absorbed in the atmosphere. So, in the near future, they may very well be restricted to use within buildings; however, there have been some new developments in virtual fiber, which is discussed in Chapter 15.

HALEs

A slightly different orbit is being introduced: *high-altitude, long-endurance (HALE) satellites*, which the ITU also calls *high-altitude platform stations (HAPS)*. HALEs are in extremely low orbit, actually circling a city or metro area. They are about 11 miles (17.8 km) overhead, and they operate at about 47GHz, although the ITU has also designated other bands of operation, including 3G bands. The main applications are Internet access, resource monitoring, and data networking in metropolitan areas. In essence, they are aircraft that hover over a city area, providing network capacity for metropolitan area networking. Some may be dirigibles, and others may have wings and fly like conventional aircraft.

The key advantage associated with HALEs is a very moderate launch cost compared to the cost associated with traditional satellites. By applying what we are learning to do with phased-array antennas (discussed in Chapter 13) to HALEs, we can provide a wide capacity: Some 3,500 beams could enable mobile two-way communications and video distribution in an area about 300 miles (about 500 km) across.

Advantages and Disadvantages of Satellite

The advantages of satellite include the following:

- Access to remote areas
- Coverage of large geographical areas
- Insensitivity to topology
- Distance-insensitive costs
- High bandwidth

The disadvantages of satellite include the following:

- High initial cost
- Propagation delay with GEO systems

- Environmental interference problems
- Licensing requirements
- Regulatory constraints in some regions
- Danger posed by space debris, solar flare activity, and meteor showers

■ Fiber Optics

In the late 1950s and early 1960s, a number of people were working in the realm of fiber optics simultaneously. Charles Kao, who was a scientist with ITT, is often acknowledged as being one of the fathers of fiber optics. Kao theorized that if we could develop a procedure for manufacturing ultrapure, ultrathin filaments of glass, we could use them as a revolutionary new communications pipeline. Thus began the move toward researching and developing optical technology.

In 1970 came the developments that have allowed us to deploy large amounts of fiber. Corning Glassworks introduced the first development, broomsticking, a procedure for manufacturing ultrapure filaments of glass. Glass that has an inner core etched into it is melted at extremely high temperatures, and as the glass melts and drops down the tube, it begins to cool and form a strand. By the time it gets to the bottom of the tube, it is a fiber-optic thread. Being able to create the fiber cable itself solved half the equation. Because the fiber's diameter is minuscule (measured in micrometers, or microns, abbreviated μ), the light source that pulses energy on this tiny fiber also has to be minuscule. In 1970, Bell Labs completed the equation by introducing the first laser diode small enough to fit through the eye of a needle.

Characteristics of Fiber Optics

Fiber optics operates in the visible light spectrum, in the range from 10^{14}Hz to 10^{15}Hz. Wavelength is a measure of the width of the waves being transmitted. Different fiber-optic materials are optimized for different wavelengths. The EIA/TIA standards currently support three wavelengths for fiber-optic transmission: 850, 1,300, and 1,550 nanometers (nm). Each of these bands is about 200 nm wide and offers about 25THz of capacity, which means there is a total of some 75THz of capacity on a fiber cable. The bandwidth of fiber is also determined by the number of wavelengths it can carry, as well as by the number of bits per second that each wavelength supports. (As discussed in Chapter 1, each year, wavelength division multiplexers are enabling us to derive twice as many wavelengths as the year before, and hence they enable us to exploit the underlying capacity of the fiber cables.)

With fiber, today we can space repeaters about 500 miles (800 km) apart, but new developments continue to increase the distance or spacing. Trials have been successfully completed at distances of 2,500 miles (4,000 km) and 4,000 miles (6,400 km).

Components of Fiber Optics

The two factors that determine the performance characteristics of a given fiber implementation are the type of cable used and the type of light source used. The following sections look at the components of each.

Fiber-Optic Cable

Fiber-optic cable is available in many sizes. It can have as few as a couple pairs of fiber or it can have bundles that contain upward of 400 or 500 fiber pairs. Figure 2.8 shows the basic components of fiber-optic cable. Each of the fibers is protected with cladding, which ensures that the light energy remains within the fiber rather than bouncing out into the exterior. The cladding is surrounded by plastic shielding, which, among others things, ensures that you can't bend the fiber to the point at which it would break; the plastic shielding therefore limits how much stress you can put on a given fiber. That plastic shielding is then further reinforced with Kevlar reinforcing material—material that is five times stronger than steel—to prevent other intrusions. Outer jackets cover the Kevlar reinforcing material, and the number and type of outer jackets depend on the environment where the cable is meant to be deployed (e.g., buried underground, used in the ocean, strung through the air).

There are two major categories of fiber: multimode and single mode (also known as monomode). Fiber size is a measure of the core diameter and cladding (outside) diameter. It is expressed in the format *xx/zz*, where *xx* is the core diame-

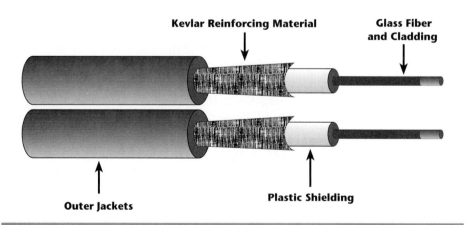

Figure 2.8 Fiber-optic cable

ter and *zz* is the outside diameter of the cladding. For example, a 62.5/125-micron fiber has a core diameter of 62.5 microns and a cladding diameter of 125 microns. The core diameter of the fiber in multimode ranges from 50 microns to 62.5 microns, which is large relative to the wavelength of the light passing through it; as a result, multimode fiber suffers from modal dispersion (i.e., the tendency of light to travel in a wave-like motion rather than in a straight line), and repeaters need to be spaced fairly close together (about 10 to 40 miles [16 to 64 km] apart). The diameter of multimode fiber also has a benefit: It makes the fiber more tolerant of errors related to fitting the fiber to transmitter or receiver attachments, so termination of multimode is rather easy.

The more high-performance mode of fiber, single-mode fiber, has a fiber diameter that is almost the same as the wavelength of light passing through it—from 8 microns to 12 microns. Therefore, the light can use only one path: It must travel straight down the center of the fiber. As a result, single-mode fiber does not suffer from modal dispersion, and it maintains very good signal quality over longer distances. Therefore, with single-mode fiber, repeaters can be spaced farther apart (as mentioned earlier, they are currently about 500 miles [804 km] apart, with the distances increasing rapidly). But because single-mode fiber has such a small diameter, it is difficult to terminate, so experienced technical support may be needed to perform splices and other work with single-mode fiber.

The bottom line is that multimode fiber is less expensive than single-mode fiber but offers lower performance than single-mode fiber. Single-mode fiber is more expensive and offers higher performance, and it has been used in most of the long-distance networks that use fiber.

Light Sources

In the realm of light sources, there are also two categories: light-emitting diodes (LEDs) and laser diodes. The cheaper, lower-performer category is LEDs. LEDs are relatively inexpensive, they have a long life, and they are rather tolerant of extreme temperatures. However, they couple only about 3% of light into the fiber, so their data rates are low, currently about 500Mbps.

Laser diodes are capable of much higher transmission speeds than LEDs. A laser diode is a pure light source that provides coherent energy with little distortion. Therefore, laser diodes are commonly used for long-haul and high-speed transmission. Laser diodes offer better performance than LEDs, and they are more expensive, although the cost of these components has been dropping about 40% per year. As the costs drop, performance is also improving; in the very near future, we should see the introduction of light sources that pulse one trillion bits per second and beyond, although this, of course, will require a lot more power.

To carry traffic over the long haul, the best combination is single-mode fiber with laser diodes. For very short implementations, such as in a campus network environment, the cost-efficiencies of multimode fiber and LEDs may make this combination a more appropriate solution. But in general, as we look forward to the new developments in optical equipment—such as wavelength division multiplexers, optical cross-connects, and optical switches—we will need higher-quality fiber to interface to. It appears that roughly 95% of the world's fiber plant is not prepared to operate at the high speed that we are evolving to with optical equipment. Even though we have been actively deploying fiber for years, it is not all compatible with the next generation of optical equipment. This means that we will see new companies laying new highways and using the latest and greatest in fiber, as well as older companies having to upgrade their plants if they want to take advantage of what optical equipment has to offer.

How Fiber-Optic Transmission Works

As shown in Figure 2.9, in fiber-optic transmission, the digital bitstream enters the light source, in this case the laser diode. If a one bit is present, the light source pulses light in that time slot, but if there is a zero bit, there is no light pulse (or vice versa, depending on how it is set up). The absence or presence of light therefore represents the discrete ones and zeros. Light energy, like other forms of energy, attenuates as it moves over a distance, so it has to run though an amplification or repeating process. As mentioned earlier, until about 1994, electronic repeaters were used with fiber, so the optical signal would have to stop; be converted into electri-

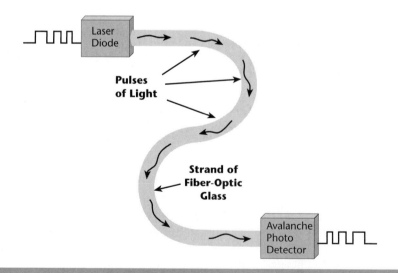

Figure 2.9 Fiber-optic transmission

cal energy; be resynchronized, retimed, and regenerated; and then be converted back into optical energy to be passed to the next point in the network. This was a major problem because it limited the data rate to 2.5Gbps. But some developments introduced in the early 1990s dramatically changed long-distance communications over fiber. The next section talks about those innovations.

Innovations in Fiber Optics: EDFAs and WDM

As mentioned in Chapter 1, erbium-doped fiber amplifiers (EDFAs) are optical repeaters made of fiber doped with erbium metal at periodic intervals (normally every 30 to 60 miles [50 to 100 km]). The introduction of EDFAs made it possible for fiber-optic systems to operate at 10Gbps. EDFAs also opened the way for Wavelength Division Multiplexing (WDM), the process of dividing the optical transmission spectrum into a number of nonoverlapping wavelengths, with each wavelength supporting a single high-speed communications channel. Today, undersea cables need to be designed with WDM in mind; until 1998 or so, most were not, which means they have inappropriate repeater spacing. So, again, for the next generation of fiber communications over undersea cables, many systems will have to be replaced or upgraded.

Since the development of WDM, several categories have been introduced, including Dense Wavelength Division Multiplexing (DWDM) and Coarse Wavelength Division Multiplexing (CWDM). There have also been developments in new generations of fiber and amplifiers; all these are discussed in Chapter 11.

Fiber All Around the World

Some years ago there was a fascinating story in *Wired* magazine, chronicling a project called FLAG that involved a 28,000-km fiber loop around the globe. I encourage you to read it. Its title is "Mother Earth Mother Board: The Hacker Tourist Ventures Forth Across the Wide and Wondrous Meatspace of Three Continents, Chronicling the Laying of the Longest Wire on Earth," and it is available at http://wired-vig.wired.com/wired/archive/4.12/ffglass_pr.html.

An optical multiplexing hierarchy was the predecessor to WDM: Synchronous Digital Hierarchy (SDH) and Synchronous Optical Network (SONET). SDH/SONET is a time division multiplexed system, and SDH/SONET fiber cables make use of just one wavelength. (SDH/SONET is discussed in detail in Chapter 4, "The PSTN.") DWDM can operate over 16 or more wavelengths. Products that are currently shipping support upward of 192 wavelengths and operate at data rates of

2.5Gbps to 10Gbps. New systems have emerged that operate at 40Gbps. Mean-while, research is also under way with dense wavelength division multiplexers that will be capable of supporting as many as 15,000 wavelengths. These developments are just the tip of the iceberg of what we can expect in coming years. (WDM and DWDM, as well as many other aspects of optical networking, are discussed in more detail in Chapter 11.)

Forecasting Optical Developments

The basic equation in assessing the development of optics is that every year, the data rate that can be supported on a wavelength doubles and the number of wavelengths that can be supported on a fiber doubles as well.

Applications of Fiber Optics

Fiber has a number of key applications. It is used in both public and private net-work backbones, so the vast majority of the backbones of the PSTNs worldwide have been upgraded to fiber. The backbones of Internet providers are fiber. Cable TV systems and power utilities have reengineered and upgraded their backbones to fiber as well.

Surprisingly, electric power utilities are the second largest network operator after the telcos. They have vast infrastructures for generating and transmitting elec-tricity; these infrastructures rely on fiber-optic communications systems to direct and control power distribution. After they have put in fiber, electric companies have often found themselves with excess capacity and in a position to resell *dark fiber* to interested parties—including several telcos! When you lease dark fiber, you're basically leasing a pair of fibers without the active electronics and photonics included, so you are responsible for acquiring that equipment and adding it to the network. But with dark fiber, you're not paying for bandwidth—you're paying for the physical facility—and if you want to upgrade your systems to laser diodes that pulse more bits per second, or if you want to add a wavelength division multi-plexer to access more wavelengths, these changes will not affect your monthly cost for the fiber pair itself. Power utilities have been big players in the deployment of fiber throughout the world.

Another application of fiber is in the local loop. There are numerous arrange-ments of fiber in the local loop, including HFC (i.e., fiber to a neighborhood node and then coax on to the subscribers); fiber to the curb with a twisted-pair solution to the home; fiber to the home that terminates on its own individual optical unit; and passive optical networking, which greatly reduces the cost of bringing fiber to the home. Chapter 12 covers the details of these various arrangements.

Another application for fiber is in LANs. Fiber Distributed Data Interface (FDDI) was the first optical LAN backbone that offered 100Mbps backbone capacity, but today it has largely been displaced by the use of twisted-pair 100Mbps Ethernet. Fiber is now used in Gigabit Ethernet and 10 Gigabit Ethernet, although some of the newer revisions also allow the use of twisted-pair (see Chapter 6).

Another application of fiber involves the use of imagery or video when extremely high resolution is critical (e.g., in telemedicine). Consider an application that involves the transmission of images between an imaging center and a doctor's office. Say you went to the imaging center to have an x-ray of your lungs, and in the transmission of your lung x-ray, a little bit of noise in the network put a big black spot on your lung. If that happened, you would likely be scheduled for radical surgery. So, for this type of application, you want a network that ensures that very little noise can affect the resolution and hence the outcome of the analysis. A lot of this use of fiber occurs in early-adopter scenarios where there are applications for imaging, such as universities, health care environments, and entertainment applications.

Another frontier where fiber is now of great interest is in home area networks (HANs). This is a very interesting area because when broadband access comes into your home, you see a shift in where the bottleneck resides, from the local loop to inside the home. Broadband access into the home requires a broadband network within the home to properly distribute the entertainment, data, and voice services that are collectively transported over that broadband access. Many new homes are now being wired with fiber from the start, but it is also possible to retrofit an older home to provide high-quality entertainment and data networks. (HANs are discussed in more detail in Chapter 12.)

Advantages and Disadvantages of Fiber Optics

The advantages of fiber optics are as follows:

- **Extremely high bandwidth**—Fiber offers far more bandwidth than any other cable-based medium.
- **Elastic traffic-carrying capacity**—Without having to change the fiber, assuming that it's the correct generation of fiber, you can add equipment that provides additional capacity over the original fiber alone. This, along with DWDM's capability to turn various wavelengths on and off at will, enables dynamic network bandwidth provisioning to accommodate fluctuations in traffic.

- **Not susceptible to electromagnetic impairments or interference**—Because fiber is not susceptible to electromagnetic impairments or interference, it has a very low bit error rate, 10^{-13}, which means fiber-optic transmissions are virtually noise free.

- **Secure transmission and early detection**—By constantly monitoring an optical network and measuring the time of light reflection, you can detect splices in the cable.

- **Low in weight and mass**—Because fiber is low in weight and mass, much less human installation power is needed than with traditional copper cable or coax bundles.

The disadvantages of fiber optics include the following:

- **High installation costs, but dropping**—Fiber installation is still relatively costly, although the cost has been dropping by about 60% per year, depending on the components. As the cost keeps dropping and the performance increases, fiber is finally moving out of its major application in the carrier backbone realm and into the local loop, supporting subscriber broadband access via techniques such as FTTx and PONs. (Fiber broadband access solutions are covered in Chapter 12.) For example, the capital cost of bringing fiber to the home, including the construction efforts, can be less than US$1,000 when using a PON arrangement. (PONs are covered in Chapter 12.)

- **Special test equipment required**—When you start putting in fiber, you have to acquire specialized test equipment because none of the test equipment you use on an electrical network will work with fiber. You need an OTDR, and when you get into more sophisticated optical networks, you need highly specialized optical probes that can be quite costly—and you need one at each location.

- **Vulnerability to physical damage**—Fiber is a small medium, so it can very easily be cut or otherwise damaged during construction activities. Similarly, because many railroad companies sell rights-of-way for fiber installation, railroad car derailments pose a threat, potentially affecting large numbers of service providers and users. When you choose fiber as the primary medium, you have to address backup, restoration, and survivability from the start because the likelihood of damage is great.

- **Vulnerability to damage caused by wildlife**—A number of flora and fauna cause damage to fiber. Some birds really like the Kevlar reinforcing material and think it makes lovely nests for their babies, so they peck away at fiber-optic cables to get at that Kevlar material. Rodents such as beavers like to sharpen their teeth on exposed cable. Several different types of ants seem to enjoy the plastic shielding in their diet, so they nibble at the underground fibers. Sharks have been known to chomp on cable near the repeating points. A plant called the Christmas tree plant thinks that fiber-optic cable is a tree root and wraps itself around it very tightly and chokes it off.

Chapter 3

Establishing Communications Channels

This chapter discusses the key definitions and characteristics associated with establishing communications channels. It covers networking modes and switching modes, including the differences between routing and switching. It also covers the details of circuit switching and its particular applications, where it shines, and where it has fallen short in the past. This chapter also looks at packet switching—why it has become such a darling in recent years, what its potential prospects are, and what challenges it faces in the future. The chapter ends with a quick comparison between the public switched telephone network (PSTN) and the Internet.

■ Establishing Connections: Networking Modes and Switching Modes

For messages to travel across a network, a transmission path must be established to either switch or route the messages to their final destinations. Therefore, network providers need a mechanism that allows them to deliver the proper connections when and where a customer requests them. *When,* as you can imagine, is ideally now, or bandwidth on demand. *Where* has two components: path calculation, which entails establishing the proper physical or logical connection to the ultimate destination, and forwarding, which is concerned with how to actually guide the traffic across the backbone so that it uses the physical and logical connections to best advantage.

The networking techniques that have evolved over time to handle the *when* and *where* have come about because, traditionally, relatively few high-capacity backbone cables existed. Those few backbone cables had to be manipulated to meet the needs of many individual customers, all of whom had varied bandwidth needs and varying budgets, affording (or not) higher-priority service. Two networking techniques arose:

- **Networking modes**—There are two networking modes: connection oriented and connectionless.

- **Switching modes**—There are two switching modes: circuit switching and packet switching. Both of these switching modes offer forms of bandwidth on demand. (But remember that the connection speed can never be greater than the speed of the customer's access line; the fastest connection you can get into the network is what your access line supports.) As you'll learn later in this chapter, circuit switching and packet switching have different ways of performing path calculations and forwarding functions.

The following sections describe networking modes and switching modes in detail.

Networking Modes

When telecom, network, and IT professionals are evaluating a network, deciding on proper solutions to implement, they often have to consider the choice between circuit switching and packet switching. But it's also very important to consider the networking mode, which can be either connection oriented or connectionless.

Connection-Oriented Networking

As time-sensitive applications become more important, connection-oriented networks are becoming increasingly desirable. In a connection-oriented network, the connection setup is performed before information transfer occurs. Information about the connections in the networks helps to provide service guarantees and makes it possible to most efficiently use network bandwidth by switching transmissions to appropriate connections as the connections are set up. In other words, the path is conceived at the outset, and after the path is determined, all the subsequent information follows the same path to the destination. In a connection-oriented network, there can be some delay up front while the connection is being set up; but once the path is established (and the same path is always followed), the delay is fixed and predictable at intermediate nodes.

Connection-oriented networks can actually operate in either switching mode: They can be either circuit switched or packet switched. Connection-oriented circuit-switched networks include the PSTN (covered later in this chapter and in detail in Chapter 4, "The PSTN"), SDH/SONET (covered in more detail in Chapter 4), and DWDM (covered in detail in Chapter 11, "Optical Networking") networks. Connection-oriented packet-switched networks (covered later in this chapter and in detail in Chapter 7, "Wide Area Networking") include X.25, Frame Relay, and ATM networks.

Connection-oriented networks can be operated in two modes:

- **Provisioned**—In provisioned networks, the connections can be set up ahead of time based on expected traffic. These connections are known as *permanent virtual circuits* (PVCs).

- **Switched**—In switched networks, the connections are set up on demand and released after the data exchange is complete. These connections are known as *switched virtual circuits* (SVCs).

Connectionless Networking

In a connectionless network, no explicit connection setup is performed before data is transmitted. Instead, each data packet is routed to its destination based on information contained in the header. In other words, there is no precomputed path. Rather, each packet of the overall traffic stream is individually addressed and individually routed. In a connectionless network, the delay in the overall transit time is increased because each packet has to be individually routed at each intermediate node. Time-sensitive applications suffer on a connectionless network because the path is not guaranteed, and therefore it is impossible to know where in the range of best to worst the network will perform. As a result, it is difficult to anticipate the actual latency, and the delay may change from packet to packet.

Connectionless networks imply the use of packet switches, so only packet-switched networks are connectionless. An example of a connectionless packet-switched network is the public Internet—that wild and woolly place over which absolutely no one has any control. It's a virtual network that consists of more than 183,052 separate autonomous systems and more than 10,000 ISPs, so being able to guarantee performance is nearly impossible at this time. One solution is to use private internets (i.e., Internet Protocol [IP] backbones), which achieve cost-efficiencies but, because they are private, provide the ability to control their performance and thereby serve business-class services. For example, a large carrier might own its own Internet infrastructure, over a very wide geographic area. Because it owns and controls those networks end to end, the company can provision and engineer the networks so that business customers can get the proper service-level agreements and can guarantee the performance of their virtual private networks and streaming media networks. The downside in this situation is reliance on one vendor for the entire network.

Switching Modes

Let's start our discussion of switching modes by talking about switching and routing. *Switching* is the process of physically moving bits through a network node, from an input port to an output port. (A *network node* is any point on the network where communications lines interface. So a network node might be a PBX, a local exchange, a multiplexer, a modem, a host computer, or one of a number of other devices.) Switching elements are specialized computers used to connect two or more transmission lines. The switching process is based on information gathered through a routing process. A switching element might consult a table to determine, based on the number dialed, the most cost-effective trunk over which to forward a call. This switching process is relatively straightforward compared to the type of path determination that IP routers in the Internet might use, which can be very complex.

Routing, on the other hand, involves moving information from a source to a destination across an internetwork, which means moving information across networks. In general, routing involves at least one intermediate node along the way, and it usually involves numerous intermediate nodes and networks. This implies an understanding of hierarchical addressing structure and switching. A router performs two basic activities: determining the optimal path and transporting information through an internetwork. Routing algorithms are necessary to initialize and maintain routing tables. Routing algorithms work with a whole slew of information, called *metrics*, to determine the best path to the destination. Some examples of the metrics that a routing algorithm might use are path length, destination, next-hop associations, reliability, delay, bandwidth, load, and communication cost. A router could use several variables to calculate the best path for a packet, to get it to a node that is one step closer to its destination. The route information varies depending on the algorithm used, and the algorithms vary depending on the routing protocol chosen. Most manufacturers today support the key standards, including Routing Information Protocol (RIP), Open Shortest Path First (OSPF), Intermediate System to Intermediate System (IS-IS), Enhanced Interior Gateway Routing Protocol (EIGRP), Border Gateway Protocol 4 (BGP4), and Multiprotocol Label Switching (MPLS). Network engineers generally decide which of these protocols to use. Routing protocols can also be designed to automatically detect and respond to network changes. (Protocols and metrics are discussed in detail in Chapter 8, "The Internet and IP Infrastructures.")

Routers can contain two types of network accessibility maps: static maps, which are manually configured and do not change, and dynamic maps, which can build routes automatically, as needed. A *static router* knows only its own table; it has no idea what the routing tables of its upstream neighbors look like, and it cannot communicate with its upstream neighbors. If a link goes down in a network that uses static routers, the network administrator has to manually reconfigure the static routers' routing tables to take the downed trunk out of service. This reconfiguration would require changes in the upstream routers, so technicians at those locations would then also have to include or accommodate the changes. Static routers are used only in tiny networks that do not change.

A *dynamic router*, on the other hand, can communicate with its upstream neighbors, so if a change occurred to its routing table, it would forward that change so that the other routers could also adjust their routing tables. Furthermore, a dynamic router has a view of its own routing table, and it can also see those of its neighbors, or the entire network or routing area, depending on the protocol. It therefore works much better in addressing the dynamic traffic patterns that are common in today's networks. Dynamic routers use the various routing protocols mentioned earlier to communicate route topology changes to each other. Static routers do not use routing protocols. A router can use either static or dynamic routes, or both.

As noted earlier in this chapter, there are two switching modes: circuit switching and packet switching. Circuit switches are position based; that is, bits arrive in a certain position and are switched to a different position. The position to which bits are switched is determined by a combination of one or more of three dimensions: space (i.e., the interface or port number), time, and wavelength. Packet switching is based on labels; addressing information in the packet headers, or labels, helps to determine how to switch or forward a packet through the network node.

Circuit Switching

Circuit switching has been the basis of voice networks worldwide for many years. You can apply three terms to the nature of a circuit-switched call to help remember what it is: continuous, exclusive, and temporary.

One of the key attributes of a circuit-switched connection is that it is a reserved network resource that is yours and only yours for the full duration of a conversation. But when that conversation is over, the connection is released. A circuit-switched environment requires that an end-to-end circuit be set up before a call can begin. A fixed share of network resources is reserved for the call, and no other call can use those resources until the original connection is closed. A call request signal must travel to the destination and be acknowledged before any transmission can actually begin. As Figure 3.1 illustrates, you can trace the path from one end of the call to the other end; that path does not vary for the full duration of the call, and the capacity provisioned on that path is yours and yours alone.

Advantages and Disadvantages of Circuit Switching   Circuit switching uses many lines to economize on switching and routing computation. When a call is set up, a line is dedicated to it, so no further routing calculations are needed.

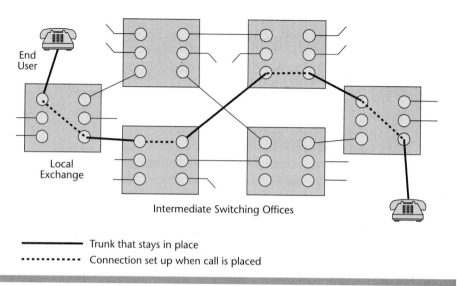

Trunk that stays in place
·············· Connection set up when call is placed

Figure 3.1 A circuit-switched call

Since they were introduced in the mid-1980s, digital cross-connect systems (DCSs) have greatly eased the process of reconfiguring circuit-switched networks and responding to conditions such as congestion and failure. DCSs create pre-defined circuit capacity, and then voice switches are used to route calls over circuits set up by these DCSs. DCSs are analogous to the old patch panels. You may have seen a main distribution frame (MDF) on which twisted-pair wiring is terminated. The MDF is a manual patch panel, and before DCSs were introduced, when it was necessary to reconfigure a network based on outage, congestion, or customer demand as a result of shifting traffic patterns, technicians had to spend days or even weeks manually making changes at the MDF. The DCS is a software patch panel, and within the software are databases that define alternate routes—alternate connections that can be activated if the network encounters a condition that requires some form of manipulation. DCSs are one of the elements of the PSTN that contribute to its reliability: When network conditions change, in a matter of minutes, a DCS can reconfigure the network around those changes. With such tools, the PSTN can offer five-nines reliability—in other words, 99.999% guaranteed uptime. (DCSs are discussed in more detail in Chapter 4.)

Circuit switching offers the benefits of low latency and minimal delays because the routing calculation on the path is made only once, at the beginning of the call, and no more delays are incurred subsequently in calculating the next hop that should be taken. Traditionally, this was sometimes seen as a disadvantage because it meant that the circuits might not be used as efficiently as possible. Silence accounts for around half of most voice calls. Most people breathe and occasionally pause in their speech. So, when voice communications are conducted over a circuit that's being continuously held, and half the time nothing is being transmitted, the circuit is not being used very efficiently. But remember that this issue is important mainly when bandwidth is constrained. And as mentioned earlier in the book, bandwidth is growing at an astounding rate, through the widespread deployment of fiber optics, so the efficient use of circuits because of bandwidth constraints will not present the same sort of issue in the future that it once did. Hence, the low latencies or delays that circuit switching guarantees are more important than its potential drawbacks in bandwidth efficiency, and therefore, emerging models for optical networking use circuit switching in the core (see Chapter 11).

Circuit switching has been optimized for real-time voice traffic for which quality of service (QoS) is needed. Because it involves path calculation at the front end, you know how many switches and cables you're going to go through, so you can use a pricing mechanism based on distance and time. The more resources you use, either over time or over distance, the greater the cost. Again, developments in fiber economics are changing some of the old rules, and distance is no longer necessarily an added cost element. (QoS is discussed in more detail in Chapter 10, "Next-Generation Networks.")

Generations of Circuit Switches   Circuit switches have been around for quite some time. They have already been through three basic generations, and we're beginning to see a fourth generation.

The History of the Strowger Switch

The Strowger switch has a rather amusing history. Once upon a time in the Wild West, there was a young man named Alman B. Strowger who wasn't a telecommunications engineer by trade. He was a mortician. As life would have it, he had a competitor in town. During this period, there were no dial pads to use when making a telephone call. Instead, you had to talk with the town telephone operator, who would extend the connection on your behalf. Mr. Strowger's competitor's wife was the town telephone operator. So, needless to say, anytime there was gossip about a gun battle about to brew on Main Street, she let her husband know, and he was there to collect the bodies before Mr. Strowger got a chance. Mr. Strowger decided to use technology to get a competitive advantage, and he invented the Strowger switch. The new switch meant that you could dial a number directly from your phone, bypassing the town telephone operator.

The first generation of circuit switches was introduced in 1888. It was referred to as the step relay switch, the step-by-step switch, or the Strowger switch, in honor of the man who invented it (see Figure 3.2).

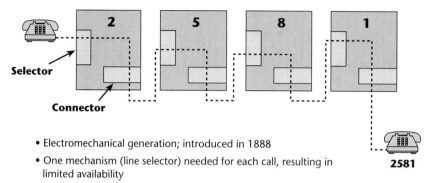

- Electromechanical generation; introduced in 1888
- One mechanism (line selector) needed for each call, resulting in limited availability
- Line selector listens for each digit and sets a separate selector and connector for each digit
- The four-part switch is occupied during the entire call
- Electromechanical is very labor intensive and requires a large amount of space

Figure 3.2 A step relay switch

In 1935 the second generation of circuit switches was introduced: crossbar switches (see Figure 3.3). Crossbar switches were electromechanical, but each one could service a larger number of subscribers than could a step relay switch. Both step relay and crossbar switches still exist in the world. Of course, they are generally in underdeveloped areas, but they're not all relegated to museums quite yet. Every year you hear about one or two being decommissioned somewhere in the world.

The third generation of circuit switches—stored program control (also referred to as electronic common control)—was introduced in 1968. A stored program control is a computer-driven software-controlled switch (and it was for this purpose that the UNIX operating system was originally developed). Because this type of switch is electronic, there are no moving parts, and the switch has a longer life than earlier generations of switches. Because it is software controlled, it offers more guarantees against obsolescence, easier upgradability to enhanced feature sets, and better control over user features and cost features because everything can be programmed into databases that facilitate the call control process (see Figure 3.4).

The three generations of circuit switches are in place and operating at various levels of activity. Each new generation of switches has brought with it more connection-oriented features, features that help in making connections (e.g., customer features such as call forwarding and call waiting). Circuit switches in the future will likely be able to define connections based on a requested service class. Examples of variables that define a service class are the amount of delay that can be tolerated end to end, as well as between components, and the maximum loss that can

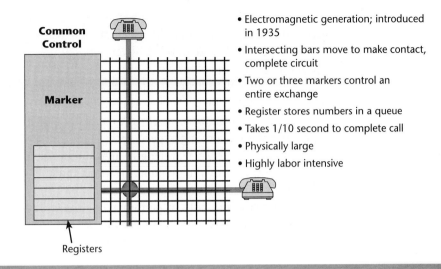

Common Control

Marker

Registers

- Electromagnetic generation; introduced in 1935
- Intersecting bars move to make contact, complete circuit
- Two or three markers control an entire exchange
- Register stores numbers in a queue
- Takes 1/10 second to complete call
- Physically large
- Highly labor intensive

Figure 3.3   A crossbar switch

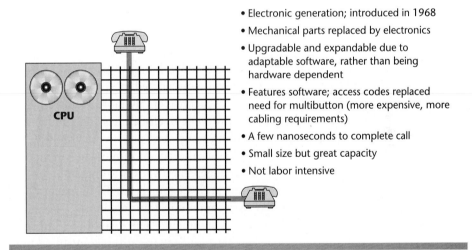

CPU

- Electronic generation; introduced in 1968
- Mechanical parts replaced by electronics
- Upgradable and expandable due to adaptable software, rather than being hardware dependent
- Features software; access codes replaced need for multibutton (more expensive, more cabling requirements)
- A few nanoseconds to complete call
- Small size but great capacity
- Not labor intensive

Figure 3.4   A stored program control

be tolerated before the transmission is greatly hampered. Hence, we will be able to build connections to meet a particular service class and thereby aid in ensuring the proper performance of an application.

Customer premises equipment (CPE) circuit switches include PBXs. In the PSTN, circuit switches include the local exchanges with which subscribers access the network, the tandem or junction switches that interconnect numbers of local exchanges throughout a metro area, the toll or transit switches used for national long-distance communications, and the international gateways used for cross-country communications. A large number of vendors sell these circuit switches, as well as more specialized niche products.

A fourth generation of switches—optical networking switches—is emerging now (see Chapter 12, "Broadband Access Alternatives"). Often, these optical networking elements are referred to as *wavelength routers* or *optical switches*. The idea is to be able to provision a very high-speed path, at OC-48 (i.e., 2.5Gbps), end to end across a network of dense wavelength division multiplexers. This will be increasingly important in providing communications interfaces to the high-speed switches that have become available.

With circuit switches, the ratio of performance to cost doubles approximately every 80 months to 40 months (i.e., normally the performance improves every 80 months, although sometimes new generations are created more rapidly—every 40 months). Major architectural changes in circuit switches occur relatively infrequently.

Network switches are responsible for doing all the work of setting up and tearing down calls, as well as for addressing and providing the features requested. They provide a very high level of functionality on a very centralized basis within the network, and that enables the end stations to be very cheap and very dumb (e.g., a single-line telephone). Again, when intelligence was extremely expensive, there was something to be gained by centralizing it in a monolithic switch because that allowed consumers to access the network and to participate as users with a very low entry point. Until recently, if you wanted to spend time on the Internet, you had to have a PC, and a PC costs considerably more than a single-line telephone. On the other hand, costs are dropping in electronics and appliances all the time, so this is also becoming less of an issue, and perhaps in this way, too, distributing intelligence makes sense. This is the age-old argument about smart core/dumb edge versus dumb core/smart edge, and it speaks to the differences in philosophies between classic telecommunications engineers (affectionately referred to as "bell heads") and modern-day data communications engineers ("net heads"). The seminal paper that gave rise to this argument, "The Rise of the Stupid Network," is an excellent resource and can be found at www.isen.com/stupid.html. Chapter 10 talks more about the evolution of the intelligent edge.

Packet Switching

Whereas circuit switching was invented to facilitate voice telephony, packet switching has its origin in data communications. In fact, packet switching was developed specifically as a solution for the communications implications of a form of data processing called *interactive processing*.

The first generation of data processing was batch processing, in which a data entry clerk would sit down at a job entry terminal and key a volume of data onto some medium—initially key punch cards, and later tape or disk. The data was then preaccumulated on an intermediate medium, and at some later point, a job would be scheduled and a link would be established to the host that would be responsible for processing the data. When this preaccumulated volume was transmitted, it was a steady stream of continuous high-volume data, so batch processing made quite effective use of a circuit-switched environment.

In contrast to batch processing, in interactive processing, data entry occurs online, so, in essence, data is transmitted only when you press the Enter key, but when you're looking at the screen or filling in a spreadsheet, nothing is being transmitted. Thus, interactive processing involves a traffic stream that's described as being *bursty* in nature, which implies long connect times but low data volumes. Therefore, interactive processing does not make efficient use of circuit-switched links: The connection would be established and held for a long period of time, with only little data passed. Packet switching was developed to increase the efficiencies associated with bursty transmission. Packet switching involves the multiplexing of multiple packets over one virtual circuit (i.e., the end-to-end logical connection that creates a complete path across the network from source to destination node; see Chapter 1, "Telecommunications Technology Fundamentals"). It also involves decentralizing the network intelligence—not only the intelligence for maintaining and tearing down the connections in centralized switches but also the endpoints that participate in the control of the end-to-end session.

Packets   A *packet* is basically a container for bits. We also use terms such as *blocks*, *frames*, *cells*, and *datagrams* to depict the same general concept, although there are differences in what type of information each contains. A packet can be a number of sizes, contain different numbers of bits, and have varying amounts of navigational control that the network nodes can use to navigate and route the packet. (Chapter 7 discusses some of the different types of packets and the techniques that use them.) In general, the features of a packet depend on several considerations. Each protocol, as it's developed over time, makes certain assumptions about whether bandwidth is available, or whether there's too much noise and therefore too much retransmission needed, or whether the key issue is latency. Packets of different sizes may therefore perform differently in different environments.

A packet is, in essence, a store-and-forward mechanism for transmitting information. Packets are forwarded through a series of *packet switches*, also known as *routers*, that ultimately lead to the destination. A *packet header* contains two very important pieces of information: the destination address and the sequence number. The original forms of packet switching (developed in the late 1960s and early 1970s) were connectionless infrastructures. In a connectionless environment, each packet is routed individually, and the packets might not all take the same path to the destination point, and hence they may arrive out of sequence. Therefore, the sequence number is very important; the terminating point needs it to be able to reassemble the message in its proper order.

Generally, in packet switching, packets from many different sources are statistically multiplexed and sent on to their destinations over virtual circuits. Multiple connections share transmission lines, which means the packet switches or routers must do many more routing calculations. Figure 3.5 illustrates a packet-switched network that uses virtual circuits. Packets are queued up at the various nodes, based on availability of the virtual circuits, and this queuing can impose delays.

The first generation of packet-switched networks could support only data, not voice or video, because there was so much delay associated with those networks. As packet-switched environments evolve, we are developing techniques for separating and prioritizing the various traffic types. (Chapter 10 talks about these issues in depth.)

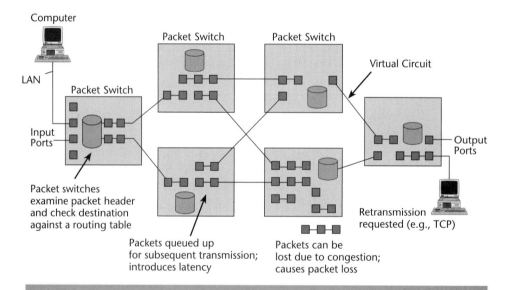

Figure 3.5 A packet-switched network

A Transportation Analogy to Packet Switching

Sometimes it helps to think about telecom networks in the context of something familiar, such as the transportation system. First, consider the physical roadways. A standard plain old telephone service (POTS) line or traditional twisted-pair alternative is equivalent to a gravelly, potholed alley—allowing only one lane of traffic in each direction that can travel at low speed due to various physical impairments. That alley, when widened and repaved, can allow vehicles to travel more quickly, improving performance, much as DSL does for twisted-pair. These alleyways may feed into a main street, with a couple lanes of traffic in each direction; we can think of this as the coaxial network. The main street, in turn, may feed into a highway with multiple lanes of traffic in each direction, and this would be our fiber-optic highway. As the air serves airplanes, the air also serves our wireless systems.

The next step in this comparison is to consider the various points at which roadways need to intersect and merge. This is the province of switches and routers. A switch is analogous to a four-way intersection: It connects separate roadways, much as a switch connects two individual transmission lines (indeed, rail yards have numerous switches that direct trains among different tracks). A router is more like an access road off the highway, directing you one step closer to your destination (e.g., go right to points east; go left to points west).

The final element is the vehicles, which are the packets in the telecom realm. Some vehicles are large and can carry a lot of passengers with only one driver, such as a bus; in the case of telecom, this is analogous to IP. Others offer high performance and advanced navigational controls but can carry only one passenger along with the driver, such as a Ferrari; in the communications context, this is ATM. The bus has the benefits of carrying more passengers with less overhead, but it is larger, and there's a longer period of time from the point at which the bus's nose enters an intersection and its tail exits, resulting in more latency. On the other hand, the Ferrari will take much less time to make it through the intersection. Similarly, if there is mass congestion at the intersection, the bus will have to wait until the traffic clears before it can cross, while the police officer is likely to let the Ferrari use the shoulder to bypass the congestion. Similarly, in packet switching, each packet basically defines the number of passengers that can be carried (the number of bits) and the level of navigational controls (the control information in the overhead defining how to handle congestion and loss).

Connectionless Versus Connection-Oriented Packet-Switched Networks   There are two forms of packet-switched networks: connectionless and connection oriented.

Connectionless Packet-Switched Networks   You can picture connectionless networks by using a postal service analogy: Bob writes a letter, puts it in an envelope, and addresses the envelope. His carrier does not care in the least what it says on the envelope because she knows where she is taking that envelope. It's going to the next point of presence, which is the local post office. The local post office will be concerned with the destination zip code, but it doesn't care at all about the name or street address on the envelope. It simply wants to know what regional center to route it to. The regional center cares about the destination city, and the destination local post office cares about the actual street address because it needs to assign the letter to the right carrier. The carrier cares about the name so that the letter finds its way into the right mailbox. If the letter ends up in someone else's mailbox, the unintended recipient holds the ultimate responsibility for error control because he or she is the endpoint. In comparison, if Bob sends that letter via fax, it is connection-oriented: The connection to the destination address is established prior to transmission, and there are no intermediate stops.

A connectionless environment worries about getting a packet one step closer to the destination (see Figure 3.6). It doesn't worry about having an end-to-end view of the path over which the message will flow; this is the fundamental difference between connection-oriented and connectionless environments, and, hence, between infrastructures such as the PSTN and the Internet. Examples of connectionless packet-switched networks include the public Internet, private IP backbones or networks, Internet-based VPNs, and LANs. Again, each packet (referred to as a *datagram transmission*) is an independent unit that contains the source and destination addresses, which increases the overhead. That's one of the issues with connectionless packet-switched networks: If we have to address each packet, the overall percentage of control information relevant to the actual data being transported rises.

Each router performs a path calculation function independently, and each makes use of various routing protocols (e.g., OSPF, IS-IS, BGP). Each router calculates the appropriate next hop for each destination, which is generally based on the smallest number of hops (although some routing protocols use an abstract notion of cost, as defined by the network administrator, in making decisions). Packets are forwarded on a hop-by-hop basis rather than as part of an end-to-end connection.

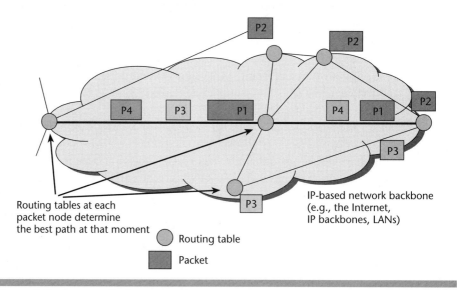

Figure 3.6 A connectionless network

Each packet must be individually routed, which increases delays (due to queuing delays), and the more hops, the greater the delay. Therefore, connectionless environments provide less control over ensuring QoS because of unknown latencies, unknown retransmissions, and unknown sequences in which the packets will arrive.

Connection-Oriented Packet-Switched Networks The connection-oriented packet-switched environment is something like a telephone network, in which a call setup is performed end to end. X.25, Frame Relay, ATM, and MPLS are all connection-oriented techniques. In a connection-oriented packet-switched network, only one call request packet contains the source and destination address (see Figure 3.7). Therefore, the subsequent packets don't have to contain the address information, which reduces the overall overhead. The call request packet establishes the virtual circuit. Each individual switch along each path, then, forwards traffic to the appropriate next switch until packets all arrive at the destination. With connection-oriented networks, each individual packet does not need to be routed. Instead, each packet is marked as belonging to some specific flow that identifies which virtual circuit it belongs to. Thus, the switch needs only to look at the mark and forward the packet to the correct interface because the flow is already set up in the switch's table. No repeated per-packet computation is required; consequently, connection-oriented networks reduce latencies, or delays.

In the connection-oriented environment, the entry node contains the routing table, where the path is calculated and determined, and all packets follow that same path to the destination node, thereby offering a better guarantee of service.

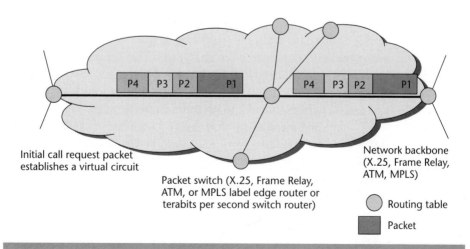

Figure 3.7 A connection-oriented network

Advantages and Disadvantages of Packet Switching   Packet-switching techniques have a number of limitations, including the following:

- Latencies occur because connection-oriented packet switching is a store-and-forward mechanism.

- Jitter occurs. *Jitter* refers to variable delay, to the delay in moving bits along the entire path, or, more specifically, to the variable arrival of packets. There are two main types of delay: jitter and entry-to-exit-point delay. Say that your end-to-end delay might meet the desired minimum of 150 milliseconds, but between switches 1 and 2, the delay is 20 milliseconds and between switches 2 and 3, it's 130 milliseconds. That variation will hamper some applications, so it needs to be controlled so that the network can support demanding applications.

- Packet loss occurs as congestion occurs at the packet switches or routers, and it can considerably degrade real-time applications. For example, if a few packets of a voice call are lost, you'll hear pops and clicks, but if the loss climbs into the 30% to 40% range, the voice might sound like "ye ah ng ng ah mm mm ah." This is the experience that some people today find at times when using the public Internet for telephony, where at peak periods of day, packet loss can be as great as 40%. But it is important to note that this varies greatly around the world; in some countries and locations, the loss is close to zero on the average, whereas other regions or providers may suffer double-digit packet loss during peak hours.

Given these drawbacks and the way packet-switched networks evolved, these networks originally gave no QoS guarantees—they offered only best-effort QoS. But they guaranteed high reliability because you would be able to route packets through alternate nodes or pathways if they encountered link-resistant failures along the way; thus, you were guaranteed that information would be transported, but not within metrics such as latency and packet loss. Currently, protocols are being developed that will enable real-time applications such as voice, video, audio, and interactive multimedia to perform properly on packet-switched networks.

The pricing mechanism that evolved with packet-switched networks was a bit different from that used for circuit-switched networks. It was not based on time and distance but on usage: Billing is based on the volume of packets or the amount of bandwidth subscribed to. Distance insensitivity is a part of the packet-switched networking environment.

Generations of Packet Switches   Similar to circuit switches, packet switches have gone through several basic generations: X.25 switches (first generation), routers (second generation), Frame Relay and cell switches (third generation), and

MPLS and tag-switched switches (fourth generation). Each generation of packet switching has increased the efficiency of packet processing and the speed of the interfaces it supports. In effect, the size of the pipes and the size of the interfaces dictate how effectively the packet-switched network performs. In packet switching, the processing is being pushed outside the network to the end nodes, so you need to have more intelligent software at the end nodes that get involved in the session setup, maintenance, and teardown, as well as flow control from end to end.

Besides X.25 switches, routers, and Frame Relay switches, packet switches include ATM switches and a new breed, called Tbps (terabits per second) switch routers. A large number of vendors sell these packet switches, and it seems that more companies jump on the bandwagon each day.

With packet switches, the ratio of performance to cost doubles every 20 to 10 months, so we see the evolution of new entries in the product line much more rapidly in this environment than in the circuit-switched world. However, again we rely on expensive end stations—PCs or other computers—to finish the job of communication in packet switching. These end stations have to rely on protocols such as Transmission Control Protocol/Internet Protocol (TCP/IP), an open standard for internetworking that performs the equivalent of call setup/teardown and correct receipt of data. (TCP/IP is discussed in Chapter 8.) These end stations also have to ensure that all the data has been received and that it has been received correctly.

Comparing Circuit Switching and Packet Switching

What does the future hold for circuit switching and packet switching? Circuit switching is superior to packet switching in terms of eliminating queuing delays, which results in completely predictable latency and jitter in the backbone. Given the trend toward real-time visual and sensory communication streams, this seems to be the most important characteristic for us to strive toward. With the large capacities afforded by the new DWDM systems and other optical network elements, minimizing latency becomes more important than optimizing bandwidth via statistical multiplexing. (DWDM and other forms of multiplexing are discussed in Chapter 1.) We're likely to see the use of statistical multiplexing continue to increase at the edge and at the customer premises, as a means of economically integrating and aggregating traffic from the enterprise to present it over the access link to the network. In the core, fiber-based and circuit-switched networks are likely to prevail.

Table 3.1 briefly compares circuit switching and packet switching. As you look at the table, keep in mind that as we get more bandwidth, circuit-switched networks do not have to be so concerned with bandwidth efficiency. And as QoS is added to packet-switched networks, these networks are able to support real-time applications. Again, the prevailing conditions have a lot to do with what is best in a given network.

Table 3.1 Circuit Switching Versus Packet Switching

Characteristic	Circuit Switching	Packet Switching
Origin	Voice telephony	Data networking
Connectionless or connection oriented	Connection oriented	Both
Key applications	Real-time voice, streaming media, videoconferencing, video-on-demand, and other delay- and loss-sensitive traffic applications	Bursty data traffic that has long connect times but low data volumes; applications that are delay and loss tolerant
Latency/delay/jitter	Low latency and minimal delays	Subject to latency, delay, and jitter because of its store-and-forward nature
Network intelligence	Centralized	Decentralized
Bandwidth efficiency	Low	High
Packet loss	Low	Low to high, depending on the network

▪ The PSTN Versus the Internet

In one very important fashion, the PSTN and the public Internet are one and the same thing: They both exist on the same physical infrastructure. There would be no Internet without the PSTN. The communications links, or backbones, that ISPs run on are delivered over the PSTN, and the access lines for entry into the Internet are all subscriber lines that are part of the PSTN. But what differentiates the PSTN and the Internet is the equipment attached to each network, its use, and how it formats the information it carries.

PSTN Characteristics

The PSTN basically includes telephones, fax machines, and circuit switches that set up continuous but temporary connections. In the PSTN, a circuit is established between two subscribers and kept open for the duration of the call, including periods of silence. This provides guaranteed QoS and minimal latencies, and it means that the PSTN is optimized for voice and other real-time applications. It also means that the PSTN uses bandwidth inefficiently, making services more expensive. But we are constantly finding ourselves able to provide more bandwidth and derive more channels over that bandwidth.

Internet Characteristics

The Internet basically includes clients, which are the user interface and the input/output device for information; servers, which are the centralized repositories of wisdom that you are seeking; and packet switches, which route the packets of information between the clients and servers. Whereas the PSTN connects two subscribers, the Internet connects networks. As on the PSTN, messages on the Internet are routed to specific end devices. These messages take various forms, such as e-mail, instant messaging, and real-time audio/video communications. Unlike the PSTN, however, the Internet breaks down a message into packets of data, whose routing information guides the packets to their destination. Individual packets may take different routes, but they are reassembled in the proper order at the destination. This system is optimal for the most efficient use of transmission facilities, particularly when you're supporting bursty traffic that involves long periods of silence. In turn, this results in less expensive services. However, the tradeoff is that you get only best-effort QoS. Progress is being made on introducing QoS to the Internet, though, and in the next two or three years, this will change more. However, note that there is greater progress in introducing QoS on private networks than on the public Internet.

What Is Meant by *Next-Generation Network*?

The term *next-generation network* is used throughout this book with a very specific meaning. The decreasing cost of bandwidth, combined with the availability of low-cost and powerful chip technology, favorably highlights the economies of statistical multiplexing and packet switching, as long as latencies and loss can be controlled. From that standpoint, next-generation networks embody two fundamental concepts. First, a next-generation network is a high-speed packet-based network capable of transporting and routing a multitude of services, including voice, data, video, and multimedia, while supporting QoS. Second, a next-generation network is a common platform for applications and services that the customer can access across the entire network as well as outside the network.

Converging Networks: Next-Generation Networks

Networks are evolving so that they can address the growing demand for QoS. The two different infrastructures—circuit switching and packet switching—are not trying to replace each other. Instead, they are converging. This marriage is required between the existing legacy environment (the circuit-switched network) and the new and unique IP marketplace (the packet-switched network). To address this convergence, a number of devices have emerged that have a number of names, including Voice over IP gateways, media gateways, next-generation switches, and softswitches. These elements are discussed in Chapter 9, "IP Services." These new devices in essence allow interoperability to exist seamlessly between the PSTN and packet-switched networks, whether IP or ATM or MPLS.

Chapter 4

The PSTN

This chapter talks about the public switched telephone network (PSTN). It discusses what comprises the PSTN, what sorts of technologies have been used to complete the connections, how the signaling systems operate, and the typical components and transmission capacities of the basic backbone architecture. This chapter also discusses what intelligent networks (INs) provide in terms of service logic and feature availability. Finally, this chapter describes some of the trends in the evolution of the PSTN that will support the new generation of applications.

■ The PSTN Infrastructure

Views about what a network should be designed to support and what the infrastructure should be composed of have changed quite a bit over the years, as applications and technology have changed. Before discussing what is needed in a network today, this chapter takes a look at how the PSTN infrastructure evolved and where it is now.

The traditional PSTN infrastructure was specifically designed to support only continuous, real-time voice communications. At the time this infrastructure was being designed, we had no notion of data communications or, indeed, notions of bursty communications or long-duration conversations.

The length of calls is an important variable in the design of the PSTN. Most voice calls are quite short, so the circuit switches in the PSTN are engineered for call durations of three minutes or less, and only a small percentage of subscribers off-hook at any time. The average Internet session, on the other hand, lasts around an hour. This means that increased Internet access through the PSTN has, in some locales, put a strain on the local exchanges. If a circuit switch is blocked because it is carrying a long Internet session, people may not be able to get a dial tone. There are several solutions to this problem. For example, as discussed in Chapter 10, "Next-Generation Networks," we can apply intelligence in front of some exchanges so that calls destined for ISPs can be diverted over a packet-switched network to the ISP rather than being completed on a circuit-switched basis through the local exchange.

Yet another variable that's important to the design of the PSTN has to do with what it was designed to support. The capacities of the channels in the PSTN are of the narrowband generation—they are based on 64Kbps channels. The worldwide infrastructure to accommodate voice communications evolved to include a series of circuit switches. Different switches are used based on the locations to which they connect. The switches have a high degree of intelligence built into them, both for establishing the communications channels and for delivering the service logic to activate a growing array of features. In the traditional framework, the monolithic switches in the network had all the smarts. The switch manufacturer and the carrier worked together very closely, and the carrier couldn't introduce new features and services into a particular area until a software release was available for the switch platform through which the neighborhood was being serviced. Thus, carriers were often unable to roll out new services and features because they hadn't yet received the new software releases from the switch manufacturers. Over time, we have separated the functions of switching and connection establishment from the functions involved in the intelligence that enables various services and features to be activated.

The traditional PSTN is associated with highly developed, although not necessarily integrated, operational support systems (e.g., billing systems, provisioning systems, network management systems, customer contact systems, security systems). These systems have very well-developed business processes and techniques for managing their environments. But the various systems' databases still do not always speak to one another to give one comprehensive view. In the IP world, the operational support systems are relatively new and are generally no more integrated than those found in the PSTN.

The backbone of the traditional PSTN was largely based on a generation called the Plesiochronous Digital Hierarchy (PDH), which includes the T-carrier, E-carrier, and J-carrier standards, depending on the country the system is deployed in. The local loop of the PSTN was provisioned as a twisted-copper-pair analog subscriber line.

Service Providers

Many abbreviations and acronyms are used to define the various players and the parts of the network in which they play. Some telcos can and do fulfill more than one of these functions, depending on the policy, regulatory, and licensing conditions that prevail in the area. The following terms are largely used in the United States, but they are important to the discussion in this chapter because they illustrate the functions service providers are addressing:

- **PTO**—PTO stands for *public telecommunications operator*, which is the name for an incumbent carrier in places other than the United States. Often, these are government owned or controlled. In some countries, the more proper term is *PT&T*, for *post, telegraph, and telephone*.

- **VAN provider**—VAN stands for *value-added network*. The term *VAN provider* originated around 1970 and was applied to companies competing to provide telecommunications services, specifically with offerings focused on data communications and data networking. VANs provided more than a simple pipe from point A to point B. They provided some additional intelligence in the network, to, for example, perform error detection and correction, or to convert protocols or languages that different computers speak so that you could have interoperability across the network. *Value-added services (VAS) provider* is another term used to define such providers.

- **LEC**—In the local environment we use the acronym LEC for *local exchange carrier*. There was originally no competition among LECs, but as soon as competition in the local loop picked up, LECs were segmented into ILECs, CLECs, and DCLECs.

- **ILEC**—The ILEC is the *incumbent local exchange carrier*, the original common carrier that either once had or, in some countries, still has monopoly rights in the local loop. For most residents in the United States, this would be one of the three "baby Bells"—Qwest Communications International, AT&T, and Verizon Communications.

- **CLEC**—The CLEC is the *competitive local exchange carrier*. CLECs came about as a result of the Telecommunications Act of 1996, which opened up competition in the local loop. The CLEC is the competitor to the ILEC. Although the decline of the telecommunications economy in 2000 and 2001 forced several CLECs out of business, or made some ripe for acquisition by ILECs, there are still some CLECs in the United States, and they currently focus on delivering dial tone to business customers.

- **DCLEC (or DLEC)**—DCLEC stands for *data competitive local exchange carrier*. A DCLEC is a company specifically focused on supporting data services (e.g., providers that offer DSL services to end users). Most of these providers have ceased operating.

- **ELEC**—ELEC stands for *Ethernet local exchange carrier.* The ELEC specializes in providing Ethernet solutions in the local loop and metro area.

- **IXC**—The *interexchange carrier* is the carrier for long-distance and international communications. AT&T Corporation, MCI (now part of Verizon), Sprint, Qwest, and Verizon are the primary IXCs in the United States. Unless certain stringent requirements imposed by the Federal Communications Commission are met, an IXC cannot offer long-distance services in the areas where it is also the ILEC.

- **SP**—Because so many lines are being blurred today by bundled services and bundled territories of operation, the basic term *service provider* is commonly used to refer generically to providers of different types of services.

Network Access

Figure 4.1 is a simple diagram that shows network access. On the left-hand side is the customer environment, which includes residences (single-line instruments being served by an access line) and business premises (with onsite telephone systems such as private branch exchange [PBX] or key telephone systems—smaller site systems for installations where there are 50 or fewer employees). Those in the customer environment are connected to the PSTN via access lines. The *access net-*

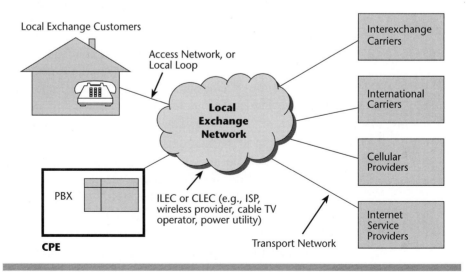

Figure 4.1 Network access

work, also called the *local loop*, includes the network interface at the premises (also referred to as the *demarcation point*), the access line leading to the local exchange, the outside plant (e.g., telephone poles, drop lines), the components at the local exchange on which those access lines terminate (e.g., the line cards with a port associated with each telephone line), and the logic used to help control the flow of traffic over the access lines. Where competition is allowed in the local loop, a myriad of players may be interested in owning the local loop (e.g., ISPs, wireless operators, cable TV companies, power utilities). However, worldwide, the incumbent local providers continue to dominate the local loop, and, as usual, politics and economics are principal factors in delaying the mass deployment of high-speed residential access.

The local exchange, in the center of Figure 4.1, provides access to the backbone, or the core, of the network, which begins with the tandem switch and includes toll and international exchanges. From the local exchange, connections are established with the other providers, such as IXCs for long distance, international carriers for overseas calls, mobile providers, and ISPs.

Services Beyond the Local Loop

Traditionally, we have thought of the local loop as leading to the home or to the business and ending there. But the need for additional bandwidth and capability is now shifting: We need these things within the premises as well as on the local loop. It is therefore a logical extension for the service provider to not only give the customer access lines and termination but also to provide the home area networking facilities needed for the customer to have an end-to-end broadband package. Chapter 12, "Broadband Access Alternatives," talks more about home area networking.

The underlying network access facilities can be either analog or digital loops, and they connect the exchanges to the customer premises. At the customer premises there are the network interfaces, customer premises equipment (CPE), premises distribution systems where wiring is cross-connected, and network interfaces. The equipment for providing switch access services includes line-termination cards, carrier and multiplexer equipment, and local exchange switching capabilities that support addressing, supervisory alerting, call progress, and other signaling functions.

Access Services

The main categories of access services are trunks, business lines for key telephone systems, centrex service, leased lines, and residential subscriber lines.

Trunks are used to provide connections into the PBX environment. There are three subcategories of trunks:

- **Two-way local exchange trunks**—On these trunks, traffic flows in both the incoming and outgoing directions.
- **DID trunks**—Direct inward dialing (DID) trunks are designed for only incoming calls. A benefit of DID trunks is that they enable the dialed number to ring directly on a user's phone rather than having to go through a centralized attendant, with the connection being established within the PBX switch. If people know whom they want to call directly, this can be a very useful feature to ease the process of connecting the call. Another benefit of DID trunks is that they make it seem like a private line goes directly to the user, but DID can support perhaps 100 different numbers with a group of only 25 to 35 trunks (traffic engineering is used to determine the proper number of trunks).
- **DOD trunks**—Direct outward dialing (DOD) trunks are used specifically for outgoing calls. DOD trunks are used when you dial an access code such as the number 9 or the number 8 to get an outside-line dial tone before you can dial the actual number that you want to reach.

To service the key telephone systems, business lines connect the network termination at the user end to the local exchange. Users who want to use the local exchange as if it were their PBX rent centrex trunks on a monthly basis. Large companies often access the network via leased lines, which can be a very expensive solution, and home users access the network via residential subscriber lines.

Access lines can be either analog facilities or digital carrier services. Analog transmission is often called *plain old telephone service* (POTS). Three main types of digital services are offered over twisted-pair cable:

- Digital services involving T-1 access (at 1.5Mbps), E-1 access (at 2.048Mbps), and J-1 access (at 1.544Mbps)
- Narrowband ISDN (N-ISDN) services, including Basic Rate Interface (BRI) for residences and small businesses and Primary Rate Interface (PRI) for larger businesses
- xDSL services, including high-speed lines that enable the all-important applications of Internet access and multimedia exploration

Chapter 2, "Traditional Transmission Media," describes these types of access in more detail.

Transport Services

Transport services are the network switching, transmission, and related services that support information transfer between the originating and terminating access facilities. The underlying facilities include local exchanges and tandem switches, toll and transit switches, international gateways, and interoffice transmission equipment. Transport services include switched services, nonswitched services, and virtual private networks (VPNs).

Switched Services

There are two main types of switched services: public and private. Switched public services include local calling, long-distance calling, toll-free calling, international calling, directory assistance, operator assistance, and emergency services.

Switched private services can be switchable either because they are deployed within the CPE or because they are deployed on a carrier basis. With CPE-based services, you can add capabilities to the telephone systems onsite in the PBXs—a feature called *electronic tandem networking*. For example, you can use electronic tandem networking to gain some flexibility in routing around congestion points: If the preferred leased line from switch A to switch B is occupied or not available, the switch can decide how to reroute that traffic to still reach switch B, but through a different series of leased lines. However, because leased lines (also referred to as *tie trunks*) are mileage sensitive and dedicated to individual customers, they are very expensive; thus, not much private voice networking is done over tie trunks because there are several more attractive solutions, such as VPNs, which are discussed shortly.

With carrier-based switched private services, a centrex customer could partition and implement extensions across multiple local exchanges and thereby be able to switch traffic between those locations.

Nonswitched Services

Nonswitched services include leased lines, foreign exchange (FX) lines, and off-premises extensions (OPXs). With leased lines, two locations or two devices are always on, using the same transmission path.

FX lines enable a toll call to appear to be a local call. For example, you might have a dedicated leased line that runs from your customer premises to a local exchange in a distant area where you call large numbers of customers. When anyone behind your PBX dials a number associated with that foreign local exchange, the PBX automatically selects the FX line. The dial tone the caller receives is actually coming from the distant local exchange, and the call proceeds as if it were a local call. The tradeoff with FX lines is that although you are not charged per call for your long-distance calls to the specified exchange, you pay a flat monthly fee for the leased line, and you have to apply some traffic engineering to ensure that you're not making people wait for the FX line to become available. So with FX lines, you need to find the right balance between reducing costs and ensuring a high level of service.

OPXs are used in distributed environments, such as a city government. Say that the city government has public works stations, libraries, fire stations, and parks and recreation facilities that are too far from the PBX to be served by the normal cabling. The city uses an OPX setup: It connects a leased circuit from the PBX to the off-premises location and ties it in as if it were part of that PBX. City government employees can then call one another, using their normal extension plan, their call accounting information can be accumulated so that cost allocations can be performed, and the employees can access the full suite of features that a business PBX offers.

VPNs

Although you might think that VPNs are related to the Internet or to Internet Protocol (IP) and are a somewhat new development, they actually originated in the circuit-switched network environment, with AT&T's software-defined network (SDN) in the early 1980s. A VPN is a *concept*, not a technology platform or a set of networking techniques. A VPN defines a network in which customer traffic is isolated over shared-service provider facilities; as more customers share the same facilities, their costs go down. The purpose of a VPN, then, is to reduce the high cost of leased lines while still providing high quality of service and guaranteeing that private traffic has capacity between locations. Figure 4.2 shows an example of a VPN.

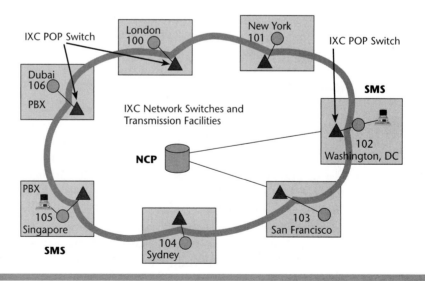

Figure 4.2 An example of a VPN

The underlying facilities of a VPN include the carrier public network, augmented by network control programs (NCPs) and service management systems (SMSs). Under computer control, the traffic is then routed through the public network in a manner that makes the VPN service seem like a facilities-based private network. Access to the VPN can occur via dedicated access, leased lines, or carrier-switched access, using either an analog or a digital carrier.

The NCP represents a centralized database that stores a subscriber's unique VPN information. The NCP screens every call and then applies call processing in accordance with the customer-defined requirements. A common-channel signaling network connects the various network elements so that they can exchange information with each other in real-time. (Common-channel signaling is discussed later in this chapter, in the section "Signaling Systems.")

An SMS is used to build and maintain the VPN database. It allows customers to program specific functions to accommodate their particular business applications. It transmits information to the NCPs, with important instructions on a customer-by-customer basis. Thus, VPNs introduce to the realm of the PSTN a lower-cost alternative to building a private voice network.

PSTN Architecture

The PSTN includes a number of transmission links and nodes. There are basically four types of nodes: CPE nodes, switching nodes, transmission nodes, and service nodes.

CPE Nodes

The term *CPE node* generally refers to equipment located at the customer site. The main function of CPE nodes is to transmit and receive user information. The other key function is to exchange control information with the network. In the traditional realm, this equipment includes PBXs, key telephone systems, and single-line telephones.

Switching Nodes

Switching nodes interconnect transmission facilities at various locations and route traffic through a network. They set up the circuit connections for a signal path, based on the number dialed. To facilitate this type of switching, the ITU standardized a worldwide numbering plan (based on ITU E.164) that essentially acts as the routing instructions for how to complete a call through the PSTN. The switching nodes include the local exchanges, tandem exchanges (for routing calls between local exchanges within a city), toll offices (for routing calls to or from other cities), and international gateways (for routing calls to or from other countries). Primary network intelligence is contained in the Class 4 switches (i.e., toll offices switches) and Class 5 switches (i.e., local exchange switches). The Class 4 switches provide long-distance switching and network features, and the Class 5 switches provide the local switching and telephony features that subscribers subscribe to. Figure 4.3 shows where the types of telephone exchanges are located.

The Local Exchange The local exchange (also called the Class 5 office or central office) is where communications common carriers terminate customer lines and locate the switching equipment that interconnects those lines. The local exchange represents the local network. Every subscriber line location in a local exchange is assigned a number, generally 7 digits (in the United States) or 8 digits (in many other countries). The first 3 (or 4) digits represent the exchange and identify the local exchange switch that serves a particular telephone. The last 4 digits identify the individual line number, which is a circuit that is physically connected from the local exchange to the subscriber. Some areas have gone to 10-digit dialing for local calls, meaning the area code must be included even when dialing a local number.

The traditional local exchange switch can handle one or more exchanges, and each exchange is capable of handling up to 10,000 subscriber lines, numbered 0000 to 9999. In large metropolitan areas, it is common to find one local exchange

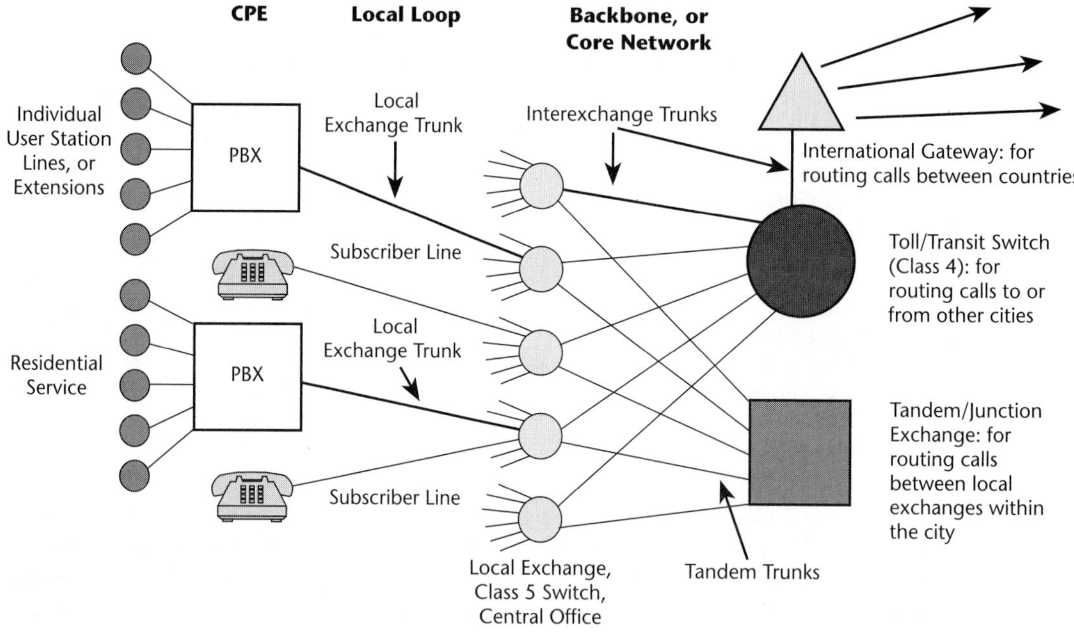

Figure 4.3 Types of telephone exchanges

building that houses more than one local exchange switch and for each switch to handle five or more exchanges. These offices are sometimes referred to as *multi-entity buildings.*

The Tandem Office   The tandem office, or junction network, is an exchange used primarily as a switching point for traffic between local exchanges in a metropolitan area. It is an office used to interconnect the local end offices over tandem trunks in a densely settled exchange area where it is not economical for a telephone company to provide direct interconnection between all end offices. The tandem office completes all calls between the end offices but is not directly connected to subscribers.

The Toll Office   The toll office (also called the trunk exchange or transit switch) is a telephone company switching center where channels and toll message circuits terminate—in other words, where national long-distance connections are made. This is usually one particular exchange in a city, but larger cities may have several exchanges where toll message circuits terminate.

The International Gateway   The international gateway is the point to and from which international services are available in each country. Protocol conversion may take place in the gateway; in ITU terminology, this is called a *centre de transit* (CT). CT1 and CT2 international exchanges connect only international circuits. CT2 exchanges switch traffic between regional groups of countries, and CT1 exchanges switch traffic between continents. CT3 exchanges connect switch traffic between the national PSTN and the international gateway.

Transmission Nodes
Transmission nodes, which are part of the transport infrastructure, provide communications paths that carry user traffic and network control information between the nodes in a network. The transmission nodes include the transmission media discussed in Chapter 2 as well as transport equipment, including amplifiers and/or repeaters, multiplexers, digital cross-connect systems, and digital loop carriers.

Service Nodes
Service nodes handle *signaling,* which is the transmission of information to control the setup, holding, charging, and releasing of connections, as well as the transmission of information to control network operations and billing. A very important area related to service nodes is the ITU standard specification Signaling System 7 (SS7), which is covered later in this chapter.

■ The Transport Network Infrastructure

The transport network includes two main infrastructures. The first is the PDH, also known as T-carrier, E-carrier, and J-carrier wideband transmission standards. This infrastructure was first introduced in the early 1960s. The second infrastructure of the transport network is the Synchronous Digital Hierarchy (SDH; ITU terminology), also known as Synchronous Optical Network (SONET; ANSI terminology), which was first formalized and standardized in 1988. SDH/SONET is the second generation of digital hierarchy, and it is based on a physical infrastructure of optical fibers.

PDH and SDH/SONET are voice-centric circuit-switched network models that switch millions of 64Kbps circuits between various switching points. Each circuit is multiplexed numerous times for aggregation onto transmission facilities. Aggregation occurs at many points in the network: in the access network, within the local exchange, and throughout the interexchanges. Hence, a significant portion of the cost of a network goes to the equipment that performs this aggregation—the multiplexers and cross-connects in both the PDH and SDH/SONET environments.

The PDH Infrastructure

The term *Plesiochronous* makes PDH sound like a dinosaur, and in a way, it is—it's an outdated architecture from the standpoint of the data rates it offers. But the word *Plesiochronous* means "minute variations in timing," which refers to the fact that PDH is an *asynchronous infrastructure*. Each network element—that is, each exchange, multiplexer, cross-connect, repeater, and so on—gets its clocking pulse from a different clocking source, and even though those clocking sources are synchronized, there are minute fluctuations in timing. To differentiate the beginning and the end of a conversation, PDH must channelize conversations.

PDH was the first system designed to use digitized voice transmission. It was born of the telcos' desire to better use their cable facilities and to enhance the quality of calls. PDH was first used by telcos as a means of aggregating multiple voice channels into a single high-speed digital backbone. Standards used today for all-digital switching and transmission come from the original PDH specifications.

PDH is an integrated digital network, so it can carry a range of traffic, as long as that traffic is presented in a digital manner. Therefore, PDH represented the first opportunity for users and carriers to combine voice and data traffic over the same pipes. In addition, it specifies the different transmission levels or data rates, some of which are available for customers to subscribe to and others of which are used by operators internally within the backbones. Finally, it defines within each of the transmission levels how many channels can be made available.

The T-, E-, and J-Carrier Standards

Various PDH standards are followed in different regions of the world: J-carrier (Japanese-carrier) in Japan, T-carrier (Terrestrial-carrier) in North America, and E-carrier (European-carrier) in Europe and most of Asia, Latin America, the Middle East, and Africa. Figure 4.4 compares these three standards. They all share one increment as a common denominator: A single channel carries 64Kbps. But each of the three standards multiplexes together a different number of these 64Kbps channels to derive higher transmission rates.

Having three separate standards—T-, E-, and J-carrier—necessitates crossing between systems that use different standards, which causes additional overhead.

Elements of the PDH Infrastructure

As shown in Figure 4.5 and described in the following sections, the following are the key elements of the PDH infrastructure:

- Transmission media
- Repeaters
- Channel service units (CSUs)/data service units (DSUs)
- Multiplexers
- Digital loop carriers (DLCs)
- Digital cross-connect systems (DCSs)

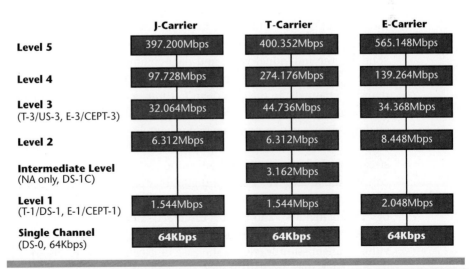

	J-Carrier	T-Carrier	E-Carrier
Level 5	397.200Mbps	400.352Mbps	565.148Mbps
Level 4	97.728Mbps	274.176Mbps	139.264Mbps
Level 3 (T-3/US-3, E-3/CEPT-3)	32.064Mbps	44.736Mbps	34.368Mbps
Level 2	6.312Mbps	6.312Mbps	8.448Mbps
Intermediate Level (NA only, DS-1C)		3.162Mbps	
Level 1 (T-1/DS-1, E-1/CEPT-1)	1.544Mbps	1.544Mbps	2.048Mbps
Single Channel (DS-0, 64Kbps)	64Kbps	64Kbps	64Kbps

Figure 4.4 T-carrier, E-carrier, and J-carrier standards

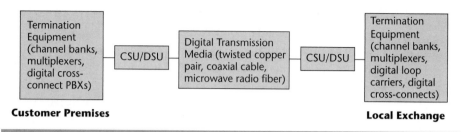

Figure 4.5 PDH components

Transmission Media PDH can include a wide variety of transmission media, and the type you use is contingent on the bandwidth you want to support. You could use copper pairs to provision T-1, E-1, or J-1 services, but if you wanted to get into the higher-bandwidth capacities afforded under T-3, E-3, or J-3, you would deploy a higher-bandwidth medium, such as coax, microwave, or fiber. PDH operates on four-wire circuits, which means it operates in full-duplex and you can communicate in both directions simultaneously.

CSUs A CSU terminates each end of a T-, E-, or J-carrier facility. It equalizes the received signal, filters the transmitted and received waveforms, and interacts with customers' and carriers' test facilities. You use a CSU to perform diagnostic tests on span lines and to set up a T-1, E-1, or J-1 line with a PBX, a channel bank, a multiplexer, or any other compliant data terminal equipment.

Multiplexers A series of time division multiplexers enables us to move up the hierarchy of the PDH infrastructure. The first in the series of multiplexers is generally referred to as *channel banks*. A channel bank has several purposes. First, it consolidates the individual voice and data channels so that they can travel over the higher-speed transmission line. In the case of a T-1 line, a channel bank consolidates 24 channels; in the case of an E-1 line, a channel bank consolidates 32 channels. Channel banks can accept analog inputs, which means they can digitize analog voice. If you're using an analog switch—either a local exchange or a PBX—the channel bank should be equipped with the codecs that run an analog voice stream through a process of digitization called Pulse Code Modulation (PCM) to convert the analog voice into a digital bitstream that can be transported over the digital carrier. (Codecs are discussed in Chapter 1, "Telecommunications Technology Fundamentals," and PCM is discussed later in this chapter.)

Beyond the channel bank, the multiplexing hierarchy steps through the individual transmission levels. In the case of T-carrier, the levels are T-1 through T-4; for E-carrier, they are E-1 through E-5; and for J-carrier, they are J-1 through J-5.

DLCs   DLCs—also called remote terminals, concentrators, or remote concentrators—were introduced in the mid-1970s, specifically as a way to economically expand the telco network. They were deployed to improve efficiency and to lower costs. DLCs reduced analog facilities by up to 80%, and they led to building, real estate liquidation, and maintenance efficiencies as well. They also eliminated the need for loading coils, which are used to improve transmission on wire pairs for distances greater than 3.4 miles (5.5 km). DLCs also reduced the number of pairs of copper wires required between the local exchange and the subscriber; they did this by sharing pairs or transmission facilities among many multiplexed conversations. Essentially, the DLC architecture, shown in Figure 4.6, reduces the loop lengths and makes more effective use of high-capacity trunks from a neighborhood into the local exchange.

DLCs continue to evolve, and as they do so, they become smaller systems. The original DLCs were built so that an individual system could service around 600 subscribers, but these boxes achieved only about a 50% fill ratio, which meant that half of the capacity was not being used. Now, given the distribution and density of neighborhoods and populations, smaller DLCs are being created. These systems service up to about 96 subscribers, and utilization is at around a 90% level. These smaller DLCs allow for faster service rollout and a shorter payback period for the deployment. They also facilitate quick response to growth in services and competition.

With ever-increasing interest in high-speed broadband access, DLCs could be a tool for shortening loop length, thereby bringing more bandwidth to the customer. Consequently, some of the additional changes that have occurred with the newer generations of DLCs also provide interfaces for SDH/SONET or optical fibers. However, the vast majority of DLCs deployed are incompatible with the xDSL services. It is imperative that the proper generation of DLC be deployed in order to meet the customer's demand for broadband residential access via twisted-pair.

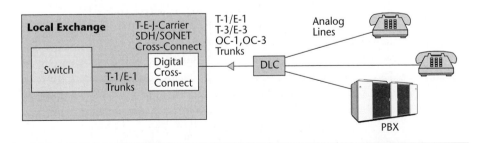

Figure 4.6   DLC architecture

DCSs   DCSs, developed in 1981 and officially introduced in 1985, basically automated the process of circuit provisioning and replaced the use of manual patch panels. The key feature of DCSs is called *drop and insert*, which refers to the capability of the cross-connect to exchange channels from one facility to another. It is used to implement appropriate routing of traffic, to reroute around congestion or failure, and to allow customers to dynamically reconfigure their own networks. Generally, drop and insert keeps communications paths in place for continuous use over a period of months, or sometimes even years, but it does allow change as demand warrants.

Essentially, a DCS is a computer system with a variety of software databases that describe first-choice routes and alternate routes (see Figure 4.7). If channel 7 normally goes out over line 1 and then goes out over trunk 1, but trunk 1 fails, the DCS can consult its alternate routing table, which might say to reroute that particular line over trunk 2. A reconfiguration can take place in a matter of minutes.

DCSs provide for different levels of switching. You can switch between DS-3s and DS-3s or between E-3s and E-3s. You can switch between DS-1s and DS-1s or between E-1s and E-1s. You can switch between DS-0s and E-0s, and you can also

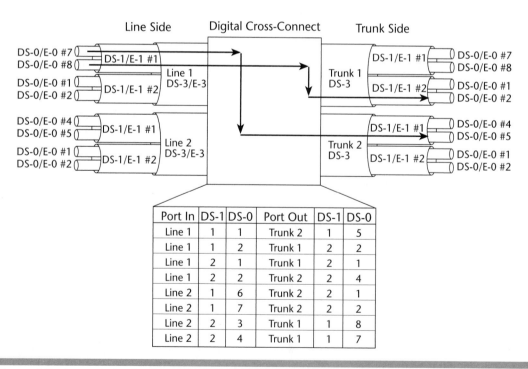

Port In	DS-1	DS-0	Port Out	DS-1	DS-0
Line 1	1	1	Trunk 2	1	5
Line 1	1	2	Trunk 1	2	2
Line 1	2	1	Trunk 1	2	1
Line 1	2	2	Trunk 2	2	4
Line 2	1	6	Trunk 2	2	1
Line 2	1	7	Trunk 2	2	2
Line 2	2	3	Trunk 1	1	8
Line 2	2	4	Trunk 1	1	7

Figure 4.7   An example of a DCS

E-Carrier: Separate Signaling Channels

The E-carrier system is different from the T-carrier and J-carrier systems in an important way: In the E-carrier system, the framing and signaling information travels in separate channels from the voice and data traffic. Two of the 32 channels are devoted to carrying signaling and framing information, and the other 30 channels are available to carry customer payload at 64Kbps. In T-carrier and J-carrier, because the signaling information flows in the conversation channel, voice channels are 64Kbps, but data channels are 56Kbps, with the remaining capacity reserved for signaling.

The SDH/SONET Infrastructure

SDH/SONET, created in the mid-1980s, is the second generation of digital hierarchy. Whereas PDH involves a lot of overhead because it includes three standards throughout the world, SDH/SONET uses one common standard that applies to networks worldwide. SDH, originally defined by the European Telecommunication Standards Institute (ETSI) for Europe, is now the most common form, used everywhere except for Japan and North America. Japan uses a version of SDH that varies slightly in some details. SONET is the American National Standards Institute (ANSI) standard, which is part of SDH, and it is used in North America. SDH/SONET was created to be an industry standard for high-speed transmission over optical fiber. It was actually part of a much bigger standard in the works at that time—Broadband ISDN. Broadband ISDN was envisioned for use with advanced applications (e.g., tele-education, telesurveillance, telemedicine, the ability to collaborate, HDTV). Two technologies were required in order to support such applications: a transport infrastructure (SDH/SONET) that had the significant bandwidth needed to support the applications and a switching technology (ATM) that could ensure that latencies could be controlled and kept very low. Consequently, SDH/SONET and ATM, as modern broadband technologies, were both born out of the Broadband ISDN standard and a desire to deliver advanced applications.

SDH/SONET is a family of transmission standards designed to achieve compatibility between different fiber-optic transport products as well as to provide compatibility with the existing digital hierarchy, PDH. A lot of fiber-optic systems have been deployed since 1984, but they're not all compatible with one another. They use different forms of cables with different diameters, and they use different types of light sources. And where there are physical incompatibilities, you can't achieve *midspan meet*—where two carrier services have to come together. A railroad analogy can be used here. Think back to when people had just begun to build railroads. Often, one provider was building tracks going east to west that were a certain width, and another provider was building tracks going west to east that were a different width.

When the providers met in the middle, their cars couldn't cross each other's tracks. The same thing happens when there's a lack of physical compatibility in fiber-optic transport, and that means you lose the ability to carry network management information on an end-to-end basis. You may not be able to do end-to-end monitoring and control of a network that is multivendor or multicarrier in nature if the vendors or carriers use incompatible physical fiber-optic equipment.

It's always important to develop and have available very strong network management tools. The goal of network management is not to *eliminate* downtime because we know that would be impractical; rather, it is to *minimize* the resolution time. So the ability to do end-to-end testing remotely is very critical to quick recoverability. SDH/SONET provides the physical layer (i.e., Layer 1) framework for broadband applications. It provides a standardized list of optical parameters that define the allowed types of cables and light sources. It defines a new table of data rates that are much higher than older transmission rates. It redefines how the multiplexing process occurs as you move within the different transmission levels. It also affords very robust operations capabilities, such as service restoration.

The SDH/SONET specifications define a *frame format*—that is, how the bits are packaged together to be transported over the fiber. As mentioned earlier, they define the nature of the physical interfaces (e.g., couplers, light sources). They define the optical carrier line rates, or transmission levels, and they define the sorts of messages that are exchanged in order to support operations, administration, maintenance, and provisioning.

An important aspect of SDH/SONET is that it introduced the notion of a ring topology to address network survivability by providing rapid restoration. SDH/SONET uses a dual-counter-rotating ring. Imagine that you have four network nodes. As shown in Figure 4.8, with a dual-counter-rotating ring, you link each of these four network nodes together by using one pair of fibers; that pair of fibers becomes the primary fiber, and information flows over it in a clockwise manner. You run another pair of fibers, which may actually be housed in the same cable as the first pair of fibers, to join the four nodes. The second pair of fibers becomes the protect fiber, which is designed to carry information in a counterclockwise manner. In theory, if a cable is cut between node A and node B, you can still move a message from A to B by reversing the information flow and going from A to D to C to B. This enables you to recover almost immediately—within 50 milliseconds—from outages that occur.

The survivability of an SDH/SONET ring depends on how the cables are engineered; if both cables share a common housing, then it's likely that a cable cut by a construction crew will stop operating in both directions. Similarly, if a major earthquake hits and all the streets are broken up, a counter-rotating ring will not necessarily ensure survivability, but for smaller-scale problems, it can very adequately handle a backup. This is one of the greatest strengths of SDH/SONET and will

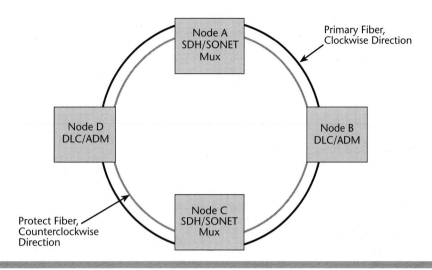

Figure 4.8   SDH/SONET ring architecture

likely keep it operational in networks for another 10 to 20 years. But these types of capabilities are also being introduced in the new generations of standards, such as WDM, and when that occurs, we will start to move away from SDH/SONET because SDH/SONET is a Time Division Multiplexing (TDM) system that does not take advantage of the fact that light can be spatially multiplexed, allowing multiple wavelengths to be carried over one fiber pair. Still, at this point, the flexibility of adding and dropping payload is one of the main reasons telcos still prefer SDH/SONET over other options: They can more easily integrate SDH/SONET into their billing systems. Although more and more customers are requesting Gigabit Ethernet, few telcos provide it.

SDH/SONET is also important because it grooms and routes traffic. *Grooming* means that SDH/SONET selectively removes channels from a digital facility for routing to a designated remote location via another digital facility; basically, it enables you to drop and add payload flexibly. SDH/SONET also provides for performance monitoring so that you can understand the performance of the network, its components, and the congestion levels.

The SDH/SONET Signal Hierarchy

The SDH/SONET signal hierarchy deals with *optical carrier (OC) levels,* which refer to the optical aspect of the transmission—the optical pulse as it travels through the fibers. These optical pulses go through electronic muxes, and when the signal is going through these network elements, the bits are packaged in a frame for transport across the fiber. In the case of SONET, this frame is called the Synchronous

Table 4.3 The SDH/SONET Signal Hierarchy

OC Level	SONET	SDH	Data Rate (Mbps)	Payload Rate (Mbps)
OC-1	STS-1	STM-0	51.48	50.840
OC-3	STS-3	STM-1	155.52	150.336
OC-9	STS-9	STM-3	466.56	451.008
OC-12	STS-12	STM-4	622.08	601.344
OC-18	STS-18	STM-6	933.12	902.016
OC-24	STS-24	STM-8	1,244.16	1,202.688
OC-36	STS-36	STM-12	1,866.00	1,804.032
OC-48	STS-48	STM-16	2,488.32	2,405.376
OC-96	STS-96	STM-32	4,876.64	4,810.752
OC-192	STS-192	STM-64	9,953.28	9,621.504
OC-768	STS-768	STM-256	39,813.12	1,327.104

Transport Signal (STS), and in SDH, the frame is called the Synchronous Transport Module (STM). Two types of rates are important in the realm of SDH/SONET: The *payload rate* refers to the capacity available to carry customer content, and the *data rate* refers to the total capacity available for customer content as well as network management information.

Table 4.3 shows the SDH/SONET signal hierarchy. You don't have to memorize all these levels, but you'll consistently encounter four or five of them in your readings that you should commit to memory. The following are the levels of the SDH/SONET signal hierarchy that you need to be familiar with:

■ OC-1—OC-1 offers about 51Mbps and is generally used as customer access lines. Early-adopter types of customers—such as universities, airports, financial institutions, large government agencies, and ISPs—use OC-1.

■ OC-3—OC-3 provides about 155Mbps. End users such as companies in the aerospace industry and high-tier ISPs need this extensive level.

- **OC-12**—OC-12 provides about 622Mbps. It is another capacity toward which high-tier ISPs are moving. It was originally deployed for the metropolitan area fiber rings built out across cities worldwide, although those rings are now moving to OC-48.

- **OC-48**—OC-48 offers about 2.5Gbps. This capacity has been deployed for backbone, or core, networks. Today the metropolitan area rings are moving from OC-12 to OC-48, and the backbone links are moving from OC-48 to OC-192.

- **OC-192**—OC-192 supports about 10Gbps and is being used for backbone networks.

Although there are more levels in the SDH/SONET signal hierarchy, the ones discussed here are the ones for which equipment is currently manufactured. We are in the early stages of deploying new muxes that operate at OC-768 and support 40Gbps. As of mid-2006, use of OC-768 connections outside research or testing networks was very rare, largely due to the fact that they are very expensive. However, given that it is the next logical speed step in the SDH/SONET hierarchy, it is predicted that there will be greater adoption of this standard going forward. On the other hand, some people feel that electronic muxes really are not suitable for the higher data rates being made possible by advances in optical technologies and that we should concentrate on moving to all-optical muxes and switches instead.

How do the high optical carrier levels relate to all the lower-level signals out there—such as those from a 1.5Mbps T-1 or a 2Mbps E-1? There are mechanisms that enable us to map signal levels below DS-3 (i.e., below 45Mbps) into what SDH calls *virtual containers* or what SONET calls *virtual tributaries*. A virtual container or tributary basically defines the data structure for the transport and switching of sub-51Mbps network services such as DS-1, E-1, DS-2, and E-3. Table 4.4 shows the various line rates that are supported and what existing standard each refers to. For most people, this type of detail won't make or break success in the industry, but it's important to know that a virtual tributary or virtual container can provide a highway for lower-rate data signals to coexist in high-speed optical pipes.

In contrast to PDH, SDH/SONET is a *synchronous* infrastructure. This means that each of the network elements draws its clocking pulse from one clocking source—so everybody is marching to the beat of the same drummer. Instead of using special framing bits to delineate channels, SDH/SONET uses a special pointer bit in front of each conversation that essentially says "start of a new conversation." When it's time to drop that channel off at a customer's premises, it is possible to identify it by its pointer bit and extract it without having to disturb any of the other traffic. This reduces the overhead associated with multiplexers by a factor of 10.

Table 4.4 Virtual Container/Virtual Tributary Line Rates and Standards

Virtual Container/ Virtual Tributary Level	Line Rate	Standard
VC-11/VT-1.5	1.728Mbps	DS-1/E-1
VC-2/VT-2	2.304Mbps	E-1
VT-3	3.456Mbps	DS-1C
VC-2/VT-6	6.912Mbps	DS-2
VT-6-N	$n \times 6.9$Mbps	(Future)
Async DS-3/VC-3	44.736/34.368Mbps	DS-3/E-3
VC-4	139.264Mbps	DS-4/E-4

SDH/SONET Muxes and Cross-Connects

SDH/SONET was built for and largely relies on fiber-optic transmission media. It also includes a variety of multiplexers and cross-connects, as well as equipment that could be placed at the customer's premises. There are two main categories of SDH/SONET multiplexers (see Figure 4.9):

- **Terminal muxes**—Terminal muxes enable signals to move through the hierarchy of optical carrier levels. They act as access nodes and support current services by accepting electrical interfaces and lower-level signals, including DS-1/E-1, DS-2, and DS-3/E-3. They concentrate one or more optical carrier signals and represent one of the optical carrier levels.

- **Add/drop muxes (ADMs)**—ADMs facilitate easy dropping and adding of payload and are therefore the building blocks of the SDH/SONET network. An ADM converts one or more lower-level signals, such as T-1 or E-1 signals, into and from one of the optical carrier levels. It can drop lower-rate signals to be transported on different facilities, or it can add lower-rate signals into the higher-rate optical carrier levels, and basically it allows telcos to add and drop traffic easily and conveniently all along the network.

There are also two categories of SDH/SONET cross-connects:

- **Wideband DCSs**—These terminate SDH/SONET and DS-3/E-3 signals. Switching occurs at the DS-0, DS-1/E-1, and VT/VC levels.

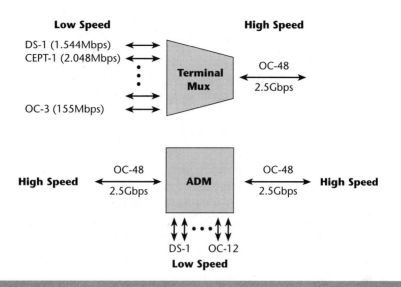

Figure 4.9 Terminal muxes versus ADMs

- **Broadband DCSs**—Broadband **DCSs** interface at the various SDH/SONET signal levels as well as the legacy DS-3/E-3 levels, but they then switch at the optical carrier levels. They can make cross-connections at DS-3/E-3, OC-1, and concatenated levels (i.e., where several frames of an OC-1 are combined). Generally, a broadband **DCS** is used as an SDH/SONET hub that grooms the optical carrier levels for broadband restoration purposes or for routing traffic.

■ Signaling Systems

The signaling system is the nervous system of the network. A great deal of information needs to pass back and forth between the network elements in the completion of a call and also in the servicing of specialized features. Four main types of signals handle this passing of information:

- **Supervisory signals**—Supervisory signals handle the on-hook/off-hook condition. For instance, when you lift a telephone handset (i.e., go off-hook), a signal tells the local exchange that you want a dial tone, and if you exist in the database as an authenticated user, you are then delivered that service; when you hang up (i.e., go back on-hook), you send a notice that says you want to remove the service. A network is always monitoring for these supervisory signals to determine when someone needs to activate or deactivate service.

■ **Address signals**—Address signals have to do with the number dialed, which essentially consists of country codes, city codes, area codes, prefixes, and the subscriber number. This string of digits, referred to as the telephone number, is, in effect, a routing instruction to the network hierarchy.

■ **Information signals**—Information signals are associated with activating and delivering various enhanced features. For instance, a call-waiting tone is an information signal, and pressing *72 on your phone might send an information signal that tells your local exchange to forward your calls.

■ **Alerting signals**—Alerting signals are the ringing tones, the busy tones, and any specific busy alerts used to indicate network congestion or unavailability.

Signaling takes place in two key parts of the network: in the access network, where it's called *loop signaling*, and in the core, where it's called *interoffice signaling* (see Figure 4.10).

With analog loop signaling, two types of starts exist:

■ **Ground start**—*Ground start* means that when you seize a particular line, it is immediately grounded so that no other call can potentially conflict with it. Ground start is used with a contentious system, perhaps a PBX at a corporate enterprise, to avoid collisions. For example, say you seize a trunk and place a call, and now you're in the ringing state. There are short periods of silence between ringing tones. The local exchange could mistake one of these periods of silence to mean that the trunk is available and try to send in a call over that same trunk over which you're trying to place a call out;

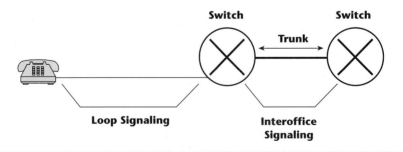

Figure 4.10 Customer loop and interoffice signaling

this would cause a collision (referred to as *glare*). Consequently, when you're dealing with systems and contention for the resource, grounding the trunk up front is the most efficient procedure.

■ **Loop start**—Pay telephones and residential phones use *loop start,* which means that the circuit is grounded when the connection is completed.

There are various start standards for digital subscriber signaling, and they are defined in accordance with the service being provided.

Interoffice signaling has evolved through several generations of signaling approaches. In the first generation, called *per-trunk signaling,* the complete path— all the way to the destination point—is set up in order to just carry the signaling information in the first place (see Figure 4.11). This method uses trunks very inefficiently; trunks may be put into place to carry 20 or 30 ringing tones, but if nobody is on the other end to take that call, the network trunk is being used but not generating any revenue. Also, when a call is initiated and begins to progress, you can no longer send any other signaling information over that trunk; for instance, passing a call-waiting tone would not be feasible.

We have moved away from the per-trunk signaling environment to what we use today—common-channel signaling (CCS; see Figure 4.12). You can think of CCS as being a separate subnetwork over which the signaling message flows between intelligent networking components that assist in the call completion and in the delivery of the service logic needed to deliver the requested feature. Today, we predominantly use the ITU-T standard SS7 for CCS. SS7 refers to a group of telephony signaling protocols used to set up the majority of the world's PSTN telephone calls.

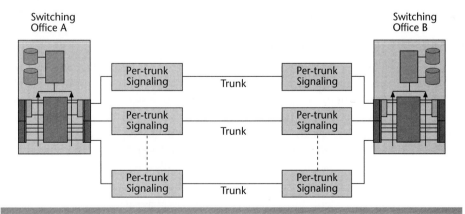

Figure 4.11   Per-trunk signaling

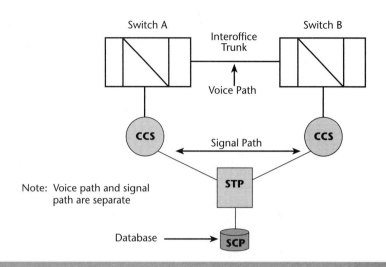

Figure 4.12 Common-channel signaling

While it is generally referred to as SS7, in North America it is also sometimes called CCS7 for Common Channel Signaling System 7, and in Europe, particularly the United Kingdom, it is referred to as C7 (for CCITT 7).

SS7 Architecture

SS7 is critical to the functioning and operation of the modern network. With SS7, a packet data network overlays and controls the operation of the underlying voice networks; signaling information is carried on an entirely different path than voice and data traffic. Signaling does not take a great deal of time, so it is possible to multiplex many signaling messages over one channel—and that's why the signaling system is a packet network. The signaling system takes advantage of the efficiencies of statistical multiplexing for what is essentially bursty data. The SS7 signaling data link is a full-duplex digital transmission channel that operates at either 56Kbps or 64Kbps, depending on the standards under which the network is operating (e.g., T-carrier and J-carrier operate at 56Kbps, E-carrier operates at 64Kbps).

SS7 is an entire architecture that performs out-of-band signaling (i.e., signaling in which the conversation and the signaling take place over different paths) in support of the information-exchange functions necessary in the PSTN, such as call establishment, billing, and routing. Database access messages convey information between toll centers and centralized databases to permit real-time access to billing-related information and other services. The SS7 architecture defines the procedures for the setup, ongoing management, and clearing of a call, and it enables the passing along of customer-related information (e.g., the identity of the caller, the primary carrier chosen) that helps in routing calls. The efficiency of the network also results in faster call setup times and provides for more efficient use of the circuits when carrying the voice or data traffic. In addition, SS7 supports services that require signaling during a call as it is occurring—not in the same band as the conversation.

SS7 permits the telephone company to offer one database to several switches, thereby freeing up switch capacity for other functions, and this is what makes SS7 the foundation for intelligent networks (INs) and advanced intelligent networks (AINs). (INs and AINs are discussed later in this chapter.) It is also the foundation for network interconnection and enhanced services. Without SS7, we would not be able to enjoy the level of interoperability we have today. SS7 is also a key to the development of new generations of services on the Internet, particularly those that support traditional telephony services. To be able to accommodate features such as call forwarding, call waiting, and conference calling, you must be able to tap into the service logic that delivers those features. Until quite recently, the Internet has not been able to do this, but the year 2000 saw the introduction of SS7 gateways, which allow an interface between circuit-switched networks (with their powerful SS7 infrastructure) and the emerging packet-switched networks that need to be capable of handling the more traditional type of voice communications on a more cost-effective basis.

As Figure 4.13 shows, there are three prerequisite components in the SS7 network:

- **Service-switching points (SSPs)**—SSPs are the switches that originate and terminate calls. They receive signals from the CPE and perform call processing on behalf of a user. The user, by dialing particular digits, triggers the network to request certain services. For instance, if you preface a number with a toll-free prefix, that toll-free arrangement triggers the local exchange, or SSP, to initiate a database lookup to determine the physical address of that toll-free number (i.e., where it resides in the network). The SSP reaches into the network to find the database that can translate the toll-free number into a physical address in order to then complete the toll-free call. The SSP does this by interacting with the SCP, as discussed shortly.

  SSPs are typically implemented at local exchanges, access tandem offices, or toll centers that contain the network-signaling protocols. The SSP serves as the source and destination point for the SS7 messages.

- **Service control points (SCPs)**—The SCP is the network element that interfaces with the SSP as well as the STP. Most importantly, the SCP is

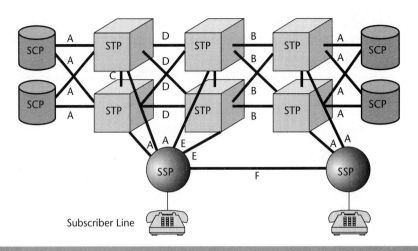

Figure 4.13 An SS7 network

the network element that contains the network configuration and call-completion database; in other words, it contains the service logic to act on the types of calls and features the users are requesting. SCPs are centralized nodes that contain service logic—basically software and databases—for the management of the call. They provide functions such as digit translation, call routing, and verification of credit cards. The SCPs receive traffic from the SSP via the STP and return responses, based on that query, via the STP.

■ **Signal transfer points (STPs)**—The STP is responsible for translating the SS7 messages and then routing those messages between the appropriate network nodes and databases. Notice in Figure 4.13 that the SCPs and the STPs are both redundant and that the links running between them are also redundant.

If a network loses its signaling system, it loses the capability to complete calls, as well as to do any form of billing or passing along of management information. This makes SS7 critical. The SS7 signaling data link, as mentioned earlier in the chapter, is a full-duplex digital transmission channel that operates at either 56Kbps or 64Kbps. A variety of other SS7 links are defined as well, and each has specific uses within the signaling network:

■ **A (access) links**—An A link interconnects an STP with either an SSP or an SCP. The SSP and SCP, collectively, are referred to as the *signaling endpoints*. A message sent to and from the SSPs or SCPs first goes to its home STP, which, in turn, processes or routes the message.

- **B (bridge) links, D (diagonal) links, and B/D links**—A B link connects an STP to another STP. Typically, a quad of B links interconnect peer (or primary) STPs (e.g., the STPs from one network to the STPs of another network). The distinction between a B link and a D link is rather arbitrary, and such links may be referred to as *B/D links*.

- **C (cross) links**—C links interconnect mated STPs.

- **E (extended) links**—E links provide enhanced reliability by providing a set of links from the SSP to a second STP pair.

- **F (fully associated) links**—F links are links that directly connect to signaling endpoints.

Intelligent Networks

The ITU's standardization of SS7 in 1980 began the evolution toward the concept of intelligent networking. An IN includes a set of nodes that rely on widespread distribution of call-handling functions and capabilities (see Figure 4.14). Before the advent of INs, customers could have only the services and features available from their local exchanges. Their ability to demand and achieve new services from the operator was very much tied to the generation of software in the local exchange and whether it had yet incorporated the feature of interest. With INs,

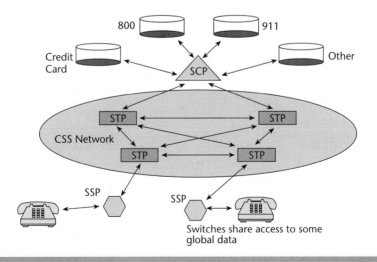

Figure 4.14 An IN

you can centrally place this type of service and feature logic on a node (such as an SCP), and then any switch can reach it and make use of that feature. The objective of intelligent networking was initially to ease the introduction of new services into the network. It also provided a foundation for complex services that would be required and desirable on a networkwide basis, such as the automation of the operator-assistance function. Because of INs and specialized peripherals—again, computing systems loaded with specific software—we no longer have to use operators to place a credit card call or a collect call.

Intelligent networking gives carriers the capability to directly develop network functionality on outboard processors connected to the switches instead of being tied to their switch manufacturer and relying on the internal software. A main feature developed for intelligent networking during the early and mid-1980s was *digit translation*, which was applied to toll-free number translation and VPNs. Customers could develop a unique calling plan that identified their location. They could invent their own numbering plan so that they could dial numbers that were easy for them to remember, and in the network, the IN infrastructure would translate those private numbers into network physical addresses (e.g., country code, city code, area code).

Intelligent networking also enables operator-assistance features such as eliminating credit card calling and collect calling as manual fulfillment processes. In addition, intelligent networking enables the identification of primary carriers (where competition exists) so that customers can select their primary carriers. *Local number portability*—which allows you to keep your own telephone number when you move to a new location—can be delivered thanks to the sophistication of this IN infrastructure (and thanks to important legislation vociferously objected to by the telcos). With local number portability, although your physical address will be different at your new location, you may want to keep your old phone number so your friends and colleagues can easily recall it. But for calls made with your old number to reach your new physical address, there must be translation tables in the network that can identify your correct physical address and properly route incoming calls to you.

AINs

Around the mid-1980s, Bellcore (which is now Telcordia) pioneered the second generation of INs, called AINs (see Figure 4.15). AINs move the service logic outside the switch and onto an independent SCP. An AIN has a service-independent network architecture that allows carriers to create and uniformly support telecom services and features via a common architectural platform, with the objective of allowing for rapid creation of customizable telecommunication services.

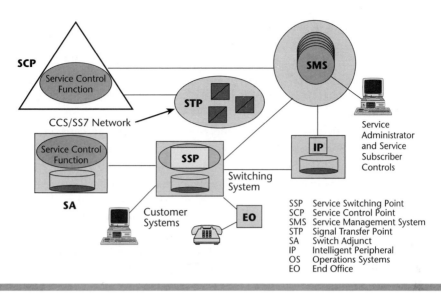

SCP

Service Control
Function

CCS/SS7 Network

STP

SMS

Service
Administrator
and Service
Subscriber
Controls

IP

Service Control
Function

SSP

Switching
System

SA

Customer
Systems

EO

SSP	Service Switching Point
SCP	Service Control Point
SMS	Service Management System
STP	Signal Transfer Point
SA	Switch Adjunct
IP	Intelligent Peripheral
OS	Operations Systems
EO	End Office

Figure 4.15 AIN architecture

An AIN is composed of intelligent nodes that are linked via SS7 to support a variety of services and advanced call-handling features across multiple vendor domains. With the introduction of the AIN architecture, a few additional components were needed. First, the SMS is a service-creation environment that facilitates the technical and customer service representatives' interface with the provisioning and network management systems. Second, intelligent peripherals are computing platforms that serve a very specific purpose but have a very widespread demand across the network (e.g., voice recognition and voice synthesis capabilities to process third-party-assisted calls).

AINs can be used for a number of applications, including intelligent call routing, visitor location registration, virtual number service, voice-activated dialing, voice response, speech recognition, and text-to-speech conversion. The AIN infrastructure is critical in mobile communications. The reason you can roam across cellular networks is that IN databases are able to log whether you are present in your home network or in a visitor network, and they can identify whether you're authenticated to use the network. If you are authenticated to use the network, IN databases can identify which services should be made available to you. Virtual number services are also an important application of AINs; for example, a 700 number can identify and locate you within a footprint rather than requiring you to be at a specific telephone to receive a call.

■ SS7 and Next-Generation Networks

The SS7 network acts as the backbone for the PSTN and INs; it provides access to the IN features, allows for efficient call setup and teardown, and interconnects thousands of service providers under one common signaling network. The capability to communicate with SS7 networks is essential for all service providers because SS7 networks give next-generation local exchange carriers access to an existing base of service features. Operators and service providers have begun the migration to IP-based network architecture (see Chapter 8, "The Internet and IP Infrastructures"). However, no one expects an overnight transition; instead, we need to find a way to support both traditional circuit-switched and contemporary IP-based services on a single network infrastructure. There is little doubt that circuit-switched services will continue to have a fruitful life for some years to come, but they will have to increasingly live with IP services, so the obvious solution is a hybrid architecture that enables a low-risk evolution while allowing for new service offerings.

There are now new genres of equipment and protocols to ensure that packet-based telephony switching gateways can in fact support key legacy services and signaling features. For example, a next-generation gateway switch supports the traditional Class 4, or toll switch, services and the Class 5, or local exchange switch, services. It is designed to support a wide variety of traffic—data, voice, fax, multimedia, and other emerging media types—over a data backbone. The next-generation gateway switch provides seamless interoperability between the circuits that network the PSTN and packet-switching networks, such as IP backbones, ATM networks, Frame Relay networks, and emerging MPLS networks. We can use these gateway switches to connect with the SS7 network and to handle the IP services that are so popular today. These gateway switches can support a variety of telephony signaling protocols (e.g., H.323, Session Initiation Protocol [SIP], and Media Gateway Control Protocol [MGCP]) for communicating with the underlying SS7 architecture. (Chapter 9, "IP Services," discusses all the call control signaling standards.)

As shown in Figure 4.16, there are different forms of these next-generation gateway switches for different purposes. In the bottom right of Figure 4.16 is an ILEC and its resident circuit-switched network, which is a series of Class 5 offices at the perimeter. These Class 5 offices are connected to the SS7 network or the STPs via A links. These Class 5 offices then connect into a CLEC's packet-switched network, and their first point of interface is a gateway switch. Among other things, this gateway switch is responsible for digitizing and packetizing the voice to prepare it for transport over the packet-switched network. The CLEC's packet-switched network also has an SS7 gateway, which is capable of communicating with the underlying ILEC's SS7 network so that it can map the appropriate IP

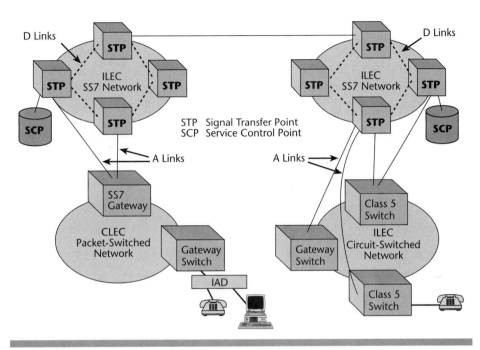

Figure 4.16 Next-generation gateway switches

addresses associated with the destination telephone number, which is served by a given destination media gateway. The next-generation gateway switch, therefore, provides a means to seamlessly interoperate between two very important and existing infrastructures. Signaling gateways allow both legacy and new equipment to seamlessly operate over high-bandwidth, scalable, and available IP-based core networks instead of taxing the TDM-based legacy SS7 network.

Figure 4.17 is an end-to-end view of a next-generation network. It shows an interconnected environment between the legacy circuit-switched network and the emerging packet-based networks. A subscriber at the customer premises (e.g., a residence, a business site) is connected to the local exchange, known as the *end office*, by access lines. From there, trunks link to a media gateway switch, which, through SS7 interfaces, can reach into the underlying intelligence within the SS7 network and further add the necessary information to process the call as requested. The call then goes out on a packet basis throughout a series of switches or routers (depending on what the provider is using as the backbone) and reaches a destination media gateway switch that unpackages the voice, undigitizes it, and delivers it to the destination phone.

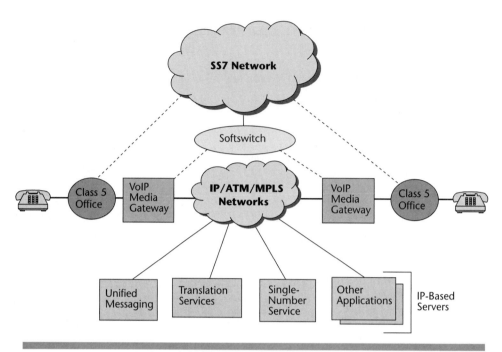

Figure 4.17   An end-to-end next-generation network

Next-Generation Networks and the PSTN

Although tremendous amounts of time and money have been spent in developing the intelligence that provides the PSTN telephony features we know today, operators are seeking ways to consolidate voice and data traffic, platforms, and services in order to reduce the operational, maintenance, and initial costs of the network. IP-based networks are now considered the best path to building converged networks from which integrated services can be offered. There are many benefits associated with an IP network, including less expensive equipment, easier deployment, higher bandwidth, and the opportunity for many enhanced services. These new IP-based services include unified messaging, IP telephony, IP-based virtual private networks (IP VPNs), IPTV, and mobile IP, among many others. Both fixed and mobile operators are choosing to deploy such all-IP infrastructures, which include support for SS7 signaling protocols.

Given the substantial presence of circuit-switched networks that continue to deliver high-quality voice and data connections and still have plenty of useful life, it is clear that an integration solution is required to interconnect the PSTN and the growing number of IP networks. The charter of the IETF Signaling Transport (SIGTRAN) Working Group, established in 1999, is to develop and standardize the messages and protocols necessary to carry mobile and PSTN signaling over IP networks (i.e., SS7 over IP). The SIGTRAN Working Group has defined a new architectural model that enables the evolution to an all-IP network. This new model defines the appropriate protocols required for converging the PSTN and IP networks. The SIGTRAN protocols provide all the functionality needed to support SS7 signaling over IP networks, including flow control; in-sequence delivery of signaling messages within a single control stream; identification of the originating and terminating signaling points; identification of voice circuits; error detection, retransmission, and other error-correcting procedures; recovery from outages of components in the transit path; control to avoid congestion on the Internet; detection of the status of peer entities (i.e., in service, out of service); support for security mechanisms to protect the integrity of the signaling information; and extensions to support security and future requirements.

The characteristics of next-generation networks are very different from what the traditional PSTN was aiming at. Next-generation networks are not designed for just voice, data, or video. They are designed for multimedia and streaming media, and this requires capacities that are broadband in nature, networks that are engineered for extremely low and controllable latencies, and infrastructures that provide the ability to administer quality of service on a very granular level.

This book has talked about the explosion of bandwidth that's occurring because of developments in optics. As the availability of bandwidth increases, bandwidth becomes cheaper and cheaper. When bandwidth becomes very inexpensive or almost free, a carrier needs to find other ways to generate revenue, such as by offering a large variety of value-added services (e.g., reliability, priority, customer service, and encryption or security). But to administer all these services and to provide differentiated pricing, which can result in handsome revenue streams, there must be mechanisms for controlling, monitoring, and billing.

The next-generation network infrastructure has a number of important features that are covered in detail in later chapters:

- It has very fast packet switching, with capacities that we're beginning to need to measure in terabits per second (Tbps) and soon in petabits per second (1Pbps = 1,000Tbps), and on its heels, in exabits per second (1Ebps = 1 billion Gbps). (See Chapter 10.)
- It places great emphasis on optical networking elements to take advantage of the abundant bandwidth inherent in the visible light spectrum. (See Chapter 11, "Optical Networking.")
- Multiservice agnostic platforms have been created, so we will not have separate devices for voice and data as we do today, but we'll have nodes that can accommodate any traffic type and protocol. We're also introducing

intelligent edges—where the smarts for processing service requests, delivering features, and accommodating advanced applications are deployed at the edge rather than in the core network. This allows for more rapid introduction, as well as more customization of the feature sets. The core also has to be multiservice because it needs to differentiate between the requirements of the different traffic streams, but more importantly, the next-generation core must be ultrafast and ultrareliable. (See Chapter 10.)

■ Next-generation telephony is very important for new entrants, particularly because of the costs of deploying normal local exchanges. A regular local exchange costs in the neighborhood of US$3 million to US$5 million, whereas a media gateway will be on the order of US$100,000. For those seeking to become competitors in the local loop environment, next-generation telephony offers a very cost-effective means of gaining entry. (See Chapter 9.)

■ Intelligent networking is being applied to the public data infrastructure as well as the Internet. From an architectural standpoint, the ITU's next-generation network relies heavily on the IP Multimedia Subsystem (IMS) framework (see Chapter 10). IMS creates a telephony-oriented signaling network that overlays an underlying IP network, replacing traditional telco SS7 signaling and acting as a control plane for both wireless and wireline networks.

■ Network operators are introducing video and multimedia elements, video servers, media farms, video compression, and decompression devices, all of which become part of what constitutes the entire communications network. (See Chapter 10.)

■ Access is moving toward the broadband realm on both a wired basis and a wireless basis. (See Chapter 12.)

Part II

Data Networking
and the Internet

Chapter 5

Data Communications Basics

This chapter explores some of the basics of data communications. It starts with a discussion of the evolution of data communication and then discusses the terminology used to describe different aspects of data networking. It's important to have a good grasp of these basics before wading into deeper waters.

■ The Evolution of Data Communications

Data communication, or *data networking*, is the exchange of digital information between computers and other digital devices via telecommunications nodes and wired or wireless links. To understand the evolution of networking services, it is important to first understand the general computing architectures and traffic types, both of which have changed over time.

Data Communications Architectures

In the rather brief history of data networking, a variety of architectures have arisen, and each has had unique impacts on network characteristics. Table 5.1 shows a basic time line of the architectures that have prevailed during different periods. Each architecture has slightly different traffic characteristics and requirements in terms of security and access control, and each has presented a different volume and consistency of traffic to the network. As described in the following sections, each new computing architecture has created a demand for new generations of network services.

Table 5.1 Time Line of Data Networking Architectures

Time	Architecture
1970s	Standalone mainframes
Early 1980s	Networked mainframes
Early 1980s	Standalone workstations
Early to late 1980s	Local area networking
Mid-1980s to mid-1990s	LAN internetworking
Mid-1990s	Internet commercialization
Mid- to late 1990s	Application-driven networks
Late 1990s	Remote-access workers
Early 2000s	Home area networking
Mid-2000s	Personal area networks and the Internet as corporate backbone

Standalone Mainframes

The 1970s was the era of standalone mainframes. These were very hierarchical networks, where certain paths needed to be taken. It was a time of terminal-to-host connectivity. At the bottom of the heap were smart terminals; a group of these terminals would report to an upper-level manager, often referred to as a *cluster controller*. The cluster controller was responsible for managing the traffic flows in and out of its underlying terminals and for scheduling resources upstream from those terminals. In turn, a number of cluster controllers would be managed by yet another level of manager, called the *front-end processor*, which served as the interface between the underlying communications network and the applications stored in the host. That front-end processor ultimately led to the host, where the users' applications resided.

In that era, a given terminal could have access only to the host upstream from it. To make use of applications that resided on another host, a user either needed a different terminal or had the pleasure of working with a variety of cables under his or her desk, changing the connections as needed.

Networked Mainframes

A major change occurred in the early 1980s: People began networking the mainframes. This was called *multidomain networking*, and it enabled one terminal device on a desktop to access numerous hosts that were networked together.

Standalone Workstations

Also in the early 1980s, standalone workstations began to appear in the enterprise. This did not generally happen because the data-processing department had decided that it would move to workstations; rather, it happened because technically astute users began to bring their own workstations into the firm, and then they would ask the data-processing or management information services (MIS) department to allow connectivity into the corporate resources from their workstations, which was generally accommodated via dialup modems or X.25.

LANs

As independent workstations began to penetrate the corporate environment, people started to study how data was actually being used. They found that 80% of the information used in a business was coming from within that location and only 20% was exchanged with other locations or other entities. This let businesses know that for the majority of their communications, they needed networks that had limited geographical span, and hence evolved the local area network (LAN). LANs were defined as serving a business address—a given building or at most a campus environment.

A shift began to occur in how the network needed to accommodate data. In the mainframe environment, with its single-terminal-to-host communications, traffic volumes were predictable. The traffic levels between a given terminal and its host were known, so it was possible to make some fairly adequate assumptions about the amount of capacity to provision between those two points. However, in the LAN environment, the traffic patterns were very unpredictable. For example, in a business with 100 PCs on one LAN and 50 PCs on another LAN, the level of traffic on each LAN might change throughout the day. Sometimes it was extremely high volume, sometimes there was nothing going on, and sometimes it was a steady, average stream. This unpredictability introduced a requirement for network services that could be flexible in how they addressed bandwidth requirements (i.e., services that could introduce bandwidth on demand). Frame Relay, which is discussed in Chapter 7, "Wide Area Networking," is one such network service. Frame Relay has the capability to provide more bandwidth than the user subscribes to, but because the traffic patterns fluctuate, the overall usage should balance out at the end of the day.

Throughout the mid- to late 1980s, the major design emphasis was on deploying LANs, which help to speed up corporate communications, to make the workforce more productive, and to reduce costs associated with sharing software and hardware resources.

LAN Internetworking

As LANs were popping up in enterprises all over, it became necessary to come up with a tool for internetworking them. Otherwise, islands of knowledge existed on a given LAN, but those islands couldn't communicate with other departments, clusters, or divisions located elsewhere in the enterprise. LAN internetworking therefore took place throughout the late 1980s and early to mid-1990s, bringing with it the evolution, introduction, and rapid penetration of interconnection devices such as hubs, bridges, routers, and brouters, whose purpose is to internetwork between separate networks.

Internet Commercialization

In the mid-1990s, yet another alternative for data networking came about with the commercialization of the Internet. Before about 1995, the Internet was mainly available to the academic, research, and government communities. Because it presented a very cost-effective means for data networking, particularly with text-based, bursty data flows, it held a significant appeal for the academic and research community. However, until the introduction of the World Wide Web, the Internet remained largely an academic platform. The intuitive graphical interfaces and navigational controls of the WWW made it of interest to those without UNIX skills—that is, anyone with a PC running some version of Windows—and hastened the demise of just about every other form of Internet communications, including Archie, Gopher, WAIS, and Veronica. The Internet was particularly useful for applications such as e-mail, for which there was finally one standard that was open enough to enable messaging exchanges between various businesses that used different systems.

Application-Driven Networks

The mid- to late 1990s began to see the development of advanced, bandwidth-hungry applications, such as videoconferencing, collaboration, multimedia, and media conferencing. This caused another shift in how people thought about deploying networks. In the days of hierarchical networks, decisions about network resources were based on the number of devices and their distance from one another. But when advanced applications—which had great capacity demands and could not tolerate delays or congestion—began to be developed, these applications began to dictate the type of network needed. Therefore, the architecture shifted from being device driven to being application driven.

Remote-Access Workers

In the late 1990s, with the downsizing of IT departments, both in terms of physical size and cost, it became much easier to deploy IT resources to the worker than to require the worker to come to the IT resources. Remote access, or teleworking, became a frequently used personnel approach that had advantages in terms of enhanced employee productivity, better morale, and savings in transportation costs. Also, as many large corporations downsized, workers became self-employed and worked from small offices or home offices. This architecture featuring remote-access workers focused on providing appropriate data networking capabilities to people in their homes, in hotels, in airports, and in any other place where they might need to access the network. Facilities were designed specifically to authenticate and authorize remote users and to allow them access to corporate LANs and their underlying resources.

HANs

Today, individuals are increasingly using their residences as places to carry out professional functions, and they need to network intelligent devices used for work, educational, or leisure activities. Therefore, home area networks (HANs) are becoming a new network domain that needs to be addressed; these days, we don't need to think about just the last mile, but about the last 328 feet (100 m)! Of course, what this really means is that we are bringing LAN technology into the home, with the likes of Wi-Fi being extremely popular at this time. (HANs are discussed in more detail in Chapter 12, "Broadband Access Alternatives.")

PANs

A personal area network (PAN) is a network that serves a single person or small workgroup and is characterized by limited distance, limited throughput, and low volume. PANs are used to transfer data between a laptop or PDA and a desktop machine or server and a printer. They usually support virtual docking stations, peripheral sharing, and ad hoc infrared links. An increasing number of machine-to-machine (m2m) applications are emerging, as are applications involving wearables and even implants; their key benefits cannot be realized without PANs. In the case of wearables and implants, the PAN exists on, or even in, the person. In fact, when talking about wearables, some refer to fabric area networks (FANs), in which the network is embedded in the fabric a person wears.

The Internet as Corporate Backbone

Another trend, just beginning to emerge, is the disappearance of the corporate LAN. In areas of the world where bandwidth is plentiful and cheap, some forward-thinking organizations have begun shrinking their LANs and relying on the Internet to play the role of corporate backbone. These companies have migrated many of their applications to Web-based services housed in (often outsourced) data centers. The applications are owned and maintained by the corporation; all access is via Internet-connected Web browser and is authenticated against a corporate directory server. These organizations no longer face the burden and expense of maintaining complicated corporate networks sprawling with various "extranets" and multilevel demilitarized zones (DMZs). The rise of high-speed ubiquitous Internet connections and reliable portable authentication has finally made such "deperimeterization" possible.

Data Communications Traffic

As the architecture of data networks has changed, so have the applications people use, and as applications have changed, so has the traffic on the network. This section talks about some of the most commonly used applications today and how much bandwidth they need, how sensitive they are to delay, where error control needs to be performed, and how well the applications can tolerate loss.

The most pervasive, frequently used applications are Web surfing and e-mail. Various forms of Web applications have dramatically different network requirements. With standard text-based exchanges (i.e., the downloading of largely text-based pages), Web surfing is not a highly challenging application. But as mentioned in the Introduction and emphasized throughout Part III, "The New Generation of Networks," the introduction of applications that include images, animation, real-time voice, real-time video, streaming media, and interactivity creates the need for greater capabilities in the network. This includes the need for more bandwidth to support the demanding interactive audio/video realm and mechanisms that address quality of service (QoS), which enables the control of priorities, latencies (delays), and packet losses. As discussed in Part III and Part IV, "Wireless Communications," optical and wireless broadband technologies are delivering more and more bandwidth, and QoS techniques are increasingly finding their way into networks.

Today, it's possible to append an entire family vacation photo album to an e-mail message, and such a massive file requires a lot of bandwidth. But e-mail in its generic text-based form is a low-bandwidth application that is delay insensitive. If an e-mail message gets trapped somewhere in the Net for several seconds, its understandability will not be affected because by the time you view it, it will have all been put on the server where your e-mail resides, waiting for you to pick it up. Another important issue with e-mail is error control. Networks today rarely perform error control because it slows down the traffic too much, so error control and recovery need to be handled at the endpoints. Instead, internetworking protocols deployed at the end node, such as TCP, detect errors and request retransmissions to fix them.

Another prevalent data networking application is transaction processing. Examples of transaction processing include a store getting approval for a credit card purchase and a police officer checking a database for your driver's license number to see whether you have any outstanding tickets. Transaction processing is characterized by many short inputs and short outputs, which means it is generally a fairly low-bandwidth application, assuming that it involves text-based messages. Remember that if you add images or video, the bandwidth requirements grow substantially. Thus, if a police officer downloads a photo from your license, the bandwidth required rises. Transaction processing is very delay sensitive because with transactions, you generally have a person waiting for something to be completed (e.g., for a reservation to be made, for a sales transaction to be approved, for a seat to be assigned by an airline). Users want subsecond response time, so with transaction processing, minimizing delays is very important, and increased traffic contributes to delay. For example, say you're at an airport and your flight is canceled. Everyone queues up to get on another flight. The agents work as quickly as they can, but because of the increased level of traffic as more people try to get on the one available flight, everything backs up, and you have to wait a long time for a response. With transaction processing, you have to be aware of delay, and error control is the responsibility of the endpoints. Transaction processing is fairly tolerant of losses because the applications ensure that all the elements and records associated with a particular transaction have been properly sent and received before committing the transaction to the underlying database.

Another type of application is file transfer, which involves moving a large amount of data from one computer to another. File transfer is generally a high-bandwidth application because it deals with a bulk of data, particularly if you are in a hurry to receive the entire file. File transfer is machine-to-machine communication, and the machines can work around delay factors, as long as they're not trying to perform a real-time function based on the information being delivered. File transfer is a passive activity—that is, it does not drive process control—and it can tolerate delay. File transfer can also tolerate losses because a reliable protocol such as TCP ensures that any errored or lost data is retransmitted, hence no data is lost. With file transfer, error control can be performed at the endpoints.

Two other important applications are interactive computing and information retrieval. With these applications, bandwidth is dependent on the objects being retrieved: If it's text, it's low bandwidth; if it's streaming or interactive video, the experience may not always be satisfactory. Interactive computing and information retrieval are delay sensitive when it comes to downloads, so higher speeds are preferred. Real-time voice is a low-bandwidth application but is extremely delay sensitive. Real-time audio and video require medium, high, and even very high bandwidth, and they are extremely delay sensitive (both end-to-end delay and jitter), and the applications work much better if the packets arrive in their original sequence. Multimedia traffic and interactive services require very high bandwidth, and they are also extremely sensitive to end-to-end delay and jitter, perform better if the packets arrive in their original sequence, and are extremely loss sensitive.

Anything that is text-based—such as e-mail, transaction processing, file transfer, and even the ability to access a database for text-based information—is fairly tolerant of losses. But in real-time traffic—such as voice, audio, or video—losses cause severe degradation in the application. For new generations of networks, the ITU (www.itu.int) suggests that packet loss should not exceed 1%; that's far from the case in today's networks. The public Internet, being a global infrastructure, has a wide range of experiences. In some parts of the world, generally in developing countries, packet losses can surpass 40% during peak hours, while developed nations have an average of approximately 5% during the day. To take a look at Internet traffic statistics, including measurements for response times (delays) and packet losses, you can visit www.internettrafficreport.com.

■ Data Flow

As discussed in the following sections, a number of important issues affect data flow in a network:

- The parts of the data circuit that comprises every network, including data terminal equipment (DTE), the data communications (or channel or circuit-terminating) equipment (DCE), the transmission channel, and the physical interface
- Modems and modulation
- Simplex, half-duplex, and full-duplex data transmission
- Coding schemes
- Asynchronous and synchronous transmission modes
- Error control

The DTE, the DCE, the Transmission Channel, and the Physical Interface

Every data network is a data circuit that has seven parts: the originating DTE, its physical interface, the originating DCE, the transmission channel, the receiving DCE, its physical interface, and the receiving DTE (see Figure 5.1). The transmission channel is the network service that the user subscribes to with a carrier (e.g., a dialup connection with an ISP).

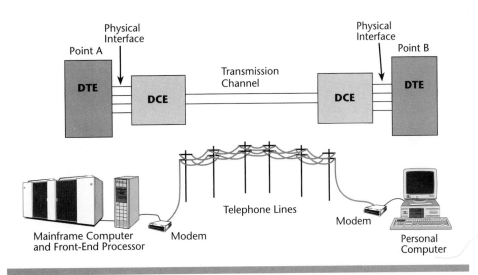

Figure 5.1 The DTE, DCE, transmission channel, and physical interface

The DTE transmits data between two points without error; its main responsibilities are to transmit and receive information and to perform error control. The DTE generally supports the end-user applications program, data files, and databases. The DTE includes any type of computer terminal, including PCs, as well as printers, hosts, front-end processors, multiplexers, and LAN interconnection devices such as routers.

The DCE, on the other hand, provides an interface between the DTE and the transmission channel (i.e., between the carrier's networks). The DCE establishes, maintains, and terminates a connection between the DTE and the transmission channel. It is responsible for ensuring that the signal that comes out of the DTE is compatible with the requirements of the transmission channel. So, for instance, with an analog voice-grade line, the DCE would be responsible for translating the digital data coming from the PC into an analog form that could be transmitted over that voice-grade line. A variety of different conversions (e.g., digital-to-analog conversion, conversion in voltage levels) might need to take place in a network, depending on the network service. The DCE contains the signal coding that makes these conversions possible. For example, a DCE might have to determine what voltage level to assign to a one bit and what level to assign to a zero bit. There are rules about how many of one type of bit can be sent in a row, and if too many of them are sent in sequence, the network can lose synchronization, at which point transmission errors might be introduced. The DCE applies such rules and performs the needed signal conversions. DCEs all perform essentially the same generic function, but the names differ depending on the type of network service to which they're attached. Examples of DCEs include channel service units (CSUs), data service units (DSUs), network termination units, PBX data terminal interfaces, and modems.

Another part of a data network is the physical interface, which defines how many pins are in the connector, how many wires are in the cable, and what signal is carried over which of the pins and over which of the wires, to ensure that the information is viewed compatibly. In Figure 5.1, the lines that join the DTE and DCE represent the physical interface. There are many different forms of physical interfaces.

Modems and Modulation

No discussion of data communications is complete without a discussion of modulation. As mentioned in Chapter 1, "Telecommunications Technology Fundamentals," the term *modem* is a contraction of the terms *modulate* and *demodulate*, and these terms refer to the fact that a modem alters a carrier signal based on whether it is transmitting a one or a zero. Digital transmission requires the use of modulation schemes, which are sometimes also called *line-coding techniques*. Modulation schemes convert the digital information onto the transmission medium (see Figure 5.2). Over time, many modulation schemes have been developed, and they vary in the speed at which they operate, the quality of wire they require, their immunity to noise, and their complexity. The variety of modulation schemes means that incompatibilities exist.

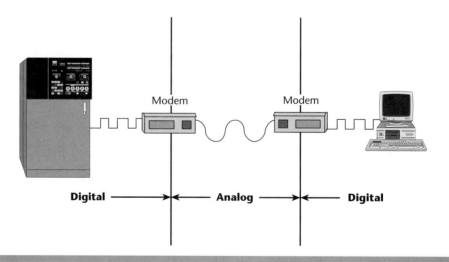

Figure 5.2 Modems

Components of Modulation Schemes

Modems can vary any of the three main characteristics of analog waveforms—amplitude, frequency, and phase—to encode information (see Figure 5.3):

- **Amplitude modulation**—A modem that relies on amplitude modulation might associate ones with a high amplitude and zeros with a low amplitude. A compatible receiving modem can discriminate between the high and low amplitudes and properly interpret them so that the receiving device can reproduce the message correctly.

- **Frequency modulation**—A frequency modulation–based modem alters the frequency value; in Figure 5.3, zero represents a low frequency and one represents a high frequency. A complementary modem decodes the original bit patterns, based on the frequency of the received signal.

- **Phase modulation**—Phase modulation refers to the position of the waveform at a particular instant in time (e.g., a 90-degree phase, a 180-degree phase, a 270-degree phase). A phase modulation–based modem uses the phases to differentiate between ones and zeros, so, for example, zeros can be transmitted beginning at a 90-degree phase, and ones may be transmitted beginning at a 270-degree phase.

By using the three characteristics of a waveform, a modem can encode multiple bits within a single cycle of the waveform (see Figure 5.4). The more of these variables

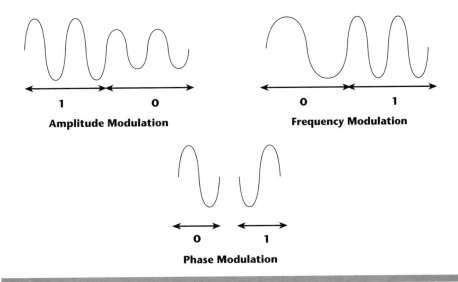

Figure 5.3 Amplitude, frequency, and phase modulation

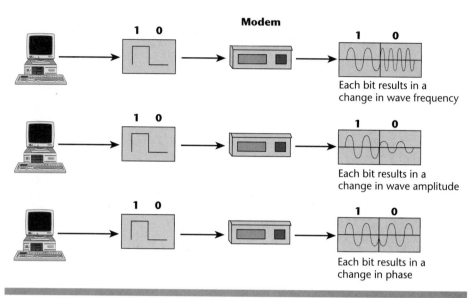

Figure 5.4   Signal modulation

the modem can detect, the greater the bit rate it can produce. Clever modulation schemes that vary phase, amplitude, and frequency at the same time are possible today, and they can offer higher bit rates because multiple bits can be encoded at the same instant.

Modulation schemes vary in their *spectral efficiency,* which is a measure of the number of digital bits that can be encoded in a single cycle of a waveform. A *bit* is a unit of information, while a *baud* is a unit of signaling speed—the number of times a signal on a communications circuit changes. The ITU-T now recommends that the term *baud rate* be replaced by the term *symbol rate*. Each signal, or symbol, can contain multiple bits, based on the modulation scheme and how many variables can be encoded onto one waveform. In the simplest of examples, where there is one bit per baud, the bit rate equals the baud or symbol rate. However, with contemporary techniques, which enable multiple bits per symbol (such as 64-QAM, which encodes 8 bits per symbol), the bps rate is much higher than the baud or symbol rate. To get more bits per Hertz, many modulation techniques provide more voltage levels. To encode k bits in the same symbol time, 2^k voltage levels are required. It becomes more difficult for the receiver to discriminate among many voltage levels with consistent precision as the speed increases. So it becomes a challenge to discriminate at a very high data rate. (Chapter 13, "Wireless Communications Basics," talks more about spectrum reuse.)

Categories of Modulation Schemes

There are two main categories of modulation schemes:

- **Single-carrier**—In the single-carrier modulation scheme, a single channel occupies the entire bandwidth.

- **Multicarrier**—The multicarrier modulation scheme uses and aggregates a certain amount of bandwidth and then divides it into subbands. Each sub-band is encoded by using a single-carrier technique, and bitstreams from the subbands are bonded together at the receiver. Therefore, no bits need to be placed on portions of the frequency band that may be subject to noise and might result in distortion. Multicarrier techniques became popular as a result of developments in digital signal processing (DSP).

Table 5.2 lists some of the most commonly used modulation schemes, and the following sections describe them in more detail.

Table 5.2 Single-Carrier and Multicarrier Modulation Schemes

Scheme	Description
Single-Carrier	
2B1Q	Used with ISDN, IDSL, and HDSL.
64-QAM	Used with North American and European digital cable for forward (i.e., downstream) channels.
256-QAM	Used with North American digital cable for forward (i.e., downstream) channels.
16-QAM	Used with North America digital cable for reverse (i.e., upstream) channels.
QPSK	Used in North American digital cable for reverse (i.e., upstream) channels, as well as in direct broadcast satellite.
CAP	Used in older ADSL deployments.
Multicarrier	
OFDM	Used in European digital over-the-air broadcast, including 802.11a, 802.11g, 802.11n, 802.16x, 802.20x, and Super 3G; it is the basis of 4G and 5G visions.
DMT	Used with xDSL and is a preferred technique because it provides good quality.

Single-Carrier Modulation Schemes   There are a number of single-carrier schemes:

- **2 Binary 1 Quaternary (2B1Q)**—2B1Q is used in ISDN, HDSL, and IDSL. 2B1Q uses four levels of amplitude (voltage) to encode 2 bits per Hertz (bits/Hz). It is well understood, relatively inexpensive, and robust in the face of telephone plant interference.

- **Quadrature Amplitude Modulation (QAM)**—QAM modulates both the amplitude and phase, yielding a higher spectral efficiency than 2B1Q and thus providing more bits per second using the same channel. The number of levels of amplitude and the number of phase angles are a function of line quality. Cleaner lines translate into more spectral efficiency or more bits per Hertz. Various levels of QAM exist, referred to as nn-QAM, where nn indicates the number of states per Hertz. The number of bits per symbol time is k, where $2^k = nn$. So, 4 bits/Hz is equivalent to 16-QAM, 6 bits/Hz is equivalent to 64-QAM, and 8 bits/Hz is equivalent to 256-QAM. As you can see, QAM has vastly improved throughput as compared to earlier techniques such as 2B1Q, which provided only 2 bits/Hz.

- **Quadrature Phase-Shift Keying (QPSK)**—QPSK is equivalent to 4-QAM, with which you get 2 bits per symbol time. QPSK is designed to operate in harsh environments, such as over-the-air transmission and cable TV return paths. Because of its robustness and relatively low complexity, QPSK is widely used in cases such as direct broadcast satellite. Although QPSK does not provide as many bits per second as some other schemes, it ensures quality in implementations where interference could be a problem.

- **Carrierless Amplitude Phase Modulation (CAP)**—CAP combines amplitude and phase modulation, and it is one of the early techniques used for ADSL. However, portions of the band over which ADSL operates conduct noise from exterior devices such as ham radios and CB radios, so if these devices are operating while you're on a call over an ADSL line, you experience static in the voice call or corrupted bits in a data session. Consequently, CAP is no longer the preferred technique with ADSL because it provides a rather low quality of service. (ADSL is discussed in Chapter 2, "Traditional Transmission Media," and in Chapter 12, "Broadband Access Alternatives.")

Multicarrier Modulation Schemes   There are two multicarrier schemes:

- **Orthogonal Frequency Division Multiplexing (OFDM)**—OFDM, which is growing in importance, is used in European digital over-the-air broadcast and in many new and emerging wireless broadband solutions, including 802.11a, 802.11g, 802.16x, 802.20x, and Super 3G, and it is the basis of 4G and 5G visions. It is also used in xDSL, where it is known as DMT. OFDM is a combination of two key principles: multicarrier transmission and adaptive modulation. Multicarrier transmission is a technique that divides the available spectrum into many subcarriers, with the transmission rate reduced on each subcarrier. OFDM is similar to FDM in that multiple-user access is achieved by subdividing the available bandwidth into multiple channels that are then allocated to users. However, OFDM is a special case of FDM. An FDM channel can be likened to the water flow out of a faucet, where the water comes out as one big stream and can't be subdivided. The OFDM channel, on the other hand, can be compared to a shower, where the water flow is composed of a lot of little streams of water. This analogy also highlights one of the advantages of OFDM: If you put your thumb over the faucet, it stops all the water flow, but that is not the case with the shower, where some of the streams of water will still get through. In other words, FDM and OFDM respond differently to interference, which is minimized in the case of OFDM. (OFDM is discussed in more detail in Chapter 15, "WMANs, WLANs, and WPANs.")

■ **Discrete Multitone (DMT)**—DMT is a multicarrier scheme that allows variable spectral efficiency among the subbands it creates. Therefore, it is used in wireline media, where noise characteristics of each wire might differ, as in the wires used to carry xDSL facilities. Because spectral efficiency can be optimized for each individual wire with DMT, DMT has become the preferred choice for use with xDSL.

Simplex, Half-Duplex, and Full-Duplex Data Transmission

Information flow takes three forms: simplex, half-duplex, and full-duplex (see Figure 5.5).

With *simplex* transmission, information can be transmitted in one direction only. Of course, simplex does not have great appeal to today's business communications, which involve two-way exchanges. Nonetheless, there are many applications of simplex circuits, such as a doorbell in homes. When someone presses a doorbell button, a signal goes to the chimes, and nothing returns over that pair of wires. Another example of a simplex application is an alarm circuit. If someone opens a door he or she is not authorized to open, a signal is sent over the wires to the security desk, but nothing comes back over the wires.

Half-duplex provides the capability to transmit information in two directions but in only one direction at a time (e.g., with a pair of walkie-talkies). Half-duplex is associated with two-wire circuits, which have one path to carry information and a second wire or path to complete the electrical loop. Because half-duplex circuits can't handle simultaneous bidirectional flow, there has to be a procedure for

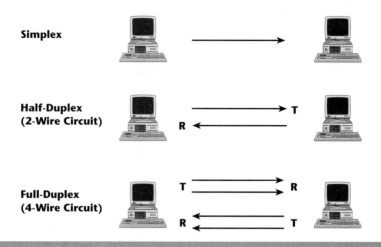

Figure 5.5 Simplex, half-duplex, and full-duplex data transmission

manipulating who's seen as the transmitter and who's seen as the receiver, and there has to be a way to reverse who acts as the receiver and who acts as the transmitter. Line turnarounds handle these reversals, but they add overhead to a session because the devices undertake a dialog to determine who is the transmitter and who is the receiver. For communication that involves much back-and-forth exchange of data, half-duplex is an inefficient way of communicating.

Full-duplex, also referred to simply as *duplex*, involves a four-wire circuit, and it provides the capability to communicate in two directions simultaneously. There's an individual transmit and receive path for each end of the conversation. Therefore, no line turnarounds are required, which means full-duplex offers the most efficient form of data communication. All digital services are provisioned on a four-wire circuit and hence provide full-duplex capabilities.

You may be wondering how you can conduct a two-way conversation on your telephone, which is connected to a two-wire local loop. The answer is that the telephone set itself is a full-duplex device, containing a circuit called the *network interface* or *telephony hybrid*, which connects the microphone and speaker to the telephone line and performs the conversion between the two-wire transmission link and the four-wire telephone set, separating the incoming audio from the outgoing signal.

Coding Schemes: ASCII, EBCDIC, Unicode, and Beyond

A *coding scheme* (or *collating sequence*) is a pattern of bits used to represent the characters in a character set, as well as carriage returns and other keyboard or control functions. Over time, different computer manufacturers and consortiums have introduced different coding schemes. The most commonly used coding schemes are ASCII, EBCDIC, and Unicode.

The American Standard Code for Information Interchange (ASCII) is probably the most familiar coding scheme. ASCII has seven information bits per character, and it has one additional bit that's a control bit, called a *parity bit*, used for error detection. In ASCII, seven ones or zeros are bundled together to represent each character. A total of 128 characters (i.e., 2^7, for the seven bits of information per character and the two possible values of each character) can be represented in ASCII coding.

At about the same time that the whole world agreed on ASCII as a common coding scheme, IBM introduced its own proprietary scheme, called Extended Binary Coded Decimal Interchange Code (EBCDIC). EBCDIC involves eight bits of information per character and no control bits. Therefore, you can represent 256 possible characters (i.e., 2^8) with EBCDIC. This sounds like a lot of characters, but it's not enough to handle all the characters needed in the languages throughout the world. Complex Asian languages, for instance, can include up to 60,000 characters.

In Table 5.3, you can see that the uppercase letter A in ASCII coding looks quite different than it does in EBCDIC. This could be a source of incompatibility. If your workstation is coded in ASCII and you're trying to communicate with a host that's looking for EBCDIC, you will end up with garbage on your screen because your machine will not be able to understand the alphabet that the host is using.

In the mid-1980s, a coding scheme called Unicode was formed. Unicode assigns 16 bits per character, which translates to more than 65,000 possible characters (i.e., 2^{16}). (Can you imagine a terminal with 60,000 keys to press?) Unicode has become the key encoding scheme for Chinese and Japanese, and new techniques have made the keyboards easy to use.

Table 5.3 ASCII Versus EBCDIC

Character or Symbol	ASCII	EBCDIC
A	1000001	11000001
K	1001011	11010010
M	1001101	11010100
2	0110010	11110010
Carriage return	0001101	00010101

Most people now believe that the best way to handle coding is to use natural language interfaces, such as voice recognition. Natural language interfaces are ultimately expected to be the most common form of data entry. But until we get there, the various coding schemes could be a potential source of incompatibility in a network, and you therefore might need to consider conversion between schemes. Conversion could be performed by a network element on the customer premises, or it could be a function that a network provider offers. In fact, the early packet-switched X.25 networks provided code conversion as a value-added feature.

Transmission Modes: Asynchronous and Synchronous Transmission

Another concept to be familiar with is the distinction between transmission modes. To appreciate the distinction, let's look at the historical time line again. The first introduced type of terminals were dumb terminals. They had no processing capabilities and no memories. They had no clocking references, so the only way they could determine where to find the beginning or the end of a character was by framing the character with start and stop bits. These systems used *asynchronous transmission*, in which one character is transmitted at a time, at a variable speed (i.e., speed depending on things such as how quickly you type or whether you stop to answer the phone). Asynchronous communication typically deals with ASCII-encoded information, which means a third control bit, a parity bit, needs to be accounted for. These extra control bits add up to fairly significant overhead. In essence, asynchronous transmission has 30% inefficiency because for every seven bits of information, there are at least three bits of control, and it can be higher as there can be 1, 1.5, or 2 stop bits used. Another disadvantage of asynchronous transmission is that it operates at comparatively low speeds; today, in general, it operates at no higher than 115Kbps.

Synchronous transmission emerged in the late 1960s, when IBM introduced its interactive processing line, which included smart terminals. These smart terminals could process information and use algorithms; for example, a terminal could use an algorithm on a message block to determine what it was composed of and in that way very succinctly check for errors. Smart terminals had buffers, so they could accumulate the characters being typed in until they had a big block that they could send all at one time. Smart terminals also had clocking devices, whereby on one pair of wires, a clocking pulse could be sent from the transmitter to the receiver. The receiver would lock in on that clocking pulse, and it could determine that with every clocking pulse it saw on one wire, it would have a bit of information present on the other wire. Therefore, the receiver could use the clocking pulse to simply count off the bits to determine where the beginning and the end of the character were, rather than actually having to frame each character with a start bit and a stop bit. Synchronous transmission in classic data communications implied sending information a block at a time at a fixed speed.

Another benefit of synchronous transmission is very tight error control. As mentioned earlier, smart terminals have processors and can apply mathematical algorithms to a block of data. By calculating the contents of that block, the terminal comes up with a 16- or 32-bit code that identifies the structure of the block's contents. The terminal adds this code to the end of the block and sends it to the receiver. The receiver performs the same mathematical algorithm on the block, and it comes up with its own 16- or 32-bit code. The receiver then compares its code with the one the terminal sent, and if they match, the receiver sends an ACK, a positive acknowledgment that everything's okay, and it moves on to sending the next block. If the two codes don't match, the receiver sends a NACK, a negative acknowledgment, which says there was an error in transmission and the previous block needs to be resent before anything else can happen. If that error is not corrected within some number of attempts that the user specifies, the receiver will disengage the session. This ensures that errors are not introduced. Yet another benefit of synchronous transmission is that it operates at higher speeds than asynchronous transmission, and today you commonly see it performing at 2Mbps.

These two types of transmission make sense in different applications. For machine-to-machine communications where you want to take advantage of high speeds and guarantee accuracy in the data flow—such as electronic funds transfer—synchronous communication is best. On the other hand, in a situation in which a human is accessing a database or reading today's horoscope, speed may not be of the essence, and error control may not be critical, so the lower-cost asynchronous method would be appropriate.

Keep in mind that things are never simple in telecom, and you rarely deal with simple alternatives; rather, you deal with layers and combinations of issues. For example, you can think of an escalator as being a synchronous network. The steps are presented at the same rate consistently, and they all travel up the ramp at the same speed. Passengers alight on steps, and all passengers are carried through that network at the same speed; therefore, the network is synchronous. However, each passenger alights on the escalator at a different rate, which makes the access to the network asynchronous. For example, an eight-year-old child might run up to the escalator at high speed and jump straight onto the third step. Behind that child might be an injured athlete with a cane, who cautiously waits while several stairs pass, until confident of stepping on the center of the stair. So people get on the escalator at varying rates and in different places; no consistent timing determines their presence.

The escalator scenario describes the modern broadband network. SDH/SONET is a synchronous network infrastructure. When bits get into an SDH/SONET frame, they all travel at OC-3 or OC-12 or one of the other line rates that SDH/SONET supports. But access onto that network might be asynchronous, through an ATM switch, where a movie might be coming in like a fire hose of information through one interface and next to it a dribble of text-based e-mail is slowly passing through. One stream of bits comes in quickly, and one comes in slowly, but when they get packaged together into a frame for transport over the fiber, they're transported at the same rate.

Error Control

Error control, which is a process of detecting and/or correcting errors, takes a number of forms, the two most common of which are parity checking and cyclic redundancy checking.

In ASCII-based terminals, which use asynchronous transmission, most often the error control is parity checking. *Parity checking* is a simple process of adding up the bit values to come up with a common value, either even or odd. It doesn't matter which one, but once you've selected either even or odd, every terminal must be set to that value. Let's say we're using odd parity. If you add up the bits for character #1 in Figure 5.6, you see that they equal 2, which is an even number. We need odd parity, so the terminal inserts a 1 bit to make that a 3, which is an odd number. For character #2 the bits add up to 3, so the terminal inserts a 0 as a parity bit to maintain the odd value. The terminal follows this pattern with each of the six characters, and then it sends all the bits across the network to the receiver. The receiver then adds up the bits the same way the terminal did, and if they equal an odd number, the receiver assumes that everything has arrived correctly. If they don't equal an odd number, the receiver knows there is a problem but cannot correct it. This is the trouble with parity checking; to determine that an error had occurred, you would have to look at the output report, and therefore errors can easily go unnoticed. Thus, parity checking is not the best technique when it comes to ensuring the correctness of information.

Bit Position	Information Character					
	#1	**#2**	**#3**	**#4**	**#5**	**#6**
1	0	1	0	0	1	0
2	1	0	0	0	0	1
3	0	0	1	1	0	1
4	0	1	1	1	1	0
5	0	0	0	0	1	1
6	1	1	1	1	1	0
7	0	0	0	1	1	0
Parity Bit	**1**	**0**	**0**	**1**	**0**	**0**

Figure 5.6 Parity checking

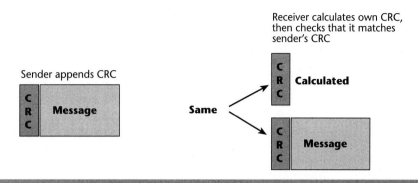

Figure 5.7 Cyclic redundancy checking

Synchronous terminals and transmission use a type of error control called *cyclic redundancy checking* (see Figure 5.7). This is the method mentioned earlier in the chapter, whereby the entire message block is run through a mathematical algorithm. A cyclic redundancy check (CRC) code is appended to the message, and the message is sent to the receiver. The receiver recalculates the message block and compares the two CRCs. If they match, the communication continues, and if they don't match, the receiver either requests retransmissions until the problem is fixed or it disengages the session if it is not capable of being fixed within some predetermined time frame.

The OSI Reference Model and the TCP/IP Reference Model

Before two computers or network devices can exchange information, they must establish communication, and this is where protocols come in. A network protocol enables two devices to communicate by using one set of rules. The OSI model and protocol standards help to ensure that networking devices are capable of working together over a network.

Protocols are the hardware or software components that carry out the OSI model guidelines for transferring information on a network. A protocol may be one component or a collection of components that carry out a task. A *protocol stack*, or *protocol suite*, is made up of multiple protocols used to exchange information between computers. One protocol in the stack might specify how network interface cards (NICs) communicate, and another might specify how a computer reads information from the NIC.

> ## For More Protocol Information
> The Web site www.protocols.com provides easy-to-understand information about protocols.

A *layer* is a section of a protocol stack that is responsible for performing one particular aspect of information transfer. Because some protocols are capable of performing more than one function, one layer in a protocol stack may not necessarily correspond to one layer in the OSI model. *Tunneling* describes the process of using a protocol to transfer information through a network, using a different type of protocol.

The OSI Seven-Layer Reference Model

In the early 1970s, a problem was brewing. There were many different computer manufacturers, and there were many incompatibilities among them. Furthermore, each manufacturer created different product lines, and even within one company, there were often incompatibilities between product lines. So the International Organization for Standardization (ISO; www.iso.org) got involved and created the Open Systems Interconnection (OSI) reference model, which is a blueprint for device manufacturers and software developers to use when creating products.

The OSI model, shown in Figure 5.8, has seven layers that describe the tasks that must be performed to transfer information on a network. When data is being transferred over a network, it must pass through each layer of the OSI model. As the data passes through each layer, information is added to that data. At the destination, the additional information is removed. Layers 4 through 7 occur at the end node, and Layers 1 through 3 are the most important to telecommunications networks.

It is important to understand that the OSI model is exactly that—a model. It is a conceptual framework useful for describing the necessary functions required of a network device or member. No actual networking product implements the model precisely as described.

Layer 7, the application layer, is responsible for exchanging information between the programs running on a computer and other services on a network. This layer supports application and end-user processes. It acts as a window for applications to access network services. It handles general network access, flow control, error recovery, and file transfer. Examples of application layer protocols include File Transfer Protocol (FTP), Telnet, Simple Mail Transfer Protocol (SMTP), and Hypertext Transfer Protocol (HTTP).

Layer 6, the presentation layer, formats information so that a software application can read it. It performs transformations on the data to provide a standardized

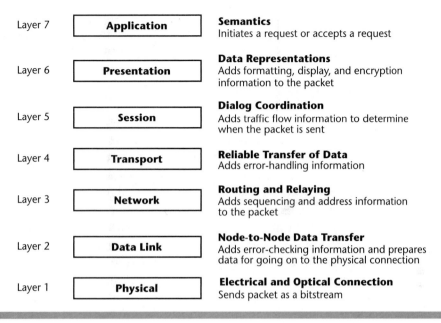

Figure 5.8 The OSI reference model

application interface and common communication services. It offers services such as encryption, compression, and reformatting. The presentation layer adds a field in each packet that tells how the information within the packet is encoded. It indicates whether any compression has been performed and, if so, indicates what type of compression so that the receiver can decompress it properly. It also indicates whether there has been any encryption, and if there has, it indicates what type so that the receiver can properly decrypt it. The presentation layer ensures that the transmitter and receiver see the information in the same format. Typically, Layer 6 processing is handled by an application rather than by a separate process running on a computer. In some cases, Layer 6 processing is handled by a process running at Layer 5.

Layer 5, the session layer, supports connections between sessions and handles administrative tasks and security. It establishes and monitors connections between computers, and it provides the control structure for communication between applications. Examples of session layer protocols include Network Basic Input/Output System (NetBIOS) and Lightweight Directory Access Protocol (LDAP).

Layer 4, the transport layer, corrects transmission errors and ensures that the information is delivered reliably. It provides an end-to-end error recovery and flow control capability. It deals with packet handling, repackaging of messages, division of messages into smaller packets, and error handling. Examples of transport layer protocols include Transmission Control Protocol (TCP), User Datagram Protocol (UDP), and Sequenced Packet Exchange (SPX).

Layer 3, the network layer, identifies computers on a network and determines how to direct information transfer over that network. In other words, it is a routing and relaying layer. It defines how to move information between networks, providing the functional and procedural means of transferring variable-length data sequences from a source to a destination via one or more networks while maintaining the QoS requested by the transport layer. The key responsibility of this layer is to perform network routing, flow control, segmentation/desegmentation, and error control functions. Examples of network layer protocols are X.25, Internet Protocol (IP), Internetwork Packet Exchange (IPX), and Message Transfer Part (MTP; part of the PSTN).

Layer 2, the data link layer, groups data into containers to prepare that data for transfer over a network. It puts the ones and zeros into a container that allows the movement of information between two devices on this same network. The protocols at this layer specify the rules that must be followed in transmitting a single frame between one device and another over a single data link. Bits are packaged into frames of data, and they include the necessary synchronization, error control, and flow control information. Examples of data link layer protocols in a LAN environment include Ethernet, Token Ring, and Fiber Distributed Data Interface (FDDI). Examples of data link layer protocols in a WAN environment include Frame Relay and Asynchronous Transfer Mode (ATM). Examples of data link layer protocols within the PSTN are Signaling System 7 (SS7) and MTP2.

Layer 1, the physical layer, defines how a transmission medium connects to a computer as well as how electrical or optical information is transferred on the transmission medium. The physical layer defines the types of cables or wireless interfaces that are allowed, the voltage levels used to represent the bits or the optical levels, the types of connectors that are allowed, and the types of transmission rates that can be supported. Every network service and every network device has definitions at the physical layer in terms of what it can physically interface with. For example, the physical layer deals with unshielded twisted-pair (UTP) and shielded twisted-pair (STP), coax, 10BASE-T (an Ethernet standard that allows the use of twisted-pair to support 10Mbps to the desktop, largely for legacy systems), 100BASE-T (the standard enterprises currently favor), multimode fiber and single-mode fiber, xDSL, ISDN, and the various capacities in PDH (e.g., DS-1/DS-3, E-1/E-3) and SDH/SONET (e.g., OC-1 through OC-192) networks.

The TCP/IP Four-Layer Reference Model

TCP/IP, which is an entire set of internetworking protocols, is described by its own layered model—somewhat like the OSI model but also unique. Whereas OSI defines seven layers, the TCP/IP model is a four-layer network architecture (see Figure 5.9).

TCP/IP Layer 1, the network access protocols, relates to OSI Layers 1 and 2. It defines the range of networks that can be interconnected with IP and through which an IP datagram can be forwarded on the way to its destination. The many options include the following:

- Ethernet LANs (10Mbps, 100Mbps, 1Gbps, and 10Gbps)
- Token-ring LANs (4Mbps and 16Mbps)
- Wireless LANs (802.11x, better known as Wi-Fi)
- 2.5G and 3G wireless WANs
- Private line or dialup links (using Point-to-Point Protocol [PPP])
- Frame Relay networks (Frame Relay interface)
- ATM-user network interface

TCP/IP Layer 2 deals with internetworking protocols and is analogous to OSI Layer 3. This layer is the key to the architecture: It realizes the interconnection of remote (heterogeneous) networks without establishing an end-to-end connection. Its role is to inject packets into any network and deliver them to the destination independent of one another. Because no connection is established first, packets may not be received in order; the delivery order control process is the responsibility of the upper layers. Because of the major role of this layer in the packet delivery process, the critical point of this layer is routing. That is why this layer compares to the network layer of the OSI model. IP is the official implementation of this layer, and all transmissions are sent in IP messages, referred to as *datagrams*. The datagrams

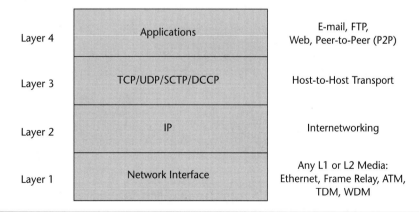

Figure 5.9 The TCP/IP four-layer reference model

are forwarded to their destinations by routers. IP defines an unreliable, best-effort packet-forwarding service. It does not provide error checking, sequencing, or guaranteed delivery.

TCP/IP Layer 3 handles the host-to-host protocols and has the same role as the transport layer of the OSI model (Layer 4). It is used to enable peer entities to talk with one another. These are terminal-to-terminal protocols that run in the end devices, such as the user's PC and the server. There are four possible implementations: TCP, UDP, and two newer transport protocols, Stream Control Transmission Protocol (SCTP) and Datagram Congestion Control Protocol (DCCP) (which are discussed in Chapter 8, "The Internet and IP Infrastructures"). TCP is a connection-oriented protocol that provides reliable, error-free delivery; mind you, sometimes conditions in the network can cause it to fail, and the network connection can be lost. Its role is to split up the message to be transmitted into a form the IP layer can handle. On the receiving side, TCP places packets in order to reconstruct the initial message. TCP is also in charge of the flow control of the connection. In comparison, UDP is a very simple protocol; it is connectionless and not guaranteed to be reliable, although in practice it works quite well. UDP assumes that there is no need for control of flow of the packets; instead, it relies on some other mechanism to assure quality control. It is used, for example, in support of Voice over IP (VoIP), where the delay associated with retransmissions is not tolerable and instead the end user must ask a person to repeat himself or herself when there is a problem with the delivery of the voice packets.

TCP/IP Layer 4 is the realm of applications protocols and relates to OSI Layers 5, 6, and 7. These are utilities that allow applications to access particular network services:

- Telnet for remote terminal access
- File Transfer Protocol (FTP) for batch transmission
- Simple Mail Transfer Protocol (SMTP) for sending e-mail
- Post Office Protocol (POP) for receiving e-mail
- Hypertext Transfer Protocol (HTTP) for accessing and downloading Web-based (HTML-formatted) information
- Simple Network Management Protocol (SNMP) for network management
- Real-Time Transport Protocol (RTP) for transport of real-time audio and video

The TCP Stack Versus the OSI Model

Figure 5.10 shows the TCP stack and how it relates to the OSI model.

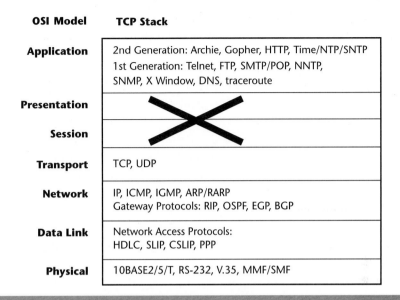

OSI Model	TCP Stack
Application	2nd Generation: Archie, Gopher, HTTP, Time/NTP/SNTP 1st Generation: Telnet, FTP, SMTP/POP, NNTP, SNMP, X Window, DNS, traceroute
Presentation	
Session	
Transport	TCP, UDP
Network	IP, ICMP, IGMP, ARP/RARP Gateway Protocols: RIP, OSPF, EGP, BGP
Data Link	Network Access Protocols: HDLC, SLIP, CSLIP, PPP
Physical	10BASE2/5/T, RS-232, V.35, MMF/SMF

Figure 5.10   The TCP/IP–OSI hybrid model (five layers)

Chapter 6

Local Area Networking

This book uses terminology that comes from the domain of local area networking, and in this chapter, you'll become familiar with the basics of local area network (LAN) components—the history of LANs, the key issues in the various architectures, and issues related to LAN interconnection and internetworking.

■ LAN Basics

In the early 1980s, when most businesses were still using networked mainframes, two changes took place in computing infrastructures. First, there was a general growth in the number of devices in organizations, which created traffic growth. Second, skilled, technically oriented users began sneaking their own workstations in to work, and they would ask the company's MIS department to provide networking to the host computer; this created additional challenges for enterprise networking.

The increased traffic made companies step back to figure out how all the information that was creating all the traffic was being used. They found that about 80% of the information used by people within a given business address also came from within that address. Only 20% was being exchanged with a location outside the enterprise's physical perimeter. This was a clue that a networking option was needed to focus on a rather limited geographical span—a building or a campus at most—and the solution that emerged became known as the LAN.

LAN Concepts and Benefits

One key concept associated with the traditional LAN is that it acts as a common data highway that allows the linking of internal information resources. This common highway provides a great economic advantage because it allows resources—both software and hardware—to be shared.

Another key concept associated with local area networking is that the LAN is responsible for connecting the senders and the receivers, and it discriminates between all the nodes on the network. Traditionally, LANs relied on a shared medium (see Figure 6.1). Everyone was basically connected to the same cable (until about 1987, the medium was generally coax cable, and then other media were built into the recommendations, as well). Due to the increasing demand for bandwidth to the desktop to support multimedia applications, we have moved away from these shared-media environments to configurations that use hubs or switches. Those devices enable each workstation to have its own dedicated connection, increasing the bandwidth available to the workstation.

Finally, LANs can be deployed to serve either peer-to-peer arrangements, where essentially every node is equal (i.e., capable of processing and storing in its own right), or server-based networks, in which one computer is the repository (i.e., the *server*) and provides services on request and the other computers (i.e., the *clients*) request services from the server.

There are a number of benefits associated with creating these internal LAN infrastructures. First, they allow very timely access to data. Knowledge is a com-

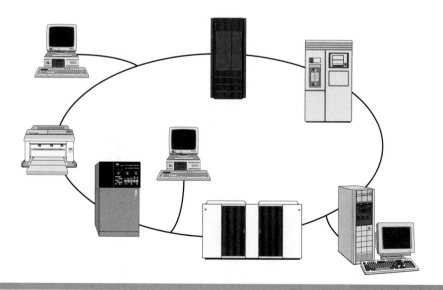

Figure 6.1   An example of a shared-medium LAN

petitive edge, and the faster you have access to the newest and latest information, the better off you will be in servicing customers and developing products. Second, LANs allow standardization of applications. Over time, departments acquire different computing platforms, depending on the cycles between centralized and decentralized management. Instead of having to go through the labor hours and cost of porting applications to reside in different platforms, you can use LANs to enable sharing of an application over the common data highway, resulting in savings and convenience. Third, because of the resource sharing, these internal LAN infrastructures provide great cost reductions. One of the simplest yet greatest benefits of having a LAN is the ability to share devices, such as printers and scanners. Finally, they promote speedy and functional communication within an organization.

LAN Components

Typically, a LAN is made up of several key elements:

- **Network nodes**—A network node is not a specific device; it is a single, addressable entity. It is an element to which a communications line interfaces. These interfaces can exist on a personal computer, a multiplexer, a modem, and so on. In the context of a LAN, a unique address is associated with each network interface card (NIC). Therefore, a server with many MAC addresses is considered to have multiple nodes.

- **NICs**—A NIC, sometimes referred to as a network adapter card, fits inside a computer and connects it to the underlying physical transport. Today the NIC is often built into the computer and is not a separate adapter card, making it a LAN interface device.

- **Transmission system**—The transmission system (which can be either wired or wireless media) performs the actual connection.

- **Software and data**—Software creates data and moves it from computer to computer by packaging the data packets, also known as protocol (or packet) data units (PDUs) that contain proper addressing and control information. These are the instructions that implement the LAN functionality according to published specifications (if a standard is being used).

- **User interface**—The user interface provides a way for the user to operate the software.

- **Operating system**—The operating system services the users' needs for files and devices such as printers and manages computer resources such as the disk, memory, and display functions. It also provides network management functions.

■ LAN Characteristics

LANs are grouped according to four key characteristics:

■ The types of transmission media over which they can operate

■ The transport technique they use to transmit data over the network (i.e., broadband or baseband)

■ The access method, which is involved in determining which device or network node gets to use the network and when it gets to use it

■ The topology, or mapping, of the network (i.e., the physical and logical connections between the nodes on the network)

The following sections describe each of these four characteristics in detail.

LAN Transmission Media

This section talks specifically about the considerations in selecting the appropriate media for a LAN. For information on the characteristics and the advantages and disadvantages of the media types, see Chapter 2, "Traditional Transmission Media."

First and foremost, when selecting transmission media for a LAN, you need to think about bandwidth. You must evaluate the kind of capacity you need: How much do you need per client? How much do you need per server? Typically, servers require more capacity than clients because they service multiple simultaneous sessions, but some clients in an organization might use applications such as three-dimensional modeling and simulation and therefore require as much capacity as some of the shared servers. You should also evaluate the bandwidth based on traffic inside workgroups and traffic over the backbone between workgroups. Clusters or workgroups are made up of users who form a community of interest, and therefore the majority of traffic sharing occurs within each cluster. However, there are reasons to have interdepartmental or interworkgroup communications as well, and therefore you need the backbone to provide connectivity between all the distinct clusters. The backbone should be engineered for great future capacity—provisioned to meet user needs in peak times with the ability to be upgraded as needed—and the workgroups should be set up so that they can easily be adjusted for moves, adds, and other changes.

The second consideration regarding LAN transmission media has to do with cost and ease of connectivity, and that speaks specifically to the installation, as well as to moves, adds, and other changes. In the average, rather stable environment, the majority of the employees are relocated at least once a year, so equipment, features, and services must move along with them. And, of course, some environments have many reorganizations and require yet more consideration in this area.

For example, in an enterprise where reorganization is common, using a wireless LAN is probably the easiest way to support such a dynamic environment. (Of course, if every desktop has an RJ-45 in place, moving may be just as easy as with wireless.) The tradeoff is that wireless media provide less bandwidth than, say, fiber, and with a wireless LAN, you have to create smaller clusters. Again, what media you choose depends greatly on the application.

The third consideration regarding LAN transmission media is sensitivity to interference and noise. If a LAN is being deployed in a manufacturing plant where other equipment emits interfering levels of noise, the noise could play havoc with a twisted-pair or wireless LAN, whereas coax and fiber would be much less susceptible to the interference.

Finally, of course, you need to consider security requirements. Again, there is no such thing as complete security, and each situation needs a different amount of security. You need to add encryption and other security mechanisms in almost any environment, but in some cases, you need to take the extra step of choosing a medium that's more difficult to tap into, such as coax or fiber. Mind you, both can be breached; it's a matter of how easy it is to do so (based on physical access) and how quickly unauthorized taps can be detected (with the help of testing equipment).

Most of the LAN standards today support the full range of media types. They vary in terms of factors such as the distances allowed between the devices and their backbones, so you need to choose the media appropriate to your situation.

LAN Transport Techniques and Standards

An important feature of a LAN is its transport technique: whether it is broadband or baseband (see Figure 6.2). *Broadband* means multichannel, so a broadband LAN implies that, through Frequency Division Multiplexing (FDM), multiple

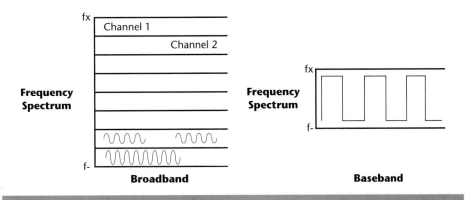

Figure 6.2 Broadband versus baseband

independent channels can carry analog or digital information, depending on the interfaces. This is essentially the way traditional cable TV operates: There are multiple channels of programming, and each one runs over a different portion of the frequency band. When you request a particular channel from the interface device (the set-top box), the device selects the frequency band on which that channel is allocated. Cable TV is a multichannel coaxial system.

Baseband implies a single-channel digital system, and this single channel carries information in containers—that is, packets or frames—that are specified by the LAN standard in use. The traditional LAN standards are Ethernet, Token Ring, and Fiber Distributed Data Interface (FDDI). Table 6.1 compares these three standards.

The vast majority of LANs—probably 85% or more—are baseband Ethernet LANs. IEEE 802.3 is the working group that creates and defines the entire family of Ethernet standards (see Table 6.2). The major milestones include the first generation, which emerged in 1983 as the IEEE 802.3 standard and defines 10Mbps Ethernet over thick coax. Later, in 1995, 802.3u introduced 100Mbps or Fast Ethernet. The next major leap occurred in 1998, producing the 1Gbps Ethernet standard, 802.3z. The latest formalized standard, 802.3ae, approved in 2003, specifies 10Gbps Ethernet. In 2004, 802.3ah specified 1Gbps Ethernet for use in the local loop. Ethernet is now also making inroads into the metro and long-haul networking spaces. Full-duplex operation and Ethernet switching have lifted the CSMA/CD distance limitation restrictions, so Ethernet is no longer technically restricted to just

Table 6.1 Traditional LAN Standards

Characteristic	Ethernet	Token Ring	FDDI
Standard	IEEE 802.3	IEEE 802.5	ANSI X3T9.5, IEEE 802.6
Logical topology	Bus	Ring	Ring
Physical topology	Bus, star	Ring, star	Dual ring, dual bus
Media	Coax, UTP, STP, fiber	Coax, UTP, STP	Fiber (CDDI)
Transmission mode	Baseband	Baseband	Baseband
Bandwidth	10Mbps, 100Mbps, 1Gbps, 10Gbps	4Mbps, 16Mbps, 100Mbps, 1Gbps	100Mbps
Media access	Nondeterministic	Deterministic	Deterministic
Control	CSMA/CD, CSMA/CA	Token passing	Token passing

Table 6.2 802.3 Ethernet Standards

Ethernet Standard	Date Completed	Description
Experimental Ethernet	1972 (patented in 1978)	2.94Mbps over coaxial cable bus.
Ethernet II (DIX v2.0)	1982	10Mbps over thick coax. Frames have a Type field. The Internet Protocol suite uses this frame format on any media.
IEEE 802.3	1983	10BASE5 10Mbps over thick coax; this is the same as DIX except the Type field is replaced by Length and LLC fields.
802.3a	1985	10BASE2 10Mbps over thin coax (thinnet or cheapernet).
802.3b	1985	10BROAD36.
802.3c	1985	10Mbps repeater specs.
802.3d	1987	FOIRL (Fiber-Optic Inter-Repeater Link).
802.3e	1987	1BASE5 or StarLAN.
802.3i	1990	10BASE-T 10Mbps over twisted-pair.
802.3j	1993	10BASE-F 10Mbps over fiber.
802.3u	1995	100BASE-TX, 100BASE-T4, and 100BASE-FX Fast Ethernet at 100Mbps (with autonegotiation).
802.3x	1997	Full-duplex and flow control; also incorporates DIX framing, so there's no longer a DIX/802.3 split.
802.3y	1998	100BASE-T2 100Mbps over low-quality twisted-pair.
802.3z	1998	1000BASE-X Gigabit Ethernet over fiber at 1Gbps.
802.3-1998	1998	A revision of the base standard that incorporates the preceding amendments and errata.
802.3ab	1999	1000BASE-T Gigabit Ethernet over twisted-pair at 1Gbps.
802.3ac	1998	Maximum frame size extended to 1522 bytes (to allow Q-tag). The Q-tag includes 802.1Q virtual LAN (VLAN) information and 802.1p priority information.

continued

Table 6.2 802.3 Ethernet Standards *(continued)*

Ethernet Standard	Date Completed	Description
802.3ad	2000	Link aggregation for parallel links.
802.3-2002	2002	A revision of the base standard that incorporates the three prior amendments and errata.
802.3ae	2003	10GBASE-SR, 10GBASE-LR, 10GBASE-ER, 10GBASE-SW, 10GBASE-LW, and 10GBASE-EW 10Gbps Ethernet over fiber.
802.3af	2003	Power over Ethernet.
802.3ah	2004	Ethernet in the first mile.
802.3ak	2004	10GBASE-CX4 10Gbps Ethernet over twin-axial (twinax) cable.
802.3-2005	2005	A revision of the base standard that incorporates the four prior amendments and errata.
802.3an	In progress	10GBASE-T 10Gbps Ethernet over unshielded twisted-pair (UTP).
802.3ap	In progress	Backplane Ethernet (1Gbps and 10Gbps over printed circuit boards).
802.3aq	In progress	10GBASE-LRM 10Gbps Ethernet over multimode fiber.
802.3ar	In progress	Congestion management.
802.3as	In progress	Frame expansion.

LANs. Long-haul Ethernet is now being applied to metropolitan area networks (MANs) and wide area network (WANs), as well. (MAN and WAN applications of Ethernet are discussed further in Chapter 11, "Optical Networking.")

The 802.3 standards are not complete yet; the 100Gbps Ethernet prototypes are in the early stages, and they promise all the benefits of a ubiquitous and inexpensive technology for use in metro and wide area service provider networks.

Due to the pervasive use of Ethernet and the extremely low cost of the hardware required, most manufacturers today build the functionality of an Ethernet NIC directly into PC motherboards. Even though Ethernet has gone through quite a few generational changes, from thick coax supporting 10Mbps in traditional LAN environments to the emerging use of Gigabit Ethernet in the local loop and 10Gbps point-to-point links in MANs and WANs, from the programmer's perspective, the variations are pretty much the same Ethernet and are easily interconnected using inexpensive and readily available hardware. Many Ethernet cards and switch ports support multiple speeds, using autonegotiation to set the speed and duplexing to match the best parameters supported by both devices. In the event that autonegotiation fails, a device designed to support multiple speeds senses the speed used by the other device but assumes half-duplex mode. For example, a 10/100 Ethernet port supports 10BASE-T and 100BASE-TX, while a 10/100/1000 Ethernet port supports 10BASE-T, 100BASE-TX, and 1000BASE-T.

Token Ring originated in the IBM environment in the early 1980s. Although it was very successful initially, after the Ethernet twisted-pair standard emerged in the early 1990s, the use of Token Ring declined. IBM no longer uses or promotes the Token Ring technology, but Madge Networks (www.madge.com) continues to provide it. The IEEE 802.5 working group has standardized token-ring LAN speeds of 4Mbps, 16Mbps, 100Mbps, and 1Gbps.

Despite the fact that FDDI was the first LAN standard to provide 100Mbps for use in a backbone application, it did not capture a major market share. The transition to a higher grade of Ethernet is much simpler for companies than is a transition to an entirely new protocol.

The prevailing standard in the world is Ethernet, which generally appears as Fast Ethernet or Gigabit Ethernet in the backbone, connecting individual Fast Ethernet or 10Mbps Ethernet LAN segments (see Figure 6.3).

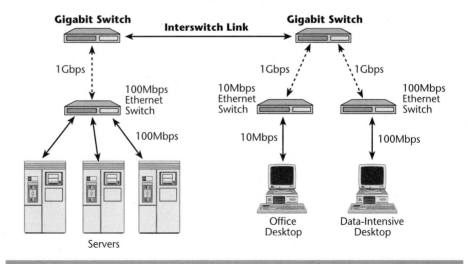

Figure 6.3 An example of Gigabit Ethernet

LAN Access Methods

The third main LAN characteristic is the access methods, which are involved in determining who gets to use the network and when they get to use it. There are two main approaches to LAN access: token passing and Carrier Sense Multiple Access/Collision Detection (CSMA/CD).

Token Passing

Token passing, shown in Figure 6.4, is used with the token-ring and FDDI architectures. Here is how token ring works:

1. The active master, chosen through a process called *beaconing*, inserts a token (i.e., a specially formatted packet) into the ring.

2. The token circulates around the ring and is regenerated by each workstation it passes. (In token-ring networks, a workstation obtains data from only its upstream neighbor, regenerates it, and sends it to its downstream neighbor.)

3. When a workstation has data to send, it waits for the token to pass by and grabs it off the wire, holding it until it has finished its transmission. The station then injects its data packets onto the wire.

4. The packets circulate around the ring and are examined and regenerated by each workstation. When the receiving workstation receives the packets, it marks them as received when it regenerates and reinjects them. This marking notifies the sender that the data was in fact received when it finally returns to the sender. The sender then generates a new token and injects it into the ring.

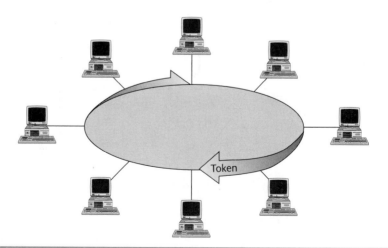

Figure 6.4   Token passing

To prevent any particular workstation from hogging the ring, a transmitting station can hold the token (and thus transmit data packets) for a specific interval, called the *token hold time*. If the time expires before the station has transmitted all its information, it must stop transmitting and put a new token back on the ring so that other stations have a chance to communicate. When the token gets back to the waiting workstation, it can resume transmitting.

A benefit of token passing is that it is a *deterministic* technique: You can always calculate the maximum delay that you'll encounter in moving information between any two points on that network, and this is especially important for applications with defined response times, such as process control. For example, an oil pipeline may have sensors in the pipelines to detect minute leakage. The oil company wants to know exactly how long it will take for the alarm from the sensor to reach the control station to shut off the valve, in order to avoid leaking oil into the community. In a LAN where there's a need to determine the delay, token passing works very well. The disadvantage of token passing is that it occurs in a unidirectional ring, so it takes time to pass the tokens. A device has to wait until it receives a token before it can send it, and if the ring is broken because a device goes down, the ring is then unable to send tokens until the ring is recovered (i.e., the failed device is either taken out of commission or reinitiated). Today, almost all token-ring interfaces include an electrical shunt to prevent this from happening.

CSMA/CD

CSMA/CD is used with the Ethernet standard. CSMA/CD is a *nondeterministic* access method, meaning that any device can send whenever it determines that the network is clear. However, each device must listen to the network at all times because there is the potential for a collision. If a collision occurs, both sending devices back off the network and wait a random number of nanoseconds or milliseconds before attempting to retransmit.

As shown in Figure 6.5, CSMA/CD works as follows:

1. The terminals listen to the network.

2. Both of the terminals assume that the network is clear. They both start sending, but they continue listening because they know there's a chance that their messages will collide.

3. The messages do collide, so both terminals produce a jam signal, which carries a bit pattern sent by a data station to inform the other stations that they must not transmit.

4. One terminal waits 20 milliseconds, and the other waits 50 milliseconds, and then they again attempt to transmit, assuming that their messages won't

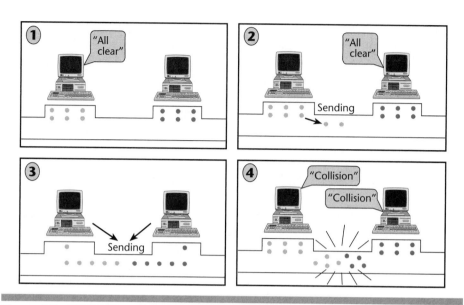

Figure 6.5 CSMA/CD

bump into each other. Because the terminals waited different amounts of time, most likely the messages don't collide and therefore get transmitted. However, if the messages collide again, the terminals repeat the back-off and random-wait procedure up to 16 times before the frames are dropped.

In this type of environment, the more devices added and the greater the traffic volumes, the more likely collisions will occur. When collisions start to exceed the available throughput, you need to start segmenting the LAN into smaller clusters, called *collision domains* in Ethernet parlance, or consider making the move to switched Ethernet LANs.

Shared Versus Switched Ethernet

With traditional Ethernets, all the hosts compete for the same bandwidth, and for this reason they are referred to as *shared Ethernets*. A *switched Ethernet* is an Ethernet LAN that uses switches to connect individual hosts or segments; that is, the network is controlled by a switch instead of a shared hub. The switch cross-connects all clients, servers, and network devices, giving each sending–receiving pair the full-rated transmission speed.

Switched Ethernet, unlike shared Ethernet, provides a private connection between two nodes on a network, speeding up the rate at which data is sent along the network and eliminating collisions. Switched connections allow full-duplex, which means network nodes can send and receive data at the same time. This doubles the theoretical speed of Ethernet and Fast Ethernet (offering a maximum of 200Mbps for Fast Ethernet). Switched Ethernets have gained in popularity because they provide a dramatic increase in throughput, offering an effective and convenient way to extend the bandwidth of existing Ethernets.

LAN Topologies

The final characteristic of a LAN is its *topology*—the physical and logical mapping of the network. The most common LAN topologies are the tree, bus, ring, and star topologies, which are illustrated in Figure 6.6. The tree topology is commonly used in broadband LANs, and the bus, ring, and star topologies are used in baseband LANs. In today's environment, the most common physical topology is the star, and the most common logical topology—that is, how the signals are exchanged between stations—is the bus.

Tree Topology
In the tree topology, the root of the tree is the headend, or the central retransmission facility. The trunk cable is attached to this root. Various branch cables are

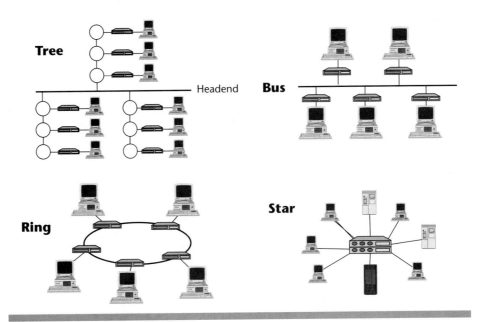

Figure 6.6 LAN topologies

attached to the trunk cable. From there, user devices can be connected. Although most broadband networks use a single cable, some use a dual-cable system—one cable for each direction to and from the headend. All transmissions must pass through the headend because each device transmits on one frequency and receives on another. The headend is responsible for translating the device's transmit frequency to the receive frequency of another device, and this frequency translation is called *remodulation*.

Bus Topology

The bus topology, which is the oldest topology, functions like a multipoint circuit. All stations are attached via cable taps or connections to a single length of cable—a wire with two open ends that are terminated by a resistor. The single cable is referred to as a *trunk*, *backbone*, or *segment*.

Each station can detect and place signals on the bus according to the access method. Only one computer at a time can send data on a bus network. Signals travel in both directions along the bus, from the point of insertion. Any other station on the network can receive a transmission from the station. Because the data is sent to the entire network, it travels from one end of the cable to the other. If the signal were to be allowed to continue uninterrupted, it would keep bouncing back and forth along the cable, preventing other computers from sending signals. Therefore, the signal must be stopped after it has had a chance to reach the proper destination address. A component called a *terminator* is placed at each end of the cable to absorb free signals and to clear the cable so that other computers can send data.

The bus topology is a *passive* topology. Computers only listen for data being sent on the network; they are not responsible for moving data from one computer to the next. An advantage of the bus topology is that it uses short cable lengths, and therefore it uses cable economically. Because the transmission media are inexpensive and easy to work with, the network is easy to extend. A disadvantage of the bus topology is that problems are difficult to isolate. A cable break can affect many users, and the network can become slow when traffic is heavy.

Ring Topology

In the ring topology, the nodes are connected by point-to-point links that are arranged to form an unbroken loop configuration. At each station the signal is received, regenerated, and transmitted to the next station on the ring, and data is transmitted in one direction around the ring. The ring is an *active* topology. That is, each computer acts like a repeater to boost the signal and send it on to the next computer. Because the signal passes through each computer, the failure of one computer can affect the entire network—but in practice this rarely occurs because the ring interfaces contain passive electrical shunts that allow the ring to remain intact in case a station goes down or malfunctions.

An advantage of the ring topology is that it can spread over long distances because each station regenerates the signal. Another advantage is ease of implementing distributed control and checking facilities; all computers have equal access, and the performance is even, despite the fact that there are many users. A potential disadvantage is sensitivity to station failures (i.e., one failed station might break the ring). Also, problems in a ring network are difficult to isolate, and network reconfiguration disrupts the operation of the entire network.

Star Topology

In the star topology, all stations are connected by cable segments to a centralized component called a *hub*. Devices can communicate with each other only through the hub. The star topology offers centralized resources and management. The advantages of the star topology include ease of fault isolation, ease of bypassing and repairing faulty stations, and high cost-efficiencies. Also, it's much easier to modify or add new computers in a star network than to do so in other topologies. Disadvantages include the need for a lot of cable to interconnect all the stations and the potential for total network disruption if the central hub facility fails.

There are a number of variations on star networks. The star bus, for instance, is a combination of the bus and star topologies. It involves several star networks linked together with linear bus trunks. The star ring, sometimes referred to as the star-wired ring, looks similar to a star bus, except that the hubs in the star ring are connected in a star pattern, and the main hub contains the actual ring.

■ LAN Interconnection and Internetworking

The realm of LAN interconnection devices offers a number of options, including hubs, LAN switches, virtual LANs (VLANs), bridges, routers, and IP switches. These options are described in the following sections.

Hubs

Hubs interconnect the wiring that is connected to workstations. They are a building block of most networks, although these days, they have largely been replaced by LAN switches. There are three major types of hubs:

- **Active**—Active hubs regenerate and retransmit signals, just as a repeater does. Because hubs typically have 8 to 12 ports for network computers to connect to, they are sometimes called *multiport repeaters*. Active hubs require electrical power to run (that's why they're called *active*).

■ **Passive**—Passive hubs serve as connection points and do not regenerate the signal; the signal simply passes through the hub. They do not require electrical power to run (that's why they're called *passive*). Wiring panels and punchdown blocks are examples of passive hubs.

■ **Hybrid**—Hybrid hubs accommodate several different types of cables.

You can connect hubs to expand a hub network. The advantages of hubs are that they make it easy to change or expand wiring systems, they use different ports to accommodate different cabling types, and they centralize the monitoring of network activity and traffic. Hubs are also sometimes called *concentrators* or *multistation access units* (MSAUs).

A group of transceivers can all be located in and managed by an *intelligent hub*. Intelligent hubs are modular and chassis based, with slots that accommodate the user's choice of interface modules—such at Ethernet, Token Ring, or FDDI—for connectivity to LANs, WANs, or other network devices. The number of ports on the NIC determines the number of users in the particular star. Intelligent hubs often provide integrated management and internetworking capabilities, as well as Simple Network Management Protocol (SNMP)–based network management. New generations also offer bridging, routing, and switching functions.

Figure 6.7 shows a network that uses a combination of interconnection devices. Intelligent hubs provide connectivity between workstations that comprise

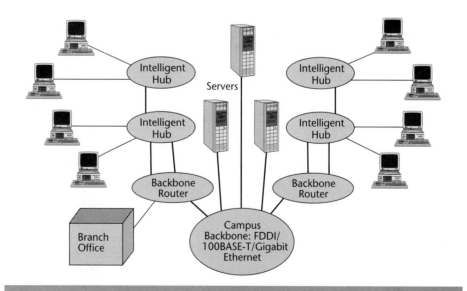

Figure 6.7 Using interconnection devices

a given cluster. An internal backbone is used to internetwork the intelligent hubs to move between different clusters. Those intelligent hubs then connect into a backbone router for purposes of WAN, or campuswide, connectivity. (Note that today switches are preferred over hubs.)

LAN Switches

LAN switches are a very cost-effective solution to the need for increased bandwidth in workgroups. Each port on the switch delivers a dedicated channel to the device or devices attached to that port, thereby increasing the workgroup's total bandwidth and also the bandwidth available to individual users.

Figure 6.8 shows a simple example of a switched Ethernet configuration. One workstation requires 100Mbps on its own, so it has the full services of a 100Mbps port on the switched Ethernet card. Five workstations, on the other hand, each need 20Mbps, so one 100Mbps port serves all five workstations. These five workstations connect into a hub, and that hub connects into the actual port. (Today such configurations are largely managed by the local switches.) Servers have extra bandwidth requirements—the ones in Figure 6.8 require 200Mbps—so they are each served by a bonding of several 100Mbps ports.

The key applications for LAN switches are to interconnect the elements of a distributed computing system, to provide high-speed connections to campus backbones

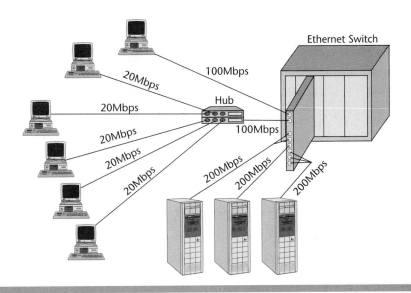

Figure 6.8 An example of a switched Ethernet configuration

and servers, and to provide high bandwidth to individual users who need it. Instead of sharing a 10Mbps or 100Mbps LAN among a number of terminals in a workgroup, a LAN switch can be used, and an individual workstation can get the entire 10Mbps or 100Mbps. LAN switches provide great scalability because they enable the network to increase in bandwidth with the fairly simple addition of more switched ports. In addition, switches operate in full-duplex mode and as such use dedicated outgoing and incoming channels to allow full-speed transmission in both directions at the same time. Thus, LAN switches have many benefits, including scalability in terms of bandwidth, flexibility, and high performance.

Figure 6.9 shows how an Ethernet switch can be used to connect devices that are on the same segment, some of which are served by one shelf of the Ethernet switch and others of which are served by connecting shelves. On the backplane, you can provide internetworking between the Ethernet segments, so you can provide internetworking on a campuswide basis.

As the amount of traffic has grown in enterprises and as the nature of applications has become more sophisticated, we have been increasing the bandwidth associated with LANs. Today, it is common to see 10Mbps being delivered to an individual desktop and 100Mbps serving as the cluster capacity. To facilitate internetworking between these high-capacity desktops and Fast Ethernet clusters, Gigabit Ethernet is increasingly being used in the backbone. As shown in Figure 6.3 earlier in the chapter, Gigabit Ethernet switches can connect underlying 100Mbps

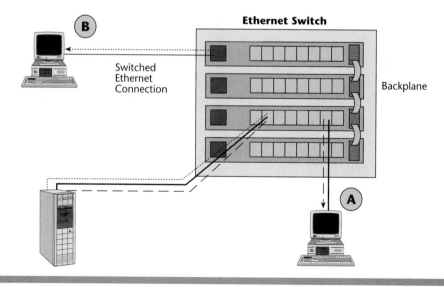

Figure 6.9 An Ethernet switch

or 10Mbps LAN segments, and the 10Mbps or 100Mbps LAN switches can deliver 10Mbps to the desktop and 100Mbps to the segment.

VLANs

Switched LANs enable us to create VLANs. A VLAN does not completely fit the earlier definition of a LAN as being limited in geographical scope; with a VLAN, geography has no meaning. A VLAN is a logically independent network, and multiple VLANs can coexist on an individual physical switch. VLANs are used extensively in campus networks, allowing users to be part of the same broadcast domain while being physically separated, on different floors of a building, or in different buildings on a campus. This is because a VLAN is defined by software rather than by hardware and physical location. The major difference is that VLANs can restrict the broadcast and collision domain to members of a particular VLAN. Figure 6.10 shows an example of a VLAN.

A switched VLAN is a high-speed, low-latency broadcast group that unites an arbitrary collection of endstations on multiple LAN segments. Switched virtual networking eliminates the bottlenecks normally associated with a physical LAN topology by creating high-speed switched connections between endstations on

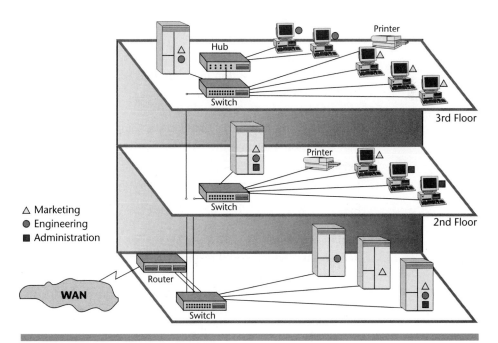

Figure 6.10 An example of a VLAN

different LAN segments. Users who want to belong to a particular broadcast domain do not have to be physically located on that LAN segment.

VLANs provide a software-based, value-added function by enabling the creation of a virtual broadcast domain, a shared LAN segment within a switched environment. Switching latencies on VLANs are typically one-tenth those of fast routers. However, routers are still required for inter-VLAN communications.

Bridges

Bridges, which entered the networking scene before routers, are used for connecting network segments (e.g., by creating the appearance of a single logical VLAN out of 5 to 10 individual clusters). A bridge can also be used to increase the number of computers on a network or to extend the distance of a segment beyond what the specifications allow. Similarly, a bridge can be used for network segmentation in order to reduce traffic bottlenecks or to control the flow of network traffic. Bridges can connect similar as well as dissimilar networks, which is their main application.

Bridges have several important functions:

- **Learning**—When a bridge is first connected to the network, it sends an announcement that says, "Hello. I'm your new bridge. What's your address?" All the other devices respond with, "Hello. Welcome to the neighborhood," along with their addresses. The bridge builds a table of local addresses, called the *Media Access Control (MAC) sublayer addresses*. The MAC sublayer (which is equivalent to OSI Layer 2) controls access to the shared transmission medium. It is responsible for making the data frames and putting bits in fields that make sense, and it works with the physical layer (Layer 1 of the OSI model). MAC standards, including IEEE 802.3, 802.4, and 802.5, define unique frame formats. Every NIC has a globally unique burned-in MAC address.

- **Performing packet transfer**—Bridges either filter, ignore, or forward packets.

- **Using the Spanning Tree Protocol (STP)**—Bridges and switches use STP to provide a loop-free topology for any bridged LAN. Loops occur when there are alternate routes between hosts, creating multiple active paths between stations. Without STP, it is possible that two connections might be simultaneously live, which could result in an endless loop of traffic on the LAN. STP works by creating a tree that spans all the switches in an extended network and disables all alternate or redundant links that are not part of that tree. However, the disabled or blocked redundant links are available as a backup in case the initial link fails, supporting path redundancy. Bridge PDUs (BPDUs) are the frames that carry the STP information.

Figure 6.11 illustrates a local bridge installed between two LAN segments located at the same local premises. When the bridge is plugged in, it sends out a hello message to its community and learns addresses by snooping on other traffic, and then the bridge builds an addressing table. Say that PC A wants to send a document to printer 1. The bridge realizes that the printer resides within its community. It knows the address and it therefore does not do anything except filter the packet. On the other hand, if PC A is attempting to communicate with server Z, the bridge says, "I don't know where that server is. It's not part of my local community, so it must be somewhere else on the other side of this bridge." The bridge then broadcasts that information to the other side of the bridge. In essence, the bridge creates broadcast storms.

Bridges are not networkable devices; that is, they can't target a destination network. They can only determine whether a destination is or is not on its segment, and if the destination is somewhere else, the bridge sends a message to every somewhere else that it knows about. This can be an especially big problem if you use a bridge in a remote mode, as shown in Figure 6.12, because, in essence, you are trying to connect remote locations by using a WAN link, which is expensive in terms of bandwidth. You pay for every bit sent, so sending messages to LAN segments that don't need to see them across a WAN link that doesn't need to be congested is inefficient.

Although bridges can operate in local and remote areas, today they are mostly used in the local environment. They operate at OSI Layer 2, and they are point to point—they do not understand networking or routing and relaying through a series of nodes. Bridges are protocol independent (Layer 3 and up), which keeps

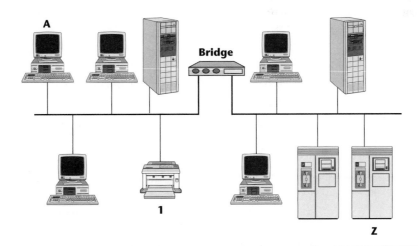

Figure 6.11 An example of a local bridge

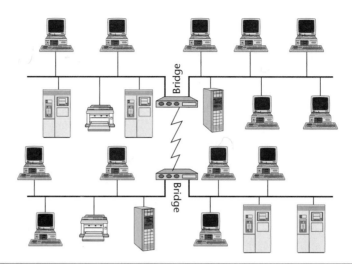

Figure 6.12 An example of remote bridges

the software simple and inexpensive. Bridges cannot translate between different Layer 2 protocols (e.g., between Ethernet and Token Ring). They are primarily used to isolate traffic loads in the local environment because they offer fast throughput; because a bridge doesn't have to do intelligent routing, it is faster and less expensive than a traditional router. Over time, the best features of bridges and routers have been merged so that some of the problems with each have begun to disappear.

Flat Networks

Flat networks are constructed by using bridges or Layer 2 LAN switches. This type of network is easy to configure, and it promises better performance than hierarchical networks because it offers higher throughput with lower latencies. However, the scalability of a flat network is limited, and a flat network is subject to broadcast storms.

Routers

The most popular internetworking device today is the router (see Figure 6.13). The applications for routers are quite similar to those for bridges. You use them for network segmentation and connection; that is, you use them either to segment larger networks into smaller ones or to connect smaller networks into a larger virtual whole. You can use a router to switch and route packets across multiple communications paths and disparate Layer 2 network types, and because it is a Layer 3

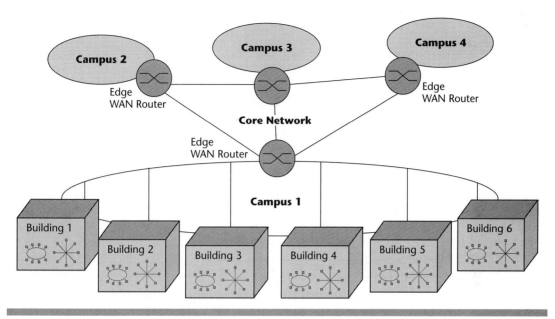

Figure 6.13 An example of routers in a network

device, a router is networkable—it understands how to read network addresses and how to select the destination or target network, so it limits broadcast storms by not propagating them. This capability allows routers to act as firewalls between LAN segments. Routers can be associated with traffic filtering and isolation, and because they can read information about the network and transport protocols used, they can make forwarding decisions.

Routers can make linking and rerouting decisions, which makes possible selective routing of individual packets over multiple communication paths. Remember that bridges have to disable all but one path, whereas a router can decide on-the-fly between numerous communications paths. The path a router selects depends on the user's requirements, including cost, speed, and priority.

Routers are protocol specific, but modern routers support multiple protocols, such as TCP/IP or IPX/SPX (the network and transport layer protocols used in Novell's NetWare network operating system). The key is that each of the protocols a router supports for internetworking requires its own separate routing table, so the more protocols the router supports, the more complex, memory intensive, and expensive it is due to the size and stability of the associated routing tables. Routers can be used as bridges to connect similar and dissimilar networks, and they are often applied as firewalls.

The functions of a router are as follows:

- **Learning**—A router learns who its neighbors are and builds a forwarding table based on their addresses.
- **Filtering**—A router forwards traffic by looking at its routing table for the next hop.
- **Routing and switching**—A router selects the best destinations based on the network addresses, distance, cost, and availability.
- **Adapting to network conditions**—A router adapts to network conditions by changing what it considers to be the best or optimum paths, depending on the network traffic status.

How do routers actually work? A router has input ports for receiving packets and output ports for sending those packets toward their destination. When the packet comes to the input port, the router examines the packet header and checks the destination against a *routing table* (i.e., a database that tells the router how to send packets to various destinations). Based on the information in the routing table, the router sends the packet to a particular output port, and the output port sends the packets—possibly to the destination, or possibly to another router that is one step closer to that packet's destination. Packets are delivered from node to node (i.e., router to router) because, at each node, the router modifies the MAC address to be that of the next node. The destination network address does not change, of course, but the destination MAC changes at each node; this is the only way the packet can travel from one node to the next.

If packets come to the input port more quickly than the router can process them, they are sent to a holding area called an *input queue*. The router then processes packets from the queue in the order in which they were received. If the number of packets received exceeds the length of the queue, packets may be lost due to the router running out of available memory. When this happens, an error control mechanism (such as TCP) that is housed on the sending and receiving computers has the packets resent. (You'll learn more about TCP in Chapter 8, "The Internet and IP Infrastructures.")

Types of Routing Tables
There are two types of routing tables:

- **Static**—The simpler kind of routing table is the static routing table. In a static routing table, there are specific ways of routing data to other networks, and only those paths can be used. New routes can be added to the routing table, but they have to be manually programmed. Static routing can't adjust routes as network traffic changes, so it isn't an optimal option for many applications today. A static router knows only its own routing table and does not communicate changes to any of its neighbors.

■ **Dynamic**—Dynamic routing is much more useful than static routing. It allows a packet to take one of multiple routes to reach its final destination, and individual packets in a stream from one destination to another might follow different routes. Dynamic routing also allows routers to change the way they route information, based on the amount of network traffic on some paths and routers. In dynamic routing, the routing table changes as network conditions change. A dynamic router communicates with other routers so that they can all update their tables to reflect any changes.

Routing Protocols

There are two broad types of routing protocols: interior and exterior. Interior routing protocols are typically used only in the routers of an enterprise's intranet (i.e., its internal network). Interior routing protocols include Routing Information Protocol (RIP) and Open Shortest Path First (OSPF). Exterior protocols are typically used for routers located in the Internet, which is composed of many different providers. Another application for exterior protocols is where routers are connecting systems between different organizations. Whereas there may be many different interior routing schemes, a single exterior routing system manages the whole global Internet, called Border Gateway Protocol 4 (BGP4). (Routing protocols are discussed in detail in Chapter 8.)

Hierarchical Networks

Routers, when built into an enterprise internetwork, create a hierarchical network (i.e., subnetworks interconnected by routers). They control traffic flow through segmentation, but this can degrade network performance because of delays, and it adds complexity to the overall network configuration. Hierarchical networks are typically used at the edge of a network to interconnect LANs or to provide WAN connectivity to remote LANs. Again, within the customer premises, the simpler bridge-based flat networks were traditionally used. However, most campus networks today are primarily switched, and large campuses use routers to segment their broadcast domains. As traffic levels keep growing and LANs keep getting busier, both the edge and the core network are becoming loaded, resulting in network slowness and unacceptable delays.

Routers use a hierarchical addressing scheme, whereby the address includes both the network address and the node address. Routers operate at Layer 3, so they are networkable—you can route and relay traffic through a series of routers. Routers are protocol sensitive, so the more internetworking protocols they support, the more complex the software and the greater the number of routing tables and algorithms required to support those protocols.

IP Switches

The network core is responsible for providing interconnectivity, server access, and network management to the edge devices on the network periphery. At the edge of a LAN, a shortage of network capacity, coupled with proliferation of broadcasts and multicasts, can create significant network problems. When the edge demand exceeds the capacity of the core, buffer overruns create capacity overload and lead to lost packets, reducing the availability and reliability of the network. As a result, users today suffer from congestion, inadequate server access, and slow response times. (But to be truthful, this is often a symptom of poor design and planning rather than technological inferiority.) People want to see information in a matter of a few seconds, so these problems are increasingly frustrating.

The solution to the problem of these increases in traffic in the core and at the edge is the IP switch. The IP switch was designed to speed up choked networks. IP switches replace the slower, more processing-intensive routers. Routers, in general, are slower than switches because they must examine multiple packet fields, make substitutions in the packet headers, and then compute the routes on a packet-by-packet basis. All this activity introduces congestion and latency. The idea behind IP switching is to make what is essentially a connectionless data technology behave like the more reliable circuit-switched network. The goal is to make networks—intranets, extranets, and the Internet—faster, as well as to enable the deployment of new genres of applications, including voice, video, and other streaming traffic.

IP switching has two major objectives. One is to add quality of service (QoS) support to IP. (QoS is discussed in detail in Chapter 8.) If we can make a network behave in a connection-oriented fashion, we can allocate resources end to end that promise to meet the required service level. (In the LAN domain, today's 1Gbps and 10Gbps Ethernet standards provide a great deal of bandwidth, so QoS is less of an issue. But when you get to the WAN edge, QoS becomes a greater concern.) The second objective of IP switching is to provide a way to scale economically because we know that data traffic is growing at a substantial rate (about 30% to 40% per year). IP switching basically replaces a network that consists entirely of Layer 3 hop-by-hop routing and the subsequent associated delays with a route-once/switch-everything-else scenario. That is, the first packet between any two nodes is routed, and then all the subsequent packets between the nodes are switched at Layer 2 to the destination over the selected virtual circuit. This is referred to as a *cut-through technique*. IP switches vastly improve the performance at LAN/WAN

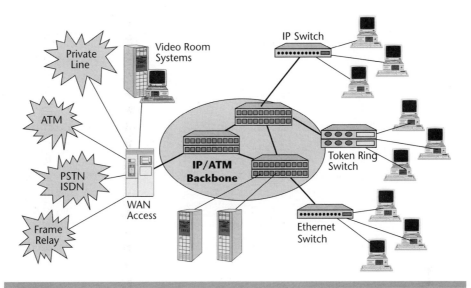

Figure 6.14   A switched LAN infrastructure with an IP/ATM backbone

integration points. As more routing lookup functions are moved from software into the ASIC chips, Layer 3 switches can inspect each packet just like a router at high speed, without using proprietary cut-through methods.

Figure 6.14 shows a switched LAN infrastructure that makes use of a high-speed packet backbone, which could be IP, ATM, or MPLS. An Ethernet switch serves a cluster, and a token-ring switch serves another cluster. An IP switch serves a high-demand cluster. The infrastructure also includes individual servers as well as WAN access devices, all connected to the WAN edge devices, which in this case are the IP switches that help connect or establish a connection-oriented link end to end and thereby guarantee latencies and improve the performance associated with the internetwork.

LANs and WANs

There is a growing commonality between LANs and WANs. The ongoing evolution and introduction of advanced applications requires high bandwidth and has driven the LAN standards to evolve to high-speed specifications. At the same time, with the introduction of very high-speed Ethernet, the applications for what was a LAN technology have progressed beyond building and campus networks to include use in the local loop as a first-mile technology, in MANs as high-speed citywide networks, and even in WAN backbones.

One major advantage of using Ethernet across the various network domains is that it bridges the gap between LANs and WANs, and it provides the opportunity to use one common architecture and protocol on an end-to-end basis. Ethernet has long been the number-one choice for LANs, and as it is improving in performance over longer distances, it has become a viable solution in the MAN space, with metro-Ethernet; there are even some who see it as an alternative in the WAN environment. (These perspectives are discussed in Chapter 11.)

Meanwhile, it is important to note that the service provider hosting sites are looking a great deal like enterprise data centers. Service providers and large enterprises alike are taking advantage of many developments in the optical realm, including dark fiber, wavelength services, and Coarse Wavelength Division Multiplexing (CWDM). There is a common emphasis on user service-level management, accounting, and rapid deployment. Finally, IP and Ethernet are becoming more pervasive in both the LAN and WAN worlds. Chapter 7, "Wide Area Networking," discusses WANs in detail.

Chapter 7

Wide Area Networking

A *wide area network* (WAN) is a group of computer networks connected over long distances by telecommunications links, which can be either wireline or wireless. A number of WAN links can be used, each of which was developed to address specific requirements in data communications. To meet specific network and application needs, a number of WAN techniques (whether deployed over public or private networks) have been developed and become popular over the years.

Leased lines offer the greatest network management control. With leased lines, a known amount of bandwidth is provisioned to you, and no one else has access to it; also, you know who the users are. One disadvantage of leased lines, depending on the carrier, is that you often pay for capacity not used. So if you lease a DS-3 circuit and use only a part of it, you may still pay for the full 45Mbps. The main disadvantage is that leased lines are very costly; you pay a premium for the comfort of having control over your own destiny.

To reduce the costs associated with leased lines, in the late 1990s, many customers migrated to Frame Relay services and today are choosing to implement converged networks based on IP. Frame Relay was introduced in the early 1990s and was largely designed as an application for LAN-to-LAN interconnection. Because numerous subscribers share its virtual circuits, Frame Relay offers great cost-efficiency compared to leased lines. Another WAN alternative to leased lines is Asynchronous Transfer Mode (ATM), which has been perhaps the best solution in environments that have intensive multimedia or other high-bandwidth applications. Most recently, IP-based networks have taken an increasingly important role, offering the benefits of a converged network and relatively low cost. Virtual private networks (VPNs) are being used more and more in WANs as well, with increased emphasis on IP-based VPNs. (See Chapters 8, "The Internet and IP Infrastructures," and 9, "IP Services," for discussions of IP and VPNs.)

A *data service* is a digital service offered for data communications at subscriber locations. Remember that data communication was essentially an add-on to the public switched telephone network (PSTN). As options designed for data were introduced, networks needed specialized equipment meant for such service (see Figure 7.1). The end user needed data terminal equipment (DTE) at the customer premises, as well as a physical interface to data communications (or channel or circuit-terminating) equipment (DCE). From that DCE there would be an access link into a specific access node, designed to facilitate the data service in question (e.g., a digital switching hub for a digital data service [DDS] over leased lines, a unique X.25 packet switch for X.25 services, a Frame Relay switch for Frame Relay, an ATM switch for ATM, an IP router for IP, or the latest entrant—a multiservice provisioning platform [MSPP] that supports multiple protocols).

Despite the fact that there are numerous WAN options, all of which can offer various cost-efficiencies or performance improvements, the many separate networks in use translate into high costs associated with the overall infrastructure—for both the end user and the operator. One goal of WANs today is to integrate voice, data, and video traffic so that it runs through a common platform (in terms of access nodes) and through a common core network (in terms of the transport infrastructure). For example, the goal of ATM was to provide an integrated broadband infrastructure that minimizes the range of required equipment that must be maintained on an ongoing basis. Similarly, IP networks are today seen as the road to converged (what we used to refer to as *integrated*) networks.

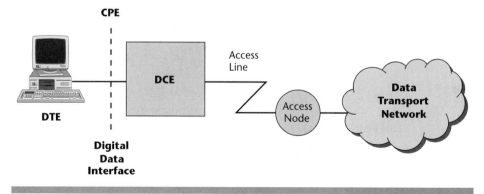

Figure 7.1 Data service components

All the various WAN options can be put into two major categories of data networks: circuit-switched and packet-switched networks. This chapter discusses the categories and characteristics of traditional WANs. It covers the use of circuit-switched WAN options—leased lines and Integrated Services Digital Network (ISDN)—as well as packet-switching WAN options—X.25, Frame Relay, and ATM. Given their significant impact, Internet and IP services are covered in separate chapters (see Chapters 8 and 9).

Circuit-Switched Networks

There are two main types of circuit-switched WANs: those based on leased lines and customer premises equipment (CPE) to manage the leased lines and those based on ISDN, including both Basic Rate Interface (BRI) and Primary Rate Interface (PRI).

Networks Based on Leased Lines

Leased lines can be configured in two different ways. The first approach uses point-to-point leased lines, as shown in Figure 7.2. In this approach, a communications

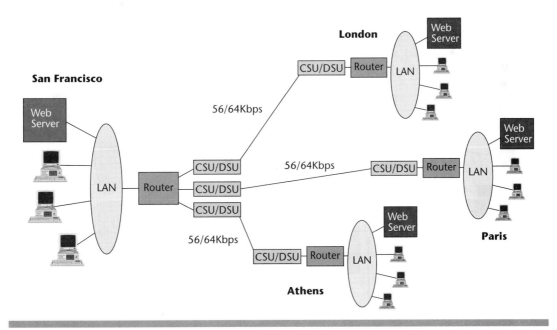

Figure 7.2 A point-to-point leased-line network

the computer, the one bits are positive voltages, and the zero bits are no voltages or low-level voltages. The *ones density rule* says that if more than 15 zeros in a row are transmitted, the network may lose synchronization, which means transmission errors could occur. Therefore, the DSU performs a bipolar variation—it alternates the one bits as positive and as negative voltages. The DSU also supplies the transmit and receive logic, as well as the timing. The CSU provides a means to perform diagnostics.

DDS facilities can be used for LAN interconnection, access to the Internet, and remote PC access to local hosts. One thing to bear in mind with a traditional DDS approach is that it is a leased-line service. If the leased line goes down, the network is out of service, and recovering the service can be a lengthy process, depending on how many network providers are associated with the link end to end. The mere process of troubleshooting and identifying within whose network the problem lies can often lead to resolution times of 24 to 48 hours—or even more, if network managers do not cooperate with one another. If you rely on a DDS network for critical applications, you need a backup in case the leased line fails at some point, and the best backup option is generally *switched digital access*, a dialup option in which facilities are allocated based on demand rather than associated with a specific customer all the time. Switched digital access supports transmission rates of 56Kbps, 64Kbps, 384Kbps, and 1,536Kbps. Another potential backup is ISDN, which is described later in this chapter.

T-, E-, or J-Carrier Backbone

In the 1980s, as networks, traffic, and applications were evolving and growing, customers saw a rise in the amount of data traffic they were carrying, and they began to institute various data services in response. This resulted in a hodgepodge of single-purpose networks based on leased lines that included unique universes of equipment or specific applications.

For example, assume that your company owns the networks shown in Figure 7.5. Both point-to-point and multipoint leased lines are being used to provide connectivity between LANs in various cities around the world. The PBXs for the most part rely on the PSTN, but there is a leased line between San Francisco and London because of the volume of traffic and security requirements. The videoconferencing systems between San Francisco and London use a specially provisioned satellite link. In essence, there are four separate networks, you're paying for four different infrastructures, and you don't have complete connectivity between all the locations, users, and resources. You therefore want to build an enterprise backbone network that ties together everybody with one common infrastructure and that provides for more fluid connectivity between the various locations and applications. This requires intelligent equipment at each location, to manage the transmis-

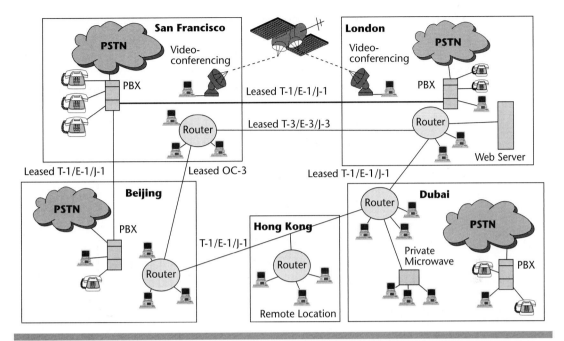

Figure 7.5 Single-purpose leased-line networks

sion resource and to properly allocate the capacity to voice, data, image, video, fax, or other forms of transmissions.

Fractional Services

Some locations may be too small to justify a full T-1 or E-1 facility. In those cases, fractional services can be used; they allow you to subscribe to capacity in small bundles of 56Kbps or 64Kbps channels, which are generally provided in increments of four channels. These services are referred to as fractional T-1 (FT-1) and fractional E-1 (FE-1) services. However, even though fractional services are technically available, many places do not have them tarriffed, and they are therefore unavailable from a regulatory perspective.

The facilities used to transport the information on this revised network can be combinations of privately owned and leased facilities, but you, the customer, own and are responsible for the equipment to manage those transmission facilities. You might be leasing a T-1 or an E-1 from a network operator, or you might be leasing dark fiber from a railroad company. Between some locations, you might deploy a privately owned digital microwave system. By whatever means you choose, you can integrate what used to be four separate networks into one cohesive backbone (see Figure 7.6). In terms of the capacities and components that would then be used within that backbone, the majority of customers today would rely on the dimensions deliverable from the T-, E-, and J-carrier infrastructure, although those with very large data centers and high levels of multimedia and visual applications have already migrated to the optical carrier levels of the SDH/SONET hierarchy.

A customer needs the following equipment to manage transmission facilities (refer to Figure 4.5 in Chapter 4):

- **Transmission media**—The customer might be using copper twisted-pairs with T-1 or E-1 and might be using higher-bandwidth media such as coax, microwave, or fiber with T-3 or E-3 capacities. These are four-wire circuits operating in full-duplex, which means that you can communicate in both directions simultaneously.

- **CSUs**—A CSU terminates each end of the T-1/E-1/J-1 carrier facility. A CSU equalizes the received signal, filters the transmitted and received waveforms, and interacts with the customer's and the carrier's test facilities so that diagnostics can be performed. Essentially, the CSU is used to set up the

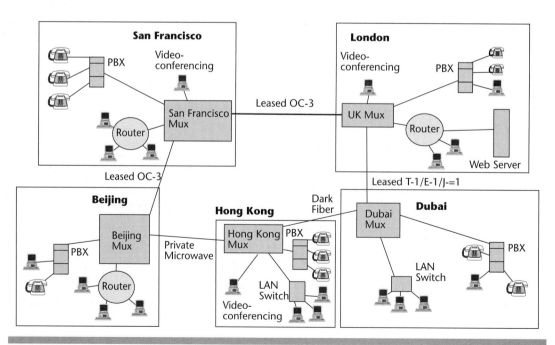

Figure 7.6 An enterprise backbone network

T-1/E-1/J-1 line with a customer-owned PBX, channel banks as standalone devices, intelligent multiplexers (e.g., T-, E-, or J-carrier multiplexers), and any other DS-*x*/CEPT-*x*-compliant DTE, such as digital cross-connects.

■ **Multiplexers**—A channel bank is a type of mux that consolidates the individual channels: 24 channels are associated with T-1, and 32 channels are associated with E-1. These voice and data channels are 64Kbps each, and they can be aggregated onto a higher-speed transmission line. Channel banks were designed to accept analog input, so if there is an analog switch either at the PBX or at the local exchange, that analog signal can be digitized, using Pulse Code Modulation (PCM), as described in Chapter 4. The channel banks provide a first level of aggregation. Beyond that, the customer might want to migrate to higher bandwidth, which would involve using T-1/E-1 or T-3/E-3 multiplexers. (Refer to Chapter 4 for a description of the rates associated with the various digital signal levels.)

Intelligent multiplexers are the most important equipment in building the enterprise backbone network because they act dynamically to manage transmission resources. They allow you to make on-the-fly decisions about who is allocated the capacity, how much capacity needs to be allocated to each user, and whether individual users have rights to access the resource they want to access. In Figure 7.7, the intelligent muxes basically form a smart computer. An intelligent mux has a port side to which you interface the universe of information resources, which could

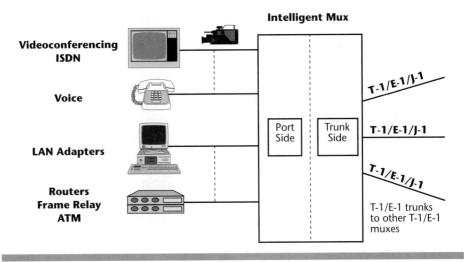

Figure 7.7 T-1/E-1 and T-3/E-3 muxes

be the videoconferencing systems, or the voice systems, or the variety of data universe that you have. On the trunk side, you terminate the T-1s/E-1s or T-3s/E-3s.

Inside the muxes are databases that allow you to make decisions in real-time. One of the greatest benefits of managing your own bandwidth between locations is that you can use that bandwidth as you need it. There are two ways you can use T-, E-, or J-carrier facilities. First, you can use them as an access pipe. For example, you can use a T-1 to access the local exchange and to replace combined voice and data trunks. When you are using it to access the PSTN, you have to work within the subscribed standards. For example, with T-1 you get 24 channels at 64Kbps per channel, so if you have only a little bit of data to send, you can't reallocate your extra bandwidth to another application. You are stuck with static bandwidth allocation (see Figure 7.8), either 24 64Kbps channels or 1 1,536Kbps channel.

A second way in which you can use T-, E-, or J-carrier facilities is to build a private network. For example, if you use a T-1/E-1 to tie together two of your own locations, you can basically do as you wish with that pipe. You're in control of it, and you have the intelligent equipment at either end that can manage it on your behalf. For example, you can dynamically assign bandwidth; you can allocate only as much capacity as is necessary for an application, which more efficiently uses the capacity available on the digital facility. When you use a T-1/E-1 to build a private network, you can also perform dynamic alternative routing. For example, in Figure 7.9, the primary route between Los Angeles and New York City is the direct diagonal line between them. But say there is a problem and that link fails. The multiplexer in Los Angeles will be smart enough to know to reroute its highest-priority traffic through Denver to get it to New York. And in Denver, it may reduce the second-priority traffic to third priority in order to make room for the incoming high-priority traffic from Los Angeles. When the primary link is recovered, the net-

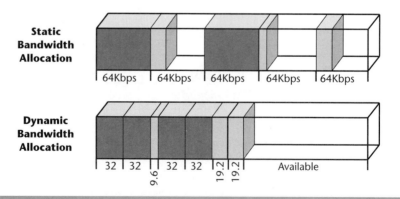

Figure 7.8 Static versus dynamic bandwidth allocation

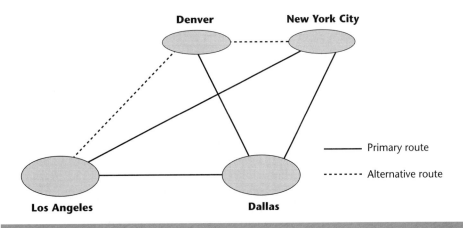

Figure 7.9 Dynamic alternative routing

work will revert to the original routing mechanisms. Dynamic alternative routing is useful in the face of congestion, failure, and a customer's need to reconfigure capacities based on activities and personnel at given locations at random times.

Another element that a customer can use in creating a comprehensive enterprise backbone is a digital cross-connect. This purpose of this device, introduced in 1985, was to automate the process of provisioning circuits—in essence, to replace the use of manual patch panels. The key feature of the digital cross-connect system (DCS) is its capability to "drop and insert," which means the cross-connect can exchange channels from one facility to another (refer to Figure 4.7 in Chapter 4). It is used to implement appropriate routing of traffic, to reroute around congestion or failure, or to allow customers to dynamically reconfigure their networks. With digital cross-connects, network configurations are defined entirely in software, which gives the customer great control and allows reconfigurations to be implemented in a matter of minutes rather than hours or days. The levels at which switching can be performed are at the DS-3/CEPT-3 level, DS-1/CEPT-1 level, and DS-0/CEPT-0 level. Sub-DS-0 and sub-CEPT-0 levels are also possible. This capability is also offered by some of the intelligent multiplexers—the T-1/E-1 and T-3/E-3 multiplexers—so the functionality can be bundled.

The main applications for digital cross-connects are recovering after disasters, bypassing systems during scheduled maintenance, addressing peak traffic demand, and implementing temporary applications. For customers who need to support even more advanced applications—such as computer-aided design, three-dimensional modeling and simulation, visualization, and multimedia—the capacities of the T-, E-, and J-carrier infrastructure may not suffice. The next step is to migrate to the SDH/SONET signal hierarchy.

SDH/SONET Backbone

As discussed in Chapter 4, SDH/SONET is the second generation of digital infrastructure, based on the use of fiber optics. With SDH/SONET, an enterprise today might subscribe to OC-1 (51Mbps) and OC-3 (155Mbps) in order to build an enterprise backbone. Service providers, like ISPs, often use the OC-12 (622Mbps) and OC-48 (2.5Gbps) levels, while the largest of carriers rely on OC-192 (10Gbps) backbones. In today's environment, given the high cost of such leased lines, the customers that use the SDH/SONET levels include airports, aerospace companies, universities that have medical campuses or significant art schools, entertainment companies, large government agencies such as the U.S. Internal Revenue Service, and the military. These organizations typically have a greater use of multimedia and visualization applications, requiring this type of bandwidth.

To build a private SDH/SONET network, a customer would need two types of multiplexers: terminal muxes and add/drop muxes (ADMs). A customer would also need two types of cross-connects to build such a network: wideband cross-connects and broadband cross-connects. (Chapter 4 describes these muxes and cross-connects.)

Dark Fiber

With dark fiber, the customer leases the fiber itself and buys the necessary equipment to actually activate the fiber. The customer pays for the physical media, not for bandwidth, and as the customer adds equipment that can either pulse more bits per second or extract more wavelengths out of the underlying fiber, the bandwidth essentially becomes cheaper and cheaper.

Networks Based on ISDN

Another circuit-switched WAN option is ISDN. The International Telecommunication Union Telecommunications Standardization sector (ITU-T) formalized the ISDN standard in 1983. According to the ITU-T (www.itu.org), ISDN is "a network evolved from the telephony integrated digital network that provides end-to-end connectivity to support a wide range of services, including voice and nonvoice services, to which users have access by a limited set or standard multipurpose customer interfaces."

One of the ideas behind Narrowband ISDN (N-ISDN), as the first generation of ISDN was called, was to give customers one access into the network, from which they could then engage in circuit-switched, leased-line, or packet-switched options. Although all these options were available before ISDN, each one generally required its own special access line and device, which meant extra costs and administrative responsibilities because of the large number of options. The goal of

ISDN was to provide one plug into the network, from which you could then go out over multiple alternatives.

ISDN Networks

A couple key elements are required to form an ISDN network (see Figure 7.10). First, you must have a digital local exchange, and that digital exchange must be loaded with ISDN software. This is an expensive proposition. The ISDN software alone costs around US$1 million, and each exchange costs in the neighborhood of US$3 million to US$5 million. Along with a digital exchange and the proper ISDN software, you also need a Signaling System 7 (SS7) network and CPE that is compatible with the ISDN network. (SS7 is discussed in detail in Chapter 4.)

As discussed in Chapter 2, "Traditional Transmission Media," N-ISDN has two interfaces (see Figure 7.11):

- **BRI**—BRI is primarily used for residential service, small businesses, and centrex environments. BRI is offered only by local telcos, and how they offer it varies greatly. It can be configured as either 1B, 2B, 1B+D, or the full 2B+D; 128Kbps transmission requires that two B-channels be used. One application for this is Internet access, so you might have a BRI device, such as an ISDN modem, that would bond two B-channels (and possibly the D-channel) to provide the 128Kbps (or 144Kbps) access to the ISP.

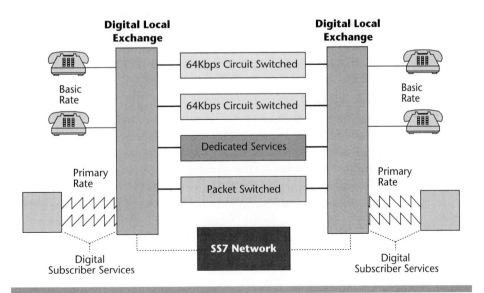

Figure 7.10 ISDN components

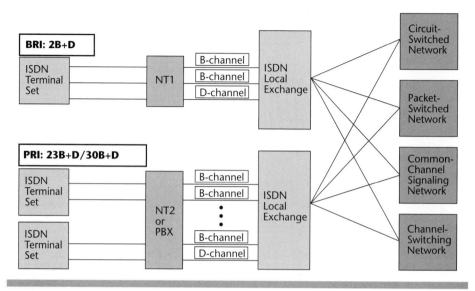

Figure 7.11 N-ISDN network interfaces

- **PRI**—PRI is primarily used for business applications, and both local and interexchange carriers offer it. In support of the voice environment, PRI applications would include access to PBX and call center networks, replacement of existing analog trunk groups, and configuration of PBX tie-lines. Q-Sig, a standard that's an enhanced version of the D-channel signaling protocol, supports feature transparency between different vendors' PBXs. A key data application of PRI is LAN/WAN integration.

ISDN Applications

ISDN can be used in a number of different situations. The following are the main applications for N-ISDN:

- **Internet access**—You could use N-ISDN to increase the speeds otherwise supported by your analog voice-grade line when you do not have other broadband access options, such as DSL, cable modems, or broadband wireless.

- **Remote access**—You could use N-ISDN to give teleworkers or telecommuters access to corporate resources.

- **LAN/WAN connections**—As mentioned earlier, N-ISDN is a technique for LAN interconnection, so you could bridge multiple LANs across a WAN over ISDN connections.

- **High-capacity access**—You could use N-ISDN if you needed to increase your capacity for things such as graphics, file transfer, video, and multimedia networking. N-ISDN does not provide motion as good as what you would get with the higher-capacity services, but it is much better than what you get with an analog facility.

- **Private-line backup**—You could use N-ISDN as a backup to the private-line services discussed earlier (e.g., DDS).

- **Dialup Frame Relay access**—Frame Relay is a very popular data networking option, particularly for LAN-to-LAN interconnection. You could use ISDN to provide measured-use dialup access to Frame Relay services in which the user dials in to a remote access port on the carrier's Frame Relay switch at either 64Kbps or 128Kbps. You could do this at smaller sites and for remote access (e.g., for telecommuters).

- **BRI 0B+D for packet data**—One 16Kbps D-channel can be shared by up to eight devices. BRI 0B+D makes use of 9.6Kbps of D-channel capacity to support low-speed data terminals. This requires a terminal adapter that encapsulates the user data in D-channel frames. Applications for BRI 0B+D include credit card terminals and automatic teller machines.

- **ISDN DSL (IDSL)**—IDSL delivers full-duplex, dedicated data services; it does not support voice services. It is provided either on a 1B or a 2B configuration (i.e., 64Kbps or 128Kbps). IDSL is compatible with existing digital loop carrier systems, which serve 30% to 40% of the U.S. population. Digital loop carriers are especially common in remote rural areas. Some of the DSL services (which are discussed in Chapter 12, "Broadband Access Alternatives") are incompatible with these older-generation digital loop carriers. IDSL, however, is compatible with them, so it can be used to deliver digital private-line service at speeds up to 128Kbps. In today's environment, 128Kbps is definitely not a desired speed, so even though IDSL can facilitate some speedier communications than standard dialup, it is nowhere near what other broadband access options have to offer, making it an antiquated solution.

Packet-Switched Networks

Packet switching was developed as a solution for the communications implications of interactive processing; it was designed to support bursty data traffic, which stays connected for a long time but is associated with low data volumes. Packet switching involves the application of statistical multiplexing, whereby numerous conversations can make use of one common communications channel, which significantly increases transmission efficiency. (Chapter 1, "Telecommunications Technology Fundamentals," discusses statistical multiplexing in more detail.) However, sharing a communications link introduces latency. A key issue that we are currently addressing is how packet-switched networks can support latency- and loss-sensitive traffic such as real-time streams. As discussed in Chapter 8, "The Internet and IP Infrastructures," and Chapter 10, "Next-Generation Networks," quality of service (QoS) mechanisms are a major requirement, and that is where much of our attention is currently focused.

With packet switching, packets are routed through a series of intermediate nodes, often involving multiple networks; they are routed in a store-and-forward manner through a series of packet switches (i.e., routers) that ultimately lead to the destination. Information is divided into packets that include a destination address and a sequence number.

The secret to understanding the various packet formats is realizing where their strengths and weaknesses lie. They vary as to the number of bits they contain, how much control they give you over delays or losses, and the rules they use to address the highways and the destination points. (See the simple analogy between transportation and communications networks in the sidebar "A Transportation Analogy to Packet Switching" in Chapter 3, "Establishing Communications Channels.")

Remember from Chapter 3 that packet switching deals with containerized, labeled entities we generically call *packets*, which vary in size. Packets come from different sources—from different users at one customer site or from different users at different customer sites. All these different packets are statistically multiplexed and sent to their destinations over virtual circuits. Also remember from Chapter 1 that a virtual circuit is a set of *logical* connections that create a pathway between two points; they are not a *physical* connection that you can trace end to end that belongs to just one conversation. A virtual circuit is therefore a shared communications link that is set up on demand based on negotiated communications parameters.

Because packet switching is a store-and-forward process of relaying through a series of intermediate nodes, latency and packet loss can considerably degrade real-time (i.e., time-sensitive) applications. In fact, the first generation of packet switching, X.25, dealt with data only. It could not handle voice or video. As discussed later in this chapter, newer generations can handle data because we have found ways to design the network to handle the requirements of voice and video applications.

In general, in the traditional mode, packet switching offered no QoS guarantees; QoS simply was not a design objective. It did, however, offer the knowledge that packets would usually make it to their destination because they could be rerouted around trouble points. But because they could be rerouted around trouble points, which might mean congestion points or failed points, there could be no guarantees about the latencies or losses that you would experience. Therefore, it is a relatively new concept to try to build in QoS as a metric in packet-switched networks. New packet networks can provision QoS by means of resource management and allocation techniques, such as RSVP-TE. (QoS techniques are discussed in more detail in Chapters 8 and 10.)

A packet-switched network is a data-centric environment, and instead of switching millions of physical circuits, as happens in the circuit-switched environment, the data-centric network switches packets, or switched virtual circuits. Circuit switching makes individual paths from the source to the destination, and in the case of the telephone network, millions of individual paths are created. Packet switching provides a dynamically determined route (hopefully a good route) for each packet presented to the network from the source to the destination. In Figure 7.12, multiple packets are statistically multiplexed as they come in through the packet switch, a routing table is consulted, an appropriate path is selected, and the packets are sent over the correct virtual circuit, leading to the next most logical stop in the network.

The capacity of the transmission facilities between the switches directly affects the performance of packet-switched networks; this is why many new-generation packet switches—IP routers and ATM switches, for instance—now come with high-speed interfaces, such as OC-48 (i.e., 2.5Gbps) interfaces. OC-48 interfaces on a switch could potentially eliminate the need for an entire layer of aggregation that we currently do according to the traditional model of 64Kbps channels. By eliminating that layer of aggregation, we can actually allow direct connection to an optical network by using DWDM at the full rate of the service and interface. (See Chapter 1, "Telecommunications Technology Fundamentals," and Chapter 11, "Optical Networking," for information on DWDM.) With data traffic growing all

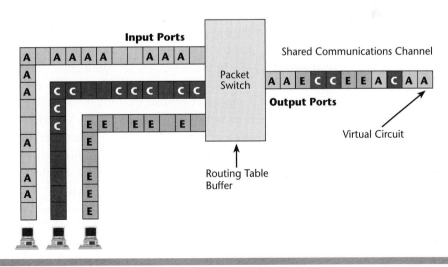

Figure 7.12 Packet switching

the time, transport networks will increasingly rely on data switches to manage and aggregate the traffic, and the transport network will be providing low-cost and reliable connections between these switches.

Remember from Chapter 3 that there are two main types of packet-switched networks: connection-oriented and connectionless networks. In a connection-oriented environment (such as X.25, Frame Relay, ATM, and VPNs that are based on Frame Relay or ATM networks), a call is set up end to end at the onset of the communication. Only one call request process that contains the source and destination address is necessary. That initial call request packet establishes a virtual circuit to the destination so that subsequent packets need only be read for the marking information that defines the virtual circuit to be taken. The intermediate nodes do not need to look at the addressing information in order to calculate a path for each packet independently. This reduces delay because routing decisions do not have to be made at the intermediate nodes. Where the error control is performed depends on the generation of the network. With X.25, error detection and correction was a necessary feature of the network because the links were almost all analog and had high error rates.

A provision of X.25 was to detect and correct for errors while they were in transport, hence improving data communications. But as networks became more digital and fiber based, noise became less of a problem; thus, the subsequent generations of packet switching—Frame Relay and ATM, for instance—give the endpoints the responsibility for error detection and correction. Not having to stop packets and investigate them in the throes of transmission greatly decreases the delays that would otherwise be encountered. Of course, today this is not so much a problem because there are fast processors and hardware to assist in this. In a connection-oriented environment, a virtual circuit defines the path end-to-end, and all packets follow the same path throughout the course of the session.

As discussed in Chapter 3, the connectionless environment (which includes X.25 networks, the public Internet, private IP-based backbones, and LANs) can be likened to the postal service, in which a message is relayed from point to point, with each relay getting one step closer to its ultimate destination. In a connectionless environment, each packet of a message is an independent unit that contains the source and destination address. Each packet is independently routed at each intermediate node it crosses. The more hops it goes through, the greater the accumulated delays, which greatly affects delay-sensitive applications, including any form of real-time voice, real-time audio, real-time video, video-on-demand, and streaming media. But connectionless environments can work around problems, which is why they were so strong in the early days, when there were frequent system failures and links that were too noisy to perform correctly. Connectionless packets could circumvent system failures or noisy conditions and still meet at the destination point with high integrity. The connectionless environment offered the flexibility of routing around problem areas, but at the risk of greater overhead associated with the overall transmission because addressing had to be included in each packet, and also at the risk of greater delays because each packet had to be independently routed.

X.25

In 1970 Tymnet introduced X.25, which was the first generation of packet switching. X.25 packet-switching networks evolved as an option for data communications and therefore did not compete directly with the telephony providers. The providers of such networks were put in a special category, called value-added network (VAN) providers.

The X.25 packet-switching technique emerged out of a need to address the bursty data flow associated with interactive processing which emerged in the late 1960s. Because bursty data implies long connect times but low data volumes, the key advantage of X.25 was that it provided a technique for many conversations, or data sessions, to share a communications channel.

Because of when X.25 was created, it was based on an analog network infrastructure. A big problem with analog networks is the accumulation of noise through the amplification points, which leads to the very high error rate associated with analog networks. One of the value-added services provided by X.25 networks was error control as a function within the network. Because packet switching is a store-and-forward technique, at every intermediate node at which an X.25 packet would be halted, the packet would undergo an error check. If everything in the packet was correct, the intermediate node would return an acknowledgment to the original transmitting node, requesting it to forward the next packet. If the packet the node received was not correct, the node would send a message requesting a retransmission. Thus, at any point in the routing and relaying of those packets, if noise contributed to errors, the errors could be resolved, which resulted in a much more accurate data flow.

Remember that what is beneficial or not beneficial about a particular network depends on the prevailing conditions, so in an analog infrastructure where noise was an issue, error control was a highly desirable feature. But performing that error control procedure on every packet, at every node, in addition to looking up the proper routing instructions at each intermediate node for the next point to which to relay the packet, increased the delays encountered end to end during transmission. Because X.25 packet-switching networks were for data only, it was not important to be able to tightly control delays or losses; the endpoints would resolve any such problems.

While X.25 networks are still found around the world, their use is in dramatic decline, and they are being replaced by newer technologies, including Frame Relay, ATM, and the much-favored IP. However, in many portions of the developing world, X.25 is still often the only available reliable service and is used mainly in legacy transaction systems. Another common application has been automated teller machines (ATMs), but as more and more of these banking kiosks today involve multimedia interfaces, many of them are moving to higher-speed connections.

Packet Size in X.25, Frame Relay, and ATM

An early attribute of X.25 was the size of its packet. It used relatively small packets, generally 128 bytes or 256 bytes long. Small packets were desirable in the X.25 generation because of the noise factor. If there was noise in the network, there would be errors, and hence fairly frequent retransmissions were necessary. Retransmitting a smaller packet is more efficient than retransmitting very long blocks of information, so X.25 was specifically designed to use small packets.

In the next generation of packet-switched networks, Frame Relay, the packet sizes are variable, but they can be up to 4,096 bytes. Frame Relay operates over a digital network, where noise is not much of an issue because regenerative repeaters eliminate the noise that may accumulate on the signal during transmission. In addition, there is greater use of fiber optics as the transmission media, and fiber is impervious to many of the impairments that affect electrical systems. As a result, all the error control procedures are removed from Frame Relay networks in order to make them faster. Furthermore, in Frame Relay we're not very concerned about having to retransmit information. There's less likelihood that errors or noise in the network will cause the need for retransmission. Thus, Frame Relay uses a larger packet size than X.25, and the result is improved bandwidth efficiency. A Frame Relay packet contains less control information for a larger group of bytes of information, and this means the packet makes better use of the available bandwidth.

If we jump ahead one more generation, to ATM switching, we find that packets are called *cells*. They're small—only 53 bytes—which gives them the capability to cross intersections quickly (i.e., it reduces the latency). And, more importantly, the cells are all the same size, which is particularly important to multimedia and interactive applications. They can transition through network nodes very quickly, but because they are so small and each cell still requires basic control information, the result is a greater percentage of overhead, which is sometimes referred to as *cell tax*. However, with ATM, there's an underlying assumption that bandwidth isn't an issue due to the presence of high-speed fiber infrastructures, so you're not trying to conserve on bandwidth; instead, the prevailing condition that you're trying to satisfy is low latencies and guaranteed QoS.

You can see that the optimum size of packets depends on a number of factors, such as the performance of the network, the cost of the bandwidth, and the demand of the applications involved.

Frame Relay

The second generation of packet switching, Frame Relay, was introduced in 1991. Frame Relay assumes that there's a digital infrastructure in place and that few errors will result from network transmission problems, such as noise or jitter. Therefore, the entire error detection and correction process has been removed from the Frame Relay network, and error control is done entirely in the endpoints. This means that traffic is not delayed by being stopped and checked, which translates to much faster throughput over Frame Relay networks than over X.25 networks.

The lack of error control in the network also means that it is possible to carry voice and video over a Frame Relay network. However, Frame Relay is not innately designed to do that. The packet sizes enabled under Frame Relay are large—up to 4,096 bytes—and variable, which means that there could be a 100-byte packet going through a network node, with a 4,000-byte packet right behind it. When you have packets of varying sizes, you can't predict the delay in processing those packets through the network, and when you can't predict the delay, you can't properly address the latency requirements of real-time voice or video. Yet it is possible, in fact, to run voice and video over Frame Relay networks by tweaking the system in one of several ways. For example, we could provision separate links to carry the voice and the data traffic, and thus some excess data bursting wouldn't affect any real-time telephony, for instance, that is under way. We could prioritize traffic by application and in that way enable access to bandwidth, based on priority. In public Frame Relay networks, we often convert frames to equal-sized cells. At the core of the Frame Relay network is ATM because ATM currently offers the strongest suite of tools for traffic management. Thus, many networks, including IP backbones, the Internet, and Frame Relay, have ATM at their core. We can trick the system in order to get added utility out of Frame Relay networks, but keep in mind that when we do this, we lose a little bit of the cost-efficiencies we would otherwise have by running all our traffic in the same manner over the same link.

The types of links that connect the Frame Relay switching points operate at high speeds—they run the full range of the wide band of the PDH hierarchy. Where a Frame Relay network is running over a T-carrier infrastructure, the links can operate at 1.5Mbps to 45Mbps; for networks being served by E-carrier platforms, the links can operate at 2Mbps to 34Mbps.

The standards for Frame Relay come from the ITU-T, which defines Frame Relay as "a conversational communication service provided by a subnetwork for high-speed bursty data." This definition implies that Frame Relay has two-way capability (it is "conversational") and that it is not an end-to-end solution (it is a "subnetwork"). So we don't look for a Frame Relay device such as a Frame Relay telephone; instead, we look at Frame Relay to serve as the cloud—that is, the WAN solution that links computer networks distributed across a country or across the world. And "high-speed bursty data" suggests that Frame Relay's preliminary application is in support of data and, specifically, LAN-to-LAN internetworking.

Frame Relay Applications

One environment that might be a candidate for Frame Relay is a hub-and-spoke network, in which traffic from remote locations travels through a central site. This is similar to the airline system, in which key airports serve as main hubs; the largest of the 777s travel between the main hubs, and to get to a smaller city, you go through a hub to get on a smaller aircraft that then takes you to your destination. Frame Relay is also used to replace the use of expensive leased lines. Depending on the network topology, Frame Relay could potentially reduce costs up to 50% compared to using leased lines.

Frame Relay is also used to give a network some bandwidth flexibility—that is, bandwidth-on-demand. Because the main application of Frame Relay is LAN internetworking, and because LANs produce highly unpredictable traffic flows, paying for a subscribed set of bandwidth whether or not you're using it may not be very cost-effective. Frame Relay provides the capability to burst above what you've committed to financially. (This is discussed in the next section "Frame Relay Networks.")

Frame Relay is also useful in a multiprotocol environment. Although IP seems to rule the world, it is not the only protocol in use. There are SNA networks in place, still making use of IBM's Synchronous Data Link Control (SDLC). The largest legacy networks today are some of the billing systems run by the world's telco operators. Frame Relay is used by more than 60,000 enterprises worldwide, and those that are highly focused on multimedia applications use ATM. Few customers use only one protocol. They have multiple protocols in their networks, and Frame Relay can handle them all because it simply encapsulates another protocol into a Frame Relay envelope and carries it through the network—it doesn't care what's inside the envelope.

Closed user groups—where you want to know who has access in and out of the network—can be achieved with Frame Relay, unlike with the public Internet, where you have no idea who's on there at any point in time. Frame Relay also allows you to predict the level of the network's performance, so it enables you to set metrics. This makes it an especially attractive solution if you are operating with countries where there are good carrier infrastructures.

Frame Relay Networks

Frame Relay is an interface specification that defines how information must be packaged in order for a Frame Relay network to act on it and deliver it to its destination. Therefore, it is not necessarily associated with a specific piece of equipment. The Frame Relay interface could reside on multiple platforms. In Figure 7.13, for example, the Frame Relay interface resides on the DTE, which is most likely a router but could also be a Frame Relay access device (FRAD), used to provide access for Voice over Frame Relay (VoFR). It could be a T-1 or an E-1 multiplexer with a Frame Relay interface. One of the things that is so valuable about Frame Relay is that it doesn't represent an investment in altogether new technology. You can use it to upgrade existing platforms, which can make a lot of economic sense. Frame Relay can be deployed on a wide range of platforms, and predominantly it is seen today on routers.

The Frame Relay interface takes the native data stream, no matter what the protocol (e.g., TCP/IP, SDLC, X.25), and puts it inside a Frame Relay envelope. Essentially, Frame Relay uses Link Access Protocol D (LAPD) to put the native data into an encapsulated form that the Frame Relay switches can act on.

Figure 7.14 shows the Frame Relay header format, LAPD. A beginning flag essentially starts the communication. A Frame Relay header is the very important part of the envelope that contains the addressing information. The user data is the native block of information. Next, the frame check sequence performs a cyclic redundancy check (CRC), and an ending flag closes the frame. An expanded view of the Frame Relay header includes the data link connection identifier (DLCI), which is a 10-bit field that represents the address of the frame and corresponds to a PVC. A few fields can be used for purposes of managing a minimal amount of QoS. The forward explicit congestion notification (FECN) and backward explicit congestion notification (BECN) fields are used to manage the traffic flow. The FECN

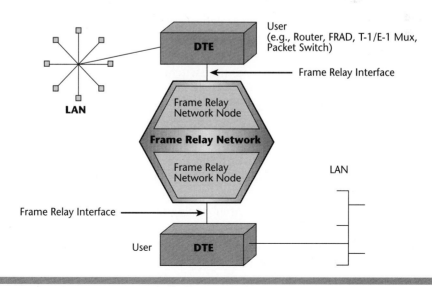

Figure 7.13 An example of a Frame Relay interface

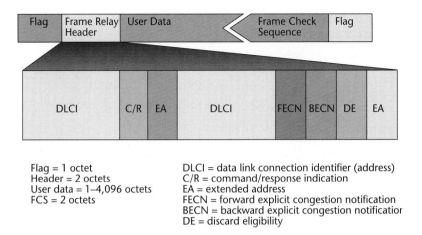

Flag = 1 octet
Header = 2 octets
User data = 1–4,096 octets
FCS = 2 octets

DLCI = data link connection identifier (address)
C/R = command/response indication
EA = extended address
FECN = forward explicit congestion notification
BECN = backward explicit congestion notification
DE = discard eligibility

Figure 7.14   Frame Relay frame format (LAPD)

tells the receiver, "I'm experiencing delays getting to you, so anticipate those delays. Don't time-out the session." FECN is rarely used. BECN tells the transmitter, "Whoa! We've got delays ahead. Throttle back or slow down on your introduction of data, or we'll end up losing those frames because of congestion." In other words, BECN indicates that all discard-eligible traffic is about to get dumped. You use the discard eligibility field to mark a frame as being either discard eligible or not and to control what occurs between voice and data in, for instance, a period of congestion. Frame Relay enables you to control the traffic flow a bit, and you can determine whether to drop a frame. But notice that there is no place in the frame for defining latency requirements or loss tolerances—the stricter QoS traffic measurements. Nonetheless, the switches will read the DLCIs to determine how to properly forward the frame.

In a Frame Relay network, the customer environment includes the full complement of information resources that the customer wants to use on the network. Next, the CPE—which could be a router, bridge, FRAD, mux, or switch—contains the interface that formats packets into the Frame Relay frames. From the CPE, an access line (called the User-to-Network Interface [UNI]) connects to the Frame Relay provider switch. That UNI could be a leased line, such as 56Kbps/64Kbps or T-1/E-1, an ISDN line, or an analog dialup line. The UNI then leads to the Frame Relay switch, which is basically a statistical multiplexer. Based on the type of subscription in place, the traffic is sent over either a permanent virtual circuit (PVC) or a switched virtual circuit (SVC). Recall from Chapter 1 that a PVC is analogous to a leased line. It is predetermined, and it is manually configured and entered into a network management system so that it stays between two locations until it is reprogrammed. SVCs, on the other hand, are like the dialup scenario; they are dynamically provisioned via signaling on an as-needed basis. (The reality is that PVCs are predominant, and SVCs are rare.)

Figure 7.15 illustrates the use of PVCs. When a packet goes through the interface in the DTE (probably a router or a FRAD), it is put into the LAPD format, and then the LAPD frame is passed to the switching point. The switching point looks at the DLCI and then looks it up in its table to determine over which particular circuit or virtual circuit to send the message.

Subscribers specify the port speed and the committed information rate (CIR) in a Frame Relay network. Port prices are based on bandwidth, which determines the speed of the interface into the network. The PVC charges are based on the CIR and the distance. (The CIR generally refers to the PVC's minimum bandwidth under normal conditions. Generally, the CIR is less than the access rate into the network, and the access rate into the network determines the maximum amount of usable bandwidth.)

Figure 7.16 illustrates the concept of bandwidth-on-demand mentioned earlier in this chapter. Say you have an access line, an E-1, that allows 2.048Mbps to your carrier's switching point. Between these two locations of the network, you have contracted for a PVC that is essentially 1Mbps. In this environment, bandwidth-on-demand works like this: You are allowed to burst above your PVC's CIR of 1Mbps, up to the rate of your access line, or port speed, which is 2Mbps. In other words, you are paying for 1Mbps, but you're actually allowed to transmit at 2Mbps for short periods of time. However, note that the contracted-for 1Mbps has a discard eligibility of zero (DE = 0), ensuring that these frames do not get dropped.

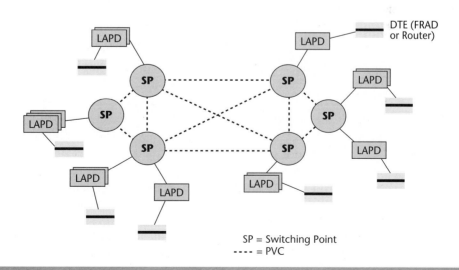

Figure 7.15 PVCs in a Frame Relay network

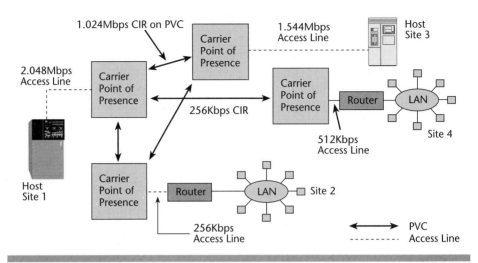

Figure 7.16 Frame Relay bandwidth-on-demand

When you burst above your CIR, everything else is DE = 1, which means those frames could get dropped.

If you try to keep transmitting at your burst rate over a sustained period, the network will do one of two things. It might start dropping frames, which is another reason voice and video might suffer over Frame Relay. Or there might be a software mechanism that allows the excess traffic to be captured so that you can be billed for overtime. But the carrier is banking on the fact that not everybody is making use of the CIR at all times. Again, LAN traffic is quite unpredictable, so there are lulls in the day when you're not transmitting anything and other times when you need twice your CIR, and, ideally, at the end of the day it all balances out. But the carrier is playing the same gamble, assuming that not everybody is going to try to exercise their CIR at the same time. If they do, whether you still experience your CIR depends on the integrity of the Frame Relay provider's engineering. In other words, if the provider oversubscribes a PVC and if everyone attempts to burst at the same time, somebody is not going to have capacity available. This is a big issue in terms of vendor selection. Frame Relay networks are much less expensive than other options because the operators save on how they carry the traffic.

With SVCs, the connections are established on demand, so the routing tables do not store path identifiers—just the address of each site. Users can connect to any site, as long as the address is programmed into the router and SVC capacity is available. Subscribers control call setup via their own routers or FRADs. The router programming, then, controls allocation of the aggregate bandwidth. SVCs share bandwidth, and they do so either on a first-come, first-served basis or on a custom basis, where chosen SVCs are disconnected when a higher-priority application needs bandwidth.

Frame Relay Performance Issues

You need to consider a number of performance issues with Frame Relay:

- **Likelihood of bottlenecks**—This depends on whether the operator has oversubscribed the backbone.

- **Ability to handle bursts**—The operator may let you burst above your CIR for sufficient periods, or the bursts may be so limited that you really don't get bandwidth-on-demand.

- **Level of network delay**—Operators commit to different maximum delays on different routes, so if you are going to be handling delay-sensitive traffic, you especially need to address this issue.

- **Network availability guarantees**—You need to determine to what level you can get a service-level agreement (SLA) that guarantees network availability. This depends on the vendor, not on technology.

As far as Frame Relay QoS goes, you can expect to be able to have classes of service (CoSs), where you specify your CIR and your maximum burst rate, as well as some minor traffic parameters, such as the discard eligibility bits and the congestion notification bits. Otherwise, Frame Relay has no provisions for controlling latencies and losses.

VoFR

VoFR is of interest among both carriers and users. The main driver behind VoFR is more efficient use of Frame Relay bandwidth. The average full-duplex voice conversation consists of about half silence, so voice has a bursty quality. Data networks have been sharing bandwidth for many years. Voice is just another protocol, so why not let it also share bandwidth and in this way achieve better use of the Frame Relay resource? The goal of VoFR is not to replace existing voice networks but rather to make use of what is already available in Frame Relay to carry overflow traffic or additional voice traffic. Voice is compressed in Frame Relay and then encapsulated into the Frame Relay protocol via a FRAD. Again, the main advantage of this is better use of a single data network and the cost savings derived from this efficiency. But remember that if you run everything over a single network, voice quality may suffer, and, even worse, data performance may suffer.

The Frame Relay Forum has specified the FRF.11 standard for how to deploy VoFR. It provides bandwidth-efficient networking of digital voice and Group 3 fax communications over Frame Relay. It defines multiplexed virtual connections, up to 255 subchannels on a single Frame Relay DLCI, and it defines support of data subchannels on a multiplexed Frame Relay DLCI.

The ITU has defined some VoFR compression standards:

■ **ITU G.711 PCM**—Regular PCM is the compression standard that was part and parcel of the PDH hierarchy, which carried voice at 64Kbps. That's a very high rate, given what we can achieve today.

■ **ITU G.726/G.727 ADPCM**—Adaptive Differential PCM (ADPCM) compression reduces the data rate to 32Kbps, allowing for more efficient use of bandwidth.

■ **ITU G.723.1 MP-MLQ**—With Frame Relay networks, we can apply Multi-pulse Maximum Likelihood Quantization (MP-MLQ), which reduces voice to 4.8Kbps and can permit up to 10 voice channels on a single 64Kbps connection.

Another important feature of VoFR is voice activity detection (VAD). VAD algorithms reduce the amount of information needed to recreate the voice at the destination end by removing silent periods and redundant information found in human speech; this also helps with compression.

Another quality issue related to VoFR is *jitter*, the variation in delays on the receive side of the transmission from one packet to the next. Delay varies, depending on the traffic in the switch, and severe jitter can make conversations very difficult to understand. Dropped packets can cause clicks or pops, and a great deal of packet loss results in altogether unintelligible conversation.

FRF.12 addresses the fragmentation of both data frames and VoFR frames. It reduces delay variation, segments voice signals into smaller data bundles, and, ultimately, provides better performance. Because bundles are smaller, when some get lost, the network feels less impact.

Another VoFR consideration is the ability to prioritize voice traffic, which, of course, is very delay sensitive. The need for echo cancellation caused by round-trip delay is another consideration. Echo cancellation is required on voice circuits over 500 miles (800 km) long. A final consideration is voice interpolation. Equipment is needed to recreate lost voice information so that retransmissions don't need to be performed because voice retransmissions would be ineffective. Unlike data, voice cannot wait for retransmissions to occur.

Advantages and Disadvantages of Frame Relay
The advantages of Frame Relay are as follows:

■ Provides cost savings compared to leased lines

■ Runs on multiprotocol networks

- Provides control over the user community
- Gives predictable performance and reliability (although with congestion, performance can be, at best, uneven)
- Provides minimum guaranteed throughput
- Allows for network management and control
- Provides greater bandwidth flexibility

Disadvantages of Frame Relay include the following:

- Provides weak network management ability
- Is inherently unsuitable for delay-sensitive traffic, such as voice and video
- Requires high-quality digital circuits, so it does not work everywhere
- Is not entirely standardized

Overall, Frame Relay represents a viable and cost-effective solution for data networking, particularly where LAN-to-LAN interconnection is the main goal. However, recently, Frame Relay has begun to be displaced by ATM and IP. Also, the introduction of IP VPNs and dedicated broadband services such as DSL and cable modems may signal the end of Frame Relay's popularity. Nonetheless, there are still locations, such as rural areas, where DSL and cable modems are not available, and in those cases the Frame Relay alternative still presents the least costly approach to an always-on connection, allowing an enterprise with rural branches to connect those offices to the corporate WAN.

ATM

ATM is a series of standards that the ITU-T introduced in 1988 as part of a larger vision for the future of networks called Broadband ISDN. Broadband ISDN defined a new genre of applications, and most of those applications, not surprisingly, involved video or multimedia content, and this is where ATM shines. ATM was designed to be a master integrator: one platform, one infrastructure over which voice, data, video, multimedia, images, and other forms of traffic that we may have not thought of yet can all coexist and all be assigned the appropriate network resources based on their needs. ATM wasn't designed to be a technique for voice; it wasn't designed as a new solution for data. It was designed for multimedia, but it hasn't yet had a chance to really demonstrate its greatest strengths in today's environment.

A huge number of networks—roughly 80% to 85% of all Internet backbones and Frame Relay networks—have ATM at their core. Today, ATM is still the only WAN approach that provides an architected QoS, which then gives network operators the opportunity to manage the traffic inside the network, which is a prerequisite to being able to offer business-class services, such as VPNs, VoFR, Voice over IP (VoIP), and Voice over ATM (VoATM). (However, it is important to note that today, MPLS, combined with RSVP-TE or CR-LDP, provides vastly improved QoS capabilities to the IP world, approaching that of ATM's structured architecture.) ATM has the capability to provide the appropriate guarantees to delay-sensitive traffic. ATM is working on your behalf more than may be evident in what you read and hear, especially as IP is the public's current darling. (Later in this chapter, the section "IP and ATM" discusses the possibility and benefits of marrying ATM and IP.)

By definition, ATM is a high-bandwidth, fast packet-switching and multiplexing technique that enables the seamless end-to-end transmission of voice, data, image, and video traffic. It's a high-capacity, low-latency switching fabric that's adaptable for multiservice and multirate connections. The capacities it affords, including low latency, are absolutely prerequisite to supporting the advanced applications for which this switching technology was designed.

ATM switches characteristically have large capacities. They range from 10Gbps to 160Gbps, and there are new products in the Tbps range. (In comparison, IP routers typically offer capacities ranging from 4Gbps to 60Gbps, although there are also new Tbps switch routers.)

The best advantages of ATM include the robust QoS and high-speed interfaces. ATM was the first networking approach to support high-speed interfaces, both 155Mbps and 622Mbps. Therefore, when an enterprise wanted to reengineer its campus network to higher bandwidth, ATM presented a viable solution. But the 1997 introduction of Gigabit Ethernet presented a more economical approach for obtaining high bandwidth, so today ATM is implemented in the enterprise because it offers the capability to administer QoS for multimedia and real-time traffic. Of course, over time, other solutions and architectures also begin to incorporate the features that people seek, so new-generation IP routers and switches accommodate the same high-speed interfaces that ATM does. Both ATM and IP today ship with 2.5Gbps (i.e., OC-48) interfaces. Today, ATM can administer QoS, and IP is getting close. (QoS and ATM's service classes are discussed in detail in Chapter 10.)

ATM enables access bandwidth to be shared among multiple sources, and it enables network resources to be shared among multiple users. It allows different services to be combined within a single access channel (see Figure 7.17).

ATM Applications

There are many key applications for ATM. The ATM standard began in the carrier community as a means of reengineering the PSTN to meet the demands of future applications. As Frame Relay networks began to see the demand to accommodate voice and video, they also began to institute ATM in their core in order to administrate service guarantees. The same goes for the Internet backbone, especially where

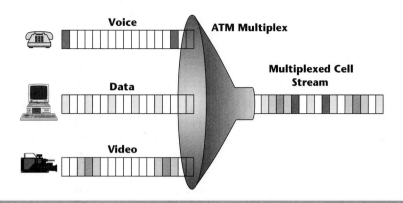

Figure 7.17 Mapping services into ATM

there's an interest in providing more than just consumer Internet access but also business-class services, where the customer wants some SLAs tied to QoS and network performance.

There's also a need for ATM in VPNs that carry multimedia traffic, and you can also use it when you want to reengineer the network environment to be integrated—for example, replacing individual PBXs for voice and LAN switches for data with an enterprise network switch that can integrate all your traffic into one point at the customer edge.

Finally, ATM can be used to enhance or expand campus and workgroup networks; that is, it can be used to upgrade LANs. In the early days of ATM, one of the first marketplaces where it saw adoption was in the LAN community. If you wanted to make a move to a campus network that could support 155Mbps or 622Mbps, the only solution was to go to an ATM environment. However, Gigabit Ethernet is a much less expensive technology and transition path than ATM. To go from 100Mbps Ethernet to ATM means going to an entirely new technology. It's an investment in an entirely new generation of equipment, with a requirement for an entirely new set of technical skills. Many more applications developers are knowledgeable in other techniques, such as IP, than in ATM. However, Gigabit Ethernet doesn't require learning a new protocol, which is a benefit for network engineers. Gigabit Ethernet also has a much lower cost in terms of the actual components and boards. Therefore, with the formalization of Gigabit Ethernet, people turned away from using ATM in the LAN and decided they would simply throw bandwidth at the problem in the campus network. But remember that Ethernet does not within itself address QoS, so we can't continue to throw bandwidth at this problem much longer because when applications truly turn to the visual and multimedia realm, Gigabit Ethernet will not suffice, and QoS will need to be included. (But to be fair, this is an area of great debate, with many feeling that throwing cheap bandwidth at the problem will suffice.)

Organizations such as the U.S. Navy, universities, and health care campuses have deployed ATM, mainly due to the large amount of multimedia and visualization applications they use. ISPs are the biggest customers of ATM, followed by financial institutions, manufacturers, health care, government, education, research labs, and other enterprises that use broadband applications.

ATM drivers include the capability to consolidate multiple data, voice, and video applications onto a common transport network with specified QoS on a per-application basis. ATM is also being used to replace multiple point-to-point leased lines, which supported individual applications' networks. In addition, Frame Relay is being extended to speeds above T-1 and E-1.

The major inhibitor of ATM is the high service cost. Remember that one of the benefits of Frame Relay is that it is an upgrade of existing technology, so it doesn't require an entirely new set of skills and an investment in new equipment. ATM requires you to acquire an entirely new generation of equipment and build up skill sets to properly implement and manage ATM, and this may have a big financial impact on the overall picture. However, it is important to note that today IP networks are of most interest and are slowly but surely replacing existing deployments of both Frame Relay and ATM. (Given the importance of IP in the current environment, two chapters are dedicated to IP: Chapters 8 and 9.) As a result of these various problems, many vendors have dropped out of the market.

ATM Interfaces

ATM is a very high-bandwidth, high-performance system that uses a uniform 53-byte cell: 5 bytes of addressing information and 48 bytes of payload. The benefit of the small cell size is reduced latency in transmitting through the network nodes. The disadvantage of the small cell size is the increased overhead. But remember that ATM was built in support of the vision of Broadband ISDN, and the second set of standards in support of Broadband ISDN was SDH/SONET. This means that ATM was created with an eye toward the deployment of fiber, which offers tremendous capacities and hence makes bandwidth less of an issue.

An ATM network is connection oriented, which for purposes of real-time, multimedia, and time-sensitive traffic is very important because it allows controlled latencies. It operates over a virtual circuit path, which leads to great efficiency in terms of network management. Payload error control is done at the endpoints, and some limited error control procedures are performed on the headers of the cells within the network itself. ATM supports asynchronous information access: Some applications consume a high percentage of capacity (e.g., video-on-demand) and others consume much less (e.g., e-mail); thus, ATM allows multirate connections.

Finally, ATM has a highly defined and structured set of QoS definitions, as discussed later in this chapter.

The ATM Layers

As discussed in the following sections, ATM has three main layers (see Figure 7.18): the physical layer, the ATM layer, and the ATM adaptation layer.

The Physical Layer   The physical layer basically defines what transmission media are supported, what transmission rates are supported, what physical interfaces are supported, and what the electrical and optical coding schemes are for the ones and zeros. Like the OSI model's physical layer, it's a definition of the physical elements of getting the ones and zeros over the network.

The ATM Layer   An ATM switch performs activities at the ATM layer. It performs four main functions: switching, routing, congestion management, and multiplexing.

The ATM Adaptation Layer   The ATM adaptation layer (AAL) is the segmentation and reassembly (SAR) layer. The native stream (whether it's real-time, analog, voice, MPEG-2 compressed video, or TCP/IP) goes through the adaptation layer, where it is segmented into 48-byte cells. Those 48-byte cells are then passed up to the first ATM switch in the network, which applies the header information that

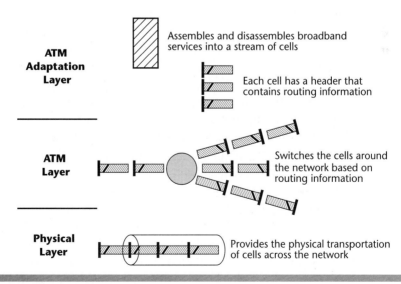

Figure 7.18   ATM layers

defines on which path and which channel the conversation is to take place. (This speaks, again, to the connection orientation of ATM.)

At the onset of the call, there is a negotiation phase, and each switch that's required to complete the call to the destination gets involved with determining whether it has a path and channel of the proper QoS to deliver on the requested call. If it does, at that time it makes a table entry that identifies what path and channel the call will take between the two switches. If along the way one of the switches can't guarantee the QoS being requested, the session is denied. ATM provides an end-to-end view of the network and an assurance that all along the way, the proper QoS can be met. Again, the AAL segments the information into 48-byte cells, and each switch, in turn, applies the headers that contain the routing information, and at the receiving end, the AAL again reassembles the cells into the native stream that is understood by the end device.

There are adaptation layers for various traffic types—for real-time traffic, for connection-oriented data, for connectionless data, for compressed video, and so on:

- **AAL 0**—When a customer's network equipment takes care of all the AAL-related functions, the network uses a Null AAL (also known as AAL 0). This means that no services are performed and that cells are transferred transparently between the service interface and the ATM network.

- **AAL 1**—AAL 1 is designed to meet the needs of isochronous, constant-bit-rate (CBR) services, such as digital voice and video, and is used to support applications that are sensitive to both cell loss and delay and to emulate conventional leased lines. It requires an additional byte of header information for sequence numbering, leaving 47 bytes for payload. This adaptation layer corresponds to fractional and full T-1/E-1 and T-3/E-3. AAL 1 provides a timing recovery functional to maintain the bit timing across the ATM network and to avoid buffer overflow/underflow at the receiver.

- **AAL 2**—AAL 2 is for isochronous variable-bit-rate (VBR) services such as packetized video. It allows ATM cells to be transmitted before the payload is full to accommodate an application's timing requirements.

- **AAL 3/4**—AAL 3/4 supports VBR data, such as LAN applications, or bursty connection-oriented traffic, such as error messages. It is designed for traffic that can tolerate delay but not cell loss. This type performs error detection on each cell by using a sophisticated error-checking mechanism that consumes 4 bytes of each 48-byte payload. AAL 3/4 allows ATM cells to be multiplexed, and it supports the process of segmentation and reassembly required to carry variable-length frames over the ATM network. It also provides a per-cell CRC to detect transmission errors and a per-frame length check to detect loss of cells in a frame.

■ **AAL 5**—AAL 5 is intended to accommodate bursty LAN data traffic with less overhead than AAL 3/4. It is also known as SEAL (simple and efficient adaptation layer). Its major feature is that it uses information in the cell header to identify the first and last cells of a frame, so it doesn't need to consume any of the cell payload to perform this function. AAL 5 uses a per-frame CRC to detect both transmission and cell-loss errors.

The speed- and traffic-shaping requirements of converged networks are increasingly challenging ATM, however. The fastest SARs known run at 2.5Gbps and have limited traffic-shaping capabilities, imposing performance bottlenecks at high speeds.

The ATM Transmission Path

The ATM transmission path includes two elements called the virtual path and the virtual channel (see Figure 7.19). You can think of the virtual channel as an individual conversation; each voice, video, data, and image transmission has its own unique virtual channel. The number of that channel will change between any two switches, depending on what was assigned at the time the session was negotiated.

All similar virtual channels—that is, all those that have the same QoS request—are bundled into a common virtual path. Virtual path 1 might be all real-time voice that has a very low tolerance for delay and loss; virtual path 2 might be for streaming media, which requires continuous bandwidth, minimum delay, and no loss; and virtual path 3 might be for non-mission-critical data, so best-effort service is fine.

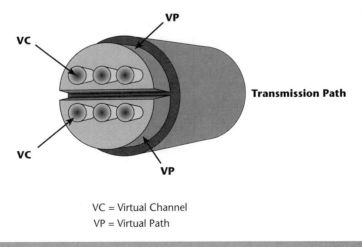

VC = Virtual Channel
VP = Virtual Path

Figure 7.19 The relationship of the virtual path, virtual channel, and transmission path

Current ATM Status

With the growing popularity of networks based on IP, ATM has a declining future. Nonetheless, the majority of telcos have implemented ATM in their WANs over the years, and most ADSL implementations use ATM. ATM is therefore not going away anytime soon. After all, significant investments were made, and still today, ATM offers the best way to ensure QoS and traffic management. The problem is that most vendors have dropped out of the ATM marketplace in favor of MPLS and other native IP solutions. ATM will continue to be used where it is deployed, in higher-speed interconnects, unifying PDH/SDH traffic and packet-switched traffic under a single infrastructure; in multiplexing services in support of DSL networks; and in carrying the majority of IP traffic. Interestingly, MPLS, the latest IP enhancement, borrows many of its technically sound ideas from ATM, enabling similar QoS capabilities without the cost and complexity of ATM. (MPLS is discussed in Chapter 10.)

Where ATM failed to gain widespread use was in the LAN environment, largely due to the emergence of Gigabit Ethernet, which provides high speeds at a much lower cost than ATM and without the complexity associated with ATM. Therefore, ATM did not realize its intended goal of being the single integrating network technology. As a result, most telcos are now planning to integrate voice and video traffic onto their IP networks, using MPLS to address the growing need for QoS to manage real-time traffic flows such as voice, video, and multimedia. Based on current trends, it is also likely that 10 Gigabit Ethernet will begin to replace ATM in many locations, enabling the convergence of voice, data, and video on one network, with one control plane. (The term *control plane* refers to infrastructure and distributed intelligence that sets up and releases connections and may restore a connection in case of a failure. It also includes protocols and mechanisms required to disseminate this information, as well as algorithms for engineering optimal paths between endpoints.)

IP and ATM

As discussed earlier in this section, ATM is used to support a great deal of Internet backbones. IP is also used in next-generation networks. (IP is discussed in detail in Chapter 8.) Approximately 85% of all IP backbones currently use ATM in the core, although MPLS is gradually being introduced in place of ATM.

Features of IP

IP was designed to work in the LAN world. It is a connectionless environment, which means it provides the capability of having information moved between network elements without a preconceived path between the source and destination. In a LAN environment, bandwidth is relatively inexpensive, and the deployment, by definition, is over a small geographic area. Because of the small coverage area, transit delay is typically not an issue in a LAN.

In the event of congestion, IP discards packets. TCP retransmits the lost packets quickly and transparently to the users, and because of the short transit delay, discarded packets are quickly detected, so users don't perceive delays in downloads. But WANs, by definition, are typically deployed over longer distances than LANs, and in WANs, transit delays become a major issue in two ways: in controlling the QoS and in identifying the loss of packets that may have occurred because of congestion. Also, bandwidth is more expensive in a WAN than in a LAN; you pay for every bit sent over a WAN link, so packet discards that create retransmissions can make the expense of retransmission alone significant.

Problems with IP Networks   Traditional IP routers were not intended to handle the large-scale type of networking that we are now demanding from IP. In IP router-based networks, the core, like the core in the PSTN, is responsible for providing interconnectivity. But in the IP router network, the core also provides server access and network management to the edge devices on the network periphery.

Because of the increased traffic that networks are seeing today, the core network is becoming loaded, and that is resulting in increased latency and unacceptable delays. At the edge of the LAN, a shortage of network capacity, coupled with proliferation of broadcasts and multicasts, can create significant network problems. However, those problems go away if the network is properly designed with VLANs that limit broadcast domains. When the edge demand exceeds the capacity of the core, queue overruns create capacity overload and lost packets, thereby reducing the availability and reliability of the network. As a result, users are suffering from congestion, inadequate server access, and slow response times.

Traditional IP routers cannot deliver the service quality that is increasingly demanded. The shortcomings of traditional routers include poor path calculation and slow rerouting. Routers usually use the shortest-path metric to calculate their routes, so IP routers send traffic over a shorter path, even if it's congested, instead of over a more desirable, longer, or uncongested path. But this depends on the routing protocol used. RIP uses the shortest-path metric, whereas OSPF, EIGRP, and BGP allow for load balancing and do not always take the shortest path but instead take the "best" path, as defined by the administrator. This is one of the reasons that there is increased use of ATM or MPLS in the core for backbone traffic-engineering purposes. Also, in the event of a backbone circuit or router failure, IP routers can take a long time—up to a minute—to calculate the new paths around the failure. This has led to more reliance on the resilient SDH/SONET backbone infrastructure, where there is a backup path—a protect fiber—which can ensure that the data is diverted to the protect fiber within a 50-millisecond time frame. SDH/SONET is now being replaced with WDM-based networks, but while early

WDM systems did not provide for network restoration, the new generation of products do address this critical feature. (See Chapter 11 for discussion of optical networking technologies and trends.)

Recent introductions of VoIP services and streaming media have exposed two other limitations of IP networks: latency and jitter. IP doesn't provide a way to control latency and jitter. For a packet-based IP network to successfully support voice services, minimum transit delay must be achieved, and so must minimum packet loss. High-quality voice demands less than 100 milliseconds for total one-way latency, including all processing at both ends, which implies digitization, compression, decompression, queuing, playback, and so on—and that must also include the network delay. Voice compression and decompression alone normally take about 30 to 50 milliseconds. Network latency must be tightly controlled to support these services properly.

One immediate solution to the problems of latency and jitter is to increase the amount of available bandwidth. If there's no congestion, there's no problem. And technologies such as DWDM provide relief initially, but history has taught us that the amount of data continues to increase significantly and rapidly, and while throwing bandwidth at the problem provides a quick fix, it does not address the growing need for detailed traffic and network management. Increasing bandwidth also does not provide the control mechanisms necessary for providing, tracking, and accounting for multiple and granular levels of service that the service provider can offer and guarantee for the customer. Therefore, simply providing more bandwidth is a short-term relief measure but not a long-term solution that addresses the need to differentiate traffic and its requirements on a very granular level. Hence the key to success for large-scale IP networking lies in delivering the flexibility of IP routing with a switched packet-forwarding mechanism that offers the highest possible performance and maximum control: IP switching.

IP Switching   IP switching was designed to speed up increasingly choked networks by replacing slower, more processing-intensive routers with switches. IP routers that provide connection-oriented services at the IP layer are referred to as *IP switches*. Routers are slower than switches because they must examine multiple packet fields, make substitutions in the packet headers, and compute routes on a packet-by-packet basis, which introduces latency and congestion.

The idea with IP switching is to make a connectionless data technology behave similar to a circuit-switched network. An IP switch routes the first packet, and then it switches all subsequent packets. The goal is to make intranet and Internet access faster and to enable the deployment of new voice, video, and graphics applications and services. Therefore, IP switching has two objectives: to provide a way for internetworks to scale economically and to provide effective QoS support for IP. In essence, IP switching replaces Layer 3 hops with Layer 2 switching, which leads to good hardware-based forwarding performance.

Even with the advantages of IP switching, IP still doesn't allow us to properly administer all the QoS parameters that are part of traffic definitions, and this is where ATM comes in.

Features of ATM

As discussed earlier in this chapter, ATM was created in the WAN environment. It came out of the carrier community as a means by which to reengineer the PSTN for multimedia and real-time streaming applications. Because ATM comes from the carrier environment, where traffic engineering is essential, it is a connection-oriented technique. It provides a means to establish a predefined path between the source and the destination, which enables greater control of network resources. Overallocation of bandwidth becomes an engineered decision; it offers a deterministic way to respond to changes, on a dynamic basis, to network status. A great benefit of ATM is that it provides for real-time traffic management. It enables policing and traffic shaping: It can monitor (i.e., police) the cells and determine, based on congestion, which cell should be dropped (i.e., perform traffic shaping).

ATM allows networkwide resource allocation for CoS and QoS provisioning. Again, because it is connection oriented, it looks ahead to the destination point to ensure that each link along the way can deliver on the requested QoS. If it can't, the session is denied. Therefore, ATM also makes possible deterministic transit delay because you can specify and calculate the end-to-end delays, as well as the variations in delays (jitter). This is all administered through multiple QoS levels.

Remember that a lot of IP takes place over ATM. Because it is connection oriented, ATM gives service providers the traffic-engineering tools they need to manage both QoS and utilization. ATM's virtual circuits control bandwidth allocation on busy backbone routes. In provisioning a network, the service provider can assign each virtual circuit a specific amount of bandwidth and a set of QoS parameters. The provider can then dictate what path each virtual circuit takes. Basing these decisions on overall traffic trends reduces the likelihood of network hot spots and wasted bandwidth, and this is why so many service providers turn to ATM to transport IP traffic. However, the service provider has to deal with two control planes—managing both IP routers and ATM switches. Using ATM virtual circuits to interconnect IP routers leads to scaling problems because every router needs a separate virtual circuit to every other router. As the network grows, the number of routes and virtual circuits can increase exponentially, eventually exceeding the capacity of both switches and routers. Network operators can work around this in one of two ways: either they can forgo a full-mesh architecture or they can move to MPLS, which is discussed in Chapter 10.

IP Versus ATM

Table 7.1 is a simple overview comparison of IP and ATM.

An upside of IP is that it is pervasive at the desktop. The downside is that it has no QoS built in. It supports data, voice, and fax. IP packet size is variable. It can be up to 64,000 bytes, but packets are segmented into 1,500-byte frames for transport, and 40 bytes of each packet is for the header information.

The upside of ATM is that it is an architected QoS approach that defines key service classes (as described in Chapter 10). The downside is that it uses a small cell size (only 53 bytes, 5 bytes of which is the header information), which means it has a lot of overhead (i.e., cell tax), which could be construed as inefficient—for data transport, for voice transport, or for other traffic types—and this is an issue when bandwidth is constrained and expensive. Remember that ATM was built based on the assumption of Gbps trunks and generous bandwidth, so the cell tax is less relevant if the prevailing condition is abundant bandwidth. ATM supports a wide variety of services, including voice, IP, Frame Relay, X.25, and leased lines.

We don't really have to choose between IP and ATM. At least for the time being, we can use them together quite effectively. IP has become the universal language of computer networking, especially in the desktop environment. IP-based services—including VPNs, e-commerce, outsourced remote access, application hosting, multicasting, and VoIP, along with fax and video over IP—are used in a number of areas. A benefit of IP is that there is a much larger pool of knowledgeable applications developers for IP than there is for ATM. However, all these wonderful applications that the programmers are developing for IP tend to require a lot of CoS and QoS, as well as controlled access. IP standards for QoS are not yet as effective as ATM's, and ATM therefore continues to be used to switch IP traffic because of its network management, restoration, and reliability capabilities.

Table 7.1 IP Versus ATM

Transport	Benefit	Drawback	Services Supported	Packet Size	Header
IP	Pervasive at the desktop	No QoS	Data, voice	Variable, 40–64,000 bytes	40 bytes
ATM	Multiple service classes	Small cell size that is inefficient for data transport	Data, voice, IP, Frame Relay, X.25, leased lines	Fixed cells, 53 bytes	5 bytes

The MFA Forum

The MFA Forum (www.mfaforum.org) is an international, industrywide, nonprofit association focused on advancing the deployment of multivendor, multiservice packet-based networks, associated applications, and interworking solutions. The MFA Forum Web site is the best resource for finding information on existing and planned standards and specifications for the three main contemporary packet-switched networks: Frame Relay, ATM, and MPLS. (MPLS is discussed in Chapter 10.)

Chapter 8

The Internet and IP Infrastructures

This chapter explores the Internet, including how today's Internet actually works, the protocols—such as Internet Protocol (IP)—that make the Internet what it is, how addressing works on the Internet, the organization and characteristics of the variety of service providers, and how IP QoS can be used to ensure maximum network performance. It also takes a glimpse at some of the exciting developments that spell the future of the Internet.

■ Internet Basics

Figure 8.1 is an astounding graph that speaks to the pace of Internet development. It shows the number of years it took several technologies to reach 50 million users worldwide. As you can see, whereas it took 74 years for the telephone to reach 50 million users, it took the World Wide Web only 4.

A number of forces are propelling our interest in the Internet. One main force is that usage continues to grow at an impressive rate. Today, more than 1 billion people actively use the Internet, although there are vast differences in the penetration and usage rates around the world. Recent statistics provided by Internet World Stats (www.internetworldstats.com) show that the greatest penetration (i.e., the percentage of the population with access to the Internet) is in North America, with 68.1% of the population online, followed by Oceania/Australia at 52.9%, and Europe at 35.9%. After these regions, the penetration drops off dramatically, with

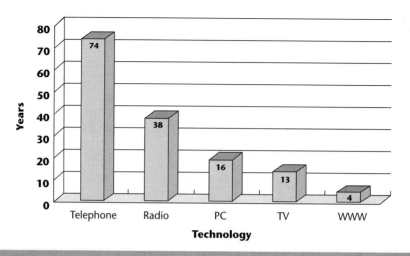

Figure 8.1   Internet pace: Years to reach 50 million users worldwide

Latin America/the Caribbean at 14.3%, Asia at 9.9%, the Middle East at 9.6%, and Africa at 2.5%. However, the picture isn't complete without also looking at the actual usage rates (i.e., usage as a percentage of world traffic). Here Asia leads with 35.7%, followed by Europe with 28.5%, North America with 22.2%, Latin America/ the Caribbean at 7.8%, Africa with 2.2%, and the Middle East and Oceania/Australia with 1.8% each.

Statistics also show that usage growth continues to be strong. For the period from 2000 to 2005, the percentage of growth was 454.2% in the Middle East, 403.7% in Africa, 337.4% in Latin America/the Caribbean, 218.7% in Asia, 176.1% in Europe, 132.2% in Oceania/Australia, and 108.9% in North America, with a global average of 182%. In general, the rate of Internet backbone growth has varied dramatically by region. Mature Internet markets in the United States and Europe have seen relatively slow growth, just 30% to 40% in 2005. Asian network backbones have grown much more rapidly—over 70% in 2005—and show no signs of slowing. (Although it is indeed very useful to have a reference to such statistics, remember that there can be a wide variety of research results, and any such statistics are not cast in stone; rather, they should be considered as a simple guide to general usage trends.)

The Internet is very useful and easy to use, and for a growing number of people, it is now the first place to look for information. Electronic commerce (e-commerce) is also increasing, in both the business-to-consumer and business-to-business sectors. Another contributor is the major shift toward the use of advanced applications, including pervasive computing, which introduces a wide range of intelligent appliances ready to communicate through the Internet, as well as applications that include the more captivating visual and sensory streams; the entertainment industry in particular expects large growth in this space. Finally, the availability of broadband or high-speed access technologies further drives our interest in and ability to interact with Web sites that use these advanced applications and offer e-commerce capabilities.

A Brief History of the Internet

To help understand the factors that contributed to the creation of the Internet, let's look very briefly at the history of the Internet. The ancestor of the global Internet was the Advanced Research Projects Agency Network (ARPANET), developed by the U.S. Department of Defense Advanced Research Projects Agency (ARPA). Introduced in 1969, ARPANET was the world's first operational packet-switched network. There were several reasons for the development of ARPANET. First, the project was launched during the Cold War era, when the government wanted to build a network that had no single point of failure and that could sustain an attack and continue to function. As my colleague, Steve Riley of Microsoft, expresses, "The launch of Sputnik really galvanized the U.S. government into action. Before then, we were somewhat complacent, not really looking toward much future technological development."

For More Information
The Internet Society offers "A Brief History of the Internet," written by the "fathers" of the Internet, at www.isoc.org/internet/history/brief.shtml.

Second, there was great interest in creating a computer communications network that would enable ARPA-sponsored researchers, scattered around the nation, to use various ARPA computers, making research results and new software quickly and widely available to all concerned parties. The initial thought, in 1966, was to simply connect the large time-sharing mainframe computers to each other via telephone lines. However, some participants felt that having telephone lines terminating directly on their computers would create unwanted loads. Another idea then surfaced, calling for small independent computers to manage the communications links, and to then connect to the large time-sharing machines. This approach allowed the task of running the network to be offloaded from the ARPANET computers, while also allowing ARPA to have complete control over the network. These smaller computers came to be called interface message processors (IMPs). The initial ARPANET consisted of four IMPs, installed at four universities:

University of California, Los Angeles; the Stanford Research Institute's Augmentation Research Center; the University of California, Santa Barbara; and the University of Utah's Graphics Department. The first ARPANET link was established on October 29, 1969, between the IMP at UCLA and the IMP at Stanford, and the entire four-node network was connected by December 5, 1969.

Internet Time Line

The following time line shows some of the important dates in the history of the Internet:

1969	ARPANET created
1973	TCP/IP created
1980	TCP/IP required on ARPANET
1983	Updated version of TCP/IP introduced
1986	NSFNet funded by National Science Foundation (NSF)
1988	NSFNet backbone based on T-1 connections
1990	ARPANET officially dissolved
1992	NSFNet backbone converted from T-1 to T-3
1995	NSFNet dissolved, Internet commercialized

Toward the mid-1970s, ARPA was renamed the Defense Advanced Research Projects Agency (DARPA), and while it was working on the distributed, or packet-switched, network, it was also working on local area networks (LANs), paging networks, and satellite networks. DARPA recognized the need for some form of internetworking protocol that would allow open communications between disparate networks. Internet Protocol (IP) was created to support an open-architecture network that could link multiple disparate networks via gateways—what we today refer to as *routers*.

Jonathan Postel and the Internet

Jonathan Postel played a pivotal role in creating and administering the Internet. He was one of a small group of computer scientists who created the ARPANET, the precursor to the Internet. For more than 30 years he served as editor of the Request for Comments (RFC) series of technical notes that began with the earliest days of the ARPANET and continued into the Internet. Although intended to be informal, RFCs have often laid the foundation for technical standards governing the Internet's operation.

Also for 30 years, Postel handled the administrative end of Internet addresses, under the auspices of the Internet Assigned Numbers Authority (IANA), a U.S. government–financed entity. As part of the effort to hand over administration of the Internet to an international private corporation, Postel delivered a proposal to the U.S. government for transforming IANA into a nonprofit corporation with broad representation from the commercial and academic sectors. That organization is today known as the Internet Corporation for Assigned Names and Numbers (ICANN), which still manages IANA.

In 1980, Transmission Control Protocol/Internet Protocol (TCP/IP) began to be implemented on an experimental basis, and by 1983, it was required in order for a subnetwork to participate in the larger virtual Internet.

The original Internet model was not based on the telephone network model. It involved distributed control rather than centralized control, and it relied on cooperation among its users, which initially were largely academicians and researchers. The original Internet had no regulation, no monopoly, and no universal-service mandate, although these issues are being considered seriously now.

Regulation of the Internet

The lack of regulation and mandates in the original Internet brings up myriad interesting questions: Did that lack actually *accelerate* the growth of the Internet? Did it also mean that Internet access is largely divided across economic ability? Why are people now considering adding regulation and universal-service mandates to the Internet? What problems will this solve? What problems will it exacerbate? Is it a good idea? Will such regulation fundamentally change the Internet from what it is today into something else?

Although there are no concrete answers to these questions at the moment, it is a wonderful topic of discussion. A very good resource for many papers and studies on regulatory issues is the Cato Institute, at www.cato.org/tech, which can serve as a starting point in studying the impacts of regulation.

Today, no one agency is in charge of the Internet, although the Internet Society (ISOC; www.isoc.org) is a nonprofit, nongovernmental, international organization for Internet professionals that focuses on Internet standards, education, and policy issues. ISOC serves as the organizational home of the Internet Engineering Task Force (IETF; www.ietf.org), which oversees various organizational and coordinating tasks. The IETF is an international community of network designers, operators, vendors, and researchers whose job is to evolve the Internet and smooth its operation by creating technical standards through consensus. In addition to the IETF, ISOC is composed of a board of trustees, the Internet Architecture Board (IAB; www.iab.org), the Internet Research Task Force (IRTF; www.irtf.org), the Internet Engineering Steering Group (IESG; www.ietf.org), and the Internet Research Steering Group (IRSG; www.irsg.org).

Another organization that is critical to the functioning and management of the Internet is the Internet Assigned Numbers Authority (IANA; www.iana.org), which is currently operated by the Internet Corporation for Assigned Names and Numbers (ICANN; www.icann.org) under a contract with the U.S. Department of Commerce, which also provides ongoing oversight. IANA oversees IP address allocation, the Domain Name System (DNS), root zone management, and other numerical assignments, such as protocol and port numbers. (DNS, top-level domains, and root servers are all discussed later in this chapter.) In its role of administering the data in the root name servers (at the top of the DNS hierarchy), IANA works closely with top-level domain (TLD) and root name server operators, as well as those involved with policy decisions at ICANN.

The registration of IP addresses around the world is delegated to five regional Internet registries (RIRs), which as a group are called the Number Resource Organization (NRO; www.nro.net):

- American Registry for Internet Numbers (ARIN; www.arin.net) for North America
- Asia Pacific Network Information Centre (APNIC; www.apnic.org) for the Asia-Pacific region
- Reseaux IP European Network Coordination Center (RIPE NCC; www.ripe.net) for Europe, Central Asia, and the Middle East
- Latin American and Caribbean Internet Addresses Registry (LACNIC; www.lacnic.net/en) for Latin America and the Caribbean
- African Network Information Centre (AfriNIC; www.afrinic.net) for Africa

Each RIR is responsible for overseeing the allocation and registration of Internet number resources within its region of the world. The resources the RIRs manage include both IPv4 and IPv6 addresses and autonomous system numbers. (Autonomous systems are discussed later in this chapter.) IANA delegates large groups of IPv4 addresses to the various RIRs, which then reallocate smaller groups of addresses in their regions to ISPs and other organizations. A process has also been established for the allocation of IPv6 addresses, although at this time there is little pressure in this area as the supply of IPv6 addresses greatly exceeds the demand. The NRO has entered into an agreement with ICANN to establish an organization, referred to as the Address Supporting Organization (ASO; www.aso.icann.org) to deal with the coordination of global IP addressing policies within the ICANN framework.

Since the formation of ICANN, the relationship between ICANN, the country code TLDs (ccTLDs), and the RIRs has been politically charged. As a result, a number of proposals have suggested the complete separation of the IANA function from ICANN, but at the same time, it has been deemed unwise to make any major changes to the control structure of the Internet as that could possibly risk "breaking" the Internet.

The section "Political and Regulatory Forces in Telecommunications" in Chapter 1, "Telecommunications Technology Fundamentals," provides more information on Internet regulation.

What the Internet Is and How It Works

To understand the Internet, it is important to first understand the concept of a computer network (see Figure 8.2). A network is formed by interconnecting computers, typically referred to as *hosts*, in such a way that they can communicate. Connecting hosts involves two major components: hardware (i.e., the physical connections) and software. The software can be run on the same or dissimilar host operating systems, and it is based on standards that define its operation. These standards, referred to as *protocols*, provide the formats for passing packets of data, specify the details of the packet formats, and describe how to handle error conditions. The protocols hide the details of network hardware and permit computers of different hardware types, connected by different physical connections, to communicate despite their differences. (Protocols are discussed in detail later in this chapter.)

In the strictest sense, the Internet is an internetwork composed of a worldwide collection of networks, routers, gateways, servers, and clients linked by a common

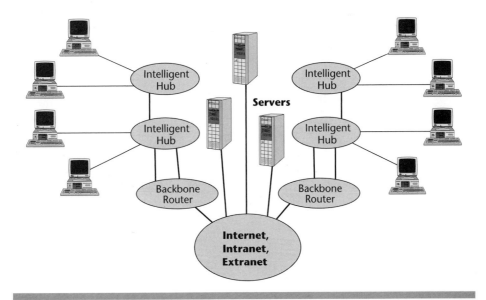

Figure 8.2 Network components

set of telecommunications protocols—the IP family (see Figure 8.3). The term *client* is often used to refer to a computer on a network that takes advantage of the services offered by a server. It also refers to a user running the client side of a client/server application. The term *server* describes either a computer or a software-based process that provides services to network users or Web services to Internet users.

Networks connect servers and clients, allowing them to share information and computing resources. Network equipment includes cable and wire, network adapters, hubs, switches, and various other physical connectors. In order for a network to be connected to the Internet, the network must send and retrieve data by using TCP/IP and related protocols. Networks can also be connected to form their own internets: Site-to-site connections are known as *intranets*, internal networks that are generally composed of LANs interconnected by a wide area network (WAN) that uses IP; and connections between partnering organizations, using IP, are known as *extranets*.

The Internet is a complex, highly redundant collection of more than 10,000 interconnected autonomous systems, composed of telecommunications circuits connected with internetworking equipment, including routers, bridges, and switches. The level of redundancy varies, depending on how the autonomous systems are connected. In an environment consisting of several network segments with different protocols and architectures, the network needs a device that not only knows the address of each segment but also can determine the best path for send-

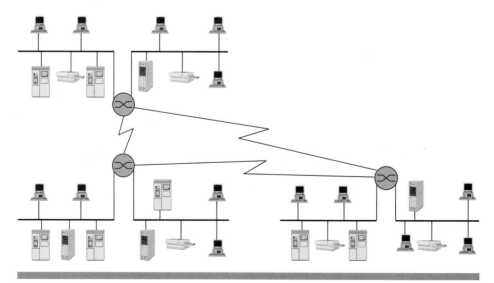

Figure 8.3 An internetwork

ing data and filtering broadcast traffic to the local segment. The Internet moves data by relaying traffic in packets from one computer network to another. If a particular network or computer (i.e., router) is down or busy, the network is smart enough to reroute the traffic automatically. Routers make decisions about how to route the data or packets, they decide which path is best, and then they use that best path. Routers work at the network layer, Layer 3, of the OSI model, which allows them to switch and route packets across multiple networks. Routers build comprehensive sets of best routes to all locations that they know about. These routing tables can be quite large for complex networks. Routers can share status and routing information with one another and use that information to bypass slow or malfunctioning connections.

Routing is the main process that an Internet host uses to deliver packets. As shown in Figure 8.4, the Internet uses a hop-by-hop routing model, which means that each host or router that handles a packet examines the destination address in the packet's IP header, computes the next hop that will bring the packet one step closer to its destination, and delivers that packet to the next hop, where the process is repeated. To make this happen, routing tables must match destination addresses with next hops, and routing protocols must determine the content of these tables. The next hop is determined from looking up the next hop in the routing table, and routers must build and maintain these tables containing the "best routes." This routing is most often dynamic, scalable, and robust (assuming that the network is designed correctly).

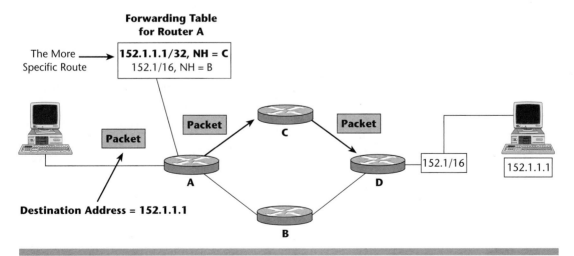

Figure 8.4 Basic IP routing

The Internet and the public switched telephone network (PSTN) operate quite differently from one another:

■ The Internet uses packet switching, where there's no dedicated connection and the data is fragmented into packets. Packets can be delivered via different routes over the Internet and reassembled at the ultimate destination. Historically, back-office functions such as billing and network management have not been associated with the Internet, although today these mechanisms are in place. But, in general, the Internet emphasizes flexibility—the capability to route packets around congested or failed points.

■ As discussed in Chapter 4, "The PSTN," the PSTN uses circuit switching, so a dedicated circuit is set up and taken down for each call. This allows charging based on minutes and circuits used, which, in turn, allows chain-of-supply dealings. The major emphasis of the PSTN is on reliability.

Although the Internet and the PSTN have different models and different ways of managing or routing traffic through the network, they share the same physical foundation in terms of the transport infrastructure, or the types of communication links they use. (Chapter 3, "Establishing Communications Channels," discusses packet switching and circuit switching in detail.)

Internet Protocols

The Internet is a collection of networks that are interconnected logically as a single large, virtual network. Messages between computers are exchanged by using packet switching. Networks can communicate with one another because they all use an internetworking protocol. *Protocols* are formal descriptions of messages to be exchanged and of rules to be followed in order for two or more systems to exchange information in a manner that the parties will understand.

The following sections examine the Internet's protocols: IP (Internet Protocol), TCP (Transmission Control Protocol), User Datagram Protocol (UDP), Stream Control Transmission Protocol (SCTP) and Datagram Congestion Control Protocol (DCCP), Internet Control Message Protocol (ICMP), Internet Group Management Protocol (IGMP), Address Resolution Protocol (ARP) and Reverse Address Resolution Protocol (RARP), routing protocols, and network access protocols. This collection of protocols is often referred to as the *TCP/IP suite*, although it contains much more than just TCP and IP. The IETF has technical responsibility for the suite, which is the most popular and widely used of the internetworking protocols. The nonproprietary nature of the suite is a major advantage, permitting the connection of hardware and operating systems of many different computers.

IP

IP handles packet forwarding and transporting of datagrams across a network. With packet forwarding, computers can send a packet on to the next appropriate network component, based on the address in the packet's header. IP defines the basic unit of data transfer, the *datagram*, also referred to as the *packet*, and it also defines the exact format of all data as it travels across the Internet. IP works like an envelope in the postal service, directing information to its proper destination. With this arrangement, every computer on the Internet has a unique address. (Addressing is discussed later in this chapter.)

Figure 8.5 shows the various components of a datagram. The entire datagram has four entities—the Payload field, the next protocol field (usually TCP or UDP), the IP field, and the L2 (Layer 2) field—which, combined, are referred to as the *Layer 2 packet (or protocol) data unit* (PDU), or frame. *Datagram*, or *packet*, refers to the combination of the payload, the TCP/UDP information, and the IP address. Finally, the *TCP maximum segment size* (MSS) refers to the size of the payload and the next protocol header.

IP provides software routines to route and to store and forward data among hosts on the network. IP functions at Layer 3 (the network layer), and it provides several services, including host addressing, error notification, fragmentation and reassembly, routing, and packet timeout. The Layer 4 protocol, usually TCP or UDP, presents the data to IP in order to provide basic host-to-host communication. IP then attaches to the packet, in a protocol header, the address from which the data comes and the address of the system to which it is going.

Under the standards, IP allows a packet size of up to 64,000 bytes, but we don't transmit packets that large because they would cause session timeouts and

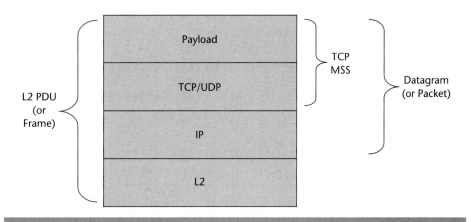

Figure 8.5 Datagram structure

big congestion problems. Therefore, IP packets are currently segmented into 1,500-byte-maximum chunks—because this is what can fit inside a typical 1,536-byte Ethernet frame and because it is a pretty efficient size, helping to keep retransmission times down. This size is likely to increase, however, to improve performance over high-speed links.

Packets between a particular source and destination might not always travel the same route. IP does its best to make the delivery to the requested destination host along the best route currently available, but if it fails for any reason, it just drops the packet. Upper-level protocols should therefore not depend on IP to deliver the packet every time. Because IP provides connectionless, best-effort service and because packets can get lost or arrive out of sequence, TCP provides a way to recover from these problems.

TCP

Many network applications present data to TCP, the most common Layer 4 (transport layer) protocol. TCP divides the data into packets and gives each packet a *sequence number* that is not unique but is nonrepeating for a very long time. These packets could represent text, graphics, sound, or video—anything digital that the network can transmit. The sequence numbers help to ensure that the packets can be reassembled correctly and in the proper order at the receiving end. Thus, each packet consists of content, or data, as well as the *protocol header*, the information that the protocol needs to do its work.

TCP uses another piece of information to ensure that the data reaches the right application when it arrives at a system—the *port number*, which is within the range 1 to 65,535. In an IP network, it is a number assigned to user sessions and server applications. The port number resides in the TCP header as well as in the UDP header for applications such as VoIP and videoconferencing. The source port, which can be a random number, is assigned to the client and is used to keep track of user sessions. The combination of port number and IP address is called a *socket*. The destination port is used to route packets on a server to the appropriate network application. On servers, port numbers identify running applications that are waiting for incoming connections from clients. Port numbers distinguish one listening application from another. Numbers between 1 and 1,023 are reserved for well-known server applications (e.g., Web servers run on port 80, FTP runs on port 21). Also, many recent protocols have been assigned well-known port numbers above 1,023. Ports with higher numbers, called *ephemeral ports*, are dynamically assigned to client applications as needed. A client obtains a random ephemeral port when it opens a connection to a well-known server port. Firewalls can use port numbers and IP addresses to control the flow of information. (Firewalls are discussed in Chapter 9, "IP Services.")

TCP is the protocol for sequenced and reliable data transfer. It breaks the data into pieces and numbers each piece so that the receipt can be verified and the data can be put back in the proper order. TCP provides Layer 4 functionality, and it is responsible for virtual circuit setup, acknowledgments, flow control, and retransmission of lost or damaged data. TCP provides end-to-end, connection-oriented, reliable, virtual circuit service.

UDP

Like TCP, UDP is a Layer 4 (transport layer) protocol that operates over IP. UDP provides end-to-end, connectionless, unreliable datagram service. It is well suited for query/response applications, for multicasting, and for use with Voice over IP (VoIP). (VoIP is discussed in Chapter 9.) Because UDP does not request retransmissions, it minimizes what would otherwise be unmanageable delay; the result is that sometimes the quality is not very good. For instance, if you encounter losses or errors associated with a voice packet, the delays that would be associated with retransmitting that packet would render the conversation unintelligible. In VoIP, when you lose packets, you do not request retransmissions. Instead, you hope that the user can recover from the losses by other means. Unlike TCP, UDP does not provide for error correction and sequenced packet delivery; it is up to the application itself to incorporate error correction, if required.

So why use UDP? Multimedia applications typically can't tolerate the additional time required for establishing TCP's virtual connection and the overhead used by TCP's delivery guarantee mechanisms. You can think of UDP as an open "pipe" between two computers that simply allows for an uninterrupted flow of data. The experience of watching a movie over the Internet under UDP is much better; you won't miss the occasional dropped datagram. Over highly controlled and error-correcting TCP, the sequencing overhead most likely would result in greater congestion and more dropped packets.

SCTP and DCCP

SCTP is a new Layer 4 (transport layer) protocol designed to overcome the limitations of TCP with respect to transport of signaling messages and VoIP networks. SCTP was originally intended for the transport of telephony signaling protocols (such as SS7) over IP, with the goal of duplicating some of the reliability characteristics of SS7 in IP. Other applications may benefit as well, such as multimedia Web browsing, video over IP, and IPTV. SCTP provides many of the features of TCP, and it also includes multistreaming, which supports independent transport and delivery of multiple streams between two communicating hosts. It can apply per-stream, in-order delivery to the destination application. It also includes multihoming, which supports more than one path between hosts for resilience. Multihoming

Interior Routing Protocols *Interior routing* occurs within an *autonomous system*, which is a collection of routers under a single administrative authority that uses a common IGP for routing packets. Most of the common routing protocols, such as RIP, OSPF, and IS-IS, are interior routing protocols.

The autonomous system number is a unique number that essentially identifies a portion of the Internet—usually owned or administered by a particular organization. Autonomous system numbers are managed and assigned by the RIRs (i.e., ARIN, APNIC, RIPE NCC, LACNIC, and AfriNIC). Exterior routing protocols, such as BGP, use autonomous system numbers to uniquely define borders between various networks in the Internet. The basic routable element, the item on which the routing decision is based, is the IP network or subnetwork, or the Classless Interdomain Routing (CIDR) prefix for newer protocols. (CIDR is discussed later in this chapter.)

OSPF OSPF, which is sanctioned by the IETF and supported by TCP, is perhaps the most widely used interior routing protocol in large networks. OSPF is a link-state protocol that has a complex set of options and features. It makes use of Dijkstra's algorithm, which determines routes based on path length, calculates the shortest-path tree, and uses cost as its routing metric.

An OSPF network is divided into *areas*, or logical groupings of routers whose information can be summarized and sent toward the rest of the network. The core of the network is formed by a special area called the *backbone area*, and all interarea routing occurs via this backbone. All areas must connect to the backbone, and if no direct connection is possible, a virtual link may be established. The other areas, which vary in their ability to receive external and/or summary route information, are as follows:

- **Stub area (SA)**—The SA does not receive any external routes and needs to rely on a default route to send traffic to routes outside the immediate domain. (A *default route* is the network route used by a router or server when no other known route works for a given IP packet's destination address.) Hosts and routers in an organization generally point the default route toward the router that has a connection to a network service provider to ensure that packets destined for the Internet will be sent toward the router that has the Internet connection.

- **Totally stubby area (TSA)**—The TSA does not receive any external routes or summary routes. The only way for traffic to get routed outside the area is by using a default route that is the only link advertised into the area.

- **Not-so-stubby area (NSSA)**—The NSSA can import autonomous system external routes and send them to the backbone but cannot receive autonomous system external routes from the backbone or other areas.

OSPF defines various router types, which are also logical definitions, and a router may be classified as more than one type. The main types of routers are as follows:

- **Area border router (ABR)**—The ABR is a router that connects one or more OSPF areas to the backbone network.

- **Autonomous system boundary router (ASBR)**—The ASBR is a router that is connected to more than one autonomous system and exchanges information with routers in other autonomous systems. It is used to distribute routing information from other autonomous systems throughout its own autonomous system.

- **Internal router (IR)**—An IR is a router that exchanges routing information only with routers in the same area.

- **Backbone router (BR)**—The BR has a connection into the backbone area.

- **Designated router (DR)**—The DR is a router elected by the network based on calculating the router's priority number and router ID.

The basic building block of the OSPF routing protocol for IP is the link-state advertisement (LSA). The LSA provides a description of a router's local routing topology that the router advertises (distributes) to all other routers. Because OSPF is designed with scalability in mind, not all LSAs are flooded (i.e., advertised) on all the interfaces; instead, they are sent only to the interfaces that belong to the appropriate area. This allows the detailed information to be kept local, while summary information is provided to the rest of the network. There are 11 LSAs defined in OSPF, each applicable to a particular area and type of router.

Routers that belong to the same broadcast domain (i.e., that belong to the same network) form what are called *adjacencies*, or the relationship of being neighbors. The routers elect a DR, which acts as a hub to reduce traffic between routers. OSPF makes use of both unicast and multicast (discussed later in this chapter) to send "hello" packets and link-state updates.

In keeping with advances in Internet protocols, a number of updates have been added to OSPF, including OSPFv3 (version 3), which allows support for IPv6. Another update introduces *Nonstop Forwarding* (also referred to as *Hitless Run* and *Graceful Restart*), which means that in the event of a network disruption, routers keep forwarding packets as the OSPF process is restarted. Two more working areas are the ability to support multiple address families (IPv4 and IPv6) as well as OSPF extensions accommodating Traffic Engineering DiffServ (a statistical technique used to predict and engineer the behavior or the network) and optical technologies.

IS-IS   IS-IS is another protocol that routers can use to determine the best way to forward packets through the network (i.e., to perform routing). It is also an IGP, which means it is used within an administrative domain or network, not between networks. (Routing between administrative domains or networks is the job of BGP.) Like OSPF, IS-IS is also a link-state routing protocol and uses Dijkstra's algorithm.

One difference between IS-IS and OSPF is that IS-IS does not use IP to carry the routing information messages. They also differ in the way they define areas and routers. In IS-IS, routers are designated as being Level 1 (intra-area), Level 2 (inter-area), or Level 1–2 (both). Level 1 routers exchange information only with other Level 1 routers, Level 2 routers exchange information only with other Level 2 routers, and Level 1–2 routers exchange information with both levels and are used to connect the interarea routers with the intra-area routers. OSPF networks look somewhat like a star topology, or spider web, of many areas all attached to the backbone area. IS-IS looks more like a central spine of Level 2 routers with branches of Level 1–2 and Level 1 routers forming the individual areas or networks.

IS-IS was developed by the telecommunication group of the International Telecommunication Union (ITU-T; www.itu.int/ITU-T) around the same time that the IETF was developing OSPF. As discussed previously, OSPF is the dominant IGP routing protocol today, although IS-IS has become more widely used as a viable alternative to OSPF in the enterprise in recent years. As with OSPF, updates continue to be made to IS-IS, including revisions that support IPv6 (IS-IS for IPv6) and Restart Signaling (another name for OSPF's Nonstop Forwarding). The Multitopology (MT) routing extension to IS-IS allows for routing between a set of independent IP topologies; it can be used for a variety of purposes, such as maintaining separate IGP routing domains for isolated multicast or IPv6 islands within the backbone, forcing a subset of an address space to follow a different topology, or adding an in-band management network on top of the original IGP topology. As with OSPF, IS-IS also has extensions that accommodate Traffic Engineering DiffServ and optical technologies.

Exterior Routing Protocols   *Exterior routing* occurs between autonomous systems and is of concern to service providers and other large or complex networks. As shown in Figure 8.6, gateway protocols are used within and between autonomous systems. Whereas there may be many different interior routing schemes, a single exterior routing scheme manages the global Internet, and it is based on the exterior routing protocol BGP version 4 (BGP4). The basic routable element is the autonomous system. Routers determine the path for a data packet by calculating the number of hops between internetwork segments. Routers build routing tables and use these tables along with routing algorithms.

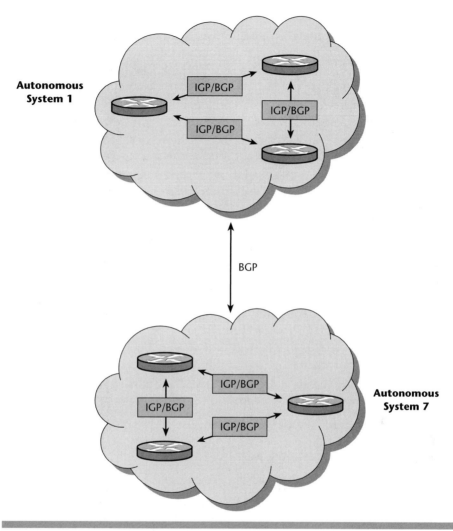

Figure 8.6 The role of gateway protocols

BGP, the core routing protocol of the Internet, works by maintaining a table of IP networks, or *prefixes*, that designate network reachability between autonomous systems. BGP makes use of a path-vector protocol, which means routing decisions are based on network policies or rules rather than on technical parameters, as is the case with distance-vector and link-state protocols. In BGP, the routing table maintains the autonomous systems that are crossed in order to reach the destination system. Very large private IP networks can also use BGP.

Although most Internet users do not use BGP directly, most ISPs must use BGP to enable routing with each other, and it is considered one of the most important protocols of the Internet. BGP is as important to the Internet as SS7 is to interprovider core call setup on the PSTN (which is discussed in Chapter 4).

Like OSPF and IS-IS, BGP is also being updated with new extensions. Current working areas include Multiprotocol BGP, which includes support for IPv6, virtual private networks (VPNs), and multicast addresses. Another working area is Graceful Restart, in which data traffic continues to be routed between the restarting router and peers. BGP is also being updated to support Layer 2 VPN and Layer 3 VPN autodiscovery as well as Virtual Private LAN Services (VPLS) signaling. (VPNs and VPLS are discussed in detail in Chapter 9.)

Network Access Protocols
Network access protocols operate at Layer 2. They provide the underlying basis for the transport of IP datagrams. The original network access protocol was Ethernet, but IP can be transported transparently over any underlying network, including Token Ring, FDDI, Fibre Channel, wireless, X.25, ISDN, Frame Relay, or ATM.

Both Serial Line Internet Protocol (SLIP) and Point-to-Point Protocol (PPP) were designed specifically for IP over point-to-point connections. PPP provides data link–layer functionality for IP over dialup/dedicated links. In other words, whenever you dial in to your ISP, you negotiate a PPP session, and part of what PPP does is to provide a mechanism to identify and authenticate the user who is dialing up and provide an IP address to the remote computer.

Internet Network Architectures

Because two key characteristics of TCP/IP are vital to the Internet, it is appropriate to say that the Internet *is* the TCP protocol suite. First, TCP/IP is a layered structure (refer to Figure 5.9 in Chapter 5, "Data Communications Basics"). It gets more comprehensive in the layers above IP, and it has become extensive in the layers below IP; that is, numerous protocols are supported at the application layer (e.g., FTP and HTTP), and increasingly more options are available at the physical layer for connectivity. Second, IP decouples applications from the transmission or transport: IP does not care what the application is, and IP does not care what transport is used.

Figure 8.7 identifies the key elements in a TCP/IP network. The TCP/IP transmission consists of the application, transport, IP, and L2 layers. The hosts deal with the application and transport layers, and the network acts on the IP and L2 information. The network is composed of IP edge routers, IP core routers, and the transmission networks between them. The routers examine the IP field to deter-

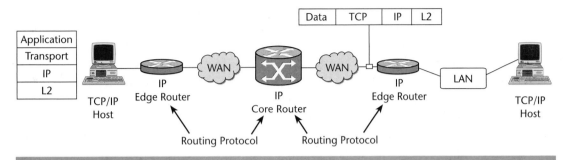

Figure 8.7 The key elements in a TCP/IP network

mine the appropriate routing of the message, and the routing protocol determines the specific technique used to determine the proper route. The hosts examine the TCP fields to ensure guaranteed service, checking for any errors or lost packets and requesting retransmissions when errors occur, and they also work with the application data.

TCP/IP is the darling of the networking world for several important reasons:

- **It provides a common internetworking paradigm**—IP enables internetworking (i.e., creating one big virtual network).

- **It supports many IP routing protocols**—The two major routing protocols are BGP and IGP. BGP distributes external network addresses within and between autonomous systems (which are discussed in more detail earlier in this chapter). BGP4 is currently the inter–autonomous system routing protocol of choice. IGP distributes internal prefixes only inside autonomous systems or to border routers leading to external networks. Examples include OSPF, IS-IS, and RIP version 2 (RIPv2).

- **It supports many transport protocols**—TCP/IP supports several main transport protocols, including TCP, UDP, DCCP, and SCTP. TCP is connection oriented, provides for flow and congestion control, and operates in a unicast mode. UDP is connectionless and therefore associated with unreliable transport. DCCP is one of the new transport protocols; it adds congestion control while still being associated with unreliable transport. SCTP is a new transport protocol that provides multistream and multihoming support.

- **It supports many link layers**—TCP/IP is data link agnostic. IP can work over many link layers, including Ethernet, IP, PPP, MPLS, ATM, optical, and wireless options. Along with being an open standard, TCP/IP also offers support for a wide variety of implementation scenarios.

IP over Birds?

For a taste of the humorous side of telecommunications and standards, you must take a look at the RFCs for "IP over avian carriers." These are classics. RFC 1149 (www.ietf.org/rfc/rfc1149.txt) was the original; it was updated by RFC 2549 (www.ietf.org/rfc/rfc2549.txt) to include quality of service.

Someone actually tried *implementing* RFC 1149. Amazing! Read about it at www.blug.linux.no/rfc1149. And be sure to check out the log of the real ping session, at www.blug.linux.no/rfc1149/pinglogg.txt.

Figure 8.8 illustrates the main aspects of an ISP's network architecture. The customers at the edge access the ISP's point of presence (POP) via an edge router that is part of the intra-POP fabric, the internal workings of the ISP's POP. (This information is covered in more detail later in this chapter, in the section "The Evolution of the POP Architecture.")

As you can see in Figure 8.8, the ISP backbone is composed of a series of core routers and the transmission links between them. Remember that the backbone may also contain ATM switches; a large percentage of ISP backbones include ATM

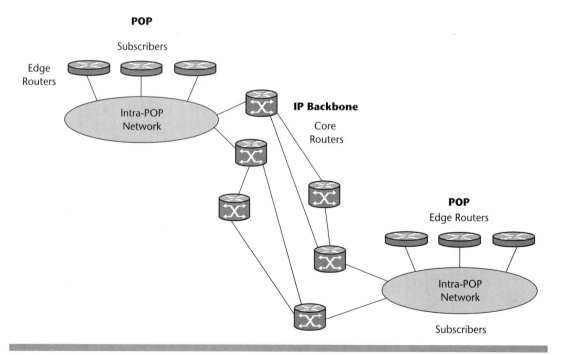

Figure 8.8 An ISP's network architecture

technology because they need to provide business-grade services with guaranteed quality of service (QoS), and they need to perform the highest class of traffic engineering to ensure maximum network performance.

From here, various ISPs are connected to create the Internet (see Figure 8.9). There are various levels of ISPs. For example, backbone ISPs serve at the highest level of the hierarchy and provide connectivity between the tens of thousands of ISPs worldwide. Below them are several classes of ISPs, including those that may cover a large area and support both business customers and basic consumers as well as local ISPs that more commonly serve small communities and focus on rock-bottom prices for consumers rather than business-class services for enterprises.

ISPs compete based on brand name, value-added services, performance, reliability, price, customer service, and other factors. Global Internet connectivity depends on private cooperation between ISPs. ISP cooperation, in turn, requires agreements about the business relationship, physical interconnection (called *peering*), ability to exchange routing information (e.g., via BGP), ability to exchange data, and the payment policy.

As Figure 8.10 shows, lower-level ISPs or local providers connect to higher-tier ISPs, which connect to the global Internet. ISPs exchange each other's customer

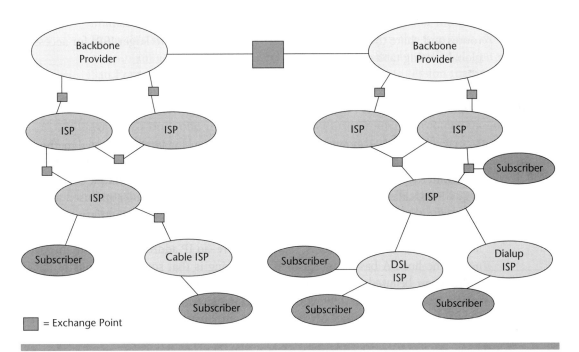

Figure 8.9 Internet composition

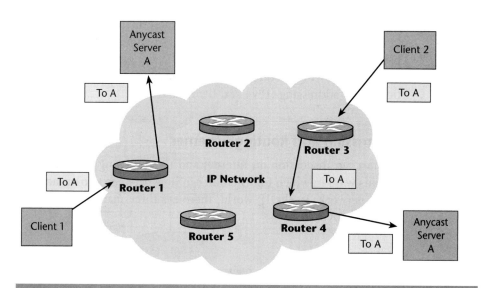

Figure 8.11   Anycast

each destination address identifies a group of receivers. However, at any given time, only one of them is chosen to receive information from any given sender.

The type of anycast is determined by the criteria for selecting the nearest server. In IP anycast, the network topology is the key criterion. In Application anycast, applications or server metrics—such as number of connections or available capacity—are the key criteria.

Anycast has several advantages. First, it offers a reduction in router and link resources because IP routing delivers packets over the shortest path to the closest available host. Another advantage is simplified configuration: The client needs to be configured with only a single IP anycast address of the server. Resiliency is another advantage: If one anycast server goes away, routing forwards the message to the next closest one with the same IP anycast address. Finally, anycast provides for load balancing, in which servers distributed over the network topology have the effect of balancing the traffic load for many clients.

There are three broad uses for IP anycast. The first use is service discovery, in which IP anycast routes the client's packets to a nearby server, which then redirects the client to a server (possibly itself), which is subsequently accessed using IP unicast. The second is query/reply services, in which the entire exchange is done using IP anycast; DNS is a popular recent example. The third use is routing services: IP anycast routes a client's packets to a routing infrastructure (e.g., IP multicast), which then continues to forward the packet by using whatever technology is appropriate.

IPv4 Addressing

The current generation of IP is called IP version 4 (IPv4). IPv4 addresses have two parts: the network ID and the host ID. Under IPv4, which was the only scheme in use until CIDR was introduced around 1995, there are five classes, which support different numbers of networks and hosts (see Figure 8.12):

- **Class A**—With Class A, there can be a total of 126 networks, and on each of those networks there can be 16,777,214 hosts. Class A address space is largely exhausted, although ICANN has reserved some Class A address space.

- **Class B**—Class B addresses provide for 16,384 networks, each of which can have 65,534 hosts. Class B space is also largely exhausted; some Class B addresses are still available at a very high cost.

- **Class C**—Class C allows for 2,097,152 networks, each of which can have 254 hosts.

- **Class D**—Class D belongs to a special aspect of the Internet called the multicast backbone (mbone). The mbone system conserves bandwidth over a distance, relieves congestion on transit links, and makes it possible to address a large population in a single multicast.

- **Class E**—Class E is address space reserved for experimental purposes.

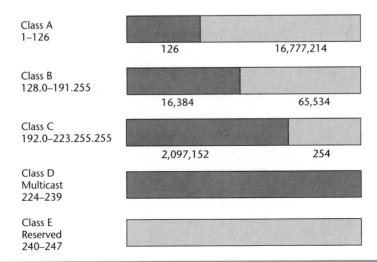

Figure 8.12 IPv4 32-bit addressing

The digits in an IP address tell a number of things about the address. For example, consider the IP address 124.29.88.7. We know this is a Class A network because the first *octet*, 124, falls in the range of numbers for Class A addresses. Thus, 124 indicates the network ID. The remaining three octets, 29.88.7, indicate the host ID. In the address 130.29.88.7, the first two octets, 130.29, comprise the network ID and indicate that this is a Class B address; the second two octets, 88.7, comprise the host ID. Figure 8.13 shows an example of IP addressing on a network.

Network IDs are managed and assigned by the RIRs (ARIN, APNIC, RIPE NCC, LACNIC, and AfriNIC). Host IDs are assigned locally by the network administrator. Given a 32-bit address field, IPv4 makes available approximately 4.3 billion different addresses. That seems like a lot, but as we began to experience growth in the Internet, we began to worry about the number of addresses left.

CIDR

In the early 1990s, the IETF began to consider the possibility of running out of IP address space. The result was the implementation of CIDR, which eliminated the old class-based style of addressing. A CIDR address is still a 32-bit IP address, but it is hierarchical rather than class based. Large national and regional service providers are allocated large blocks of contiguous Internet addresses, which they then allocate to other smaller ISPs or directly to organizations. Networks can be broken down into subnetworks, and networks can be combined into supernetworks, as long as they share a common network prefix. Basically, with CIDR, a route is no

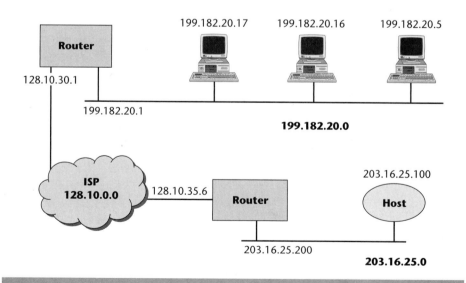

Figure 8.13 An example of IP network addressing

longer an IP address broken down into network and host bits according to its class; instead, the route becomes a combination of an address and a mask. The mask indicates how many bits in the address represent the network prefix. For example, the address 200.200.14.20/23 means that the first 23 bits of the binary form of this address represent the network. The bits remaining represent the host. In decimal form, the prefix 23 would look like this: 255.255.254.0.

Table 8.1 lists the most commonly used masks, giving their dotted-decimal and prefix values and the number of available host addresses of each type. CIDR defines address assignment and aggregation strategies designed to minimize the size of top-level Internet routing tables, which was another goal of CIDR. The national or regional ISP needs only to advertise its single supernet address, which

Table 8.1 CIDR Masking Scheme

Mask as Dotted-Decimal Value	Mask as Prefix Value	Number of Hosts
255.255.255.224	/27	32
255.255.255.192	/26	64
255.255.255.128	/25	128
255.255.255.0 (Class C)	/24	256
255.255.254.0	/23	512
255.255.252.0	/22	1,024
255.255.248.0	/21	2,048
255.255.242.0	/20	4,096
255.255.240.0	/19	8,192
255.255.224.0	/18	16,384
255.255.192.0	/17	32,768
255.255.0.0 (Class B)	/16	65,536
255.254.0.0	/15	131,072
255.252.0.0	/14	262,144
255.248.0.0	/13	524,288

represents an aggregation of all the subnets within that supernet. Routers in the Internet no longer give any credence to class; routing is entirely based on the CIDR prefix. CIDR does require the use of supporting routing protocols, such as RIPv2, OSPF version 2, Enhanced Interior Gateway Routing Protocol (EIGRP), and BGP4.

Subnetting is a term you may have heard in relationship to addressing. It once referred to the subdivision of a class-based network into subnetworks. Today, it generally refers to the subdivision of a CIDR block into smaller CIDR blocks. Subnetting allows single routing entries to refer either to the larger block or to their individual constituents, which permits a single general routing entry to be used through most of the Internet, with more specific routes required only for routers in the subnetted block.

NAT

Network Address Translation (NAT) is another technique used to deal with the shortage of IPv4 addresses. NAT was developed specifically to address this problem when the cost of extra IP addresses is an issue. NAT is therefore of particular interest in countries other than the United States where historically there have been fewer addresses allocated per capita, and also in small businesses and home offices. NAT enables a LAN to use one set of IP addresses for internal traffic and a second set of addresses for external traffic. The necessary IP address translations are performed at the NAT router, which is located where the LAN meets the Internet.

NAT allows an enterprise to use internal IP addresses, which, because they are internal, present no conflict with IP addresses employed by other enterprises. In a typical configuration, the LAN uses one of the designated "private" IP address subnets (10.0.0.0/8, 172.16.0.0/12, or 192.168.0.0/16). The router connecting this LAN to the Internet will have an address from the private subnet and a public address assigned by the ISP. The NAT function in the router translates between the public and private addresses. As far as the Internet is concerned, the router is the source and destination for any traffic. Because NAT-enabled routers do not have end-to-end connectivity, they cannot take part in some of the Internet protocols; for example, security protocols such as IPsec are complicated by the use of NAT— although the IETF has approved an extension to IPsec that encapsulates IPsec inside UDP, thus enabling it to traverse NAT devices. On the other hand, because the NAT server resides on the local network and must be used to initiate any connections to hosts on the other side of the router, the NAT server prevents some potential malicious activity coming from outside hosts. This improves the reliability of the local network, enhancing privacy by making it difficult for someone from outside the network to monitor individual usage patterns. Of course, this is less a function of NAT than a function of the rules that can be present in any router or firewall—blocking all inbound traffic unless that traffic is a reply to some previous outbound request.

There are two main types of NAT: dynamic and static. In static NAT, the public IP address is always the same, allowing an internal host, such as a Web server, to have an unregistered private IP address and still be reached over the Internet. In dynamic NAT, a private IP address is mapped to a public IP address drawn from a pool of registered public IP addresses. By keeping the internal configuration of the private network hidden, dynamic NAT helps conceal the network from outside users.

As always, it is important to also note any shortcomings. As my colleague, Dr. Art St. George of the University of New Mexico, notes, "While it is true that NAT serves many useful functions, it also serves to make end-to-end performance very difficult, if not impossible, to achieve and measure. On the LAN, use of NATs makes network diagnostics very difficult."

IPv6 Addressing

Because researchers predict that we may run out of IPv4 addresses as soon as 2009 ("IPv6: Friend or Foe," SearchNetworking.com, http://searchnetworking. techtarget.com/originalContent/0,289142,sid7_gci1156263,00.html?track=NL-81& ad=539879), a new version of IP has been developed, called IP version 6 (IPv6). IPv6 provides for an expanded address space. It uses 128-bit addressing (versus 32 bits in IPv4), which results in 340 undecillion unique addresses—that is, 340 billion billion billion billion—which is enough to supply 75 IP addresses to every square inch of the earth's surface, including oceans! IPv6 addresses typically have two parts: a 64-bit network prefix and a 64-bit host address. The host address can be assigned sequentially or automatically generated from the interface's MAC address. The IPv6 addressing structure uses hexadecimal notation, normally written as eight groups of four hexadecimal digits, and colons replace the periods used in IPv4, as in the following example:

2001:0db8:85a3:0000:1319:8a2e:0370:7344

IPv6 has four address types: unicast (one-to-one), anycast (one-to-nearest), multicast (one-to-many), and a reserved class. A single interface may be assigned multiple IPv6 addresses of unicast, anycast, or multicast addresses. Note that IPv6 does not support broadcasting.

IPv6 is designed to be an evolutionary step from IPv4. It can be installed as a normal software upgrade in Internet devices and is interoperable with IPv4. IPv6 runs well in high-performance networks, such as Gigabit Ethernet and ATM networks, and it is also efficient for low-bandwidth networks such as wireless networks. In addition, it provides a platform for new Internet functionality that will be required in the near future. IPv6 simplifies the packet header format (see Figure 8.14). It

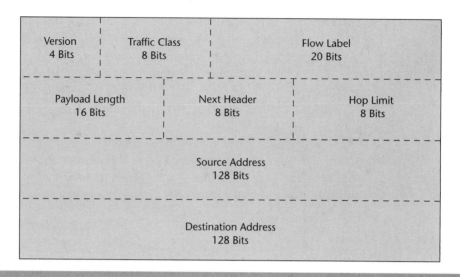

Figure 8.14 The IPv6 packet header

supports autoconfiguration and multihoming. IPv6 includes the DiffServ Code Point (DSCP) in the traffic class, and it addresses authentication and privacy capabilities.

Benefits of IPv6 include improved routing efficiency due to the streamlined header format as well as simplified administration. QoS capabilities are also enhanced because the specification includes a flow label to support real-time traffic. Finally, IPv6 offers better security mechanisms, mandating the use of IPsec and IKE (which are discussed in Chapter 9, in the section "IPsec VPNs"). The encryption extension known as the Encapsulating Security Payload (ESP) service renders the packet's payload data illegible unless the recipient has the proper key to unscramble the data. Administrators can choose to encrypt only the transport and data payload of a packet or the entire packet, including headers and extensions.

The architecture for IPv6 is defined in RFC 3513, "IP Version 6 Addressing Architecture," which is available at www.ietf.org/rfc/rfc3513.txt and provides complete information on IPv6 addressing, rules, and exceptions. IPv6 addressing rules are covered by multiple RFCs.

The Transition from IPv4 to IPv6

There are several techniques for enabling IPv4-to-IPv6 interworking and coexistence:

■ **IPv4-to-IPv6 translation**—IPv4-to-IPv6 translation, shown in Figure 8.15, involves a network address translator, or a protocol translator. It employs stateless IP and ICMP translations. It is a bidirectional translation algorithm for IPv4, IPv6, ICMPv4, and ICMPv6 packet headers.

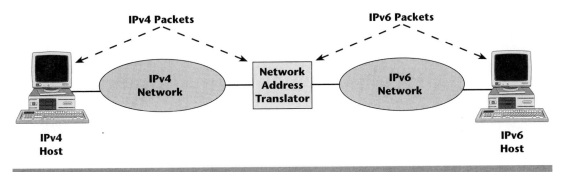

Figure 8.15   IPv4-to-IPv6 translation

■ **Dual Stack**—With Dual Stack, which is already widely deployed, IPv4 and IPv6 exist in the same host (see Figure 8.16). New Dual Stack IPv6 devices will be backward capable with IPv4, and IPv4 devices can be programmed with both IPv4 and IPv6 stacks to process respective packets appropriately.

■ **6to4**—The third alternative involves IPv6 tunneling through IPv4, referred to as 6to4 (see Figure 8.17). 6to4 specifies a new technique designed for interconnecting IPv6 networks over IPv4 networks without explicitly defined tunnels. The IPv4 address (V4ADDR) portion of the special 6to4

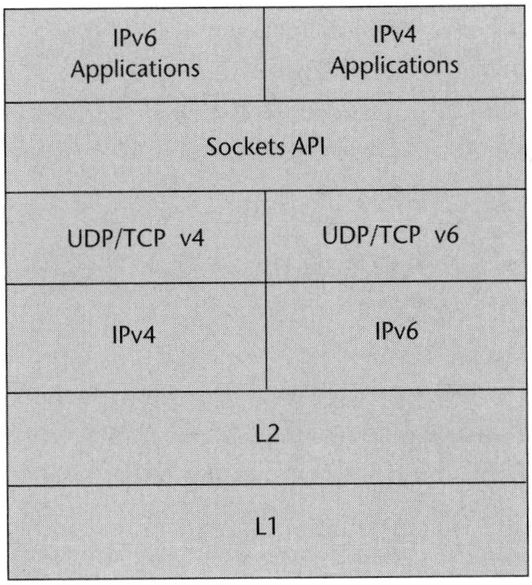

IPv6 Applications	IPv4 Applications
Sockets API	
UDP/TCP v4	UDP/TCP v6
IPv4	IPv6
L2	
L1	

Figure 8.16   Dual Stack

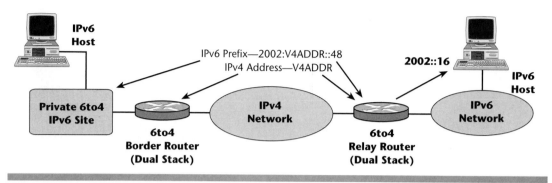

Figure 8.17 6to4

IPv6 address identifies the IPv4 tunnel endpoints. Border routers need a default route to a 6to4 relay router, or they must run IPv6 interdomain routing protocols (such as MP-BGP). 6to4 can use special anycasts advertised by 6to4 relay routers to find the nearest one.

The Status of IPv6 Deployment

The push to IPv6 was initially driven by a concern that the supply of available IP addresses would soon run out and that the addressing scheme had to be changed to allow for more addresses. However, especially in the United States, this shortage has not yet been realized. Most large enterprises have address blocks so big that they have never felt any address crunch at all. Furthermore, CIDR, NAT, network address port translation, and similar technologies have helped ease the strain on IP addresses. Fears about imminent IP address depletion were somewhat exaggerated. Nevertheless, Asia, especially China, is currently experiencing significant difficulty with IP address allocations. All of China has fewer IP addresses allocated to it than does Stanford University. Europe's IP address space issues are somewhat less pressing than Asia's but are still of concern, especially as mobile 3G networks begin to be deployed. In contrast, there is a general sense of complacency about these issues in the United States. Therefore, IPv6 had dropped off the radar screen of U.S. enterprises for a while, but now, with the government specifying that all federal agencies must deploy IPv6 by 2008, more attention is being focused on how migration to IPv6 will affect enterprises and providers alike. Again, IPv6 has also become a strategic priority in Europe and a pressing issue in Asia.

The European Union issued a consultation report on infrastructure for fully distributed mobile and shared applications. This report, which analyzes the development and deployment of IPv6, states that IPv6 will be of strategic importance to Europe for the next generation of communication systems. Meanwhile, the Japanese government has mandated that all its public networks must adopt IPv6. This is in part because Japan has embraced 3G wireless phones, which require IPv6 for networking. It is believed that the mobile market will be the greatest pusher of IPv6 because wireless is going to challenge IPv4's address availability. Currently it is not possible to expand the address range with NAT and retain functionality for wireless devices. With the proliferation of globally routable IP-aware devices—such as mobile phones, videogame consoles, PDAs, smart cars, and wearables—an accompanying demand for wireless Web access is occurring, making migration to IPv6 a necessity.

There is very little end-user or application demand for IPv6, however. The current stumbling blocks to major deployment of IPv6 networks globally include the lack of wide-scale network infrastructure deployment and a lack of killer applications that require IPv6 to function. The primary benefits of IPv6 at this time accrue at the network management level, in areas such as intradomain routing, network configuration, end-to-end security, and address space management.

In 1996 the IETF established 6bone (www.6bone.net) as an IPv6 testbed network to enable IPv6 testing as well as to assist in the transitioning of IPv6 into the Internet. It operated under the IPv6 address allocation 3FFE::/16. More than 1,173 networks in some 60 countries were connected to the 6bone IPv6 network. 6bone started as a virtual network, using IPv6-over-IPv4 tunneling/encapsulation, operating over the IPv4-based Internet to support IPv6 transport. It slowly migrated to native links for IPv6 transport. 6bone ceased to operate in June 2006, and IANA reclaimed all 6bone prefixes.

The Moonv6 Project

The Moonv6 project (http://moonv6.sr.unh.edu) is a global effort led by the North American IPv6 Task Force (NAv6TF; www.nav6tf.org), involving the University of New Hampshire InterOperability Laboratory (UNH IOL; www.iol.unh.edu), Internet 2 (www.internet2.edu), vendors, service providers, and regional IPv6 Forum (www.ipv6forum.org) task force network pilots worldwide. Taking place across the United States at multiple locations, the Moonv6 project is the largest permanently deployed multivendor IPv6 network in the world. The U.S. Department of Defense (DoD) Joint Interoperability Test Command (JITC; http://jitc.fhu.disa.mil) and other government agencies, the Defense Research and Engineering Network (DREN; www.v6.dren.net), and the High Performance Computing Modernization Program (HPCMP; www.hpcmo.hpc.mil) play significant roles in the Moonv6 demonstrations, ensuring that DoD interoperability and migration objectives are identified and demonstrated.

The Moonv6 network is a set of native IPv6 connections between sites on the global Internet that forward packets to other Moonv6 peering sites. Participants can have a native IPv6 connection to the Internet, and Moonv6 permits IPv6-in-IPv4 tunnel hops for a 90-day period to test on the Moonv6 network, provided that the requestor, not Moonv6 administration, defines and administers those tunnels. A Moonv6 site forwards packets within the Moonv6 peering network and also participates as a Moonv6 site for collaborative testing of IPv6 implementations for interoperability and verification of functions within the IPv6 protocol and architecture. To become a Moonv6 peering network, a network must be an IPv6 peer with an existing Moonv6 peering network. To become a Moonv6 site, one must connect to an existing Moonv6 peering network.

DNS

DNS is a distributed database system that operates on the basis of a hierarchy of names. DNS provides translation between host names (such as www.lidoorg.com or www.telecomwebcentral.com) and the difficult-to-remember numeric IP addresses. It identifies a domain's mail servers and a domain's name servers. When you need to contact a particular URL, the host name portion of the URL must be *resolved* to the appropriate IP address (see Figure 8.18).

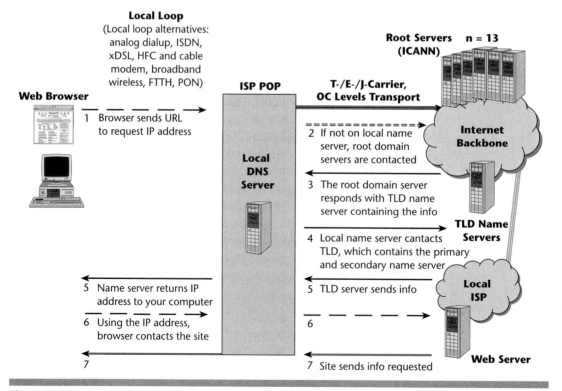

Figure 8.18 How DNS servers work

Your Web browser goes to a local name server, maintained either by your ISP, your online service provider, or your company. If the IP address is a local one—that is, if it's on the same network as the one you are on—then the name server will be able to resolve that URL with the IP address right away. In this case, the name server sends the true IP address to your computer, and because your Web browser now has the real address of the place you're trying to locate, it contacts that site, and the site sends the information you have requested.

If the local name server determines that the domain you have requested is not on the local network, it must get the information from a name server on the Internet. The local name server contacts 1 of the 13 root domain servers, each of which contains a list of the TLD name servers managed by ICANN. All 13 root servers contain the same vital information to spread the workload and back each other up. They contain the IP addresses of all the TLD registries, and they address both the global registries, such as .com and .org, and the 250 country-specific registries, such as .fr (for France). The root domain server tells the local server which TLD name server contains the domain specified in the URL.

Scattered across the Internet are thousands of computers—called *domain name resolvers* or just *resolvers*—that routinely download and copy the information contained in the root servers. These resolvers are located strategically with ISPs or institutional networks. They are used to respond to a user's request to resolve a domain name (i.e., to find the corresponding IP address).

TLD registry organizations house online databases that contain information about the domain names in that TLD. The .org registry database, for example, contains the IP address of the primary DNS server for the domain icann.org. In trying to find the Internet address of www.icann.org, your computer must first find the .org registry database. The TLD name server tells the local server which primary name server and secondary name server are authoritative for the domain in the requested URL (icann.org in our example). The local name server can then contact the domain's primary name server to resolve the full name of the host in the URL (www.icann.org in our example). If the primary name server does not respond, the local name server contacts the secondary name server. One of those name servers will have the proper information, and it will then pass that information back to the local name server. The local name server sends the information back to your browser, which then uses the IP address to contact the proper site.

Top-Level Domains
For some time, there have been seven generic TLDs (gTLDs):

.com	commercial
.gov	government
.mil	military

.edu	education
.net	for network operation
.org	nonprofit organizations
.int	international treaty organizations

gTLDs are unrestricted; this means anyone from anywhere can register as many of these domain names as they like.

In addition, 11 TLDs have been added since 2001:

.aero	air-transport industry
.arpa	infrastructure
.biz	businesses
.coop	cooperatives
.info	any use
.job	related to jobs
.museum	museums
.name	individuals
.pro	accountants, lawyers, and physicians
.root	infrastructure
.travel	travel-related sites

A few more TLDs are in the startup phase, including .cat, .mobi, .post, and .tel. In addition, some new TLDs have been proposed, including .asia, .geo, .kid, .mail, .sco, .web, and .xxx. The .nato TLD has been retired, and .example, .invalid, .localhost, and .test are held in reserve at this time.

There are also country code TLDs (ccTLDs). Each of these is a two-letter country code (e.g., .au, .ca), and there are 250 ccTLDs, including a .us domain for the United States. If you wanted to protect your domain name in the .com domain, for example, you would actually have to register it in 251 domains—.com and then .com with the appropriate two-letter country code after that—and if you really wanted to get serious about branding, you would probably want to register another 250 each in the .net, .org, and .biz domains! Of course, very few organizations actually do this.

As discussed earlier in this chapter, the overall responsibility for managing DNS falls to ICANN. In addition to governing the terms and conditions of the gTLDs with the cooperation of the gTLD registries, ICANN also controls the root domain, delegating control over each TLD to a domain name registry. When it comes to the ccTLDs, the government of a given country typically controls the domain registry. Although ICANN may consult with the domain registries, it does not regulate the terms and conditions of how the domain name is allocated or who allocates it within each of the country-level domain registries.

The Importance of Domain Names

Many new domain names are registered every minute, and it seems that all the simple one- and two-word .com names have already been taken. Therefore, there's a call for new TLDs to be added. Originally IANA, which was funded by the U.S. government, administrated the DNS. From 1993 to 1998, Network Solutions (now part of VeriSign) was the sole provider of direct domain name registration services in the open gTLDs, and registration authority over the ccTLDs was relegated to the individual countries and bodies within them.

ICANN, a nonprofit, international corporation, was formed to take over in 1998. ICANN has assumed responsibility for a set of technical functions previously performed under U.S. government contract by IANA and other groups. Specifically, ICANN coordinates the assignment of the following identifiers, which must be globally unique for the Internet to function:

- Internet domain names
- IP address numbers
- IP numbers and TCP/UPD port numbers

In addition, ICANN coordinates the stable operation of the Internet's root server system. ICANN has also introduced competition into the administration of the DNS through a policy for the accreditation of registrars and a shared registry system for the .com, .net, and .org domains. As a result of competition, numerous domain name registration service providers from around the world are providing .com, .net, .org, .biz, and .info domain name registration services. The Accredited Registrar Directory provides a listing of ICANN-accredited domain name registrars that are currently taking domain name registrations (see www.icann.org).

The Value of Domain Names

The small Pacific Islands country of Tuvalu, population 10,600, was assigned the country code .tv. Naturally, .tv is a very appealing domain. It has relevance to entertainment, streaming media, and screaming multimedia, and it also has a global context: Once you registered something as .tv, you would no longer be able to alter it by appending another country code because it already is a country code. Of course, many entrepreneurs developed an interest in Tuvalu, and many companies approached the country to acquire its domain name, so Tuvalu auctioned the name. A company called .tv bought the name for roughly US$1 million quarterly—adjustable for inflation—with a US$50 million cap over 10 years. In addition, Tuvalu holds a 20% stake in the company. This auctioning of the country's domain name produced four times the country's GDP. The island is richly developing its transportation, educational, and health care facilities.

On the .tv domain, some domain names are quite expensive, with bidding starting at US$250,000 for broadband.tv, for instance. On the other hand, some creative and descriptive domains haven't yet been registered, and you could acquire those for as little as US$50. A lot of money is tied up in domain names, and the process of creating new domains will make identifying the best branding strategy a further challenge.

■ The Organization of the Internet

It is important to understand what the Internet infrastructure is composed of and how it is structured in terms of the large variety of players represented in the Internet space. It is also important to keep in mind that similarly to the PSTN, the Internet was not originally structured for what we're asking it to do now.

Initially, the Internet was designed to support data communications—bursty, low-speed text data traffic. It was structured to accommodate longer hold times while still facilitating low data volumes, in a cost-effective manner. (With the packet-switching technique, through statistical multiplexing, long hold times do not negatively affect the cost structure because users are sharing the channel with other users.) The capacities of the links initially dedicated to the Internet were narrowband: 56Kbps or 64Kbps. The worldwide infrastructure depended on the use of packet switches (i.e., routers), servers (i.e., repositories for the information), and clients (i.e., the user interfaces into the repositories). The Internet was composed of a variety of networks, including both LANs and WANs, with internetworking equipment such as routers and switches designed for interconnection of disparate networks. The Internet relied on TCP/IP to move messages between different subnetworks, and it was not traditionally associated with strong and well-developed operational support systems, unlike the PSTN, where billing, provisioning, and network management systems are quite extensive, even if they are not integrated.

The traditional Internet relied on the PSTN for subscriber access to the Internet. So the physical framework, the roadways over which a package travels on what we know as the Internet, is the same type of physical infrastructure as the PSTN: It uses the same types of communications, links, and capacities. In order for users to actually access this public data network, they had to rely on the PSTN. Two types of access were facilitated: dialup for consumers and small businesses (i.e., the range of analog modems, Narrowband ISDN) and dedicated access in the form of leased lines, ISDN Primary Rate Interface (PRI), and dedicated lines based on T-1/E-1 capacities for larger enterprises, and, in some cases, even T-3/E-3.

The Evolution of the POP Architecture

The early Internet point-of-presence (POP) architecture was quite simple, as illustrated in Figure 8.19. Either 56Kbps or 64Kbps lines came in to access ports on a router. Out of that router, T-1/E-1 trunks led to a UNIX host. This UNIX environment was, for most typical users, very difficult to navigate. Until there was an easier way for users to interface—the World Wide Web—the Internet was very much the province of academicians, engineers, and computer scientists.

The architecture of the Internet today is significantly different from its early days. Figure 8.20 shows some of the key components you would find in a higher-level network service provider's (NSP's) or a high-tier ISP's POP today. (Of course, a local service provider with just one POP or one node for access purposes, perhaps to a small community, looks quite different from this because it is much simpler.)

First, let's look at the support for the dialup users. Today, we have to facilitate a wide range of speeds; despite our admiration of and desire for broadband access, it's not yet widely available. As of year-end 2005, only 15.7% of the world's population had any type of Internet access (www.internetworldstats.com). In the next several years, we should see more activity in terms of local loop modernization to provide broadband access to more users, using both fiber and wireless broadband alternatives

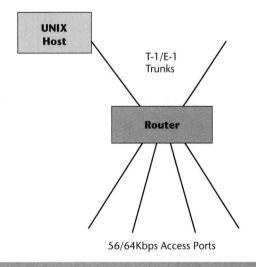

Figure 8.19 POP architecture in the 1980s

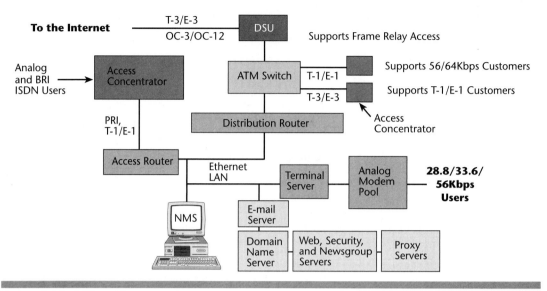

Figure 8.20 POP architecture today

(see Chapter 12, "Broadband Access Alternatives"). But for the time being, we still have to accommodate a wide range of analog modems that operate at speeds between 14.4Kbps and 56Kbps. Therefore, the first point of entry at the POP requires a pool of analog modems that complement the ones that individuals are using.

Also, as we add broadband access alternatives, additional access devices are required (e.g., for DSL modems or cable modems). The analog modem pool communicates with a terminal server, and the terminal server establishes a PPP session. PPP does two things: It assigns an IP address to a dialup user's session, and it authenticates that user and authorizes entry. By dynamically allocating an IP address when needed, PPP enables us to reuse IP addresses, helping to mitigate the problem of the growing demand for IP addresses. A user is allocated an address when she or he dials in for a session; when the session terminates, the IP address can be assigned to another user. PPP supports two protocols that provide link-level security:

■ **Password Authentication Protocol (PAP)**—PAP uses a two-way handshake for the peer to establish its identity upon link establishment. The peer repeatedly sends the password to the authenticator until verification is acknowledged or the connection is terminated. PAP is insecure, though, in that it transmits passwords in the clear, which means they could be captured and replayed.

■ **Challenge Handshake Authentication Protocol (CHAP)**—CHAP uses a three-way handshake to periodically verify the identity of the peer throughout the life of the connection. The server sends to the remote workstation a random token (a challenge) that is encrypted with the user's password and sent back to the server. The server performs a lookup to see if it recognizes the password. If the values match, the authentication is acknowledged; if not, the connection is terminated. A different token is provided each time a remote user dials in, which adds more robustness. Although an improvement over PAP, CHAP is still vulnerable. If an attacker were to capture the clear-text challenge and the encrypted response, it is possible to statistically determine the encryption key—which is the password. CHAP is strong when the password is complex or, better, at least 15 characters long.

The terminal server resides on a LAN, which is typically a Gigabit Ethernet network today. Besides the terminal server, the ISP POP houses a wide range of other servers. It also contains network management systems that the service providers can use to administer passwords and to monitor and control all the network elements in the POP, as well as to remotely diagnose elements outside the POP. As shown in Figure 8.20, the following are possible elements in the ISP POP architecture, and not all POPs necessarily have all these components (e.g., ATM switches are likely to be found only in larger ISPs):

- **E-mail servers**—These servers route e-mail between ISPs and house the e-mail boxes of subscribers.

- **Domain name servers**—These servers resolve DNS names into IP addresses.

- **Web servers**—If an ISP is engaged in a hosting business, it needs a Web server, most likely several.

- **Security servers**—Security servers engage in encryption, as well as in authentication and certification of users. Not every ISP has a security server. For example, those that want to offer e-commerce services or the ability to set up storefronts must have them. (Security is discussed in detail in Chapter 9.)

- **Newsgroup servers**—Newsgroup servers store the millions of Usenet messages that are posted daily, and they are updated frequently throughout the day.

- **Proxy servers**—A proxy server provides firewall functionality, acting as an intermediary for user requests and establishing a connection to the requested resource either at the application layer or at the session or transport layer. Proxy servers provide a means to keep outsiders from directly connecting to a service on an internal network. Proxy servers are also becoming critical in support of edge caching of content. People are constantly becoming less tolerant of lengthy downloads, and information streams (such as video, audio, and multimedia) are becoming more demanding of timely delivery.

Say you want to minimize the number of hops that a user has to go through. You could do this by using a tracing product to see how many hops it takes to reach a Web site. You'll see that sometimes you need to go through 17 or 18 hops to get to a site. Because the delay at each hop can be more than 2,000 milliseconds, if you have to make 18 hops when you're trying to use a streaming media tutorial, you will not be satisfied. ISPs can also use proxy servers to cache content locally, which means the information is distributed over 1 hop rather than over multiple hops, and that greatly improves the streaming media experience. Not all proxy servers support caching, however.

■ **Access router**—An access router filters local traffic. If a user is simply checking e-mail, working on a Web site, or looking up newsgroups, there's no reason for the user to be sent out over the Internet and then brought back to this particular POP. An access router keeps traffic contained locally in such situations.

■ **Distribution router**—A distribution router determines the optimum path to get to the next hop that will bring you one step closer to the destination URL, if it is outside the POP from which you are being served. Typically, in a higher-level ISP, this distribution router will connect to an ATM switch.

■ **ATM switch**—An ATM switch enables the ISP to guarantee QoS, which is especially necessary for supporting larger customers on high-speed interfaces and links and for supporting VPNs, VoIP, or streaming media applications. The ATM switch, by virtue of its QoS characteristics, enables us to map the packets into the appropriate cells, which guarantee that the proper QoS is administered and delivered. Typically, QoS is negotiated (and paid for) by an organization using the Internet as the transport between its various facilities in a region or around the world, to guarantee a minimum performance level between sites; a single ISP is used for all site connections. QoS for general public Internet access is unlikely to arise because the billing and servicing is economically infeasible. (ATM QoS is discussed further in Chapter 10, "Next-Generation Networks.") The ATM switch is front-ended by a DSU.

■ **Data service unit (DSU)**—The DSU is the data communications equipment on which the circuit terminates. It performs signal conversion and provides diagnostic capabilities. The network also includes a physical circuit, which, in a larger higher-tier provider, would generally be in the optical carrier levels.

■ **Access concentrator**—An access concentrator can be used to create the appearance of a virtual POP. For instance, if you want your subscribers to believe they're accessing a local node—that is, to make it appear that you're in the same neighborhood that they are in—you can use an access concentrator. The user dials a local number, thinking that you're located down the street in the business park, when in fact, the user's traffic is being hauled over a dedicated high-speed link to a physical POP located elsewhere in the network. Users' lines terminate on a simple access concentrator, where their traffic is multiplexed over the T-1s or T-3s, E-1s or E-3s, or perhaps ISDN PRI. This gives ISPs the appearance of having a local presence when, in fact, they have none. Later text in this chapter discusses the advantages of owning the infrastructure versus renting the infrastructure; clearly, if you own your infrastructure, backhauling traffic allows you to more cost-effectively serve remote locations. For an ISP leasing facilities from a telco, these sorts of links to backhaul traffic from more remote locations add cost to the overall operations.

You can see that the architecture of the POP has become incredibly more sophisticated today than it was in the beginning; the architecture has evolved in response to and in preparation for a very wide range of multimedia, real-time, and interactive applications.

Internet Challenges and Changes

Despite all its advances over the past couple decades, the Internet is challenged today. It is still limited in bandwidth at various points. The Internet is composed of some 10,000 service providers. Although some of the really big companies have backbone capacities that are 50Gbps or greater, there are still plenty of small backbones worldwide that have only a maximum of 1.5Mbps or 2Mbps. Overall, the Internet still needs more bandwidth.

One reason the Internet needs more bandwidth is that traffic keeps increasing at an astonishing rate. People are drawn to Web sites that provide pictures of products in order to engage in demonstrations and to conduct multimedia communications, not to mention all the entertainment content. Multimedia, visual, and interactive applications demand greater bandwidth and more control over latencies and losses. This means that we frequently have bottlenecks at the ISP level, at the backbone level (i.e., the NSP level), and at the Internet exchange points (IXPs) where backbones interconnect to exchange traffic between providers. These bottlenecks greatly affect our ability to roll out new time-sensitive, loss-sensitive applications, such as Internet telephony, VoIP, VPNs, streaming media, and IPTV. And remember, as discussed in the Introduction, one other reason more bandwidth is needed is that in the future, everything imaginable—your TV, refrigerator, electrical outlets, appliances, furniture, and so on—will have IP addresses, thus vastly increasing demand.

Therefore, we are redefining the Internet, with the goal of supporting more real-time traffic flows, real audio, real video, and live media. This requires the introduction of QoS into the Internet or any other IP infrastructure. However, this is much more important to the enterprise than to the average consumer. While enterprises are likely to indeed be willing to pay to have their traffic between ISP-connected sites routed at a certain priority, consumers are more likely to be willing to pay for simple enhanced services (such as higher bandwidth for a higher monthly fee) rather than individual QoS controls. And for the ISPs, there's little economic incentive to offer individual QoS because it is much too expensive to manage.

There are really two types of metrics that we loosely refer to as QoS: class of service (CoS) and true QoS. CoS is a prioritization scheme—like having a platinum credit card versus a gold card versus a regular card. With CoS, you can prioritize streams and thereby facilitate better performance. QoS, however, deals with very strict traffic measurements, where you can specify the latencies end to end, the jitter or variable latencies in the receipt of the packets, the tolerable cell loss, and the mechanism for allocating the bandwidth continuously or on a bursty basis. QoS is much more stringent than CoS, and what we are currently using in the Internet is really more like CoS than QoS.

Techniques such as DiffServ allow us to prioritize the traffic streams, but they really do not allow us to control the traffic measurements. That is why, as discussed in Chapter 10, we tend to still rely on ATM within the core: ATM allows the strict control of traffic measurements, and it therefore enables us to improve performance, quality, reliability, and security. Efforts are under way to develop equivalent QoS mechanisms for IP networks, such as MPLS, which is increasingly deployed and available (also discussed in Chapter 10), but we are still a couple years away from clearly defining the best mechanism, especially because we need to consider the marriage of IP and optical technologies. In the meantime, we are redesigning the Internet core, moving away from what was a connectionless router environment that offered great flexibility and the ability to work around congestion and failures, but at the expense of delays. We are moving to a connection-oriented environment where we can predefine the path and more tightly control the latencies, using techniques such as Frame Relay, ATM, and MPLS, each of which allow us to separate traffic types, prioritize time-sensitive traffic, and ultimately reduce access costs by eliminating leased-lines connections.

The other main effort in redesigning the Internet core is that we are increasing the capacity, moving from OC-3 and OC-12 (155Mbps and 622Mbps) at the backbone level to OC-48 (2.5Gbps), OC-192 (10Gbps), and even some early deployments of OC-768 (40Gbps). But remember that the number of bits per second that we can carry per wavelength doubles every year, and the number of wavelengths that we can carry per fiber also doubles every year. So the migration beyond 10Gbps is also under way in the highest class of backbones, and it will continue with the evolution and deployment of advanced optical technologies. (However, to be fair, there are issues of power consumption and customer demand to deal with, which will ultimately determine how quickly what is technically feasible gets adopted in the marketplace.)

The emergent generation of Internet infrastructure is quite different from the traditional foundation. It is geared for a new set of traffic and application types: high-speed, real-time, and interactive multimedia. It must be able to support and guarantee CoS and QoS. As discussed in Chapter 9, it includes next-generation telephony, which is a new approach to providing basic telephony services while using IP networks.

The core of the Internet infrastructure will increasingly rely on DWDM and optical networking. It will require the use of ATM, MPLS, and Generalized MPLS (GMPLS) networking protocols to ensure proper administration of performance. (Optical advances are discussed in Chapter 11, "Optical Networking.") New generations of IP protocols are being developed to address real-time traffic, CoS, QoS, and security. Distributed network intelligence is being used to share the network functionality. At the same time, broadband access line deployment continues around the world, with new high-speed fiber alternatives, such as passive optical networks (PONs), gaining interest. (PONs are discussed in Chapter 12.) An impressive number of wireless broadband alternatives are also becoming available, as discussed in Chapter 15, "WMANs, WLANs, and WPANs."

Service Providers and Interconnection

There is a wide range of service providers in the Internet space, and they vary greatly. One way they differ is in their coverage areas. Some providers focus on simply serving a local area, others are regionally based, and others offer national or global coverage. Service providers also vary in the access options they provide. Most ISPs offer plain old telephone service (POTS), and some offer ISDN, xDSL, Frame Relay, ATM, cable modem service, satellite, and wireless as well. Providers also differ in the services they support. Almost all providers support e-mail (but not necessarily at the higher-tier backbone level). Some also offer FTP hosting, Web hosting, name services, VPNs, VoIP, application hosting, e-commerce storefronts, and streaming media. Providers could service a very wide variety of applications, and as a result, there is differentiation on this basis as well. Two other important issues are customer service and the number of hops a provider must take in order to get to the main point of interconnection to the Internet.

It is pretty easy to become an ISP in a developed economy: Pick up a router, lease a 56Kbps/64Kbps line, and you're in business. But this is why there are some 10,000 such providers, of varying sizes and qualities, worldwide. And it is why there is a service provider pecking order: Research backbones have the latest technology, top-tier providers focus on business-class services, and lower-tier providers focus on rock-bottom pricing. There are therefore large variations in terms of the capacity available, the performance you can expect, the topology of the network, the levels of redundancy, the numbers of connections with other operators, and the level of customer service and the extent of its availability (i.e., whether it is a 24/7 or a Monday-through-Friday, 9-to-5 type of operation). Ultimately, of course, ISPs vary greatly in terms of price.

Figure 8.21 shows an idealized model of the service provider hierarchy. At the top of the heap are research backbones. For example, Internet 2 replaces what the original Internet was for—the academic network. Some 85% of traffic within the academic domain stays within the academic domain, so there's good reason to have a separate backbone for the universities and educational institutions involved in research and learning. Internet 2 will, over time, contribute to the next commercialized platform. It acts as a testbed for many of the latest and greatest technologies, so the universities stress-test Internet 2 to determine how applications perform and which technologies suit which applications or management purposes best. Other very sophisticated technology platforms exist, such as the Abilene Project and the Interplanetary Internet (IPN), which are discussed later in this chapter.

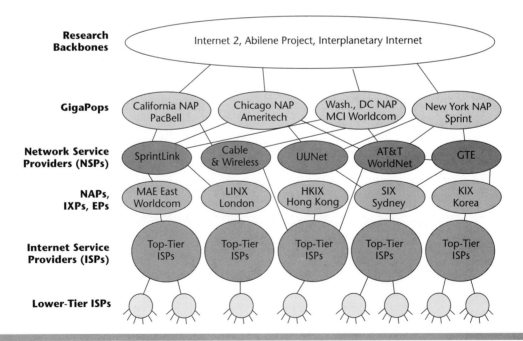

Figure 8.21 Service provider hierarchy

In the commercial realm, the highest tier is the NSP. NSPs are very large backbones, global carriers that own their infrastructures. The NSPs can be broken down into three major subsets:

- **National ISPs**—These ISPs have national coverage. They include the incumbent telecom carriers and the new competitive entrants.
- **Regional ISPs**—These ISPs are active regionally throughout a nation or world zone, and they own their equipment and lease their lines from the incumbent telco or competitive operator.
- **Retail ISPs**—These ISPs have no investment in the network infrastructure whatsoever. They basically use their brand name and outsource all the infrastructure to an NSP or a high-tier ISP, but they build from a known customer database that is loyal and provides an opportunity to offer a branded ISP service.

These various levels of NSPs interconnect, and they can connect in several ways. In the early days of the Internet, there were four main network access points (NAPs), all located in the United States, through which all of the world's Internet traffic interconnected and traveled. The four original NAPs were located in San Francisco (PacBell NAP, operated by PacBell), Chicago (AADS, operated by Ameritech), Tysons Corner, Virginia (MAE-East, operated by MCI Worldcom), and Pennsauken, New Jersey (SprintNAP, operated by Sprint) These IXPs are also called metropolitan area exchanges (MAEs). Today there are hundreds of IXPs distributed around the world.

IXPs

An *IXP* is a physical infrastructure where different NSPs and/or ISPs can exchange traffic between their networks with their counterparts. By means of mutual peering arrangements, traffic can be exchanged without cost. An IXP is therefore a public meeting point that houses cables, routers, switches, LANs, data communications equipment, and network management and telecommunications links. IXPs allow the NSPs and top-tier ISPs to exchange Internet traffic without having to send the traffic through a main transit link. This translates to decreased costs associated with the transit links, and it reduces congestion on the transit links.

The main purpose of an IXP is to allow providers to interconnect via the exchange rather than having to pass traffic through third-party networks. The main advantage is that traffic passing through an exchange usually isn't billed by any party, whereas connection to an upstream provider would be billed by that upstream provider. Also, because IXPs are usually in the same city, latencies are reduced because the traffic doesn't have to travel to another city or, potentially, continent. Finally, there is a speed advantage, so an ISP can avoid the high cost of long-distance leased lines, which may limit its available bandwidth due to the costs, whereas a connection to a local IXP might allow limitless data transfer, improving the bandwidth between adjacent ISPs.

A common IXP is composed of one or more switches to which the various ISPs connect. During the 1990s, ATM switches were the most popular type of switch, but today Ethernet switches are increasingly being employed, with the ports used by the different ISPs ranging from 10Mbps to 100Mbps for smaller ISPs to 1Gbps or 10Gbps for larger providers. The costs for operating an IXP are generally shared by all the participating ISPs, with each member paying a monthly fee, depending on the speed of its port or the amount of traffic it offers. (A good source of information showing all the IXPs around the world is www.ep.net.)

Peering Agreements

An alternative to IXPs is the use of private peering agreements. In a peering solution, operators agree to exchange with one another the same amount of traffic over high-speed lines between their routers so that users on one network can reach addresses on the other. This type of agreement bypasses public congestion points, such as IXPs. It is called *peering* because there is an assumption that the parties are equal, or peers, in that they have an equal amount of traffic to exchange. This is an important point because it makes a difference in how money is exchanged. People are studying this issue to determine whether a regulatory mechanism is needed or whether market forces will drive it. In general, with the first generation of peering agreements, there was an understanding that peers were equals. Newer agreements often call for charges to be applied when traffic levels exceed what was agreed to in negotiations.

The most obvious benefit of peering is that because two parties agree to work with one another, and therefore exchange information about the engineering and performance of their networks, the overall performance of the network is increased, including better availability, the ability to administer service-level agreements (SLAs), and the ability to provide greater security. Major backbone providers are very selective about international peering, where expensive international private-line circuits are used to exchange international routes. Buying transit provides the same benefits as peering, but at a higher price. Exchanging traffic between top-tier providers basically means better performance and involves fewer routers. Again, these types of arrangements are critical to seeing the evolution and growth in IP telephony, VoIP, IPTV, interactive gaming, and the expanding varieties of multimedia applications.

One problem with peering is that it can be limited. Under peering arrangements, ISPs often can have access only to each other's networks. In other words, I'll agree to work with you, but you can work only with me; I don't want you working with anyone else. Exclusivity demands sometimes arise.

IP QoS

QoS is one of the most important issues in networks in general, and particularly so in the Internet and other IP networks. QoS deals with the strict management of traffic such that guarantees can be made and SLAs between customers and service providers can be observed. In the case of packet switching, QoS basically guarantees that a packet will travel successfully between any two points. QoS is also of concern in circuit-switched networks, such as the PSTN, where the demands of real-time voice impose conditions that need to be tightly controlled, including availability, latency, and control of noise. In packet-switched networks, other parameters need to be controlled in order to guarantee QoS, including latency end to end (i.e., from entry to exit point), jitter (i.e., the variation in delay between any two points), loss (i.e., dropped packets), sequencing (i.e., the order of delivery of the packets), and errors (i.e., the result of various impairments that affect transmission).

When the Internet was first conceived of and IP protocols were initially created, QoS was not seen as a critical feature. In fact, the Internet was built on the principle of best effort. When the traffic flows consisted of simple, bursty data, the economies of best effort were an advantage. But today, with the introduction of more and more real-time traffic, such as VoIP or video, and interactive applications, QoS is a requirement that cannot be ignored. In fact, services cannot be offered until QoS can be guaranteed, and best effort is simply not good enough. As a result, much attention is being focused on developing QoS mechanisms and protocols that enable packet-switched networks to properly accommodate the demanding needs of the emerging era of multimedia applications and services.

QoS Mechanisms

There is a growing requirement to meet or exceed expectations of end users and applications communicating over a packet-switched network. To fulfill this requirement, we can take several approaches: We can overprovision networks so that bandwidth exceeds the demand and there are enough routers to always ensure available capacity, we can use traffic engineering to steer away from congestion, and we can use fancy queuing so that where there is contention for bandwidth, demand exceeds supply. This final approach requires QoS mechanisms.

Figure 8.22 shows the four main QoS mechanisms: classification (used for packet identification), conditioning (used for traffic shaping), queue management (used to manage the queue depth), and queue scheduling (used for packet scheduling).

Classification identifies packets for subsequent forwarding treatment. Classification is performed in routers or hosts, and it is combined with other actions. It is based on one or more fields in the packet header, the payload contents, and the input interface. Classification is generally done in hardware at line rate.

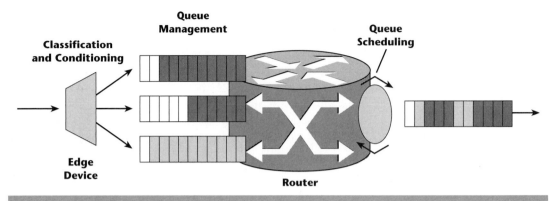

Figure 8.22 IP QoS mechanisms

Conditioning involves policing and shaping. Policing checks conformance to a configured or signal traffic profile. In-profile traffic (i.e., traffic that meets the configured profile) is injected into the network. Out-of-profile traffic may be marked, delayed, or discarded. Shaping removes jitter but at the expense of some latency. Policing and shaping are performed at the network ingress or logical policing points.

Traditional first-in, first-out (FIFO) queuing provides no service differentiation and can lead to network performance problems, such as increased delay, jitter, packet discard, and so on. IP QoS requires routers to support some form of queue scheduling and management to prioritize outbound packets and control queue depth or to minimize congestion. Several techniques are used for queue management and scheduling. The main approach to queue management is a technique called random early detection (RED). RED monitors time-based average queue length and drops arriving packets with increasing probability as the average length increases. No action is taken if the average length is less than the minimum threshold, and all packets are dropped if the average length is greater than the maximum threshold. The queue-scheduling process decides which packet to send out next. It is used to manage bandwidth resources of the outbound interface. The different solutions involve tradeoffs in function and complexity.

Queuing Mechanisms

Although there are no standards for QoS, most router implementations provide some sort of non-FIFO queuing mechanism that is implementation specific. There are four common mechanisms:

- **Fair Queuing (FQ)**—FQ has two main objectives: to provide fair access to bandwidth, resources, and routers and to ensure that no one flow receives more than its fair share. FQ assumes that queues are serviced in a bit-by-bit round-robin fashion (see Figure 8.23). FQ transmits one bit from each queue, but bits from different queues are not interleaved. FQ computes when the packet would have left the router by using bit-by-bit round robin.

- **Weighted Fair Queuing (WFQ)**—The WFQ scheduler orders packets for departure based on their weights. For example, in Figure 8.24, source 1 gets 50%, source 2 gets 33%, and source 3 gets 17% of the bandwidth. WFQ provides flow protection and can be used to bound delay.

- **Weighted Round Robin (WRR)**—WRR assigns a weight to each queue, and it then services each nonempty queue in proportion to its weight, in round-robin fashion (see Figure 8.25). WRR is optimal when using uniform packet sizes, a small number of flows, and long connections.

- **Deficit Round Robin (DRR)**—DRR does not need to know the mean packet size up front. It assigns a quantum to the queue scheduler and initializes a deficit counter to 0. DRR services each nonempty queue if the packet size is

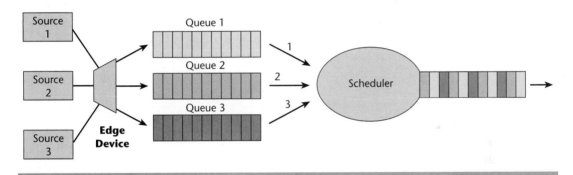

Figure 8.23 IP QoS queue scheduling: Fair Queuing

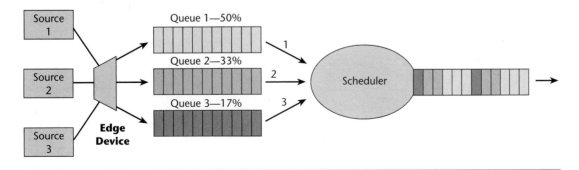

Figure 8.24 IP QoS queue scheduling: Weighted Fair Queuing

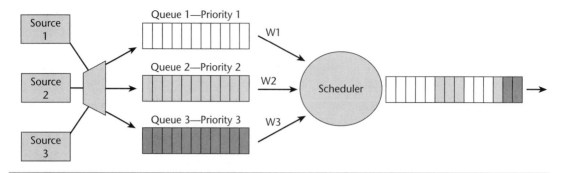

Figure 8.25 IP QoS queue scheduling: Weighted Round Robin

less than or equal to the quantum plus the deficit counter, and then it updates the deficit counter. Otherwise, it adds the quantum to the deficit counter and tries on the next pass. DRR is simple to implement. Like WRR, it is optimal with uniform packet sizes, a small number of flows, and long connections.

Figure 8.26 illustrates how DRR works. This example shows a quantum value of 1,000 bytes and three different queues. In queue 1, a packet of 1,500 bytes is waiting to be transmitted. Queue 2 has a packet of 800 bytes, and queue 3 has a packet of 1,200 bytes. On the first pass, the packet from

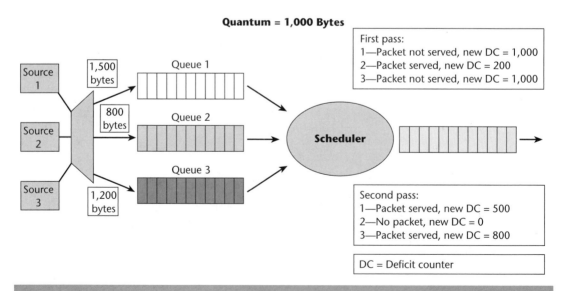

Figure 8.26 IP QoS queue scheduling: Deficit Round Robin

queue 1 is not served because it is 1,500 bytes, and the quantum is set at 1,000 bytes. We therefore create a new deficit counter of 1,000. The packet from queue 2 is served because it is less than the quantum. Because the quantum is 1,000 and the packet length is 800 bytes, the next deficit counter is reset to 200. With queue 3, the packet is not served because it is longer than the quantum. This packet is 1,200 bytes, and the quantum is 1,000, so we reset the deficit counter to 1,000, based on the quantum value.

On the second pass, with queue 1, we reset the deficit counter to 1,000 after the first pass. We add that value to the quantum, which is also 1,000, giving us 2,000 bytes. Now the packet can be served because it is 1,500 bytes, which is less than 2,000 bytes. The packet is served, and the deficit counter is then reset with the remainder, which is 500. In queue 2, we already served the packet, so there's now nothing there, and we reset the deficit counter to 0. With queue 3, on the first pass, we reset the deficit counter to 1,000, so now we add the quantum of 1000, which results in a value of 2,000 bytes. The 1,200-byte packet is now served, and the deficit counter is reset to 800.

The IP QoS Continuum

IP QoS has a continuum that involves a range of cost and complexity (see Figure 8.27). At the bottom of the range is best effort. Basically, this implies fair access to all, FIFO queuing, and no priority. Next on the scale is Differentiated Services (DiffServ), which is a bit more costly and complex. With DiffServ, packets carry a class or priority ID, and the routers use per-class forwarding. At the top of the heap is Integrated Services (IntServ). This is the most costly and most complex level, but it allows per-flow state maintenance, uses RSVP signaling, and provides for guaranteed service

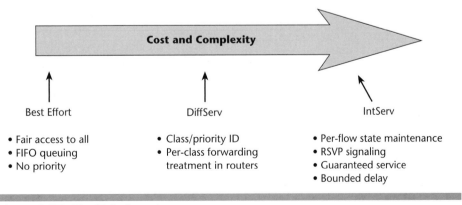

Figure 8.27 The IP QoS continuum

and bounded delay. Next Steps in Signaling (NSIS) addresses the introduction of QoS on an end-to-end basis. The following sections briefly describe the DiffServ and Int-Serv QoS schemes as well as NSIS; Chapter 10 describes the first two in more detail.

DiffServ

DiffServ is a prioritization model with preferential allocation of resources based on traffic classification. Figure 8.28 shows the DiffServ architecture, in which different packets are of different sizes and colors, suggesting that they have different priorities and queuing. DiffServ supports multiple service levels over an IP-based network. It uses a DSCP to select the service—that is, the per-hop behavior—that the packet will receive at each DiffServ-capable node. DSCP is a field in the packets transported over DiffServ networks that classifies the packets according to priority. (The DSCP field was formerly known as the Type of Service field in IPv4 and as the Traffic Class field in IPv6.) DiffServ classifies traffic by marking the IP header at the ingress to the network with flags corresponding to a small number of per-hop behaviors. The per-hop behaviors map to the DSCPs. DiffServ then sorts the packets into queues via the DSCP. The various queues get different treatment in terms of priority, share of bandwidth, and probability of discard.

There are several defined DiffServ per-hop behaviors:

■ **Default**—The Default behavior provides for best-effort service.

■ **Expedited Forwarding**—Expedited Forwarding, specified under RFC 2598, defines low latency, or delay, and controlled jitter service. It is targeted at VoIP and virtual leased lines. Expedited Forwarding is roughly equivalent to priority queuing, with a safety measure to prevent starvation, and no more than 50% of the link can use Expedited Forwarding.

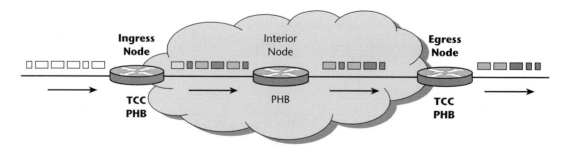

TCC = traffic classification and conditioning (classification, marking, and policing)
PHB = per-hop behavior (queuing and dropping)

Figure 8.28 The DiffServ architecture

■ **Assured Forwarding**—Assured Forwarding is specified under RFC 2597. It supports four relative classes of service, and within each class are three levels of drop precedents. A congested Assured Forwarding node discards packets with a higher drop preference first. Packets with the lowest drop preference must be within the subscribed profile.

■ **Class Selectors**—Class Selectors is backward capable with IP precedence.

IntServ

IntServ, which is specified in RFC 1633, extends the Internet model to support real-time and best-effort services. It provides extensions to the best-effort service model to allow control over end-to-end packet delays, and its key building blocks are resource reservation and admission control. IntServ, a per-flow, resource reservation model, requires Resource Reservation Protocol (RSVP). RSVP allows applications to reserve router bandwidth. Its service provides a bandwidth guarantee and a reliable upper bound to packet delay. RSVP is therefore a resource reservation setup protocol for the Internet. Its major features include the use of soft state in the routers, receiver-controlled reservation requests, flexible control over sharing of reservations and forwarding of subflows, and the use of IP Multicast for data distribution.

Unfortunately, using RSVP on the public Internet is impractical. The resource requirements for running RSVP on a router increase proportionally with the number of separate RSVP reservations, and this results in a big scalability problem. RSVP signaling has evolved into a general-purpose signaling protocol for enterprise-based IP networks, applications, and services. Classic RSVP (described in RFC 2205) is for application-requested edge-to-edge QoS signaling.

A router-based RSVP modification for MPLS traffic engineering, called RSVP Traffic Engineering (RSVP-TE), is specified under RFC 3209. RSVP-TE is in addition to the RSVP protocol for establishing label-switched paths in MPLS networks. (MPLS is covered in Chapter 10.) RSVP-TE supports the instantiation of explicitly routed label-switched paths with or without resource reservations. It also supports smooth rerouting of label-switched paths, preemption, and loop detection. There are RSVP-TE extensions for fast restoration and extensions for Generalized MPLS. (GMPLS is discussed in Chapter 11.)

Another new standard, called Aggregated RSVP, is specified under RFC 3175. Aggregated RSVP messages install an ingress-to-egress fat pipe. Normal RSVP message flow triggers the creation, expansion, or contraction of the ingress-to-egress fat pipe. Normal RSVP messages are forwarded edge to edge and ignored by interior routers inside the aggregation region. Aggregated RSVP retains the edge-to-edge RSVP signaling paradigm but employs DiffServ forwarding and Aggregated RSVP signaling in the core network.

RSVP Proxy is an extension to RSVP message processing currently in draft form at the IETF. In RSVP Proxy, an intermediate router responds, or proxies, a reservation message back to the sender. In this case, RSVP messages do not travel edge to edge as usual. Proxied reservation is generated under policy control. Applications can signal their presence and receive policy-based designation for special network treatment.

NSIS

Current QoS signaling is limited in scope and scale. Classic RSVP operates between hosts and routers but is absent in the greater Internet. RSVP-TE is edge-to-edge for traffic engineering. RSVP does not cross administrative domains, nor does it really traverse different technology regimes such as wireless or support mobility. An IETF working group has therefore been chartered to develop the requirements, architectures, and protocols for expanding and extending QoS signaling across the Internet, and a new architecture called NSIS is emerging.

The design goals of NSIS include applicability across different QoS technologies, such as DiffServ and MPLS, as well as resource availability upon request prior to a reservation request. NSIS is modular in design. It involves the decoupling of the protocol and the information carried within it. It allows reuse of existing QoS provisioning, where appropriate, and it provides independence between signaling and provisioning mechanisms. As shown in Figure 8.29, the NSIS architecture

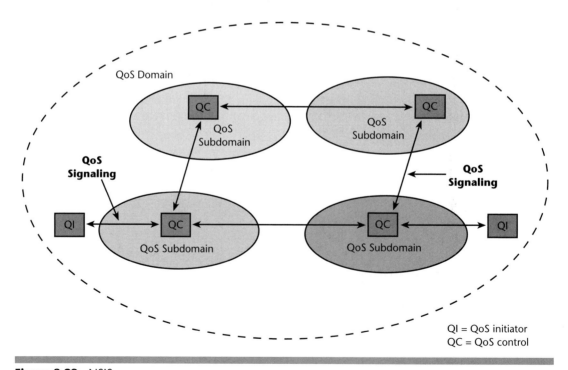

Figure 8.29 NSIS

includes a QoS service class, which specifies QoS requirements of a flow or traffic aggregate. It also includes QoS signaling, which conveys the QoS service class into the network. A QoS initiator triggers QoS signaling. QoS control interprets and acts on QoS signaling messages in the network.

RSVP version 2 (RSVPv2) defines a lighter version of RSVP signaling that addresses the NSIS requirements. It has been designed to coexist with RSVPv1 and have efficient core functionality, with service-specific extensibility. RSVPv2 allows for unicast operation, and it is sender oriented and soft-state based. It has multiple service specifications, and it accommodates raw IP transport.

■ What's Next on the Internet

An interesting way to consider what's next on the Internet, or in ICT in general, is to play a game that Vinton Cerf, one of the heralded fathers of TCP/IP and the Internet, is fond of introducing in his presentations. He calls it the "Fifty Year Game." It goes like this: "Let's go back in time from 2006 to 1956. What mistakes would we make? How would we act if we expected doors to open as we approached or faucets to run automatically and toilets to self-flush? And what would people think of our odd behavior as we walked into doors, expecting them to swing open? Now, go into the future and go back again from 2056 to 2006. What mistakes would we make? Imagine trying to talk to all the appliances and no one is listening. Or waiting for a room to recognize you and adjust to your personal configuration in terms of temperature, lighting, music, ambiance, and so on. And what would we think of their odd behavior?" If you really want to play this game well, when thinking of 2056, remember the things we talked about in understanding the broadband evolution—all the significant and dramatic developments in intelligent wearables, embedded devices, teleimmersion, virtual reality, and so forth—and make use of that in playing this game with your colleagues.

The following sections describe some of the new Internet projects under way, including the Next-Generation Internet (NGI); other Next-Generation internets (NGis), such as the Interplanetary Internet; Internet-enabled devices; RFID applications; Session Initiation Protocol (SIP) telephony; digital objects and libraries; and the Semantic Web.

The Next-Generation Internet

Next-Generation internet (NGi) is a term used by governments, corporations, and educators to describe the future network and the work under way to develop it. This Internet will be so pervasive, reliable, and transparent that we'll all just take it for granted. It will be a seamless part of life—like electricity or plumbing.

Current NGi projects include Internet 2 (www.internet2.edu), Abilene, Hybrid Optical Packet Infrastructure (HOPI; http://networks.internet2.edu/hopi), National LambdaRail (NLR; www.nlr.net), Global Lambda Integrated Facility (GLIF; www.glif.is), Manhattan Landing Exchange Point (MAN LAN; http://networks.internet2.edu/manlan), GÉANT2 (GN2; www.geant2.net), and Trans-Eurasia Information Network (TEIN2; www.tein2.net). The Advanced Research and Education Network Atlas (ARENA; http://arena.internet2.edu) project is a compendium of information about advanced research and education networks around the world. The Atlas database includes links to various types of network maps; administrative, technical, and operational contacts for networks; and information about connections between networks. It provides several tools with which to explore this information and the relationships between networks.

The Interplanetary Internet

The vision of NGis does not stop with our planet. One very interesting project involves the Interplanetary Internet (IPN), which is being designed as a network that connects a series of internets. These internets would be located on planets and moons or aboard spacecraft. The IPN will need to embody an inherent design that allows for long transmission times, bandwidth constraints, blockage, lost data, and constantly moving sources. It will form a backbone that connects a series of hubs on or around planets, space vehicles, and at other points in space. These hubs will provide high-capacity, high-availability Internet traffic over distances that could stretch up to hundreds of millions of miles.

IPN researchers have already assigned Internet addresses to all the planets, satellites, and spacecraft in our solar system. Because of the large speed-of-light delays involved with interplanetary distances, the IPN needs a new set of protocols and technologies that are tolerant of large delays. The key components of the IPN, as presently conceived, include planetary internets linked to one another by internet gateways located at various locations across the solar system, an Interplanetary Channel Protocol, functional layers of the protocol, and an interplanetary network and information systems directorate.

The standards being adopted as a basis for the IPN are the result of work done by both the IETF and the Consultative Committee for Space Data Systems (CCSDS; www.ccsds.org). The protocols that underlie the IPN will need to share many of the capabilities that the earth's Internet has required (which are embodied in TCP/IP). The IPN will work somewhat like e-mail, where information can be stored and forwarded to any hub on the system. This delay-tolerant network will provide an always-on connection between planets, spacecraft, and the terrestrial Internet. The IPN's store-and-forward approach will help minimize problems that arise due to the vast distances involved, such as high error rates and latency rates that are minutes or even hours long (versus the fractions of a second we experience on the earth-based Internet).

In early 2004, a pioneering demonstration of communications between the U.S. National Aeronautics and Space Administration (NASA; www.nasa.gov) Mars Exploration Rover *Spirit* and the European Space Agency (ESA; www.esa.int) *Mars Express* orbiter succeeded. On February 6, 2004, while *Mars Express* was flying over the area *Spirit* was examining, the orbiter transferred commands from earth to the rover and relayed data from the robotic explorer back to earth. This was the first time we had had an in-orbit communication between ESA and NASA spacecraft, and it was also the first working international communications network around another planet, both of which are significant achievements.

As of 2005, NASA had cancelled plans to launch the Mars Telecommunications Orbiter in September 2009; that orbiter had had the goal of supporting future missions to Mars and would have functioned as a possible first definitive Internet hub around another planetary body. Still, while earth-bound Internet and mobile phone users won't be surfing the IPN any time in the near future, the research that goes into the IPN is very likely to spark exciting innovations in our terrestrial networks. The InterPlaNetary Internet Project Web site at www.ipnsig.org provides ongoing information about this exciting project.

Internet-Enabled Devices

One trend affecting the future of the Internet is the growth of Internet-enabled devices. As discussed in this book's introduction, we're looking toward programmable devices, mobiles, palm devices, Web TVs, videogames, picture frames, electronic teachers, and even smart surfboards. More and more home appliances are smart, including washing machines, refrigerators, and bathroom scales. Smart vehicles are increasingly being equipped with GPS receivers, and geographical databases will become more valuable as a result. An extension of Internet-enabled devices is Internet-enabled clothing. All these products will require sophisticated authentication and cryptography mechanisms.

RFID Applications

Another technology affecting what's next on the Internet is the increasing availability and use of radio frequency identification (RFID). A growing list of RFID applications can be found in the transportation industry, consumer products, drug and food IDs and shelf life indicators, patient identification, smart houses, and intelligent wearables. RFID is discussed in detail in Chapter 15.

SIP Telephony

The concepts behind SIP promise to be disruptive, and SIP represents something much more dramatic than VoIP. Whereas VoIP basically addresses only telephony, SIP opens the door to all sorts of capabilities that are not possible in the Time Division Multiplexing world, such as presence management across both voice and instant messaging, Secure SIP–based instant messaging behind the corporate firewall, instant messaging archiving, click-to-talk voice functionality, speech-to-text functionality, and specialty modes for road warriors and telecommuters. Chapter 9 discusses SIP in detail.

Digital Objects and Libraries

Digital objects and libraries will grow in importance. Industry experts are painting a future of structured information in which data is surrounded by a layer of software, where content is encapsulated in procedures, with active object interfaces that say, "Show me your language or rendering, show me your media rendering, transcribe yourself to my media." Cataloguing and indexing of digital objects will similarly gain importance.

A whole new world of information management is arising from the growing codification of objects alone. We can also expect to see the rise of digital object identifiers, uninterpreted strings as handles, the binding of objects and controls and indexed repositories, digital signatures for authenticity and integrity protection, codification of copyright control terms and conditions, and long-term storage that can last hundreds of years.

We have many storage and media challenges to overcome. For example, memory sticks break. We seem to all be swimming in a vast sea of CDs. How long will today's digital media last? How will we approach the concept of media rewriting, going from videotape to CD to DVD? And how do we handle exabyte and attabyte archives? We're looking toward molecular memories and biological memories, as discussed in the introduction.

There are more questions to answer as well: How do we deal with indexing? How do we handle read/write rates? The solutions will no doubt involve the indexing of unstructured data; the standardization of information representation; the creation of new Web crawlers and search engines; the association of media with text; the indexing of images, video, audio, music, and so on; and the need for powerful new tools for finding otherwise unstructured information, such as blogs.

The Semantic Web

There is much talk about the next generation of the Web—a concept referred to as the *Semantic Web* (www.semanticweb.org). This is Sir Tim Berners-Lee's latest project, and it is focused on creating a universal medium for information exchange using refined indexing and searching—in other words, providing meaning (semantics) to the content of documents in a manner that machines can understand. The Semantic Web looks at enhanced processing of structure information where you can search by business documents versus scientific data, or for an author versus an entertainer. It also supports the ability for command and control of scientific instruments and the labeling of data from those instruments. This is very important to data collection and archiving of data coming from the exploding population of sensors. The Semantic Web greatly expands the utility of the World Wide Web, and it does so by using standards, markup languages, and related processing tools.

Part III

The New Generation of Networks

Chapter 9

IP Services

This chapter discusses the evolution from circuit-switched to Internet Protocol (IP)–based packet-switched infrastructures to support the variety of IP services in use today, including IP telephony (IPT), IP television (IPTV), and virtual private networks (VPNs). IPT involves the transmission of voice, fax, and related services over IP-based packet-switched networks. IPTV systems deliver digital television service to a subscriber, using IP over a broadband connection. VPNs are a critical requirement for businesses because they distribute mission-critical and sensitive traffic to remote locations; they offer networking security and performance comparable with that available at the office.

■ The Evolution to IP Services

Service providers are in the midst of a gradual evolution from circuit-switched to IP-based packet-switched infrastructures. IP is attractive for two main reasons: cost savings and revenue. Carriers expect operational and infrastructure savings from deploying new IP-based services because they believe that implementing applications on IP networks will be much less expensive than running them on circuit-switched networks. In addition, every carrier is looking for new ways to enhance its service suites, which are rapidly becoming commodities.

The evolution to IP-based infrastructures means more shared networks. Because IP emphasizes logical over physical connections, IP makes it easier for multiple carriers to coexist on a single network. This encourages cooperative sharing of interconnected networks, structured as anything from sales of wholesale circuits to real-time capacity exchanges. It also means increased competition because there are reduced barriers to entry; new companies can enter the market without the huge fixed costs associated with traditional network models.

Most of the evolution so far has taken place in the transport and access parts of the network and in the development of IP infrastructure elements, such as gateways, softswitches, and the IP Multimedia Subsystem (which is discussed in Chapter 10, "Next-Generation Networks"). The market for next-generation IP application services is beginning to take shape, and IP-based application servers have been developed to deliver actual revenue-generating services for carriers.

The problem is that IP has been positioned as a magical potion that will cure everything, and the industry has suffered from too much hype and wishful thinking. Equipment and service providers have been guilty of promoting such thinking, claiming that their products can enable multiple new services without clearly identifying just what those new services will be. While there are indeed very good reasons to transition to IP, it is important to be realistic and pragmatic about them. The migration to IP is not without risk. In terms of the IP application services market, two key questions need to be answered: Will the quality of the real-time services over IP be good enough in the next few years to drive carriers and customers to switch? To what extent will enterprises take advantage of their existing IP infrastructure and data communications expertise to implement their own services, thus avoiding additional service provider charges?

Traditional Internet applications, such as e-mail, Telnet, FTP, and the World Wide Web, are referred to as *elastic applications* because they are tolerant of network delays and packet losses. Unlike those applications, advanced real-time applications are highly sensitive to timely data delivery. Quality of service (QoS) is the most important obstacle for the Internet and IP networks to overcome, especially in light of the growing use of voice and video. As QoS emerges within the Internet, the ability to differentiate services will result in differentiated pricing. QoS capabilities will allow revenue-generating service levels to be implemented and service-level agreements (SLAs) to be negotiated.

The ability to control and manage a network effectively will allow the creation of value-added services and packages. Providing value-added IP services implies increased attention to tools and equipment that help service providers succeed. These include software that gives service providers greater network control and visibility; intrusion prevention systems that support always-on stateful inspection (i.e., a form of stateful inspection that provides cumulative data against which subsequent communication attempts can be evaluated and acted on in real-time) and deep packet analysis capabilities; software that can deliver flexible bandwidth; tools that offer granular analysis of bandwidth consumption by customers; and tools that enable creative solutions that reduce costs, such as the robots from CityNet Telecommunications (www.citynettelecom.com) that string fiber through sewers at a fraction of the cost of digging up city streets to lay the fiber.

Value-added IP services allow carriers greater differentiation from their competitors. Evolving next-generation IP services include IP virtual private networks (VPNs), IP telephony (IPT) and Voice over IP (VoIP), IP centrex and IP call centers, application hosting, mobility management/follow-me services, unified messaging, instant messaging (IM), presence management, Video over IP, IP television (IPTV), and different types of conferencing, including audioconferencing, videoconferencing, and Web/data conferencing. As carriers consolidate and wireless broadband networks are deployed, a major challenge will be developing viable business models to market, bill, provision, and provide excellent customer care for all these services.

Many incumbent carriers are choosing to initially implement IP-based services on an overlay network. Carriers that take this approach do not have to replace circuit-switched network elements, which usually have minimal ongoing operational expenses. In an overlay network scenario, the packet-switched network is isolated from the circuit-switched network, and the two are connected via a gateway.

▤ IPT

IPT has been drawing a lot of attention in the past couple years, and terminology in this area is confusing, with VoIP being the most common expression, even though there are in fact technical differences between IPT (the umbrella term), VoIP (IPT over private IP networks), and Internet telephony (voice over the Internet). The following sections cover the types of applications anticipated for IPT as well as what network elements are required in order to make IPT work and provide similar capabilities to what we are used to from the PSTN.

Although IPT has a very important place, it is not yet taking over the traditional circuit-switched approach to accommodating voice telephony. The truly exciting future of IPT, or VoIP, lies in advanced and interesting new applications, an environment where voice is but one of the information streams comprising a rich media application. While such applications are being developed, there are other compelling reasons to adopt IPT, including the reduction of toll and international calling charges, which makes a strong argument for many businesses and consumers. The network-specific cost for VoIP on dedicated networks is quite a bit lower than the cost of calls on circuit-switched networks, not to mention the benefit an average residential user, with family members and friends scattered around the globe, can gain by avoiding the normally sky-high charges associated with international calling. Many analysts expect that sales of VoIP equipment will grow rapidly in the coming months and years.

IPT Versus *Internet Telephony* Versus *VoIP*

People use several IP-related terms interchangeably. However, according to the International Telecommunication Union (ITU; www.itu.int), there are distinctions between the following terms:

- **IPT**—The transmission of voice, fax, and related services over packet-switched IP-based networks. Internet telephony and VoIP are specific subsets of IPT.
- **Internet telephony**—Telephony in which the principal transmission network is the public Internet. Internet telephony is commonly referred to as Voice over the Net, Internet phone, and net telephony, with appropriate modifications to refer to fax as well, such as Internet fax.
- **VoIP**—IPT in which the principal transmission network or networks are private, managed IP-based networks.

This chapter generally uses the encompassing term *IPT*.

With leading telecommunications carriers and cable companies unveiling major VoIP initiatives, consumers and businesses will be hearing a great deal more about VoIP in the near future. Despite the long road ahead, consumer and business migration to VoIP is on the verge of moving out of the early adoption phase and into the mainstream, and the hope is that widespread (although not ubiquitous) VoIP use will finally take off by 2007. It appears that some 20% of businesses have already adopted VoIP technology. Interestingly, companies are citing benefits other than reduced costs as the reasons for switching to VoIP. The biggest reasons mentioned have to do with strategic investments, integration with existing IP VPNs, employee mobility, and increased productivity. Reduced costs alone are not likely to propel IPT or VoIP to the pedestal envisioned by its proponents.

The IPT Evolution

We know that IPT is here for several reasons. First, we can do it effectively, and greater processing power (following Moore's Law) applied to signal processing along with lower costs makes VoIP attractive. Second, as discussed later in this chapter, standards for VoIP have made progress. Third, IP has become pervasive: It is easier now for both businesses and consumers to enter the IPT realm. Finally, the marketplace is now home to many commercial entries.

Moore's Law

Moore's Law refers to a prediction made in 1965 by Gordon Moore, cofounder of Intel. Moore said that the number of transistors occupying a square inch of integrated circuit material had doubled each year since the invention of the integrated circuit, and he predicted that this multiplication of circuitry would continue. For the most part, the prediction held true until the late 1970s, when the time span of a year increased to about 18 months. Today Moore's Law is commonly used as an expression to state that the power of microprocessor technology doubles and its cost of production halves every 18 months.

Many variations of phones, gateways, IP PBXs, and open-source PBXs are now available to both consumers and enterprises. Several key milestones have been reached. There has been a surge of Session Initiation Protocol (SIP) support and offerings for SIP-based enterprise communications, and SIP products are now widely available. Avaya (www.avaya.com), Lucent (www.lucent.com), and NEC (www.nec.com) have announced SIP enterprise product lines. Microsoft (www.microsoft.com), IBM (www.ibm.com), Novell (www.novell.com), and Sun Microsystems (www.sun.com) are all moving to SIP for their enterprise collaboration tools. Cisco (www.cisco.com) has announced the migration of its proprietary call manager technology to SIP. (SIP is discussed in detail later in this chapter.)

Most enterprises today are not using or considering IPT services, but many are using or considering migrating to Multiprotocol Label Switching (MPLS), in part because combining voice, video, and data can finally justify the cost of MPLS. Most organizations are currently using predominantly ATM or Frame Relay, with some IP VPNs here and there. The cost differential between Frame Relay or ATM and MPLS is less than 10%. But if voice and video are added, it can reach 25% and justify the move to both MPLS and IPT.

However, many unresolved issues challenge widespread deployment of IPT. For example, the connection to emergency service access systems is problematic. Callers may not know that the IPT phone they are using is not connected to emergency services, creating potentially fatal problems. Surveillance is another public safety issue. Data encryption schemes are making it more difficult for law enforcement agencies to conduct surveillance because they may not be able to listen to IPT calls in the manner that has become standard in the circuit-switched world. For example, if police officers have to decrypt an IPT call instead of listening in real-time, they may have to wait three weeks after the call took place in order to use it as a basis for arrest.

IPT is being deployed today on a trial basis. The main application is currently LAN-to-LAN or cross-enterprise solutions, typically using matched gateways linked by private lines. The cost justifications are roughly split between toll bypass or WAN savings and cost reductions in moves, adds, and changes. Justifying the move to IPT therefore is largely centered initially around cost justification. Besides the benefit of toll bypass, IPT offers a reduction in the cost associated with staff; increased efficiencies due to using the existing IP data networks to also carry voice; less expensive moves, adds, and changes; and applications benefits, such as the ability to combine the Web and computer telephony integration applications and to provide a universal desktop device.

Regulatory Issues Surrounding IPT

IPT services are not seeing large growth yet, but they are definitely affecting decisions about WAN architectures. Ultimately, whether and how quickly we move to IPT is not just a question of technical solutions; the regulatory environment may determine whether these services flourish in the long run.

In an interview he did with the *San Jose Mercury News* on December 31, 2003, then-Chairman of the U.S. Federal Communications Commission (FCC; www.fcc.gov) Michael Powell said, "To be a phone company you don't have to weave tightly the voice service into the infrastructure. You can ride it on top of the infrastructure. So if you're a Vonage, you own no infrastructure, you own no trucks, you roll to no one's house. They turn voice into an application and shoot it across one of these platforms and suddenly you're in business. And that's why if you're the music industry you're scared. And if you're the television studio, movie industry, you're scared. And if you're an incumbent infrastructure carrier, you'd better be scared because this application separation is the most important paradigm shift in the history of communications and will change things forever. I have no problem if a big and venerable company no longer exists tomorrow, as long as that value is transferred somewhere else in the economy." These are interesting words to contemplate as we try to predict what the regulatory approach toward IP communications will be, and the approach will no doubt vary around the world.

The area of international regulation has seen increasing activity, mostly from the United Nations (UN) and the ITU (which has regulated spectrum and telephony for decades and was placed under the auspices of the UN). For some time, the ITU has been considering what role it should take in relationship to the Internet, a medium that grew up completely independent of the ITU and where most activists see no positive role for the ITU. Another UN/ITU activity, the World Summit on the Information Society, has established a working group on Internet governance to look into these issues. A new set of European Union (EU) directives will significantly affect the licensing requirements of IPT in Europe. The European Commission (EC) is the driving force for determining whether IPT should be treated and licensed as conventional telephony. Member states are allowed some discretion as to the implementation of the EC's directives, but the EC does not issue telephony licenses; that is left to the member states. However, many issues still require resolution, including wire tapping, interconnection and regulatory fees, universal service contributions, and access to a system that allocates telephone numbers and a directory system.

European legislators and regulators have not finished the debate on how to treat IPT and are seeking suggestions from the industry on new developments and technical solutions. For instance, regarding wire tapping, Europeans are closely observing any new developments in the United States. In particular, at the FCC, VoIP is by default treated as an information service and currently does not contribute to the Universal Service Fund.

The next generation of IPT will offer strategic value to the enterprise by combining presence-aware communications applications with extended converged networks. This is possible thanks to two technological advances: first, the ability of extended converged IP networks to unify voice, data, wireline, and wireless domains, supporting applications that unify the end users' communications experience, and second, the continued growth and processing power of bandwidth and storage. As bandwidth and storage become less expensive and more abundant, there will be better and more choices for software services and content.

The Next Generation of IPT

The IPT evolution has so far been through three phases:

- **Point-to-point communications over IP networks**—These communications are largely based on the use of ITU H.323 standards, a philosophy of having intelligence everywhere.

- **Master/slave architectures**—These architectures rely on standards such as Megaco and Media Gateway Control Protocol (MGCP). This approach is an effective way to implement rich feature sets in dumb endpoints.

- **The integration of communications media with the Internet**—This strategy involves intelligent endpoints and a dumb network. The relevant standards include SIP and SIP for Instant Messaging and Presence Leveraging Extensions (SIMPLE).

Next-generation IPT applications are most distinguished by two specific applications: (1) synchronous communications that streamline and enrich business processes and (2) presence awareness that allows one to see who is available for collaboration and how to reach them. Key IPT productivity benefits for the field force include increased efficiencies among service employees, shortened reaction times, improved service quality, and an increase in the number of customer contacts. For the sales force, the benefits of IPT include a reduction in the number of client appointments needed, lower service costs, shortened proposal and negotiation processes, and improved transparency of the sales processes. For the supply chain, the key productivity benefits include reduction of inventory levels, improved data quality, fewer disruptions in downstream processes due to logistical errors, and lower total logistical costs.

The IPT Network

As shown in Figure 9.1, the IPT network taxonomy has three major layers:

- **Media layer**—In this layer, on the *bearer platform*, media is processed, including the media transport, QoS, and items such as tones and announcements. Two bearer platforms communicate with one another over media transport, and this is where TDM, Frame Relay, ATM, and MPLS apply.

- **Signaling layer**—Signal processing, signaling conversion, resource management, and bearer control occur on this layer, on the *signaling platform*. Signaling platforms talk with one another by using a signaling technique. This is where H.323, SIP, and other call control protocols apply.

- **Application layer**—This layer, referred to as the *application platform*, is home to call intelligence, and it is where service creation and execution as well as provisioning management occur. Application platforms talk to one another with application-specific interapplication protocols.

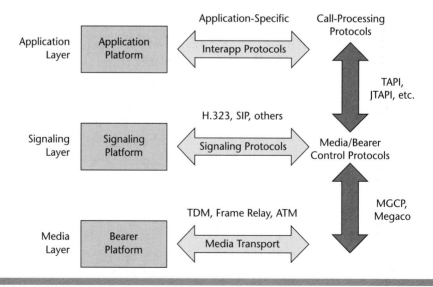

Figure 9.1 The IPT network taxonomy

Between the bearer and signaling platforms are media/bearer control protocols. This is the realm of MGCP and Megaco. Between the signaling and application layers are call-processing protocols such as Telephony Applications Programming Interface (TAPI) and Java TAPI (JTAPI).

In terms of the transport infrastructure, a number of packet network alternatives can be used, and the full range of packet-switching techniques—including IP, Frame Relay, ATM, MPLS, and GMPLS, as well as Ethernet, Voice over Wireless LAN (VoWLAN), Voice over DSL (VoDSL), and Voice over Cable—can act as the transport infrastructure.

Until recently, the IPT business model has been much like the traditional circuit-switched world, with each vendor supplying its own platform, handset, gateway, call-processing, and end-user feature sets. Convergence for the early IPT player involved converging voice onto the data network and selling telephony to the IT buyer. To this day, one of the greatest challenges is for traditional voice vendors to learn to sell what the data people buy.

Many in the industry view long-distance as the first major market disruption in the transition from TDM to IP and handsets as the second. Initially, IPT had the most disruptive effect on carriers' transmission networks. This promoted a competitive triangle between the handset, the platform, and the network. Industry analysts predict that the next few years will see battle between these three industries as each attempts to commoditize the other two.

The IPT Network Architecture

The first requirement for an IPT network is an IP local exchange or media gateway (also referred to as a VoIP gateway). Gateways are carrier-class products that reside in the service provider network. They provide PBX-like telephony service to multiple business and telecommuting customers as well as basic telephony services for consumers. Another requirement is the softswitch (also called a call server or call agent) for call-processing functions and administrative software. End-user services are delivered by IP phones and other devices. Finally, IP-based voice enterprise systems include IP PBXs, open-source PBXs, and service provider solutions. Figure 9.2 shows an example of the IPT network architecture, and the following sections describe the components.

Media Gateways   Gateways provide seamless interoperability between circuit-switching and packet-switching network domains. They interconnect with the Signaling System 7 (SS7) network and handle IP services. They support a variety of telephony signaling protocols, such as H.323, Megaco (H.248) and MGCP, and SIP. They support Class 4 (i.e., toll) switches and Class 5 switches (as in local exchange services). They operate in the classic public network environment, where call control is

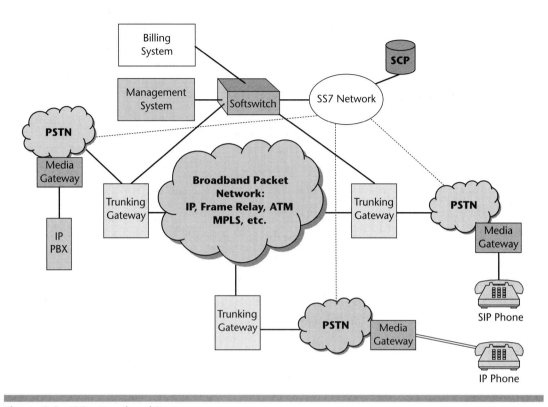

Figure 9.2 IPT network architecture

separate from media flow. They support a variety of traffic, data, voice, fax, multimedia, and so on over a data backbone.

Softswitches In enhanced applications such as network conferencing, network interactive voice response, fax serving, network voicemail, and directory services, a softswitch controls the voice or data traffic path by signaling between the media gateways that transport the traffic. The gateway provides the connection between an IP or another packet-based network (such as ATM or MPLS) and the traditional circuit-switched network, acting as a multiprotocol cross-connect. The softswitch ensures that a call's or connection's underlying signaling information gets communicated between gateways. The signaling information may include automatic number identifiers, billing data, or other call triggers.

Softswitches must communicate with packet switches, VoIP gateways, media gateways, and SS7 networks by using standardized protocols. A number of different technical specifications, protocols, and standards are involved in delivering these services and the desired end functions. As discussed in more detail later in this chapter, they include H.323, Megaco and MGCP, SIP, Real-Time Transport Protocol (RTP), Real-Time Transport Control Protocol (RTCP), RTCP Reporting Extension (RTCP XR), and Secure Real-Time Transport Protocol (SRTP).

IP Devices   A number of IP devices are available:

- **Legacy support**—Simple terminal adapters are available for standard telephones.
- **IP hard phones**—These are IP phones that look and work just like a traditional multiline business display phone. They plug in to an Ethernet RJ-45 jack. Typically, they're proprietary and part of a vendor's platform. Their original prices were similar to PBX phones, around US$300 and up, but are now down to less than US$100. Emerging IP phone-on-a-chip technologies promise dramatically lower prices in the near future.
- **IP soft phones**—IP soft phones are software that runs on a user's PC and graphically resembles a phone. The key advantage of this approach is its low price. IP soft phones are gaining acceptance because applications such as presence management and IM are much better on a PC than on other devices. The disadvantages lie in the fact that an IP soft phone relies on the PC sound card, which can create problems with the volume level when switching between the soft phone and other applications that use the PC sound card. However, products such as the Clarisys USB handset (www.clarisys.com) overcome these problems. This device replaces the headset, rings audibly, includes a speakerphone, and, as a USB device, avoids the PC sound card.
- **IP Web phones**—These devices combine a complete analog phone device and a diskless processor, providing an e-mail browser and a variety of organizer applications such as a call list and directory manager, a notepad, and a calendar.
- **SIP phones**—SIP has the potential to realize the ultimate IPT dream: low cost, feature-rich headsets from third-party phone vendors. SIP for VoIP phones is mature and solid, with at least six models passing the test. Major platform vendors continue to rely on propriety protocols for both their platforms and their handset features. This suggests that despite talk of support for SIP, complete openness and interoperability have yet to be achieved. However, vendors can test the interoperability of their SIP implementations with other vendors three times per year at the SIP Forum SIP IT events (www.sipforum.org).
- **Mobile IP devices**—This category includes 3G handsets, Wi-Fi SIP phones, PDAs equipped to handle VoIP, and game platforms.

In addition, the emerging generation of intelligent wearables, automobiles, smart appliances, smart rooms, and ultimately implants will all add to the expanding universe of IP devices.

IP-Based Voice Enterprise Systems   There are three main approaches to IP-based voice enterprise systems: IP PBXs, open-source PBXs, and service provider solutions, which include IP centrex, hosted PBX, and virtual PBX services. IP PBX and IP centrex offer network management advantages over legacy PBX solutions.

IP PBXs   What can an IP PBX environment do that a traditional PBX can't? IP PBXs boast dozens of new applications, ushering in a new era of human communications, productivity, and mobility. These enhanced and advanced applications are a very hot area, representing the potential for incredible revenue. Significant progress has been made in several key applications areas: unified messaging, which is defined today as the merger of voicemail, e-mail, and fax; conferencing applications; collaboration applications; presence awareness; multimedia packages; mobility features; and extensible SIP support.

The most notable trends include the fact that video is coming to the desktop. Point-to-point or multiparty video is being offered by the majority of leading IP PBX vendors, and the cost per desktop is now generally under US$200. Document collaboration now allows document sharing to be more than a one-way display of PowerPoint slides. Impressive new capabilities from leading vendors include real-time coediting and collaborative working on the same document. In addition, exciting new mobility capabilities are being developed, ranging from a simple SMS gateway that lets local IM users send short messages directly to coworkers' mobile phones and pagers to sophisticated call control features with which remote and traveling workers can easily place calls and set up complex conferences.

Not every product will contain each and every one of the key collaboration and conferencing features, but the following is a comprehensive list of the types of features that are available: soft phone support; the use of presence, be it dynamic or static; mobility features; conferencing, either scheduled or ad hoc; search capabilities; contacts and database access and integration; video (either point-to-point or multipoint); call control of external devices as well as call control filters that allow you to find me and follow me; recent call history; the ability to sort or quick-dial; IM, with chat or multiparty IM; document viewing and presentation; document collaboration and coediting; and whiteboarding and Web cobrowsing. As this list shows, a significant number of productivity-enhancing features are becoming available and adding a new dimension of value to IP PBX functionality.

The key unified messaging features include redundant voicemail servers; text-to-speech readout of e-mail (in multiple languages); automatic speech recognition; an inbox that shows the caller by automatic number identification and/or name;

voicemail and e-mail that indicate the message duration; the ability to reply to and forward voicemail and e-mail; the ability to add other attachments; the ability to send voicemail and e-mail via distribution lists; telephone user interface–based retrieval of voicemail or e-mail; callout of system voicemail delivery; voicemail notification options; scheduled delivery of voicemails; the ability to dial back from the inbox interfaces; and mobility features.

Early marketing efforts for IPT systems focused on a variety of cost-saving and productivity benefits, with little emphasis on the advantages of a more flexible system design. However, it is becoming evident that these two benefits are best realized by taking advantage of a third aspect of IP PBXs: their inherent ability to provide a more modular and survivable configuration compared with traditional circuit-switched TDM PBXs. Customers with multiple premises can configure an IP PBX to operate seamlessly across two or more locations at a lower cost and with greater performance capabilities than a network of standalone systems would offer.

One of the major factors in the accelerated migration to the new IP-based platforms is their ability to replace multiple standalone systems, such as key telephone systems, hybrids, or standard PBXs, with a single IP PBX system that uses survivable remote equipment to create a dispersed architecture. The ability to leverage an existing data network infrastructure for both call control signaling and voice communications transmission is a relatively recent enhancement to IPT. However, because IPT architectures are based on LAN/WAN connections, the enterprise must ensure that backup systems are in place in the event of a loss of LAN/WAN connectivity.

Several IPT design options are available to customers who favor a single-system approach to serve multiple premises. These options range from the simplicity of remote, standalone IP telephones to standalone servers coupled with fully provisioned distributed port carrier cabinets that function as media gateways between traditional station trunk connections and the LAN/WAN. The customer money saved using a distributed or dispersed IPT system solution for multiple-premises communications requirements can be substantial, and a single-system design can also provide significantly enhanced performance and operating benefits. Using an IP PBX system design that supports multiple locations allows advanced features such as station user roaming and automatic call distribution to be accessed and implemented by system subscribers, regardless of their physical location. This contributes to the enhanced performance potential of the single distributed system solution with local survivability options.

Open-Source PBXs   The theory behind open source is that too many cooks actually improve the broth. Widespread peer review finds and fixes bugs faster than the efforts of a smaller, albeit dedicated, project team. The result is often more robust software, lower support costs, and more rapid innovation. Of course, this challenges the established IP PBX pricing model while facilitating standards-based cooperation. However, customer concerns about product schedules and quality detract from trust in the open-source model.

Service Provider VoIP Solutions   The three major approaches to service provider VoIP solutions are IP centrex, hosted PBX, and virtual PBX services, such as provider-managed call servers, application servers, and media gateways.

The main driver of service provider VoIP solutions is reducing the enterprise administration and reducing capital expenditures. Voice quality is often comparable to that in the PSTN. But the greatest benefit is the cost-efficient bundling of voice, Internet access, and enhanced features, including an auto-attendant, a Web-based dashboard for each user and administrator, integrated messaging (e.g., voice-mail as e-mail file attachments), redirection to other phones, and simultaneous ringing of up to 10 phones.

Standards for IP Voice

Before we talk about the standards for IP voice, we need to discuss the characteristics of voice traffic. First of all, voice traffic is an isochronous traffic flow, meaning it involves real-time communications that are delay sensitive as well as loss sensitive. Voice has a low bandwidth requirement, but as a tradeoff, it requires very high QoS.

Digital Voice Technologies

A number of digital voice technologies are enabling IP voice as we know it today. The primary component is the codec (coder-decoder), which is used to digitize the voice stream. Two broad categories of codecs are used:

- **Waveform coders**—Waveform coders directly encode speech in an efficient way by exploiting temporal and/or spectral characteristics. There are several categories of waveform coders. The first is time domain, or predictive, coders, and these include the well-known standards G.711, known as Pulse Code Modulation (PCM; μ-Law in the North American and Japanese standards, using 56Kbps, and A-Law for those following the ITU standards, at 64Kbps), and G.726, known as Adaptive Differential PCM (ADPCM), which encodes voice at a reduced rate of 32Kbps, 24Kbps, or 16Kbps. Two other types of waveform coders are G.722 subband coders and transform coders, which are used to convert between different digitizing techniques.

- **Source coders, or vocoders**—Vocoders estimate and efficiently encode a parametric representation of speech. The standards under this category include G.728, which is also known as Low-Delay Code-Excited Linear

Prediction (Low-Delay CELP) and supports digital voice at 16Kbps; G.729, known as Conjugate Structure Algebraic CELP, which reduces voice down to 8Kbps; and G.723.1, known as Multipulse Maximum Likelihood Quantization, which carries voice at 6.4Kbps.

Another element of digital voice technologies is echo cancellers, which are used to eliminate echoes. The voice echo path is like an electrical circuit: If a break or a cancellation is made anywhere in the circuit, an echo canceller can eliminate the echo. The easiest place to make the break is with a canceller looking into the local analog/digital telephony network. The echo canceller at the local device cancels local echoes from the hybrid reflection, the echo canceller at the other end of the call eliminates the echoes you hear, and vice versa.

The last part of digital voice technologies is noise generation. As it turns out, silence is not always golden. When speech stops, we generate comfort noise to help assure people that the "circuit" is still live, that the call hasn't dropped. The simple techniques involve playing white or pink noise or replaying the last receiver packet over and over. More sophisticated techniques include options in which the transmitter measures the local noise environment. The transmitter then sends a special comfort noise packet as the last packet before silence. The receiver generates noise based on the comfort noise packet. One of the major issues in carrying voice in a packet form, be it IP, Frame Relay, ATM, or MPLS, is delay, which is discussed in the following section.

Delay, Jitter Buffers, and Error Concealment

Table 9.1 shows some of the myriad sources of delay associated with VoIP. The two columns at the right are based on different codec standards. As you can see, the device sample capture introduces a bit of delay, followed by encoding delay, packetizing and framing delay, queuing delay, access uplink and downlink as well as transmission over the backbone, and various jitters that might be associated with the transmission, the decoding process, and ultimately, the playout process. The budget that results is fairly high. In G.711 at 64Kbps, the total delay is 94.6 milliseconds, while with G.729 at 8Kbps, the total delay is 124.1 milliseconds. That's very large, especially when you consider the recommended standards for maximum delay. The ITU-T, for purposes of voice, recommends a maximum delay of 100 milliseconds end to end, with a preference, of course, for much less.

Delay is very important in real-time communications. For instance, for video, the ITU-T recommendation is 80 milliseconds maximum end-to-end delay. And when we get into some of the interactive applications such as teleimmersion or videogames, the tolerance for delay is only 30 to 50 milliseconds maximum end to end. There is a lot to consider in adequately addressing the QoS for voice from the standpoint of delay, both end to end and jitter.

Table 9.1　Standards for IP Voice Delay

Source of Delay	G.711/64Kbps Budget (in ms)	G.729/8Kbps Budget (in ms)
Device sample capture	0.1	0.1
Encode delay (algorithmic delay + processing delay)	2.5	17.5
Packetization/framing	10.0	20.0
Move to output queue/queuing delay	0.5	0.5
Access (up) link transmission	30.0	30.0
Backbone network transmission	5.0	5.0
Access (down) link transmission	10.0	10.0
Input queue to application	0.5	0.5
Jitter buffer	35.0	35.0
Decode processing delay	0.5	5.0
Device playout delay	0.5	0.5
Total	94.6	124.1

As mentioned earlier in this chapter, speech is inherently isochronous. It occurs in real-time, requires a fixed amount of bandwidth, and is not very tolerant of delays or losses. Transmitters emit packets at fixed intervals, but packet networks have queues. As a result, the receivers see interarrival jitter. What do we do about this? The solution is jitter buffers. There are two varieties: fixed jitter buffers and adaptive jitter buffers. Fixed jitter buffers work as follows: A playout point is set to some fixed number of packets in the future, and the hope is that no packets arrive later than the playout point. Late arrival equals lost packets, so there is a delicate tradeoff between delay-induced impairment and loss-induced impairment. Fixed jitter buffers are useful when delay doesn't matter, as with Internet radio, or with nonstop sources, such as fax. With adaptive jitter buffers, the ideal is to converge to minimal delay with zero loss. You need breathing room to move the playout point to address talk spurt boundaries or silence. Adaptive jitter buffers can do fancy audio processing, such as speeding up or slowing down the rate. They rely on algorithms that adapt the playout point close to measured jitter, and if loss occurs, they back off.

Another issue we have to deal with is error concealment. The techniques for this depend on the codec standards used. With waveform coders, the technique is to replay the previous packet, to interpolate, and to predict. With the CELP coders, coefficients are used to predict the gain, pitch, and so on of the missing packet. There are also some advanced adaptation techniques, such as forward error correction (FEC), in which extra packets with FEC are sent over some number of the packets. As another example, with layered coders, you send higher- or lower-fidelity or different encodings on different streams. Receivers then subscribe to appropriate layers. This is especially valuable for multicast.

Media Transport Requirements

Media transport requirements include identification of the payload, the type of codec used, the framing used, timing reconstruction, when to play out each packet within a stream, and how to synchronize multiple streams. Note that an external reference clock is needed to correlate time stamps of different RTP streams. Another requirement is sequencing—that is, how to play out in the correct order and how to detect losses.

The media transport functions include moving bits, which is accomplished with RTP and SRTP. Feedback and statistics need to be provided as well, and this is accomplished using RTCP as well as the emerging standard RTCP XR, which is a reporting extension being developed by the IETF's AVT (Audio/Video Transport) working group.

These are the main transport protocols:

- **RTP**—RTP, specified in RFC 3550, is a transport protocol for real-time applications. It is used by all VoIP signaling protocols, and it is based on User Datagram Protocol (UDP). RTP provides media transport functions as well as additional features. It is multicast friendly and easy to encrypt, it provides QoS feedback with RTCP, and it requires minimal session control.

- **RTCP**—RTCP is based on the periodic transmission of control packets to all participants in the session, using the same distribution mechanism as the data packets. RTCP provides feedback on the quality of the data distribution. This is an integral part of RTCP's role as a transport protocol and is related to the flow and congestion control functions of other transport protocols.

- **SRTP**—There is considerable interest in the use of SRTP, a relatively new protocol, to prevent eavesdropping on VoIP calls. SRTP permits the voice packet payload to be encrypted. It also allows other protocol messages, such as RTCP messages, to be protected. Encryption protects privacy. However, diagnostic troubleshooting tools cannot analyze encrypted voice payload. That's where RTCP Reporting Extension (RTCP XR) comes in. It allows information hidden by SRTP to be extracted directly from the digital signal processing software, IP phones, and gateways and reported directly in the RTCP XR message. Of course, this assumes that the RTCP XR messages themselves are not encrypted.

■ The advantages of SRTP are that it provides both privacy via encryption and authentication via message integrity checking. It uses very little bandwidth for overhead, and it uses modern and strong cryptology suites, such as Advanced Encryption Standard (AES) countermode for encryption and Keyed Hashing for Message Authentication for message integrity.

IPT QoS

QoS is managed unfairness because some users purposely get better service than others. As discussed further in Chapter 10, QoS is needed to address the stringent delay requirements of voice traffic.

Several techniques, including the following, can be used to improve various aspects of a network's QoS:

■ **Random Early Detection (RED)**—RED is a queue management algorithm and a congestion avoidance algorithm. RED monitors the average queue size and drops packets based on statistical probabilities. If the buffer is almost empty, all incoming packets are accepted. As the queue grows, the probability for dropping an incoming packet grows, too. On a shared voice/data queue, RED does not prevent large delay and jitter for voice. RED is primarily effective for avoiding congestion, and it works best for congestion-responsive flows such as TCP. But voice has constant bit rate and, hence, is not usually responsive, and it uses UDP. So although RED is a good mechanism for many network applications, it is not the most effective for IP voice.

■ **Weighted Fair Queuing (WFQ)**—With WFQ, each flow gets a share of the server link bandwidth in proportion to its weight. Per-packet delay guarantee in a WFQ scheduler depends on the accuracy of the WFQ implementation.

■ **IntServ RSVP architecture**—As discussed in Chapter 10, RSVP is the primary specification for handling multimedia traffic over IP subnets (see Figure 9.3). RSVP messages are carried over IP/UDP. RSVP enhances connectionless best-effort service by providing QoS requests and guarantees. There are two main classes of service: RFC 2211 specifies control-load or best-effort service, and RFC 2212 is the guaranteed class of service (CoS), offering bandwidth and delay guarantees. RSVP relies on a router-to-router signaling scheme, which allows IP applications to request priority, delay, and bandwidth guarantees. The connection is established link by link and

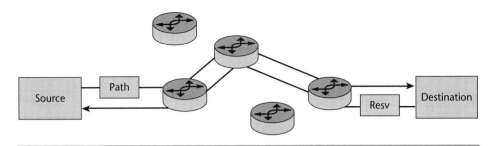

Figure 9.3 VoIP QoS: IntServ RSVP

is denied if a router cannot accept the request. Signaling is distinct from routing. Transparent operation across non-RSVP routers is possible. RSVP supports shared and distinct reservations, applies to unicast and multicast applications, and is simplex and receiver oriented. RSVP is well suited for real-time applications and delay-sensitive traffic. However, it does not scale well in large networks, so it is not used much in WANs.

- **IP precedence**—IP precedence is the poor-man's approach to QoS. The IP precedence or DiffServ Code Point (DSCP; discussed in detail in Chapter 8, "The Internet and IP Infrastructures") is set higher on voice packets. This puts them in a different queue, resulting in isolation from best-effort traffic. It can be done by the endpoint, by a proxy, or in routers through heuristics. IP precedence scales better than RSVP, and it keeps QoS control local. It pushes the work to the edges of the boundaries and can provide QoS by either customer or network. However, it has no admission control, so too much high-precedence traffic can still swamp the network.

- **DiffServ**—DiffServ employs a small, well-defined set of building blocks from which a variety of services can be built. Although DiffServ evolved from the IntServ architecture, DiffServ is a prioritization model with preferential allocation of resources based on traffic classification. DiffServ uses the DSCP to carry information about IP packet service requirements. It classifies traffic by marking IP headers at ingress to the network with flags corresponding to a small number of per-hop behaviors. In other words, queues get different treatments in terms of priority, share of bandwidth, and probability of discard. The DiffServ architecture assumes a relatively small number of feasible queue-scheduling algorithms for high link speeds. It also assumes a large number of individual flows, with many different rules, often being policy driven. The nodes at the edge of the boundaries do the hard work: They group packets explicitly by the per-hop behavior they are to receive (the queue service, the classification, and the conditioning and policing of those packets). The nodes in the middle of a cloud only have to deal with traffic aggregates. QoS is managed by local rules within the cloud, and QoS information exchange is limited to boundaries. It is bilateral, not multilateral, and it is not necessarily symmetric. Inter–service provider DiffServ and end-to-end Internet QoS need further standardization and commercial arrangements.

■ **Compressed Real-Time Transport Protocol (CRTP)**—CRTP is basically RTP compression. Normally, the IP header is 20 bytes, the UDP header is another 8 bytes, and the RTP header is 12 bytes, resulting in a 40-byte header. CRTP can reduce the header to 2 to 4 bytes, which is really useful on slow links.

■ **Multi-Class Multi-Link (MCML) PPP**—The idea with MCML PPP is that single-packet latency is unacceptable on slow links. A 1,500-byte message transfer unit takes 215 milliseconds to transmit on a 56Kbps link, which is significantly more than the recommended delay. MCML PPP allows multiple fragment streams on a multilink PPP session. It sets the fragment size to match the delay budget of the link (e.g., 128 bytes equals 18 milliseconds). Small voice packets are interleaved between the fragments of big packets by applying WFQ at the fragment level.

VoIP Call-Signaling Protocols

Three major VoIP protocols are used in call signaling. The first standard applied to support interoperability between VoIP systems was the ITU-T's H.323. While it has the advantage of being a mature standard, there are some negatives associated with it, including its complexity, its tuning for PC conferencing rather than telephony, its very bad scaling properties, and its difficulty working over firewalls. The second protocol that came into play is MGCP, which advocates a centralized control architecture. It is fairly simple: It models current PSTN call control architecture but requires high-reliability and high-availability call servers. The third protocol is SIP, which advocates a decentralized control architecture. SIP is transaction based, which means it is a good match for what's called the stupid network paradigm, where it is relatively easy to build in scalability and reliability and there are built-in security mechanisms.

H.323

H.323 is a protocol suite defined by the ITU-T for voice transmission over the Internet. First published in 1996, the latest version of H.323, Version 5, was completed in 2003. In addition to voice applications, H.323 provides mechanisms for video communication and data collaboration. H.323 defines a centralized architecture for creating multimedia applications that use VoIP, and it is an umbrella specification that includes various other ITU standards.

The H.323 architecture includes the following components (see Figure 9.4):

- **Terminals**—A terminal is the end device of every connection. It provides real-time two-way communications with another H.323 terminal, gateway, or MCU. This communication consists of speech, speech and data, speech and video, or a combination of speech, data, and video.

- **Gateways**—Gateways establish the connections between the terminals in the H.323 network and the terminals that belong to networks with different protocol stacks, such as the traditional PSTN network, SIP, or Megaco endpoints.

- **Gatekeepers**—Gatekeepers are responsible for translating between telephone numbers and IP addresses. They also manage the bandwidth and provide mechanisms for terminal registration and authentication. A gatekeeper also provides services such as call transfer and call forwarding. The main gatekeeper functions fall into two categories: mandatory services and optional services. Mandatory services address translation, admission control, bandwidth control, and zone management. Optional services include

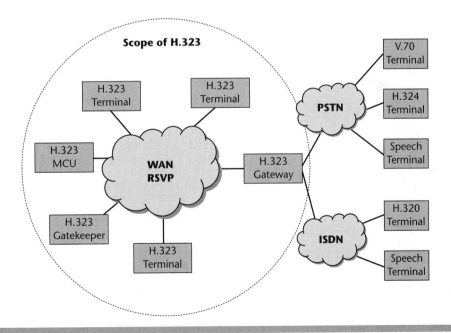

Figure 9.4 The H.323 architecture

call control signaling, call authorization, bandwidth management and reservation, call management, and directory services.

■ **Multipoint control units (MCUs)**—MCUs establish multipoint conferences. An MCU consists of a mandatory multipoint control, which is for call signaling and conference control, and an optional multipoint processor, which is for switching or mixing of media streams and sometimes real-time transcoding of the received audio/video streams.

Five types of information exchange are enabled in the H.323 architecture: audio; digitized voice; digitized video; data, including files or images; and communication control, which involves the exchange of supported functions, control of logic channels, and control of connections and sessions (i.e., the setup and teardown).

H.323 has a number of strengths. For one thing, it is an ITU standard. In addition, it is a mature protocol with many large-scale deployments. It has widespread vendor support and market acceptance, and it facilitates interoperability between vendors. Finally, it has defined standards for supplementary services, the network retains the call state for the duration of the call (providing greater call control for the user), and application services are available through the gatekeeper and best-of-breed application platforms.

H.323 suffers from some limitations as well: As mentioned earlier, it is complex, it is tuned for PC conferencing rather than telephony, it has very bad scaling properties, and getting it to work reliably over firewalls is quite a challenge, especially if both parties in a call are behind firewalls (e.g., only four TCP connections per call are allowed). Maintaining call state in the network actually increases the cost to scale. Many soft phones are proprietary, so they are not widely deployed.

Megaco and MGCP

Both Megaco (Media Gateway Controller) and MGCP (Media Gateway Control Protocol) are protocols for control of elements in a physically decomposed multimedia gateway, which enables separation of call control from media conversion. This means that the system is composed of a call agent, at least one media gateway whose function is to perform the conversion of media signals between circuits and packets, and at least one signaling gateway when connected to the PSTN. Both Megaco and MGCP are media/device control protocols. They both embrace a philosophy in which the network is smart and the endpoint is dumb. Services are provided by intelligent network elements.

So why are there two standards, Megaco and MGCP? As usually is the case, it is the result of different parties with different interests and agendas. Megaco was created by joint efforts of the IETF and the ITU. Megaco is the IETF name and is defined in IETF RFC 3525. Within the ITU it is known as ITU Recommendation H.248. MGCP originated with Cisco and is defined in an informational (nonstandard) IETF document, RFC 3435. Megaco is less widely implemented than MGCP. Megaco and MGCP are client/server protocols, so they allow service providers to have more control over subscribers through the use of more network intelligence. This is in contrast to H.323 and SIP, which are both peer-to-peer protocols. With peer-to-peer protocols, all the intelligence is distributed to the network edge, embedded in the terminating devices or endpoints, requiring only a simple core network and great scalability but reducing the network's control over the user.

Megaco addresses the relationship between a media gateway, which converts circuit-switched voice to packet-based traffic, and a media gateway controller (also referred to as a call agent or softswitch), which dictates the service logic of that traffic. Megaco instructs a media gateway to connect streams coming from outside a packet or cell data network onto a packet or cell stream such as RTP. Megaco is similar to MGCP from an architectural standpoint and in terms of the controller-to-gateway relationship, but Megaco supports a broader range of networks, such as ATM.

As shown in Figure 9.5, MGCP is a VoIP protocol used between elements of a decomposed multimedia gateway that consists of a call agent, which contains the

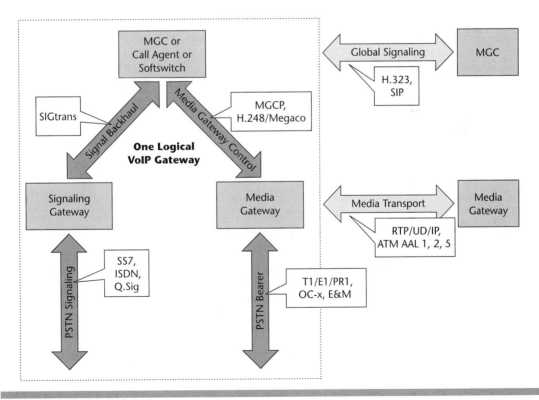

Figure 9.5 Megaco and MGCP

call control intelligence, and a media gateway, which contains the media functions (i.e., conversation from TDM voice to VoIP). Media gateways contain endpoints on which the call agent can create, modify, and delete connections in order to establish and control media sessions with other multimedia endpoints. A media gateway is typically a network element that provides conversion between the audio signals carried on telephone circuits and data packets carried over the Internet or over other packet networks. The call agent can instruct the endpoints to detect certain events and generate signals. The endpoints automatically communicate changes in service state to the call agent. Furthermore, the call agent can audit endpoints as well as the connections on endpoints. MGCP assumes a call control architecture where the call control intelligence is outside the gateways and handled by call agents. It assumes that call agents will synchronize with each other to send coherent commands and responses to the gateways under their control. MGCP does not define a mechanism for synchronizing call agents. It is, in essence, a master/slave protocol where the gateways are expected to execute commands sent by the call agent.

MGCP assumes a connection model where the basic constructs are endpoints and connections. Endpoints are sources and/or syncs of data and can be physical or virtual. Creation of physical endpoints requires hardware installation, while creation of virtual endpoints can be done by software. Connections can be either point to point or multipoint. A point-to-point connection is an association between two endpoints with the purpose of transmitting data between those endpoints. When that association is established for both endpoints, data transfer between them can take place. A multipoint connection is created by connecting the endpoint to a multipoint session. Connections can be established over several types of bearer networks. In the MGCP model, the gateways focus on the audio signal translation function, and the call agent handles the call-signaling and call-processing functions.

SIP

SIP, which is standardized under RFC 2543, is a peer-to-peer protocol in which end devices, known as *user agents*, initiate sessions. SIP is designed in conformance with the Internet model. It is an end-to-end signaling protocol, which means that all the logic is stored in end devices, except the routing of SIP messages. State is also stored in end devices only. There is no single point of failure with SIP, and networks designed this way scale well. The tradeoff for the distributiveness in scalability is the higher message overhead that results from the messages being sent end to end. The aim of SIP is to provide the same functionality as the traditional PSTN, but with an end-to-end design that makes SIP networks much more powerful and open to the implementation of new services.

SIP is an application-layer control protocol that can establish, modify, and terminate multimedia sessions. (Examples of a session include Internet telephone calls, distribution of multimedia, multimedia conferences, and distribution of computer games.) SIP can also invite participants to already existing sessions, such as a multicast conference. Media can be added to and removed from an existing session. SIP transparently supports name-mapping and redirection services, which make personal mobility possible. Users can maintain a single externally visible identifier, regardless of their network locations.

SIP support five facets of establishing and terminating multimedia communications: user location (the determination of the end system to be used for communication), user availability (the determination of the willingness of the called party to engage in communications), user capabilities (the determination of the media and media parameters to be used), session setup (the establishment of session parameters at both the called and calling parties), and session management (the transfer and termination of sessions, modification of session parameters, and invocation of services).

SIP can be used with other IETF protocols to build a complete multimedia architecture. For example, it can be used with RTP for transporting real-time data and providing QoS feedback, with Real-Time Streaming Protocol (RTSP) for controlling delivery of streaming media, with MGCP for controlling gateways to the PSTN, or with Session Description Protocol (SDP) for describing multimedia sessions. Although SIP should be used in conjunction with other protocols to provide complete services to users, the basic functionality and operation of SIP do not depend on any other protocols.

SIP, which works with both IPv4 and IPv6, operates as follows for Internet telephony sessions: Callers and callees are identified by SIP addresses. When making a SIP call, a caller locates the appropriate server and then sends a SIP request. The most common SIP operation is the invitation. Instead of directly reaching the intended callee, a SIP request may be redirected or may trigger a chain of new SIP requests by proxies. Users can register their locations with SIP servers; SIP addresses can be embedded in Web pages and, therefore, can be integrated as part of powerful applications such as click-to-talk.

The purpose of SIP is just to make the communication possible (see Figure 9.6). The communication itself must be achieved by another means and possibly another protocol. As mentioned earlier, two protocols that are most often used along with SIP are RTP and SDP. RTP is used to carry the real-time multimedia data, including audio, video, and text. RTP makes it possible to encode and split the data into packets and transport the packets over the Internet. SDP is used to describe and encode the capabilities of session participants. This description is then used to negotiate the characteristics of the session so that all the devices can participate. For example, the description is used in negotiation of the codecs used to encode media so all the participants will be able to decode it and in negotiation of the transport protocol to be used.

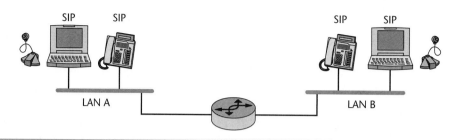

SIP   SIP   SIP   SIP

LAN A   LAN B

Figure 9.6   SIP

SIP Network Elements   Basic SIP elements include user agents, proxies, registrars, and redirect servers (see Figure 9.7). User agents usually but not necessarily
reside on a user's computer in the form of an application, but user agents can also
be cellular phones, PSTN gateways, PDAs, automated integrated voice response
systems, and so on. User agents are often referred to as the user agent server (UAS)
and user agent client (UAC). The UAS and UAC are logical entities only. Each user
agent actually contains both. The UAC is the part of the user agent that sends
requests and receives responses; the UAS is the part of the user agent that receives
requests and sends responses.

A proxy server is an optional SIP component. Proxy servers handle routing of
SIP signaling, but they don't initiate SIP messages. User agents can send messages
to a proxy server. The most important task of a proxy server is to route session
invitations closer to the callee. The session invitation usually traverses a set of

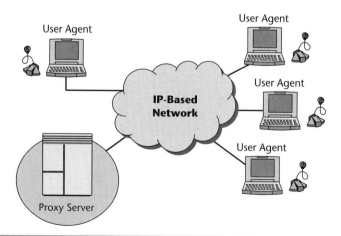

User Agent

User Agent

IP-Based
Network

User Agent

User Agent

Proxy Server

Figure 9.7   SIP network elements

proxies until it finds one that knows the actual location of the callee. Such a proxy then forwards the session invitation directly to the callee, and the callee then accepts or declines the session invitation.

A registrar server is another optional SIP component. It is a special SIP entity that handles registration from SIP user agents but does not route SIP messages. It receives registrations from users, extracts information about their current locations (such as IP address, port, and user name), and then stores the information in local databases. A registrar is very often a logical entity only and is usually collocated with proxy servers.

A redirect server is yet another optional SIP component. A redirect server receives requests and looks up the intended recipient of a request in the location database created by a registrar. It then creates a list of current locations of the user and sends this list to the request originator. The redirect server does not route SIP messages; rather, it returns a redirect to the user agent for direct routing.

SIP and Presence Systems   *Presence* is defined as the ability, willingness, desire, and capability of a user to communicate across media end devices and even time and space. Presence systems collect and distribute presence information to interested parties such as other users or applications. Policy—that is, who is allowed to see what and when—is central to presence. The value of presence is based on the richness of the data it has access to. Presence is the ability to see in real-time where someone is, how that person prefers to be reached, and even what the person is doing.

Today, only one in seven business calls is completed successfully. Instead, we get busy signals or are routed to voicemail. Users spend a lot of time trying many different numbers for the same person and calling many numbers in succession, trying to reach someone. Presence, therefore, has great value in improving the productivity of an organization because it can see ahead of time whether a call will succeed. It can tell the caller which is the best way to reach a user, and it can allow a caller to quickly see who among a set of candidates is available for a call.

Accuracy is paramount to presence. The greater the accuracy, the greater the value of presence. The worse the accuracy, the lower the value. Productivity enhancement depends on accurate presence data, and accuracy is achieved by combining multiple sources of presence data. There are many sources for presence data within an enterprise, such as detecting whether somebody is on a call or off a call, based on information from enterprise phones; determining whether a person is in a meeting or out of a meeting, based on information from the enterprise calendar systems; determining whether a person is in a conference or out of a conference, based on enterprise conferencing systems; or determining whether a person has logged in or logged out of the enterprise IM system.

Enterprise presence applications show presence on IP PBX phones and on PC-based IM applications. They can also support presence-based call routing as well as voicemail ringback. Two standards are involved in presence. The SIMPLE standard is a set of SIP extensions for IM and presence supported by Microsoft, IBM, Sun, and Novell. A competing standard, Extensible Messaging and Presence Protocol (XMPP), is an XML-based extensible open-source option that drives the Jabber IM client (www.jabber.com).

For all the good news about presence, there are also arguments against it. Most revolve around IM and the perception that it is intrusive and, at times, invasive. Most companies today use some form of IM, through mostly public services. The industry forecasts that we are only one to three years away from embedding presence in enterprise applications. Of course, standards, privacy, and security are major concerns.

SIP is creating new opportunities for platform providers that are introducing new soft phones. Proprietary soft phones incorporate SIP-based presence capabilities across both voice and IM, secure SIP-based IM behind the corporate firewall, IM archiving, click-to-talk voice functionality, speech-to-text functionality, and specialty modes for road warriors and telecommuters. There are also open-source SIP products. Not only do platform vendors have to worry about soft phones displacing their high-dollar hard phones, they have to worry about losing market share to some other open-source provider or to Microsoft.

Currently, SIP has no video specifications. When a vendor states that it uses SIP for video, it only means SIP is used for the signaling; it does not imply interoperability with other SIP video clients. In the near term, desktop video will be dominated by SIP-based endpoints, while the traditional group conferencing market will remain H.323 based; they will meet through SIP-to-H.323 gateways, as needed.

The SIP Forum (www.sipforum.org) and the IETF SIP protocol process are making it possible for many new SIP-based products to enter the market. SIP could disrupt the handset business, blurring the distinction between desk phones and mobiles because SIP can cross many boundaries, including desk phones, mobiles, PCs, PDAs, soft phones, intelligent appliances, and wearables.

SIP's Strengths and Weaknesses   SIP's strengths include tremendous industry support and widespread development. SIP soft phones, Ethernet phones, and application servers are available to integrate with IP clients and IM. SIP facilitates application development, and minimal call state duration is maintained in the network. SIP is central to all the latest solutions for telephony, ranging from hosted services to proprietary platforms, from handsets to soft phones to open-source software. The concepts behind SIP are disruptive and much more dramatic than VoIP on its own. The IETF still has a substantial amount of work to do to replicate in SIP the hundreds of TDM PBX calling features, but SIP is not just telephony: It involves many applications, such as presence, that enable capabilities that are not possible in the TDM world.

One shortcoming of SIP is a shortage of commercial and large-scale deployments at this time, resulting in a lack of real-world experience. Another problem is the lack of call state in the network, which affects billing and security issues. And of course, SIP is a moving target, with rapid development in progress. It is likely to be three to five years before presence and real-time communication standards become stabilized.

ENUM: Telephone Number Mapping

How do you find a telephone number on the Internet? How do you find islands of connectivity across domain boundaries? The answer is the Electronic Number Mapping Standard (ENUM). ENUM, defined in RFC 2916, is an IETF protocol that will assist in the convergence of the PSTN and the IP network. It maps a telephone number from the PSTN to Internet services: You put a telephone number in and get a URL out.

ENUM was developed as a solution to the question of how to find services on the Internet by using only a telephone number and how telephones, which have an input mechanism limited to 12 keys on a keypad, can be used to access Internet services. ENUM resolves a complete international telephone number to a series of URLs by using an architecture based on the Domain Name System (DNS). ENUM puts telephone numbers into the DNS, so it allows for a wide range of applications based solely on a phone number. Probably the most exciting application is an improvement in VoIP. Other applications include addressing for fax machines, e-mail, IM, and Web sites. The possibilities are enormous.

The ENUM protocol is the result of work of IETF's working group for telephone number mapping (www.enum.org). The charter of this group was to define a DNS-based architecture and protocols for mapping a telephone number to a uniform resource identifier (URI) that can be used to contact a resource associated with that number. (The syntax of the URI is defined in RFC 2396.) The protocol itself is defined in the standards-track document E.164, which describes the international public telecommunication telephony numbering plan.

How ENUM Works

ENUM makes extensive use of the Naming Authority Pointer Resource Records (which are defined in RFC 2915) in order to identify available ways or services for contacting a specific node identified through the E.164 number. In a nutshell, ENUM involves the following steps:

1. ENUM turns a phone number into a fully qualified domain name (FQDN). It does this by first adding the city, or area, and country code. For example, 555-1234 dialed in Washington, DC, becomes +1-202-555-1234, where 202

is the area code, the 1 represents the North American country code, and the + indicates that the number is a fully qualified E.164 number. Then ENUM removes all the characters except for the digits and reverses the order (e.g., +1-202-555-1234 becomes 43215552021). Finally, it places dots between the digits and appends the domain E164.ARPA to the end of the string (e.g., 4.3.2.1.5.5.5.2.0.2.1.E164.ARPA).

2. ENUM issues a DNS query on the FQDN created in step 1.

3. DNS returns a list of URIs that contain information about what resources, services, and applications are associated with that specific phone number.

An important feature of the ENUM protocol is that more than one type of contact information can be stored in the DNS record that belongs to a specific ENUM number. An ENUM record associated with The LIDO Organization might contain instructions for a VoIP call (e.g., h323:info@server.lidoorg.com or sip:info@sip.lidoorg.com), a fax call (e.g., fax:office@fax.lidoorg.com), and e-mail communications (e.g., mailto:info@lidoorg.com). Additional services can be developed in the future and included in the ENUM name records. The phone number in ENUM can therefore be the single contact number for multiple types of communication, such as voice, fax, e-mail, mobile, text messaging, location-based services, and Web pages.

ENUM does not replace the numeric IPv4 or IPv6 addresses that will be used to interact within IP directly. ENUM performs no conversion of signaling messages and media streams. Instead, ENUM is a framework for mapping and processing addresses of different network types. ENUM provides another way to determine the desired destination to be used to initiate communication over a next-generation network. Although ENUM will help facilitate VoIP calls, it is important to understand that VoIP phone calls do not require ENUM, and ENUM implementation is not mandatory, at least not at this point. VoIP calls can be made wholly without ENUM by using their defined Internet addressing scheme (e.g., sip:*user@host*.com).

The Future of ENUM

The Internet Architecture Board (IAB; www.iab.org) and ITU Study Group 2 are discussing a collaboration on the operational administration and delegation issues related to deployment of ENUM-based services. As you can imagine, this requires extensive consultation with administrators of resources derived from the international E.164 numbering plan, including national and international numbering plan administrators.

Under current practice, service providers generally develop their own address-mapping solutions and negotiate their own traffic exchange arrangements among themselves. Experts predict a gradual shift toward public ENUM as the number of IP voice endpoints grows. The following ENUM structures are possible:

- **Private ENUM**—Service and equipment providers are finding ways to make money on private ENUM, or ENUM-like, proprietary mapping and signaling. ENUM creates and enables the opportunity for a third party to enter and build the technology and then make money by charging fees to all the different providers who have numbers stored in the system. In this scenario, the third party would make fractions of a penny per number, per month. A grander vision would include transport service between VoIP providers, combining call routing and transmission. The service providers would have to have a sufficient number of customers and amount of traffic to warrant such services.

- **User ENUM**—User ENUM gives end users on the Internet and end users on the PSTN a possibility to find services of other end users on the public Internet. In this case, ENUM service providers provide a form of electronic business card or basic buddy list. The phone number becomes a universal key that is globally accessible by all potential correspondents of the user. With user ENUM, the data is public. Anyone who knows the universal key—that is, the phone number—can have access to the information, which may have privacy implications. Even if the user subscribes to several applications and services, the user would remain the only party who has complete control over the set of identifiers. User ENUM is a capability provided for end users and is optional both for the calling user and for the called user.

- **Infrastructure ENUM**—Network operators using IP-based technology within their networks cannot rely on an optional technology used by end users. They need an independent routing mechanism to find the ingress points to their networks. Using DNS and ENUM technology for this purpose, as described in RFC 3761, is called *infrastructure ENUM*, or carrier, or operator, ENUM. The basic premise of infrastructure ENUM is to provide information only to IP service providers and, in some cases, only to selected peers. The end user typically cannot use this information or has no access to it. This type of system must be implemented as an independent system.

  If every IP communications service provider is only providing data for numbers hosted by the operator itself, a later merging of trees should not be a problem. If, on the other hand, providers are entering data for numbers they are not hosting themselves (e.g., data for numbers where they provide transit services), a later merging of trees will cause problems. Therefore, it is not recommended to use infrastructure ENUM for providing transit information.

Another application for infrastructure ENUM technology is to provide access to national number portability information, which is currently stored in databases. However, this information will have only national significance (e.g., national routing numbers). As a result, this data cannot be used in supranational infrastructure ENUM implementations.

The reality is that ENUM is not currently required in networks, based on the type of applications that carriers and service providers are supporting. In terms of U.S. domestic policy, the U.S. government endorses moving forward with ENUM based on the concept of an industry management limited liability corporation similar to that used with number portability. It involves an arm's-length contractual relationship with an administrative entity. This is similar to existing relationships with ICANN (www.icann.org) for IP address space, top-level domain names, and root server management; with NeuStar (www.neustar.com) for numbering plan and portability management; and with VeriSign (www.verisign.com) for .com and .net registries.

The U.S. ENUM Forum (www.enumf.org) is developing policies and taking steps to implement ENUM in the United States. Some early participants include AT&T, Sprint, SBC, Verizon, Neustar, Cox Cable & Wireless, Cisco, and Telcordia. However, it is anticipated that it will be a while before the United States sees public ENUM. Several national forums are under way in the United Kingdom, Austria, Sweden, Japan, the Netherlands, Germany, Brazil, Austria, Poland, and elsewhere. A number of resources are available on the Web, including the approved ENUM delegation list (www.ripe.net/enum/request-archives) and the ITU ENUM Web page (www.itu.int/osg/spu/enum/index.html).

■ IPTV

IPTV is generally described as a system that delivers digital television service to a subscriber using IP over a broadband connection, often provided in conjunction with video-on-demand (VOD), Internet services, and VoIP, as part of *triple-play services* (a combination of voice, data, and video services over the same infrastructure). In its simplest definition, IPTV is the delivery of television content through technologies used for the World Wide Web rather than traditional formats.

Some say that incumbent telcos have developed their current interest in offering video or TV services as a result of fear—fear that cable operators are beginning to encroach on their territory with residential voice services, fear that competition is eroding the number of access lines being deployed, and fear that traditional landline revenues will continue to fall even further. IPTV therefore holds great promise for telcos. But more importantly, with IPTV, telcos and cable providers alike can offer triple-play services. It is also important to note that IPTV is not just a replication of the passive cable TV viewing environment of old; instead, it offers services including interactive gaming, access to massive libraries of video content on demand, and e-commerce activities, with a view to future features such as energy management and security services.

IPTV was not possible in the dialup era, when the download speeds were far too slow to allow any type of video content to be received, let alone enjoyed. With the penetration of broadband growing daily, IPTV is becoming available to more households. The market research firm Research and Markets expects the number of global IPTV subscribers to grow from 4.3 million in 2005 to 36.8 million in 2009, at a compound annual growth rate of 72%. Europe is leading the market for subscriber numbers, while Asia and North America have fallen off slightly due to a slower-than-expected rate of fiber deployment ("Global Users Tune In to IPTV," www.vnunet.com/vnunet/news/2154560/iptv-set-rocket). Needless to say, many if not most of the world's leading telecom providers are investigating IPTV, in the search for a new revenue-generating opportunity and as a defensive measure against the ever-increasing encroachment of cable TV operators. Because IPTV relies on IP, it promises lower costs for providers and lower prices for consumers—what appears to be a win–win situation.

IPTV supports both live TV (multicasting) and VOD (stored video). IPTV is viewed on a TV and requires a set-top box. The video content is usually in MPEG-2 TS (Transport Stream) format, delivered via IP Multicast. IPTV was specifically designed to deliver high-quality content to a traditional TV through the Internet. From the consumer's point of view, the experience with IPTV is very similar to the experience with cable or satellite.

One of the main advantages of IPTV is its two-way capability, which traditional TV distribution technologies do not have. Another benefit is its point-to-point distribution, which allows each viewer to view individual broadcasts. This functionality enables stream control (pausing, forwarding, rewinding, and so on) and a free selection of programming similar to what the Web offers. As mentioned earlier, IPTV enables providers to offer more services over the same pipe (e.g., triple-play services).

Of course there are alternatives to IPTV, encompassing traditional TV distribution technologies such as terrestrial, satellite, and cable TV. Because cable can be upgraded to two-way capability, it can also carry IPTV.

IPTV Versus Streaming Media

Streaming media is an almost identical server-side technology to IPTV, but it terminates on a PC rather than on a TV. Streaming media is still difficult to sell to broadcasters and is not a hot topic of discussion because it does not leverage the TV sets already out there. The general perspective is that if you're a television professional, computers are not really part of your world. In fact, from a broadcaster's point of view, it would be better if computers simply disappeared because they take away traditional TV viewers.

With IPTV, the network operator controls the entire path—from the time the content is assembled to the delivery of that content to the consumer's TV set. The operator can set the QoS and control the security. In the streaming media model, the signal is likely to traverse different providers' networks, so the network operator doesn't have the same control over bandwidth and QoS. The deployment of IPTV is greatly affected by the need for end-to-end control. IPTV does not involve a signal being sent from one end of the world to the other; it is regional or local, and IPTV is therefore being implemented by companies that own entire networks.

Because IPTV is a closed, managed network, it can deliver full-screen, high-quality video content, unlike streaming media, which is most often still relegated to small-screen and relatively low-quality video. For streaming media, network capacity is a critical issue that needs to be resolved if it is to have any hope of not only keeping up with but converging with IPTV. High-definition TV (HDTV) is setting another benchmark that streaming media might struggle with.

For telcos in particular, IPTV is laying the foundation for the future, allowing the provider to serve the customer with a bundle of offerings, as well as establishing a position in the nascent market for online video distribution. Aside from TV, there are a multitude of opportunities for future multimedia applications that involve the integration of voice, data, and video. Examples of these types of services include displaying caller ID on a TV set to being able to program a personal video recorder (PVR) remotely from a handheld device.

The IPTV Architecture

Using IPTV requires either a PC or a set-top box connected to a TV (see Figure 9.8). The primary underlying protocols used for IPTV are Internet Group Management Protocol (IGMP) version 2 for channel-change signaling for live TV and RTSP for stored video (i.e., VOD).

Protocols that use peer-to-peer technology to distribute live TV are just starting to emerge. Their primary advantage over traditional distribution models is that they provide a way to share data delivery workloads across connected client systems as well as the distributor's own server infrastructure, which drastically decreases the operational costs for a stream provider. Video compression formats used for IPTV include MPEG-2, MPEG-4, H.264, WMV (Windows Media Video 9 and VC-1), XviD, DivX, and Ogg Theora. (Compression techniques are discussed in Chapter 10.)

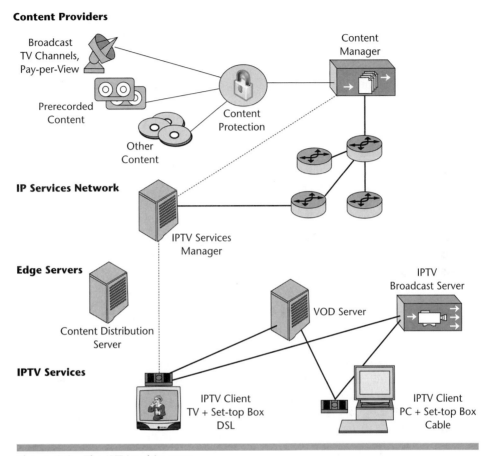

Figure 9.8 The IPTV architecture

VPNs

VPNs are a crucial requirement for businesses because they distribute mission-critical and sensitive traffic to remote locations. More and more often, customers are looking at mechanisms for securing traffic and for extending the reach of the enterprise to geographically dispersed locations. VPN technology is also being extended to the home office, providing telecommuters with networking security and performance comparable with that available at the office.

A big driver of interest in VPNs has been that customers need to communicate with people outside their enterprise, not just those inside the enterprise. As mentioned in Chapter 5, "Data Communications Basics," in the 1980s, about 80% of the information that was used within a given address of a business came from within that address. Only 20% was exchanged outside the walls of that location. Today, the relationship has reversed: As much as 80% of information exchanged is with points outside a given business address.

Another reason for interest in VPNs has been that customers want to quickly and securely change their access points as changes occur in their businesses. Many strategic alliances and partnerships require companies to exchange messages quickly. Some of these are temporary assignments—for example, a contractor building a fiber-optic loop or an applications developer building a new billing system—that might last a few months, during which time the individuals involved need to be incorporated into the network. Leased lines are infamous for requiring long waits for provisioning—often 6 to 18 months. VPNs allow rapid provisioning of capacity where and when needed.

Traffic has steadily migrated away from traditional networks based on leased lines (see Figure 9.9) to public networks. As a result, we're seeing a steady growth in the pseudoprivate realm of the VPN (see Figure 9.10). A *VPN* is a logical network that isolates customer traffic on shared service provider facilities. In other words, the enterprise's traffic is aggregated with the traffic of other companies. VPNs have been around for quite some time—since X.25 closed user groups on the packet-switched network and the AT&T Software-Defined Network (SDN) on the circuit-switched networks. A VPN looks like a private network, but it runs across either the public circuit-switched network or public packet-switched data net-

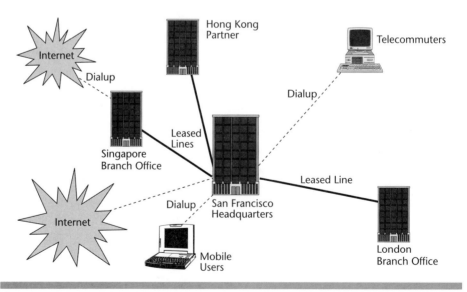

Figure 9.9 An enterprise network based on leased lines

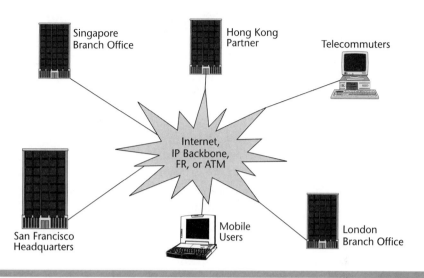

Figure 9.10 An enterprise network using a VPN

works. Thus, a VPN is not just a solution within the IP realm; a VPN is a concept, not a specific set of technologies, and it can be deployed over a wide range of network technologies, including circuit-switched networks, X.25, IP, Frame Relay, ATM, and MPLS.

With the advances in VoIP and Video over IP, consumers have realized that they can converge real-time applications such as voice, video, and data into one access circuit. Carriers have realized that with the evolution of converged technologies, they no longer need to deploy, maintain, and support both TDM and IP backbones. However, carriers' IP backbones provide neither segmentation of customer traffic nor the security normally associated with that segmentation. Under the initiative of service providers, the standards organizations have recognized the value of starting work on the standardization of VPN technology, through ITU-T Study Group 13 and the IETF Provider Provisioned VPNs (PPVPNs) group. These standardization efforts have focused on the provider-provisioned class of VPNs. Today's provider-provisioned and provider-managed VPNs are intended to emulate whatever LAN or WAN connectivity a customer desires.

The following sections discuss key VPN concepts, types of VPNs, and VPN security.

Key VPN Concepts

A VPN uses a shared carrier infrastructure. It can provide additional bandwidth on demand, which is an incredible feat, compared to the weeks it normally takes to add bandwidth to dedicated networks. Carriers build VPNs with advanced survivability and restoration capabilities, as well as network management tools and support, so that QoS can be considered and service-level agreements (SLAs) can be administered and met.

There are two major models of VPNs:

- **Customer edge model**—This customer-based model requires the CPE to be fully capable of configuring and provisioning the VPN and thereby results in higher operating expenses for the enterprise user. The routing intelligence resides at the end-user's site. Service providers install gateways, routers, and other VPN equipment on the customer's premises. Because this requires the service provider to manage onsite equipment, the cost associated with the onsite visits from field engineers can be high. This approach is generally preferred where the customer wants to have control over all aspects of security.

- **Provider edge model**—In this model, the VPN intelligence resides at the provider's edge, where it can be extended out to many end-user locations. The carrier houses all the necessary equipment at a point of presence (POP) near the customer's location. This offers the advantages of scalability, support of an increasingly diverse range of IP-based services, and efficient prioritization of traffic. It provides the foundation needed to integrate fixed and mobile VPN communications into one seamless framework. This approach is generally preferred by customers who want to take advantage of the carrier's VPN economies of scale.

VPN Frameworks

Contemporary VPNs can be described as belonging to one of three categories: Internet-based VPNs, provisioned VPNs, and IP-based VPNs. The following sections define the nature of these types of VPNs.

Internet-Based VPNs In an *Internet-based VPN* (see Figure 9.11), smaller ISPs provide local access services in defined geographical regions, requiring an enterprise to receive end-to-end services from multiple suppliers. An Internet-based VPN uses encryption to create a form of closed user group, thereby isolating the enterprise traffic and providing acceptable security for the enterprise across the public shared packet network. However, because it involves multiple ISPs in the delivery of the VPN, the performance is unpredictable. The biggest problem of having multiple suppliers is the inability to define and meet consistent end-to-end bandwidth or performance objectives.

Figure 9.12 shows what is involved in providing an Internet-based VPN. The customer has on the premises a wide variety of servers that dish up the corporate content, the finance systems, the customer service systems, and so on. A VPN is

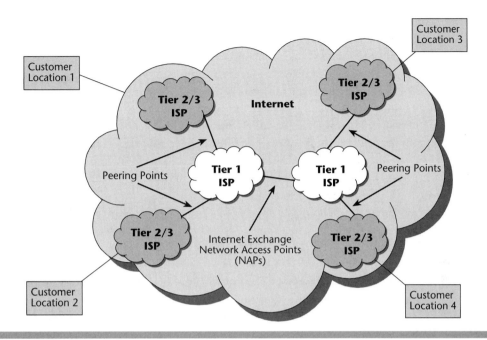

Figure 9.11   An Internet-based VPN

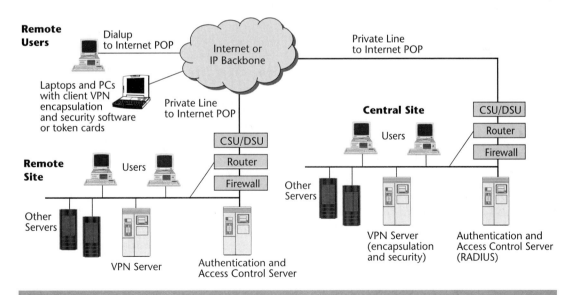

Figure 9.12   The parts of an Internet-based VPN

responsible for the encapsulation of the information and hence the security aspects. *Remote Authentication Dial-in User Services* (RADIUS), an authentication and access control server, is used to authenticate a user who wishes to access corporate resources. The RADIUS server connects to a directory server, which contains the user accounts of those allowed to access the network. Traffic from the VPN server usually passes through a firewall, which determines whether traffic is allowed into or out of the network. The router selects the optimum path for the messages to take, and the circuit physically terminates on a channel service unit/data service unit (CSU/DSU). A private line interfaces with the Internet provider's POP. From that point, the VPN either uses the public Internet that comprises multiple ISPs or relies on IP backbones provided by an individual provider or at least a small group of providers. Users who are working on mobile devices have laptops equipped with the client and VPN services necessary for encapsulation and for administration of security.

Provisioned VPNs   VPNs rely on the capability to administer preferential treatment to applications, users, and so on. The public Internet does not support preferential treatment because it is subject to delay, jitter, and loss; it is therefore unsuitable for next-generation services that require high performance. In most cases, to accommodate business customers that are interested in such advanced services and that demand SLAs, the underlying transport is Frame Relay or ATM. Frame Relay and ATM VPNs offer greater levels of QoS and can fulfill the SLAs that customers and vendors agree to. However, they require that the customer acquire an integrated access device (IAD) to have on the premises, which can increase the deployment cost significantly. IADs enable the enterprise to aggregate voice, data, and video traffic at the customer edge.

A *provisioned VPN* (see Figure 9.13) is a packet-switched VPN that runs across the service provider's backbone, generally using Frame Relay or ATM. This type of VPN is built on OSI model Layer 2 virtual circuits, such as those used by Frame Relay, ATM, or MPLS, and it is provisioned based on customer orders. Virtual circuits based on predetermined locations create closed user groups and work well to carve out a VPN in a public shared network by limiting access and usage to the provisioned VPN community. However, encryption is still required to securely protect the information from theft or modification by intruders.

A provisioned VPN is differentiated from an IP-based VPN by its ability to support multiple protocols and by the fact that it offers improved performance and management. These VPNs are characterized as having excellent performance and security, but the negative is that a single vendor may not offer the necessary reach and breadth in terms of service offerings.

Figure 9.14 shows what the CPE looks like for a VPN based on Frame Relay or ATM. The customer has an IAD that allows voice and data to be converged at the customer premises. The IAD feeds into the data communications equipment, over

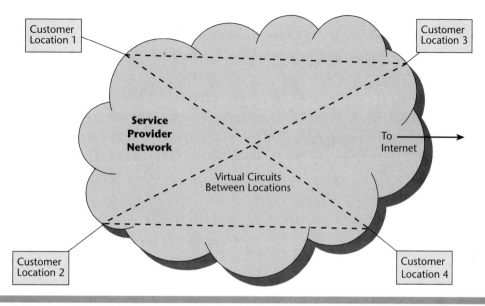

Figure 9.13 A provisioned VPN

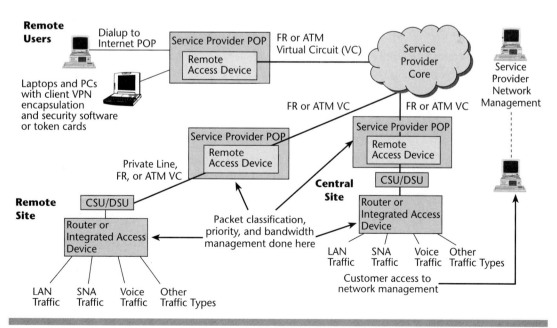

Figure 9.14 A Frame Relay– or an ATM-based provisioned VPN

which a circuit goes to the service provider's POP. At the service provider's POP is a multiservice access device that enables multiple protocols and interfaces to be supported and that provides access to the service provider's core network, which is based on the use of Frame Relay or ATM. To differentiate Frame Relay– and ATM-based VPNs from IP-based VPNs, service providers stress that multiple protocols are supported and that they rely on the use of virtual circuits or MPLS labels to facilitate the proper path, thereby ensuring better performance and providing traffic management capabilities.

To further differentiate Frame Relay– or ATM-based VPNs from regular Frame Relay or ATM services, additional functions—such as packet classification and traffic isolation, the capability to handle multiple separate packet-forwarding tables and instances of routing protocols for each customer—reside at the edge.

IP VPNs   Whereas Internet-based VPNs tend to involve numerous ISPs, IP-based VPNs tend to involve IP backbones that are under the control of a given service provider or a customer-owned enterprise network. An IP VPN is basically a private, or restricted, communications network constructed over shared IP-based networks, usually serviced on the providers' backbones, but with connections to the public Internet. IP-based VPNs have traditionally been referred to as networks of secure links over a public IP infrastructure. However, today an IP VPN is likely to be an MPLS-based infrastructure. (BGP MPLS VPNs are discussed later in this chapter.) However, as far as the user is concerned, the experience is the same, regardless of the technique. IP VPN services provide secure access for connecting intranets to other intranets, support mobile and teleworker access to their enterprise intranets, and provide for the connection of extranets to private enterprise, education, and government networks.

As discussed later in this chapter, there are two broad categories of IP VPNs:

- **Network-based VPNs**—With a network-based VPN, all the routing intelligence and VPN topology for the VPN are provided on the carrier's provider edge. Network-based IP VPNs make life much easier for users: Because all of the VPN topology is stored on the carrier's provider edge, the provider has the responsibility of managing all the complexity of the VPN topology. All the customer needs is a single connection from the CPE to the provider edge.

- **CPE-based VPNs**—In the case of CPE-based VPNs, which are most often based on IPsec, the network topology is defined at the customer's edge router. Obviously, with large or highly meshed networks, the management of so many tunnels and VPN rules can be overwhelming and can severely affect the capabilities of customers' edge routers.

IP VPNs are discussed in detail later in this chapter.

VPN Tunneling

The goal of a VPN is to provide connectivity over a shared infrastructure that is as secure and cost-effective as a dedicated private network such as a Frame Relay or ATM network. In addition, a VPN solution must be scalable, highly available, and easy to manage. And of course, QoS is a required feature. A VPN works by using the shared public infrastructure while maintaining privacy through security procedures and tunneling protocols, such as Point-to-Point Tunneling Protocol (PPTP), Layer 2 Tunneling Protocol (L2TP), Generic Routing Encapsulation (GRE), and IP Security (IPsec).

In effect, the protocols, by encrypting data at the sending end and decrypting it at the receiving end, send the data through a tunnel that cannot be entered by data that is not properly encrypted. An additional level of security involves encrypting not only the data but also the originating and receiving network addresses. *Tunneling* is the transmission of data intended for use only within a private, usually enterprise, network through a public network in such a way that the routing nodes in the public network are unaware that the transmission is part of a private network.

As shown in Figure 9.15, tunneling is generally done by encapsulating the private network data and protocol information within the public network transmission units so that the private network protocol information appears to the public network as data. Tunneling allows the use of the Internet, which is a public network, to convey data on behalf of a private network. VPN tunneling is not intended as a substitute for encryption and decryption. In cases where a high level of security is necessary, the strongest possible encryption should be used within the VPN, and tunneling should serve only as a convenience. Some tunneling protocols include

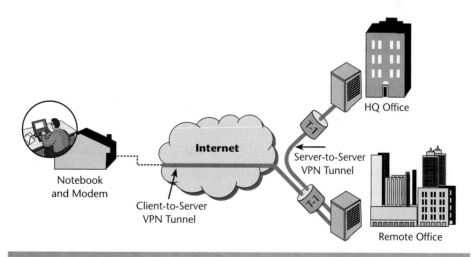

Figure 9.15 VPN tunneling

encryption: PPTP includes MPPE (Microsoft Point-to-Point Encryption, based on RC-4), and IPsec specifies a tunnel mode typically used in gateway-to-gateway (but not client-to-gateway) communications. (VPN security is covered in detail later in this chapter.)

Customers and providers can employ various flavors of point-to-point tunnels to serve as logical links in an IP VPN. An IP VPN tunnel connects two sites or a user to a site by imposing a separate tunnel header on the VPN data packet at the source site and disposing of the tunnel header at the destination site. This lets VPN data packets travel opaquely through the public Internet, independent of their payload or header content.

Applications of VPNs

A VPN is an architecture, a series of products and software functions tied together and tightly calibrated. Managing a VPN entails dealing primarily with two issues: monitoring security policies and parameters, and ensuring that applications function within the latency requirements. It is important to be able to effectively and easily manage the VPN environment. You need to consider how easy it is to track a VPN's tunnel traffic, support policy management, track QoS, track security infractions, and support public key certificate authorities (CAs). Managed VPN services—the one-stop-shopping approach to VPNs—are designed to lock in users and to reduce costly customer churn, but with this approach, interoperability is very restricted. Managed VPNs provide capabilities such as IP connection and transport services, routers, firewalls, and a VPN box at the customer site. Benefits of this approach include the fact that it involves a single service vendor, SLAs, guaranteed latency and bandwidth, and the security of traffic being confined to one network.

VPN applications provide maximum opportunities to save money and to make money—by substituting leased lines with Internet connectivity, by reducing costs of dialup remote access, and by stimulating new applications using extranets. These savings can be substantial.

The three major applications of VPNs—intranets (i.e., site-to-site VPNs), remote access, and extranets—are examined in the following sections.

Intranet VPNs   Intranet VPNs are site-to-site connections (see Figure 9.16). The key objective of an intranet VPN is to replace or reduce the use of leased-line networks, traditional routers, and Frame Relay services. The cost savings in moving from private networks to Internet-based VPNs can be very high, in the neighborhood of 50% to 80% per year. Remember that Internet-based VPNs allow less control over the quality and performance of applications than do provisioned VPNs; this is a bit of a deterrent, and many clients still want to consider Frame Relay– or ATM-based VPNs, which provide better QoS. The savings might drop a bit, but the cost of a provisioned VPN would still be substantially less than the cost of using leased lines.

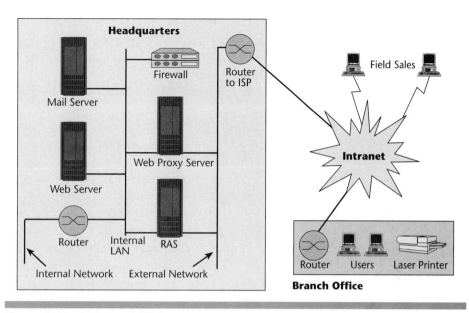

Figure 9.16 An intranet VPN

There are two key barriers to building more intranets based on VPNs: First, there is a variance between vendors' products that leads to interoperability problems, and second, today's Internet is unable to provide end-to-end QoS.

Remote Access VPNs   The most interesting and immediate VPN solution for most customers is the replacement of remote access servers. VPN remote access implementations can save customers from 30% to 70% over traditional dialup remote access server deployment. Remote access servers provide access to remote users, generally via analog plain old telephone service (POTS) lines, or, perhaps, ISDN connections, including dialup protocols and access control for authentication (administered by the servers). However, a remote access server requires that you maintain racks of modems, the appropriate terminal adapters for ISDN services, or DSL-type modems for DSL services. You also need remote access routers, which connect remote sites via a private line or public carriers and provide protocol conversion between the LANs and WANs. To have an internal implementation of remote access, you have to acquire all these devices, as well as the talent to maintain them.

If an enterprise needs remote access connections outside local calling areas, and/or if it needs encrypted communications, it is generally fairly easy to justify a VPN service rather than an enterprise-based remote access server. The initial cost of hardware for a VPN approach is about 33% less than the cost of hardware for a traditional dialup remote access server deployment. The customer also saves on charges for local access circuits, and costly toll and international charges are eliminated.

By virtue of supporting a greater range of customers, a service provider that offers VPN-based remote access is more likely to support a wider variety of broadband access options, including xDSL, cable modems, and broadband wireless. VPN-based remote access also reduces the management and maintenance required with modem banks and remote client dial-in problems. For these reasons, remote access represents the primary application for which customers turn to VPNs. Figure 9.17 shows an example of a remote access VPN.

Extranet VPNs   Extranet VPNs allow an external organization to have defined access to an enterprise's internal networks and resources (see Figure 9.18). There are three major categories of extranets: supplier extranets, which focus on speeding communications along the supply chain; distributor extranets, which focus on the demand side and provide great access to information; and peer extranets, which create increased intraindustry competition.

The key applications for extranets include distribution of marketing and product information, online ordering, billing and account history, training policies and

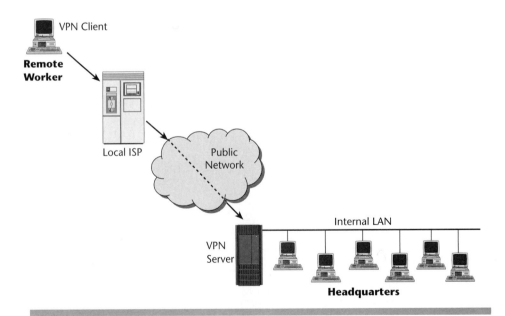

Figure 9.17   A remote access VPN

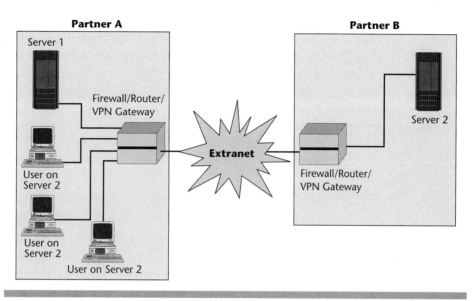

Figure 9.18 An extranet VPN

standards, inventory management, collaborative research and development, and e-mail, chat, news, and content.

Benefits and Evolution of VPNs

The main benefit of VPNs as compared to leased-line or Frame Relay networks is cost savings. VPNs also optimize environments that use IP; they have less overhead than Frame Relay, and tunneling protocols may eliminate the need for proprietary encapsulation of protocols. Provisioned VPNs also have the additional benefits of Frame Relay and ATM in the administration of virtual circuits and QoS. VPNs also provide the capability to support dialup access, and greater redundancy is achieved in the network by virtue of meshed nets. In addition, VPNs do not necessarily demand an end-to-end digital fiber infrastructure.

VPNs are undergoing an evolution, and various parameters still need to be addressed. Among those are the QoS guarantees. Effective traffic prioritization is at the heart of QoS, and currently available mechanisms include Differentiated Services (DiffServ), Class-Based Queuing (CBQ), Common Open Policy Service (COPS), and MPLS. (These mechanisms are covered in Chapter 10.) Other areas of evolution in VPNs are tiering of VPN services (i.e., bandwidth tiering and different policy management), the capability to support autoprovisioning, and the emphasis on security.

QoS and security are the two most important considerations in administering VPNs, so uptimes, delays, and SLAs need to be structured. For example, QoS guarantees could promise 100% premises-to-premises network availability, with a maximum latency of 80 milliseconds. Some vendors offer separate SLAs for dedicated and remote access. For dedicated access, the SLA may offer an availability guarantee of 99.9% and a maximum latency guarantee of 125 milliseconds. On remote access SLAs, a busy-free dial availability guarantee of 97% may be stipulated, and the latency guarantee would depend on the initial modem connection speed.

Today, three basic types of carrier-managed IP VPN services are offered:

■ **CPE-based IPsec VPNs**—These VPNs are generally used to support site-to-site enterprise VPNs and have, in many ways, become the gold standard for VPN security, especially when traffic is running over the public Internet.

■ **Network-based IPsec VPNs**—These VPNs may run over the Internet or the service provider's private IP facilities. Customers use leased-line connections from the premises router to the service provider's POP.

■ **Network-based MPLS VPNs**—These VPNs are receiving the most attention today. Service providers' VPN solutions can be deployed using partial mesh, full mesh, and hub-and-spoke designs. They can provide point-to-point and multipoint connectivity. They support a multitude of services and are available from multiple providers around the world.

VPN Standards

The initial VPN service standardization efforts focused on service provider Layer 3 solutions, where multiple competing implementations had already been developed. The main driving forces of the standards initiatives included multivendor interoperability and applicability scenarios of each of those Layer 3 solutions. Later, the interest in Layer 2 provider edge–based solutions was driven by the growing attractiveness of the metro-Ethernet market and the capability to offer relatively simple migration paths from traditional Layer 2 ATM and Frame Relay services to network-based VPNs over an IP infrastructure.

The ITU-T has been mainly developing requirements, architecture elements, and Layer 1 architectures and is currently working on generalized VPN architectures and QoS aspects. The IETF has focused on Layer 3 and Layer 2 solutions and related applicability scenarios. Finally, the Ethernet-based Layer 2 VPN domain covers areas of interest for various standards communities. The Metro Ethernet Forum (www.metroethernetforum.org) is one of the major groups working on solutions to offer Ethernet Layer 2 VPNs using Ethernet metro or core networks.

Types of IP VPNs

IP-based VPNs were initially deployed to address two specific market segments:

■ **Virtual private dial networks (VPDNs)**—VPDNs were developed for tele-commuters and road warriors who needed secure and convenient access to their enterprise servers (see Figure 9.19). This approach has included the use of PPTP, L2TP, or IPsec. With a VPDN, the end user establishes a user-to-corporate-gateway point-to-point session that travels over a combination of two links: a dialup data link to the Internet service provider edge and a VPN tunnel (sometimes called a voluntary tunnel) from the user to the enterprise gateway (less common is a compulsory tunnel, established from the ISP edge to the enterprise gateway). L2TP supports the tunneling of PPP sessions containing user data through the Internet, but by itself isn't secure; L2TP connections are clear text. L2TP is usually combined with IPsec to achieve the required privacy. Residential dialup access to the Internet uses similar technology. Broadband provides additional options, including the use of cable links, DSL links, or 802.11 in the wireless realm.

■ **Site-to-site VPNs**—Site-to-site VPNs were developed for enterprises desiring to communicate over the public Internet but requiring data integrity authentication and privacy. The main approach has included the use of IPsec or GRE. However, many more options are now available, especially in the provider edge–based arena. As shown in Figure 9.20, provider edge–based VPNs are available as Layer 3 VPNs and Layer 2 VPNs. Layer 3 VPNs offer two choices: RFC 2547 and virtual routers. Layer 2 VPNs also offer two choices: virtual private wire service (VPWS) and Virtual Private LAN Services (VPLS).

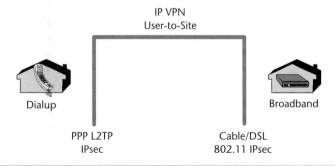

Figure 9.19 VPDN solutions

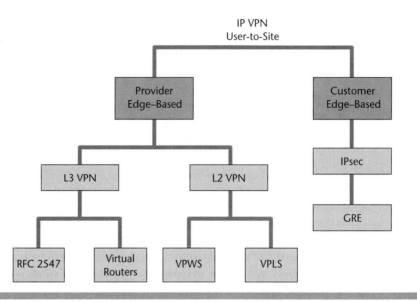

Figure 9.20 Site-to-site VPN solutions

The following sections describe the various types of site-to-site VPNs.

IPsec VPNs

IPsec has been around for quite some time and is offered by most service providers as a mechanism for tunneling traffic across the Internet to areas where the provider does not have POPs. In order to address the heightened security requirements, the customer or the provider managing the CPE routers can build IPsec security associations (not called *tunnels* unless using a specific type of security association, known as *tunnel mode*, described shortly) across the Internet to interconnect CPE. In order to authenticate and encrypt the user data, packets are forwarded across the shared Internet. IPsec uses a variety of protocol exchanges and encapsulations at the endpoints.

IPsec is an IETF protocol suite that addresses basic data integrity and security. It covers encryption, authentication, and key exchange. It supports key sizes of varying lengths, depending on the capabilities of each end of the connection. IPsec emphasizes security by authenticating both ends of the connection, negotiating the encryption protocol and key for the encrypted session, and encrypting and decrypting the session establishment data. IPsec provides secure transmission of packets at the IP layer, including authentication and encryption of the packets. This is accomplished by using the authentication header and encapsulating security payload features of IPsec.

IPsec uses transport and tunnel modes. In transport mode, only the IP payload is encrypted. There is no change to the original IP header. This is generally used between hosts or routers and also in client/server VPNs. In tunnel mode, the entire IP datagram is encrypted; the original packet is encapsulated in IPsec and given a new IP header. This mode is generally used between gateways.

IPsec and IKE in IPv4 and IPv6

Internet Key Exchange (IKE), which is defined in RFC 2409, is the key exchange protocol that IP Security (IPsec) uses in computers that need to negotiate security associations—that is, connections between systems, established for the purpose of securing the packets transmitted across the connections—with one another. Although IPsec is optional in IPv4, in IPv6, providing security through IPsec and, in turn, IKE is mandatory.

With IKE, public key techniques are used to mutually authenticate the communicating parties. IKE supports both digital certificates and preshared keys for authentication. IKE uses a Diffie-Hellman key exchange to set up a shared session secret from which the bulk cryptographic keys are derived. If you use preshared keys, then every node must be linked to every other node by a unique key, and the number of keys needed can grow out of control (e.g., two devices need 1 key, and eight devices need 28 keys). That's why most production implementations of IPsec use digital certificates issued most often by internal certificate authorities. IKE version 2 (IKEv2), defined in RFC 4306, expands upon IKEv1. (Public keys, digital certificates, and CAs are discussed later in this chapter.)

Initially, IPsec became the predominant mechanism for providing the underlying VPN architectures. This technology works at OSI Layer 3 to create a connection into the network so that as a device logs on, it can act as if it is physically attached to the LAN. By encrypting the traffic, the customer can build VPN networks over the Internet. A customer's traffic is encrypted but not necessarily segmented. IPsec provides encryption and authentication, but there is a tradeoff in performance, although most modern hardware can handle the cryptographic requirements well enough. In general, IPsec is inefficient because it requires significant overhead to encrypt the traffic. This may be acceptable on low-speed links, but throughput is significantly affected on high-speed links. Most router vendors provide IPsec capabilities embedded in the operating systems, but there is a significant performance degradation in the routers.

Line-speed IPsec processing is still not where most customers would like it to be. You need to take this into consideration when choosing a routing platform that will be initiating IPsec security associations. In addition to the performance impact, there is the additional management overhead of configuring, maintaining, and managing IPsec across the IP cloud. IPsec, key distribution, key management, and peering configuration can become complex in a large IPsec deployment.

GRE VPNs

RFC 2784 and RFC 1702 specify the GRE protocol for using IP as both the delivery and payload protocol. In the most general case, a system has a packet that needs to be encapsulated and delivered to some destination, referred to as the *payload packet*. The payload is first encapsulated in a GRE packet. The resulting GRE packet can then be encapsulated in some other protocol and forwarded. This outer protocol is referred to as the *delivery protocol*.

GRE is a simple stateless protocol that allows for the tunneling of IP in IP. GRE tunnels can be used to form VPNs, connecting remote sites by using private IP addresses via a public network. These tunnels are configured between provider edge routers and are transparent to the rest of the network. GRE VPNs currently have simple support for QoS. By default, the DSCP value in each payload header is copied into the tunnel header. This means that any QoS policy for IP packets can be applied to GRE-encapsulated packets as well. An added benefit is that GRE VPNs provide adjacencies directly between customer routers.

GRE VPNs provide a complete separation between customer and provider routing (see Figure 9.21). Customers can run their own routing protocols across the VPN and have no interaction with provider protocols. An internal gateway protocol dedicated to customers, such as OSPF or IS-IS, can be run across a provider network with strict separation from the provider's internal or external routing protocols. If customers are transitioning from a private enterprise network, they may be able to use this approach to preserve much of their internal gateway protocol configuration.

Key concepts in GRE VPNs include multiple contexts and multiple interfaces:

■ **Contexts**—A GRE router's VPN solutions all rely on *contexts*, which are virtual routers running within single physical devices. A context has its own IP address space, routing table, user authentication, logging and

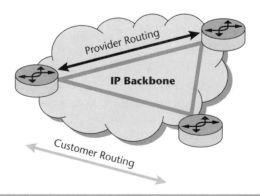

Figure 9.21 IP GRE VPNs

debugging functions, and other attributes. Customers get a dedicated context for each VPN.

- **Interfaces**—Virtual or logical interfaces enable physical ports or circuits to be individually mapped to different contexts through simple configuration commands. An *interface* is a logical entity that holds an IP address and is configured as part of a context. Interfaces are independent of physical ports and circuits. An interface can pass traffic only when it is bound to, or associated with, a physical port or circuit. This binding process can be changed at any time so that a customer port can easily be mapped to one context and then remapped to another with only one line of configuration code.

GRE routers can carry multicast traffic in GRE tunnels. Carriers can, therefore, distribute multicast traffic, such as video, in GRE VPNs or use GRE tunnels to carry multicast traffic through a unicast network. The latter application is ideal when a carrier wants to support multicast capability in only certain select routers or segments of the network. A provider can support GRE VPNs as only the first step in its VPN strategy. If the provider wants to eventually offer Border Gateway Protocol (BGP) and MPLS VPNs, it can continue to offer GRE VPNs while the network is migrated to MPLS and the BGP mesh between provider edge routers is configured. Then the provider can migrate GRE VPN customers to be BGP MPLS VPNs (which are discussed later in this chapter, in the section "RFC 2547 (BGP MPLS) VPNs").

Layer 3 VPNs

The objective of Layer 3 VPNs is to virtualize multiple per-VPN forwarding instances within a single physical platform. This offers new customer IP VPN services, reduces capital and operational expenditures, offers scalability, and provides per–control plane protection, isolation, and security. The provider forwards packets based on customer Layer 3 addresses, and the customer does less routing because the provider assists in distributing customer routes to VPN sites.

The basic components of a Layer 3 VPN are the provider, provider edge, and customer edge routers. The *provider routers* are IP or MPLS routers found in the core, and they interconnect the provider edge routers at the edge. A *provider edge router* sits at the edge of the provider's network and provides the interface between the customer edge router and the IP or MPLS backbone. The *customer edge routers* exchange their routing tables with the provider edge routers via standard routing protocols, such as RIP, OSPF, Enhanced Interior Gateway Routing Protocol (EIGRP), and BGP.

As shown in Figure 9.22, the provider edge devices that implement the VPN functionalities implement a set of per-VPN virtual forwarding instances (VFIs). A VFI is a logical entity that resides at a provider edge that includes the router information base and forwarding information base for a VPN instance. A separate

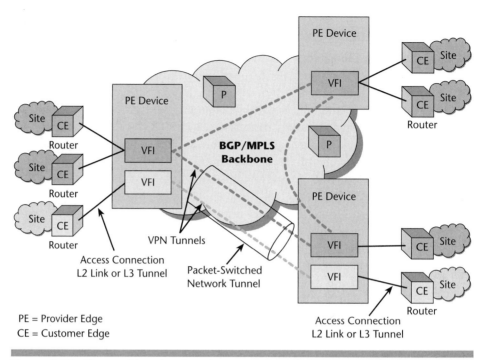

Figure 9.22 The provider edge–based Layer 3 reference model

forwarding or switching instance is dedicated to one specific VPN. Customer edge–sourced packets are forwarded across the provider backbone in a tunnel based on a per-VPN VFI lookup of destination customer Layer 3 addresses. VFIs make forwarding decisions based on the VPN customer packet Layer 3 information (i.e., the packet destination IP address).

VFI entities implemented in different provider edge devices on the same service provider network and belonging to the same VPN are interconnected via VPN tunnels. As mentioned earlier in this chapter, a *VPN tunnel* is a virtual link between two entities that belong to the same VPN. This virtual link is implemented by means of adding an encapsulation header to each forwarded packet, and that header is understood by the packet-switched network backbone in such a way that the encapsulated traffic can be forwarded from the packet-switched network source entity to the packet-switched network destination entity. The source entity is responsible for adding the encapsulation header, and the destination entity is responsible for removing it. Multiple VPN tunnels established between the same two provider edge devices are often multiplexed in a provider edge–to–provider edge packet-switched network tunnel and transparently carried over the packet-switched network's provider core devices.

The customer site is a local private network—that is, a set of communication devices that do not use a shared backbone to communicate with each other. The edge devices of a site, the customer edge routers, are connected to one of the service provider's provider edge devices via an access connection or attachment circuit through the access network. An access connection in this context is a dedicated Layer 2 connection, such as an ATM virtual circuit, a Frame Relay data link connection identifier (DLCI), a PPP connection, an Ethernet interface, or a virtual LAN. It could also be a Layer 3 tunnel, such as an IPsec security association over the Internet. The customer edge–to–provider edge access connection is configured to be associated with the specific VFI in the provider edge, depending on which VPN the site belongs to.

Layer 3 VPNs are implemented in two ways:

- **RFC 2547 (BGP MPLS) VPNs**—RFC 2547 is an IETF informational document that describes BGP MPLS. RFC 2547bis—the second version of RFC 2547—is an Internet Draft. RFC 2547bis VPNs are also known as BGP MPLS VPNs because BGP is used to distribute VPN routing information across the provider's backbone and MPLS is used to forward VPN traffic from one VPN site to another. RFC 2547bis multiplexes many VPN routes through a single BGP system. In this approach, customer routing is terminated at the provider edge.
- **Virtual router VPNs**—With these types of VPNs, each virtual router runs an instance of a routing protocol that is responsible for disseminating VPN reachability information between virtual routers. In this model, customer routing is extended across the provider network.

The following sections describe these two types of Layer 3 VPNs in detail.

RFC 2547 (BGP MPLS) VPNs   IP VPNs based on RFC 2547 are becoming increasingly popular. As shown in Figure 9.23, they use a combination of BGP and MPLS to pass IP traffic through an MPLS core. Offering this type of VPNs requires a provider to configure MPLS on all core and edge routers. Furthermore, all provider edge routers need to have Multiprotocol BGP (MP-BGP) sessions established between them to communicate VPN information. The provider edge routers store the routing updates from each customer's customer edge router in what is termed a *virtual routing forwarding (VRF) instance*; simply put, it is a routing table populated with VPN routes.

Because there may be a great number of provider edge routers in a network, carriers might also need to configure BGP route reflectors to simplify the internal BGP mesh. Route reflectors reduce the size of the internal BGP mesh. Route reflector

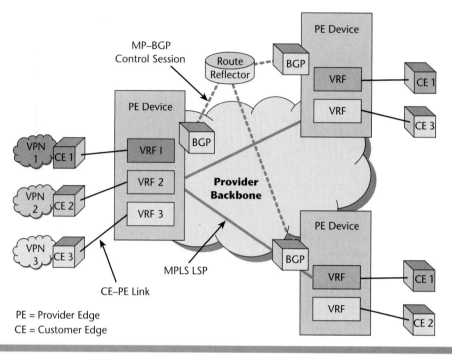

Figure 9.23   The RFC 2547bis model

clients propagate routes up to the route reflectors, which, in turn, send the routes to other route reflector clients. Route reflectors are useful in partitioning total routing table space across multiple devices. This allows the route reflector clients to receive only routes they need—not all the routes.

Each customer edge router has its own VRF on the provider edge. The customer advertises all routes associated with that location to the provider edge. When all the provider edge routers that connect to a particular customer have the customer's routing information in a VRF, the provider edge routers exchange information by using MP-BGP. These routes and the corresponding VRFs make up the customer VPN.

To the customer, from a routing perspective, the customer edge routers appear as if they are connected via a traditional VPN. The customer can view the routing table on the customer edge router and see routes to remote sites, just as it would with a traditional VPN. The routing adjacencies formed are between the customer edge and the provider edge, not the customer edge and the customer edge. The customer edge has one interface to the MPLS cloud, and the MPLS provides full or partial meshing with the customer edge router attached to the network.

One of the benefits of Layer 3 MPLS VPNs is that the provider handles all the meshing and can provide any-to-any connectivity over a multitude of interface types. Previously, if a customer wanted to mesh its remote locations, it had to purchase leased lines and build a mesh of permanent virtual circuits (PVCs). The routing architecture and propagation of routes was up to the customer; the provider only ensured connectivity. With Layer 3 MPLS VPNs, all that is required is the advertisement of the routes to the provider edge, and the provider handles the rest. The only drawback to this solution is that the provider may not have the geographic footprint to reach all the customer locations; it can be cost-prohibitive for the customer to purchase a local loop to the nearest provider edge router in the provider's POP. This is a limiting factor with MPLS deployment, especially for organizations that have international locations.

Virtual Router VPNs   The objective of a Layer 3 virtual router VPN, which is currently an IETF Internet Draft, is to provide per-VPN routing, forwarding, QoS, and service management capabilities. This VPN service is based on the concept of a *virtual router*, which has exactly the same mechanisms as a physical router and, therefore, can inherit all existing mechanisms and tools for configuration, deployment, operation, troubleshooting, monitoring, and accounting. Multiple virtual routers can exist in a single physical device, and virtual routers can be deployed in various VPN configurations.

Direct virtual router–to–virtual router connectivity can be configured through Layer 2 links or through a variety of tunnel mechanisms, using IP- or MPLS-based tunnels. Also, multiple virtual routers can be aggregated over a backbone virtual router. This architecture accommodates various backbone deployment scenarios, including situations in which the VPN service provider either owns the backbone or obtains backbone service from one or more other service providers.

As shown in Figure 9.24, a VPN customer site is connected to the provider backbone by means of a connection between a customer edge device—which can be one or more hosts and/or routers—and a virtual router. Customer edge devices are preconfigured to connect to one or more virtual routers. Multiple virtual routers may coexist on the same service provider edge device or provider edge. Customer edge devices can be attached to virtual routers over any type of access link (e.g., ATM, Frame Relay, Ethernet, PPP) or IP tunneling mechanisms (e.g., IPsec, L2TP, or GRE tunnels). Customer edge sites can be statically connected to the provider network via dedicated circuits or can use dialup links. Routing tables associated with each virtual router define the site-to-site reachability for each VPN. The internal backbone provider routers are not VPN aware and do not keep VPN state.

In general, the backbone is a shared network infrastructure that represents either a Layer 2, ATM, or Frame Relay network; an IP network; or an MPLS network. Not all VPNs existing on the same provider edge are necessarily connected

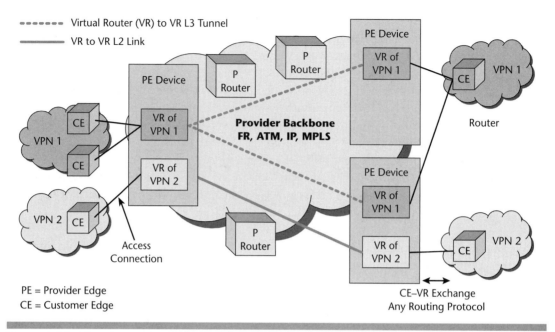

Figure 9.24 Virtual router VPNs

via the same backbone, so a single provider edge can be connected to multiple backbones. Individual virtual routers on the provider edge may also connect to multiple backbones. Thus, a single VPN can be built from multiple transport technologies in the virtual router architecture.

Virtual routers have independent IP routing and forwarding tables, and they are isolated from each other. This means that two virtual routers on a provider edge can serve two different VPNs that may have overlapping address space. The addresses need only be unique within a VPN domain. A virtual router has two main functions: constructing routing tables for the paths between VPN sites, by using any routing technology (such as OSPF, RIP, or a border gateway protocol), and forwarding packets to the next hops within the VPN domain.

From a VPN user's point of view, a virtual router provides the same functionality as a physical router. Separate routing and forwarding capabilities provide each virtual router with the appearance of a dedicated router that guarantees isolation from the traffic of other VPNs while running on shared forwarding and transmission resources. To the customer edge access device, the virtual router appears as a neighbor router in the customer edge–based network.

Three main virtual router deployment scenarios can be used for building VPNs: virtual router–to–virtual router connectivity over a Layer 2 connection, virtual router–to–virtual router connectivity tunneled over an IP or MPLS network, and aggregation of multiple virtual routers over a backbone virtual router to provide connectivity over a Layer 2 IP or MPLS network. These virtual router deployment scenarios can coexist on a single provider edge or within a single VPN.

RFC 2547 VPNs Versus Virtual Router VPNs   Table 9.2 compares the RFC 2547 VPN and virtual router VPN architectures.

The standards debate is ongoing, with high-profile companies on both sides of the argument. For now, the choice of a network-based VPN implementation is up to the provider. All these IP VPN services are more complicated to configure and require more attention from both carriers and customers than Frame Relay, private-line, or ATM services. Without any application or architectural triggers for the customer to move to IP VPN service, the shift may be very gradual.

Layer 2 VPNs

Carriers need to continue to benefit from legacy services such as TDM private lines, Frame Relay, and ATM while they introduce new Ethernet metro-transport and Ethernet access services. They need a common edge infrastructure that supports both new and legacy services and allows all the services to seamlessly communicate. To accomplish this goal, most carriers are planning to simplify their network infrastructures over a common MPLS core and introduce MPLS-based services.

Table 9.2   Summary of RFC 2547 and Virtual Router VPNs

Characteristic	RFC 2547 VPNs	Virtual Router VPNs
Is simple to implement	No	Yes
Is scalable	Yes	No
Is easy to provision new services	Yes	No
Provides high security	No	Yes
Is a securable network	Yes	Yes
Supports many subscribers	Yes	No
Requires MPLS/BGP	Yes	No
Supports interoperability	Yes	No
Provides end-to-end QoS	Yes	No
Reduces CPE complexity	Yes	Yes
Reduces CPE processing	Yes	No

MPLS was first deployed in the core of carrier networks to enhance the performance and capabilities of connectionless IP routing. Today, there is increased interest in MPLS Layer 2 VPN services. With MPLS Layer 2 VPN services, carriers can transport protocols such as SNA, DECnet, or IPX and keep legacy TDM private lines as well as Frame Relay and ATM services. With Layer 2 VPNs, the provider forwards packets based on Layer 2 information or port information. It emulates Layer 2 WAN or LAN connectivity between customer sites. In this case, the customer is responsible for the Layer 3 routing. Layer 2 MPLS VPNs are identical to private network VPNs in that the customer attaches its customer premises router to the MPLS cloud via traditional Layer 2 circuits and builds a Layer 3 routing topology over the provisioned circuits. The management of the routing is handled by the customer in the same fashion as it would be with a traditional private VPN.

In a Layer 2 VPN solution, there is no exchange of routing information between the provider edge and the customer edge. The IP/MPLS service provider core network transports customer Layer 2 frames from ingress provider edge to egress provider edge. The VPN tunnels that transport this traffic between provider edges are called *pseudo-wires*, as they emulate the behavior of a connection or wire over a connectionless infrastructure. The provider edges implement Layer 2 VFIs that forward the customer traffic based on Layer 2 information (e.g., ATM virtual path identifiers and virtual circuit identifiers, or Ethernet MAC addresses, or Frame Relay DLCIs). This is beneficial for organizations that need legacy protocol support and those that feel they can efficiently and cost-effectively manage their own routing environment. They are, in effect, purchasing bandwidth, not the additional services offered by a Layer 3 MPLS VPN. Customers still have the PVC mesh, provisioning, and routing issues, as before, and there may be limitations on what interfaces a carrier will support. Carriers that are evaluating Layer 2 VPNs are challenged by the interconnectivity issues associated with Layer 2 VPNs. Support for any-to-any connectivity over Layer 2 MPLS backbones is not widely deployed by any of the major carriers. In most instances, the customer edge routers require common access types, such as Frame Relay–to–Frame Relay or ATM-to-ATM. Ultimately, however, Layer 2 MPLS VPNs will allow customers to attach any Layer 2 access circuit to the MPLS cloud, allowing for diverse and cost-effective interface options.

Multiple Layer 2 VPN service models are being analyzed in the industry and by the Provider Provisioned Virtual Private Networking (PPVPN) working group and the Pseudo-Wire Emulation Edge-to-Edge (PWE3) working group. The PPVPN group is working on the Kompella draft, named after Cureda Kompella. The Kompella draft makes use of BGP to allow provider edge routers to communicate with one another about their customer connections. The PWE3 group is working on a draft named the Martini draft, after Luca Martini. The Martini draft makes use of the Label Distribution Protocol (LDP) between provider edge routers. Two of the most important Layer 2 VPN models, VPWS and VPLS, are described in the following sections.

VPWS   VPWS VPNs are also known as point-to-point pseudo-wires. A pseudo-wire emulates a point-to-point link and provides a single service perceived by its user as an unshared link or circuit of the chosen service. Using encapsulated pseudo-wire tunnels, customers' sites can be connected via point-to-point circuits as if they were using their own private leased lines (see Figure 9.25). VPWS VPNs support traffic types such as Ethernet, ATM, Frame Relay, SDH/SONET, and TDM. VPWS provides a mesh of point-to-point customer edge–to–customer edge Layer 2 connections over a packet-switched network. The provider edge does the mapping between the attachment circuit and the pseudo-wire.

VPWS is seen largely as an appropriate approach for point-to-point connection-oriented services, such as ATM, Frame Relay, and point-to-point Ethernet. For multipoint-to-multipoint connectionless services such as Ethernet and VLANs, VPLS is required.

VPLS   A number of vendors have adopted the VPLS approach, and deployments of VPLS are mushrooming worldwide. VPLS is a growing solution for providing Ethernet services. It combines the benefits of Ethernet and MPLS for both customers and carriers.

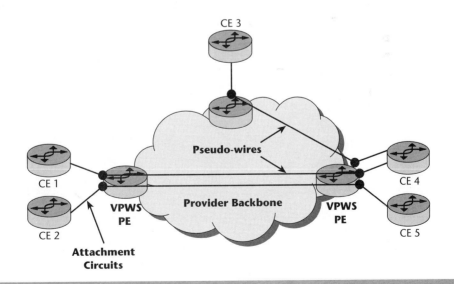

Figure 9.25   VPWS

VPLS offers at Layer 2 what IP VPNs offer at Layer 3: a service with multipoint connectivity (see Figure 9.26). The main difference is the interface used between the customer edge equipment and the provider edge equipment. With IP VPNs, customer edge equipment is IP routers, whereas with VPLS, it can be an Ethernet bridge, a switch, a hub, or a router, allowing non-IP traffic as well as IP traffic to be exchanged between sites. Apart from this essential difference, MPLS Layer 2 VPNs and Layer 3 VPN-based approaches are very similar in other areas. Both share the same common MPLS protocols and the underlying IP/MPLS infrastructure. In the past, these services were most commonly delivered on TDM, Frame Relay, and ATM networks. VPLS is one of the most innovative and easily manageable ways of providing Ethernet MPLS VPNs. Each customer location is attached to a node on the MPLS network. For each customer or VPN, a full mesh of logical point-to-point connections is set up over the backbone MPLS network. This allows a customer location to have direct visibility to every other location belonging to that customer.

Unique MPLS labels are used to segment one customer's traffic from another's and to segment one service from another. This segmentation allows a customer to acquire a bundle of services from its provider, each of which is tailored for the end application. For example, a customer's bundle could comprise VoIP, Internet access, and maybe two or more VPN services. The first VPN service could be to provide broad data connectivity between all corporate locations, accessible to all employees. The second VPN service could be restricted to some financial transactions conducted between a subset of locations. Each of these services would be uniquely configured over VPLS, thus allowing them to have unique quality and security attributes.

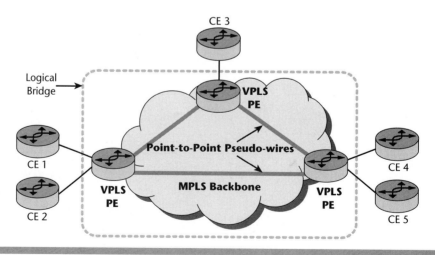

Figure 9.26 VPLS

VPLS provides logical LAN bridging or switching functions over a packet-switched network. The provider edge performs virtual bridging or switching for LAN-attached customer edge nodes. VPLS supports both point-to-multipoint and multipoint-to-multipoint service using PWE3. PWE3 specifies the encapsulation, transport, control, management, interworking, and security of services emulated over packet-switched networks.

The benefits to carriers of combining Ethernet and MPLS are numerous. Carriers immediately benefit from the lower capital expenditure required for deploying Ethernet infrastructure. However, a simple Ethernet switched network has limitations on service scalability due to VLAN ID restrictions as well as limitations on reliability (e.g., Spanning Tree Protocol does not scale well). These limitations are solved by MPLS, which offers a portfolio of solutions that provide massive scalability and multiple reliability options and also bring other benefits. For example, MPLS's dynamic signaling is instrumental in providing quicker changes and reconfigurations of service. Its traffic engineering capabilities allow providers to support service-level guarantees across the entire network. Thus, it not only meets their needs for scalability and reliability but also provides operational advantages that can further reduce expenditures.

The advent of the Internet and the resulting productivity gains spurred by the adoption of new technologies are leading to a demand for increased bandwidth and services. Corporations are demanding customized services at greater bandwidth, and consumers are looking for services such as broadband connectivity and VOD. Carriers have to balance the demands of their target markets with the realities of their business. Traditional technologies (such as ATM and SDH/SONET), while being familiar, simply do not match the vision that carriers have for their networks. They are built on expensive infrastructure that cannot scale without large investments. Moreover, the complex management and multiple handoffs between all these technologies cause significant operating overhead. The market opportunity for Ethernet services is clear and exists today. Numerous early adopters have been successful in deploying these services. Carriers are facing a challenge in how to respond to these market dynamics. VPLS with an Ethernet infrastructure can present an optimal solution for carriers to roll out new services profitably. The benefits from reduced capital and operating expenditures add up quickly to improve the bottom line. In addition, the ability to leverage existing networks ensures carriers that the investments made in older technologies can be preserved and that more returns can be generated from them. There are, however, potential disadvantages associated with the use of Ethernet in MANs and WANs. The biggest concern is the lack of QoS capabilities, leading some industry observers to view Ethernet solutions as one of throwing bandwidth at the problem and therefore a short-term strategy at best.

VPN Security

Security is very important to the proper operation of VPNs. The following sections describe the available security mechanisms, including firewalls; authentication, authorization, and accounting (AAA); encryption; and digital certificates.

Firewalls

A *firewall* is typically defined as a system or a group of systems that enforces and acts as a control policy between two networks. It can also be defined as a mechanism used to protect a trusted network from an untrusted network—usually while still allowing traffic between the two. All traffic from inside to outside and vice versa must pass through the firewall. Only authorized traffic, as defined by the local security policy, is allowed to pass through it. The system itself is highly resistant to penetration. A firewall selectively permits or denies network traffic.

There are several variations of firewalls, including the following:

- A firewall can use different protocols to separate Internet servers from internal servers.

- Routers can be programmed to define what protocols at the application, network, or transport layer can come in and out of the router—so the router is basically acting as a packet filter.

- Proxy servers can separate the internal network users and services from the public Internet. Additional functions can be included via proxy servers, including address translation, caching, encryption, and virus filtering.

Viruses

The term *virus* broadly refers to a program designed to interfere with computers' normal operations. The term also can be used more narrowly to refer to malicious software programs that move from one file to another and can be transmitted to other PCs via an infected file. They generally don't seek out the Internet or e-mail to spread.

Another type of malware is a *worm*. Worms make use of a LAN or the Internet (especially via e-mail) to replicate and forward themselves to new users. Many worms target humans, not software.

Finally, a *Trojan horse* hides within another program or file and then becomes active when someone opens the unwitting host.

A big part of administrating security involves reducing the threat of malware. The fact that we can deploy malware detection and removal technologies on a proxy server is very attractive.

Authentication, Authorization, and Accounting

An important aspect of security is the authentication of users and access control, which is commonly handled by an AAA server. An AAA server is a network server used for access control. *Authentication* identifies the user, *authorization* implements policies that determine which resources and services a valid user may access, and *accounting* keeps track of time and data resources used for billing and analysis. The AAA server, also called 3A software, typically interacts with a network access server (NAS) and gateway servers, as well as with databases and directories that contain user information.

RADIUS, the current standard by which devices or applications communicate with an AAA server, is an AAA protocol for applications such as network access or IP mobility. This UDP-based protocol is intended to work in both local and roaming situations and is considered suitable for high-volume service control applications, such as regulation of dialup or VPN services. Increased use of RADIUS is occurring due to the introduction of 802.1X port security (discussed in Chapter 15, "WMANs, WLANs, and WPANs") for wired and wireless LANs. In fact, Microsoft has included 802.1X security in Windows TCP/IP, and every enterprise PC might require authentication before being granted access to the LAN.

RADIUS servers are designed to block unauthorized access by remote users, and they rely on authentication schemes such as Challenge Handshake Authentication Protocol (CHAP), which means there's a back-and-forth dialog to verify a user's identity. In fact, RADIUS makes use of CHAP, which uses a three-way handshake to periodically verify the identity of the peer throughout the connection. The server sends a random token to the remote workstation. The token is then encrypted, using the user's password, and sent back to the server. The server performs a lookup to see whether it recognizes the password. If the values match, the authentication is acknowledged; if the values do not match, the connection is terminated. Because a different token is provided each time a remote user dials in, CHAP provides robust authentication.

A newer protocol, called DIAMETER, serves as a replacement for RADIUS. DIAMETER is also an AAA protocol for the same applications of network access and IP mobility. The major change is that DIAMETER extends RADIUS to provide AAA services to new access technologies.

Encryption

The best way to protect electronic data is to use encryption—that is, to encode the data so as to render a document unreadable by all except those who are authorized to have access to it. Encryption and decryption are performed by using a *cipher*, which is an algorithm, or a series of well-defined steps that can be followed as a procedure. The content of an original document is referred to as *plaintext*. When encryption is applied to the document, the plaintext is scrambled, through the use of an algorithm and a variable, or key; the result is called *ciphertext*. The key is a randomly selected string of numbers. Generally, the longer the string, the stronger the security.

Although encryption may ensure privacy, other techniques are required for full communications security, including a message authentication code or digital signatures, both used to verify the authenticity and integrity of the message. The message authentication code is a tag, or short piece of information, used to authenticate a message. Using a secret key and an arbitrary-length message, a message authentication code algorithm calculates a hash value, which protects the message's integrity and authenticity by allowing those who also have the secret key to detect any changes that may have been made to the message content. The same secret key is used to both generate and verify the message authentication code values. Digital signatures, on the other hand, use two complementary algorithms: one for signing the message and the other for verification. Digital signatures rely on public key cryptography (discussed later in this chapter).

There are two major categories of encryption algorithms: symmetric and asymmetric.

Symmetric Encryption   In symmetric encryption, the sender and the receiver use the same key or machine setup. There are two approaches to encoding data using symmetric encryption: block cipher and streaming cipher. With the block cipher approach, the algorithm encodes text in fixed-bit blocks, using a key whose length is also fixed in length. With the streaming cipher approach, the algorithm encodes the stream of data sequentially, without segmenting it into blocks. Both of these techniques require a secure method of reexchanging keys between the participants.

Symmetric encryption algorithms include the following:

- **Data Encryption Standard (DES)**—DES, which was developed in the 1970s, is very popular in the banking industry. It is a block cipher that encodes text into fixed-bit blocks (typically 64 bits), using a 56-bit key. DES has been replaced by Advanced Encryption Standard (AES).
- **Triple DES (3DES)**—3DES is 168-bit encryption that uses three 56-bit keys. 3DES applies the DES algorithm to a plaintext block three times.
- **Rivest Cipher 4 (RC4)**—RC4 is a streaming cipher technique; a stream cipher adds the output of a pseudorandom number generator bit by bit to the sequential bits of the digitized plaintext.
- **Blowfish**—Blowfish is a 64-bit block code that has key lengths of 32 bits to 448 bits. Blowfish is used in more than 100 products and is viewed as one of the best available algorithms.

- **International Data Encryption Algorithm (IDEA)**—IDEA, developed by ETH Zurich (www.ethz.ch), is free of charge for noncommercial use. It is viewed as a good algorithm and is used in Pretty Good Privacy (PGP) and in Speak Freely, a program that allows encrypted digitized voice to be sent over the Internet.

- **Twofish**—Twofish, developed by Bruce Schneier of Counterpane Internet Security (www.counterpane.com), is very strong, and it was one of the five initial candidates for AES.

- **Advanced Encryption Standard (AES)**—AES was adopted by the National Institute of Standards (NIST; www.nist.gov) in November 2001 after a five-year standardization process.

According to NIST, it would take 149 trillion years to crack the U.S. government's AES, which uses the Rijndael algorithm and specifies three key lengths—128 bits, 192 bits, and 256 bits. In comparison, DES, which uses a 56-bit key, would take only a matter of hours using a powerful computer, but, of course, this is totally dependent on the speed of the hardware used for cracking the code; a typical desktop PC would require much more than a few hours to crack a 56-bit DES key.

Asymmetric Encryption   Key encryption requires a secure method for exchanging keys between participants. The solution to key distribution came, in 1975, with Diffie and Hellman's public key cryptography scheme. This permits the use of two keys, one of which can be openly published and still permit secure encrypted communications. This scheme later became known as *asymmetric key cryptography* (also called *public key encryption* [PKE]).

Asymmetric cryptography can be used for authentication. After encrypting a signature by using a private key, anyone with access to the public key can verify that the signature belongs to the owner of the private key. As shown in Figure 9.27, the following are the steps in PKE:

1. User A hashes the plaintext.

2. User A encrypts the plaintext with user B's public key and encrypts the hash value with user A's private key.

3. User B decodes the ciphertext with user B's private key.

4. User B decodes the hash value with user A's public key, thereby confirming the sender's authenticity.

5. User B calculates the hash value of the just-encrypted plaintext.

6. User B compares the decrypted hash value with the value calculated locally, thereby confirming the message's integrity.

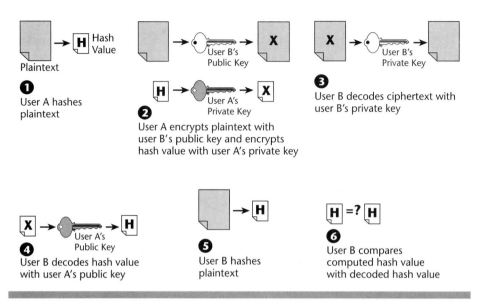

Figure 9.27   Encryption and authentication

Public key management involves the exchange of secrets that both ends use to produce random short-term session keys for authenticating each other. It is a method of encrypting data by using two separate keys or codes. The sender uses a public key generally provided as part of a certificate issued by a CA to scramble data for transmission. The receiver then uses the corresponding private key to decrypt the data upon receipt. The CA issues certificates that contain data about individuals or enterprises that has been verified to be authentic (although not all public CAs do this). In essence, the CA vouches for the authenticity of other parties so that their communications are secured.

Message authentication verifies the integrity of an electronic message and also verifies that an electronic message was sent by a particular entity. Before an outgoing message is encrypted, a cryptographic hash function—which is like an elaborate version of a checksum—is performed on it. The hash function compresses the bits of the plaintext message into a fixed-size digest, or hash value, of 128 or more bits. It is then extremely difficult to alter the plaintext message without invalidating the hash value.

Message authentication mechanisms include Message Digest-5 (MD5) and Secure Hash Algorithm-1 (SHA-1). MD5 hashes a file of arbitrary length into a 128-bit value. SHA-1 hashes a file of arbitrary length into a 160-bit value; it is more processor intensive, but it renders greater security.

Public key management provides a secure method for obtaining a person's or an organization's public key, with sufficient assurance that the key is correct. There are three main public key algorithms: RSA (named for its creators, Rivest, Shamir, and Adelman), Diffie-Hellman, and PGP. RSA is the oldest of the three algorithms, and its security derives from the difficulty of factoring the product of two large prime integers. Diffie-Hellman is used mostly for exchanging keys; its security rests on the difficulty of computing discrete algorithms in a finite field, generated by a large prime number. PGP (www.pgp.com), which was created in 1991, is one of the most popular PKE schemes.

Public Key Infrastructure Without a functioning universal public key infrastructure (PKI), we cannot reliably and easily acquire certificates that contain public keys for persons or organizations we want to communicate with. One of the biggest hurdles e-commerce companies face is confirming the identity of the parties involved. Ensuring identity requires an encrypted ID object that can be issued by a mutually trusted third party (i.e., a CA) and then verified and accepted by a user's browser. Personal digital IDs contained in the user's browser accomplish this. Historically, these client certificates have been used to control access to resources on a business network, but they can also contain other user information, including identity discount level or customer type. The user's browser reads the server certificate, and if it's accepted, the browser generates a symmetric session key, using the server's public key. The server then decrypts the symmetric key, which is then used to encrypt the rest of the transaction. The transaction is then signed, using the user's digital ID, verifying the user's identity and legally binding the user to the transaction.

PKI is a system that provides protocols and services for managing public keys in an intranet or Internet environment; it involves distributing keys in a secure way. PKI secures e-business applications such as private e-mail, purchase orders, and workflow automation. It uses digital certificates and digital signatures to authenticate and encrypt messages. It permits the creation of legally verifiable identification objects, and it also dictates an encryption technique to protect data transmitted over the Internet.

Usually, PKI involves client software, server software such as a CA, hardware (e.g., smart cards), and operational procedures. Using his or her private key, one user digitally signs a message, and the receiver, using the public key contained in the sender's certificate, issued by a CA within the PKI, can check that signature. In this fashion, two or more users can establish confidentiality, message integrity, and user authentication without having to exchange any special information in advance. PKI systems used in the enterprise are generally closely linked to the enterprise directory system, where each employee's public key is often stored, along with his or her general contact information. The leading directory technology is LDAP, which is discussed in Chapter 10.

Standards are absolutely vital to proper PKI operation, given that there is a certificate hierarchy composed of at least several computers and often more than one organization, using interoperating software from different sources. The group responsible for developing standards in this area is the IETF PKIX working group (www.imc.org/ietf-pkix). This group's purpose is to develop the Internet standards needed to support an X.509-based PKI. (X.509 is discussed in the next section.)

Overall, the market for commercial PKI operations has not bloomed as its pioneers imagined. Too many differences in enacted laws and regulations, not to mention technical and operational problems, have slowed progress tremendously.

PKI Alternatives

There are some alternatives to PKI, including Web of Trust, Simple Public Key Infrastructure, and Robot Certificate Authorities.

The Web of Trust scheme makes use of self-signed certificates and a third party that attests to those certificates. Two examples of the Web of Trust are GNU Privacy Guard (GPG) and PGP, which has been extensively used in e-mail and is widely deployed.

Simple PKI (SPKI) came out of three independent efforts to overcome the growing popularity of PGP's Web of Trust and the complexities of X.509. With SPKI, users and systems are bound directly to keys, using a local trust model, somewhat like the Web of Trust, but with the addition of authorization.

As the name suggests, Robot Certificate Authorities (Robot CAs) are automated programs that validate certain aspects of a public key's validity and then sign it to attest that those aspects are indeed valid. The common aspects validated include the following: the use of the key is current, the holder of the destination e-mail address is aware that his or her key is published, and a secret key corresponding to the public key is in possession of the holder of the e-mail address. At this point, the most successful PKI implementations are in government.

Digital Certificates

Digital certificates, based on the ANSI X.509 specification, have become a de facto Internet standard for establishing a trusting relationship by using technology. X.509 comes from the X.500 specification on directory services, which serves as an electronic phonebook, allowing enabled applications to look up included entities. Each entity has an identifying record or certificate, and that certificate follows the ITU X.509 recommendation. Using digital certificates is a method for registering user identities with a third party, a CA (such as Entrust or VeriSign). A digital certificate binds a user to an electronic signature that can be trusted like a written signature and includes authentication, access rights, and verification information.

CAs prepare, issue, and manage the digital certificates, and they keep a directory database of user information, verify its accuracy and completeness, and issue the electronic certificates based on that information. A CA signs a certificate, verifying the integrity of the information in it.

By becoming their own digital CAs, service providers can package electronic security with offerings such as VPN and applications services. Server certificates ensure Internet buyers of the identity of the seller's Web site. They contain details about the Web site, such as the domain name of the site and who owns it. Third parties, such as Thawte (www.thawte.com), then guarantee this information. Sites with server certificates post the CA, and Internet browsers accept their certificates for secure transactions.

There are still many security developments to come, especially with the constant introduction of new networking technologies and systems. Standards need to be defined and formalized for the likes of the various IP services and wireless/mobile networks before e-commerce will truly be able to function with the security that it mandates. For now, these are the types of mechanisms necessary to ensure that your data remains with you.

Chapter 10

Next-Generation Networks

This chapter explores the current perspectives and developments with respect to next-generation infrastructures. It is a very important chapter for both service providers and end users who need to understand how the forces of convergence and emerging next-generation technologies will affect the evolution of their networks. The information covered in this chapter will help those attempting to make investment decisions, develop strategic plans, or choose what to do regarding business development and marketing. This chapter covers the essentials of how architectures are shifting, and the driving forces and trends behind the new infrastructures.

As discussed in this book's introduction, some evolutionary ICT trends are well on their way to making a profound impact on life as we know it, affecting communications of all sorts—human-to-human, human-to-machine, machine-to-machine, and even human-to-animal. Broadband applications are redefining our notion of education, health care, government, environment, arts and entertainment, and science. The network environment is seeing the rapid growth of a new genre of users. We're quickly becoming a world populated with things that think: embedded devices, intelligent wearables, human–machine interfaces, grid computing, and real-time communications. In order for these applications to flourish, we need a new generation of converged infrastructure, one based on bandwidth abundance, the use of intelligent optical networks, protocols that can guarantee performance in service levels, and devices that can engage across a complete realm of voice, data, video, rich media, and sensory media—all on a mobile basis when needed.

This chapter describes the key architectural changes required to meet the demands of the emerging world of broadband applications, devices, and infrastructures. The topics covered include the broadband evolution, multimedia networking requirements, the broadband infrastructure, next-generation networks and convergence, and the next-generation network infrastructure.

■ The Broadband Evolution

One primary driver toward broadband is the increasing demand for information. Today's key competitive edge is two-fold: It includes both intellectual property (i.e., how valuable the information assets are and how smart your people are) and the ability to develop and sustain relationships well (i.e., the soft skills to maintain customer loyalty). To perform well in both of these aspects, you need an ongoing stream of the latest information with which to build your knowledge base, and you need effective communications tools to engage your customers and business associates. In an attempt to remain competitive and to grow, it is important to create an infrastructure that encourages fast and effective knowledge exchange.

Another driver toward broadband is the shifting traffic patterns we're seeing. This chapter looks at which of the traffic types are becoming dominant on the network and what they mean to the network characteristics they call on. Networks are being used more and more, and we're experiencing rapid technology advances that present us with different strategies and architectures. It becomes increasingly difficult to make a commitment to a set of technologies today because, after all, tomorrow might introduce a vastly improved architecture. With products and protocols developing so quickly, it is difficult for a given solution to become widely embraced, and without mass appeal, many products and services never have the opportunity to develop in the marketplace.

We're experiencing a wild unleashing of bandwidth, largely driven by developments in both optical networking and wireless communications. We're also seeing a trend toward advanced applications that include high degrees of visualization as well as sensory streams. Finally, convergence is driving the move to broadband, as industries, devices, and applications find natural synergies in the digital world and merge platforms with one another.

The following sections examine some of these trends in more detail and explore the ways they affect next-generation networks.

Communications Traffic Trends

For a decade, the Internet demonstrated tremendous growth rates. According to TeleGeography's 2005 survey of Internet backbone providers (www.telegeography.

patient videoconferences, remote monitoring of vital signs, and remote-control use of diagnostic and surgical instruments.

Yet another key area is broadband's support of teleworking. The key teleworking applications include fast data access, enhanced communications, and videoconferencing with remote locations. Teleworking enables employees and students to work more productively from home or other remote locations. The benefits to be gained encompass reducing traffic congestion, affecting the investment needed in reengineering the transportation grid, alleviating pollution, reducing dependence on fossil fuels, improving the quality of life, and generating potentially enormous cost savings to our society.

Broadband is also vital to providing an effective national security system. Broadband contributes to national security by supporting real-time interagency coordination, monitoring, and mobilization. Because a broadband infrastructure is characterized by multiple carriers, facilities, and decentralization, it is relatively resilient and reliable in the event of disruption, and if disruptions do occur, teleworking will allow communications and work to continue from remote locations. In defense applications, broadband is vital to battlefield logistics, intelligence gathering and distribution, data tracking, and equipment maintenance.

There are endless examples of the necessity of broadband in retail, field services, transportation, mining, oil, and many other fields; the list of industries that are changing and benefiting due to broadband applications and transport is limited only by the imagination.

■ Multimedia Networking Requirements

Today's networks simply were not built for multimedia and, in particular, for applications that involve video communications, multimedia collaboration, and/or interactive-rich media. Curiously, it is through the use of sophisticated computer applications and devices that we have been able to determine what the human information-processing model comprises: There is a very strong tendency for us to rely on the visual information stream for rapid absorption and longer retention. More than 50% of a human's brain cells are devoted to processing visual information, and combined with the delights of sound, smell, and touch—despite our enormous dependence on the written word—we're very active in processing the cues from the physical world. By changing the cues, we can change the world. Digital-rich media, in every conceivable sort of format—including audio, animation, graphic, full-motion video, application, whiteboards, and communities—will increasingly depend on multimedia. Video and multimedia applications require substantial bandwidth, as well as minimal latencies and losses. The table on the following page is a snapshot of the per-user bandwidth requirements for various services.

Application	Bandwidth Requirement
E-mail and Web (not optimum support)	56Kbps
Web as an always-on utility, crude hosted applications, 15-second video e-mail	500Kbps
Hosted applications, reasonable videophone	5Mbps
Massive multiplayer/multimedia communities	10Mbps
Scalable NTSC/PAL-quality video	100Mbps
Digital high-definition video-on-demand (uncompressed)	1Gbps
Innovation applications (3D environments, holography, and so on)	10Gbps

Digital video and digital audio also require minimal, predictable delays in packet transmission, which conventional shared-bandwidth, connectionless networks do not offer. (Chapter 3, "Establishing Communications Channels," discusses connectionless networks in detail.) They also require tight controls over losses, and again, connectionless networks do not account for this. As more people simultaneously access files from a server, bandwidth becomes a significant issue. Correct timing, synchronization, and video picture quality are compromised if the bandwidth is not sufficient. As discussed in the following sections, two key issues relate to multimedia communications: the nature of digital video and the role of television.

Digital Video

One of the fascinating areas driving and motivating the need for broadband access is television. Although TV has a tremendous following throughout the world—more than computing and even telecommunications—it remained untouched by the digital revolution until recently. Despite major advances in computing, video, and communications technologies, TV has continued to rely on standards that are more than 55 years old. The biggest shortcoming with the existing TV standards—that is, National Television Standards Committee (NTSC; used in North America and Japan), Phase Alternating Line (PAL; used throughout the majority of the world), and Systeme Electronique Couleur Avec Memoire (SECAM; used in France and French territories)—is that they are analog systems, in which video signals degrade quickly under adverse conditions. Most of this signal degradation occurs along the path the picture travels from the studio to a TV.

Digital TV (DTV) offers numerous advantages over the old analog TV signal, among which is the fact that it is nearly immune to interference and degradation. Another advantage of DTV is the ability to display a much better range of colors.

The human eye can discriminate more than 16 million colors, and sophisticated computer monitors and DTVs can display those 16 million colors and more. DTV can transmit more data in the same amount of bandwidth, and it can also transmit more types of data. Combined with high-definition TV (HDTV) and digital sound, what this means to the end user is a better picture, better sound, and digital data. However, digital broadcasters are not restricted to just sending a high-definition picture; they can still broadcast a standard-definition picture over DTV, referred to as standard-definition TV (SDTV). But why would they want to do that? The answer is simple: In the same amount of bandwidth, they can deliver four standard-definition programs instead of only one high-definition program. But most importantly, digital technology is converting television from a mechanism that supports passive viewing to an interactive experience—an environment in which you choose when, where, and how you engage with the world at your disposal. Of course, you can still passively watch TV, but you can also customize the experience and make it your own. DTV is already offering us more choices, and it's going to make our viewing experience even more interactive.

People have only so much time and money to spend on electronic goods and services. In many parts of the world, the first thing people seem willing to spend their time and money on involves entertainment. Therefore, the television industry, as well as the content, entertainment, and application worlds, will be increasingly important to how the local loop develops and how this further demands the introduction of home area networking. Of course, TV and networks will deliver more than entertainment. They will deliver edutainment and infotainment, too, and the presentation of the information and knowledge you need will be in a format that is palatable and ensures assimilation and retention on a rapid and effective basis. Video and multimedia facilitate our ability to understand and retain information and therefore will become the basis of much information delivery. This will drive the need for more bandwidth not just to the home but also within the home, to network the growing variety of computing and entertainment systems. Very importantly, it will also drive the need to deliver programming and content on a mobile basis—yet another argument for fixed-mobile convergence (FMC)—and fuel the broadband wireless arena to new generations of wireless technology and spectrum utilization.

What is required to carry a digitized stream to today's TVs? In the North American system, a 6MHz NTSC channel requires approximately 160Mbps; a digitized PAL stream, used throughout Europe, requires about 190Mbps (the PAL system uses an 8MHz channel); and HDTV requires 1.5Gbps. Videoconferencing needs much less bandwidth than TV, but it still requires a substantial amount; the H.323 standard from the ITU allows videoconferencing to be carried at bandwidths ranging from 384Kbps to 1.5Mbps. Streaming video requirements vary, depending on the quality: Low quality requires 3Mbps, medium quality requires 5Mbps, and high quality requires 7Mbps.

An important driver behind broadband access is content, and much of the content for which people are willing to pay is entertainment oriented. The television industry is now beginning to undergo the revolution that digital technology has caused in other communications-related industries, and it is now starting to capitalize on the potential new revenue-generating services that personal digital manipulation may allow. One example is digital video recording (DVR), also called personal video recording (PVR), in which television programs are digitally recorded onto a hard disk, letting viewers pause live TV, watch programs on their own schedule, and even skip commercials. With the introduction of DTV and the mandate by spectrum management agencies to phase out or decommission analog broadcasting, we will need a much greater amount of bandwidth in our homes to feed the new generations of televisions.

In terms of information transfer, television has generally been associated with the concept of broadcast, terrestrial or satellite, or cable delivery of someone else's programming on someone else's timetable. Video is associated with the ability to record, edit, or view programming on demand, according to your own timetable and needs. Multimedia promises to expand the role of video-enabled communications, ultimately effecting a telecultural shift, with the introduction of interactive television.

Before we begin our detailed discussion of video compression and DTV standards, it makes sense to provide a brief explanation of the key parameters that determine not only the viewing experience but the bandwidth required:

- **Number of pixels on a screen**—A *pixel* (which is short for *picture element*) is one of the thousands of small rectangular dots that comprise television and computer screen images. Basically, the more pixels per screen, the greater, or better, the resolution—that is, the more defined, detailed, and crisp the image appears.

- **Frame rate**—The frame rate is a measure of how fluid or natural the motion onscreen appears. As a quick reference, motion pictures use 24 frames per second (fps), the North American NTSC television standard uses 30fps, and the European PAL standard uses 25fps. (Television standards are discussed later in this chapter.)

- **Number of bits per pixel**—The number of bits per pixel is a measure of the color depth; the more bits per pixel, the more colors can be represented. Remember that the human eye can perceive more than 16 million colors. A digitally encoded image, using 24 bits per pixel, can display more than 16 million colors, providing a rich and natural experience.

As we talk about compression techniques and digital television standards, you will notice that most of the standards define the number of pixels and frames per second that can be supported.

Video Compression

To make the most of bandwidth, it is necessary to apply compression to video. Full-motion digital video needs as much compression as possible in order to fit into the precious spectrum allocated to television and wireless communications, not to mention to fit on most standard storage devices. Moving Picture Experts Group (MPEG; www.chiariglione.org/mpeg) is a working group of the International Organization for Standardization (ISO; www.iso.ch) and the International Electrotechnical Commission (IEC; www.iec.ch) that is in charge of developing standards for coded representation of digital audio and video. It has created the MPEG compression algorithm, which reduces redundant information in images. One distinguishing characteristic of MPEG compression is that it is asymmetric: A lot of work occurs on the compression side, and very little occurs on the decompression side. It is offline versus real-time compression. Offline allows 80:1 or 400:1 compression ratios, so it takes 80 or 400 times longer to compress than to decompress. Currently, MPEG-2 generally involves a compression ratio of 55:1, which means it can take almost an hour to compress 1 minute of video. The advantage of this asymmetrical approach is that digital movies compressed using MPEG run faster and take up less space.

There are several MPEG standards, in various stages of development and completion, and with different targeted uses. The following are some of the most common MPEG standards:

- **MPEG-1**—MPEG-1 is a standard for storage and retrieval of moving pictures and audio on storage media. MPEG-1 is the standard on which such products as Video CD and MP3 are based. MPEG-1 addresses VHS-quality images with a 1.5Mbps data rate. MPEG-1 can play back from a single-speed CD-ROM player (150Kbps or 1.2Mbps) at 352×240 (i.e., quarter-screen) resolution at 30fps.

- **MPEG-2**—MPEG-2 is the standard on which such products as DTV set-top boxes and DVD are based, and at this point, it is the compression scheme of choice. It addresses DTV- or computer-quality images. MPEG-2 carries compressed broadcast NTSC at a 2Mbps to 3Mbps data rate, broadcast PAL at 4Mbps to 6Mbps, broadcast HDTV at 10Mbps to 12Mbps, and professional HDTV at 32Mbps to 40Mbps. MPEG-2 supports both interlaced and progressive-scan video streams. (Interlaced and progressive-scan techniques are discussed later in this chapter.) MPEG-2 on DVD and Digital Video Broadcasting (DVB) offers resolutions of 720×480 and $1,280 \times 720$ at up to 30fps, with full CD-quality audio. On MPEG-2 over Advanced Television Systems Committee (ATSC), MPEG-2 also supports resolutions of $1,920 \times 1,080$ and frame or field rates of up to 60fps.

- **MPEG-4**—MPEG-4 is a standard for multimedia applications. MPEG-4, an evolution of MPEG-2, features audio, video, and systems layers and offers variable-bit-rate encoding for both narrowband and broadband delivery in a single file. It also uses an object-based compression method, rather than MPEG-2's frame-based compression. MPEG-4 enables objects—such as two-dimensional or three-dimensional video objects, text, graphics, and sound—to be manipulated and made interactive through Web-like hyperlinks and/or multimedia triggers. The best feature of MPEG-4 is that the RealNetworks players, Microsoft Windows Media Player, and Apple QuickTime all support MPEG-4. MPEG-4 is intended to expand the scope of audio/visual content to include simultaneous use of both stored and real-time components, plus distribution from and to multiple endpoints, and also to enable the reuse of both content and processes.

- **MPEG-4 Advanced Video Compression (AVC)**—MPEG-4 AVC, also called Part 10 or ITU H.264, is a digital video codec standard noted for achieving very high data compression. It is the result of a collaborative partnership effort between the ITU Video Coding Experts Group (VCEG) and the ISO/IEC MPEG known as the Joint Video Team (JVT). AVC contains a number of new features that allow it to compress video much more effectively than older standards and to provide more flexibility for application to a wide variety of network environments. H.264 can often perform radically better than MPEG-2 video compression, typically achieving the same quality at half the bit rate or less. It is planned to be included as a mandatory player feature in an enormous variety of implementations and standards.

- **MPEG-7**—MPEG-7 is a multimedia content description standard for information searching. Thus, it is *not* a standard that deals with the actual encoding of moving pictures and audio, like MPEG-1, MPEG-2, and MPEG-4. It uses XML to store metadata and can be attached to timecodes in order to tag particular events, or, for example, to synchronize lyrics to a song.

- **MPEG-21**—Today, many elements are involved in building an infrastructure for the delivery and consumption of multimedia content. However, there is no big picture to describe how these elements relate to each other. MPEG-21 was created to provide a framework for the all-electronic creation, production, delivery, and trade of content. Within the framework, we can use the other MPEG standards, where appropriate. The basic architectural concept in MPEG-21 is the digital item. *Digital items* are structured digital objects, including a standard representation and identification, as well as metadata. Basically, a digital item is a combination of resources (e.g., videos, audio tracks, images), metadata (such as MPEG-7 descriptors), and structure (describing the relationship between resources).

MPEG-1, MPEG-2, and MPEG-4 are primarily concerned with the coding of audio/visual content, whereas MPEG-7 is concerned with providing descriptions of multimedia content, and MPEG-21 enables content to be created, produced, delivered, and traded entirely electronically.

Faster compression techniques using fractal geometry and artificial intelligence are being developed and could theoretically achieve compression ratios of 2,500:1. Implemented in silicon, this would enable full-screen, NTSC-quality video that could be deliverable not only over a LAN but also over the traditional PSTN as well as wireless networks. Until better compression schemes are developed, we have standardized on MPEG-2, which takes advantage of how the eye perceives color variations and motion. Inside each frame, an MPEG-2 encoder records just enough detail to make it look like nothing is missing. The encoder also compares adjacent frames and records only the sections of the picture that have moved or changed. If only a small section of the picture changes, the MPEG-2 encoder changes only that area and leaves the rest of the picture unchanged. On the next frame in the video, only that section of the picture is changed.

MPEG-2 does have some problems, but it is a good compression scheme, and it is already an industry standard for digital video for DVDs and some satellite television services. One problem with MPEG-2 is that it is a *lossy* compression method. This means that a higher compression rate results in a poorer picture. There's some loss in picture quality between a digital video camera and what you see on your TV. However, MPEG-2 quality is still a lot better than the average NTSC or PAL image. By applying MPEG-2 encoding to NTSC, we can reduce the bandwidth required.

Another important video compression technique is Windows Media 9 (WM9). The WM9 series codec standard, implemented by Microsoft as Windows Media Video (WMV) 9 Advanced Profile, is based on the VC-1 video codec specification currently being standardized by the Society of Motion Picture and Television Engineers (SMPTE; www.smpte.org) and provides for high-quality video for streaming and downloading. By making use of improved techniques, VC-1 decodes high-definition video twice as fast as the H.264 standard while offering two to three times better compression than MPEG-2. WM9 is supported by a wide variety of players and devices. It supports a wide range of bit rates, including high-definition at one-half to one-third the bit rate of MPEG-2, as well as low-bit-rate Internet video delivered over a dialup modem. (More detailed information is available at www.microsoft.com/windows/windowsmedia/9series/codecs/video.aspx.)

Even if we achieve the faster data rates that MPEG-2 offers, how many of us have 20Mbps pipes coming into our homes? A 1.5Mbps connection over DSL or cable modem cannot come close to carrying a 20Mbps DTV signal. Therefore, broadband access alternatives will shift over time. We will need more fiber, we will need that fiber closer to the home, and we will need much more sophisticated compression techniques that can allow us to make use of the even more limited wireless spectrum to carry information. We will also need to move forward with introducing new generations of wireless technologies geared toward the support of multimedia capacities—a combination of intelligent spectrum use and highly effective compression—with support for the requisite variable QoS environment and strong security features. We will also need better compression techniques. Improvements in compression are on the way, as Table 10.1 illustrates.

Delay and Jitter

Along with their demands for so much capacity, video and other real-time applications such as audio and voice also suffer from delay (i.e., latency) and bit errors (e.g., missing video elements, synchronization problems, complete loss of the picture). Delay in the network can wreak havoc with video traffic. The delay in a network increases as the number of switches and routers in the network increases. The ITU recommends a maximum delay of 150 milliseconds, and evolving agreements promise packet loss of 1% or less per month and a round-trip latency guarantee of 80 milliseconds. However, the public Internet has as much as 40% packet loss during peak traffic hours and average latencies of 800 to 1,000 milliseconds. Although we really can't control the delay in the public Internet, we can engineer private IP backbones to provide the levels we're seeking.

Jitter is another impairment that has a big impact on video, voice, and so on. Jitter is introduced when delay does not remain the same throughout a network, so packets arrive at the receiving node at different rates. Video can tolerate a small amount of delay, but when congestion points slow the buffering of images, jitter causes distortion and highly unstable images. Reducing jitter means reducing or avoiding the congestion that occurs in switches and routers, which in turn means having as many priority queues as the network QoS levels require.

Television Standards

Given the importance of the new era in television, the following sections establish some reference points for television standards, both analog and digital.

Table 10.1 Improvements in Compression

2006 MPEG-2	2006 MPEG-4/VC-1	2007 MPEG-4/VC-1 Enhancements	2009 MPEG-4/VC-1 Improvements
Standard definition	2.5–3Mbps	1.5–2Mbps	<1–1.5Mbps
High definition	15–19Mbps	1–12 Mbps	<7–10Mbps

Analog TV

In 1945, the U.S. Federal Communications Commission (FCC; www.fcc.gov) allocated 13 basic VHF television channels, thus standardizing the frequencies and allocating a broadcast bandwidth of 4.5MHz. The NTSC was formed in 1948 to define a national standard for the broadcast signal itself. The standard for black-and-white television was finally set in 1953 and ratified by the Electronic Industries Association (EIA; www.eia.org) as the RS-170 specification. Full-time network color broadcasting was introduced in 1964, with an episode of *Bonanza*.

The NTSC color TV specification determines the electronic signals that make up a color TV picture and establishes a method for broadcasting those pictures over the air. NTSC defines a 4:3 horizontal:vertical size ratio, called the *aspect ratio*. This ratio was selected in the 1940s and 1950s, when all picture tubes were round, because the almost-square 4:3 ratio made good use of round picture tubes. An NTSC color picture with sound occupies 6MHz of frequency spectrum, enough bandwidth for 2,222 voice-grade telephone lines. To transmit this signal digitally without compression requires about 160Mbps.

The English/German PAL system was developed after NTSC and adopted by the United Kingdom, Western Germany, and The Netherlands in 1967. The PAL system is used today in the United Kingdom, Western Europe (with the exception of France), Asia, Australia, New Zealand, the Middle East, Africa, and Latin America. Brazil uses a version of PAL called PAL-M. The PAL aspect ratio is also 4:3, and PAL channels occupy 8MHz of spectrum. Uncompressed PAL, digitally transported, requires approximately 200Mbps.

The SECAM system is used in France and the former French colonies, as well as in parts of the Middle East. Russia and the former Soviet-allied countries use a modified form of SECAM. There are two versions of SECAM: SECAM vertical and SECAM horizontal.

The PAL and SECAM standards provide a sharper picture than NTSC, but they display a bit of a flicker because they have a slower frame rate. Programs produced for one system must be converted in order to be viewed on one of the other systems. The conversion process detracts slightly from the image quality, and converted video often has a jerky, old-time-movie look.

DTV

DTV represents the ongoing convergence of broadcasting and computing. Simply put, DTV makes use of digital modulation and compression to broadcast audio, data, and video signals to TV sets. Thanks to MPEG-2, studio-quality images can be compressed and transformed into a digital stream. DTV is the next generation of television; its development has improved the audio and video quality of broadcast television, and it has in many cases replaced the film cameras used in movie production.

The difference between analog TV and DTV is profound in terms of picture quality as well as special screen effects, such as multiple-windowed pictures and interactive viewer options. The quality of DTV is almost six times better than what analog TV offers, delivering up to 1,080 lines of resolution and CD-quality sound. But the real promise of DTV lies in its huge capacity: the ability to deliver, during a single program, information equivalent to that contained on dozens of CDs. The capacity is so great that whole new industries are being created to use this digital potential for whole new revenue streams. Recognizing that the Web and other Internet services may grow to rival television, it is highly likely that new generations of television system infrastructure design will include this medium as part of the total system—making television a critical aspect of convergence on all fronts, including devices, applications, fixed networks, wireless infrastructure, and service providers.

The Move to DTV and HDTV One main application of DTV is to carry more channels in the same amount of bandwidth, either 6MHz or 8MHz, depending on the standard in use. The other key application is to carry high-definition programming, known as HDTV. Because DTV makes use of a digital signal, many common analog broadcasting artifacts can be eliminated, including static in the audio, snow on the screen, and the presence of ghost images (called *multipath distortion*). However, digital signals can also suffer from artifacts. For example, when the data rate is too low, MPEG compression results in artifacts such as *blocking*, or blocky images. In addition, while analog TV may produce an impaired picture under some circumstances, it is still viewable, whereas DTV may not work at all in the same situation. Basically, depending on the level and sophistication of error correction defined by the standard and chosen by the provider, DTV may work either perfectly or not at all.

The move to DTV systems is generally associated with a switch in picture format, going from the aspect ratio of 4:3 to one of 16:9, although both HDTV and SDTV are available in both formats. However, the aspect ratio is only part of HDTV.

The History of Aspect Ratio

The 4:3 aspect ratio was originally developed by W. K. L. Dickson in 1889 while he was working at Thomas Edison's laboratories. Dickson was experimenting with a motion-picture camera called a Kinescope, and he made his film 1 inch wide with frames 0.75 inch high. This film size, and its aspect ratio, became the standard for the film and motion-picture industry because there was no apparent reason to change. In 1941, when the NTSC proposed standards for television broadcasting, they adopted the same ratio as the film industry.

In the 1950s, Hollywood wanted to give the public a reason to buy a ticket to attend the theater rather than sit at home watching the TV. Because our two eyes give us a wider view, a wider movie makes more sense. Widescreen formats are formatted much closer to the way we see. Our field of vision is more rectangular than square. When we view movies in widescreen format, the image fills more of our field of vision and has a stronger visual impact. Wider screens gave the theater audience a more visually engulfing experience. The 16:9 aspect ratio allows TV to move closer to the movie experience.

Besides being formatted for a wider screen, an HDTV picture has more detail and crisper images. With the bigger pictures comes a finer resolution. TV images are made up of pixels, each of which is a tiny sample of video information, one of the little squares that make up an overall picture. Each pixel is composed of three close dots of color: red, green, and blue. Combined on the phosphor screen, the three separate colors appear to blend into a single color. Each phosphor emits light in proportion to the intensity of the electron beam hitting it. On a standard TV screen, the electron beam has about 256 levels of intensity for each of the three colored phosphors. Therefore, each pixel has a spectral range of about 16.8 million colors. From a distance, each pixel ends up looking like a single dot of color, but up close, you can see that each pixel is really a rectangular trio of red, green, and blue; this is most visible on projection televisions, where the colors separate a little more. HDTV uses smaller pixels that are closer together, and they are square, just like on most computer monitors. Digital pixels are also smaller. HDTV has 4.5 pixels in the area taken up by a single pixel on standard NTSC TVs. The more pixels in a given area, the more detailed and better the picture. A quick comparison will help you appreciate the vastly improved resolution offered by HDTV. The maximum resolution of an NTSC TV is a display that is 720 pixels wide by 486 active lines, resulting in a total of 349,920 pixels. A high-end HDTV display is 1,920 pixels wide by 1,080 active lines, resulting in 2,073,600 pixels—six times more pixels than the older NTSC resolution.

DTV not only improves the visual experience, it also improves the sound quality, using advances in digital sound. HDTV broadcasts sound by using the Dolby Digital/AC-3 audio encoding system, which is the same digital sound used in most movie theaters, in DVDs, and in many home theater systems. It can include up to 5.1 channels of sound: 3 in front (left, center, and right), 2 in back (left and right), and a subwoofer bass for a sound you can feel (the .1 channel). Sound on DTV is CD quality, with a range of frequencies lower and higher than most people can hear.

DTV Implementations and Distribution   Service providers are increasingly interested in providing service bundles—a strategy often referred to as *triple play* (voice, data, and video) or *quadruple play* (voice, data, video, and wireless/mobile).

DTV, which is a big part of this service strategy, can be implemented and distributed in a number of ways. The following are some of the possible implementations:

- **Terrestrial DTV**—A number of countries are in the process of deploying digital terrestrial television (DTT), which offers many advantages. Governments see DTT as an opportunity to free up existing TV frequencies for resale, as well as a technology that ensures that the country is on the forefront of the digital revolution. Broadcasters see DTT as a means by which they can fight the growing competition from cable DTV, satellite providers, and telcos, not to mention emerging digital program distribution technologies such as PVR/DVR and video-on-demand (VOD). Manufacturers see DTT as an opportunity to sell new equipment, ranging from digital set-top boxes to new DTV sets. Consumers view the move to DTT as a way to get new and exciting programming. At the moment, however, HDTV sets are still very expensive, and there is not much HDTV programming available.

- **Satellite DTV**—In the satellite TV market, DTV is mainly used to multiplex large numbers of channels, including pay TV, onto the available bandwidth. Because satellite operators have much more bandwidth available to them, they often can compete very effectively with terrestrial DTV providers in terms of both number of channels and picture quality.

- **Cable DTV**—For cable TV providers, the main advantage of replacing their analog systems with digital cable was initially the ability to offer users more channels and better picture quality. Of course, in today's era of convergence and service bundles, a digital two-way system is absolutely required to support the emerging modern services such as VoIP, IPTV, VOD, and interactive HDTV. In addition, an expanding range of set-top boxes and middleware software also makes many new features possible. Depending on the choices an operator makes in hardware and software, features such as TV guides, program reminders, content censorship, interactive Web-style content viewing, gaming, voting, and on-demand services such as VOD can add significantly more value and ultimately revenues.

- **IP television (IPTV)**—The Internet is starting to be adapted for use with DTV deployments as part of triple play. When combined with advances in new compression standards, such as MPEG-4 H.264 or WM9, and in the picture quality supported by HDTV, IPTV represents a big step forward as a new approach to distributing television programming. (IPTV is discussed in Chapter 9, "IP Services.")

Telcos of all sorts, far and wide, are helping to lead the way into the video space. Many are using new IP-based technologies, while others are tapping older, but known and reliable, techniques such as radio frequency (RF) broadcasting to deliver a full-service menu of high-definition programming, VOD, DVR, music channels, interactive gaming, and more. Combined with voice and data services, telco TV is expected to become serious business.

Some analysts suggest that telcos' success will hinge on video, which means telcos face many challenges ahead. The move to becoming a video provider means spending billions on network upgrades, rolling out services with unproven IPTV platforms, and navigating the difficult content acquisition process. Telcos are in transition, and the basic building blocks are there for the packet networks and transport needed to move video around. However, telcos will need to develop content relations and appropriate bandwidth to support high-definition channels and interactivity with in-home wiring. According to the Consumer Electronics Association (www.ce.org), HDTV is the compelling device at retailers and the roadmap to the future, with IP driving it. Without it, telcos won't be able to compete. But key issues need attention, including the integration of billing and operational support systems. In addition, set-top manufacturers and other vendors must support the service, and new compression technologies and a new generation of set-top boxes will make a big difference. The transformation is under way, but telcos must have the right software, content streams, and security provisions, and that will take a while. More and more small telcos, cities, and electric companies are deploying fiber delivery systems that will serve smaller communities, so we're likely to see many variations with telco TV.

Mobile TV constitutes another new and fascinating approach to distributing television programming and entertainment content. Mobile is the fourth screen, after movies, TV, and the PC. Production costs for a big-budget film run about US$1 million per minute, while production costs for the mobile world range from US$2,000 to US$8,000 per minute. Set-top boxes are not only becoming more intelligent but will also interact with other devices, such as PDAs, mobile phones, and the Internet, to provide a truly flexible solution that allows local information (weather, traffic, news, and so on) to be tailored to specific regions. Industry analysts predict that broadcast mobile TV has undoubted potential, with interactive TV and the extension of advertising at the forefront of that success. These beliefs are based on the fact that TV plays in the lives of people worldwide, mobile subscriber penetration has reached (and sometimes exceeded) a high saturation level in many markets, and the subsequent convergence of the broadcast and mobile industries is inevitable. But it is important to keep in mind that not everyone feels joyful about watching TV on a tiny screen; the young generation is most likely to embrace this new viewing experience.

Some feel the mobile phone is the most exciting software platform in history; it has become an essential part of just about everyone's lifestyle, and it is truly global. As a result, the simple mobile phone is morphing into a futuristic entertainment system and the most exciting new technology platform since the Internet. There are more than 1.5 billion mobile phones in use worldwide, compared to just 690 million PCs and laptops. Needless to say, entertainment giants and newly inspired entrepreneurs are rushing to develop songs, graphics, games, and videos to populate millions of tiny screens. (Mobile TV is discussed in more detail in Chapter 16, "Emerging Wireless Applications.")

DTV Standards   Initially, an attempt was made to prevent the fragmentation of the global DTV market into different standards, as was the case with the NTSC, PAL, and SECAM analog standards. However, as usually seems to be the case, the world could not reach agreement on one standard, and as a result, several major standards exist today. These standards fall into two categories:

- **Fixed reception**—The fixed-reception digital broadcasting standards include the U.S. Advanced Television Systems Committee (ATSC; www. atsc.org) system, the European DVB-Terrestrial (DVB-T; www.dvb.org) system, the Japanese Integrated Services Digital Broadcasting (ISDB) system, and the Korean Terrestrial Digital Media Broadcasting system. The most widely adopted standard worldwide is DVB-T. Argentina, Canada, Mexico, and South Korea have followed the United States in adopting ATSC. Digital Multimedia Broadcasting-Terrestrial (DMB-T) is the youngest major broadcast standard and provides the best reception quality for the power required. The DMB standard is derived from the Digital Audio Broadcast (DAB) standard that enjoys wide use in Europe for radio broadcasts. DAB and DMB-T are the preferred Chinese standards. Korea has since renamed its preferred standard T-DMB to differentiate it from the Chinese standard DMB-T. T-DMB is currently used in Korea but will also go into trial in 2006 in Germany, France, Switzerland, and the United Kingdom. A related Korean standard, S-DMB, exists for satellite television services, allowing for TV reception over larger areas than can be served with T-DMB. There could also be additional high-resolution digital formats for markets other than home entertainment introduced in the future. One such format being proposed by Japan's public broadcaster, NHK, is Ultra High Definition Video (UHDV). UHDV provides a resolution that is 16 times greater than that of HDTV.

- **Mobile reception**—As far as mobile standards go, DVB-Handheld (DVB-H) is the selected standard in Europe, India, Australia, and southeast Asia. North America also uses DVB-H, as well as the MediaFLO standard proposed by Qualcomm. MediaFLO, used only in North America at this time, supports relatively fast channel switching and uses its own broadcast towers as well as available bandwidth in the cellular network. Japan is adopting the ISDB-T Mobile Segment standard. Korean is embracing T-DMB. China may follow DVB-H or something else, and for the time being, it is unknown which standard South America and Africa will follow. The mobile broadcast market is nascent, and many developments are in store before a winner emerges in this arena.

As far as the broadband evolution goes, the importance of entertainment content and DTV is significant, so being aware of what constitutes DTV is mandatory to understanding the requirements of the next-generation network. The following sections describe the most commonly followed DTV fixed-reception standards, and Chapter 16 discusses the details of mobile TV standards. A comprehensive list of DTV deployments around the world is available at http://en.wikipedia.org/wiki/List_of_digital_television_deployments_by_country.

ATSC Standards   The ATSC, an international, nonprofit organization, develops voluntary standards for DTV. It was formed in 1982 by the member organizations of the Joint Committee on InterSociety Coordination (JCIC): the Electronic Industries Association (EIA), the Institute of Electrical and Electronics Engineers (IEEE), the National Association of Broadcasters (NAB), the National Cable Television Association (NCTA), and the Society of Motion Picture and Television Engineers (SMPTE). Today, approximately 140 ATSC members represent the broadcast, broadcast equipment, motion picture, consumer electronics, computer, cable, satellite, and semiconductor industries.

The ATSC's DTV standards include high-definition TV (HDTV), enhanced-definition TV (EDTV), standard-definition TV (SDTV), data broadcasting, multichannel surround-sound audio, direct-to-home satellite broadcast, and interactive television. On December 24, 1996, the U.S. FCC adopted the major elements of the ATSC DTV standard (Standard A/53). The ATSC DTV standard has since been adopted by the governments of Argentina, Canada, Mexico, and South Korea.

Types of Scanning

One of the biggest issues in TV standards involves how DTV images are drawn to the screen. There are two perspectives: those of the broadcast TV world and those of the computer environment. The broadcasters would rather initiate DTV with interlaced scanning, which is used by today's TV sets; computer companies want progressive-scanning DTV signals, similar to those used by computer monitors. The source of the conflict is different historical bandwidth limits.

Originally, the NTSC decided that the best way to fit a 525-line video signal into a 6MHz broadcast channel was to break each video frame into two fields, each holding half of the picture. *Interlacing* is a technique cameras use to take two snapshots of a scene within a frame time. During the first scan, the camera creates one field of video, containing even-numbered lines, and during the second, it creates another, containing the odd-numbered lines. The fields are transmitted sequentially, and the receiver reassembles them. This technique makes for reduced flicker and therefore greater brightness on the TV receiver for the given frame rate (and bandwidth). Interlacing is rough on small text, but moving images look fine.

Progressive, or *noninterlaced, scanning* is a method for displaying, storing, or transmitting moving images in which the lines of each frame are drawn in sequence. This type of scanning is used in most computer monitors. There are a number of advantages associated with progressive scanning, such as a subjective perception of an increased vertical resolution. With interlaced images, the perceived vertical resolution is usually equivalent to 60% of the active lines. This is why HDTV standards such as 1080i (1,920 × 1,080, interlaced) are generally perceived as a poorer quality than 720p (1,280 × 720, progressive). Additional benefits include the absence of flickering of narrow horizontal patterns, easier compression, and simpler video-processing equipment.

The ATSC high-definition standard includes three basic formats: HDTV, EDTV, and SDTV. EDTV is largely a marketing term, referring to low-resolution TVs with minor enhancements. Digital TVs often have a 16:9 widescreen format and can display progressive-scan content. Each of these formats is defined by the number of lines per video frame, the number of pixels per line, the aspect ratio, the frame repetition rate, and the frame structure (i.e., interlaced scan or progressive scan). The ATSC standard recommends that the receiver seamlessly and without loss of video continue to display all these formats in the native format of the television receiver.

ATSC signals are designed to work on the same bandwidth as NTSC (6MHz) or PAL (8MHz) channels. The video signals are compressed using MPEG-2, and the data stream is then modulated. The modulation technique varies, depending on the transmission method. Because any terrestrial TV system must overcome numerous channel impairments such as ghosts, noise bursts, signal fades, and interference in order to reach the home viewer, the selection of the right RF modulation format is critical. In the case of terrestrial broadcasters, the technique used is 8-VSB (Vestigial Sideband), with a maximum transfer rate of 19.39Mbps. This is sufficient to carry several video channels and metadata. Because cable TV operators usually have a higher signal-to-noise ratio (SNR), they can use 16-VSB or 256-QAM to achieve a throughput of 38.78Mbps using the same size channel. (Modulation techniques are discussed in Chapter 5, "Data Communication Basics.") Table 10.2 shows the details of the various ATSC DTV standards.

Table 10.2 ATSC DTV Standard

Lines of Resolution	Pixels per Line	Aspect Ratio	Frame Rate	Scanning Sequence
		HDTV—NTSC		
1,080	1,920	16:9	30, 24	Progressive
1,080	1,920	16:9	60	Interlaced
1,080	1,440	4:3	30, 24	Progressive
1,080	1,440	4:3	60	Interlaced
720	1,280	16:9	60, 30, 24	Progressive
720	1,280	16:9	60	Interlaced
720	960	4:3	60, 30, 24	Progressive
720	960	4:3	60	Interlaced
		HDTV—PAL		
1,080	1,920	16:9	25	Progressive
1,080	1,920	16:9	50	Interlaced
1,080	1,440	4:3	25	Progressive
1,080	1,440	4:3	50	Interlaced
720	1,280	16:9	50, 25	Progressive
720	1,280	16:9	50	Interlaced
720	960	4:3	50, 25	Progressive
720	960	4:3	50	Interlaced
		EDTV—NTSC		
480	720	16:9, 4:3	60	Progressive
		EDTV—PAL		
576	720	16:9, 4:3	50	Progressive

continued

Table 10.2 ATSC DTV Standard *(continued)*

Lines of Resolution	Pixels per Line	Aspect Ratio	Frame Rate	Scanning Sequence
SDTV—NTSC				
480	704	16:9	60, 30, 24	Progressive
480	704	16:9	60	Interlaced
480	640	4:3	60, 30, 24	Progressive
480	640	4:3	60	Interlaced
SDTV—PAL, SECAM				
576	1024	16:9	50, 25	Progressive
576	1024	16:9	50	Interlaced
576	768	4:3	50, 25	Progressive
576	768	4:3	50	Interlaced

ATSC requires about half of the power for the same reception quality, in absence of errors, as the more widely used DVB-T standard, but it is more suscepti-ble to errors. One recognized limitation with ATSC is that unlike DVB-T and ISDB-T, which are able to dynamically change the error correction modes, code rates, inter-leaver mode, and randomizer, ATSC cannot be adapted to changes in propagation conditions. However, despite ATSC's fixed transmission mode, under normal con-ditions, it is still a very robust waveform.

DVB Standards DVB is a suite of internationally accepted, open standards for DTV maintained by the DVB Project (www.dvb.org). Services using the DVB stan-dards are available on every continent, with more than 110 million DVB receivers deployed. Formed in 1993, the DVB Project is responsible for designing global standards for the global delivery of DTV and data services. The DVB Project's 270+ membership includes broadcasters, manufacturers, regulatory bodies, software developers, network operators, and others from more than 35 countries. DVB stan-dards are published by the European Telecommunications Standards Institute (ETSI; www.etsi.org), and there is considerable day-to-day cooperation between the two organizations. ETSI, the European Committee for Electrotechnical Stan-dardization (CENELEC; www.cenelec.org), and the European Broadcasting Union

(EBU; www.ebu.ch) have formed a joint technical committee to handle the DVB family of standards.

DVB standards are very similar to ATSC standards—including MPEG-2 video compression, packetized transport, and guidelines for a 1,080-line-by-1,920-pixel HDTV format—but they provide for different audio compression and transmission schemes. DVB embraces four main standards that define the physical and data link layers of a distribution system:

- **DVB-S and DVB-S2 (satellite TV)**—DVB-S is an open standard for digital video broadcast over satellites, defined by ETSI and ratified in 1994. DVB-S supports only MPEG-2 encoded video streams. DVB-S2 is an open standard for digital video broadcast over satellites, defined by ETSI and ratified in 2005. It has improved quality over DVB-S and allows for coded video in H.264 (AVC) or VC-1 bitstreams.

- **DVB-C (cable TV)**—DVB-C is an open standard for digital video transmission over cable that was defined by ETSI and ratified in 1994.

- **DVB-T (terrestrial TV)**—DVB-T, an open standard defined by ETSI and ratified in 1997, is used as the de facto standard for terrestrial TV broadcasts in many nations, particularly those in Europe. It supports only MPEG-2 compression.

- **DVB-H (terrestrial TV for handhelds)**—The DVB-H standard is an adaptation of DVB optimized for mobile handheld devices. It is widely used in Europe and is starting to see adoption in North America.

These four distribution systems vary in their modulation schemes, based on the technical constraints associated with the different operating environments. DVB-T and DVB-H use Coded Orthogonal Frequency Division Multiplexing (COFDM), DVB-S uses Quadrature Phase-Shift Keying (QPSK), and DVB-C uses QAM, especially 64-QAM. (Modulation schemes are covered in Chapter 5.)

The DVB Project has also designed an open middleware system for DTV, called the DVB-Multimedia Home Platform (DVB-MHP, www.mhp.org), which is being used to support interactive applications in many countries. DVB-MHP enables the reception and execution of interactive, Java-based applications on a TV set, including applications such as e-mail, SMS, information services, shopping, and games. Although the European Commission has not mandated EU-wide standards for interactive DTV middleware, there is clear support for the continued development of DVB-MHP in the commitment to continue to promote and support open and interoperable standards and to monitor the use of proprietary technologies. As of mid-2005, the largest deployments of DVB-MHP were in Italy (DVB-T) and Korea (DVB-S), with other small deployments or trials taking place in Australia, Finland,

Germany, and Spain. In the United States, CableLabs has specified its own middle-ware system called OpenCable Applications Platform (OCAP), which is based on DVB-MHP.

ISDB Standards ISDB is the DTV and DAB format that Japan has created to allow radio and television stations there to convert to digital. ISDB is maintained by the Association of Radio Industries and Businesses (ARIB; www.arib.or.jp). ARIB is a standards organization in Japan, designated as the center of promotion of the efficient use of the radio spectrum and frequency change support.

ISDB incorporates several standards:

- **ISDB-S (digital satellite TV)**—ARIB developed the ISDB-S standards to meet a number of requirements Japanese broadcasters were asking for, including HDTV capability, interactive services, network access, and effective frequency utilization. ISDB-S, operating in the 12GHz band, uses PSK modulation. ISDB-S allows 51Mbps to be transmitted through a single transponder, making it 1.5 times more efficient than DVB-S, which can handle a bitstream of approximately only 34Mbps. This means the ISDB-S system can carry two HDTV channels using one transponder, along with other independent audio and data. ISDB-S was commercially launched in 2000 and today is used by several service providers.

- **ISDB-T and ISDB-Tsb (terrestrial)**—In the 1980s, Japan started research on and development of a completely digital system that led to the introduction of ISDB. ISDB-T began commercial operation in Japan in December 2003. ISDB-T specifies OFDM transmission with one of four modulation schemes: QPSK, DQPSK, 16-QAM, or 64-QAM. With ISDB-T, an audio program and TV for both fixed and mobile reception can be carried in the same multiplex. For example, ISDB-T can transmit three SDTV streams in one channel or carry an HDTV and a mobile phone channel in the same 6MHz usually reserved for TV transmission. The combination of services can be changed at any time, as can the modulation schemes. ISDB-T can support HDTV on moving vehicles at over 62 mph (100 kph), and it can be received on mobile phones moving at over 250 mph (400 kph). (DVB-T can only support SDTV on moving vehicles, and ATSC cannot be used on moving vehicles at all.) ISDB-T is applicable to all 6MHz, 7MHz, and 8MHz bandwidth systems, so it could be adopted worldwide.

  ISDB-Tsb refers to the terrestrial digital sound broadcasting specification and is the same technical specification as ISDB-T. ISDB-Tsb can also be used for mobile reception.

- **ISDB-C (digital cable TV)**—ISDB-C is the cable digital broadcasting specification. It supports terrestrial digital broadcasting services over cable using the OFDM scheme with a 6MHz channel. It employs 64-QAM modulation.

- **2.6GHz band (mobile broadcasting)**—The mobile broadcasting 2.6GHz band uses Code Division Multiplexing (CDM). A Japanese company named MobaHO! began using mobile broadcasting in October 2004, constituting the world's first satellite digital multimedia broadcasting for personal and mobile device use. Users throughout Japan can listen to and view the same programs from 30 audio channels (including overseas FM radio and genre-specific music programming) and from 7 video channels (including news, sports, and entertainment programming).

All these standards are based on MPEG-2 video and audio coding and are capable of HDTV.

Brazil is currently the only country considering adopting ISDB-T for its DTV standard.

The Broadband Infrastructure

We are in an era of new networks that we loosely term *next-generation networks*. Data traffic in these networks is equal to or surpassing voice as the most mission-critical aspect of the network. Remember that when all the traffic is ones and zeros, everything is data, and voice is just another data application. Integration of voice, data, and video without protocol conflicts greatly simplifies the migration of legacy communication systems and network applications to next-generation transport technologies. The undeniable appeal of interactive multimedia applications, content, and programming also signals the need for a convergent infrastructure that offers minimum latencies to ensure the responsiveness that customers need.

Traffic is growing at an alarming rate. More human users, more machine users, and more broadband access are all contributing to the additional traffic. Established carriers and new startups are deploying huge amounts of fiber-optic cable and wireless broadband, introducing new possibilities, and optical technology is revolutionizing the network overall. This new era of abundant capacity stimulates development and growth of bandwidth-hungry applications and demands service qualities that can allow control of parameters such as delay, jitter, loss ratio, and throughput. Bandwidth-intensive applications are much more cost-effective when the network provides just-in-time bandwidth management options. Next-generation networks will provide competitive rates due to lower construction outlays and operating costs.

Converging Public Infrastructures

Public infrastructures are converging on a single set of objectives. The PSTN looks to support high-speed multimedia applications, and therefore it also looks to provide high levels of QoS and the ability to guarantee a granular diversification of QoS. The PSTN has traditionally relied on a connection-oriented networking mode as a means of guaranteeing QoS, initially via circuit switching and now incorporating ATM as well.

The public Internet is also intended to support high-speed multimedia applications, and it must deal with providing QoS guarantees. But we are investigating slightly different options for how to implement this in the Internet than in the PSTN (see Chapter 8, "The Internet and IP Infrastructures"). Included in the IETF standards are Integrated Services (IntServ), Differentiated Services (DiffServ), and the new panacea, Multiprotocol Label Switching (MPLS), all of which are described later in this chapter.

Broadband Service Requirements

For next-generation networks to succeed, they must offer a unique set of features, including the following:

- **High speed and capacity**—All next-generation networks must offer very high capacities, today measured in terabits per second (1Tbps = 1 trillion bps) and already moving into the range of petabits per second (1Pbps = 1,000Tbps). Higher-bandwidth broadband access (such as 100Gbps) will drive the need for additional core bandwidth, and discussions are beginning about network cores needing to support capacities measured in exabits per second (1Ebps = 1 billion Gbps) when 100Gbps broadband access becomes a reality.

- **Bandwidth-on-demand**—Next-generation networks must be able to provide or provision bandwidth-on-demand, as much as is needed, when it is needed—unlike today's static subscription services.

- **Bandwidth reservation**—Next-generation networks must be able to offer reserved bandwidth, so that when you know you will need a high-capacity service for streaming media, you can reserve the network resources so that they are guaranteed at the time and place that you need them. Mind you, the major application for reserved bandwidth is videoconferencing; for other applications, most people don't plan ahead.

- **Support of isochronous traffic**—Isochronous traffic is time-bounded information that must be transferred within a specific time frame, and it therefore has a low tolerance for delay and loss.

- **Agnostic platforms**—Agnostic devices support multiple data protocols (e.g., IP, Frame Relay, ATM, MPLS) and traffic types (e.g., voice, data, and video), so that all traffic can be aggregated and administered at a single point.

- **Support for unicasting and multicasting**—In unicasting, streams from a single origination point go directly to a single destination point. In multicasting, streams from a single origination point flow to multiple destination points. This reduces traffic redundancy by limiting the access to a selected group of users.

- **QoS**—As discussed later in this chapter, next-generation networks must provide variable QoS parameters and ensure that those service levels can be guaranteed and that service-level agreements (SLAs) can be honored.

A number of developments have been key to allowing us to deliver on this set of requirements. One important area is photonics and optical networking. Chapter 11, "Optical Networking," describes the revolution that started with the ability to manufacture glass wires; went further to introduce erbium-doped fiber amplifiers (EDFAs); grew to encompass Wavelength Division Multiplexing (WDM), Dense Wavelength Division Multiplexing (DWDM), and Coarse Wavelength Division Multiplexing (CWDM); and is proceeding to introduce new generations of high-performance fiber, reconfigurable optical add/drop multiplexers (ROADMs), optical cross-connects, optical switches and routers, and the optical probes and network management devices that are very important for testing networks. We're looking forward to a future of end-to-end optical environments.

A number of broadband access technologies, both wireline and wireless, have been developed to facilitate next-generation networking. Chapter 12 covers these options, which include the twisted-pair DSL family; hybrid fiber coax (HFC) alternatives that make use of cable modems; fiber-to-the-node and fiber-to-the-home/fiber-to-the-premises; broadband wireless, including direct broadcast satellite, Wi-Fi, and WiMax; Free-Space Optics; and innovative new uses of powerlines to support high-speed communications. As discussed later in this chapter, multiservice core, edge, and access platforms—including the IP Multimedia Subsystem (IMS), multiservice provisioning platforms (MSPPs), and the MPLS architecture—are being developed.

■ Next-Generation Networks and Convergence

A next-generation network is a high-speed packet- or cell-based network capable of transporting and routing a multitude of services, including voice, data, video, and multimedia, and it is a common platform for applications and services that is accessible to the customer across the entire network as well as outside the network. The main physical components of the next-generation network are fiber and wireless media, routers, switches, gateways, servers, and edge devices that reside at the customer premises. A next-generation network is designed for multimedia communications, which implies that it has broadband capacities, multichannel transport with high data rates, low latencies (80 milliseconds or less is the target), low packet loss (less than 5%, with the target being less than 1%), and QoS guarantees.

A next-generation network has a worldwide infrastructure that consists of fast packet-switching techniques, which make maximum use of transport and provide great transmission efficiencies. A next-generation network involves optical networking. Today's electronic systems are going to be the bottlenecks to delivering tomorrow's applications, so we will see a replacement of the electronic infrastructure with optical elements that will provide end-to-end optical networking.

A next-generation network has a multiservice core, coupled with a multiservice intelligent edge. The application of next-generation telephony in the edge environment may potentially replace the existing architectures associated with the PSTN. Next-generation networks will be characterized by intelligent networking for rapid service delivery and provisioning. They will also have video and multimedia elements, to deliver the content for which the broadband infrastructure exists. Their access media are broadband in nature and encompass both wired and wireless facilities.

Next-generation networks stand to change how carriers provision applications and services and how customers access them. End-user service delivery from a single platform provides many benefits: It decreases time to market; it simplifies the process of moves, adds, and changes; and it provides a unique connection point for service provisioning and billing. Full-service internetworking between the legacy circuit-switched network and the next-generation packet networks is mandatory going forward. Next-generation networks also must be interoperable with new emerging structures, which implies that they have to be able to support the most up-to-date transport and switching standards. They also must support advanced traffic management, including full configuration, provisioning, network monitoring, and fault management capabilities. In a next-generation network, it is important to be able to prioritize traffic and to provide dynamic bandwidth allocation for voice, data, and video services, and this enables management of delay-tolerant traffic and prioritization of delay-sensitive traffic.

Convergence in Different Industry Segments

One of the central themes in next-generation networks is the notion of convergence. What convergence is depends on who you are and what segment of the industry you represent because convergence is actually occurring in a number of different areas. As discussed in the following sections, the concept behind convergence varies a bit depending on whether you're a service provider, an equipment manufacturer, or an applications developer. In the end, though, they all focus on one thing: bringing together voice, data, and video to be happily married at the network level, at the systems level, at the applications level, and at the device level.

Convergence in Transport

Convergence in transport refers to voice, data, and video traffic all sharing a common packet-based network, generally based on IP at present. This can apply to LANs, MANs, WANs, and wireless alternatives to each of those domains. From the standpoint of a service provider, convergence has to do with the idea of bringing together all the different technologies we've known in the past to come up with one common infrastructure, rather than working in today's world that consists of a separate voice network, the PSTN, separate data solutions, the Internet, IP backbones, Frame Relay, and ATM—a variety of different packet-switched alternatives—and then generally also separate networks engineered specifically for video and broadcast. The problem is that each of these represents a separate control plane, which means separate network management systems and procedures. It means technicians who are trained and knowledgeable in those specific systems, services, and products; and, of course, it means greater cost because there's duplication among platforms, and you have to make redundant components available and power backups to a large number of what, in essence, are overlays. So, to the service provider community, convergence means the convergence of the transport network.

Convergence in Systems

There has to be some convergence from the standpoint of the systems. To equipment manufacturers, this means creating systems that allow voice, data, and video traffic to all be commonly served through one device. In the context of next-generation network infrastructures, this most commonly refers to the use of softswitches, also known as call servers, to replace the use of traditional circuit switches, allowing the support of voice communications over IP backbones rather than the circuit-switched PSTN. From the standpoint of an enterprise network, this can also involve the use of IP PBXs at the customer premises or a service provider making IP centrex available to the enterprise, as well as integrated access devices (IADs) that combine voice and data traffic before presenting it to the external network.

Convergence in Applications

In the realm of applications, convergence refers to the integration of voice, data, and video at the desktop or in servers. Examples of this include integrated messaging, instant messaging, presence management, real-time rich-media e-learning and training products, multimedia sales presentations, and a variety of interactive programs, such as videogames. A host of such applications are unique and specific to various vertical industries, including health care, education, entertainment, government, and warfare.

Arguments for Convergence

One of the primary arguments for convergence has to do with cost reductions. As discussed earlier, packet switching is a more efficient approach than circuit switching for carrying conversations, particularly those that may be bursty in nature. With the continuing reduction in the cost of electronics, with the growth in traffic levels, and with the emergence of an increasing number of competitors, the price of delivering a packet on the backbone has been dropping by about 45% to 50% per year. Of course, we're now approaching a stabilizing point; nevertheless, packet switching has continually become more cost-efficient than the traditional circuit-switched network, or PSTN.

Another cost-reduction argument for convergence is in support of VoIP, and the major savings here occur through bypassing normal toll operations. Of course, this is most dramatic on international calls.

There are some other arguments for convergence as well. One is that you get improved productivity, from both user operations and the ICT staff. Another benefit is easier administration of the network. Again, you have a single network infrastructure and a single system that needs to be administered versus a number of separate platforms and networks consolidating the network management systems.

However, the real value in and the real argument for convergence lies in the applications. There are many synergies between converged transport, IP telephony, and converged applications. As functions such as instant messaging, presence, video communications, and streaming media merge with IP telephony, it becomes something greater than a cheaper voice solution: It becomes an integrated application. When you have an application that integrates voice, data, video, and streaming media, you most certainly require converged transport.

Regulatory Effects on Convergence

While we can achieve advances in technology very rapidly, what tends to delay their deployment is both a human factor and a political factor: We have to resolve the regulatory issues that surround the argument for convergence.

The integration of all communication modes under the control of IP has a powerful impact on regulatory models. Regulation has historically been quite different for various parts of the industry (e.g., voice versus broadcast versus cable). The way our regulatory system and regulations have been structured and still currently operate is that they are largely based on a service definition. If you offer telephone service, telephone regulations apply. Cable TV regulations apply if you offer cable TV service. But IP and converged networks part with the vertical model traditionally used in regulation. How do we regulate within a converged network? One idea considers a horizontal model, whereby regulations would be applied to the layers of activity versus the service definition. However, this is an area very much under hot debate, and ideas vary around the world. The main point is to remember that before you proceed to make decisions based on technology platforms and promises, you need to make sure you also consider what your regulatory agency is thinking and doing.

Converging Public Infrastructures

Today we have converging public infrastructures. The PSTN and the Internet are well on the path to convergence. There has been a steady, albeit slow, migration to packet-based networks. Today there are many networks running converged voice, data, and video over a common WAN infrastructure. Meanwhile, new developments, especially in the optical era, stand to alter the path of migration for all concerned. Truly magnificent new network designs are facilitated through the introduction of optical elements end to end. As a result, a new generation of networks is emerging.

If we look at where the PSTN and the Internet stand, side by side, we see that they both have the same goal (see Figure 10.1). Where originally the PSTN was a voice solution and the Internet was a data solution, they have now converged their objectives—that is, both are striving to become high-speed networks capable of

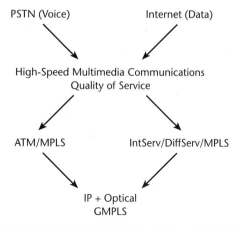

Figure 10.1   Converging public infrastructures

accommodating interactive multimedia applications. Both are also striving to apply QoS guarantees, for two reasons. First, the performance of applications is critical to customers, and without QoS guarantees, we are not able to guarantee the performance of interactive rich-media applications. Second, and perhaps more importantly in the mind of the service provider, having differentiated levels of service allows differentiated levels of pricing, and in an era where the cost of transporting a bit continues to drop dramatically, revenues have to be gained from new sources. One of those sources is potentially to offer customers a wide range of service levels and prices, from best-effort/lowest-cost to platinum service, with the highest QoS resulting in the highest cost.

Where there is a difference between the PSTN and the Internet is that in the 1980s, the PSTN took the approach of deploying ATM to support multimedia and QoS. Interestingly, the telco community is now looking toward one of the newer standards developed by the IETF, MPLS, as a means of reducing some of the costs traditionally associated with ATM. (MPLS is covered at the end of this chapter.) The ultimate goal, at least based on what we know today, is to marry IP and the optical realm via a control plane based on a more robust version of MPLS called Generalized MPLS (GMPLS).

The Internet has the same objective as the PSTN: to support high speeds, accommodate multimedia traffic, and support QoS guarantees. But the Internet community took a slightly different approach than the PSTN. Rather than rely on ATM and its QoS architecture, it began developing various architectures that address class of service (CoS) and QoS. Included in these is an overall umbrella architecture known as Integrated Services Architecture (ISA). ISA encompasses various solutions, including IntServ and DiffServ, along with MPLS; these strategies have the ultimate goal of blending IP and optical and migrating to GMPLS.

Convergence in the Service Environment

An important perspective of convergence lies in the operating assumptions of both service providers and enterprises. Let's look at both the traditional assumptions and current thinking.

Traditional Operating Assumptions

In the service environment, the operating assumptions are those of the traditional carrier mindset. Much of the carrier's business operations have been driven by industry regulations. Voice is a regulated environment, whereas data is not, and because more than 70% of carrier revenues come from voice, most of the traditional carrier's attention has been focused on that world. For example, network engineering has been focused on the requirements of voice traffic, and the network has been optimized to support voice. Before the current era of bandwidth abundance, controlling latency was an easier task than providing bandwidth. Bandwidth was considered to be at a premium, requiring high utilization and oversubscription by customers. Because QoS was a prerequisite to supporting voice, controlling latency was the dominant traffic-engineering issue. In the traditional world, all carriers and some enterprises desired measured use for network chargeback, so accountability was a critical concern. In terms of network ownership, traditional thinking was that carriers should own the facilities to maintain control. Finally, the basic business model was one where transport was considered to be the business.

In the traditional enterprise, the main goal of an enterprise network was seen to be the linking of enterprise sites. The network staff was generally divorced from the Web site developers. The main objective of network management was to manage the network as a cost center, with the major focus being on controlling the size of the "phone bill." In terms of network architecture, the traditional enterprise saw the use of separate voice and data networks, with most traffic being local to a nearby server. The key consideration was to provide high availability, first and foremost for voice, with data being a secondary consideration. Network optimization activities were supported by predictable traffic, predictable service providers, and predictable rates and tariffs. The preference in terms of network infrastructure was to build private networks; they were the norm and favored over public networks, whose use was the exception.

Current Operating Thinking

The assumptions at play with the new enterprise are vastly different from the traditional thinking. Today, using the public Internet for communications is considered as important as using enterprise networks. More often than not, the networking staff works with the Web site and e-commerce operations. The new network management objective is to manage the network as an application-enabling infrastructure, with flexibility being more important than cost. The new network architecture consists of converged voice/data applications and transport, with most traffic destined for remote servers. Given the increasing emphasis on data and multimedia, data network availability is today the key consideration. Network optimization, however, is more challenging and can be said to be nondeterministic due to unpredictable traffic, changing service providers, and changing pricing. When it comes to network infrastructure, the preference is for utilization of public networks and outsourcing, relying on private networks only where necessary.

In the mind of the new-era service provider, voice, data, and video in converged networks are all just bits—they are all the same thing to service providers and regulators alike. However, although regulatory changes are indicated, they have yet to be fully articulated and instituted. The revenue stream is seen to come primarily from data and advanced applications involving multimedia. Voice is likely to move to wireless or may become "free," as part of IP service. With the focus shifting to data, the main network concern is to optimize the infrastructure for IP traffic. Traffic engineering in the current environment is governed by the philosophy that providing bandwidth is easy but controlling QoS is much more difficult, with the need to provide various levels of service designed to control latencies, losses, and bandwidth allocation. In terms of bandwidth, optical bandwidth has been driving down the cost and price of long-haul WAN transport. Lots of bandwidth, made available through optical technologies such as DWDM, beats the complexity of QoS-based service levels. Many of today's strategies therefore involve throwing bandwidth at the problem. However, QoS is increasingly emphasized as one of the main objectives behind building next-generation networks. When it comes to accountability, usage-based chargeback is being replaced by multiple flat-rate service levels. From the standpoint of network ownership, today extensive wholesaling and reselling of other carriers' facilities replace the view that complete network ownership is required for success. Finally, the business model is also changing: New-era service providers don't want to be just transport businesses any longer.

In the new service environment, there is a growing commonality between the network infrastructures of both service providers and enterprises. Fewer and fewer networks will be 100% facilities based. The service provider hosting sites are looking a great deal like enterprise data centers. As discussed in Chapter 11, service providers and large enterprises alike are taking advantage of many developments in the optical realm, including dark fiber, wavelength services, and WDM. There is a common emphasis on user service-level management, accounting, and rapid deployment. Finally, IP and Ethernet are becoming more pervasive in both worlds.

■ The Next-Generation Network Infrastructure

The vision of next-generation networks originated in the Internet community over 20 years ago. The development and growth of packet-switching networks provided the basis for the concept of next-generation networks. The key principles defining this vision included connectionless datagram transport, best-effort packet delivery, and the separation of service creation from IP transport.

Today, virtually all service providers recognize the need to evolve their infrastructures to support multimedia and content delivery services. Telecommunications service providers, both wireline carriers and mobile operators, face the challenge of providing seamless migration of the circuit-switched voice services onto an IP-based backbone while retaining all the important traditional features, particularly those required by law. The key PSTN capabilities that must be preserved include public safety, law enforcement, fraud prevention, precedence and preemption of traffic during emergencies, assistance for the hearing and speech impaired, privacy and data protection, consumer protection against intrusion, and issues of billing and settlement. In addition, seamless interoperability is critical.

In response to this challenge, carriers and service providers, with the participation of vendors and governments, are working with an ITU study group on developing a new interpretation of the next-generation network. The main objective of these efforts is to ensure the integration and interoperability of IP networks with the PSTN and mobile networks. The ITU's next-generation network is a packet-based network capable of providing telecom services and making use of multiple broadband, QoS-enabled transport technologies in which service-related functions are independent of the underlying transport-related technologies. Furthermore, the ITU's vision encompasses the need to support generalized mobility while allowing consistent and ubiquitous provisioning of services to users. The objective of the ITU-defined next-generation network is to support much more than simple voice communications, including services such as presence management, instant messaging, push-to-talk, voicemail, video communications, and a wide range of multimedia applications, including both real-time and streaming modes.

Many industry observers believe the ITU next-generation network effort is an attempt by the ITU to take control of the Internet. Carriers and governments have the equally strong view that the Internet today is not serving the interests of consumers or businesses well. The current Internet world is plagued by infrastructure vulnerabilities as well as the rapidly growing problems of fraud, cybercrime, spamming, and phishing. This reality lends strength to the argument that there is a need for greater control by operators, and the ITU next-generation network standard could serve this purpose. On the other hand, it also suggests a highly controlled world, one many of us may not feel comfortable in. To be fair, there are potential evils of such control, including limited choices, a favoring of the wealthy, and reduced democracy, without a definite guarantee of any more security. There are arguments for both sides of the issue, and you need to be aware of them to ensure open discussion and a voice in the decisions that will ultimately be made.

In addition to gaining control, there are other potential benefits for carriers choosing to implement infrastructure based on the ITU next-generation network. Operators implementing that architecture will benefit from the QoS features inherent in next-generation networks and will therefore be positioned to give preferential treatment to their own multimedia services as well as have the opportunity to create walled gardens. In so doing, operators can reduce competition by virtue of mediating users' access to applications or content.

As discussed in the following sections, the evolving next-generation network infrastructure is composed of several key elements, including IMS, a new three-tiered architecture, a multiservice core, QoS, and an MPLS architecture.

The IP Multimedia Subsystem

The architecture of the ITU's next-generation network relies heavily on the IP Multimedia Subsystem (IMS) framework. Originally developed by the 3G Partnership Project (3GPP; www.3gpp.org) for 3G/UMTS networks, IMS was based on standards work that started in mid-1999 for an all-IP network. IMS has been extended to cover wireline networks as well, and it now facilitates FMC, eliminating the distinction between wired and wireless networks. (IMS for wireless networks is discussed in more detail in Chapter 16.) FMC speaks to the vision of being able to use one phone with one number, address book, and voicemail bank while enjoying the benefits of low-cost, high-speed connectivity in the office or fixed-line residential environment—of course, still enjoying the freedom of mobility in the WAN. Seamless handoff between fixed and mobile networks is also included.

Defined by 3GPP and 3GPP2 (www.3gpp2.org), IMS is a service infrastructure that relies on Session Initiation Protocol (SIP) to establish and maintain call control. IMS is an internationally recognized standard that defines a generic architecture for offering VoIP and other multimedia services in wireline and wireless applications. By adopting SIP as the signaling protocol, service providers have a standard that works well for both voice and data. In fact, VoIP has now become the foundation of almost every service provider's next-generation network architecture, including wireless, wireline, and cable/MSP operators. As we examine the role of VoIP in these providers' networks, it is clear that it constitutes a vital part of their strategies for differentiation, reduced costs, and increased competitiveness.

IMS gives carriers the opportunity to build a single and common IP service infrastructure independent of the access method. Building the infrastructure only once causes the cost per service to go down over time and increases the opportunity to offer a more integrated, richer, and more seamless environment. The IMS architecture offers a number of benefits, including enhanced person-to-person communications; improved interaction between media streams, which enables easy integration and interworking of different IP-based services; improved service mobility, which enables services to be offered over various access networks; and the ability of third-party developers and vendors to easily create and integrate new solutions through well-defined APIs and standards.

IMS applications include voice telephony, video telephony, multimedia streaming, HTTP and TCP/IP browsing, instant messaging, file sharing, gaming, push-to-talk/push-to-media, and presence-based services. Major vendors, including Ericsson, Lucent, Nortel, and Siemens, have made substantial investments in IMS software.

Four basic principles are associated with IMS:

- **Access independence**—As the name implies, *access independence* means that IMS is intended to enable work with any network—be it fixed, wireless, or mobile—and includes all the access options, such as UMTS, GPRS,

CDMA2000, WLAN, WiMax, DSL, and cable. Gateways are used to accommodate older systems such as circuit-switched telephone networks and GSM cellular systems. The fact that open interfaces are used between the control and service layers (discussed later in this chapter) allows the elements and sessions from various access networks to be combined.

- **Different network architectures**—IMS allows service providers and carriers to employ a variety of underlying network architectures.

- **Terminal and user mobility**—Terminal mobility is supported by roaming via the mobile network, and user mobility is enabled via IMS and SIP.

- **Extensive IP-based services**—Supporting a wide range of IP services is the ultimate goal, and IMS can enable support of applications ranging from VoIP to Push-to-Talk over Cellular (PoC), messaging, presence management, multiparty gaming, and content sharing.

IMS Protocols

IMS creates a telephony-oriented signaling network that overlays an underlying IP network. IMS uses Session Initiation Protocol (SIP), with specific extensions for IMS. As discussed in Chapter 9, SIP is a peer-to-peer protocol in which end devices, known as user agents, initiate sessions. It is an end-to-end signaling protocol, which means that all the logic is stored in end devices, except the routing of SIP messages. State is also stored in end devices only; there is no single point of failure, and networks designed this way scale well. An IMS network comprises many SIP proxy servers that mediate all customer/user connections and access to network resources. The tradeoff for the distributiveness and scalability is higher message overhead because the messages are sent end to end. The aim of SIP is to provide the same functionality as the traditional PSTN, but because of their end-to-end design, SIP networks are much more powerful and open to the implementation of new services.

Although IMS is SIP based, it includes enhancements and exceptions to the SIP specification, particularly for registration, authentication, and session policy. IMS uses DIAMETER rather than RADIUS for authentication, taking advantage of DIAMETER's additional support for charging and billing functions, such as prepaid calling services. IMS also uses the Common Open Policy Service (COPS) protocol for mobile operators to enforce security and QoS policies across network elements.

IMS initially required the use of IPv6 (discussed in Chapter 8), but given the number of transport networks using IPv4, this requirement has been relaxed. IMS terminal devices are centrally and tightly controlled, unlike the IP networks that provide the underlying network transport for IMS.

IMS assumes that each user is associated with a home network, and it supports the concept of roaming across other wired or wireless networks. Network services and applications are implemented in the user's home network. Because visited networks act primarily as vehicles for multimedia IP packets sent or received by the roamer, service knowledge is not required in visited networks. IMS also includes a policy engine and an authentication, authorization, and accounting (AAA) server for operator control and security.

The IMS Architecture

The IMS standard defines a generic architecture that offers VoIP and other multimedia services within wireline and wireless infrastructures. As shown in Figure 10.2, the IMS architecture is divided into three layers: service (or application), control, and transport (or access).

The IMS architecture consists of various components, including SIP proxies, media gateways, and various types of servers. The key components, as shown in Figure 10.3, include the following:

■ Service- or application-layer components:
  - **Application servers**—Application servers are IMS-compliant multimedia application servers. The application server can provide service capability interaction manager (SCIM) functions to manage interactions.

■ Control-layer components:
  - **Call session controller function**—The call session controller function (CSCF) provides call control similar to that of a VoIP softswitch. There are three types of CSCFs: the proxy CSCF (P-CSCF), which is a SIP

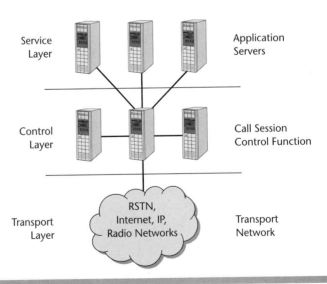

Figure 10.2 The IMS layers

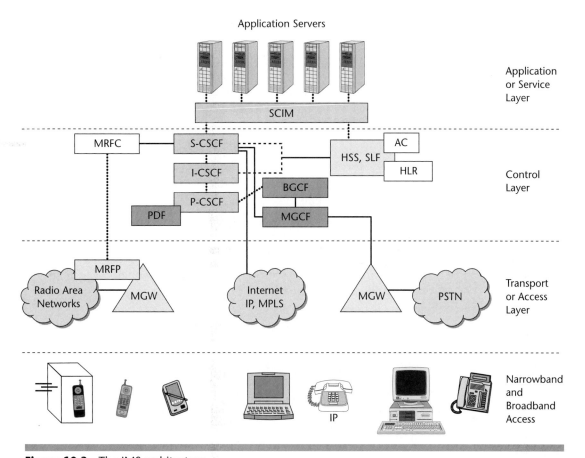

Application Servers

Figure 10.3 The IMS architecture

proxy that provides subscriber access to network-based services and sits in front of the serving CSCF; the serving CSCF (S-CSCF), which is the primary call controller for the operator network; and the interrogating CSCF (I-CSCF), which is a SIP proxy that can be optionally used by a network operator to hide internal configurations.

- **Home subscriber servers (HSSs)**—An HSS handles centralized provisioning, management, and authentication/authorization. CSCFs consult with the HSS before initiating SIP connections. The HSS includes the home location register (HLR) and the authentication center (AC). The HLR is a database used for storage and management of subscriptions; storage of permanent information about subscribers, including the subscriber's service profile; location information; and activity status. The AC is used to protect subscribers from unauthorized access (by providing authentication and encryption parameters that verify the user's identity) and to ensure the confidentiality of each call. It also protects network operators from different types of fraud found in today's mobile networks.

- **Subscription locator function (SLF)**—The SLF locates the database that contains subscriber data in response to queries from the I-CSCF or application server.
- **Policy controllers**—A policy controller is a server that performs the policy decision function (PDF) for QoS and security. It checks the HSS database and uses COPS to control policy enforcement points embedded in other network elements.
- **Border gateway control function (BGCF)**—The BGCF handles control/signaling messages to other IMS domains.
- **Multimedia resource function controller (MRFC)**—The MRFC interprets information coming from an application server and S-CSCF and controls the multimedia resource function processor (MRFP) accordingly. It also generates CDRs.
- **Multimedia gateway controller function (MGCF)**—The MGCF, also known as a softswitch or call agent, communicates with the CSCF and controls the connections for media channels in an IMS media gateway. The MGCF performs protocol conversion between ISUP (ISDN, User Part) and the IMS call control protocols. (ISUP is a part of SS7 that is used to set up calls in the PSTN.)

■ Transport- or access-layer components:

- **Multimedia resource function processor (MRFP)**—The MRFP provides a wide range of functions for multimedia resources, including provision of resources to be controlled by the MRFC, mixing of incoming media streams, sourcing media streams (for multimedia announcements), and processing of media streams.
- **Media gateway (MGW)**—The MGW functions as a translation device between different networks (e.g., by performing the conversions between VoIP and TDM-based voice on the PSTN). A related signaling gateway (SGW) may be included for exchanging control messages with the PSTN's SS7 control network. MGWs are controlled by the MGCF, and they communicate with one another using protocols such as MGCP or Megaco.

The History and Future of IMS

The base IMS functionality was first defined in the 3GPP Release 5 (R5) standards, finalized in March 2003. This standard was optimized for use by GSM UMTS wireless networks.

The second phase of IMS standards development ended in September 2004 with the publication of 3GPP Release 6 (R6) standards. R6 adds support for SIP forking and multiway conferencing and the group management capabilities necessary for instant messaging and presence services. R6 also allows for interoperability between the IMS variant of SIP and the IETF SIP standard (RFC 3261). Finally, R6 adds interworking with WLANs.

3GPP Release 7 (R7), working together with TISPAN (Telecoms and Internet converged Services & Protocols for Advanced Networks) R1, adds support for fixed networks. TISPAN is a standardization body of ETSI that specializes in fixed network and Internet convergence. The TISPAN architecture is based on the concept of cooperating subsystems sharing common components.

IMS products began to be introduced in 2005, and IMS-based consumer and entertainment services are expected in 2006 or 2007. One of the first applications to use IMS is likely to be Push-to-Talk over Cellular. (Push-to-talk is discussed in Chapter 16.)

The Next-Generation Network Architecture

Network architectures are in transition. In today's environment, time division and statistical multiplexers gather customer traffic for additional circuit-based aggregation through a stable hierarchy of edge (i.e., local), tandem, and core switching offices in the carrier networks. Overlay networks, such as X.25, Frame Relay, ATM, and the Internet, have been put in place and have created the need to internetwork services, thereby eroding traditional network borders. As additional access in transport options—including cable, DSL, fiber, and wireless—began to be introduced, they joined traditional modems and brought their own high-density access aggregation devices into the picture. Meanwhile, in the core, SDH/SONET transport has been layered over DWDM, adding capacity and producing a variety of vendor-specific switching, routing, and management options.

Figure 10.4 puts today's networks into a visual context. Residential customers on POTS connect through their first point of access, the Class 5 (i.e., local exchange) switch. Some users are serviced by xDSL, and these lines terminate on a DSL access multiplexer (DSLAM). The DSLAM links back to the local exchange for regular voice traffic, which is diverted out over the PSTN, and it also has connections into the packet-based backbone (which could be a core or backbone network based on IP, ATM, Frame Relay, or MPLS) for data traffic.

Some users have dialup modems that terminate on remote access devices; through digital access cross-connects and routers, they use private lines to access their corporate facilities to work with internal LANs and resources. Customers who have optical networks have a series of multiplexers onsite that multiplex sub-optical carrier levels up to levels that can be introduced into an SDH/SONET

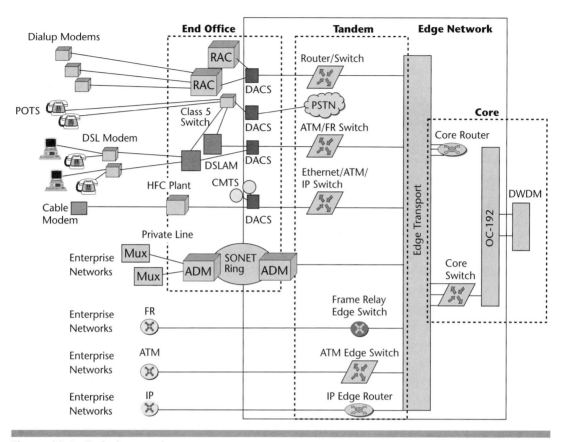

Figure 10.4 Today's networks

add/drop multiplexer to carry that traffic through the SDH/SONET ring, or today they may even have connections directly into DWDM systems. Customers also have Frame Relay, ATM, and IP switches and routers that interface into complementary equipment within the carrier network. Between the access and the edge is a plethora of different equipment, requiring different interfaces; different provisioning, billing, and network management systems; and different personnel to handle customer service and technical support and maintenance.

The core network is increasingly becoming optical. Therefore, there is access into the high-speed optical multiplexers via routers or switches, and then those optical carrier levels in the SDH/SONET hierarchy are further multiplexed via DWDM systems to take advantage of the inherent bandwidth available in those fibers.

The broadband architecture is an increasingly complicated arena. Many different alternatives in the network have been engineered to support specific voice, data, or video applications, meeting certain performance characteristics and cost characteristics. When we add up all the different platforms and networks we have, it's quite a costly environment and one that is difficult to maintain and manage cohesively. By building the overlay networks and separating access and transport functions, carriers manage to add capacity and new services without interrupting their existing services. However, the downside of this system is that the new services rarely use the same provisioning management and troubleshooting systems as the old network. These operations and management costs can amount to as much as half of the carrier's total cost to provide a service.

The Three-Tiered Architecture

The broadband architecture has three tiers. The first tier involves the access switches; it is the outer tier, associated with delivering broadband to a customer. The second tier involves the edge switches and is associated with protocol and data service integration. The third tier, the inner tier, involves the core switches and handles transmission of high-speed packet data throughout the backbone. Figure 10.5 shows the components that comprise these three tiers, and the following sections describe them.

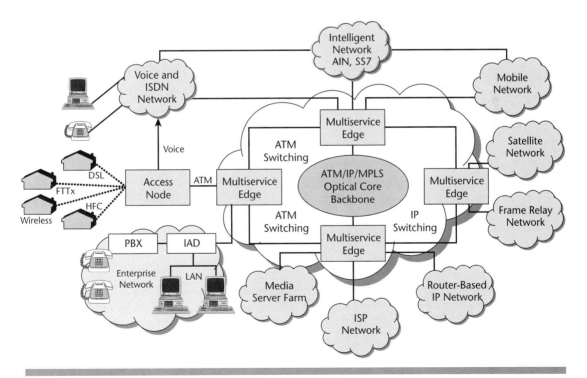

Figure 10.5 A multiservice network

The Outer Tier: The Broadband Access Tier Access tier devices include legacy network infrastructure devices such as Class 5 local exchanges and digital loop carriers. The access tier also includes DSLAMs, which are designed to concentrate hundreds of DSL access lines onto ATM or IP trunks and then route them to routers or multiservice edge switches.

Also in the access environment are IADs, which provide a point of integration at the customer edge, integrating voice, data, and video networks and supporting broadband access options. The access tier also contains remote access servers, which typically provide access to remote users via analog modem or ISDN connections and include dialup protocols and access control or authentication schemes. Remote access routers are used to connect remote sites via private lines or public carriers, and they provide protocol conversations between the LAN and the WAN.

The Middle Tier: The Intelligent Edge The second tier involves the intelligent edge devices. These can include next-generation switches, VoIP gateways, media gateways, trunking gateways, ATM switches, IP routers, IP switches, multiservice agnostic platforms, optical networking equipment, and collaborating servers. This tier is also home to the network management stations that manage all those devices.

The edge devices and the intelligent edge generally handle AAA functions. They identify the specific levels of performance required and map the proper QoS levels into the packet according to the backbone protocol. The intelligence keeps moving closer and closer to the customer, and it is actually being extended to CPE. We're trying to get away from an environment that has a lot of single-purpose networks associated with single-purpose boxes and their own individual access lines (see Figure 10.6). As mentioned previously, there are complexities involved with acquisition, with ongoing maintenance, and with the talent pool to administer and maintain these systems.

The ideal situation would be a multipurpose WAN switch that could facilitate the termination of any type of data protocol as well as facilitate aggregation at high speeds to the various optical levels (see Figure 10.7). This is what we're striving for with the intelligent edge.

Traditionally, networks have employed two types of devices at the edge:

- **Access-oriented devices**—These devices include MSPPs, which can handle all the popular data protocols and interfaces, except that not all of them are designed to be optical aggregators.

- **Transport-oriented devices**—These optical aggregations systems support a full range of hierarchical aggregation, from DS-3 to OC-192. They offer electrical-to-optical conversion as well. But they don't offer all the data interfaces.

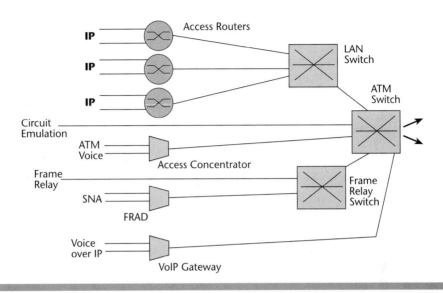

Figure 10.6 Complexities with single-purpose boxes

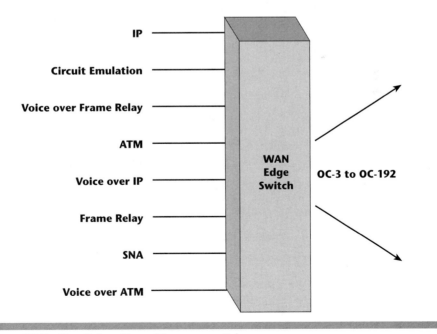

Figure 10.7 Simplicity with multipurpose switches

Successful edge devices need to handle multiprotocol data services as well as multispeed aggregation. Emerging solutions for the intelligent network edge therefore have to meet four critical objectives. First, there's a need to bridge the bandwidth bottleneck that currently exists between user LANs and the optical core. We have LANs that operate at 1Gbps (Gigabit Ethernet, or GigE) and even 10Gbps (10 Gigabit Ethernet, or 10GigE), and 100Gbps Ethernet is in development. We have optical cores that operate at 10Gbps (OC-192) and are moving beyond that, to 40Gbps (OC-768), with some hoping to introduce even 80Gbps. By applying multiple wavelengths in a fiber, we can achieve terabits per second. But the WAN link between the LAN and the optical core is still often limited to a link that can handle only 56Kbps to 2Mbps. So a severe bottleneck is occurring at the LAN/WAN integration point, and that needs to be addressed. Second, we need to improve the serviceability of the carrier networks; we need to make it easier to define, provision, bill, and manage services and equipment across a converged area. Third, we need to enable converged carrier infrastructures to simplify the carrier networks and to simplify the support of end-user services. Fourth, having multiple options for broadband access brings with it the challenge and complication of supporting multiple access techniques. Therefore, we must provide media-agnostic service interworking between multiple access technologies at the edge. The intelligent edge must be able to support each converged service, recognizing and properly handling all the voice, data, video, and multimedia traffic.

New network designs are promising to facilitate a number of issues—above all to eliminate all the service-specific and hierarchical aggregation layers that reside in today's edge network. All those layers contribute to cost and complexity over time. Figure 10.8 depicts what the next-generation access edge might look like. You can see that we've replaced separate platforms throughout the edge with more integrated environments; for example, we might have softswitches that enable traditional PSTN call telephony-type features, but over packet backbones. Circuit switches are predicted to continue to be present in the network for another 10 to 20 years, depending on location. Trunking gateways are used to attach multiple media gateways that are putting voice into IP packets to the underlying SS7 network. Remote access concentrators enable remote access for telecommuters and people who need to access remote corporate hosts. New generations of broadband access switches enable the multialternative broadband access environment—cable modems, Frame Relay, xDSL, wireless alternatives, and so on. We want to reduce the edge environment to a simpler set of agnostic, multiplatform, multiprotocol intelligent edge devices.

The main responsibilities of the intelligent edge include broadband access, adaptation of the native traffic to the underlying backbone technique, and concentration of many customer streams onto the bigger pipes within the core. This is the point at which the service attributes are mapped to QoS mechanisms in order to

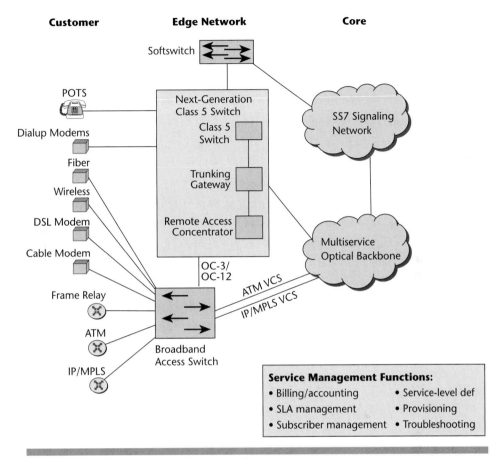

Figure 10.8 The next-generation network edge

deliver the requested performance and thereby live up to the SLAs. One of the major benefits is that it allows rapid and dynamic service provisioning, and it even allows customization for individual users. These service changes can be made without affecting the core, so as new service logic is required and as market segments find demand for new services, we will not necessarily have to reengineer the entire core network to accommodate those changes. Service provisioning is therefore decoupled from service specification and service delivery.

The Inner Tier: The High-Speed Core   The access and edge switches are designed to be scalable, both in port counts and in their ability to deliver multiservice support, and they are evolving to include more and more intelligence and features that would enable policy-based service management. In contrast, core switches are designed to be incredibly big and incredibly fast but generally quite dumb. Their main objective is to transport traffic as reliably and quickly as possible, at the highest available rate.

So in the emerging environment, we see a reversal. In the traditional PSTN, the edges served the network core, and the network core had all the intelligence. Now, the network core is serving the edges, and intelligence is being distributed closer and closer to the customer premises (see Figure 10.9).

The Multiservice Intelligent Edge

As discussed in the preceding section, the evolution of a multiservice intelligent edge is a key element of the next-generation infrastructure. Service providers face the challenge of supporting their existing data services while transitioning to a new IP world. They need a service edge platform that will allow them to achieve this goal. Multiservice switches can now support Layer 3 services while continuing to support traditional Layer 2 ATM and Frame Relay services, DSL aggregation, and voice and wireless applications. They also support Packet over SDH/SONET (PoS) and Ethernet interfaces, as well as interfaces for Frame Relay, ATM, Circuit Emulation Service, and TDM.

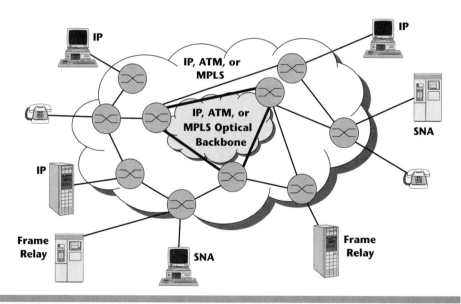

Figure 10.9 The network core serving the edges

Most of today's Tier 1 service providers have ATM-based networks that support Frame Relay, ATM, and private-line services. These services continue to show growth. For example, IP traffic growth in the United States is expected to be approximately 75%, while non-IP data is expected to grow at approximately 40%. Service providers are looking for new IP and Ethernet revenue streams while continuing to support and grow their current private-line, Frame Relay, and ATM services. However, service providers don't know how the service mix will change over time and therefore need the flexibility to manage changing demand.

An additional complication comes from the fact that while non-IP data represents a decreasing percentage of traffic, the revenues associated with these services remain significantly higher than those for IP. Revenues for IP are expected to be only 5% of total Frame Relay and ATM revenues. (But bear in mind that customers are used to paying more for Frame Relay and ATM data services, and of course the service providers are more than happy to maintain the status quo.)

The trend is to accommodate a full mix of services. Service providers will use a combination of Layer 2 and Layer 3 networks to deliver new services, and the choice will depend on many variables. Proper components, including service routers and routing switches, are necessary to migrate existing networks. Servicing this market completely requires an end-to-end approach that includes components, interworking, and end-to-end management.

Attributes of the Multiservice Edge

The multiservice edge has the following attributes:

- **Support for traditional and emerging Layer 2 and Layer 3 services**— These services include IP VPNs, broadband remote access servers, Internet access, Virtual Private LAN Services (VPLS), virtual private wire service (VPWS), ATM, Frame Relay, and security services. The multiservice edge is required to support today's revenue streams and emerging services over a cost-reduced infrastructure.

- **High reliability**—The multiservice edge must support true carrier-grade reliability at the nodal, network, and service levels to provide high service availability and support mission-critical, converged voice, video, and data traffic.

- **A modular, flexible hardware and software architecture**—The multiservice edge must have distributed input/output, and it needs a control and data plane that has the ability to independently scale switching capacity and the control plane. This is required to enable pay-as-you-grow deployment in any size POP, flexible sparing (or backup) strategies, and performance improvements. Multiservice optimized traffic management must have very granular integrated Layer 2/Layer 3 traffic management that is consistent across all media and services. This is required to enable differentiated services through service bundling and unique SLAs.

■ **Intelligent integration into the existing architecture**—The multiservice edge must provide interworking with existing platforms, management systems, and operational support systems, and it must support current SLAs and service definitions.

Service and Protocol Integration at the Intelligent Edge
Multiservice edge platforms are a new category of product designed to deliver convergence, revenue generation, and cost reductions on a single edge device. The multiservice edge is an emerging market segment of edge devices optimized for converging Layer 2/Layer 3 services over IP/MPLS.

A multiservice edge device must be designed from inception for full multiservice convergence. This includes the requirement to deliver high reliability, provide a modular and flexible architecture, enable multiservice optimized traffic management, and support intelligent integration into existing infrastructures. The multiservice edge involves two key components: routing switches, which perform full routing and switching and offer scalability and full IP functionality distributed to the line cards, and service routers, which perform full Internet routing with the mechanisms to enforce VPNs based on SLAs.

Service edge router requirements include combining routed and switched data services, particularly because new services do not necessarily replace old services. Another requirement is an interface to TDM and packet access networks (see Figure 10.10). Again, access networks are not readily replaced. The service edge router must adapt multiple services for delivery across a common packet core, with the core being transparent to the customer, and it is a key point for mapping services into network QoS. Finally, it must manage a large number of customer interfaces, both physical and logical.

Service providers also want to allow their customers to determine the rate at which they move from Frame Relay and ATM to IP/MPLS. Ideally, service providers would like to allow their customers to use any access method they want and operate as a single VPN. This means enterprise customers could keep low-speed Frame Relay at some sites while upgrading other sites to Ethernet services. For the service providers, this means the potential for better service margins, greater customer retention, and the potential to increase the share of enterprise spending by bringing additional locations into the VPN service.

The multiservice edge must support mission-critical applications. As the IP network moves from a best-effort network to one that supports more mission-critical business applications and real-time consumer and business applications,

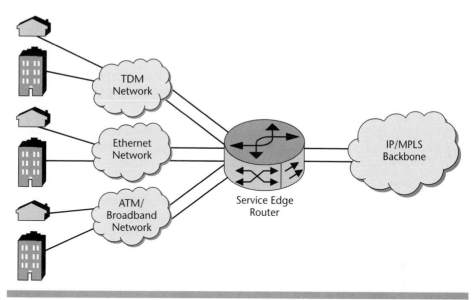

Figure 10.10 The multiservice edge

the requirements for edge equipment change. Today, applications such as gaming, streaming media, and VoIP represent only a small percentage of U.S. IP traffic, but it is expected that the volume will grow as IP networks add the requisite QoS and high-availability capabilities.

While these mission-critical applications allow service providers to increase the revenues from their IP networks, they also demand a higher level of service reliability. The gradual migration to voice-over-packet also introduces the requirement for stringent QoS, further emphasizing the need to provide the predictability and control that TDM networks offer. Five-nines reliability (i.e., 99.999%, or less than 5 minutes of downtime per year) will become an increasingly critical component of IP networks.

The Architecture of the Multiservice Edge

The multiservice edge has three main architectural requirements:

- **High reliability**—We can address the need for reliability by providing for built-in redundancy in the form of redundant switch fabrics and components, stable software that offers five-nines reliability, support for in-service upgrades, and the ability to easily integrate into the service provider's operational support systems. In the realm of availability, the ability to perform hitless software upgrades is a necessity, as are hot-swappable components and modules. Modular software code is required for maximum flexibility. Finally, the ability to detect failures and reroute traffic while detecting and reporting faults is required.

■ **Scalability**—The multiservice edge must support increasing amounts of traffic, increasing numbers of users, and the ability to add capacity as needed.

■ **Flexibility**—The multiservice edge must be able to handle any protocol type with equal ease, to upgrade software seamlessly, and to support a wide and diverse range of interfaces.

A multiservice network is a single network solution that delivers common services end to end. It is a fully managed solution that provides interworking and native services as well as best-of-breed routing switches and service routers.

The multiservice edge also involves feature requirements such as the following (see Figure 10.11):

■ **Multiservice support**—The multiservice edge must support Frame Relay, ATM, IP, and MPLS services.

■ **Support for multiple standards**—The multiservice edge must support multiple standards, including ATM's User-to-Network Interface (UNI), the Private Network-to-Network Interface (PNNI), Border Gateway Protocol (BGP), Intermediate System to Intermediate System (IS-IS), and Open Shortest Path First (OSPF), as well as VPN standards such as RFC 2547

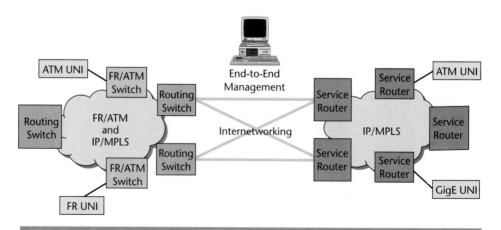

Figure 10.11 Migrating to a multiservice network

and pseudo-wire emulation edge to edge, along with interworking standards for Frame Relay and ATM.

- **Support for a wide variety of interfaces**—The multiservice edge must support various protocols, such as Frame Relay, ATM, GigE, and PoS.

- **Support for both network and service interworking**—The multiservice edge must support both network and service interworking. Multiservice switches support interworking of Frame Relay and ATM services today. Multiservice edge devices must also support network interworking, such as the ATM–MPLS network interworking specification, allowing them to act as gateways between Layer 2 and Layer 3 networks. (For detailed information and updates on the various service and network interworking specifications available for Frame Relay, ATM, and MPLS, consult the MFA Forum site, at www.mfaforum.org.)

Quality of Service

As mentioned throughout this chapter and others, QoS issues play a very important role in next-generation networks. It is becoming increasingly important to provide for very granulated levels of service, thereby allowing very high performance and at the same time creating platforms for multitudes of new revenue-generating services.

QoS is the ability to provide different levels of service to differently characterize traffic or traffic flows. It constitutes the basis for offering various classes of service to different applications or segments of end users. This then allows the creation of different pricing tiers that correspond to the different CoS and QoS levels. QoS is essential to the deployment of real-time traffic, such as voice or video services, as well as to the deployment of tiered data services.

QoS includes definitions of the network bandwidth requirements, the user priority control, control of packet or cell loss, and control of delay—both transit delay (which is end to end) and traffic delay variations (i.e., jitter). Traffic characterizations include definitions of the delay tolerance and elasticity for that application. They can also associate delay tolerance and elasticity with applications and users and potentially even time-of-day, day-of-week scenarios. It is necessary to be able to ensure various levels of service; the availability of bandwidth, end-to-end delay, delay variances, and packet losses that support the application in question; and the relative priority of traffic. Also, QoS is associated with policy admission control and policing of traffic streams.

There are two ways of implementing QoS. *Implicit QoS* means that the application chooses the required QoS. *Explicit QoS* means that the network manager controls that decision.

There are three main approaches to QoS. The first is an architected approach, and ATM falls under this category. The second is per-flow services, where the QoS is administered per flow, or per session. This includes the reservation protocol (Resource Reservation Protocol [RSVP]) that is part of the IETF IntServ specification, as well as MPLS. The third approach is packet labeling, in which each individual packet is labeled with an appropriate QoS or priority mark; the techniques that use this approach include IEEE 802.1p and 802.1pq, as well as the IETF DiffServ specification.

The following sections describe various QoS tactics, including ATM QoS, IP QoS, and Class-Based Queuing (CBQ), as well as policy-based management and related protocols, such as COPS and Lightweight Directory Access Protocol (LDAP).

ATM QoS

ATM QoS includes four different service levels (one of which has two variations) that define a series of specific QoS parameters that tailor cells to fit video, data, voice, or mixed-media traffic. The following are the four service classes:

- **Constant bit rate (CBR)**—CBR provides a constant, guaranteed rate to real-time applications such as streaming video—so it is continuous bandwidth. It emulates a circuit-switched approach and is associated with minimum latencies and losses. CBR is the highest QoS you can get, and it is for very demanding applications, such as live media, streaming media, streaming audio, streaming video, and VOD. Initially, CBR was to be used for applications such as voice and videoconferencing, but we have found that those applications do not necessarily need the continuous bandwidth. As mentioned previously, much of a voice conversation is silence. If we were carrying that voice over CBR service, whenever there was silence, the ATM switches would be stuffing in empty cells to maintain that continuous bandwidth, and of course that would be overkill and a waste of network resources.

- **Variable bit rate (VBR)**—VBR has two subsets: real-time (VBR-RT) and non-real-time (VBR-NRT). VBR provides a fair share of available bandwidth according to a specific allocation policy, so it has a maximum tolerance for latencies and losses. VBR is the highest QoS in the data realm, and it is also an adequate QoS for real-time voice. VBR-RT can be used by native ATM voice with bandwidth compression and silence suppression. So when somebody is silent, VBR-RT makes use of the available bandwidth to carry somebody else's cells, and therefore, VBR is also appropriate for multimedia functions such as videoconferencing. VBR-NRT can be used for data transfer where response time is critical (e.g., transaction-processing applications such as airline reservations, banking transactions).

■ **Available bit rate (ABR)**—ABR supports VBR data traffic with average and peak traffic parameters (e.g., LAN interconnection and internetworking services, LAN emulation, critical data transfer that requires service guarantees). Remote procedure calls, distributed file services, and computer process swapping and paging are examples of applications that would be appropriate for ABR.

■ **Unspecified bit rate (UBR)**—You could call UBR poor-man's ATM. It provides best-effort service. UBR offers no service guarantee, so it is used for text data and image transfer, messaging, and distribution of noncritical information, where there is no need for a set response time or service guarantee.

ATM provides a very well-planned approach to providing QoS. Table 10.3 shows how each service class allows you to define or not define certain parameters. The parameters boil down to two major categories:

■ **QoS parameters**—These parameters include cell error rate (CER; the percentage of errored cells), cell loss ratio (CLR; the percentage of lost cells), cell transfer delay (CTD; the delay between the network entry and exit points), cell delay variation (CDV; the jitter), and cell misinsertion rate (CMR; the number of cells inserted on the wrong connection).

■ **Traffic parameters**—These parameters include peak cell rate (PCR; allows you to specify the maximum amount of bandwidth allowed on a connection), sustainable cell rate (SCR; allows you to specify guaranteed bandwidth during the variable transmissions—used only by VBR), maximum burst size (MBS; allows you to specify the maximum number of cells that will be transmitted at PCR—used only by VBR), cell delay variation tolerance (CDVT; allows you to specify the maximum allowable jitter), minimum cell rate (MCR; allows you to specify the rate in cells per second that the source can transmit—used only in ABR), and allowed cell rate (ACR; works with ABR's feedback mechanism that determines cell rate).

As Table 10.3 shows, UBR allows you to define very little, whereas CBR allows you to tightly control most of these parameters.

Depending on the service class, you have the option of defining or not defining certain parameters, and that gives you control over the performance of an application within a service level. The transmission path in a virtual circuit with ATM is composed of virtual paths and its virtual channels (refer to Figure 7.19 in Chapter 7, "Wide Area Networking"). You can think of the virtual channel as an individual conversation path and the virtual path as a grouping of virtual channels

Table 10.3 ATM Classes of Service

Parameter	CBR	VBR-NRT	VBR-RT	ABR	UBR
Cell loss ratio	Yes	Yes	Yes	No	No
Cell transfer delay	Yes	Yes	Yes	No	No
Cell delay variation	Yes	Yes	Yes	No	No
Peak cell rate	Yes	Yes	Yes	Yes	Yes
Sustained cell rate	No	Yes	Yes	No	No
Minimum cell rate	No	No	No	Yes	No
Maximum burst size	No	Yes	Yes	No	No
Allowed cell rate	No	No	No	Yes	No

that all share the same QoS requirement: All CBR streaming video traffic may go over virtual path 1, all bursty TCP/IP data traffic may go over virtual path 2, and all MPEG-2 compressed video traffic may go over virtual path 3. In this way, we can organize all the virtual channels that have the same demands from the network into a common virtual path, thereby simplifying the administration of QoS and easing the network management process for the carrier. Within the cell structure, the key identifier in the header is which path and which channel is to be taken between any two ATM cells. The channel assignments change, depending on what channels were reserved at the time the session was negotiated.

Remember that because it is connection oriented, ATM gives service providers the traffic-engineering tools they need to manage both QoS and utilization. In provisioning a network, the service provider can assign each virtual circuit a specific amount of bandwidth and set the QoS parameters. The provider can then dictate what path each virtual circuit takes. However, it does require that the service provider manage the ATM switches and whatever else is running over that ATM network (e.g., IP routers).

IP QoS

There are two IP schemes for QoS: IntServ and DiffServ. The following sections describe each of these schemes; IP QoS mechanisms are also discussed in Chapter 8.

IntServ   IntServ was the IETF's scheme to introduce QoS support over IP networks. It provides extensions to the best-effort service model to allow control over end-to-end packet delays. In essence, IntServ is a bandwidth reservation technique that builds virtual circuits across the Internet so that applications running in the hosts can request bandwidth.

IntServ was introduced first as a setup protocol, used by hosts and routers to signal QoS in the network. It also introduces flowspecs, which are definitions of traffic flow according to traffic and QoS characteristics. Finally, IntServ introduces traffic control, which delivers on QoS by controlling traffic flows within the hosts and routers. IntServ is a per-flow resource reservation model that requires RSVP. Its key building blocks include resource reservation and admission control. In IntServ, data transmissions are built around a flow, a unidirectional path with a single recipient. In routing, traditional routers examine packets and determine where to send them and then switch them to output ports. With IntServ, routers must also apply the appropriate queuing policy if packets are part of a flow.

IntServ routers usually use first-in, first-out (FIFO) queuing. This is fast and easy, but it can make delay-sensitive applications wait behind long bursts of delay-insensitive data. IntServ uses Fair Queuing to ensure that a single flow does not use all the bandwidth and to provide minimal guarantees to different flows.

The IntServ model involves a classifier. Packets are mapped to a service class, and they are forwarded by a packet scheduler, based on their service class (see Table 10.4). Admission control determines whether the requested QoS can be delivered, and, as mentioned earlier, the setup protocol is RSVP. RSVP relies on router-to-router signaling schemes, which allow IP applications to request priority delay and bandwidth guarantees. Connections are established link by link, and a connection can be denied if a router cannot accept the request (see Figure 10.12). RSVP is particularly well suited for real-time applications and delay-sensitive traffic. RSVP allows applications to reserve router bandwidth. RSVP-guaranteed service provides bandwidth guarantees and a reliable upper bound to packet delays. But the resource requirements for running RSVP on a router increase proportionately with the number of separate RSVP reservations. This scalability problem makes using RSVP on the public Internet impractical, so it has largely been left to campus and enterprise-type networks.

Several other protocols are associated with RSVP (see Figure 10.13). Real-Time Transport Protocol (RTP) is for audio, video, and so on. It is based on UDP, to cut down on overhead and latency. RTP is specified as the transport for H.323, and receivers can sequence information via the packet headers. Real-Time Transport Control Protocol (RTCP) provides status feedback from senders to receivers. Both RTP and RTCP are standardized by the ITU under H.225. Real-Time Streaming Protocol (RTSP) runs on top of IP Multicast, UDP, RTP, and RTCP.

Table 10.4 IntServ Service Classes

Service Class	Guaranteed Service	Controlled Load Service	Best-Effort Service
End-to-end behavior	Guaranteed maximum delay	Best effort on unloaded network	Best-effort only
Intended applications	Real-time	Sensitive to congestion	Legacy
ATM mapping	CBR or VBR-RT	VBR-NRT or ABR with MCR	UBR or ABR

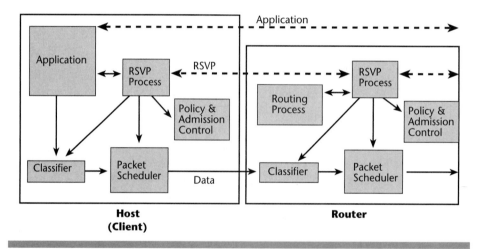

Figure 10.12 RSVP in hosts and routers

RSVP is simplex (i.e., it is a reservation for unidirectional data flow), it is receiver driven (i.e., the receiver of data flows initiates and maintains the resource reservation for that flow), and it supports both IPv4 and IPv6. RSVP is not a routing protocol. Key issues regarding RSVP include scalability, security, and assurance that policy-based decisions can be followed. RSVP and related protocols are discussed in more detail in Chapters 8 and 9.

DiffServ   Today we concentrate more on DiffServ than on its parent, IntServ. The DiffServ approach to providing QoS in networks uses a small, well-defined set of building blocks from which a variety of services can be built (see Figure 10.14). A small bit pattern in each packet in the IPv4 Type of Service (ToS) octet, or the IPv6

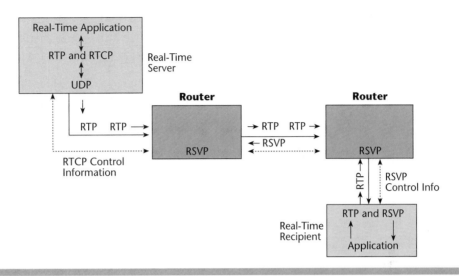

Figure 10.13 RSVP and related protocols

Traffic Class octet, is used to mark a packet to receive a particular forwarding treatment or per-hop behavior at each network node. For this reason, DiffServ is really a CoS model: It differentiates traffic by prioritizing the streams, but it does not allow the specification and control of traffic parameters. DiffServ differentiates traffic by user, service requirement, and other criteria. It then marks the packets so that the network nodes can provide different levels of service via priority queuing or bandwidth allocation, or by choosing dedicated routes for specific traffic flows. DiffServ scheduling and queue management allow routers to act on the IP datagram. Service allocation is controlled by a policy management system. Routers can do four things after receiving an IP datagram: manage a queue, schedule interfaces, select which datagram is the logical choice for discard, and select an outbound interface.

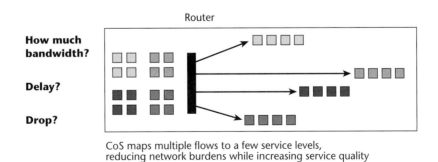

Figure 10.14 DiffServ

DiffServ is a prioritization model with preferential allocation of resources based on traffic classification. As discussed in Chapter 8, DiffServ uses a DiffServ Code Point (DSCP) to select the service—that is, the per-hop behavior—that the packet will receive at each DiffServ-capable node. Queues then get different treatment in terms of priority, share of bandwidth, or probability of discard.

CBQ

Class-Based Queuing (CBQ) is a QoS tactic based on traffic management algorithms deployed at the WAN edge. CBQ is a fully open, nonproprietary technology that brings bandwidth-controlled CoS to IP network infrastructures. It allows traffic to be prioritized according to IP application type, IP address, protocol type, and other variables. It allocates unused bandwidth more effectively than other QoS mechanisms do, and it uses priority tables to give critical applications the most immediate access to unused bandwidth.

Policy-Based Management, COPS, and LDAP

A few additional concepts are relevant to QoS: policy-based management, COPS, and LDAP.

Policy-Based Management   The idea behind policy-based networking is to associate information about individual users, groups, organizational units, entire organizations, and even events (such as the beginning of the accounting department's month-end closing) with various network services, or classes of service. So on a very granular basis, and on a time-sensitive basis, you can ensure that each user is receiving the QoS needed for the particular application at a specific time and place.

COPS   COPS is an IETF query-response-based client/server protocol for supporting policy control over QoS signaling protocols, such as RSVP. It is part of the Internet Protocol suite, as defined by IETF RFC 2748. COPS addresses how servers and clients on a network exchange policy information, and it transmits information between a policy server and its clients, which are policy-aware devices such as switches.

COPS is composed of policy decision points (PDPs), which are servers on which policies are stored, and policy enforcement points (PEPs), the clients on which the policies are enforced. There are two COPS models:

- **Provisioning Model**—In the Provisioning Model, the PEP reports its decision-making capabilities to the PDP, which then downloads the pertinent policies onto the PEP. The PEP uses these policies to make its own decisions. In this model, the policy information base is the repository of the policies.

- **Outsourcing Model**—With the Outsourcing Model, the simplest mode, all policies are stored at the PDP. When a PEP needs to make a decision, it sends the relevant information to the PDP, which then analyzes the information and forwards a decision to the PEP. All the PEP has to do is enforce the decision.

An Internet Draft called COPS-MAID introduces QoS extensions for multi-access environments. The main benefits of COPS are that it creates efficient communication between policy servers and policy-aware devices, and it increases interoperability among different vendors' systems.

LDAP   LDAP, a standard directory server technology for the Internet, allows retrieval of information from multivendor directories. More specifically, it is a networking protocol for querying and modifying directory services running over TCP/IP. LDAP version 3 (LDAPv3) provides client systems, hubs, switches, and routers, as well as a standard interface to rewrite directory information. Equipment and directory vendors use LDAP for accessing and updating directory information. The current version, LDAPv3, is specified in IETF RFC 3377.

QoS and Prevailing Conditions

There are quite a few potential approaches to implementing QoS. Which one makes sense often depends on what is available and what the prevailing conditions are. At this point, ATM is used most frequently because it offers the strongest abilities to address traffic engineering and resource utilization. Right now, high hopes are also pinned on MPLS because it does a good job of marrying the best qualities of IP with the best qualities of ATM. But once again, we are in an era of many emerging technologies. This chapter should give you an appreciation of how many issues there are to understand in the proper administration of the emerging business-class services that promise to generate large revenues.

The MPLS Architecture

MPLS was created to address the weaknesses in traditional IP networks. Remember that IP was designed to support best-effort service. Routers do not see rings or connections; they see ports and addresses via the routing tables and proprietary priority cues. IP routing lacks intelligence. Least-cost routing causes traffic to take the shortest number of hops, which means traffic takes shorter, congested paths rather than longer, uncongested paths, leading to network hotspots and inconsistent performance.

A lot of attention is being focused now on the MPLS environment, which was born out of Cisco's tag switching. MPLS, which was designed with large-scale WANs in mind, was originally proposed by the IETF in 1997, and core specifications were completed in 2000. By plotting static paths through an IP network, MPLS gives service providers the traffic-engineering capability they need, and it also helps them build a natural foundation for VPNs. Remember that traffic engineering allows service providers to control QoS and optimize network resource utilization.

MPLS is one of the most significant developments in IP. MPLS is not an IP network, although it uses IP routing protocols such as OSPF and IS-IS and can run in routers. MPLS is not an ATM network, although it can use repurposed ATM cell switch hardware. MPLS is yet another type of network: It is a service-enabling technology. MPLS is a general-purpose tunneling mechanism that can carry IP and non-IP payloads. It uses label switching to forward packets or cells through the network, and it can operate over any data link layer.

MPLS separates the control plane from the forwarding plane. It thus enables the IP control plane to run on devices that cannot understand IP or recognize packet boundaries. The *MP* part of MPLS means it's *multiprotocol*—it is an encapsulating protocol that can transport a multitude of other protocols. *LS* indicates that the protocols being transported are encapsulated with a label that is swapped at each hop. A *label* is a number that uniquely identifies a set of data flows on a particular link or within a particular logical link. The labels are of only local significance. They must change as packets follow a path—hence the *switching* aspect of MPLS.

Another benefit of MPLS is its potential to unite IP and optical switching under one route-provisioning umbrella. Because IP is a connectionless protocol, it cannot guarantee that network resources will be available. In addition, IP sends all traffic between the same two points over the same route. During busy periods, therefore, some routes become congested and others remain underutilized. Without having explicit control over route assignments, the provider has no way to steer excess traffic over less busy routes. One key difference between MPLS and IP is that in MPLS, packets sent between two points can take different paths based on different MPLS labels.

How MPLS Works

MPLS is connection oriented, like ATM and Frame Relay, and it makes use of label-switched paths (LSPs). MPLS tags, or adds a label to, IPv4 or IPv6 packets so they can be steered over the Internet along predefined routes. MPLS also adds a label that identifies the type of traffic, the path, and the destination. This allows routers to assign explicit paths to various classes of traffic. Using these explicit routes, service providers can reserve network resources for high-priority or delay-sensitive flows, distribute traffic to prevent network hotspots, and preprovision backup routes for quick recovery from outages.

As shown in Figure 10.15, an MPLS network is composed of a mesh of label-switching routers (LSRs). These LSRs are MPLS-enabled routers and/or MPLS-enabled ATM switches. They are core routers that ignore the IP packet header. LSRs forward packets based on labels, running IP routing protocols and some form of MPLS Label Distribution Protocol (LDP) to allocate and distribute the Forwarding Equivalence Class (FEC) and label bindings. Labels are contained in the packets or cells. They are used by the LSR to index the Label Information Base (LIB) during the label swap. The format is link-layer dependent. As each packet enters the network, an ingress LSR assigns it a label, based on its destination, VPN membership, ToS bits, and other considerations. At each hop, an LSR uses the label to index a forwarding table. The forwarding table assigns each packet a new label and directs the packet to an output port. To promote scaling, labels have only local significance. As a result, all packets with the same label follow the same LSP through the network.

MPLS traffic engineering enables tunneling through an IP network. With FEC, a group of IP packets are forwarded in the same manner—that is, over the same path and with the same forwarding instructions. LDP refers to the control protocols that operate between the LSRs. The LSP is established through a contiguous set of LSRs. The FEC allows treatment of traffic to be based on application, destination, or other parameters. It allows traffic to be grouped together and allows priorities to be established. The end result is that the responsibility is split between ingress, egress, and transit routers; heavy processing is done at the edges, and label forwarding is done at the core.

Service providers can specify explicit routes by configuring them into edge LSRs manually, or they can use one of two new signaling protocols: RSVP-TE, which is RSVP with traffic-engineering extensions, or MPLS LDP, which is augmented for constraint-based routing. Most equipment vendors support both.

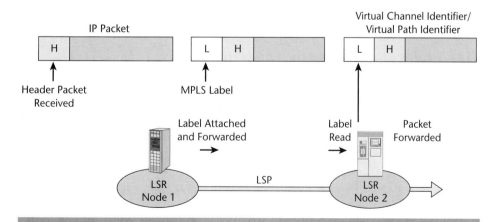

Figure 10.15 How MPLS works

With MPLS, network operators don't have to use explicit routing—and they are not likely to in networks that have plenty of bandwidth. Instead, they can let ingress LSRs use LDP without any constraint-based extensions, to automatically associate labels with paths. With plain LDP, MPLS packets follow the same routes as ordinary routed packets. With MPLS, you can support all applications on an IP network without having to run large subsets of the network with completely different transport mechanisms, routing protocols, and addressing plans.

MPLS can switch a frame from any kind of Layer 2 link to any other kind of Layer 2 link, without depending on any particular control protocol. Compare this to ATM, for example: ATM can switch only to and from ATM and can use only ATM signaling protocols, such as PNNI or Interim Interface Signaling Protocol. MPLS supports several types of label formats. On ATM hardware, it uses the well-defined virtual channel identifier (VCI) and virtual path identifier (VPI) labels. On Frame Relay hardware, it uses a data link connection identifier (DLCI) label. Elsewhere, MPLS uses a new generic label, known as a *shim*, which sits between Layers 2 and 3. Because MPLS allows the creation of new label formats without requiring changes in routing protocols, extending technology to new optical transport and switching could be relatively straightforward.

MPLS Stacks

Label stacking is a powerful feature of MPLS that enables LSRs to insert an additional label at the front of each labeled packet, creating an encapsulated tunnel that can be shared by multiple LSPs. At the end of the tunnel, another LSR pops the label stack, revealing the inner label. An optimization in which the next-to-last LSR peels off the outer label is known in IETF documents as *penultimate hop popping*.

Whereas ATM has only one level of stacking (virtual channels inside virtual paths), MPLS supports unlimited stacking (see Figure 10.16). An enterprise could

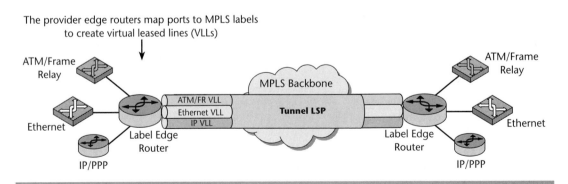

Figure 10.16 MPLS stacks

use label stacking to aggregate multiple flows of its own traffic before passing the traffic on to the access provider. The access provider could then aggregate traffic from multiple enterprises before handing it off to the backbone provider, and the backbone provider could aggregate the traffic yet again before passing it off to a wholesale carrier. Service providers could use label stacking to merge hundreds of thousands of LSPs into a relatively small number of backbone tunnels between points of presence. Fewer tunnels mean smaller routing tables, and smaller routing tables make it easier for providers to scale the network core.

Why MPLS?

MPLS adds two important elements to IP: virtual circuits and capacity reservation. Virtual circuits, in this context, are referred to as LSPs. LSPs provide security similar to that found in Frame Relay: Tunnels are used to isolate customer traffic. (But true security is not simply guaranteed through the use of tunnels; rather, true security means that customer traffic must be encrypted end to end.) MPLS also allows for capacity reservation, enabling the support of SLAs. Typical parameters might include a packet loss of less than 1% and a round-trip delay of less than 55 to 70 milliseconds.

Constraint-based routing is superior to IP because it bases routing decisions on more than just a shortest-path calculation. Hence, using MPLS may be the best way for service providers to provision VPNs that meet customer service quality metrics and permit ISPs to scale their networks and meet traffic-engineering requirements without having to resort to using ATM permanent virtual circuit (PVC) overlay networks.

In summary, MPLS adds QoS and virtual tunnels; it provides a common control plane between Layer 2 and Layer 3; it can support multiple Layer 2 protocols such as Frame Relay, ATM, and Ethernet; and it provides Layer 2 performance, which means it has the benefits of connection-oriented networks. MPLS is a compromise between connectionless Layer 3 and connection-oriented Layer 2, which means it provides deterministic behavior.

Using MPLS is the most effective way to integrate IP and ATM in the same backbone network. It reduces the processing overhead in IP routers, improving packet-forwarding performance. MPLS is also another way to provide QoS in network backbones, competing with or being complementary to DiffServ, IntServ's RSVP, and the ATM QoS architecture. Finally, it solves the n-squared route propagation problem in large backbones, where routers have to be interconnected with a mesh of ATM or Frame Relay virtual circuits.

Major efforts are under way to adapt the control plane of MPLS to direct the routing of not just LSRs but also an expanded universe of devices, including optical switches and other optical elements. This will allow optical switches, optical cross-connects, LSRs, regular IP routers, and even time division multiplexers to recognize each other and exchange information. The same routing system can control optical paths in the DWDM core, LSPs across the MPLS backbone, and paths involving any IP routers at the edge of the network. This is the realm of GMPLS, which is discussed in detail in Chapter 11. Whether with MPLS or GMPLS, service providers can simplify their operational procedures, deliver more versatile IP services, and, most importantly to customers, sign meaningful SLAs.

Chapter 11

Optical Networking

The recent inventions and developments in optical networking will no doubt yield a new, radical perspective on communications. We are beginning to see some exciting applications being developed as a result of the bandwidth that we are unleashing. This chapter discusses end-to-end optical networking, the optical edge, the optical core (and the overlay and peer-to-peer networking models), the IP+optical control plane, and the migration to optical networking.

■ Optical Networking Today and Tomorrow

The performance improvements—in speed, cost, and capacity—of fiber have been fast and furious. The number of bits per second that fiber can carry doubles every 9 months for every dollar spent on the technology. The number of bits per second per lambda (λ), or wavelength, doubles every 12 months. The cost of transmitting a bit of information optically drops by 50% every 9 months, and fiber prices, on a per-megabits-per-second basis, are falling by 60% each year. In comparison, the number of transistors on a computer chip doubles only every 18 months. Therefore, over a 5-year period, optical technology far outpaces silicon chips and data storage. New fiber networks are increasing long-distance transmission capacity incredibly quickly and relatively inexpensively.

Falling Prices in Optical Networking

Developments in optical networking have caused the cost of transport to drop dramatically in recent years. Over the past decade, the cost of moving bits has dropped so dramatically that if the automotive industry could match it, you could buy a BMW for just a dollar or two.

The following sections discuss the factors driving the optical networking boom, what today's networks actually look like, and the abundance of bandwidth.

Drivers of Optical Networking

A number of factors are driving the interest in and deployment of optical networking. First, carriers want to boost capacity by orders of magnitude. Dense Wavelength Division Multiplexing (DWDM) enables multiple wavelengths of light to be carried over a single strand of fiber, which allows for the elegant expansion of capacity. We're also seeing developments in the application of Frequency Division Multiplexing (FDM) to WDM systems, whereby we can combine more streams of traffic onto the same wavelength, promising a several-fold boost to the carrying capacity of fiber. (DWDM, FDM, and other multiplexing techniques are discussed in Chapter 1, "Telecommunications Technology Fundamentals.") Thus, we can extract more wavelengths, and over each wavelength we can derive more channels, and on each channel we can achieve more bits per second.

Second, carriers want to slash costs. Advances are being made in eliminating the need for regeneration stations on long-haul networks. Because many optical networks still use electronic repeaters, every 200 miles (320 km) a light signal has to be converted back into an electrical signal in order to be reshaped, resynchronized, and retimed. Then the signal is again converted back into a light pulse. This process accounts for about half the cost of optical networking. Advances in optical amplifiers, solitons (laser pulses that retain their shape in a fiber over long distances), and optical add/drop multiplexers (OADMs) and cross-connects (which eliminate the need for any conversions for signals passing through the nodes) are vastly improving the performance of optical infrastructures while also reducing the costs of deployment and ongoing operation.

Third, the provisioning of services needs to occur in minutes. But at this point, a carrier may have to wait six to nine months for an OC-3 (i.e., 155Mbps) circuit to be provisioned. Optical switches will automate the provisioning process while also boosting capacities to handle thousands of wavelengths; that is the promise of end-to-end optical networking.

As described in Chapter 2, "Traditional Transmission Media," today's networks maintain mostly separate electronic connections for voice and data (see Figure 11.1). They achieve reliability in the network by using dual-counter-rotating rings based on the SDH/SONET communications standard (which is discussed in Chapter 4, "The PSTN"). With dual-counter-rotating rings, traffic normally flows in a clockwise direction over the primary fiber. A protect fiber is designed to carry traffic in a counterclockwise direction. An SDH/SONET multiplexer aggregates traffic onto the rings. If the primary link is cut, traffic is switched to the protect fiber very quickly—in about 50 milliseconds. This ensures a high degree of network survivability, and it is a major strength of SDH/SONET. The first generations of WDM equipment did not address network restoration, but newer equipment now possesses such features as well.

Optical networks in the near future will channel all traffic over a single fiber connection and will provide redundancy by using the Internet's mesh of interlocking pathways. When a line breaks, traffic can flow down a number of different pathways. Optical switching will become the foundation for building these types of integrated networks (see Figure 11.2).

Network Reality Today

Today's network reality involves a complex layering of many different architectures and their individual control planes. As shown in Figure 11.3, today's network has

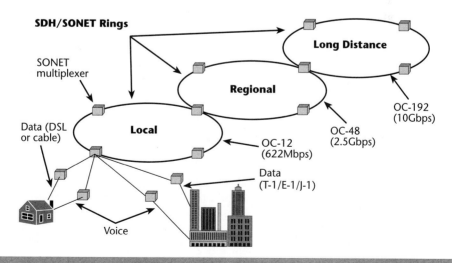

Figure 11.1 An example of today's optical networks

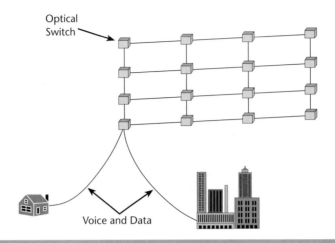

Figure 11.2 An example of tomorrow's optical networks

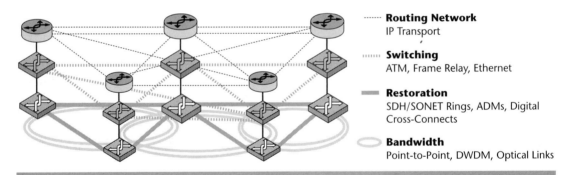

Figure 11.3 Network infrastructure today

many layers of packet data networks—including IP, Frame Relay, ATM, and MPLS—all operating over mesh topologies. These packet networks sit on top of SDH/SONET rings. The rings themselves are stacked, addressing the specific requirements of access networks, metro networks, or core networks. They facilitate fast restoration in the event of failure, but adding capacity is an intensive manual process. The SDH/SONET rings further sit on top of DWDM networks, which are point-to-point systems that involve link-by-link management and massive traffic connections at the tandem offices. The management and traffic problems will get worse as systems grow in capacity. Today's systems carry 160 wavelengths or more, and at 10Gbps per wavelength, a 160-wavelength system offers 1.6Tbps of traffic;

the capacities—that is, the number of wavelengths and bits per second per wavelength—are increasing every year.

Multiple packet data networks run over SDH/SONET, which runs over DWDM. Packet networks are naturally resilient. Therefore, the cost of overbuilding SDH/SONET may not be justified. Some services still expect 50-millisecond restoration, but not all require it. In order to remain profitable and retain market share, most service providers must offer voice, private-line, and packet data services on the same infrastructure.

Service providers are experiencing a new dilemma. In order to understand the problem, we must first examine where the bandwidth demand is coming from: the Internet, other data protocols, and voice. Packet traffic has overtaken circuit-switched voice as the dominant source of demand. Data traffic today constitutes some 90% of all traffic. Data unit growth is approximately 100% per year, and IP is the dominant form of data growth. However, other data protocols are also still being used, such as ATM and Frame Relay. The greatest bandwidth demand is coming from the Internet, yet voice represents about 80% of the revenues and dwarfs the data revenue, which is estimated at just 20%. So, while the Internet is the largest source of traffic growth, at the same time, the Internet is today a low-margin service. For example, in the United States, revenues for IP are expected to be only 5% of total Frame Relay and ATM revenues. To address this dilemma, service providers are moving from time and distance orientation to bandwidth and services orientation. They are also recognizing that the ability to deploy and support tomorrow's high-value services requires a new generation of network, an intelligent optical network platform.

The carriers are taking a number of steps to find new high-margin services. The traditional approach has been to offer new services, such as Frame Relay VPNs, IP VPNs, and MPLS offerings. Premium service revenue is driven by value. The offer of higher bandwidth is added value, as is the offer of guaranteed and measurable performance via service-level agreements (SLAs) or the offer of expedited service installation. However, even these advanced services eventually become commodities, and prices begin to drop.

Carriers need to migrate to an intelligent optical network, a new infrastructure composed of intelligent optical switches, reconfigurable optical add/drop multiplexers (ROADMs) that include the functionality of SDH/SONET restoration, DWDM and Coarse Wavelength Division Multiplexing (CWDM) systems, optical cross-connects, and new maintenance and management tools for optical networks. In an intelligent optical network, these devices can communicate with each other to discover the topology, enabling simple A-through-Z provisioning. The strategic direction is to migrate to mesh topology where and when appropriate, choosing expenses that reflect revenue margins. For example, carriers should continue to dedicate a source of restoration for those services that expect it, such as private line or voice, but rely on shared mesh protection or even unprotection for resilient protocol services such as IP, Frame Relay, or ATM.

The new-generation service provider's solution is to offer new, high-bandwidth services, optical VPNs, and public services that act like private networks. Optical networks are the only architecture that can allow IP to scale to meet the demands of the new generation, and this implies the marriage of IP and optical networks, which is discussed later in this chapter.

Bandwidth Abundance

As mentioned earlier in this chapter, service providers may choose to pursue the strategy of migrating to intelligent optical networks to guarantee growing revenues. Optical technology is revolutionizing networking and introducing a new era of abundant capacity, stimulating developments and growth of bandwidth-hungry applications. These bandwidth-intensive applications, however, are much more cost-effective when the network provides just-in-time bandwidth management options as well. And, of course, these advanced applications demand more than bandwidth; they look for service qualities that allow control of parameters such as delay, jitter, loss ratio, and throughput.

Next-generation SDH/SONET quadruples the bandwidth per channel about every two years. In addition, DWDM improvements are resulting in twice the number of wavelengths per fiber every year. Also, light sources can pulse more bits per second all the time. To top it off, new generations of fiber cable are growing in size, with more than 100 fibers per cable becoming the norm. The result is that optical bandwidth is even outpacing Moore's Law governing growth and processing power.

Internet backbones now account for over 85% of the world's cross-border capacity used in fiber-optic networks. The balance of used capacity is dedicated to private corporate networks and international telephone traffic. The submarine capacity currently deployed worldwide provides on the order of 40Tbps of capacity. Not all of this capacity is being used. Only some 11% to 25% of current fiber capacity is lit. The remainder lies idle, either unpurchased or unused by service providers, although recent trends suggest that bandwidth demand is growing and the unlit fibers will soon be put into action. Nonetheless, the increase in capacity has resulted in dramatic declines in prices. Customer demand for broadband is growing as prices are falling, and carriers are constantly investing in newer technology.

■ End-to-End Optical Networking

At this point in the optical networking revolution, we're striving for what will be an *end-to-end optical architecture*, which means that nowhere in the network is the optical signal converted into an electronic signal. This reduction in the processing of signals would reduce costs and ultimately provide better performance.

No other transmission medium can unlock the same level of available bandwidth as can the visible light spectrum. But today, electronic network equipment acts as the bottleneck. Fibers now can carry terabits per second (Tbps), but they terminate on equipment that, at best, can handle gigabits per second (Gbps). Before we can unleash the possibilities and realize the savings of end-to-end optical networking, we need to replace all the existing electronic equipment with optical equipment, which, of course, will be costly. It will involve not only new hardware but also new skill sets and network management solutions.

An end-to-end optical network includes the following components:

- Optical line amplifiers, such as erbium-doped fiber amplifiers (EDFAs), Raman amplifiers, and semiconductor optical amplifiers (SOAs)
- WDM equipment
- OADMs, including ROADMs
- Optical switches
- Integrated photonic circuits

Figure 11.4 shows an example of an optical network that incorporates these components. The following sections describe them, as well as the role of network management systems, in more detail.

Optical Line Amplifiers: EDFAs, Raman Amplifiers, and SOAs

As mentioned in Chapter 1, EDFAs, which were introduced in 1994, were a key innovation in the fiber world because they meant that an optical signal could be amplified without having to undergo any conversions. Before EDFAs, electronic

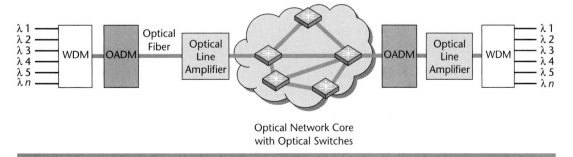

Figure 11.4 Optical network components

regenerators had to extract signals, retime them, and then regenerate them. This conversion limited data rates to 2.5Gbps. EDFAs quadruple this speed, providing data rates of 10Gbps. EDFAs have also opened the door to the development of wavelength division multiplexers, which enable incredible expansion of capacity on fiber optics. (Wavelength division multiplexers are discussed in detail later in this chapter.)

Composed of erbium metal and doped with special atoms, EDFAs are incorporated in optical fiber at periodic intervals, generally 30 to 60 miles (50 to 100 km), to boost communication signals. The components in an EDFA include an erbium-doped fiber, a laser-pump diode, couplers, and isolators. The light to be amplified is coupled in a section of erbium-doped fiber together with light from a laser-pump diode, normally about 980 nm. The EDFA itself operates in the range of 1,550 nm. The light from the laser-pump diode boosts the 1,550-nm light and is separated on the exit route. An isolator at each end protects the system from unwanted reflections.

Just as EDFAs were critical to the development of WDM, future advances in WDM capacity also require new developments in amplifiers. One approach to increasing the capacity of WDM systems is to expand the usual frequencies to make room for more channels. However, EDFAs present a problem: They boost light only in the C-band (1,530 to 1,565 nm) and L-band (1,565 to 1,625 nm), and a different EDFA is required in each band. To use both bands, a 5-nm separation is required between bands, and the unused bandwidth represents about 120Gbps of lost capacity. One solution to the problem posed by EDFAs is to use Raman amplifiers. A Raman amplifier uses a powerful laser source to boost the signal power in standard optical fiber. A single Raman amplifier can boost both C- and L-bands, eliminating the need for the 5-nm separation, thereby increasing capacity.

Another development in amplifier technology is the emergence of the SOA, which is built on a single chip. SOAs can be integrated into multifunction optical chips and can be less expensive than EDFAs. The disadvantage of SOAs is a higher signal-to-noise ratio. However, SOAs are attractive for optical signal processing (e.g., all-optical switching, wavelength conversion). Much research is therefore being done on SOAs as optical computing components.

WDM Equipment

WDM works by spatially separating, or multiplexing, different wavelengths of light down a single optical fiber. Current fiber-optic systems use only a fraction of the available bandwidth. They carry just one wavelength, when, in fact, thousands of wavelengths can be derived. The data rate supported by each wavelength depends on the type of light source. Today, each wavelength can carry from 2.5Gbps (OC-48) to roughly 10Gbps (OC-192). Recently we have seen some deployment of 40Gbps (OC-768) systems, but we are in the early stages of deploying that level. Nonetheless, in the very near future, we're expecting the delivery of Tbps light sources, and by 2010, we expect to see lasers operating in the petabits per second (Pbps) range. (With speeds in the Pbps range, the time between bursts is the same time that light takes to travel one-eighth the width of a human hair.)

WDM furnishes separate channels for each service at the full rate. The idea is not to aggregate smaller channels into one larger channel but to provide a very high-speed channel that can terminate on today's switches and routers that, in fact, support 2.5Gbps and 10Gbps interfaces.

WDM systems are generally divided into two market segments: dense (DWDM) and coarse (CWDM). While the definitions often overlap, generally a DWDM system supports more than 8 wavelengths and is used in long-haul transport networks. Both the WDM and DWDM terminology are used to describe this network element. DWDM systems today support in the range of 1 to 192 wavelengths, but every year, new systems are introduced that support increasing numbers of wavelengths.

CWDM was specifically developed for metro area applications. It supports fewer wavelengths than DWDM, but it uses less expensive lasers, making it cost-effective for metro deployments, cable TV, and enterprise networks. While both DWDM and CWDM are based on the same principle of accommodating multiple wavelengths on a single fiber, they differ in terms of the type of light source used, the spacing between wavelengths, the total number of channels supported, the distance over which they operate, and the type of amplifiers used. And it is important to note that at this time, DWDM and CWDM systems are not interoperable; they are incompatible when operating on the same network, but because CWDM is less expensive, it is often used. This remains an issue that needs to be resolved.

The potential exists for transmitting thousands of channels—potentially as many as 15,000 wavelengths on a single fiber—with developments such as Bell Labs' chirped-pulse WDM. The idea of chirped pulse involves a specialized mode-locked laser, which rapidly emits very wide pulses of light. Because each part of a fiber interacts differently with varying frequencies of light, the result of chirped-pulse WDM is unequal dispersion. The pulse is stretched out when it enters the fiber, and data can be put on the discrete frequencies that emerge. You can think of this process in terms of a horse race: When a race starts, horses emerge together from the gate, but because each horse keeps a separate pace, spaces soon develop between the horses. This is the same type of stretching out that happens to the laser light in chirped-pulse WDM.

If we couple the potential for 15,000 wavelengths on one fiber with each of those wavelengths supporting Pbps, we have an explosion of bandwidth that is like nothing we have known before. As fantastic as all this sounds, we're likely to see even greater achievements; after all, we are still in the very early stages of knowledge about what we can achieve with optical networking. Before any real progress can be made, the realm of microphotonics, or integrated photonic circuits, must mature.

DWDM Developments and Considerations

As the number of wavelengths increases and the difference between the wavelengths gets smaller, the need for wavelength stability becomes greater to ensure that the optical carriers do not bump into each other. Getting this stability requires either a stock of boards for each wavelength (maintained by network operators) or tunable lasers. If you have 320 wavelengths, you need 320 separate boards, each tuned to the appropriate wavelength. For redundancy purposes, you need a backup for each of those boards. And you need this at each location where you have a wavelength division multiplexer. You can see that a tunable laser that could adopt the behavior of a specific frequency as needed would greatly reduce the operating cost and the costs of spare parts and inventory.

DWDM is beginning to be able to address network survivability requirements. It is also now capable of incorporating highly valued SDH/SONET-like capabilities, including monitoring performance, providing protection, and provisioning optical channels. As mentioned in Chapter 4, SDH/SONET introduced the network survivability tactic. The dual-counter-rotating rings provide a protected fiber path over which information can be shunted in the opposite direction if a fiber ring is broken. Until recently, DWDM had no such capability. It was deployed as a point-to-point link; if the fiber was cut, communication between the two DWDM systems was lost. But now we are beginning to see the introduction of restoration capabilities in DWDM platforms, which means that SDH/SONET will have a more limited life in the future. Industry forecasts predict that SDH/SONET has perhaps a 10-year lifespan left, after which the benefits of DWDM will override the reliability factors that we today associate with SDH/SONET. Remember that SDH/SONET is a TDM system, and therefore it cannot take advantage of the capacity gains that DWDM systems provide.

A different consideration emerges as DWDM systems continue to develop. Because of a combination of nonlinearities and dispersion, the majority of the fiber currently in place around the world—possibly 95% of it—would have trouble carrying very fast (Tbps speed and Pbps pulses) signals for long distances in a DWDM system. These impairments that exist in current fiber can lead to crosstalk among the different wavelengths, interference between consecutive pulses on any signal wavelength, and degradation in the overall signal-to-noise ratio. This means that much of the fiber we have deployed over the past two decades will have to be replaced in order to take advantage of the new generation of optical equipment. Fiber solutions exist today, but time and financial resources will be needed to deploy them.

Where DWDM Fits in the Network Architecture

The core network was the first place DWDM was deployed because that is where the economics made the most sense. Increases in intercity traffic required carriers to expand the capacity of their long-haul pipes. The response was to deploy those point-to-point links with DWDM. This resolved the bandwidth problem, but it did nothing to address the routing issues. WDM and DWDM currently lack the intelligence required to really deliver meshed network configurations, and thus we have a need for optical switches. The main benefit of DWDM in the core is that it reduces deployment costs by eliminating the need for expensive amplifiers. Current DWDM products can operate successfully over about 300 to 450 miles (480 to 725 km), and there are examples of successful transmission up to 4,000 miles (6,400 km) without signal boosting. As mentioned earlier in this chapter, the process of regenerating signals represents as much as half of the overall cost of an optical deployment. Therefore, developments in extending distances are very promising.

In the quest for expanding the capacity of WDM systems, in addition to employing new generations of amplifiers, such as Raman amplifiers, another strategy is to pack channels together more closely. This applies primarily to long-haul systems. Current DWDM systems space channels at 50GHz, but tighter spacing is also possible, including 25GHz and 12.5GHz spacing. Tighter spacing requires precise lasers and channel separators.

CWDM

A vital application for WDM is in metropolitan area networks (MANs). MANs are becoming saturated, and network expansion is costly: Pulling fiber along existing conduits costs about US$30,000 per mile. But traditional DWDM systems are not well suited to MANs. For one thing, they were designed to work well on point-to-point links, but MAN traffic must be dropped and added frequently. DWDM does not present the same cost justifications in the MAN as it does in the core.

The great savings that can come with DWDM in the MAN are due to the reduction in the need for expensive amplifiers because, by definition, a MAN spans a fairly short distance. You can spend US$20,000 to US$30,000 or more for an amplifier that is capable of operating over a range of 300 to 450 miles (480 to 725 km). However, runs in MANs are typically no longer than 70 miles (110 km), so these expensive amplifiers are often overkill. As a result, the next generation of MAN products, designed to address the MAN core—that is, metro access, cable TV, and enterprise networks—has been introduced. These CWDM products are used for building citywide rings, covering distances of up to 37 miles (60 km). They generally support longer distances and greater capacity than do metro access products. Metro access products, such as passive optical networks (PONs), are designed to bring fiber closer to the customer. Enterprise products address building high-capacity campus networks. In all three of these MAN sectors, the issues are the same: pricing, scalability, access, and flexibility.

As far as pricing and scalability issues go, the lower carrying capacity and distance requirements in the metro area allow providers to reduce costs by using less expensive lasers. The price of a transponder board, which represents 90% of the cost of a laser, can vary by 25%, depending on the quality of the laser. Shorter-distance lasers use less-expensive modulation and amplification techniques. Whereas long-haul lasers are externally modulated, enabling the signal to travel up to 450 miles (725 km), shorter distances may allow direct modulation, where the laser runs only 50 to 60 miles (80 to 100 km) but costs 30% to 40% less than a long-haul laser. But less expensive lasers also mean less capacity. The lower grade of light sources requires greater spacing between the wavelengths, thereby reducing the number of channels or wavelengths that can be derived by up to 50%.

To meet these new demands, we need a very dynamic network that has the capability to accommodate huge capacity requirements and to change the configuration of that capacity dynamically. Subscribers want to connect at the current speed of their backbone. They want to make a direct connection through MANs and long-haul networks, with the associated protocols. And, of course, they want guaranteed QoS.

IP over WDM

Today, bandwidth reservation and intelligent IP switches can prioritize voice and video traffic to ensure that high-priority traffic gets the first shot at the underlying bandwidth. New generations of IP-based switches provide the capability to meet QoS commitments. Layer 3/Layer 4 switching services allow the switch to prioritize and guarantee packets, based on predetermined criteria within a switch. Higher-level protocols (such as RSVP) can reserve bandwidth across an entire network. This creates a value proposition for the service provider: The ISP can deliver high bandwidth in a format that users want, for less cost, while approximating the QoS guarantees that the end user expects for high-priority traffic.

As discussed in Chapter 4, the PSTN was not built to be dynamic. It was based on a system of 64Kbps channels, or DS-0s/CEPT-0s, aggregated by time division multiplexers into DS-1/CEPT-1 or DS-3/CEPT-3 facilities that would deliver traffic into cross-connects and switches at the network core. More time division multiplexers were required at the other end to reverse the process and to distribute the DS-0s/CEPT-0s. Time division multiplexers are expensive, and they often require manual configuration, which slows provisioning and further increases costs.

Whereas TDM is reaching its limits in terms of network elements and switching technologies, DWDM is just beginning. But with any new technology, obstacles arise, and in the case of DWDM, the obstacles include management and performance impedance mismatches between networks. The International Telecommunication Union (ITU; www.itu.int) has formed a study group that will look into the interoperability standards to ensure that traffic can move between vendor networks despite the underlying differences in the many different vendors' equipment.

Emerging WDM Applications

Emerging WDM applications—for example, extensive data (Ethernet) services, such as broadband access and video delivery (e.g., VOD) in cable networks—address the growing desire for wavelength-on-demand, where individual wavelengths are assigned either to specific protocols, such as ATM, IP, or MPLS, or to specific customers. Alternatively, some providers might lease an entire dark fiber to each client, and the client would then purchase the CPE to route different protocols over each individual wavelength. This is opening the door to a whole new way of thinking about providing wavelengths to the long-haul carriers, to the MAN market, and to the customer.

The development of managed wavelength services depends on the development of wavelength changers and optical switches. A *wavelength changer* converts an optical signal to an electronic signal and then sends it to a laser that produces an optical signal at a different wavelength than the original. *Optical switches* give carriers the ability to provision bandwidth automatically, enable them to build mesh optical restoration, and allow them to establish QoS levels associated with restoration. (Optical switches are discussed later in this chapter.)

OADMs

Next-generation network services must be easily reconfigurable, and they must support real-time provisioning. Demultiplexing all the wavelengths at each node is costly, it introduces delay, and it reduces the distance over which a signal can travel. OADMs, as shown in Figure 11.5, work much more inexpensively than

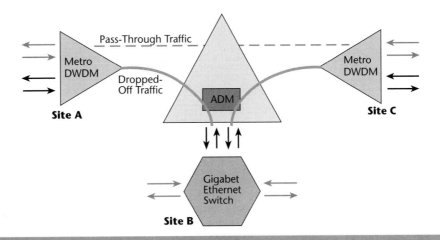

Figure 11.5 Optical add/drop multiplexing

demultiplexing all the wavelengths because they simplify the process—they eliminate the costly electronics used to convert between light and electricity. Most
OADMs use special filters to extract the wavelengths that need to be dropped off at
a given location. For most vendors, the wavelength is fixed, so at the time of configuration, the carrier designates the individual wavelengths to be dropped at each
location.

The ROADM is a fairly new variety of add/drop mux (ADM). This software-
based enabler adds the capability to switch between different networks. ROADMs
also make it easier for service providers to separate, add, and drop traffic being
transported over optical rings to and from customers. One of the distinguishing
features of an ROADM compared to a standard OADM is its ability to switch traffic
at both the SDH/SONET and wavelength layers.

The function of an ROADM has been available in DWDM systems for a short
time (since 2005), but the most significant advance is its presence in optical equipment designed for MANs. Driven by the need for more bandwidth to support growing packet data traffic as well as the emergence of triple-play services (i.e., voice,
data, and video/TV) that telcos and MSOs are intent on providing, today more
attention is being focused on the MAN domain, and many optical technologies
have been introduced specifically for this market, including coarse wavelength
division multiplexers and ROADMs.

ROADMs offer several key advantages. First, as the name suggests, they enable
bandwidth assignment to be configured on an as-needed basis rather than having
to be determined in advance, prior to rollout. Second, remote configuration and
reconfiguration are possible. Finally, ROADMs accommodate automatic power balancing, a much-needed capability because it is not always known in advance where
a signal may be routed, and power balancing of the signals is therefore not only
required but necessary.

Optical Switches

Optical switches, sometimes referred to as *optical cross-connects* or *wavelength routers*,
are devices that reside at junction points in optical backbones and enable carriers to
string together wavelengths to provide end-to-end connections (see Figure 11.6).
They link any of several incoming lines to any of several outgoing lines and automatically reroute traffic when a network path fails. An optical switch is the optical
version of a general-purpose switch that provides flexibility and reliability in
today's PSTN. Optical switches move transmissions between fiber segments and
also enable some network management activities, including optical-layer restoration
and reconfiguration, dynamic wavelength management, and automated optical-layer
provisioning.

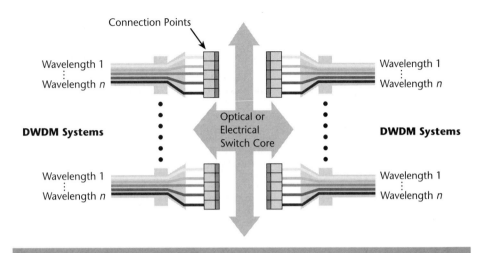

Connection Points

Wavelength 1

Wavelength n

DWDM Systems

Wavelength 1

Wavelength n

Optical or
Electrical
Switch Core

Wavelength 1

Wavelength n

DWDM Systems

Wavelength 1

Wavelength n

Figure 11.6 An example of an optical switch

There are three key issues in selecting optical switches:

- **Number of ports**—Carriers are looking for devices that can scale to more than 1,000 ports.
- **Automation**—Carriers want to provision strings of wavelengths from a remote console in real-time.
- **Granularity**—Carriers want a switch to handle small as well as large bandwidths so that they can eliminate multiplexers.

First- and Next-Generation Optical Switches

Two types of optical switches are currently being produced: switches with electrical cores (i.e., first-generation optical switches) and switches with optical cores (i.e., next-generation optical switches). The electronics in first-generation switches slow their capability to work with the very high rates that the fiber itself can support. The future lies in the pure optical switches, but we still have to fully develop the microphotonics industry; thus, integrated photonic circuits (discussed later in this chapter) are really the next key technology required to drive the optical networking industry forward.

Optical switches fall into two main categories. First, the multiservice provisioning platform (MSPP) enables carriers to get a quick start on offering a full range of services. It resides either in the carrier's point of presence (POP) or at the customer site, and it incorporates DWDM and offers customers different grades of IP service, telephony, and other offerings. (MSPPs are discussed in detail later in this chapter.) Second, big switches can be deployed at the carrier's local exchange. These switches act as on-ramps, funneling large volumes of traffic from IP, ATM, and MPLS backbones on and off the optical core.

Challenges in Deploying Optical Switches

Because we are in the early stages with optical switches, we have to deal with issues such as how to quickly provision services, how to accommodate billing, and how to elegantly separate services. In the next three to five years, we should start seeing these more sophisticated elements become available in pure optical form.

As mentioned earlier, with end-to-end optical networking, because transmission rates are reaching the Tbps, Pbps, and even the Ebps levels, the bottleneck is moving to the network elements. The faster the light pulses are emitted—that is, the faster the data rates on the line get—the more technically challenging it is to handle optical-electrical-optical conversions at line speed. Therefore, to fully take advantage of the capacity being created by WDM, fiber networks need switches capable of rerouting light. The good news is that the cost of optical components has decreased by 40% in recent years, and it is expected to continue to drop by 40% to 60% per year.

The biggest problem that converged telcos are now facing is how to accurately forecast their future bandwidth requirements. Transmission speeds are doubling every 12 months, so it is essential that we have infrastructures capable of providing a large amount of bandwidth on short notice and at reasonable cost. Without intelligent optical networking, adding an OC-48 circuit over existing dark fiber can take between 6 and 9 months. To automate provisioning, we need to also address how we can look into a wavelength to determine how to properly act on it.

Optical switches enable improved reliability, improved scalability, and flexible service provisioning. They also reduce the capital required to add additional capacity, and the overall savings can then be passed on to the customer. Deploying optical networking technology in the metro area can bring the benefits of converged networks down to the customer's premises. The end-to-end optical infrastructure can then support advanced services such as true bandwidth-on-demand.

Optical Switching Fabrics

Optical switches are components in a fiber-optic network that direct light beams from one fiber to another, and they are used as an alternative to hubs for routing connections. Optical switching fabrics, such as the following, can provide subsystems that connect one wavelength to another:

- **Microelectromechanical system (MEMS) switches**—A MEMS switch uses an array of microscopic mirrors to reflect light from an input port to an output port.

- **Bubble switches**—Similar to inkjet printers, bubble switches use heat to create small bubbles in fluid channels that then reflect and direct light.

- **Thermo-optical switches**—With thermo-optical switches, light passing through glass is heated up or cooled down by using electrical coils. The heat alters the refractive index of the glass, bending the light so that it enters one fiber or another.

- **Liquid crystal display (LCD) switches**—LCDs use liquid to bend light.

- **Tunable lasers**—Tunable lasers pump out light at different wavelengths, and they can switch from one wavelength to another very quickly.

MEMS-based optical switches were among the first technology to be deployed (see Figure 11.7), with several companies offering a new generation of optical high-capacity switches. Unfortunately, the market for optical switches in general has been fraught with difficulties, with service providers yet to make big, bold commitments to adopt the technology. However, developments and announcements are continuing. For example, in early 2006, Lambda OpticalSystems (www.lambdaopticalsystems.com) unveiled its LambdaNode 2000, an all-optical switch

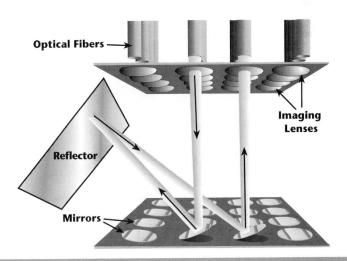

Figure 11.7 A MEMS switch

including silica, silicon, polymer, and rare earths. Each material has unique advantages and disadvantages in terms of the performance of the chip and the ease and cost of manufacturing it. In these early days for this technology, vendors are producing relatively simple components, such as DWDM chips, small switch modules, and passive splitters.

Indium phosphide (InP) is the material of choice for optoelectronic integration. It is likely to revolutionize the communications industry, much as silicon revolutionized the computer industry. InP is a compound made of binary crystals produced by combining one element from the metallic Group III of the periodic table with an element from the nonmetallic Group V. InP has photonic properties that allow for the large-scale integration of components such as lasers, detectors, dynamic components, passive waveguides, and electronics onto the same chip. Its qualities make InP a good fit for circuits in wireless devices as well. Components built with InP consume very little power, permitting them to remain connected to the Internet over high-speed wireless networks for extended periods. InP's shortcomings include low yields of InP wafers in manufacturing (less than 40%) and the labor-intensive effort to build optical networking equipment, which make these components expensive.

Integrated optical circuits could lower costs of components by 90%. Currently, components account for as much as 50% of the cost on a long-haul US$100,000 DWDM device and 15% of the cost on a US$40,000 metro WDM system. Innovations in optical chip making will make possible 100Mbps network connections for homes at less than $10 per month.

Optical Network Management

One of the most important areas of any networking technology is network management, which in the case of optical networks involves network restoration, wavelength services, and performance.

As discussed earlier in this chapter, most optical networks today are based on an existing SDH/SONET architecture. One of the great strengths of SDH/SONET is, in fact, its network restoration capabilities. However, as new elements such as WDM systems are added, it can be difficult to ensure that restoration techniques are not in conflict. At the very least, the network management system must enable the service provider to identify any possible conflicts (not to mention resolve them). Along with managing the overall network, the network management system performs some specific tasks, such as monitoring the signal performance for each wavelength. And the more elements there are—including WDM/DWDM/CWDM, OADMs, ROADMs, optical cross-connects, and optical switches—the more difficult the job. Also, as the number of wavelengths grows, there has to be a facility to monitor and manage each one of them. Of course, the ability to provision services quickly is also a key requirement, and a proper network management system can help providers not only manage their own networks efficiently but also offer end-to-end managed wavelength service.

The Optical Edge

Today, SDH/SONET channels are used for voice and time-division-multiplexed private-line traffic where the equipment typically involves ADMs and digital cross-connects (see Figure 11.11). Optical networks today are also used to support Layer 2 services, such as ATM, Frame Relay, and Ethernet, and switch equipment. In addition, they are used to support Layer 3 services, such as routed IP; IP routers are the most typical equipment type at Layer 3.

Vast changes are occurring at the optical edge. As discussed in the following sections, three categories of optical access products (i.e., specialized access equipment) are being introduced at the optical edge: next-generation digital loop carrier systems, PONs, and MSPPs.

Next-Generation Digital Loop Carriers

The main feature of a next-generation digital loop carrier is its support for SDH/SONET fiber as well as copper connections to the local exchange. These devices allow the integration of DSL modem support without requiring the installation of DSL access multiplexers (DSLAMs). In other words, the DSLAM functionality is built into the next-generation digital loop carrier. Also, the new digital loop carriers can support ATM multiplexing for DSL services along with the traditional TDM

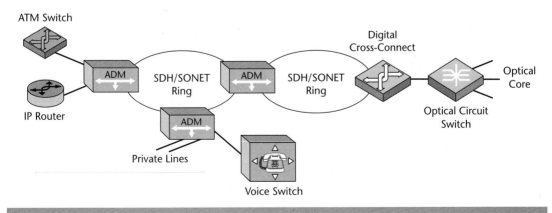

Figure 11.11 The optical edge

interfaces for voice. Voice channels are multiplexed in the traditional TDM style and sent over the PSTN, and data traffic is combined and sent on one shared ATM trunk, with each customer assigned a separate ATM virtual circuit.

Along with support for plain old telephone service (POTS), ISDN, and DSL interfaces, new interfaces are also being added to support a wider range of services. These include 10Mbps and 100Mbps Ethernet in support of emerging metro area Ethernet services, PON headends in support of PON service, and OADMs that support the provisioning of wavelength services.

Ultimately, the biggest issue facing the deployment of next-generation digital loop carriers is regulation. Regulation adds a level of complexity due to disputes over which portions of the local loop the incumbent local exchange carriers (ILECs) are required to wholesale to their competitors.

PONs

A PON is basically a fiber-to-the-premises (FTTP) arrangement in which a single optical fiber serves multiple (up to 32) premises. It is, in essence, a point-to-multipoint configuration that reduces the amount of fiber required. Taking advantage of WDM, PONs allow for two-way traffic on a single fiber pair by making use of one wavelength for downstream traffic and another for upstream traffic. PONs work by using passive (i.e., unpowered) optical splitters to split the power of the optical signal and route it to multiple subscribers. (Figure 12.8 in Chapter 12, "Broadband Access Alternatives," shows an example of a PON.)

A PON shares one fiber channel among up to 32 customers to deliver voice, data, and potentially video. PONs reduce costs by distributing costs across more endpoints and replacing expensive ADMs or DWDM nodes with optical splitters and couplers at each fiber connection in the network. Downstream signals, broadcast to each premise by using a shared fiber, are encrypted to prevent eavesdropping. Upstream bandwidth is allocated by assigning a time slot to each subscriber when the user has traffic to send.

PONs have started to be of more interest to local telcos because they significantly reduce the cost of provisioning fiber to the subscriber compared to approaches such as fiber-to-the-curb or fiber-to-the-home. (Chapter 12 provides a comprehensive discussion of fiber-to-the-x and PONs.)

MSPPs

MSPPs are specialized optical access systems that enable carriers to get a quick start in offering a full range of services. Typically, MSPPs reside at the carrier's POP or at the customer's site. They incorporate WDM, allowing service providers and customers to take advantage of the fact that a fiber can carry much more than the single wavelength that SDH/SONET fibers today carry. With MSPPs, carriers can also offer customers different grades of service, as well as telephony and other multimedia offerings.

Today's MSPPs are based largely on proprietary technology, so they vary from provider to provider, but they all share some basic characteristics, including the following:

- **Fiber access**—Optical interfaces can use SDH/SONET, Gigabit Ethernet (GigE), or 10GigE, and they can include an automatic restoration capability.

- **Digital multiplexing**—MSPPs can use TDM, a form of packet access, or a combination of both.

- **Support for WDM**—Many MSPPs incorporate CWDM, so a single fiber pair can support multiple customers. Coarse wavelength division multiplexers were developed for metro and campus environments. They use a less powerful laser source, reducing their capabilities but also reducing their costs and making it easier to justify using them for the type of short-haul applications metro and campus environments represent. Because the laser sources are less powerful with CWDM, the channels need to be spaced further apart (at 100GHz or 200GHz intervals), and one result of this is that fewer channels can be derived. Generally, CWDM is limited to no more than 64 channels. But because of the lower cost of the light sources, CWDM devices are much less costly to build and can be more justified in their deployment in the metro network.

The Optical Core: Overlay Versus Peer-to-Peer Networking Models

Today's advanced networks maintain mostly separate electronic connections for voice and data and achieve reliability by using rings based on the SDH/SONET communication standard. In this configuration, if one link is cut, traffic flows down the other half of the ring. The SDH/SONET multiplexer aggregates the traffic onto the ring, so there's a stack, or hierarchy, of rings, depending on the scope of the network they're serving (refer to Figure 11.1).

In the local realm, which might be a small city or metro area environment, traditionally the rings are based on a capacity of OC-12, or 622Mbps. For slightly larger-scale rings, such as regional rings, OC-48, or 2.5Gbps, is often the capacity. Core backbone rings provide OC-192, or 10Gbps. Currently, as metro capacity requirements are increasing, we're migrating from OC-12 to OC-48. Similarly, some of the regional rings are migrating from OC-48 to OC-192, and we're looking at ways to expand the capacity of the backbone core, generally through the addition of dense wavelength division multiplexers, which allow multiple 10Gbps streams to coexist on one fiber. Although some systems can now offer up to 40Gbps, they are in early stages of deployment.

Rather than using rings, tomorrow's networks will channel all traffic over the same fiber connection and will provide redundancy by using the Internet's mesh approach of interlocking pathways. In that case, when a line breaks, traffic can flow down several alternating pathways. Optical switches will be the foundation for building these integrated networks. Optical switches all have point-to-point links between them (refer to Figure 11.2). If there is a failure in a given link or node, traffic can be quickly rerouted over any other alternative in the network configuration.

There are several problems with the first generation of optical networks. Bandwidth efficiency is an issue at the higher capacities of SDH/SONET. The SDH/SONET hierarchy is not optimized for large data transfers, mainly because it is a single-wavelength solution. SDH/SONET is a TDM scheme, so it does not take advantage of WDM and the resident ability to carry multiple wavelengths (hundreds today and thousands in the future). As a result, operators have to manage two layers today—SDH/SONET and WDM—and riding on top of those, both Layer 2 and Layer 3 networks.

To enable a network to request additional capacity to accommodate changes with very large traffic flows, two approaches are emerging:

■ **The overlay model**—The overlay model, shown in Figure 11.12, calls for maintaining two discreet and separately provisioned networks: a Layer 1 optical network and the client network. In this model, devices reside at the edge of the network cloud, and core network infrastructure is hidden from the routed network. The overlay model relies on the User-to-Network

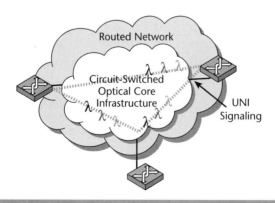

Figure 11.12 The overlay model

Interface (UNI) for signaling at the edge. The ITU and ANSI support this model. The traditional voice carriers are driving the development of a protocol that will transport all types of traffic: nonvoice over SDH/SONET as well as its high-speed successor, the Optical Transport Network (OTN). The OTN would operate across a new standard, the Automatic Switched Optical Network (ASON). (The OTN and ASON are described later in this chapter.)

- **The peer-to-peer model**—The peer-to-peer model, shown in Figure 11.13, argues for a single network in which the equipment on the network edge decides how bandwidth is allocated within the network's core. The network is fully visible to all devices, but edge devices need to know about only their closest optical switches. Routers and optical switches are peers in this model. This approach is promoted by the data community, including the IETF and the IEEE. This IP-centric approach is based on Generalized Multiprotocol Label Switching (GMPLS). GigE and 10GigE are promoted as solutions for the near to mid-term, with the long term possibly focusing on Resilient Packet Ring.

The following sections describe these two approaches to the optical core in more detail.

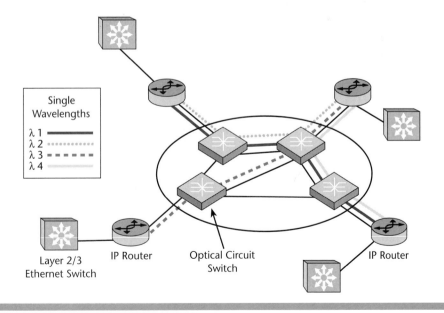

Figure 11.13 The peer-to-peer model

The Overlay Model

The overlay model, formally known as the OTN and promoted by the ITU and carrier communities, is characterized by devices residing on the edge of the cloud, the core network infrastructure being hidden from the routed network, and relying on UNI for signaling at the edge.

The ITU's next generation of optical networks is specified under a number of recommendations, including G.872, G.709, and G.959.1. The OTN defines a new network hierarchy, the optical transport hierarchy, whose base unit is the optical transport module (OTM), which has a 64-byte frame. The OTN comprises all optical elements. The initial clients of the OTN are SDH/SONET and data services, including Ethernet, IP, ATM, and Fibre Channel. Management capabilities are defined for conductivity verification, performance assessment, and fault sectionalization.

The OTN has three main elements:

■ **Optical channel**—The optical channel is similar to SDH/SONET's path component. It defines the logical connection between stations or end-to-end networking, and it transports clients' signals between two endpoints on the OTN.

■ **Optical multiplex section**—The optical multiplex section, which is similar to SDH/SONET's line component, describes the WDM portions that underpin the optical channels and consists of many aggregated optical channels.

■ **Optical transmission section**—The optical transmission section is similar to SDH/SONET's section component. It defines a physical interface that details optical parameters such as frequency, power level, and signal-to-noise ratio.

The OTN reaches higher speeds by bundling wavelengths. OTMs, which can span multiple wavelengths of different capacities, are described with two suffixes: n refers to the maximum number of wavelengths supported at the lowest bit rate on the wavelength, and m indicates the bit rate supported on the interface. Together, these are written as OTM $n.m$. The OTN supports optical signals with three bit rates: When m equals 1, it refers to 2.5Gbps; when it is 2, it refers to 10Gbps; and when it is 3, it refers to 40Gbps. An interface can support combinations of these rates. For example, OTM 3.2 indicates a channel that spans three wavelengths, each operating at least at 10Gbps. OTM 5.12 indicates a channel that spans five wavelengths and can operate at either 2.5Gbps or 10Gbps.

ASON and ASTN

The OTN differs from today's networks in the types of services it can offer. Instant provisioning requires a signaling protocol to set up the paths or connections so that data can be transported. Work on SDH/SONET and OTN signaling is being defined in two ITU ANSI specifications:

- **Automatic Switched Optical Network (ASON)**—ITU G.8080 describes ASON, the set of control plane components used to manipulate transport network resources in order to provide the functionality of setting up, maintaining, and releasing connections. ASON is described further later in this chapter, at the end of the section "The IP+Optical Control Plane."

- **Automatic Switched Transport Network (ASTN)**—ITU G.807 describes ASTN, which allows traffic paths to be set up automatically through a switched network. ASTN is often used interchangeably with GMPLS. ASTN allows the user to specify the start point, endpoint, and bandwidth required. ASTN/GMPLS consists of several protocols, including routing protocols (OSPF-TE or IS-IS-TE), Link Manangement Protocol (LMP), and reservation/label distribution protocols (RSVP-TE and CR-LDP). ASTN consists of clients, with each level seeing a differing degree of network detail. Clients can be multiplexers or WDM systems, as well as Ethernet switches or other devices that implement Generic Framing Procedure (GFP), a unifying data link for both SDH/SONET and OTN networks. ANSI's GFP T1X1.5a is an SDH/SONET subprotocol that provides a standard means for packing voice traffic into an SDH/SONET frame, enabling equipment interoperability.

Clients connect to the network through one of three types of network interfaces:

- **User-to-Network Interface (UNI)**—The UNI defines how customers can access their providers' networks. It is used to request capacity from the underlying network and shields the client from network complexities. Minimal information is provided; the UNI provides only the name and address of the endpoint, the authentication and admission control of the client, and connect service messages.

- **External Network-to-Network Interface (E NNI)**—The E NNI provides summarized network address information along with authentication and admission control and connection service messages. The partner does not know the exact paths, but it does know the available clients that can be called. This is analogous to an electronic address book provided by one carrier to the next of all the available nodes.

- **Internal Network-to-Network Interface (I NNI)**—The I NNI enables devices to get topology or routing information for the carriers' network, as well as connection service messages and information necessary to optionally control network resources.

Clients can request three types of circuits in ASTN. First, *provisioned circuits* are hard or permanent circuits much like a leased line, also known as a permanent connection. Second, *signaled circuits* are established dynamically by the endpoint requesting bandwidth. This requires network addressing information and is known as a switched connection. Finally, *hybrid circuits* are a cross between provisioned and signaled circuits. They have provisioned connections into the ASTN network but rely on switched connections within the ASTN network to connect with other nodes. They are also known as soft provisioned connections.

The Ethernet Evolution

Compared to other optical networks, Ethernet is inexpensive and efficient. It has a number of advantages: It is easily provisioned, offers highly granular bandwidth for tactical applications, requires simpler centralized management (due to using a single protocol), requires less network equipment, makes it easy to upgrade network routers or nodes (one at a time), and makes fat pipes available. Basically, Ethernet makes a WAN look like a LAN to the end user.

Ethernet also has a number of disadvantages, such as lack of reliability, packet loss, minimal QoS capabilities, and bandwidth problems. Furthermore, although the 10GigE standards are now final, they are still a long way from SDH/SONET's OC-768, or 40Gbps, and the future OC-1536 of 80Gbps. Another disadvantage is the cost to deploy fiber to the customer. Finally, the lack of valid, quantifiable SLAs, compelling applications, and formal support for VoIP will slow the uptake of Ethernet. The biggest issue with Ethernet is the challenges Ethernet itself faces: the reliability and QoS issues.

The 10Mbps and 100Mbps versions of Ethernet use the access technique Carrier Sense Multiple Access/Collision Detection (CSMA/CD), which permits several network nodes to share the same link. Each node can send information only if it senses that the link is not already being used. If two nodes happen to send at once, a collision occurs, and neither message gets through. Both then have to wait a random amount of time before trying again. Although 10GigE uses separate channels for sending and receiving rather than using CSMA/CD, collisions lower down the network result in unpredictable delays and high jitter. This high jitter can lead to packets being received in the wrong order, which in turn makes Ethernet unsuitable for real-time applications. There is also no way to guarantee bandwidth because every user is competing for network access. It is therefore fair to say that the 10GigE solution basically throws bandwidth at the problem.

IEEE 802.1p, the QoS scheme typically used by Ethernet, does not offer the necessary admission control to properly ensure the service quality needed to transport voice and other real-time traffic. The IEEE has defined a new format called 802.1pq, which adds an additional four-octet header field that includes a three-bit priority indicator in the LAN header, allowing eight levels of priority. LAN switches can act on 802.1pq to define high-, medium-, and low-priority data traffic. Because of its problems with QoS, Ethernet cannot be used in the public network without the deployment of IP with MPLS or GMPLS in order to carry voice or deliver bandwidth of different sizes.

The Peer-to-Peer Model

The peer-to-peer model, promoted by the data community and the IETF and IEEE standards organizations, relies on the GigE and 10GigE standards. It is characterized by full visibility of the entire network for all devices, the edge devices needing to know only about the closest optical switches, and the routers and optical switches being peers.

Ethernet has a long and rich history and, it would appear, future. The concept of Ethernet is based on the notion that peers in a network send messages to each other over a radio system contained within a common wire or channel—which is referred to as the *ether*. Each user, or peer, has an individual and distinct 48-bit key known as the Media Access Control (MAC) address. Today, because of the pervasiveness of Ethernet and the low cost of hardware required to support it, most computers come equipped with the functionality of an Ethernet card.

One of the great benefits associated with Ethernet is the fact that, despite its many different generations, variations, and wiring plans, it is all the same, making it easy to interconnect all types of Ethernet by using highly available and inexpensive hardware. Ethernet, which is mostly standardized under IEEE 802.3, is the most widely used LAN technology, replacing other LAN standards such as IBM's Token Ring or FDDI.

The four major categories of Ethernet standards are 10Mbps Ethernet, Fast Ethernet (100Mbps), Gigabit Ethernet (1Gbps, referred to as GigE), and 10 Gigabit Ethernet (10Gbps, referred to as 10GigE). Currently, there is also work ongoing in the development of 100Gbps Ethernet. However, of the formal standards, 10GigE is quite new, and which of the standards will gain the widest commercial acceptance remains to be seen. GigE and 10GigE are the two standards of interest to access network, MAN, and WAN providers.

As discussed in the following sections, three standards from the IEEE aim to provide the core technology for the new data-centric public network of the peer-to-peer model (see Figure 11.14):

- **10GigE**—10GigE, IEEE standard 802.3ae, supports 10Gbps and is targeted at the metro core and wide area networking. Along with operating at high speeds, 10GigE networks can unite LANs and WANs under a single technology.

- **Ethernet First Mile (EFM)**—EFM, specified under IEEE standard 802.3ah, supports 1Gbps and is targeted at the first (or last) mile.

- **Resilient Packet Ring and other new standards**—Resilient Packet Ring, specified by the IEEE 802.17 working group, is a standard for the optimized

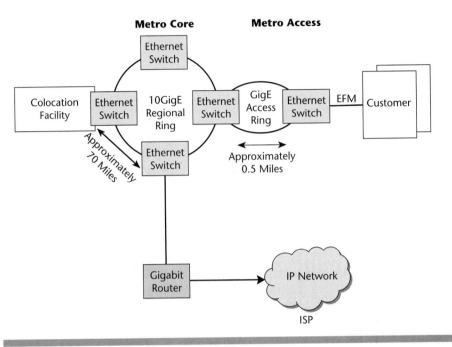

Figure 11.14 The Ethernet metro network

transport of data traffic over fiber rings. Its purpose is to provide the same resilience that SDH/SONET networks offer (50-millisecond restoration), but by using packet-based transmission rather than circuit-switched connections. The main goal is to increase the efficiency of IP services and Ethernet.

10GigE

Today, 10GigE, which is in the early stages of deployment, is the highest-bandwidth Ethernet offering. Some of the main 10GigE applications include colocation of carrier facilities, inter-POP connectivity, storage area network (SAN) connectivity, data center disaster recovery and mirroring systems, multimedia transport, computer-aided design, medical file transport, data center access, and local loop access. Therefore, the most likely environments for 10GigE are carriers, university campuses, research and development labs, and some government agencies. But, at the moment, 10GigE is not a common enterprise solution, although it may become so in the near term as companies seek more bandwidth to accommodate advanced applications while wishing to use a technology with which they have well-founded knowledge and experience.

The IEEE is setting two separate physical-layer standards for 10GigE. The first is for LANs; it offers a capacity of exactly 10Gbps and is really just a faster version of GigE. The second is targeted at WANs. Strictly speaking, it is not Ethernet, and it does not run at 10Gbps; instead, it transports Ethernet frames over an SDH or SONET link at 9.29Gbps, which makes is compatible with existing carrier networks but limits the number of GigE links that can be aggregated to nine.

There are two categories of WAN physical interfaces for 10GigE: electrical and optical. Electrical interfaces are less costly to build than optical interfaces, and the reality is that today most commercial buildings do not have fiber access. There are two electrical interfaces. 10Gbps on coax, known as 10GBASE-CX4, has about a 50-foot (15-m) range. It would most likely be used to connect devices within the same room. The other interface is 10Gbps on wire pair, using unshielded twisted-pair. Real solutions are expected sometime in 2006, with the initial definitions including 10GBASE-T over Category 7 wiring (up to 330-foot [100-m] range), screened or enhanced Category 6 wiring (up to 330-foot [100-m] range), or standard Category 6 (less than or equal to 180 feet [55 m]).

In terms of fiber options, a LAN physical interface can operate at the full 10Gbps rate up to a range of 1,000 feet (300 m). This would be suitable for local applications and could be configured to run either point-to-point links or over Resilient Packet Ring. WAN physical interfaces are designed for WANs and pack the Ethernet frames into an SDH/STM 64C payload (OC-192, or 10Gbps), providing a usable capacity of 9.29Gbps. Table 11.1 compares the various physical interfaces for 10GigE.

Table 11.1 10GigE Optical Interfaces

Characteristic	LAN Physical Layer	LAN Physical Layer	WAN Physical Layer
Interface	Serial	4-Lane LAN/WWDM*	Serial
Usable data rate	10Gbps	10Gbps	9.29Gbps
Physical media wavelength/range	1,550 nm/≤40 km 1,310 nm/≤10 km 850 nm/≤65 m	1,275.2 nm, 1,300.2 nm, 1,324.7 nm, 1,349.2 nm For multimode fiber, range ≤300 m; for single-mode fiber, range ≤10 km	1,550 nm/≤40 km 1,310 nm/≤10 km 850 nm/≤65 m
Line rate	10.3Gbps	4 × 3.125Gbps	9.953Gbps

* WWDM (Wide WDM) refers to CWDM operating at 1,310 nm, compared to traditional CWDM, which operates at 850 nm.

EFM

EFM, standard 802.3ah, addresses Layer 1 enhancements for metro and wide area Ethernet services, such as providing for an extended range. EFM allows for operation on copper wire and includes Layer 1 testing capabilities.

Three main physical options for EFM are being developed:

- **EFM fiber**—As the name implies, this option is geared toward supporting Ethernet access over point-to-point fiber-optic facilities. Although there are currently a number of point-to-point fiber options available for Ethernet, they need enhancements in the areas of operations, administration, and maintenance.
- **EFM PONs**—In the context of the EFM standards, PONs provide for point-to-multipoint shared fiber access. (PONs in general are discussed in more detail earlier in this chapter and in Chapter 12.)
- **EFM copper**—This option supports point-to-point facilities over copper wire using DSL technology. This is an interesting option, given the huge amount of installed copper wire. This option mandates operation on telco unshielded twisted-pair, not LAN cable, and there are minimum performance goals. On a short reach, the goal is 10Mbps up to 0.5 miles (750 m); on a long reach, it is 2Mbps up to 1.67 miles (2.7 km).

The EFM standards also address two modem options: Discrete Multitone (DMT), which is currently used in most DSL modems, and Quadrature Amplitude Modulation (QAM), which is used in HDSL and VDSL modems.

Finally, the EFM committee is also concerned with inverse multiplexing, one application of which is the use of multiple transmission paths to create a high-bandwidth channel (referred to as *bonding*). ADSL2 defines an ATM-based inverse multiplexing scheme, but in general, the EFM committee favors an Ethernet-oriented approach.

Resilient Packet Ring and Other New Standards Initiatives

Several major standards initiatives are under way to address the resiliency and QoS issues of Ethernet. The IEEE 802.17 working group is defining the Resilient Packet Ring access protocol for use in LANs, MANs, and WANs, for transfer of data packets at rates scalable to many gigabits per second. Resilient Packet Ring technology enables high-speed, survivable ring networks that are optimized for IP and other packet data. This new standard will use existing physical-layer specifications and will develop new interfaces, where appropriate.

Major features of Resilient Packet Ring include a dual-counter-rotating ring format, automatic discovery for adding new stations, a fairness principle that replaces the contention-based Ethernet CSMA protocol with a priority-based access protocol, destination stripping or spatial reuse, and protection whereby Resilient Packet Ring can be restored in 50 milliseconds or less. In addition, Resilient Packet Ring can carry voice and data traffic, which means it is possible to define jitter-free services with low latency for voice and video.

As mentioned earlier, Resilient Packet Ring aims to increase the efficiency of Ethernet and IP services, providing the resilience found in SDH/SONET networks as a function of their network restoration capabilities, and in this way optimizing the transport of data traffic over fiber rings. Resilient Packet Ring also employs the SDH/SONET concept of dual-counter-rotating rings, but in the case of Resilient Packet Ring, they are called *ringlets*. Ringlets connect Resilient Packet Ring stations at nodes where ingress and egress data traffic is dropped. MAC messages are used to direct the traffic in both directions around the ringlet. Bandwidth negotiation between the nodes is done by using a fairness algorithm. Furthermore, all the traffic on a given ringlet is assigned a class of service, with the standard specifying three classes: Class A (high) traffic exists to support low-latency and low-jitter applications, such as voice and video, requiring a pure committed information rate (CIR); Class B (medium) traffic combines CIR and excess information rate (EIR) metrics, introducing queuing based on fairness; and Class C (low) traffic, used for basic Internet access, covers best-effort traffic, providing whatever bandwidth may be available.

An important feature of Resilient Packet Ring is spatial reuse: Resilient Packet Ring removes the signal off the ringlet when it reaches the destination, allowing the freed space to carry additional traffic. (SHD/SONET, by comparison, uses the bandwidth around the entire ring.)

The Overlay and Peer-to-Peer Models Compared

The OTN represents a new generation of physical framework, and it will therefore undoubtedly replace the existing PDH and SDH/SONET infrastructures, supporting WDM, greater bandwidth, and instant provisioning. GigE and 10GigE, offering the benefits of both low cost and familiar protocol solutions, will be favored by those seeking economical and rapid deployments. Both models have the support of strong communities, and we are therefore likely to see evidence of both going forward. We need to be able to control these networks, and that's the realm of the IP+optical control plane, which is the subject of the following section.

■ The IP+Optical Control Plane

The optical network is becoming an ideal IP transport infrastructure in both core and metro networks due to its potentially unlimited bandwidth. However, service providers are experiencing great management costs and complexity with current architectures. As a result, we are moving toward a two-layer architecture that transports IP traffic directly over an optical network (see Figure 11.15). The challenges we face immediately include how to rapidly and effectively provision bandwidth and how to address protection and restoration.

As Figure 11.16 shows, we are taking an evolutionary path to IP+optical. Today we still operate largely with IP running over ATM running over SHD/SONET running over DWDM. The next stage is to eliminate the ATM control plane and instead run IP and MPLS together over SDH/SONET over DWDM. As we begin to add more optical elements to the network, GMPLS will replace MPLS and run over

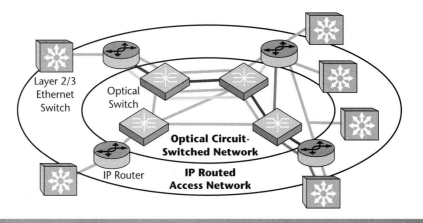

Figure 11.15 The IP+optical control plane of the next-generation optical core

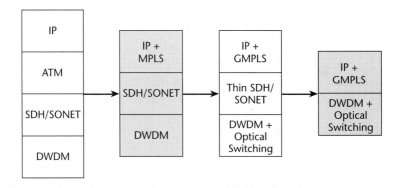

Figure 11.16 The IP+optical control plane evolution

a variation of SDH/SONET referred to as Thin SDH/SONET (meaning thin routes), which in turn will run over DWDM with optical switching. The final stage of the evolution is predicted to involved just two layers: IP and GMPLS running over DWDM and optical switches.

IP+optical networks have two major considerations that are also two major benefits. First, they provide a platform for new service revenues. Intelligent optical networks support best-effort IP but also enable voice, video, and anything else to coexist, and they do so very economically. Second, IP+optical networks can reduce the amount of equipment and the number of protocol stacks. Intelligent optical switching reduces the footprint and the operation's complexity. GMPLS and the ASTN unify the protocols and the layers.

Standards efforts are working on optical management specifications, addressing the linking of IP services directly to the optical networks that carry data, allowing these IP+optical networks to take advantage of the routing intelligence now embedded in IP headers. As described in the following sections, the three main standards efforts are IETF (www.ietf.org) GMPLS, Optical Internetworking Forum (OIF; www.oiforum.com) UNI, and ITU (www.itu.int) ASON.

GMPLS

GMPLS extends MPLS to Layer 1, which allows a coupling of the IP and optical control planes. Routers, packet switches, and optical switches become aware of each other thanks to GMPLS. GMPLS supports fiber, lambda, and TDM switching. It enables dynamic optical networks, which means paths can be established through optical networks via signaling and routing protocols; this involves the use of an optical UNI that allows the edge to signal the core for more or different bandwidth.

The GMPLS control plane is an IP-based controller that employs IP protocols to operate the underlying optical network. It is a family of protocols that includes the following:

- **Link Management Protocol (LMP)**—GMPLS introduces the concept of LMP, which accommodates neighbor identification and link verification, as well as shared-risk groups, fault isolation, and topology-aware networks.

- **Signaling protocols**—GMPLS adds signaling, which enables us to signal into the network with a request that specifies the type of connection desired, change the path to use capacity previously not used, set up direct paths where needed and appropriate, and build in restoration. It uses signaling protocols for establishing links and restoration paths. GMPLS is implemented as a signaling protocol. When the route is calculated, GMPLS uses RSVP–Traffic Engineering (RSVP-TE) or Constraint-Based Routed

Label Distribution Protocol (CR-LDP) to set up the label-switched paths as it would with MPLS. However, GMPLS extends MPLS to control not only routers but also DWDM systems, ADMs, optical cross-connects, and optical switches.

■ **Routing protocols**—GMPLS uses routing protocols for selecting paths through the network. The routing protocols used include OSPF, IS-IS, and BGP.

GMPLS deals with several interfaces: packet switch capable (the only interface supported by MPLS); Layer 2 switch capable, which recognize frames and cells; TDM, which forward data based on the data's time slot; lambda switch capable, which work on individual wavelengths much like optical cross connects; and fiber switch capable, which work on individual or multiple fibers. GMPLS is a peer-to-peer network in which every participating label-switched router sees the entire network design.

The generic functions in the GMPLS control plane are mapped into different functional modules, including the resource management module, the connection module, the protection restoration module, and the main module. The resource management module is used for routing and wavelength assignment, for topology and resource discovery, and for support of QoS. It uses an OSPF-based routing protocol similar to that of GMPLS. The connection module is used for light path signaling and maintenance. In the GMPLS control plane, RSVP-TE or CR-LDP is used for the signaling. The protection restoration module is dedicated to fault monitoring and fast protection and restoration. The objective of the main module is to receive the incoming messages and work closely with other modules to process the requests.

In summary, GMPLS allows service providers to dynamically provision resources and provide the necessary redundancy for implementing various protection and restoration techniques. As Figure 11.17 shows, we're in the midst of an evolution. Those practicing pure IP solutions today look toward MPLS and DiffServ to administer QoS and manage their networks effectively. The early optical net-

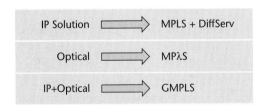

Figure 11.17 GMPLS, a unified end-to-end solution

works look toward MPLS as a control plane. In the future, the marriage of IP and optical naturally leads us to GMPLS, offering an end-to-end unified solution.

UNI

The UNI for the GMPLS specification, as discussed earlier in this chapter, allows for neighbor discovery and channel assignment at the SDH/SONET level. The control interface can be an out-of-band Ethernet interface or an in-band command carried in the SDH/SONET overhead. The UNI specifies a way for a client, called a *UNI client*, to invoke transport network services with a UNI network, a device on another provider's network. Today, UNI is limited to three actions: connection creation, connection deletion, and connection status inquiry.

ASON

As discussed earlier in this chapter, ASON is based on a technology that enables automatic delivery of transport services. Specifically, an ASON network can deliver not only leased-lines connections but also other transport services, such as soft permanent and switched optical connections. In an ASON network, each network node should be equipped with a control plane. The control plane sets up and releases connections and can restore a connection in case of a failure.

ASON optical network elements will take over a number of tasks from the Telecommunications Management Network (TMN) architecture, including routing, restoration, service provisioning, admission control, and accounting. This requires the migration of OTN from a TMN-controlled network to a distributed approach: ASON. ASON is still in its early stages but will likely complement optical UNIs as well as GMPLS. The major features of ASON include fast provisioning, easy network operation, increased network reliability, scalability, and simple planning and design.

Although current optical networks offer enormous capacity compared to their IP counterparts, they are quite inflexible. Most of the limitations are a result of the fact that they are operated manually or via complex and slow network management systems. Drawbacks of existing optical networks include error-prone manual provisioning, long provisioning time, inefficient resource utilization, difficult interoperability between packet client networks and circuit-switched optical networks, complex network management, difficult interoperability between networks belonging to different operators, and lack of protection in mesh-type optical networks.

Network operators implementing the ASON control plane can expect increased revenue-generating capabilities, reduced operational cost, and increased return on capital. Additional benefits to operators include better resource utilization, reduction of manual intervention, simplification of network management systems, support for all-optical networks, and easier internetworking. The major benefits to customers include new services, reduction of service provisioning times, VPNs and closed user groups, bandwidth-on-demand services, provisioned bandwidth services, and wider SLA support capability.

An ASON network allows for three types of connections: permanent connections (established and controlled by a TMN), soft permanent connections (established by a TMN but controlled over the ASON plane), and switched connections (established and controlled by the ASON network).

■ The Migration to Optical Networking

There are still many challenges to building a pure optical network. Optical networks are expensive and require a wide range of new equipment and systems, including Tbps switch routers, pure optical switches, DWDM and CWDM muxes, optical cross-connects, optical repeaters and regenerators, optical components and integrated photonic circuits, new generations of fiber-optic cable, new fiber construction approaches, and, of course, optical network maintenance and management tools.

Some of the challenges to building a pure optical network include the fact that incumbent carriers are not healthy financially. They traditionally build only when there's proven demand and return on investment. Many new entrants have basically gone bust. Carriers can no longer afford the "if you build it, they will come" strategy. There's a glut of optical bandwidth in the backbone already, with rapidly falling prices, and there is a lack of new, high-bandwidth killer applications (although, as discussed in Chapter 10, "Next-Generation Networks," we are finally beginning to see prices stabilize and demand for bandwidth grow). Nonetheless, many such applications are under development and increasingly entering the realm of commercial deployment. It's only a matter of time before we start to see the all-optical network come to be.

As discussed in this chapter, the goals of optical backbones include the migration from ring to mesh topologies; greater control of connections; the ability to provision circuit-switched bandwidth on demand; the extension of the reach of optical links to thousands of kilometers without amplification or regeneration; the integration of DWDM or CWDM with switches to reduce cost and complexity; support of increasingly higher speeds from OC-768, or 40Gbps, to levels we've not yet defined; and scaling of switches to hundreds or thousands of lambdas per fiber port. Given the continuing growth in processing power and storage, the development of bandwidth-hungry applications, the growing demand for broadband connectivity, and the unique properties of the optical spectrum, there is little question that the next-generation network infrastructure will be based on end-to-end optical networking.

Chapter | 12

Broadband Access Alternatives

Whereas Chapter 2, "Traditional Transmission Media," discusses each of the traditional transmission media types, this chapter focuses on the important aspects of and considerations in deploying the media types associated with broadband access. It primarily explores wired broadband solutions, including the growing xDSL family, cable TV networks, a variety of fiber alternatives, and broadband powerline telecommunications (PLT). This chapter also briefly discusses the wireless options, to put them into context; however, given the growing importance of wireless communications and mobility, not to mention the myriad technologies and systems that are emerging, Part IV, "Wireless Communications," is devoted to those technologies, including detailed discussion of wireless broadband access in Chapter 14, "Wireless WANs," and Chapter 15, "WMANs, WLANs, and WPANs." Because broadband doesn't stop at the curb, this chapter also examines the options available for the deployment of home area networks (HANs), which bring broadband deep into the premises.

■ Drivers of Broadband Access

Broadband access is incredibly important: The type of access you have may very well determine how well you're able to grow both professionally and personally, affecting your productivity, leisure time, education, health care, safety, and security.

Initially, the main drivers propelling subscribers to demand broadband access were the users' desires to find information valuable to them, to be connected, and to surf the Web. While these were initially exciting new services, we now assume them as a standard part of daily life; those who have broadband access can no longer imagine life without it. But today additional motivators—such as the desire to experience the increasingly content-rich multimedia spectacle of the Web and the desire to shuttle, share, and even stream digital photos, music, and video—are driving us to seek even more bandwidth and performance from access lines. We are really just at the beginning of an era of spectacular advanced multimedia applications, so there is still much work to be done in the area of broadband access.

Even as there has been steady growth in the number of broadband access lines around the world, the industry is also developing and introducing new high-performance options, tailored to the demands of a high-definition, on-demand multimedia world. As the world transitions to the realm of digital high-definition TV (HDTV), we will embark on a journey into the second generation of broadband access, looking upon conventional ADSL or cable modems as if they were no more than basic telephone lines. To show just how rich this field is, Table 12.1 lists the available and emerging broadband media options, all of which are covered in this chapter and in Part IV.

Broadband is to this decade what cable TV was to the 1980s, evolving from a leading-edge service to a standard offering with mass adoption. Worldwide, broadband lines—DSL, cable modem, and other broadband connections (including fiber, powerline, and wireless)—have now surpassed the 200 million mark, with over 229 million subscribers noted as of the first quarter of 2006. The current growth rate is more than one new subscriber every second. Naturally, the newest broadband markets are showing the fastest growth. According to Point Topic ("World

Table 12.1 Broadband Media Options

Medium	Deployment Examples
Twisted-pair	HDSL, SDSL, G.SHDSL, ADSL, ADSL2, ADSL2+, ADSL2-RE, RADSL, VDSL, LR-VDSL2–12MHz, SR-VDSL2–30MHz
Coax	HFC, DOCSIS1.0, DOCSIS1.1, DOCSIS2.0, DOCSIS3.0, PacketCable 1.0, PacketCable 1.5, PacketCable 2.0, OpenCable, CableHome
Fiber	FTTN, FTTH/FTTP, APON, EPON, GPON
Wireless	DBS/DTH, WiMax, FSO, VF
Mobile	UMTS HSDPA, CDMA EV-DO
Emerging	Broadband PLT

Broadband Statistics: Q1 2006," www.point-topic.com), the United States remains the largest broadband market, with more than 48.3 million lines. China comes in second place, with 41.2 million lines; Japan is third, with 23.4 million lines; and South Korea is fourth, with more than 12.4 million lines. Of the Western European countries, Germany ranks highest, with 11.5 million lines, followed by the United Kingdom and France, with 10.8 million lines each. Just as we expect the economies of China, India, and Russia to grow by leaps and bounds in the coming years, theirs are also the markets where broadband is anticipated to see the largest growth in the near term. China is expected to surpass the United States in the number of broadband subscribers by the year 2007.

The big and established broadband countries have achieved high penetration and are now growing less rapidly than in the past. The slowest-growing region in 2005 was Asia-Pacific, where countries known for their love of technology, such as Japan, Singapore, South Korea, and Taiwan, are exhibiting saturation (although Malaysia, Australia, and New Zealand are now showing rapid growth). Africa and the Middle East, while having the smallest share of broadband lines, is now the fastest-growing region of the world, percentage-wise. The next-fastest-growing regions are Latin America and eastern Europe, both of which still have a small share of the world's broadband access. Southeast Asia shows the greatest increases in terms of absolute numbers (i.e., number of new subscriber lines), with India and China responsible for the majority of the growth.

As of early 2006, DSL had 66.72% of world broadband market share, with cable operators accounting for 23.64% and fiber-to-the-x (FTTx, where x means premises, curb, building, or home) operators coming in with 8.84% of the broadband lines. Other technologies, including broadband wireless and powerline communications, account for the rest of broadband usage. The DSL Forum (www.dslforum.org) expects to see 500 million DSL subscribers by 2010. It appears that cable modems and alternative technologies are gradually losing out to DSL, and Point Topic predicts that in the short term, DSL is likely to see a boost in market share worldwide. However, due to the growth in FTTx, particularly in China, Japan, and the United States, fiber deployment, especially passive optical network (PON) technology, is on the rise worldwide, as is wireless broadband access, thanks to the many new wireless broadband systems that have emerged and are now poised to take off. To keep track of the fast-paced environment, you can check the latest Point Topic "World Broadband Statistics" reports at www.point-topic.com; published several times a year, they provide detailed statistics by country as well as region, offering the most up-to-date glimpse of broadband access deployment globally.

What drives a service provider to consider deploying broadband access in the first place? One reason it may do so is if it is experiencing slower rates of growth or even decline in its core business, whether it is fixed-line telephone services for the telco or television services for cable TV operators. Also, there's a great deal of competition going on among many alternative networks, and there's ongoing growth in the demand for high-speed data and video services. After a service provider decides to deploy broadband access, it has to decide which of the available broadband media options to deploy: twisted-pair (i.e., xDSL), coax, fiber, wireless, or one of the other options listed in Table 12.1.

What drives the strategy for deciding which of the options to deploy? One factor is the status of the embedded distribution plant—how old it is, how well it extends into the neighborhood, and whether it can support the high data rates specified with that broadband access option. Another factor is the services strategy of the network operator. Is it a legacy or new-era services provider? That is, is the service provider merely interested in providing its basic service package and perhaps some specialized relatively low-speed data types of services, or does the provider aim to deliver IP services, interactive broadband services (e.g., Internet access, remote access, teleshopping), and broadcast and interactive video? A third factor is the cost of installing the new distribution system, given the physical footprint realities, such as the terrain and environmental conditions. Finally, the service provider needs to consider the performance level of the distribution system in terms of the requirements to implement the services strategy. This also deals with the physical footprint realities.

The Best Broadband Option for the Footprint

People often want to know what the best broadband access option is. The answer is that there is no best option: What is best for a given situation depends on the footprint reality (e.g., broadband wireless may work very well in one area but provide poor performance in another because there are many trees, whose leaves act as obstacles to microwave). Multiple options are currently available. Across different terrains, across different applications, and across different politics and regulations, one of them is bound to work and prevail, allowing you to enter the broadband era.

■ DSL Technology

DSL is an entire family of technologies, all of which provide digital transmission over the copper wires used in the local loop, or last mile. The xDSL technologies offer many home users their first taste of broadband, and most users find that once they've tried broadband, they'll never go back. It's exciting how much broadband can improve performance, despite the fact that today's broadband is not as fast as the data rates we will see in the coming years. As discussed in detail in the following sections, the xDSL family of standards includes a large variety of speeds and distance specifications:

- High-Bit-Rate Digital Subscriber Line (HDSL)
- Symmetrical (or Single-Line) Digital Subscriber Line (SDSL)
- Symmetric High-Speed Digital Subscriber Line (G.SHDSL)
- Asymmetrical Digital Subscriber Line (ADSL), including ADSL2, ADSL2+, and ADSL2-RE
- Rate-Adaptive Digital Subscriber Line (RADSL)
- Very-High-Bit-Rate Digital Subscriber Line (VDSL), including LR-VDSL2–12MHz and SR-VDSL2–30MHz

Projections Versus Reality

Once in a while, there is a great lesson to be learned from reflecting on market research. The first edition of this book says the following: "According to Cahners In-Stat Group (*Business Communications Review,* July 2001), the worldwide DSL subscriber base was expected to include some 7.5 million users in 2001, 12 million in 2002, 17 million in 2003, and 23 million in 2005." Generally, we find that most forecasts are not accurate, and in fact, far from reality—and usually the reality is much lower than the predicted outcome. In the case of broadband access, I'm happy to report that reality has far exceeded early expectations: Whereas in 2001, market researchers forecast 23 million DSL subscribers by the year 2005, the reality is that, according to Point Topic ("World Broadband Statistics, Q3 2005," www.point-topic.com), we had more than 125 million DSL subscribers worldwide as of September 2005—and by the first quarter of 2006, there were more than 150 million DSL subscribers worldwide ("Thriving DSL Surges Past 150 Million Worldwide Subscribers," DSL Forum, www.dslforum.org).

How DSL Works

The history of DSL goes back to 1988, when Bellcore (which is now Telcordia; www.telcordia.com) created DSL as a technique to filter out the incessant background noise on copper wires and to allow clearer connections through the use of electronic intelligence in the form of DSL modems at either end of the twisted-pair line. In essence, the engineers came up with a way to carry a digital signal over the unused frequency spectrum available on the twisted-pair running between the local exchange and the customer. By using the unused spectrum, DSL could use the basic telephone line to carry digital data without interfering with traditional voice services. Initially, the incumbent local exchange carriers (ILECs) were not thrilled with the idea; after all, it would not be as profitable as installing a second telephone line for customers seeking to access the Internet while maintaining their voice connections. In addition, offering a broadband connection stood to cannibalize the existing ISDN customers.

In the late 1990s, when cable TV companies began to offer broadband Internet access, things changed: ILECs suddenly became very interested in DSL technology, largely due to competitive pressure. Today, DSL is the main competitor to cable modem access when it comes to providing high-speed Internet access to residential users worldwide. As discussed later in this chapter and in Chapter 10, "Next-Generation Networks," service operators are very interested in providing *triple-play* services (combining the delivery of voice, data, and video) as well as *quadruple-play* services (which adds wireless services to the mix), and in order to do so, high bandwidth is mandatory, particularly in the support of HDTV.

In general, a DSL implementation includes two main components (see Figure 12.2, on page 505):

- **DSL modem**—The DSL modem at the customer premises performs the necessary conversion between the digital signals emitted by the computer and the voltage signals required by the network. In the initial deployments of DSL, a technician was required to come to the home and make proper adjustments, including installing a splitter—whose purpose was to separate the voice and data channels—near the demarcation point. However, contemporary offerings allow subscribers to self-install the equipment. This reduces costs because there is no change required to the cable plant at the customer premises, and no "truck roll" (a physical visit from the technician) is required. Instead, the subscriber simply plugs DSL filters into each telephone outlet. This approach, while easier and less costly, can cause degradation in performance, particularly if there are many devices connected to the one DSL line, because the DSL signal will be present on all the telephone wiring throughout the home or building. Nonetheless, this is the most common approach today.

- **DSL access multiplexer (DSLAM)**—A DSLAM terminates and aggregates a large number of DSL subscriber lines, separating the voice and data traffic before handing it off to the proper network, either the PSTN for traditional circuit-switched voice calls or a packet network (ATM, IP, or MPLS) for the data and multimedia traffic.

Characteristics and Properties of DSL

A number of factors determine whether you get the kind of service that DSL promises and that you expect. The performance of any of the DSL alternatives is highly dependent on the loop length as well as the loop condition because a host of impairments can affect the performance of a given pair of copper wires. DSL modems generally range up to a maximum of about 3.5 miles (5.5 km), although new specifications are constantly being created to increase the permitted distances. The general rule of thumb with DSL is that the greater the distance, the lower the performance, and the shorter the distance, the greater the data rate possible. The original ADSL standards, using twisted-pair copper, can deliver up to 7Mbps downstream over a distance of about 1.25 miles (2 km). The latest ADSL standards, such as ADSL2+, can deliver up to 24Mbps downstream, but this rate depends on the distance between the customer and the DSLAM, the point at which numerous subscriber lines are first terminated and aggregated before connecting to the PSTN (for traditional circuit-switched voice) or packet-based backbone (for data and multimedia) local exchange and then onward to the PSTN or packet backbone; in order to deliver 24Mbps downstream, the maximum distance allowed is roughly 1 mile (1.5 km). With one version of VDSL2, VDSL2–30MHz Short Reach (SR-VDSL2–30MHz; the highest-performance DSL standard), it is possible to achieve 100Mbps in both the downstream and upstream directions, but the maximum distance is only 0.3 mile (0.5 km).

A number of factors can affect the loop condition for a subscriber, including the following:

- **Attenuation**—Attenuation is signal loss, and it is a function of frequency. As the frequency increases, the distance the signal can travel decreases, by the square root of the frequency. So higher frequencies lose power more rapidly, thereby limiting the loop length; it is necessary to use the full-frequency spectrum available on the twisted-pair to carry the promised data rates and hence, the higher frequencies must be used for DSL.

- **Resistance**—As signals are transmitted through wires at very high frequencies, a phenomenon called the *skin effect* occurs. As electricity migrates to the medium's skin, resistance increases because less of the wire is used. This increased resistance weakens the signals. Because of the skin effect, there are currently no services above 1GHz over wired media.

- **Crosstalk**—When two adjacent wires carry signals, signals from one wire might be able to enter the other wire as a result of electromagnetic radiation; this is called *crosstalk*. Crosstalk increases as frequency increases and is a principal cause of signal degradation at the frequencies required by high-speed services. This can affect how many pairs within a cable can be used to deliver DSL service. The *spectral compatibility* of two DSL systems depends on the effect of crosstalk that one DSL system has on another inside a single cable bundle.

- **Phase error**—Phase error introduces bit errors where modulation techniques depend on phase modulation.

- **Loaded pairs**—Loaded pairs, which means that loading coils are placed on twisted-pair for purposes of improving performance over 3.5 miles (5.5 km), cannot be used for DSL. A *coil* is an inductor that acts like a low-pass filter, filtering out high frequencies and improving voice frequency response on longer telephone lines. Loaded pairs cannot pass frequencies above 3,500Hz. Because ADSL uses the higher frequencies, it does not work on lines that have load coils.

- **Taps**—Taps are open points on a cable bundle that are left so that technicians will be able to easily splice off a pair to bring additional service to a home or bring service to a new home. Taps generally cause too much distortion to be used with DSL.

- **Loop carriers**—Loop carriers, or remote concentrators, are not compatible with most of the DSL family. xDSL, therefore, must work around the existing loop carrier systems, or the network operators must replace older-generation loop carriers with next-generation loop carriers designed to work with DSL modems. Currently only HDSL works with older digital loop carriers. Approximately 30% to 40% of the U.S. population is served by such digital loop carriers, and around the world, remote and rural locations are generally served with digital loop carriers. As a result, certain market territories do not have quick and easy access to DSL. DSL access in those areas depends on the operator's ability and desire to upgrade the plant.

- **Other external impairments**—Leakage, impulse noise, narrowband interference, and the general quality of the copper pair can all affect the quality of DSL service.

Another characteristic of DSL is that it is a point-to-point connection that is always on. So when you have access to your ISP through a DSL line and your computer is powered up, the connection is on throughout the day. This has security implications: It is very important that you incorporate some form of firewall and security software to prevent the potential activities of a curious or malicious attacker.

DSL provides high-bandwidth transmission over copper twisted-pair. It uses efficient modulation, or line-coding, techniques that enable it to carry more bits in a single cycle (i.e., Hertz) than older twisted-pair. It uses echo cancellation, which allows full-duplex transmission to occur over a single electrical path, and it relies on frequency splitting to enable you to derive separate voice and data channels from one wire. DSL also retains power in the event of a power failure; if the electricity goes out, you lose your high-speed data services, but you retain your voice services.

Finally, it is important to consider one more factor before selecting the broadband access technology that will work best: contention ratios. In the case of DSL, *contention ratio* refers to the fact that users of the system compete for use of the same facility at the same time—in this case, the number of people connected to an ISP who all have to share a set amount of bandwidth.

The following sections look at each of the DSL family members in turn. Table 12.2 summarizes some of the characteristics of xDSL. Keep in mind that the rates shown in Table 12.2 vary depending on the loop length, loop conditions, contention ratios, and so on.

Table 12.2 DSL Technology Options

Name	ITU Designation	Ratified	Maximum Speed	Deployment Distance	Symmetrical/ Asymmetrical	Number of Twisted-Pairs
HDSL						
HDSL	G.991.1	Late 1980s	Up to 2Mbps in each direction	2.2 miles (3.6 km)	Symmetrical	One or two
SDSL						
SDSL	N/A	N/A	Up to 2Mbps in each direction	3.5 miles (5.5 km)	Symmetrical	One
SHDSL						
G.SHDSL	G.991.2	2001; updated in 2003	5.6Mbps in each direction	3.5 miles (5.5 km)	Symmetrical	One or two
ADSL						
G.dmt	G.992.1	1999	7Mbps downstream, 800Kbps upstream	3.5 miles (5.5 km)	Asymmetrical	One
G.lite	G.992.2	1999	1.5Mbps downstream, 512Kbps upstream	3.5 miles (5.5 km)	Asymmetrical	One

continued

Table 12.2 DSL Technology Options *(continued)*

Name	ITU Designation	Ratified	Maximum Speed	Deployment Distance	Symmetrical/ Asymmetrical	Number of Twisted-Pairs
ADSL2						
G.dmt.bis	G.992.3	2002	12Mbps downstream, 1Mbps upstream	3.5 miles (5.5 km)	Asymmetrical	One
G.lite.bis	G.992.4	2002	12Mbps downstream, 1Mbps upstream	3.5 miles (5.5 km)	Asymmetrical	One
ADSL2+						
ADSL2+	G.992.5	2003	24Mbps downstream, 1Mbps upstream	3.5 miles (5.5 km)	Asymmetrical	One
ADSL2-RE	G.992.3	2003	8Mbps downstream, 1Mbps upstream	3.5 miles (5.5 km)	Asymmetrical	One
RADSL						
RADSL	N/A	N/A	600Kbps–7Mbps downstream, 64Kbps–1Mbps upstream	3.5 miles (5.5 km)	Symmetrical or asymmetrical	One
VDSL						
VDSL	G.993.1	2004	55Mbps downstream, 15Mbps upstream	1 mile (1.5 km)	Symmetrical or asymmetrical	One
VDSL2						
LR-VDSL2–12MHz	G.993.2	2005	55Mbps downstream, 30Mbps upstream	2.5–3 miles (4–5km)	Symmetrical or symmetrical	One
SR-VDSL2–30MHz	G.993.2	2005	100Mbps in each direction	0.3 miles (0.5 km)	Symmetrical or asymmetrical	One

HDSL

HDSL is the oldest of the DSL technologies. It has been in full use for over a decade, and it is most commonly used by telcos to provision T-1 or E-1 services. HDSL allows carriers to do so at a reduced cost because it does not require special repeaters, loop conditioning, or pair selection in order to deliver those services. HDSL reduces the cost of provisioning T-1/E-1 because of the way it delivers the bandwidth (see Figure 12.1). A traditional T-1/E-1 environment makes use of two twisted-pairs. Each pair carries the full data rate, which is 1.5Mbps with T-1 and 2.048Mbps with E-1. Because each pair is carrying such a high data rate, higher frequencies need to be used; as a result, repeaters need to be spaced roughly every 0.5 to 1 mile (900 to 1,800 m). Furthermore, no bridge taps are allowed in the traditional T-1/E-1 environment.

HDSL is a symmetrical service, meaning that it provides equal bandwidth in both directions. In addition, it is full-duplex, so it allows communication in both directions simultaneously. HDSL modems contain some added intelligence, in the form of inverse multiplexers. Because of these multiplexers, each pair carries only half of the data rate (and the receiver combines the two to deliver the full data rate), and as a result, those bits can ride in the lower range of frequencies, thus extending the distance over which they can flow without the need for a repeater. The allocation of bandwidth on HDSL depends on whether it is operating on T-1 or

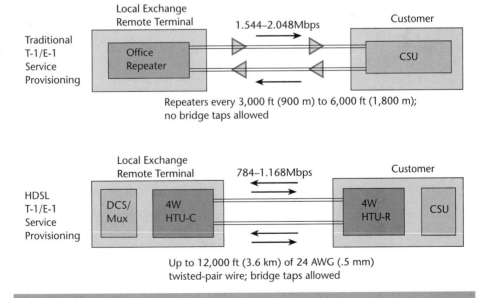

Figure 12.1 Traditional T-1/E-1 versus HDSL provisioning

E-1 capacities; in the T-1 environment, it offers 784Kbps on each pair, and in the E-1 environment, it offers 1.168Mbps on each pair. With HDSL, you need a repeater only every 2.2 miles (3.6 km) or so. In addition, bridge taps are allowed with HDSL. These factors reduce the cost of provisioning services to customers and allow more customers who are outside the range of the traditional T-1/E-1 environment to enjoy the privileges of this high-bandwidth option. Because taps can be used with HDSL, provisioning can occur rather quickly. Also, HDSL is a good solution for increasing the number of access lines via the digital loop carrier transport because it is compatible with the existing loop carriers. Key applications of HDSL include replacement of local repeatered T-1/E-1 trunks, use as a local Frame Relay option, use in PBX interconnection, and use in general traffic aggregation.

HDSL is largely used to provision digital services to business premises. It is standardized under ITU G.991.1 and ANSI T1E1.4, Tech Report 28.

The HDSL2 (two-wire) and HDSL4 (four-wire) specifications were developed in order to provide the capacities and symmetry of HDSL to residences. HDSL2 involves the use of a single twisted copper pair for distances up to 2.2 miles (3.6 km). HDSL2 is a symmetrical, full-duplex service that offers up to 1.5Mbps in each direction. HDSL2 does not support voice telephone service on the same wire pair. The main difference between HDSL2 and HDSL is that HDSL2 uses one pair of wires, whereas HDSL uses two pairs. HDSL4 makes use of two pairs and also supports 1.5Mbps in each direction. HDSL4 is the same as HDSL2 except that by using two pairs of wires, it can achieve a 30% increase in the distance allowed.

Today, newer standards than HDSL, such as G.SHDSL (discussed later in this chapter), are preferred and used in new installations.

SDSL

SDSL involves a single twisted copper pair that can be up to 3.5 miles (5.5 km) long. It is a symmetrical, full-duplex service, and it supports multiple data rates—up to T-1 or E-1 rates—so you can subscribe to varying bandwidths, up to 1.5Mbps or 2Mbps. Symmetry can be very important, depending on the application. If your only goal is to surf the Internet and browse Web sites, then most of the bandwidth you will need is in the downstream direction—from the network to you—in which case solutions such as ADSL are appropriate. But if you're telecommuting or operating in a small office/home office (SOHO) and you need to transfer large files or images or engage in videoconferencing, you need a great deal of bandwidth in the upstream direction as well as in the downstream direction, and in these cases, symmetrical services are best. So if your major purpose for wanting broadband access goes beyond Internet surfing, to a use such as increased productivity with school or professional work, then SDSL is probably a better option than ADSL. It is more costly than asymmetrical options, but it provides a better performance guarantee.

Applications of SDSL include replacement of local repeatered T-1/E-1 trunks, use as fractional T-1/E-1, interconnection of PBXs, support of multirate ISDN, support for switched 384Kbps service (and therefore appropriate bandwidth for lower-level videoconferencing), support for local Frame Relay options, traffic aggregation, and high-speed residential service.

SDSL was not standardized until the ITU-T standardized G.SHDSL (discussed in the following section). Unfortunately, this leads to some confusion because in Europe G.SHDSL was standardized by the European Telecommunication Standards Institute (ETSI) under the name SDSL. This ETSI variant is compatible with the ITU-T G.SHDSL regional variant for Europe. It is important to be aware that equipment referred to as supporting SDSL is generally proprietary equipment that talks only to SDSL equipment from the same vendor or another vendor that uses the same DSL chipset. However, most new installations use the standardized G.SHDSL equipment instead of the older SDSL.

G.SHDSL

Two main drivers influenced the introduction of G.SHDSL. First, the industry observed that there was a need for a higher-speed digital transport service for business applications. HDSL was available but had never been adopted as an international standard. Second, SDSL, which was introduced in the late 1990s as the business-class DSL service, never became a standard, and it also posed problems in that it interfered with the residential ADSL service, being very noisy and therefore spectrally incompatible with ADSL (i.e., creating difficulties when deployed in the same cable bundle as ADSL). A global standard was therefore needed. G.SHDSL was developed to incorporate the features of other DSL technologies, such as ADSL and SDSL, and it can transport T-1, E-1, ISDN, ATM, and IP signals.

G.SHDSL, often referred to as simply SHDSL, was the first international standard for DSL, originally ratified by the ITU-T in February 2001 in recommendation G.991.2. The standard was then updated in 2003, and that version is referred to as G.991.2bis. It is compatible with the ETSI SDSL and ANSI HDSL2 standards. This is more important than it may seem on the surface: A worldwide standard allows for global mass deployment, and higher volumes worldwide mean lower equipment prices.

G.SHDSL is a symmetrical service with options to operate over one pair or two pairs of copper wires, and it also has rate-adaptive capability. Symmetric bandwidth, an increasingly desirable characteristic, supports advanced applications that require high performance in both directions. G.SHDSL supports data rates up to 5.6Mbps in each direction. G.SHDSL eliminates the need for T-1/E-1 repeaters on loops under 3.5 miles (5.5 km), but because the technology supports the use of signal repeaters, users outside the range of ADSL can now be offered DSL service.

G.SHDSL also offers improved reach, providing a 20% to 30% increase compared to HDSL and SDSL. On the average, G.SHDSL provides 3,000 feet (1 km) increased reach over previous symmetric technologies such as SDSL. To be fully appreciated, this has to be put into the context of the serving area: An increased reach of that amount translates to approximately 40% increase in coverage area. Of course, a greater serving area means more customers served, which means more revenue potential for service providers.

Unlike SDSL, G.SHDSL is spectrally compatible with ADSL, causing little noise or crosstalk between cables, which means G.SHDSL can be mixed in the same cable bundles with ADSL, HDSL, HDSL2, and IDSL without much, if any, interference. This maximizes the deployment options available to service providers, allowing G.SHDSL and ADSL to be deployed from the same platform.

G.SHDSL supports a wide range of business and residential applications that demand high bit rates in both the downstream and upstream directions. The voice and data applications that businesses can benefit from include the following:

- **Multiline Voice over DSL (VoDSL)**—VoDSL service typically provides 4 to 16 voice ports in addition to the data ports on the unit. VoDSL makes use of an integrated access device (IAD), which is a device that consolidates voice, data, Internet, and video services by using ATM over T-1/E-1 lines.

- **Web hosting**—G.SHDSL can be used for Web hosting, where the Web server resides at the subscriber's premises, requiring a high-bandwidth connection in the upstream direction.

- **Videoconferencing**—With its higher data rate and symmetry, G.SHDSL provides for improved video quality as well as multiple videoconferences on the same line.

- **Virtual private network (VPN) services**—G.SHDSL can be used to provision VPN services to interconnect smaller branch offices, bypassing the high cost of T-3/E-3 or fiber access.

- **Remote LAN access**—The symmetry of SHDSL makes it an excellent vehicle for providing remote LAN access, which is used by teleworkers, SOHO environments, and campus locations.

Residential applications of G.SHDSL include the following:

- **Extended reach for remote customers**—Because G.SHDSL technology supports the use of repeaters, subscribers outside the reach of ADSL can benefit from DSL service.

- **Internet gaming**—The gaming community uses ranking levels, and every 5 milliseconds of delay (i.e., slower packet transmission response) results in a lower ranking level. Asymmetric service, with its slower upstream speed, skews the player's performance and therefore ranking. G.SHDSL, because it is symmetrical, ensures a successful Internet gaming application.

- ■ **Residential gateway access**—Use of a residential gateway allows all the residents of a household to have simultaneous access to multiple services both to and from the home.
- ■ **Peer-to-peer services**—For those engaging in information sharing with clients and colleagues, such as media file sharing, G.SHDSL enables successful two-way communication.

G.SHDSL also supports a third market, the multiunit market, generically called MxU and alternatively referring to as multiple-dwelling unit (MDU) or multiple-tenant unit (MTU). MDUs include apartment buildings, condominiums, and commercial multitenant office buildings, and MTUs are generally hotels. The G.SHDSL with Inverse Multiplexing over ATM (IMA) feature enables G.SHDSL over multiple lines multiplexed together to offer higher-speed service rates between MxU and the network without needing to install T-3/E-3 lines or pull fiber to the building.

The main drawback of G.SHDSL is that its data rates are not sufficient to support triple- or quadruple-play applications.

ADSL

ADSL was initially introduced in 1993, with the principal driver being the much-anticipated deployment of video-on-demand (VOD). However, because of some early issues with video servers, including storage capacity and processing power, VOD was largely abandoned at that time. On the other hand, Internet access was emerging as a highly desirable service, and with 80% of the traffic flow on the Internet being in the downstream direction, ADSL presented a perfect solution. ADSL, also referred to as G.dmt, was ratified by the ITU-T under recommendation G.992.1 in 1999. It is also standardized under ANSI T1.413, Issue 2.

The asymmetric operation is the key distinguishing characteristic of ADSL. Traditional ADSL, operating over a bandwidth of 1.1MHz, supports downstream data rates from 256Kbps to 7Mbps and upstream rates from 64Kbps to 800Kbps. The maximum reach is 3.5 miles (5.5 km). There is also a version of ADSL known as ADSL Lite, or G.lite. By limiting the data band to 550KHz, ADSL Lite operates at lower speeds, typically up to 1.5Mbps downstream and up to 512Kbps upstream. It is rarely used today. Again, remember that the real-world performance of ADSL, like that of any other DSL, depends on a number of factors, including the distance from the CPE to the DSLAM, the signal-to-noise ratio, the signal attenuation, the cable diameter, the line impedance (which is affected by changes in weather as well as the number of taps on the cable), and the general condition of the cable.

Because ADSL carries a mixture of traffic, including voice, data, Web access, and multimedia, a multiplexing technology is required to carry both time-critical and less time-critical data. ADSL is therefore commonly deployed with ATM, which serves this purpose. In addition, because different ATM virtual circuits (VCs) can be allocated for different services, ATM ensures that service providers can provide triple-play services. However, recently, some network operators have been moving away from the use of ATM, for reasons of cost savings, and replacing it with Ethernet-based solutions. ADSL service providers offer either static or dynamic IP addressing. Static IP addresses are preferred in cases where the subscriber wants to connect to his or her enterprise via a VPN or to host a Web server.

ADSL allows for simultaneous voice and Internet traffic on the same twisted-pair that used to be a phone line. It reserves the bottom 4KHz of spectrum for the voice traffic, and filters (known as *splitters*) at each end of the copper pair split the frequency bands. The lower frequencies are sent to the local exchange to switch the voice traffic. The higher frequencies are sent to the DSL modems, and a user is generally connected over a packet-switched backbone to the ISP.

Carrierless Amplitude Phase Modulation (CAP) was the de facto modulation scheme for ADSL deployments, used in 90% of the installations, until 1996. However, the DMT modulation scheme was selected for the first ITU-T ADSL standards, G.992.1 (also called G.dmt) and G.992.2 (also called G.lite), and CAP is no longer used. DMT, which is an Orthogonal Frequency Division Multiplexing (OFDM) technique, is a multicarrier scheme in which the spectrum is divided into 256 4KHz carriers. Variable numbers of bits are put on each carrier, and the portions of the frequency band that suffer interference from other devices don't have any bits put onto them. The result is improved performance. Compared to CAP, DMT is less prone to interference and can carry data over a longer distance.

Figure 12.2 shows an example of an ADSL environment. At the residence, a splitter is splitting off the plain old telephone service (POTS) to the telephone instrument, using the bottom 4KHz of spectrum on the twisted-pair; the remainder of the line is left for the ADSL modem and the data communications. At the top of the figure is a business environment using a DSL line to carry the voice and data traffic, on an integrated basis.

In Figure 12.2, numerous DSL lines come in from residential and business premises. Their first point of termination is the DSLAM. The DSLAM is a network device, usually located at the telco local exchange or within a neighborhood digital loop carrier configured to support DSL, although it can also reside at the customer premises in the case of a large enterprise or an MDU. The service provider generally connects all its DSLAMs, which are essentially massive ATM concentrators, over an ATM backbone network. DSLAMs are designed to concentrate hundreds of DSL access lines onto ATM or IP trunks connecting to ATM switches, routers, or multiservice edge switches that then connect the DSLs to the ISPs. Each DSLAM

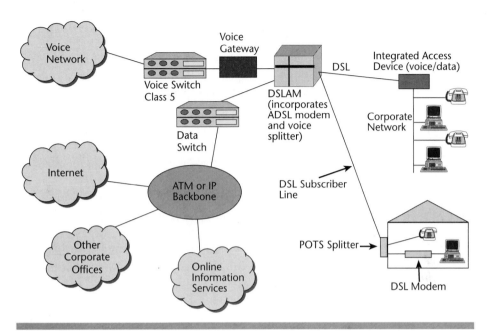

Figure 12.2 An ADSL configuration

has multiple DSLAM aggregation cards, and each card has multiple ports (typically 24, although the number can vary by manufacturer). DSLAMs typically contain power converters, DSLAM chassis, DSLAM cards, cabling, and upstream links. The upstream links are most commonly either multigigabit fiber-optic links or Gigabit Ethernet. The DSLAM splits the voice and data traffic, sending the voice traffic through traditional local exchanges onto the PSTN and sending the data traffic to the appropriate ISP or enterprise network. Each subscriber's traffic appears as a separate ATM VC (a permanent virtual circuit [PVC]). If the service provider provides access to more than one ISP, an ATM VC is created to provide the subscriber with access to his or her ISP of choice. DSLAMs also support quality of service (QoS) features such as priority queues, contention, and DiffServ.

ADSL2

In July 2002, the ITU-T approved G.992.3 and G.992.4, two new standards for ADSL technology collectively called ADSL2. The basic goal of both standards, known as G.dmt.bis and G.lite.bis, respectively, is to increase the transmission rates, increase the range, and improve the overall reliability and manageability of DSL services.

ADSL2 adds several new features and functions, all aimed at improving performance and interoperability, while adding support for new applications, services, and deployment scenarios. The key changes include improvements in the data rate and reach, rate adaptation, diagnostics, and standby mode.

ADSL2 supports higher data rates of up to 12Mbps downstream and 1Mbps upstream, depending on loop length and other factors. It also improves the reach by about 600 feet (180 m). ADSL2 introduces a number of features, including power cutback capability (i.e., two power modes that help reduce overall power consumption while maintaining ADSL's always-on functionality for the user); reduced framing overhead; better modulation efficiency (i.e., seamless rate adaptation [SRA], which allows modems to signal one another in the event of changing transmission conditions and adjust the data rates almost instantaneously); channelization capability (i.e., the ability to split bandwidth into different channels with different link characteristics for different applications); and bonding of lines (i.e., joining of several copper pairs to create one logically larger pipe). ADSL2 also defines an optional "all-digital mode" where the voice transmission band (≤25KHz) can be used to provide an additional 256Kbps of upstream transmission capacity. Other features of ADSL2 include the following:

- **Integrated diagnostics**—Extensive diagnostic capabilities greatly enhance ADSL2 transceivers, incorporating tools for trouble resolution during and after installation, performance monitoring while in service, and upgrade qualification.

- **Faster startup**—A fast startup mode reduces initialization time from about 10 seconds to less than 3 seconds.

- **IMA**—ADSL2 addresses the growing demand for even higher data rates via the ability to combine several ADSL connections, commonly referred to as *bonding*. Inverse multiplexing can be used to bond up to 32 ADSL links, although in actual practice bonding 2 or 3 lines is far more likely.

- **Ethernet support**—The latest ADSL2 standard includes a packet mode transmission convergence layer (PTM-TC), which supports packet-based services such as Ethernet.

ADSL2+

The ITU-T approved ADSL2+, or ADSL2plus, as G.992.5 in 2003. ADSL2+ doubles the downstream frequency band to 2.2MHz, increasing the DMT channel count to 512. This effectively doubles the maximum downstream data rates, achieving up to 24Mbps on phone lines as long as 1 mile (1.5 km) while supporting up to 1Mbps upstream. However, under most practical scenarios, speeds are in the 15Mbps to 20Mbps range when delivered approximately 1 mile (1.5 km) from the local exchange.

ADSL2+ solutions are most commonly multimodal, interoperating with ADSL and ADSL2, as well as with ADSL2+ chipsets. There is also an option in which customers served by digital loop carriers could be designated to operate only on the higher frequency channels (i.e., 1.1MHz to 2.2MHz) to limit interference with customers on longer loops who would be assigned the regular ADSL/ADSL2 channels (i.e., ≤1.1MHz).

ADSL2+ allows service providers to evolve their networks to support advanced services, such as video, in a flexible way, with a single solution for both short-loop and long-loop applications. ADSL2+ includes all the feature and performance benefits of ADSL2 while maintaining the capability to interoperate with legacy equipment. The other major enhancement with ADSL2+ is improvement in crosstalk and interference control. The standard specifies a set of upstream and downstream power spectrum density (PSD) masks that define methods for shaping the DSL transmission signal. Particularly important on longer loops (i.e., 2.5 to 3.5 miles [4 to 5.5 km]), the PSD masks allow the modems to optimize performance by adjusting the power levels on the various DMT channels. The operator can specify which mask to use when the link is installed, or the modems can determine which mask to use in the initialization and handshaking.

Some telcos are already beginning to use ADSL2+ to support Internet Protocol TV (IPTV) services, with an eye toward HDTV. However, despite improvements in data rates and reach, ADSL2 and ADSL2+ are still not sufficient to support applications such as multiple HDTV channels; such uses require the use of VDSL, which is discussed later in this chapter. Another problem with ADSL2+ is that although the standard is approved and chipsets are plentiful, the equipment for multiple-vendor setups still requires interoperability testing.

ADSL2-RE

To expand carriers' addressable markets, the ITU has developed a reach-extended version of the ADSL2 specification—called ADSL2-RE—that allows DSL systems to reach up to 3.75 miles (6 km). This equates to more than a 20% increase in coverage and opens the door for carriers to sign up new subscribers. The ITU-T ratified ADSL2-RE under recommendation G.992.3 in 2003. While it can support up to 8Mbps downstream and 1Mbps upstream, when taking advantage of its main feature, ADSL2-RE extends a 768Kbps downstream service by approximately 0.5 mile (1 km), to 3.5 miles (5.5 km).

RADSL

RADSL, a nonstandard version of ADSL, adapts data rates dynamically, based on changes in line conditions. It can therefore operate over a wide range of loop lengths and conditions, up to a maximum of 3.5 miles (5.5 km). With RADSL, the modem adjusts the upstream bandwidth to maintain a certain speed on the downstream channel. If there is a large amount of line noise or signal degradation, the upstream bandwidth may be significantly reduced, down to 64Kbps. RADSL can be configured to operate in either symmetrical or asymmetrical mode. The downstream rates range from 600Kbps to 7Mbps, and the upstream rates range from 64Kbps to 1Mbps. Most RADSL devices rely on Discrete Multitone (DMT) encoding.

VDSL

The ITU-T standardized VDSL, the highest-performing DSL option, under recommendation G.993.1 in 2004. Conventional VDSL relies on a single twisted copper pair, operating over very short distances. The loop length range is just 1,000 to 5,000 feet (300 m to 1.5 km), with performance degrading over longer distances. With its greater bandwidth of 12MHz, the maximum data rates are up to 55Mbps downstream and up to 15Mbps upstream. Actual speeds vary, depending on distance and configuration. The following are some possible scenarios:

Mode	Distance	Downstream Rate	Upstream Rate
Asymmetrical	3,000 ft. (900 m)	26Mbps	3Mbps
Asymmetrical	1,000 ft. (300 m)	52Mbps	6Mbps
Symmetrical	3,000 ft. (900 m)	13Mbps	13Mbps
Symmetrical	1,000 ft. (300 m)	26Mbps	26Mbps

VDSL is a very high-capacity technology, and its performance degrades rapidly over distances, so it is really meant to be almost a sister technology to fiber-to-the-node (FTTN), discussed later in this chapter, going the very short distance from the curb to the home. (Or in the case of fiber-to-the-home/fiber-to-the-premises [FTTH/FTTP] with an MDU, VDSL could be run over twisted-pair from the fiber coming into the building to each apartment.) The main application for VDSL is short-loop environments, such as MDUs or MTUs.

VDSL2

VDSL2 standardization efforts started in January 2004. Consent and approval of the ITU-T G.993.2 recommendation were reached in 2005. The key applications for VDSL2 are the next generation of TV—VOD, DTV, HDTV, and forms of interactive multimedia Internet access. (Chapter 10 provides more information on TV standards.) VDSL2 uses the same DMT modulation as ADSL, with two bandwidth options:

- **LR-VDSL2–12MHz**—Specified as G.993.2, LR-VDSL2–12MHz is the "long reach" alternative, supporting up to 55Mbps downstream and up to 30Mbps upstream. However, when it is used over longer distances, the data rates drop. For instance, at 2.5 to 3 miles (4 to 5 km), the downstream rate drops to 1Mbps to 4Mbps.
- **SR-VDSL2–30MHz**—Specified as G.993.2, SR-VDSL2–30MHz is the "short reach" option, enabling up to 100Mbps in both directions, albeit over very short distances of 0.3 miles (0.5 km) or less.

VDSL2 supports a larger variety of services, including integrated QoS features, the ability to carry ATM as well as Ethernet payload, and channel bonding for extended reach or rate. An additional benefit of VDSL2 is that it is compatible with ADSL, ADSL2, and ADSL2+, whereas the original VDSL (VDSL1) is not. ADSL2+ backward compatibility makes VDSL2 deployment much more attractive for service providers and will speed the adoption of this technology. Given its improved data rates and reach, power features, and QoS features, VDSL2 also enables triple- and quadruple-play applications. A typical VDSL2 connection can support at least three DTV channels, 5Mbps Web surfing, and Voice over IP (VoIP).

For all these reasons, VDSL2 is viewed as the ultimate DSL standard, being a natural evolution of ADSL2+, allowing continued exploitation of copper plants, and providing sufficient bandwidth for advanced applications. Rather than building fiber all the way to the premises, VDSL2 will give telcos the ability to support multiple standard-definition and high-definition video streams via copper (using advanced compression). Adoption of VDSL2 appears to be moving quickly, with major activity worldwide. The first chipsets and systems are already available. The major business decision will be whether it is less expensive to extend fiber or to shorten copper loops for performance gains.

■ Cable TV Networks

Cable operators, also referred to as *multiple-system operators* (MSOs), are in major competition with telcos because the two industries are increasingly resembling each other, offering the same range of services and fighting for the same customers: Cable providers have gone into the business of supporting data and voice communications (e.g., Internet access and VoIP), while telcos have begun to provide TV and interactive services (e.g., IPTV and VOD). Cable TV networks, which are most commonly deployed as hybrid fiber coax (HFC) arrangements, support a wide range of services, including traditional circuit-switched telephony and VoIP, Internet access, broadcast video, VOD, and interactive broadband services. HFC involves the use of fiber in the backbone and in the access network. The fiber termination point (i.e., the neighborhood node) can support anywhere from 200 to 2,000 homes, with 200 to 500 homes being the norm. From that neighborhood node, coax (normally 750MHz or 1,000MHz) is run to the home, in a two-way subsplit system. (When two cables are not used but there is a need for simulation of a dual-cable system, bandwidth on a single cable can be split up, with one portion representing one cable, and the other portion representing the second cable. Splitting the frequencies so that the lower frequencies are used for one purpose and the higher for another is called a *subsplit system*.)

In countries where there is a history of cable TV, the cable plants have traditionally been one-way analog networks, sending just downstream; after all, what more was required for the conventional broadcast of live television and video programming? However, to handle Internet access, voice communications, or any other interactive services, a two-way infrastructure is required, so the operators had to upgrade their networks. Over the past few years, the upgrade to digital two-way systems has been occurring in countries with existing cable infrastructures. In other parts of the world, where there had been no MSOs, new systems are being built with digital two-way capabilities, recognizing the need to support today's interactive services environment.

A number of elements are involved with a cable TV–based network, including the physical transport infrastructure, generally known as the HFC architecture; cable modems, which are largely standardized under the CableLabs DOCSIS specifications; and cable modem controllers, which are known as cable modem termination systems (CMTSs). The following sections discuss these elements.

HFC Architecture

Cable operators' network infrastructures are based on the HFC architecture, which is in essence a community LAN that uses a bus topology, meaning that it's a shared-access architecture. (Chapter 6, "Local Area Networking," describes bus and other LAN topologies.) Figure 12.3 shows the topology of a cable TV operator's HFC network. On the left side are the headends, from which the information is being broadcast. Those headends are tied together, generally with fiber, referred to as *fiber in the backbone*. By moving to a fiber-based backbone, the cable TV operators have also made improvements to the performance of their networks as well as the costs associated with operating and maintaining them. The backbones, then, feed into the neighborhood nodes, or the optical nodes (i.e., the access points), and

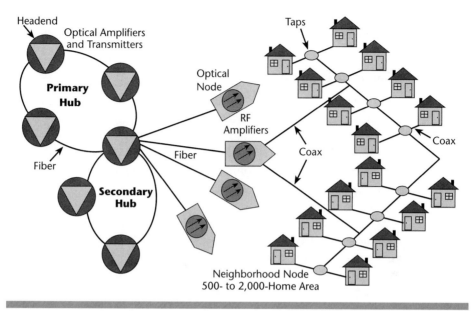

Figure 12.3 The topology of an HFC network

from there coax goes out to the homes. You can see in Figure 12.3 that HFC is a shared infrastructure; this is one of the drawbacks of the HFC architecture.

The HFC architecture uses Frequency Division Multiplexing (FDM) to derive individual channels, some of which are dedicated to the support of telephony services, others of which are reserved for analog TV, and still others of which are reserved for DTV and future interactive broadband services. This multiple-access coax system represents a bit of a hostile environment: The points where the coax connects into set-top boxes or cable-ready TV sets tend to collect noise, so the cable picks up extraneous noise from vacuum cleaners or hair dryers. If every household on a network is running a hair dryer at 6:30 AM, the upstream paths are subjected to this noise, and hence there will be some performance degradations. Extra signal processing must therefore be added to overcome the impairment in the return channel.

The major concerns with HFC include security, privacy, reliability, and return-path issues, particularly in support of telephony. With twisted-pair, we're used to having a private line to the local exchange, but that is not the case in using a shared coax system. Also, HFC faces bandwidth constraints: Given that cable modems have caught on and there are increasingly more subscribers to such services, more homes within a neighborhood are making use of their Internet access channel, and everyone's downloads and bandwidth are minimized. Subdividing the nodes can help alleviate bandwidth constraints, and it can also help reduce ingress noise. If the service provider continues to subnet, it can keep performance high for the subscribers.

Cable Modems and CMTSs

A cable modem is needed in order to support high-speed data access over HFC, using the cable TV infrastructure. Cable modems function like special-purpose routers, linking the cable network's Layer 3 to another network or device. Generally, this requires an external box with cable and Ethernet connections. Figure 12.4 illustrates cable modem connectivity. On the left side of the figure is an individual neighborhood with users attaching to the shared coax system via their cable modems. These various coax trunks then come into the headend facility, where they terminate on a CMTS. The CMTSs are linked by a common Ethernet hub, which in turn feeds into the IP router, which determines the optimum path to take over an optical backbone onto the ISP.

CMTS functions include providing QoS, allocating bandwidth, classifying packets, policing packets for Type of Service (ToS) fields, adjusting the ToS fields as needed, performing traffic shaping, forwarding packets, converting and classifying QoS parameters, handling signaling and reservation of backbone QoS, and recording call resource usage.

Cable modems provide downstream data rates of up to 36Mbps, and the downstream rates are generally supported in the frequency band 42MHz to 750MHz.

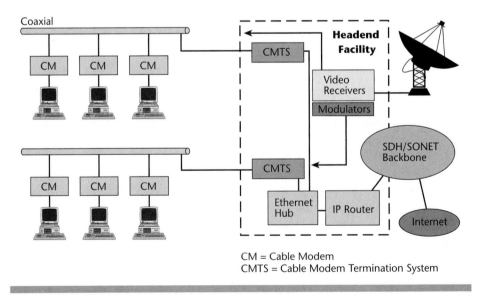

CM = Cable Modem
CMTS = Cable Modem Termination System

Figure 12.4   Cable modems: LAN-oriented connectivity

The downstream channel depends on the QAM technique used because that is what gives it the most bits per second and, hence, the fastest data rates downstream, where rapid downloads are important. Upstream data rates range from 5Mbps to 30Mbps, and the upstream direction operates in the range of 5MHz to 42MHz. As mentioned earlier, this portion of the frequency band is especially subject to noise interference, so it requires modulation techniques such as Quadrature Phase-Shift Keying (QPSK) and 16-QAM, which transport fewer bits per second than other techniques but also provide better noise resistance.

Cable Modem Standards

Many standards deal with cable modems. CableLabs (www.cablelabs.org) is an industry leader in creating cable modem standards for the cable TV industry. CableLabs has defined the following standards:

- Data Over Cable Service Interface Specification (DOCSIS)
- PacketCable
- OpenCable
- VOD Metadata
- CableHome

The Euro-DOCSIS standard was created based on the U.S. DOCSIS standard, with the goal of ensuring correct and optimal performance of Euro-DOCSIS modems and CMTSs in European networks as well as being fully compliant with the European Digital Video Broadcasting (DVB) standard in the downstream. tComLabs (www.tcomlabs.com) developed the Euro-DOCSIS annex of the DOCSIS specification in 1999, with the cooperation of equipment vendors and cable operators. The European cable community agreed on final specifications in early 2000.

ETSI has approved both DOCSIS and the Euro-DOCSIS annex as specifications. The primary difference between DOCSIS and Euro-DOCSIS is that DOCSIS employs the 6MHz channel NTSC standard used in North America, whereas Euro-DOCSIS relies on the 8MHz PAL channel spacing used in Europe. Also, Euro-DOCSIS takes advantage of a higher capacity in the upstream band, ranging from 5MHz to 65MHz, versus the North American version, which uses 5MHz to 42MHz. Japan employs other variants of DOCSIS.

DOCSIS

For several years, cable TV operators have been migrating from their traditional core business of TV (or entertainment) programming to the role of a full-service provider, offering not just video but voice and data services as well. DOCSIS has been instrumental in this shift. The main objective of DOCSIS is to provide uniform specifications to ensure compatibility with various cable operators' infrastructures and to allow cable modems to be purchased from various retail outlets.

There are two main components to the DOCSIS architecture: the cable modem, which is located at the customer premises, and the CMTS, which is located at the cable operator's headend. The customer's equipment, such as a PC, is first connected to the cable modem, which is then connected through the HFC network to the CMTS. The CMTS basically performs the same function as the DSLAM does for xDSL: hosting downstream and upstream ports and routing traffic between the HFC network and the Internet. The cable operator also uses the CMTS to configure each customer's cable modem, adjusting for different line conditions based on the customer's service requirements.

With the DOCSIS and Euro-DOCSIS standards, the downstream channel occupies the capacity of a single TV transmission channel in the cable operator's channel offerings: In the United States, it is a 6MHz downstream channel, and in the European annex to the standard, it is an 8MHz channel. In general, several hundred users can share the downstream channel and one or more upstream channels. The digital set-top box uses MPEG-2 transport stream modulation, based on either 64-QAM or 256-QAM, providing up to 40Mbps downstream. The upstream can use QPSK, 16-QAM, or 64-QAM, depending on the generation of DOCSIS standard. (See Chapter 5, "Data Communications Basics," for information on modulation schemes such as QPSK and QAM.) DOCSIS also involves an Ethernet connection to the PC, so data is transferred by using TCP/IP encapsulated in Ethernet frames between the cable modem and headend. DOCSIS includes a baseline privacy specification that relies on the use of both the 40- and 56-bit versions of DES. (See Chapter 9, "IP Services," for more information on security.)

At this point, there are several generations of DOCSIS standards, including DOCSIS 1.0, 1.1, 2.0, and 3.0. The ITU has also adopted two of the DOCSIS variants as international standards: DOCSIS 1.1 was ratified as ITU-T Recommendation J.112, and DOCSIS 2.0 was ratified as ITU-T Recommendation J.122. DOCSIS 2.0 is backward compatible with DOCSIS 1.1.

DOCSIS 1.0 DOCSIS 1.0 enables the cable TV industry to deliver high-speed data using cable modems. As with all the other DOCSIS standards, the main service with DOCSIS 1.0 is two-way access to the Internet.

With DOCSIS 1.0, the upstream rate is up to 10Mbps over a 3.2MHz channel. For downstream data, the modulation technique specified is either 64-QAM or 256-QAM, and upstream it is either QPSK or 16-QAM. It is possible to deploy DOCSIS 1.0 on a one-way HFC network by implementing the return path over traditional phone lines.

DOCSIS 1.1 DOCSIS 1.1 was created to address the cable industry's desire to offer VoIP services. DOCSIS 1.1 includes key network technologies, including dynamic QoS, which is very important to VoIP, packet fragmentation, and enhanced security. (QoS is discussed in Chapter 10.) By supporting QoS, DOCSIS 1.1 allows for the provisioning of VoIP and interactive gaming. QoS also enables tier-based services such as higher speeds to heavy users. DOCSIS 1.1 also offers improved security and privacy, both of which are necessary to support voice services. For downstream data, the modulation technique specified is either 64-QAM or 256-QAM, and upstream it is either QPSK or 16-QAM. Along with cable modems, DOCSIS 1.1 also supports VoIP phones and residential gateways.

To deploy DOCSIS 1.1 (or higher), the cable operator must have in place a two-way HFC network that supports a return path for the upstream traffic. The DOCSIS 1.1 standard addresses real-time applications such as IP telephony. The key issues in cable-based IP telephony include voice quality and how to guarantee it in terms of latency, fidelity, jitter, packet loss, and reliability at the customer end. Other issues are legacy signaling support, data security, scalability, and feature deployment at the service provider's end. Finally, there are a number of provider-specific issues, such as implementation of systems for PSTN gateways and gate-keepers, provisioning, billing, and network maintenance.

DOCSIS 1.1 enables time-sensitive voice and multimedia packets to share in HFC networks with time-insensitive pure data packets. DOCSIS 1.1 enables a node to recognize a nondata packet and switch to it instantaneously from whatever data packet it is working on. It requires a CMTS at the edge of the cable access network and a DOCSIS 1.1–compliant cable modem at the customer premises. Edge cable CMTSs need the intelligence to isolate traffic flows and apply policy-based QoS treatments in real-time. Traffic flows need to be isolated by service provider, application, and subscriber so that during times of congestion, flows within the service-level agreement (SLA) are maintained and flows that exceed the SLA are discarded first. Operators then map the DOCSIS-based flows to IP specifications such as DiffServ and MPLS, which are discussed in Chapter 10, to manage the handoff to the core network.

Figure 12.5 shows an example of using DOCSIS 1.1 for cable-based IP telephony. Considerations for cable-based IP telephony include technical architecture, achieving PSTN-level reliability (i.e., five-nines reliability, or 99.999%), being able to accommodate the same PSTN-level feature sets, and regulatory issues. Operators face challenges such as how to provide detailed, sophisticated, end-to-end SLAs; how to adjust to the need to do maintenance, which will become more critical; and how to evolve from being broadband video providers to being mission-critical service providers. Developments in the cable-based IP telephony environment are expected in the next couple years.

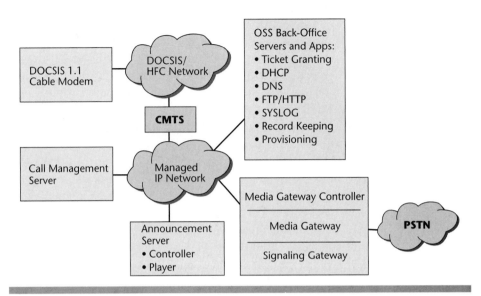

Figure 12.5 Cable-based IP telephony

DOCSIS 2.0 and 2.x DOCSIS 2.0 increases downstream speed to 40Mbps and upstream throughput to 30Mbps over channels as wide as 6.4MHz, resulting in an increase in the capacity to deliver high-speed data. DOCSIS 2.0 also supports symmetric services, which means it can serve business customers more adequately. Along with broadband Internet access, VoIP, and tiered services, DOCSIS 2.0 also supports commercial services and videoconferencing. In addition to cable modems, VoIP phones, and residential gateways, it also supports video phones.

For downstream data, the modulation technique specified is either 64-QAM or 256-QAM, and upstream it is either QPSK, 16-QAM, or 64-QAM. CableLabs and its members are working on a 2.x version of DOCSIS that will add features such as roaming, committed data rates, Media Access Control (MAC) layer improvements, and better commercial service capabilities. DOCSIS 2.x also adds support for mobile devices.

More than two years after CableLabs officially released the DOCSIS 2.0 specification, more than 60 cable modems are now DOCSIS 2.0 certified, and the technology is a must-have on modem supply contracts with major operators. However, only a handful of operators have actually deployed DOCSIS 2.0 in their networks. It is only when the cable operators are ready to offer VoIP and commercial services on a large scale that they will begin using DOCSIS 2.0. Although most operators will build it into their hardware, it will be the services—from IP voice to multimedia gaming—that will drive MSOs' decisions to implement DOCSIS 2.0.

DOCSIS 3.0 DOCSIS 3.0, currently under development, will increase the capacity up to a minimum of 160Mbps downstream to customers and a minimum of 120Mbps upstream. In DOCSIS 3.0, several downstream and several upstream channels can be bonded together to multiply the bandwidth delivered to each customer.

DOCSIS 3.0 will most likely require a new chip at the modem and at the CMTS. However, DOCSIS 3.0 will be worth the effort because it will give operators enough bandwidth to offer a wider range of IP-based offerings, including entertainment-quality media services. (Table 12.3 compares the amount of bandwidth each DOCSIS version provides.) DOCSIS 3.0 adds entertainment video on top of the services supported by DOCSIS 2.0 and 2.x, and it also adds support for IP set-top boxes to the list of equipment supported by the earlier DOCSIS versions.

DOCSIS DSG The cable industry is applying DOCSIS to many services and applications beyond just Internet access, including new applications to control the communications pathway for digital set-top boxes and to monitor the health of the cable plant, including power supplies and amplifiers.

DOCSIS Set-top Gateway (DSG) is an extension to the DOCSIS standards that gives operators a standard method to deliver out-of-band data, such as channel lineups and program guides, and more advanced streaming applications via a DOCSIS channel to the digital cable set-top box.

The DSG network consists of three main elements: the DSG gateway, which is responsible for generating the stream of out-of-band data; the DSG agent, which is the same as a CMTS and is responsible for forwarding the out-of-band data as well as publishing the out-of-band directory; and the set-top box. The set-top box contains three subcomponents: the DSG-capable cable modem, also called the DSGeCM

Table 12.3 DOCSIS Bandwidth Comparison

Bandwidth	DOCSIS 1.0	DOCSIS 1.1	DOCSIS 2.0	DOCSIS 2.x	DOCSIS 3.0
Downstream Bandwidth					
Per channel	40Mbps	40Mbps	40Mbps	40Mbps	200Mbps
Per node	5Gbps	5Gbps	5Gbps	5Gbps	6.3Gbps
Upstream Bandwidth					
Per channel	10Mbps	10Mbps	30Mbps	30Mbps	100Mbps
Per node	80Mbps	80Mbps	170Mbps	170Mbps	450Mbps

(embedded cable modem); the actual data consumer, called the DSG client; and the DSG client controller, which configures and controls the DSGeCM. The DSG specification applies equally to all versions of DOCSIS.

PacketCable

CableLabs created PacketCable (www.packetcable.com) to define standards for the cable TV industry. The PacketCable initiative aims to develop interoperable interface specifications for two-way cable networks in order to deliver advanced real-time multimedia services. PacketCable interconnects three networks, including the HFC access network, the PSTN, and IP networks. PacketCable networks, built on top of DOCSIS 1.1 or higher, use IP to enable various multimedia services, including IP telephony, videoconferencing, multiparty game playing, and other multimedia applications. By using a single high-speed, QoS-enabled broadband architecture, a DOCSIS 1.1 or 2.0 network with PacketCable extensions allows cable operators to economically and efficiently deliver data and voice traffic.

The PacketCable architecture relies on several key protocols. First is DOCSIS, which is the standard for data over cable and details the radio frequency (RF) band. For media transfer, Real-Time Transport Protocol (RTP) and Real-Time Transport Control Protocol (RTCP) are required. The signaling protocols include PacketCable Trunking Gateway Protocol (TGCP; a PSTN gateway call signaling protocol specification), which is an MGCP extension for media gateways, and the Network-Based Call Signaling (NCS) protocol specification, which is an MGCP extension for analog residential media gateways that details VoIP signaling. (RTP, RTCP, and MGCP are discussed in Chapter 9.) Finally, Common Open Policy Services (COPS) is used for controlling access. (COPS is discussed in Chapter 10.)

PacketCable is known internationally as IP Cablecom. PacketCable documents have been approved by the Society of Cable Telecommunications Engineers (www. scte.org), which ANSI recognizes as a standard-setting body for cable in North America, and have been approved by the ITU for adoption as worldwide standards. The cable industry is pursuing global standardization, with the objective of achieving worldwide interoperability of services and equipment, vendor independence, ease of interconnection with other operators, and reduced cost through scale of economies. The ITU has approved a suite of CableLabs PacketCable specifications as standards for the international version of services, including VoIP.

As discussed in the following sections, three versions of the PacketCable standard are defined today: 1.0, 1.5, and 2.0.

PacketCable 1.0 The first service defined for the PacketCable platform is VoIP. The CableLabs PacketCable 1.0 specification deals with transmitting multifeatured IP phone calls over HFC, and it allows four independent IP voice channels through a single cable modem. PacketCable 1.0 consists of 11 specifications and 6 technical reports that define the call signaling, QoS, codec, client provisioning, billing event message collection, PSTN interconnection, and security interfaces necessary to implement a single-zone PacketCable solution for residential IP voice services.

The core set of PacketCable 1.0 specifications essentially describes how to move the basic functions generally found on traditional Class 5 local exchanges onto a distributed architecture consisting of several general-purpose servers, leading to a low-cost, highly flexible, and scalable solution. PacketCable multimedia defines a generic architecture where application managers request QoS on behalf of a client and where policy servers authorize and commit these QoS requests.

PacketCable 1.5   PacketCable 1.5 supersedes previous versions (1.1, 1.2, and 1.3) and consists of additional capabilities. It consists of 21 specifications and 1 technical report that define the call signaling, QoS, codec, client provisioning, billing, message collection, PSTN interconnection, and security interfaces necessary to implement a single-zone or multizone PacketCable solution for residential IP voice services.

PacketCable 2.0   PacketCable 2.0 will replace MGCP with SIP. (The MGCP and SIP protocols are discussed in Chapter 9.)

OpenCable

Digital cable TV devices present another exciting area to watch in the coming years. The goal of the CableLabs OpenCable program (www.opencable.org) is to publish specifications that define digital cable network interfaces, as well as the nature of next-generation cable set-top boxes. CableLabs started the OpenCable initiative in 1997, with the goal of helping the cable industry deploy interactive services over cable, creating a common standard for digital cable TV within the United States, and promoting competition among licensed device manufacturers.

OpenCable has two key components: a hardware specification and a software specification. The hardware specification describes a receiver that ensures interoperability and can be sold at retail. The software specification, called the OpenCable Applications Platform (OCAP), creates a common platform on which interactive services can be deployed. The following sections describe these two components.

OpenCable Hardware   The CableLabs cable modem standard MCNS will be used with OpenCable set-top boxes, with advanced digital video compression circuitry to create terminals capable of supporting next-generation video and the entire range of current and future Internet and Web-based applications. The OpenCable effort is seen as the linchpin of the cable industry's digital future. It is independent of the processor and operating system. Compliant set-top boxes must allow both high- and low-speed bidirectional Internet service for both Internet and TV applications, and computer applications must be provided to both the television and the desktop computer through cable.

Characteristics of OpenCable digital set-top boxes will include expanded memory, powerful graphics engines, and support for one-way broadcasts (e.g., near-VOD, Web browsing, Internet e-mail) as well as two-way interactive services (e.g., Internet access via TV, high-definition video programming). Besides defining next-generation digital consumer devices, OpenCable also aims to encourage supplier competition and to create a retail hardware platform.

OCAP   OCAP is intended to enable the developers of interactive television services and applications to design such products so that they will run successfully on any cable TV system in North America, independent of set-top or television receiver, hardware, or operating system software choices.

OCAP consists of a set of technical specifications created by CableLabs and endorsed by the Society of Cable Telecommunications Engineers (www.scte.org) and other industry groups. The OCAP 1.0 specification was released in December 2001 and was followed by OCAP 2.0 in April 2002. The specifications include two main sets of software: middleware and applications software/content authoring tools. The majority of the software is based on Sun Microsystems Java, which is already used by many developers to create content for PCs, the Web, gaming devices, and TV. OpenCable's objective is to put OCAP middleware into all sorts of intelligent devices and then use OCAP authoring tools to create interactive content to run on those devices. This will allow manufacturers and retail distributors of set-top boxes, television receivers, and other appliances to build and sell to consumers interesting and highly functional next-generation digital devices aimed at supporting a host of new and exciting interactive services delivered by cable operators. Simply put, OCAP creates the opportunity to establish a standardized platform, national and international, to launch a myriad of interactive services over a wide variety of digital devices.

Supporters of OCAP believe that it will do for TV in the United States what DOCSIS has done for high-speed Internet access and what DVB–Multimedia Home Platform (DVB-MHP) is doing for TV in Europe. (DVB is discussed in Chapter 10.) In fact, much of the OCAP specification is based on or is compatible with MHP. In addition, South Korea has adopted OCAP to introduce a variety of interactive services, further strengthening its role internationally.

VOD Metadata
Another project established by CableLabs that is pertinent to the future of interactive services is VOD Metadata (www.cablelabs.com/projects/metadata). Its purpose is to examine the distribution of content assets, such as movies, coming from

multiple content providers and being sent over various networks to the cable operators.

Metadata refers to descriptive data associated with a content asset package. It can be something simple such as identifying the content title, or it can be much more complex, such as providing a complete index of different scenes in a movie. The initial efforts of VOD Metadata are focused on creating specifications for VOD and subscription VOD (SVOD) applications.

CableHome

CableLabs has a home networking initiative called CableHome (www.cablelabs. com/projects/cablehome). CableHome's objective is to deliver to subscribers high-quality, managed, value-added broadband services over any home network media. Furthermore, the objective is that by complying with CableHome, different manu-facturers can develop interoperable products, making it as convenient as possible for the consumer and reducing time to market, complexity, and costs.

Cable operators and telcos are taking advantage of revenue opportunities pro-vided by home networking services. Major cable operators are conducting trials or have rolled out services that enable and support providing broadband to multiple PCs. Consumers see value in these services and, as a result, cable operators are realizing incremental revenue now. In addition, forward-looking services, such as medical monitoring, energy management, and networked personal video recording (PVR) distribution, will be increasingly visible. (HANs and the specifics of the CableHome specification are discussed in more detail at the end of this chapter.)

The Future of Cable TV Networks

The industry perspective is that within 10 to 15 years, cable networks will have evolved to a converged platform. Analog video will have ceased, and telephone will have migrated to VoIP, leaving only QAM-modulated downstream channels carry-ing MPEG transport stream packets. Some of those packets will carry video, and others will carry IP traffic, which might include voice, computer files, video, set-top box commands, or network management traffic. All upstream communications will be based on DOCSIS, including cable modem traffic, IP voice, and communi-cations from DOCSIS-enabled set-top boxes and gateways and system-monitoring devices. Encryption modules will be portable, allowing any set-top box to decrypt any transmission if properly authorized, and headend encryption will no longer be inseparable from multiplexing and modulation.

VOD is cable TV's fastest-growing new service category. Aside from providing additional service revenue, VOD is an essential tool in cable's competition with satel-lite. It exploits three inherent advantages that HFC networks have over direct broadcast satellite networks: greater raw information capacity, a broadband two-way connection, and a customer base that can be segmented into small groups. This combination allows the network to dynamically create and manage bidirectional information sessions with individual customers or groups of customers, which enables not only VOD but telephony, Internet access, and multiplayer interactive gaming.

The initial successes of VOD launches coupled with new flavors of on-demand, such as SVOD and free-on-demand (FOD), have strained network resources and raised new issues such as how to manage very large video libraries, update commercials and advertisement-supported content, and address network scaling and redundancy protection.

The eventual cessation of over-the-air and cable-carried analog broadcast television will greatly relieve the bandwidth crunch, even if some of that bandwidth is reassigned to expanding the upstream spectrum. Current estimates, however, are that this is not likely to happen until 2009 at the earliest. We have limited options for solving the immediate bandwidth problem: increasing the downstream bandwidth, decreasing the node sizes or subdividing the nodes, using more efficient digital video encoding, more efficiently sharing bandwidth between applications, using more aggressive modulation formats (such as 1024-QAM), or moving to switched real-time broadcasting. Also, advanced codecs such as MPEG-4 and Windows Media 9 (which are discussed in Chapter 10) promise a leaner bandwidth profile with potentially better picture quality. But introducing them onto MPEG-2-dominated networks isn't going to be easy or quick.

The proposed next-generation network architecture calls for a headend with the ability to transcode video, converting content there as opposed to converting it at a video storage hub further out in the network.

■ Fiber Solutions

As you've read many times in this book, fiber is an area of rapid evolution. Few other media options promise to offer the capacities of fiber. Where its deployment is possible, fiber is the clear-cut best solution. Fiber can be used on its own or in conjunction with twisted-pair, coax, and wireless to provide broadband access.

FTTx (fiber-to-the-*x*, where *x* means premises, curb, building, or home) solutions are gaining momentum as the best means for offering bundled services. Fiber-to-the-node (FTTN) is a solution in which fiber is run very close to the home—to the curb—and coax runs from the curb to the home. In addition, all-fiber networks can be used to deliver broadband services. Fiber-to-the-home/fiber-to-the-premises (FTTH/FTTP) goes a step further than FTTN—it brings fiber into the residence. In addition, a generation of technologies called *PONs* promises to dramatically reduce the cost of deploying FTTH/FTTP.

FTT*x*

FTT*x* solutions involve some key considerations for providers, including existing infrastructure and geographical density. The current FTT*x* market is primarily composed of municipalities, utilities, smaller independent and competitive local exchange carriers, MSOs, and incumbent telcos, although it is becoming of greater interest to others, such as ISPs. Most of the sector has focused on the residential home side. On the commercial and MDU fronts, it is believed that cable operators have a keen interest in plugging fiber directly into small and medium-sized businesses and apartment buildings. Incumbent telcos are expected to warm up to FTT*x* technologies as cable operators achieve more success with the video, voice, and data bundling strategies.

High equipment and construction costs have long been a barrier for FTT*x*, but costs are declining as the technology matures. Thanks to less expensive equipment and more efficient field operations, the costs are now nearly on par with those of advanced HFC architectures. New cable designs can reduce field deployment costs. Ribbon-style cables, which eliminate the jelly found in a traditional buffer tube, cut back on the cleaning and preparation time for field technicians. This reduces cable prep time and labor costs by more than 50%. Current FTT*x* expense figures, per connected home, range from US\$800 to US\$2,000. Of course, the price depends on the technology and the footprint reality.

Because FTT*x* is best suited for greenfield environments (i.e., environments that lack any constraints imposed by prior work), some providers see their main market as the international marketplace, where traditional infrastructures are not in place. How deep into the network should fiber be placed, and what will be the cost of replacing existing copper with fiber? The main architectural difference between major service providers is how far to drive the fiber toward the home.

As described in the following sections, there are two main FTT*x* options:

- **FTTN**—FTTN uses a variety of DSL technologies to optimize the copper bandwidth. When extending FTTN, the network takes advantage of existing copper or HFC plants to deliver services.
- **FTTH/FTTP**—This approach is being used today by MSOs.

FTTN

The biggest benefit of FTTN is that it takes advantage of the enormous amount of existing copper. The most important challenge—and disadvantage—is to squeeze sufficient capacity out of that plant to deliver triple-play services (voice, data, and video services) or, more specifically, video. In order to accommodate more bits per second down the transmission path, two techniques must be applied: Increase the usable bandwidth (i.e., provide a bigger frequency band), and strive to get greater bandwidth efficiency by enhancing the signal encoding, or modulation, technique (i.e., carry more bits per second per Hertz).

In the FTTN architecture, the fiber is extended to the serving area interface—that is, the point at which the telco's feeder cable connects to the local distribution cable (see Figure 12.6). The intended range of the copper connection is 1 mile (1.5 km), with the goal of delivering 25Mbps over that range. Two alternatives can be used to achieve this objective: bonded ADSL2+ and VDSL.

Given the 20Mbps to 30Mbps local connection supported by FTTN, not many digital video channels can be accommodated. Video over FTTN will require a new architecture to deliver high-quality multimedia content over a limited-capacity copper loop. In response to this challenge, the telcos are investigating the use of a packet-based architecture for video. Two IP video proposals are being considered at this time. One solution for packet-based video is the DSL Forum's (www.dslforum.org) IP video distribution technology. In this case, video packets are given priority based on setting the DiffServ control points in the IP headers. The other solution involves proprietary vendor-defined schemes.

Those pursuing an FTTN strategy are investigating new technologies that address three key areas: new technology for wire pair transmission, video compression, and packet video with appropriate and adequate channel-changing performance.

FTTH/FTTP

FTTH/FTTP takes fiber directly to the side of each home. The selected method depends on a number of demographic and financial considerations, but FTTH/FTTP offers the greatest potential for realizing the long-term end-user service

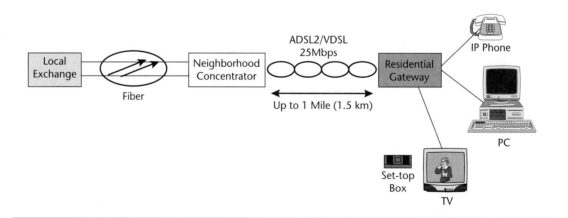

Figure 12.6 FTTN

needs. Accordingly, this is the most "future-proof" of the FTTx architectures. Basically, the closer to the subscriber the fiber is, the greater the potential bandwidth and improved performance.

A number of deployment scenarios are possible for FTTH/FTTP, but today one of the most popular is the use of PONs. The advantage of PONs is a lower cost per subscriber to provision the service initially. On the other hand, as Figure 12.7 indicates, because it is a system based on sharing wavelengths, a PON limits the bandwidth available, depending on the number of subscribers sharing the fiber. In addition, because it is a passive system (i.e., it makes use of nonpowered splitters to break out individual wavelengths to each subscriber), it also faces distance limitations. (PONs are discussed in detail in the following section.)

PONs

The most common fiber implementation today is the PON, which allows multiple buildings to share one access line. A PON is basically an FTTH/FTTP arrangement in which a single optical fiber serves multiple premises (currently up to 32). It is, in essence, a point-to-multipoint configuration, which reduces the amount of fiber required. Taking advantage of WDM, PONs allow for two-way traffic on a single fiber pair by making use of one wavelength for downstream traffic and another for upstream traffic.

PONs work by using passive optical splitters to split the power of the optical signal and route it to multiple subscribers. Eliminating active components reduces the distance the signal can travel, resulting in a theoretical range of about 12 miles (20 km) for a PON.

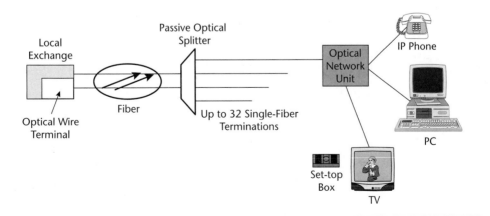

Figure 12.7 FTTH/FTTP

The concept with PONs is to share one fiber channel among up to 32 customers to deliver voice, data, and potentially video. This reduces costs by distributing the costs across more endpoints and replacing expensive add/drop multiplexers (ADMs) or DWDM nodes with optical splitters and couplers at each fiber connection in the network. Downstream signals, broadcast to each premise using a shared fiber, are encrypted to prevent eavesdropping. Upstream bandwidth is allocated by assigning a time slot to each subscriber when the user has traffic to send.

PON Architecture

As shown in Figure 12.8, the basic PON configuration includes the following components:

■ **Optical line terminal (OLT)**—This device broadcasts downstream transmissions to all premises devices. The traffic sent is a series of ATM cells or Ethernet frames. Each downstream cell or frame is addressed, and each ONU selects the cells or frames addressed to it. The OLT also handles the upstream return from subscribers. OLTs can be implemented in the local exchange or on a next-generation digital loop carrier (NGDLC) system.

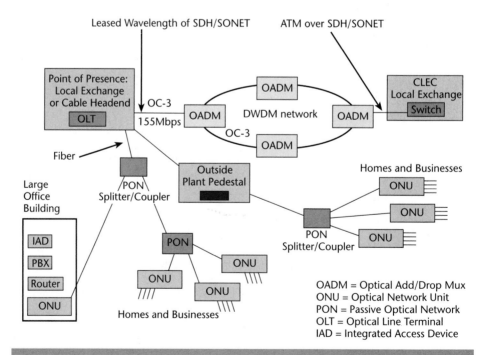

Figure 12.8 PON architecture

- **Optical network units (ONUs)**—ONUs are premises devices that share one upstream channel on a time division basis. Upstream channel access is assigned using TDMA. If a given user device has no traffic to send, it transmits idle signals.
- **End-user interfaces**—For voice services, the ONU provides a standard analog tip-and-ring interface; for data services, a 10/100BASE-T Ethernet network is used for delivery of service; and for video services, a traditional coaxial cable interface is used.

PONs bundle multiple wavelengths (up to 32) so they can be carried over a single access line from the carrier's local exchange to a manhole or controlled environmental vault (CEV) close to a group of customer sites. Passive optical splitters reside inside CEVs. As the light broadcast from the OLT hits the splitter, it is deflected onto multiple fiber connections, depending on the splitter used. (*Passive* means the splitters don't need any power—they work like a prism, splitting light into the colors of the rainbow—so there is nothing to wear out or go wrong.) Splitters feature 2 to 32 branches and can be positioned to create PON star, ring, or tree configurations. From the customer to the local exchange, each site is given a specific time slot to transmit, using a polling scheme.

Types of PONs

There are three main types of PONs:

- **ATM PON (APON)**—APONs are standardized by the ITU-T under recommendation G.983.x. The key advantage of this type of PON is that traditional telcos have already invested heavily in ATM. ITU G.983.3 adds wavelengths for video and private wavelength services.
- **Ethernet PON (EPON)**—The EPON standards are being developed in the Ethernet First Mile committee, IEEE 802.3ah. They stress cost advantages.
- **Gigabit PON (GPON)**—The GPON standards—ITU-T G.984.1, G.984.2, and G.984.3—stress significant savings in capital and operating expenditures, QoS/CoS assurance, and extensible network architecture.

APONs, EPONs, and GPONs all operate over a single fiber and use different wavelengths for transmissions upstream (around 1,300 nm) and downstream (around 1,500 nm). Multiple users share the upstream and downstream channels. In APONs, the downstream channel operates at 155Mbps or 622Mbps, and the upstream channel operates at 155Mbps. A symmetrical 622Mbps standard is being developed. The total usable capacity is 448Mbps. APONs use a separate wavelength around 1,550 nm to carry analog video, digital video, or dedicated wavelength services. EPONs typically operate symmetrically at 1.25Gbps, with a usable capacity of 612Mbps. GPONs operate at 2.5Gbps, with a usable capacity of 2.36Gbps.

Passive optical splitters/combiners are used to split the power of the optical signal and route it to multiple customers. A separate wavelength around 1,550 nm can also be used to carry analog video, as do the HFC configurations now used in cable TV. The maximum transmission range is theoretically about 12 miles (20 km). Each splitter reduces the power of the optical signal, so the range is reduced as splitters are added.

The Future of PONs

One of the key issues related to PONs is the availability of fiber; we still face a shortage of fiber in access networks. PONs also have distance limitations due to their passive nature. Eliminating active components reduces the distance the signal can travel, resulting in a theoretical range of about 12 miles (20 km). Another key issue is that users share the bandwidth, as with cable modems.

Optimizing splitter ratios is important to reducing hardware costs and saving labor time. Remember that optical splitters are used to enable a single optical fiber to serve multiple locations. The purpose of the splitter is to divide the power of an optical signal, meaning it divides the total received light into two or more outputs. Split ratios—that is, the number of subscribers that can be served by that single fiber—can range from 2 to 32, and sometimes more. This is determined by the layout of the neighborhood, including lot sizes, home placement, total development shape and size, distance from the headend, and so on. An additional factor to consider is the proximity of homes. For example, with homes placed close to each other, the fiber loss due to the distance from the headend is not an issue. In this case, using 1×8 optical splitters reduces the hardware costs while maintaining a similar quality level.

With PONs it is also important to manage the fear factor—that is, to minimize the use of underground vaults and rely more on proper placement, accurate documentation, appropriate location schemes and devices, and control of the resource mapping. Up to half the cost of a PON project is in the onsite labor. Field location must be carefully managed. For example, it is important to consider that the material may not be on the site when needed, there may not be documentation of the headend or local exchange layout, project plans may be out-of-date, splice enclosures/splitters may be placed incorrectly, installation time may be incorrectly estimated, and labor needs to be overseen to ensure proper installation.

PONs significantly reduce the cost of provisioning fiber to the subscriber. They are of increasing interest to independent and local telcos, MSOs, utilities, and municipalities. However, shared channel and bandwidth limitations may impose restrictions in terms of long-term usability.

▪ Wireless Broadband

Broadband wireless access is an increasingly exciting option, especially because cable modems and DSL are not always available as easily and as widely as we would like. Wireless broadband access provides the opportunity to make use of many new technologies, including wireless local area networks (WLANs), such as the popular IEEE 802.11x standards; and wireless metropolitan area networks (WMANs), including recent IEEE 802.16 WiMax specifications along with several proprietary systems, including Direct Broadcast Satellite (DBS), Free Space Optics, and virtual fiber (VF). Wireless systems increasingly offer more options, each of which promises greater speeds, supports QoS, and operates over a wider range of footprints.

It is likely that within the next couple years, more than half of the new fixed phone lines installed worldwide each year will be wireless. Fixed wireless is a strong contender to fill the gap where existing wiring is not up to the job or where there is no wiring at all. For example, about one in five people in the United States lives in an area that is too remote to receive any type of fast wireline access to the Internet, and this is an even more prevalent situation in vast but not densely populated parts of Africa, Asia, Eastern Europe, and Latin America. Further, millions of people work in modest industrial parks that do not have fast access and are not able to receive DSL, cable, or fiber connections. Wireless broadband can often be used in such situations.

The cost of wireless links has been halving every seven years, and the data capacity of these links has been doubling every three years. These factors combined mean that the cost-to-capacity ratio in wireless communications has been dropping by 50% about every two years. For wireless links, the construction costs account for approximately 20% of the total installation cost, and equipment accounts for the other 80%.

Wireless systems often operate in a point-to-multipoint mode. The antenna communicates with several different clients' antennas, usually installed within a well-defined region. Because the air is a shared medium, like cable, the maximum transmission rate that can be provided to any one client decreases as more clients are served. Clients that need the greatest bit rate obtainable from a system (e.g., an ISP) may need to arrange for a point-to-point system.

Because there are now so many wireless alternatives available, Part IV of this book is dedicated entirely to wireless communications. Chapter 13, "Wireless Communications Basics," introduces the history and other basics of wireless communications. Chapters 14 and 15 discuss all the wireless standards, systems, and options in detail. Chapter 16, "Emerging Wireless Applications," describes the handset revolution and the increasing number of applications driving the need for next-generation wireless technologies.

■ Broadband PLT

In an increasingly competitive market for broadband technology, powerline broadband—often referred to as powerline telecommunications (PLT), broadband over powerlines (BPL), or powerline communication (PLC)—has emerged as a darkhorse technology in a market that is becoming increasingly saturated by DSL and cable modem alternatives. PLT is a wireline technology that uses the current electricity networks for data and voice transmission. It offers a vision that would allow electrical utilities to provide high-speed Internet, voice, data, and video services to customers of all classes via power transmission and distribution lines.

The concept of PLT is not new. It came to be in the 1920s, although the application then was the protection of power transmission lines, as well as telemetry, remote system control, and voice communication. PLT today includes BPL, which infers data rates above 1Mbps, and narrowband over powerlines, which involves much lower data rates. The power company can communicate voice and data by superimposing an analog signal over the standard 50Hz or 60Hz alternating current (AC). Traditionally, electrical utilities have used low-speed powerline carrier circuits for control of substations, voice communication, and protection of high-voltage transmission lines. However, in the broadband race, high-speed data transmission has been developed using the lower-voltage transmission lines used for power distribution. There is also a short-range form of powerline carrier used for intercoms and home automation.

There are three distinct applications for powerline communication:

■ **Outdoor long-haul or broadband access**—BPL can be used as a broadband access, or local loop, alternative.

■ **Indoor short-haul or home area networking**—Home area networking refers to the use of powerline within the home or residence domain. (HANs are covered in detail later in this chapter.)

■ **Automotive applications**—Automotive applications enable in-vehicle network communications—whether voice, data, video, or music signals—by digital means over direct current (DC) battery powerline. The automotive applications include mechatronics (for functions such as obstacle detection, door control, and climate control) as well as support for telematics and multimedia.

PLT Architecture

As shown in Figure 12.9, PLT works by injecting the digital connection into the powerline on the consumer side of a low-voltage substation. The injection point

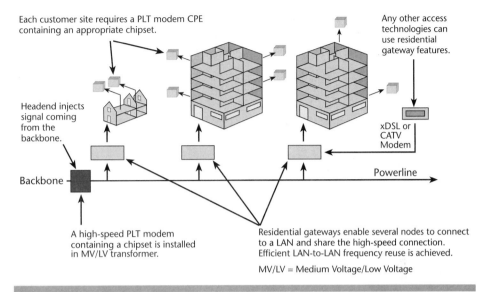

Each customer site requires a PLT modem CPE containing an appropriate chipset.

Any other access technologies can use residential gateway features.

Headend injects signal coming from the backbone.

xDSL or CATV Modem

Backbone

Powerline

A high-speed PLT modem containing a chipset is installed in MV/LV transformer.

Residential gateways enable several nodes to connect to a LAN and share the high-speed connection. Efficient LAN-to-LAN frequency reuse is achieved.

MV/LV = Medium Voltage/Low Voltage

Figure 12.9   An example of PLT

is connected to a fiber backbone by any appropriate means. This could be a wireless connection in a rural area or a DSL or cable modem in an urban area. Utility companies use conditioning units that act as multiplexers to transmit low- and high-frequency signals. The lower-frequency signals carry power, and the higher-frequency signals carry data and voice. The conditioning units are part of a high-frequency conditioned power network (HFCPN) and send signals to outlets in the home or office. These signals are received by boxes similar to cable modems in the home and can link numerous devices, from microwave ovens to PCs.

When PLT technology is used to provide broadband Internet access, it is called BPL; simply put, it is the distribution of IP-based services over powerline infrastructure. In this case, a computer or other digital device only needs to plug a BPL modem into any outlet in a facility (home or building) equipped for high-speed Internet access. The most obvious advantage of BPL over DSL or cable modems is the extensive availability of power infrastructure; while not everyone has telephone lines or cable TV installed, most everyone does have power, so PLT enables more people in more locations to gain access to the Internet. On the other hand, the lack of standards for powerline as an access technology means that there is no standard provisioning of the service—there is no well-established process that can be repeated over and over. And of course, there are differences in the physical characteristics of the electricity network. There are also questions about the total bandwidth BPL can provide as compared to DSL or cable modems.

BPL makes use of the electric circuit between the electric substations and home networks; one standard used for this application is ETSI PLT. PLT modems transmit in medium and high frequency—that is, the 1.6MHz to 30MHz electric carrier. The asymmetric speed in the modem is usually from 256Kbps to 2.7Mbps. The speed in the repeater, located in the meter room, is up to 45Mbps, and up to 256 PLT modems can be connected. In the medium-voltage stations, the speed from the headends to the Internet is up to 135Mbps. Utilities use either optical fiber or wireless links to connect to the Internet.

In the access network, current technology can deliver speeds of up to 45Mbps, while in the home networking applications, up to 200Mbps is possible using the HomgPlug AV standard. (HAN technologies and powerline standards are explored at the end of this chapter.) QoS and CoS capabilities can be implemented by using PLT technologies, which is a critical feature in support of real-time and streaming media applications.

A recent PLT development is the use of microwave frequencies that employ new propagation mechanisms that permit much higher-speed transmission using a single powerline conductor. The experimental work thus far indicates that there is potential for over 1Gbps in each direction, supporting symmetric and full-duplex communication. Trials have also demonstrated that analog TV along with multiple Wi-Fi channels can operate simultaneously in the 2.4GHz and 5.3GHz unlicensed bands over medium-voltage lines.

The Future of PLT

As with any other technology, there are weaknesses associated with PLT. It is estimated that more than 80 PLT initiatives in more than 40 countries have been launched, worldwide, by electric utilities. Pilot sites, technological or commercial trials, and deployments are numerous in Europe. The largest technology dilemma hinges on finding a reliable way to send data on powerlines without causing interference for either data or electrical signals. There are also issues with the number of users PLT can reach and the distance over which it can travel while still providing good-quality data and voice transmission.

Powerline solutions, like phone line solutions, are unintentional radiators. Emissions can potentially cause interference with radio, television, cable TV, telephone, and DSL services. There can also be disruption of the data signals due to noise interference produced by the electronic equipment already on the powerlines, not to mention signal loss over longer distances. In discussing broadband over powerline, there has been for some discussion about the extent to which this technology creates radio frequency interference (RFI). For many, this concern is irrelevant, but for those who work with sensitive instrumentation, it is a legitimate problem. Most of this RFI can be traced to high-voltage powerline solutions, but Motorola has recently produced a low-voltage solution, called Powerline LV, that the company claims eliminates RFI. From a market perspective, WLAN alternatives pose a serious competitive threat to PLT. In addition, PLT's maximum access speed depends on a shared connection, shared by all the users connected to the same local network station, so the more people simultaneously using the Internet, the lower the obtained speed.

PLT technology is still in its early stages, and there was no global technology standard for the use of PLT as a broadband access line in place until early 2006. The Open PLC European Research Alliance (OPERA; www.ist-opera.org), a European initiative to develop BPL technologies and specifications, has been busy working on developing such standards. The OPERA group links European universities and companies developing chips and equipment for broadband and utilities. The group suggests that its standard will be the only really open PLT system that ensures full interoperability for broadband access and in-building distribution systems without recourse to proprietary technologies. After two years of development, a consortium of industry specialists from 35 organizations (including 10 universities), supported by the European Commission, developed a specification based on a marketing and functional requirement blueprint ratified by OPERA. In February 2006, OPERA announced the approval of the first open global specification for PLC access, also known as BPL. This specification will accelerate mass rollout of high-speed, low-cost broadband access, voice, and audiovisual services, as well as utility applications for control and management operations. (The specification, together with an "OPERA Technology White Paper," can be freely downloaded from the Project Outputs section of the OPERA Web site.)

PLT's interference problem is being addressed by developments that use OFDM. As discussed in Chapter 13, OFDM divides available spectrum into small paths that are overlapped and spaced perpendicular to each other. The greater the overlapping, the more paths can be handled. While each path has a low data rate, together they offer a higher rate and more efficient use of the spectrum. By using small data packets inside the home—where distribution could be interrupted by electrical devices being turned on and off—only a little bit of data might be lost rather than the whole signal.

PLT suffers from distance limitations: It can reach about 2 miles (3 km) with a very low bandwidth or a few hundred yards offering several Mbps. However, unlike with DSL, most premises worldwide are within 300 yards (100 m) of an electricity substation. Vendors are working on extending the reach.

There are significant differences between the electrical distribution systems around the world, and these differences affect the implementation of BPL. For example, in North America, relatively few homes are connected to each distribution transformer, while in Europe, hundreds of homes may be connected to each substation. BPL signals do not propagate through distribution transformers, and additional equipment is therefore required in the North American market. Because of differences in the way the electrical grids are designed, Europe and Asia will most likely see PLT before the United States does. In European systems, electricity is sent to the customer at between 220 and 240 volts, as compared to 110 volts in the United States. The high power throughput means a European substation can serve 100 to 300 homes, while in the United States, a substation can reach only about 8 to 10 homes. Furthermore, U.S. interest in PLT is limited because of the proliferation of existing last-mile technologies such as DSL and cable modems, particularly in urban areas. Many people believe that DSL, cable modems, and fiber alternatives may ultimately outweigh the potential for PLT in Europe as well.

Still, with more than 3 billion users worldwide, the penetration of the electricity networks is almost ubiquitous, bringing access to a global communications infrastructure within reach of the majority of people, without the need for heavy infrastructure costs. However, xDSL and cable modems have already made significant headway, and PONs are enjoying widespread popularity at the moment, while PLT technology is still in the early stages of deployment. As mentioned at the beginning of this chapter, there are many issues to consider when attempting to determine the best solution, as a provider and as a consumer; the choice depends on the prevailing conditions.

■ HANs

Smart devices, such as the many devices discussed in this book's introduction, need channels over which to communicate, so the more computers, communications devices, entertainment vehicles, and intelligent appliances and accessories present in a home (such as home automation or security tools), the greater the likelihood that they all need a home network—a HAN—over which to exchange information in order to realize their true value.

The emergence of intelligent appliances also opens up an entirely new level of market involvement. It creates a new outlet for knowledge, content, and information services that can be offered by online experts and service providers. A smart appliance acts as a vehicle for stimulating interest in activities that benefit from using the appliance. In essence, the appliance becomes a part of a collaborative system that satisfies a much higher human need. Basically, a smart device needs a reason to exist, and that reason is a continually developing set of applications and services with which to better our lives. It is therefore important to look beyond the last mile and at technologies that apply in home area networking.

The HAN Market, Applications, and Elements

Broadband deployments are accelerating. As of early 2006, on the order of 200 million broadband access lines had been deployed worldwide. Traditionally, broadband deployments have focused on core networks and on the last mile (i.e., the local loop). But the last mile is really only half of the broadband solution. Simplicity and user-friendliness are driving rapid penetration of intelligence into all the various home elements. The HAN—which is the last 330 feet (100 m)—brings the broadband access solution closer to completion. (Ultimately, broadband access will need to extend to the individual—the domain of PANs—and then right *into* the individual—the realm of intelligent implants, as discussed in the introduction.) Therefore, we can expect to see the global market for home networking equipment rise substantially. Many expect the home data and entertainment networking market as well as the connectivity services market to be worth billions of dollars. Connectivity products will offer additional voice management, home monitoring, and entertainment services. The service provider will begin to move its area of domain into the home, offering broadband access along with home area networking technology, smart appliances, and bundled applications. Service providers today see the home network as a competitive necessity as well as a source of revenue. In fact, the home network is now considered part of the service provider network.

Home networking is substantially different from enterprise networking. The traffic patterns are different, the applications are different, and the transmission media available to carry the information are different. Home users, whether consumer or professional users, will need to network computers and peripherals, and they will need a residential gateway to access their broadband connection and allow it to be shared among multiple devices. They will also want additional services, such as VoIP, support for interactive multiplayer games, and streaming entertainment media. Although new homes are increasingly wired with Cat 5 cable or fiber, most existing homes are not. The most common choices for HAN media are generally phone lines, powerlines, and wireless technologies. As discussed shortly, each presents a unique set of advantages and disadvantages.

We will certainly be developing quite a complex HAN infrastructure, which might include the components shown in Figure 12.10. The product range includes transceivers or communications interfaces, network interface cards for the various devices participating on the network, gateways, servers, sensors, controllers, and some form of operating system. A variety of broadband services—including DSL, coax cable, fiber, wireless, and hybrid arrangements—are all possible. Those services will terminate on the home network gateway, which will connect to some form of a communications hub, a residential gateway device that can then split the signals and deliver them to the proper receivers. From the residential gateway there will then be several different networks. The automation and control network may

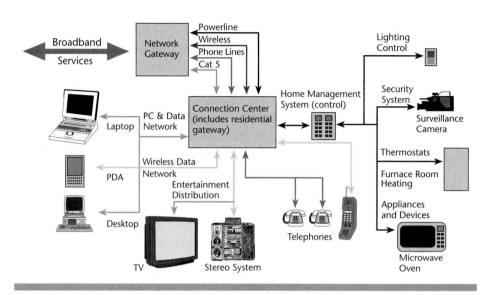

Figure 12.10 Home networking elements

include the various sensors that help automate the home to make life easier and happier. Mobility networks will be wireless networks that allow a user to roam within the range of a home and the outdoor area surrounding it.

Computer interconnection is one of the major applications of HANs. It allows access to the Internet and the connection and communication of multiple PCs with various peripherals and communications and entertainment devices. This computer connection requires very high-speed networks. Generally, homes with two or more computers are considered to be prime candidates for this type of HAN. In addition, controlling the home—including managing lights, appliances, climate control systems, and surveillance cameras—will be a huge market for HANs.

Types of HANs

Several different technologies can be applied in HANs. The home network is likely to become a layered network, just like the enterprise network, where there's a need for backbone networks, mobility networks, control networks, and wired networks, each of which is best served by one or another alternative. The success of HANs depends on standard products that are operable with a variety of physical infrastructures, so we'll see the use of voice-grade telephony wiring, coax, electric powerlines, wireless, and fiber. The wireless approach has by far the greatest penetration today, using the popular Wi-Fi standard for wireless LANs.

HANs over Phone Lines

One approach to HANs is the use of existing phone lines (see Figure 12.11). The Home Phone Networking Alliance (HomePNA; www.homepna.org) is a major interest group in this space. HomePNA, which is composed of more than 150 companies, is an incorporated nonprofit association, and more than 25% of it member companies are outside the United States. HomePNA's main objective is to work toward establishing and ensuring compatibility with standards among telecom, computer, and network products. Although HomePNA does not enforce standards, it does advise the ITU-T. And although it does not actually manufacture any products, it does endorse products as being HomePNA certified.

HomePNA develops triple-play HAN solutions, supporting multimedia home networking services, such as VoIP, data, and SDTV/HDTV, over existing phone or coax lines. The technology provides data rates up to 240Mbps, with guaranteed QoS, enabling service providers to support multimedia services in the home, including in-home distribution of broadcast IPTV and networked PVRs.

The HomePNA specification has been through several versions. The most current is HomePNA 3.0. (The 2.0 version was approved by the ITU-T as a global standard and is formally known as Recommendation G.989.1, with subsequent upgrades to G.989.2 and G.989.3.) HomePNA 3.0, announced in 2003, allows the

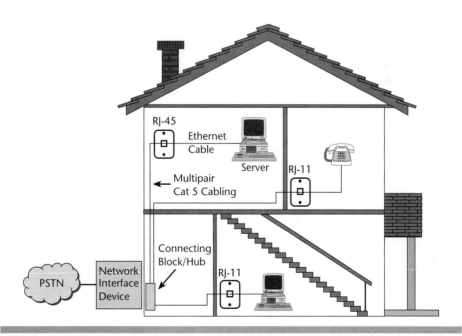

Figure 12.11   A HAN over phone lines

networking of home computers over what looks like a LAN, using existing telephone or coax wiring. Given this capability, multiple computers can share Internet access and access to various peripherals (such as printers or storage devices), files, or multiplayer games without the need for a router. HomePNA 3.0 makes use of different frequencies for the data streams than for the basic phone traffic. A frequency reserved and prioritized for phone and fax calls allows them to take precedence over any other data communications. HomePNA 3.0, standardized by the ITU-T as G.9954, has been selected by major service providers in North America and Europe. A number of companies have working products moving toward production, and manufacturers are demonstrating gateways, set-top boxes, and devices with embedded interfaces.

HANs over Powerlines

Figure 12.12 shows an example of a powerline HAN. The main advantage of the powerline approach to home area networking is that it's an ideal architecture for data networks because the majority of devices must connect to a power source in order to operate in the first place. Another advantage is that, as with phone lines, no RF conversion hardware is necessary, so the cost can be lower than that of wireless solutions. However, powerlines are considered to be a harsh environment for communications, and that is the main disadvantage of this method.

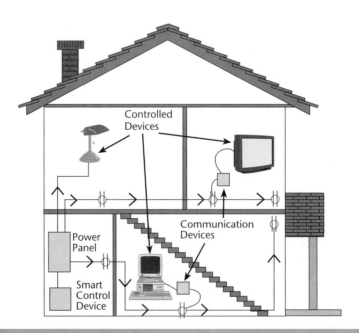

Figure 12.12 A powerline HAN

In the home network scenario, there are likely to be many stubs with terminating loads of various impedances. At some frequencies, the transmitted signal may arrive at the receiver with little loss, while at others, it may be very noisy. Typical sources of noise are dimmer switches, switching power supplies, brush motors, and halogen and fluorescent lamps. In addition, the conditions on the powerline change, for instance, as users plug in new devices. This means that the nature of the channel between outlets may vary a great deal, resulting in differences in the quality of transmission as well as the amount of bandwidth available to carry data.

Another issue is that the flexibility of a PLT HAN depends on the availability and placement of the power sources. Another important consideration is the topology of the power distribution to the home. In the United States, a distribution transformer provides power to a small number of homes (8 to 10). While the distribution transformer does a good job of blocking the powerline networking signals from crossing into the main power grid, it does not prevent signals from crossing between homes powered by the same distribution transformer. This means that the networking signals from your home could show up on the powerline in any of the other homes served by the same source, creating privacy and security concerns similar to those experienced with wireless networks. In order to provide a reliable communications channel over powerline, the proposed solution must include both robust physical layer (PHY) specifications and an efficient MAC protocol. Again, the PHY defines the basic packet formats, coding, and modulation, and the MAC protocol controls how multiple clients share the medium.

The HomePlug Powerline Alliance (www.homeplug.com) plays a critical role with its global HomePlug standard for PLT. HomePlug-certified products connect computers and peripherals that use Ethernet, USB, and IEEE 802.11. The HomePlug Powerline Alliance certifies products for HomgPlug compliance so that devices carrying its certification mark are interoperable. There are two versions of HomePlug:

- **HomePlug 1.0**—HomePlug 1.0 enables speed up to 14Mbps.
- **HomePlug 2.0**—Also known as HomePlug AV, HomePlug 2.0 promises a raw data rate of up to 200Mbps, although the practical throughput is closer to 100Mbps. This new standard, while compatible with HomePlug 1.0, can support VoIP and HDTV.

The alliance is also now working on a HomePlug BPL standard.

Through the use of OFDM modulation, which allows coexistence of several distinct data carriers in the same wire pair, HomePlug brings back the ability to use Ethernet in a bus topology. To deal with the noise problems inherent in the powerline medium, the HomePlug technology uses OFDM as the basic transmission technique. (OFDM, which is widely used in DSL technology and in numerous wireless systems, is discussed in Chapter 13.) It also makes use of a combination of sophisticated forward error correction (FEC), interleaving, error detection, and automatic repeat request (ARQ) to ensure that the channel appears reliable to the network-layer protocols.

A nonprofit organization called the Consumer Electronics Powerline Communication Alliance (CEPCA; www.cepca.org) has been formed by Sony (www.sony.com), Mitsubishi (www.mitsubishi.com), and Panasonic (www.panasonic.com). A company with a global effort, CEPCA's main mission is to promote and continuously advance high-speed PLT technology to use and implement a new generation of consumer electronics products through the rapid, broad, and open industry adoption of CEPCA specifications. It is important to note that the alliance's main purpose is to promote coexistence rather than to develop a specific technology; in fact, the founders are currently making use of four or more technologies. CEPCA will be working on promoting coexistence in the United States, Europe, and China and encouraging PLT deregulation in Japan while also submitting proposals to the IEEE, ETSI PLT, and PLC-J (in Japan).

In January 2006, Panasonic debuted its new HD-PLC Ethernet adapter, which supports up to 190Mbps data speed over a range of 500 feet (150 m). HD-PLC makes it possible to connect, over one unified network, high-definition video content, music playback, Internet gaming, VoIP phone service, color video monitoring, and computers and peripherals. The new adapter also addresses security, automatically setting AES 128-bit encryption with the push of a setup button on each unit. To address the noise and interference issues present in the powerline medium, HD-PLC uses OFDM and sophisticated error control to ensure the highest-quality transmission and reliability in the face of noise and interference. Quite a few other players are also creating hardware PLT HAN devices.

Another PLT standard is X10 Ltd.'s (www.x10.com) standard X10. X10 is a communications protocol for remote control of electrical devices and communications over standard household AC powerline wiring (with off, on, and dim functions). Manufacturers of home appliances can design and embed X10 transmitters in them, and the receiving and control devices are made by X10 Ltd. itself.

The Consumer Electronic Bus (CEBus) home networking standard is for multiple alternatives, including powerlines. The CEBus effort began in 1984, when members of the EIA identified a need for standards that included more than on, off, dim, bright, all lights on, and all units off controls. After six years of meeting on a regular basis, the engineers proposed the CEBus standard. The standard was released in 1992, presenting an open architecture set of specification documents that define protocols for how to make products communicate through powerline wires, low-voltage twisted-pair, coax, infrared, RF, and fiber. Presently, the CEBus communications hardware, language, and protocol are available on a chip produced by Intellon Corporation (www.intellon.com). Having moved out of the laboratory and into the market, the CEBus trademark is now owned by the EIA.

Ongoing developments are being conducted by the CEBus Industry Council (www. cebus.org), a nonprofit organization made up of representatives of many national and international electronics firms, such as Microsoft (www.microsoft.com), IBM (www.ibm.com), Honeywell (www.honeywell.com), Panasonic (www.panasonic. com), and Sony (www.sony.com).

Wireless HANs

Figure 12.13 shows an example of a wireless HAN. Wireless HANs have advantages as well as disadvantages. The main advantage of a wireless HAN is that it provides an untethered solution for devices that need mobility in communications. I adore my wireless LAN, specifically for that reason. I can take my work where I want it, within my grounds, and not worry about being near a phone jack, although a power connection is a consideration.

One disadvantage is that a multitude of standards address wireless HANs, including the following:

- **802.11**—IEEE 802.11, Wi-Fi, originally supported 1Mbps to 2Mbps, in the 2.4GHz range. The IEEE has since published three supplements to the 802.11 standard: 802.11a (55Mbps in the 5GHz band, with actual throughput closer to 27Mbps), 802.11b (11Mbps in the 2.4GHz band, with actual

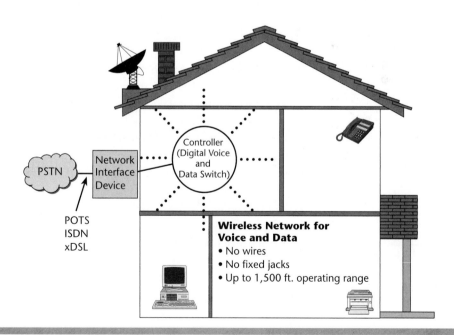

Figure 12.13 A wireless HAN

throughput closer to 5.5Mbps), and 802.11g (55Mbps in the 5GHz band, with actual throughput closer to 27Mbps). The greatest advantage of Wi-Fi is its simplicity. You can connect computers anywhere in the home or office without the need for wires. The 802.11 and other short-range wireless technologies are discussed in detail in Chapter 15.

■ **Bluetooth**—The Bluetooth Consortium (www.bluetooth.com) deals with networks that operate over very short ranges (about 100 feet [30 m]), but more and more devices are being created to work in these ranges. Approximately 2,500 manufacturers have signed up to incorporate Bluetooth into their products, which is a very important step in the growth of wireless. (Chapter 15 discusses the details of Bluetooth.)

Another disadvantage of wireless HANs is that generally, depending on the type of wireless network or standard selected, there may be bandwidth limitations. But more importantly, wireless also has unresolved security issues, network infringement issues, interference from other wireless sources, and various performance issues. (Chapter 13 discusses wireless behavior, and Chapter 15 describes the wireless communication standards applicable to home area networking in more detail.)

Control Networks

Control networks are typically low-speed powerline networks (see Figure 12.14). The most widely used technologies for home automation and control purposes are based on three standards:

■ **LonWorks**—Echelon Corporation's LonWorks (www.lonworks.com) is an open standard under EIA 709 that provides a solution to the many problems of designing, building, installing, and maintaining control networks. LonWorks networks can range in size from 2 to 32,000 devices and can be used in everything from supermarkets to petroleum plants, aircraft to railway cars, fusion lasers to slot machines, single-family homes to skyscrapers. The trend now is to move away from proprietary control schemes and centralized systems to open, off-the-shelf chips, operating systems, and parts to build products. The LonWorks protocol is now embedded in silicon neuron chips from Cypress Semiconductor (www.cypress.com), Toshiba America (www.toshiba.com), and other companies. Dozens of manufacturers are incorporating these chips into their modules for controlling household electrical equipment, providing interoperability, robust technology, faster development, and scale economics.

■ **X10**—As mentioned earlier in this chapter, X10 is a communications protocol for remote control of electrical devices and communications over stan-

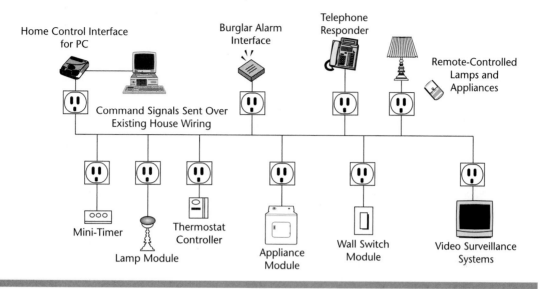

Figure 12.14 A control network

dard household AC powerline wiring (with off, on, and dim functions). X10 Ltd. publishes the specifications, manufacturers can embed the transmitters into their appliances, and X10 Ltd. manufactures and sells the receiving and control devices.

■ **CEBus**—CEBus, as discussed earlier in this chapter, is an open standard that specifies the technology and parameters for communications using powerlines, Cat 5 twisted-pair, coax, wireless, and infrared. It is based on EIA 600.

Advantages of control networks include the fact that there are existing product solutions and well-established industry standards. Control networks also have relatively low cost and simple implementation. The disadvantage is that these networks are not designed to support real-time, high-bandwidth, or mobility requirements, so the value proposition of standalone applications does not offer the incentives for the mainstream market to consume the products.

Wired HANs

Wired HANs include Universal Serial Bus (USB), Category 5 or 10BASE-T wiring, and IEEE 1394 (FireWire). The benefits of wired HANs are that wired network standards are reliable and robust. The drawbacks of wired networks are that penetrating the mass market requires a "no new wires" technology. These solutions, therefore, will primarily extend only to new homes that are making use of structured wiring and perhaps to the technophile hobbyist and professional home user market.

HAN Gateways and Servers

A HAN requires a system for identifying data and routing it to its destination, and this implies the need for gateways and servers. A residential gateway connects a HAN to the Internet. A hardware device similar in appearance to a router, it provides many features necessary in a HAN. Most residential gateways support at least the basic features of broadband connectivity (usually through DSL or cable modems), sharing of the Internet connection, and firewall security. In addition, as we progress toward support of advanced multimedia applications, the residential gateway will also interact with the home telephone, entertainment systems, kitchen and home appliances, and the entire new generation of network-enabled devices.

At this point, gateway products are in their early stages, and the technical standards are therefore evolving. One important standard is CableLabs CableHome, which has two specifications:

- **CableHome 1.0**—The CableHome 1.0 specification achieved international standardization in 2002 as ITU document J.191. CableHome 1.0 provides for handoff, authentication, and provisioning of the gateway; secure remote management and configuration; home device visibility and connectivity tests; cable and application-friendly address translation; protection of the cable network from in-home traffic; firewall management and rule set downloading; and local name service.

- **CableHome 1.1**—In 2004, the CableHome 1.1 specification also gained international standardization, as the ITU-approved document J.192. CableHome 1.1 introduced features requested by cable operators, allowing them to enhance their home networking service offerings. CableHome 1.1 improves on the features available in CableHome 1.0 and adds gateway security features; standardized prioritized QoS for HANs; support for home servers, teleworkers, and home offices; simple parental control; and LAN management messaging and LAN IP statistics monitoring.

Planning for the Future of HANs

HANs are becoming a fundamental aspect of a person's residence, and they will become more functional and important as we go forward into the realm of interactive and mobile multimedia lifestyles. In considering HANs, it is important to plan for the future. You need to plan and install an infrastructure designed to address today's needs, and you also need to understand that tomorrow you will need to support much more advanced applications and a greater range of devices. It is a good idea to stay away from permanent equipment that will become obsolete soon. You should try not to choose products that limit your ability to change or upgrade in the future, and you should try to ensure that the infrastructure stays invisible.

You should consider a number of other points going forward, as more and more intelligence surrounds you and becomes self-aware in an attempt to serve you even better:

- Who is in control in the smart house?
- Does the house's behavior act consistently with the image you would like to project?
- Does the house now have a personality of its own?
- What happens when the power goes off? More importantly, what happens when the house crashes? Do you get locked in forever?

These are issues we will resolve in time. Security is going to be quite important to all of this, and although security solutions do not abound, there has been significant progress in the areas of encryption, authentication, and key exchange. Much additional development is being done in this area, including the use of biometrics.

Part IV

Wireless Communications

Chapter 13

Wireless Communications Basics

Most people consider mobility to be one of their most cherished abilities and rights. In fact, what do we take away from those who have been deemed injurious to their fellow humans? Mobility. The freedom afforded by mobility is very precious.

One area in which we like to exercise our freedom of mobility is at work, and the mobile workforce is growing all the time. Market researchers and industry analysts expect the number of mobile workers to continue to grow worldwide. Given this trend, a company's performance and productivity will increasingly depend on understanding, managing, controlling, and securing technologies and tools that enable its mobile workers. Included in this mix of solutions are both remote and mobile network access, enabling connectivity to enterprise networks, applications, and data while away from the office, using a variety of devices, including notebooks, PDAs, and emerging mobile devices. Without reliable and secure mobile access to enterprise networks, mobile workers will not be able to be productive.

Another area in which we want to use our freedom to be mobile is with the Internet. The mobile Internet is already a reality in many places, and it will become more prevalent everywhere in the near future, as more and more Internet-ready mobile phones and other wireless devices make their way into people's pockets, accessories, and clothing. According to Ray Kurzweil, in his brilliant book *The Age of Spiritual Machines*, wireless is predicted to become the dominant form of access to the Internet by 2009. Mobile entertainment is yet another application area, with interest and services growing daily. These trends, as well as the trend toward machine-to-machine communications, sensor-based networks, and portable computing in the form of wearables, contribute to our avid interest in wireless communications and systems.

We used to think of wireline facilities as the default and of wireless as something extra that needed to be justified. Wireless was traditionally justified only in situations such as when wire could not be physically applied (e.g., in a jungle, in a desert, on a mountaintop); when wire could not be economically justified (e.g., when the expense of burying cable was too great); when time was an issue (the time to deploy a cable system can range from 9 to 18 months, while wireless systems can be deployed in 3 to 6 months); and of course, when mobility was a requirement. We are now beginning to see mixed-media approaches (including both wireline and wireless solutions), depending on the situation. For example, we may want to bring fiber as close as possible to an end node, but to engage in a more mobile lifestyle, we might use a wireless link for the last few meters.

This chapter discusses the history of wireless communication, wireless communications regulations issues, and technical issues facing wireless communications, including wireless impairments, antennas, bandwidth, signal modulation, and spectrum utilization. Chapter 14, "Wireless WANs," discusses the impressive range of standards and generations in the brief history of wireless wide area networks (WWANs). Chapter 15, "WMANs, WLANs, and WPANs," explores the various options in wireless metropolitan area networks (WMANs), wireless local area networks (WLANs), and wireless personal area networks (WPANs). Chapter 16, "Emerging Wireless Applications," delves into the emerging applications propelling the need for high-speed mobile communications.

■ A Brief History of Wireless Telecommunications

Radio is defined as the transmission and reception of electrical impulses or signals by means of electromagnetic waves without the use of wires. Basically, radio waves are electromagnetic radiation transmitted through the air to a receiver.

The history of wireless technology goes back over 200 years. It began in 1747, when Benjamin Franklin illustrated that electricity can move through air and proposed a model of electricity that proved to be correct. In 1819, Hans Christian Oersted, a Danish physicist, observed that a compass needle would move in the presence of an electric field. This established the fundamental relationship between electricity and magnetism and gave rise to the field of study we know as electromagnetics. Then, between 1865 and 1873, Scottish physicist James Maxwell identified the mathematical relationships between electricity and magnetism, developing four equations that describe the movement of electromagnetic waves through space. He illustrated the basic principle of radio transmission by showing that an oscillating electric field would produce an oscillating magnetic field that would in turn produce an oscillating electric field.

The next step in the development of wireless communications came in 1887, when German physicist Heinrich Rudolf Hertz invented the oscillator (an alternating-current generator) and was credited with the discovery of radio waves. Essentially, a radio wave is made of two fields: one electric and one magnetic. These two fields are perpendicular to each other, and the sum of the two fields is called the *electromagnetic field*. Energy transfers back and forth from one field to the other, and this is known as *oscillation*. The invention of the first radio transmitter, in 1895, is credited to Italian Guglielmo Marconi, who sent the first radio telegraph transmission across the English Channel in 1895 and across the Atlantic Ocean in 1901. In 1896, Marconi submitted an application for a patent for the world's first wireless telegraph using Hertzian waves. The use of public radio began in 1907.

Since the beginning of radio communications, there have been two key issues to address, and they are still the main goals of the industry: expanding capacity and maintaining quality.

Radio waves are classified by their *frequency*, which describes the number of times a signal cycles per second, commonly referred to as *Hertz* (Hz), in honor of Heinrich Hertz. The *wavelength* is the distance between repeating units of a wave pattern (see Figure 13.1). In a sine wave, the wavelength is the distance between any point on a wave and the corresponding point on the next wave in the wave train. As shown in Table 13.1, there is an inverse relationship between frequency and wavelength: As the frequency increases, the wavelength decreases.

There are performance differences between radio frequencies. Low frequencies can travel much further without losing power (i.e., *attenuating*), but they carry much less information because the *bandwidth* (i.e., the difference between the highest and lowest frequency carried in the band) is much lower. High frequencies (those in the HF band, from 3MHz to 30MHz) offer much greater bandwidth than lower frequencies, but they are greatly affected by interference from a variety of sources. Very high frequencies (those in the SHF band, from 3GHz to 30GHz) suffer greatly from adverse weather conditions, particularly precipitation. This problem is

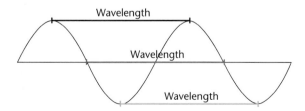

Figure 13.1 Wavelength

Table 13.1 Radio Spectrum

Class of Frequency (Abbrev.)	Frequency	Wavelength	ITU Band	Key Applications
Extremely low (ELF)	<3Hz–30Hz	100,000–10,000 km	1	Communication with submarines
Super low (SLF)	30Hz –300Hz	10,000–1,000 km	2	Communication with submarines
Ultra low (ULF)	300Hz–3KHz	1,000–100 km	3	Communication within mines
Very low (VLF)	3KHz–30KHz	100–10 km	4	Submarine communication, avalanche beaconing, wireless heart rate monitoring
Low (LF)	30KHz–300KHz	10–1 km	5	Navigation, time signaling, AM long-wave broadcasting
Medium (MF)	300KHz–3MHz	1,000–100 m	6	AM medium-wave broadcasting
High (HF)	3MHz–30MHz	100–10 m	7	Short-wave broadcasting and amateur radio
Very high (VHF)	30MHz–300MHz	10–1 m	8	FM and television broadcasting
Ultrahigh (UHF)	300MHz–3GHz	100–10 cm	9	Television broadcasting, mobile phones, WLANs, and ground-to-air and air-to-air communications
Super high (SHF)	3GHz–30GHz	10–1 cm	10	Microwave devices, mobile phones (W-CDMA), WLANs, and most modern radars
Extremely high (EHF)	30GHz–300GHz	1–0.1 cm	11	Radio astronomy, high-speed microwave radio relay

even greater in the extremely high frequencies (EHF band, from 30GHz to 300GHz). Above 300GHz, the earth's atmosphere greatly absorbs electromagnetic radiation, rendering the atmosphere basically opaque to higher frequencies of electromagnetic radiation, until it once again becomes transparent in the infrared and optical frequency ranges.

Beyond EHF, no class of frequency or ITU band is specified, but in the frequencies above 300GHz, the wavelengths are smaller than 1 mm. One application for this region is night vision. The majority of wireless data applications today are therefore handled in the band between 2GHz and 6GHz (the UHF and SHF bands). However, there is also great interest in making use of the higher bands, where the bandwidth is much greater, driven by the emergence of bandwidth-intensive multimedia applications. There is currently a great deal of discussion about what to do with the analog television channels as broadcasting is required to move to digital. That spectrum is coveted by many, especially the wireless industry.

■ Wireless Communications Regulations Issues

Regulation plays a critical role in radio communications. In the early twentieth century, the first people experimenting with radio were largely amateurs. There were no laws or regulations until 1912. The first step to regulating the U.S. radio spectrum was adopted in August 1912, referred to as "An Act to Regulate Radio Communication."

In 1927, the international community formed the Consultative Committee on International Radio (CCIR), which was responsible for creating international radio standards and coordinating the technical studies, tests, and measurements being carried out in the various fields of wireless telecommunications. In 1932, the CCIR and several other organizations (including the original ITU, which had been founded as the International Telegraph Union in 1865) merged to form what became known as the International Telecommunication Union in 1934. The ITU is organized under the United Nations. In 1992, the CCIR became the ITU Radiocommunication Sector (ITU-R), a standards body subcommittee of the ITU. The role of the ITU-R is to regulate the allocation of radio frequencies and so reduce the interference between radio stations in various countries. Although the ITU-R works on coordinating spectrum allocation on a global basis, it does not have the authority to mandate that countries comply with its recommendations. The ITU-R also has responsibility for regulating orbital positions of satellites relating to radio communications. In addition, it publishes international engineering standard documents in its area of responsibility. The ITU-R also organizes the World Administrative Radio Conference (WARC), held periodically to address major issues on an international basis.

The regulatory aspect of radio communications covers two major areas: political issues, including regulation and spectrum allocation, and spectrum management (also known as frequency management), which involves several activities, two of the most important being assignment and allocation. *Assignment* is the process of selecting operating frequencies for radio equipment, ideally in such a way as to permit each system to operate without causing harm (interference) to other systems or receiving interference from them. *Allocation* refers to the process of determining what radio services—for example, what types of station (such as radar, broadcast TV, or amateur)—should operate in a particular band of frequencies.

The radio spectrum is allocated on a country-by-country basis, so that the spectrum available to various wireless systems varies by region. Balancing competing claims is an important part of the allocation process. Within each nation, the government often claims a significant amount of spectrum for a variety of public safety and military applications. Regulatory agencies allocate radio spectrum into licensed and unlicensed bands. The use of licensed spectrum is an exclusive right to use a particular band of frequencies in a particular geographic market, with those licenses typically being sold at auction. Licensed spectrum is most commonly used by mobile telephone, wireless local loop, and wireless DSL providers. Of course, many argue that this is roughly the equivalent of having to pay for something that already belongs to the public. More healthy debate is needed about the enormous amounts of money the government earns by charging for these licenses. What value does that government income bring to citizens, who ultimately pay for it through higher rates charged by wireless operators?

Regulatory agencies also leave large portions of spectrum unlicensed. Anyone is allowed to build products that operate in unlicensed spectrum bands, as long as they conform with specified regulations that govern use, such as observing the power limits. One of the complexities of building products for use in unlicensed spectrum is that not all countries have allocated the same bands for unlicensed operation. One of the biggest questions, and opportunities, in securing more spectrum for wireless systems lies in the spectrum currently allocated to the broadcast television industry. Depending on the country, a single TV channel occupies either a 6MHz or 8MHz transmission band, which is equal to 300 or more digital cellular channels.

▪ Wireless Impairments

Wireless impairments come from many sources, including the following:

- **Path loss**—Radio signals lose power at a rate that increases with the square of the distance from the transmitter. The path loss, in decibels (dB), represents the ratio of the strength of the transmitted signal to the received strength. *Path obstacles* are materials such as water, metal, concrete, or masses of dirt that increase path loss.

■ **Multipath**—*Multipath* is the artifact of reflections and echoes. For example, with antenna televisions, when an image has a ghost figure around it, that is an echo. Multipath can create secondary and tertiary signals that compete with the primary signal. Poor connections and cabling can also induce multipath distortion in cable TV signals.

■ **Fading**—There are a number of propagation characteristics, and they vary with the different frequencies. As a mobile station moves through a cell, the multipath signals abruptly and rapidly add to and subtract from each other. As a result, very good signals are interspersed with very poor signals. This effect is referred to as a *Rayleigh fade* (named after the physicist Lord Rayleigh). The multipath delays can be predicted on a statistical basis, and components can be designed to handle the problem.

■ **Doppler effects**—As a mobile station transmitter is moving toward or away from the base station, there can be frequency shifts, called *Doppler effects*, in the received signal.

■ **Co-channel interference**—Although frequencies are not to be reused in adjacent cells, if a clear path exists, a transmission on the same channel in a non-adjacent cell might reach a user in another part of the service area and cause interference. Wireless systems operating in unlicensed spectrum are also subject to interference that may come from other wireless devices or networks.

Mobile Phones and Health Issues

Health issues related to mobile phone use are of legitimate concern. One important finding is that mobile phones may cause the blood–brain barrier—a network of tiny capillaries surrounding the brain that protects the brain from toxins—to break down. Another finding is that mobile phone radiation has shown effects on blood proteins. While there is no conclusive proof, many studies point to the need to continue research. You can watch an interesting video on the radiation effects of mobile phones and find summaries of many of the research studies conducted over the years at www.globalchange.com/radiationtv.html.

■ **Interference and noise**—Interference and noise are by-products of precipitation in the air, metals in the environment, and a variety of other anomalies. Error correction techniques are needed to fix these problems.

■ **Foliage**—Foliage can be a source of interference because the water in leaves absorbs radio signals.

- **Weather effects**—Weather can cause interference, particularly in the higher frequencies, where each radio wave is smaller than a drop of rain.

- **Environmental obstacles**—Radio signals cannot penetrate various materials, so walls, desks, buildings, hills, vehicles, and other environmental obstacles can affect the performance of radio.

- **Range and electrical power**—Range and electrical power are considerations because more radio power is required to increase the range or to compensate for poor path quality.

▪ Antennas

An *antenna* is a device through which radio frequency (RF) energy is coupled from the transmitter to the outside world and, in reverse, to the receiver from the outside world. Antennas have often been the most neglected of the components in a wireless system, yet they really are the most important part of a radio system. The manner in which energy is collected from and distributed into the surrounding air greatly influences the bandwidth efficiency, cost, and service quality of wireless networks. Antenna design is as critical as the prevailing radio conditions.

The function of an antenna is to collect or radiate electromagnetic waves. An oscillating electric field from the radio's transmitter is fed to the antenna, creating an oscillating magnetic field. Radio transmission is the propagation of electromagnetic waves through space. The electromagnetic waves create an electric current in the receiving antenna, which is then sent to the radio receiver. Antennas can be designed to handle a wide range of frequencies and power levels. They can also be designed to partially reject interference and signals coming from a direction other than that intended or, on the other hand, to focus energy in a particular direction when transmitting.

The first important consideration in antenna selection is *gain*. Antennas, as passive devices, do not create radio energy; they focus it. Focusing the energy into a narrower beam causes an increase in power, which is referred to as *antenna gain*. There are two main types of antennas:

- **Omnidirectional**—Omnidirectional antennas are used for communicating with mobile stations spread out in all directions. Examples include whip antennas, discone antennas, vertically oriented dipole antennas, and horizontal loop antennas.

- **Panel, or directional**—Panel, or directional, antennas are designed for high gain and are used to concentrate the signal both vertically and in a specific horizontal sector. Examples include Yagi antennas, parabolic dishes, and patch arrays.

Building Your Own Antenna

You can find some interesting photos of all sorts of antennas at www.seattlewireless.net/AntennaHowTo#head-6fb42901f5e11125848e5805ce715432a1d4cd20. Make sure to check out the "Build an Antenna Yourself" category, where you'll see antennas made from potato chip cans, sardine cans, and even Chinese cookware!

The past decade or so has brought a revolution in the way we communicate. The Internet and multimedia applications have fueled an enormous appetite for high-speed and high-bandwidth facilities, while mobile phones and other wireless devices have created a growing desire for ubiquitous connectivity for a large number of subscribers. Needless to say, the near future must promise a new generation of wireless high-bit-rate devices. However, we have a basic obstacle to overcome: the relatively low bit rate that current wireless systems support, limited by the information capacity between a transmitter and a receiver. This information capacity is defined by the famous formula called Shannon's Law (discussed later in this chapter). With the overcrowded frequency spectrum and limitations on maximum power, we are challenged in how to increase the information capacity.

Since 1996, multiantenna arrays have been suggested as a way to stretch the limit of Shannon's Law, making better use of the available spectrum and mitigating the effects of various impairments. It is increasingly clear that multiantenna technology is going to play an essential role in the wireless communications of the future. These newer antenna approaches include phased-array antennas, magnetic polarization antennas, and MIMO antennas, which are all described in the following sections.

Phased-Array Antennas

The simplest multiantenna array is a phased-array antenna, also called a steered-beam antenna. Intelligent antennas based on phased-array technology can be used to mitigate the effects of multipath and other environmental interactions, such as proximity to metal. A phased-array antenna is usually implemented as a flat panel with a relatively large number of active antenna elements (see Figure 13.2). The elements can be electronically steered to focus energy from the antenna in a given direction, and the steering can even be dynamic to allow for some degree of tracking of a mobile client. Phased-array antennas achieve directional selectivity by electronically imposing minute delays on the signals, referred to as a phase shift, moving from (or to) different parts of the array. Arrays can be programmed to send a grid of electronically formed radio beams to track moving targets or, alternatively, to receive signals from only certain directions.

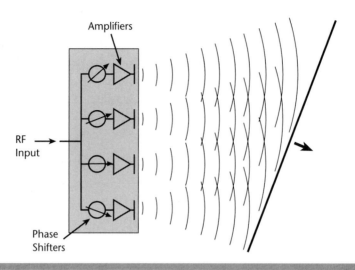

Figure 13.2 Phased-array antennas

Beam steering and intelligent antenna techniques increase the signal directed toward an intended receiver and reduce the reception of stray signals intended for other targets, which appear at the receiver as noise. Phased-array antennas enable 100-fold spectrum reuse (i.e., a capacity increase by a factor of 100) and may enable us to reach 1,000-fold reuse. Phased arrays have the additional advantage of being flat, which makes them more suitable than other antennas for many applications, particularly mobile installations.

Magnetic Polarization Antennas

Magnetic polarization antennas can be used to increase bandwidth. They work by reusing the same frequency at different polarizations. Waves vibrating in perpendicular directions cannot interfere with each other, so the same frequency can be used twice in the same place. Polarization is also applied to the magnetic waves, which are transmitted alongside their electric counterparts and have very similar properties. Different combinations of these polarizations make a sixfold capacity increase possible, and this can be achieved by simply upgrading the base stations to fit the extra antennas.

MIMO Antennas

A recent advance in antenna design is the multiple-input multiple-output (MIMO) system, which is one of the key building blocks for next-generation wireless access.

MIMO is an advanced antenna technology that can carry several times more data traffic than today's most advanced 3.5G networks (which are discussed in Chapter 14). MIMO enables a network to quickly deliver multimedia content. For example, MIMO enables a 1MB picture to be downloaded in a second and a 60MB video to be downloaded in a minute.

MIMO creates multiple parallel data streams between the multiple transmit and receive antennas. MIMO exploits phenomena such as multipath propagation to increase throughput, or reduce bit error rates, rather than attempting to eliminate the effects of multipath. It uses the multipath phenomenon to differentiate the separate signal paths from each MIMO antenna. (Telephony Online's article "Building Future Networks with MIMO and OFDM," at http://telephonyonline. com/wireless/technology/mimo_ofdm_091905/, provides a good graphic of MIMO antennas.)

MIMO is a key technology associated with most of the advanced and emerging wireless systems, including 3.5G and 4G. MIMO will also be used by IEEE 802.11n, the high-throughput 100Mbps WLAN standard expected to be finalized in 2007. By employing MIMO, 802.11n will offer up to eight times the coverage and up to six times the speed of current 802.11g networks. MIMO has also recently been added to the latest draft version of Mobile WiMax, described in IEEE 802.16e.

A conventional radio has one input, a transmit antenna, and one output, a receive antenna. A MIMO system uses at least two transmit antennas, working simultaneously in the service of a single logical channel, and at least two receive antennas at the other end of the intended connection. In reality, the number of receive antennas in a MIMO system is usually greater than the number of transmit antennas, and performance generally improves with the addition of more receive antennas. A MIMO system uses its multiple antennas to simultaneously transmit data to the receivers in small pieces, and the receivers then process the data flows and put them back together. This process, called *spatial multiplexing*, proportionally boosts the data transmission speed by a factor equal to the number of transmitting antennas (e.g., using four antennas increases the data rate by four times). In the ideal case, the throughput will be increased n-fold, where n represents the number of spatial channels in use. In addition, because all data is transmitted both in the same frequency band and with separate spatial signatures, this technique uses spectrum very efficiently.

MIMO can be combined with Orthogonal Frequency Division Multiplexing (OFDM; discussed later in this chapter) to take advantage of the multipath properties of environments by using base station antennas that do not have line-of-sight (LOS) functionality. MIMO-OFDM allows service providers to deploy a broadband wireless access (BWA) system that has non-line-of-sight (NLOS) functionality, which is a tremendous benefit for wireless communications.

■ Wireless Bandwidth

Bandwidth is determined by the range of frequencies that can be carried on a facility or the range of radio frequencies that a signal will occupy. *Bandwidth* refers to the amount of spectrum available to transport information. *Narrowband*, also referred to as *baseband*, implies a single channel. *Wideband*, also referred to as *broadband*, implies the use of multiple channels.

It is important to note that bandwidth is most often limited by regulation rather than technology. That is, the politics and business of spectrum allocation—rather than the physical attributes of a given frequency band—often determine which frequencies are made available and who obtains the licenses to use them.

The maximum physical capacity of a transmission channel can be determined by using Shannon's Law, which describes the relationship between the primary limiting factors in a transmission channel—bandwidth and noise. This formula is

$$C = W \log_2 (1 + S/N)$$

where C is the capacity of a channel (in bits per second), W is the bandwidth of the channel (in Hertz), and S/N is the signal-to-noise ratio. The more bandwidth there is available, the more bits per second can be sent on the channel. The more noise that is present, the fewer bits per second the channel will be able to carry.

As mentioned earlier in this chapter, as radio signals travel through the air, they lose power and encounter interference from other signals as well as environmental disturbances. The level of noise affects how efficiently the radio signal can be encoded and, therefore, how many bits per second can be carried on one cycle of radio bandwidth; this is referred to as the *bandwidth efficiency*. Noise is measured by the signal-to-noise ratio. As the power of the signal is reduced, the signal-to-noise ratio degrades, and the potential for error therefore increases.

■ Wireless Signal Modulation

In wireless systems, information transfer takes place through the process of *modulation*—that is, changes introduced onto the radio carrier wave. The data is combined with the carrier wave, creating the radio signal; the receiving end extracts the data, discards the carrier signal, and reconstructs the information. There are various modulation techniques for both analog and digital systems.

In order to represent the digital bitstream in analog format, one of three main characteristics of the carrier signal is altered:

- **Amplitude**—With amplitude modulation, different amplitudes or power levels are used to represent the 1 or the 0.

- **Frequency**—With frequency modulation (FM), also referred to as frequency-shift keying (FSK), different frequencies are used to differentiate between 1s and 0s.

- **Phase of the wave**—With phase-shift keying (PSK), a shift from the expected direction of the signal is used to encode the 1 or the 0.

These signal characteristics are illustrated in Figure 5.3 in Chapter 5, "Data Communications Basics." Some modulation schemes use a combination of these characteristics to alter the carrier signal, most commonly combining amplitude and phase. Modulation techniques vary in several ways, including speed, immunity to noise, and complexity. Not surprisingly, many incompatible schemes exist.

The duration of a single cycle of a waveform is called the *symbol time*. Modulation schemes vary in their spectral efficiency, which is a measure of the number of digital bits that can be encoded in a single cycle of a waveform, or symbol. To get more bits per Hertz, many modulation techniques define more amplitude levels. To encode k bits in the same symbol time, 2^k voltage levels are required. However, it becomes more difficult for the receiver to discriminate among many voltage levels with consistent precision as the speed increases. As discussed in Chapter 5, there are two categories of modulation schemes: single-carrier and multicarrier modulation. The following sections describe the modulation schemes that relate to wireless communication.

Single-Carrier Modulation Techniques

In single-carrier modulation schemes, a single channel occupies all the bandwidth. The following single-carrier techniques are commonly used in wireless systems:

- **Gaussian Minimum-Shift Keying (GMSK)**—GMSK is a kind of continuous-phase frequency-shift keying modulation. GMSK produces one bit per symbol time. Starting with a bitstream of 1s and 0s, a bit-clock assigns each bit a timeslice. The baseband signal is generated by first transforming the 0/1 encoded bits into −1/+1 encoded bits. These encoded bits are then filtered, transforming the square-shaped pulses into Gaussian-shaped (or sinusoidal) pulses. The baseband signal is then modulated, using frequency modulation. Frequency shifts can be detected by sampling the phase at each symbol period. Transmitting a 0 or 1 bit is therefore represented by changing the phase. Each shift in the phase represents a bit. This technique is used in the GSM cellular system.

- **Binary Phase-Shift Keying (BPSK)**—BPSK is the simplest form of PSK. It introduces a 180-degree phase shift (i.e., it uses two phases, separated by 180 degrees). It is able to modulate at only one bit per symbol time and is therefore unsuitable for high-data-rate applications. However, it is the most robust of all the PSK techniques because it takes a tremendous amount of distortion for the demodulator to reach an incorrect decision. For this reason, it is the best solution under noisy conditions. It is commonly used with the DSSS version of the original 802.11 radio link. (DSSS is discussed later in this chapter.)

- **Quadrature Phase-Shift Keying (QPSK)**—QPSK introduces four different phase shifts—0 degrees, 90 degrees, 180 degrees, and 270 degrees—providing two bits per symbol time. QPSK can operate in harsh environments, such as with over-the-air transmission. Because of its robustness and relatively low complexity, QPSK is widely used in situations such as with Direct Broadcast Satellite (DBS). It is also used with 802.11x WLANs. In 802.11b, it is used when operating at 5.5Mbps and 11Mbps, and in 802.11a and 802.11g, it is used when operating at 12Mbps or 18Mbps.

- **Differential Phase-Shift Keying (DPSK)**—DPSK is a form of phase-shift keying used for digital transmission in which the phase of the carrier is discretely varied in relation to the phase of the immediately preceding signal element and in accordance with the data being transmitted. The demodulator determines the changes in the phase of the received signal rather than the phase itself. DPSK can be significantly simpler to implement than ordinary PSK because there is no need for the demodulator to have a copy of the reference signal to determine the exact phase of the received signal. However, it produces more erroneous demodulations as a result. Differential Binary PSK (DBPSK) is used in low-speed 802.11 WLANs (operating at 1Mbps), and Differential Quadrature PSK (DQPSK) is used with the extended-rate 2Mbps 802.11 WLANs.

- **Quadrature Amplitude Modulation (QAM)**—QAM modulates multiple levels of amplitude or uses both amplitude and phase to yield a higher spectral efficiency. As discussed in Chapter 5, various levels of QAM are referred to as *nn*-QAM, where *nn* indicates the number of states per Hertz. The number of bits per symbol time is k, where $2^k = nn$. Therefore, 4 bits per Hertz = $2^4 = 16$-QAM, 6 bits per Hertz = $2^6 = 64$-QAM, and 8 bits per Hertz = $2^8 = 256$-QAM. QAM techniques are used in many applications, including digital cable television, cable modems, DSL modems, digital satellite systems, 802.11 (Wi-Fi), 802.16 (WiMax), and 3G W-CDMA/HSDPA systems.

Multicarrier Modulation Techniques

Multicarrier modulation techniques use an aggregate amount of bandwidth and divide it into subbands. Each subband is then encoded by using a single-carrier technique, and the bitstreams from the subbands are bonded together at the receiver. OFDM, discussed later in this chapter, is an increasingly popular multi-carrier technique. It is used in European digital over-the-air broadcast and in many new and emerging wireless broadband solutions, including 802.11a, 802.11g, 802.16x, 802.20x, and Super 3G; it is the basis of the 4G and 5G visions.

Spectrum Utilization

The wireless spectrum is limited. Wireless is like having one invisible cable in the sky that the whole world has to share. This is one of the major limitations of wireless, and we need techniques for efficiently using the spectrum that we do have. There are several steps in reusing spectrum.

The first step in spectrum reuse is to apply space division—that is, carve up the service area into smaller coverage areas. The key purpose of space division is to reuse frequencies across the coverage areas, or *cells*. The second step is to apply a multiple-access technique to allow the sharing of spectrum by multiple users. After you have delineated the space and combined multiple conversations onto one channel, you can apply spread spectrum, duplexing, and compression techniques to use the bandwidth even more efficiently. The following sections discuss these steps in more detail.

Using the Available Radio Spectrum

The first key characteristic of a radio transmission system is how it makes use of the available radio spectrum, or bandwidth. As discussed in the following sections, four major techniques are used to allocate capacity: Space Division Multiplexing, Frequency Division Multiple Access (FDMA), Time Division Multiple Access (TDMA), and spread spectrum (implemented as Code Division Multiple Access [CDMA] in 2G networks and as either W-CDMA or OFDM in 3G cellular networks).

Space Division Multiplexing
The cellular concept involves subdividing coverage areas. Mobile telephony is not a new invention. It has been around since the early 1950s, but at that time, two things limited its availability to the mass market. First, we were using very high-powered antennas. So, when we relayed a signal, it would have strength over a coverage area of perhaps 100 miles (161 km) in diameter. Second, at that time, the spectrum management agencies issued very few frequencies (perhaps one or two dozen) that could be used for purposes of mobile communications. In the relatively large coverage area of 100 miles (161 km) or so, only 12 to 24 channels were available. The majority of these few channels were reserved for critical services,

such as police and other emergency services, as well as for those who could afford a body builder to carry those big phones that operated at low frequencies over long stretches.

In the 1970s, two things changed. The first was the advent of the low-power transmitter receiver tower, which reduced the coverage area to a cell size that was only about 8 miles (13 km) in diameter. Second, the regulatory agencies made available large amounts of spectrum for use in support of mobile communications, and depending on the location, anywhere from 600 to 1,000 channels were made available to service providers.

The cellular architecture depends on cells organized into a reuse pattern. In the traditional analog cellular network, the cellular reuse pattern is $n = 7$ and is often depicted as a honeycomb configuration of what are called *seven cells* (see Figure 13.3). The idea of spectrum reuse is that you can reuse frequencies as long as they are not in adjacent cells. Say that in the honeycomb configuration, 700 channels are available. Each of the cells could make use of 100 of those channels. The next honeycomb configuration could then reuse those 100 channels, as long as those channels were not adjacent to one another between cells.

As the density of subscribers increases, the next step is to subdivide the cells into smaller coverage areas, based on accepted reuse patterns. The traditional analog cellular network uses *macrocells* (see Figure 13.4). This network was for fast-moving users, traveling distances of miles on their end-to-end journey. The coverage area was about 8 miles (13 km) in diameter, and the base station power was rather great—generally 10 watts or more. This network offered low deployment costs and a small number of handoffs. Depending on how many channels the spectrum agency gave the region, a cell could support up to about 60 users.

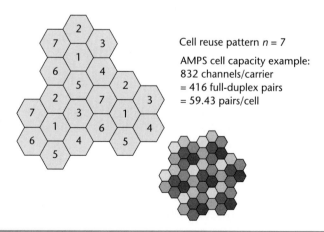

Cell reuse pattern $n = 7$

AMPS cell capacity example:
832 channels/carrier
= 416 full-duplex pairs
= 59.43 pairs/cell

Figure 13.3 Space division for spectrum reuse

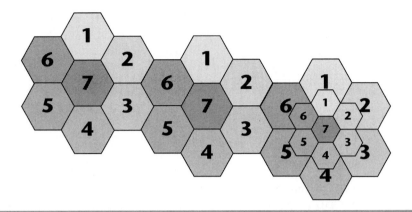

Figure 13.4 Analog cellular reuse pattern

As the demand for use increased, we started to migrate toward a *microcell* architecture. Users of this architecture were assumed to be moving more slowly than those in a macrocell approach; they were, for example, people trapped in a traffic grid, people on golf carts on a golf course, people riding bicycles in a city, or pedestrians anywhere. These users traveled distances of less than 1 mile (1.5 km) end to end. Therefore, there are not as many handoffs involved with microcells as there are with macrocells.

With macrocells and high-speed vehicles, in 1980, when processing power was significantly lower than it is today, if you were moving very rapidly through cell boundaries, there would be undue strain on the processing power of the systems, and calls might be dropped. But by the time microcells started to come about, handoffs were facilitated by more rapid processing. The coverage area of a microcell is about 0.6 miles (1 km) in diameter. Compared to macrocells, this architecture offers better frequency reuse, lower power, and better battery life, as well as smaller subscriber units.

It is not always useful to define a cell with a full coverage of 360 degrees. In some cases, cells with a particular shape and coverage are needed. These cells are called *selective cells*. A typical example of selective cells is the cells that may be located at the entrances of tunnels, where 360-degree coverage is not needed. In this case, a selective cell with a coverage of 120 degrees is used.

The demand for spectrum is growing beyond what even the microcell design can provide, and further shrinkage of the cell size is mandated, so we are now employing the *picocell*—that is, the tiny cell—architecture. This approach is for stationary or very slow-moving users—folks who dash out of a seminar during a conference and stand by a window so they can conduct a conversation, or coffee lovers who check e-mail over lattes. These users are not traveling great distances, maybe 330 to 1,000 feet (100 to 300 m) end to end. The coverage radius of a pico-cell is only about 150 feet (46 m), and because it's such a small coverage area, the base station power is also very small—10 milliwatts or less. Therefore, compared to the microcell design, the picocell design offers even better frequency reuse, even lower power, even smaller subscriber units, and even better, longer battery life. The picocell architecture does create some concerns in the engineering realm; for example, Tokyo needed to plan how to implement more than 40,000 cells for its Personal Handyphone System (PHS) deployment. There are tradeoffs with the various designs: You can serve greater densities with the picocell design than with other designs, but at the cost of a bigger engineering project.

The concept of *umbrella cells* was introduced to address the situation where a large number of handoffs occurs among many small neighboring cells. An umbrella cell covers several microcells or picocells. The power level inside an umbrella cell is increased compared to the power levels used in the microcells that form the umbrella cell. When the speed of the mobile device is too high, the mobile device is handed off to the umbrella cell. The mobile device then stays longer in the same cell (in this case, the umbrella cell), reducing the number of handoffs and the work of the network.

FDMA

With FDMA, which is used in analog cellular systems, each user is assigned to a different frequency; everybody is speaking at the same time, but each conversation is on a different portion of the frequency band. FDMA is characterized as facilitating what would today be called low capacity—approximately 60 users per cell. Given the number of users today, let alone what tomorrow will bring, FDMA alone can no longer handle the volume.

The cost of FDMA handsets is low, as these are not smart devices. For example, an FDMA-based device does not know how to search for another frequency that has a better transmission quality associated with it. This approach is inexpensive for the user, but the service operator needs to have a transceiver for each channel, which means the base station cost is high. And because it's an analog technology, FDMA also consumes a great deal of power, and the cost associated with the power consumption is greater than with digital systems.

The advantage of FDMA is that it doesn't need strict clocking devices to enable synchronization between the base stations, as would, for example, TDMA. As Figure 13.5 shows, everybody uses the system at the same time, but each user is working off a different frequency.

Although analog FDMA systems are no longer common, with most analog systems having been decommissioned at this point, the FDM technique is still very important because it is required to divide the allocated spectrum into individual

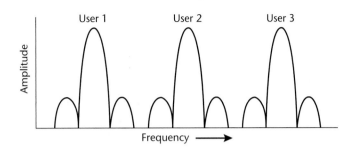

Figure 13.5 FDMA

channels to which other techniques are then applied to enable multiple users to use a channel simultaneously.

TDMA

TDMA, which is used in 2G digital cellular systems, WLANs, and Personal Communications Services (PCS) systems, is actually a combination of FDM and TDM. In TDMA systems, you first divide the available or allocated frequency spectrum into a number of channels by using FDM. Then, within each channel, you apply TDM to carry multiple users, interleaved in time. Therefore, one transceiver can support multiple channels. Various cellular network standards are based on TDMA, including Global System for Mobile Communications (GSM), Universal Wireless Communications (UWC), and Personal Digital Cellular (PDC). UWC-136 TDMA technology, also referred to as ANSI-136, provides a three-to-one gain in capacity compared to analog technology. Each caller is assigned a specific time slot for transmission. GSM supports eight users per channel, resulting in an eightfold increase in capacity. (These standards are discussed in further detail in Chapter 14.)

The digital handsets associated with TDMA are more intelligent than those used with FDMA. For example, they have scanning capabilities, and if the channel you are on is encountering anomalies that are lending themselves to transmission errors, the handset can search for an available channel that provides better performance.

The key benefits of TDMA are that it offers greater capacity and spectral efficiency than FDMA. As Figure 13.6 shows, in TDMA, everybody is talking on the same frequencies but at different moments in time. The users perceive their conversations as being continuous, even though each is actually getting very rapid samples of his or her conversation.

Spread Spectrum

Spread spectrum is a multiple-access technique that is receiving a great deal of attention today. In spread spectrum, everybody is using the same frequency at the

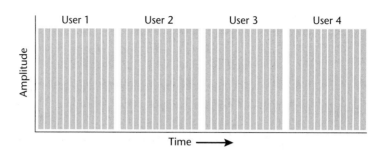

Figure 13.6   TDMA

same time. This is referred to as *universal frequency reuse*. Spread spectrum provides the ultimate in terms of the supported density of users, and it is possible because each conversation is uniquely encoded. In spread spectrum, a single spectrum of bandwidth is available for all the users. As Figure 13.7 shows, in spread spectrum, although everybody is using the same frequencies at the same time, each conversation is uniquely encoded, allowing the transceiver to pick it out from among all the conversations.

Spread spectrum has become a critical technology. It is used in 3G cellular systems as well as WLANs, and it is the basis of the majority of emerging wireless broadband solutions. There are two major benefits to spread spectrum: greater resistance to interference (and hence greater reliability) and greatly improved capacity.

There are two generations of spread spectrum. The first generation, CDMA, operates in an allocation of 1.25MHz. The second generation of CDMA, called Wideband CDMA (W-CDMA), operates over allocations of either 5MHz, 10MHz, or 15MHz. As is implied by the name, W-CDMA can support higher data rates than can CDMA. Both generations of CDMA use a unique code for each conversation, and both use spread spectrum techniques. One advantage of W-CDMA is that it

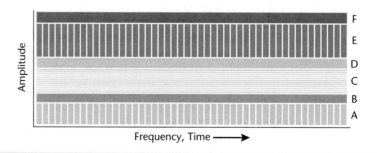

Figure 13.7   Spread spectrum

uses a bigger channel than CDMA, which means that it can carry more calls and that those calls can be encoded in longer strings. The longer strings, in turn, mean greater security and better performance.

Spread Spectrum's Military History

George Antheil and the glamorous movie star Hedy Lamarr held the original patent on CDMA technology. Hedy Lamarr had strong personal sentiments against World War II. She had recently escaped from her first husband, Fritz Mandl, who was one of Europe's largest armaments manufacturers and was selling munitions to Hitler. As his wife, Lamarr was exposed to military technology ideas.

Lamarr met George Antheil, who had been at the forefront of experimental music in the 1920s, at a party in Hollywood. Antheil was one of the first people to work with the player piano as an instrument for composed music; his famous *Ballet Mecanique* was written for 12 player pianos, an airplane propeller, and a symphony. Antheil also opposed the Nazis, and it was in this context that Lamarr told Antheil about her idea for a secret communications system that could guide torpedoes to their target without being intercepted by the enemy, by sending messages between transmitter and receiver over multiple radio frequencies in a random pattern. The only problem was how to ensure that the transmitter and receiver would stay in synchronization as they moved through the frequencies. Lamarr thought Antheil could help solve the synchronization problem.

Antheil did come up with a solution: Paper rolls perforated with a pseudorandom pattern would delineate the frequency path. Two rolls with the same pattern would be installed in the transmitter and receiver. If the two rolls were started at the same time, and one stayed at the launch point while the other was launched with the torpedo, the system would maintain the synchronization right on down to where the torpedo hit the ship. Interestingly, Lamarr and Antheil designed their system to use 88 frequencies—exactly the number of keys on a piano—just like the player piano rolls in *Ballet Mecanique*.

Today, we call this technique Frequency Hopping Spread Spectrum (FHSS), and it is one of the ways in which spread spectrum uniquely encodes its conversations.

Spread spectrum is characterized by not requiring any timing coordination, so clocking is not necessary. It offers great reliability because it is highly resistant to interference. Spread spectrum has greatly improved capacity over FDMA and TDMA; the spectral efficiency of spread spectrum, as standardized in IS-95, is 10 to 20 times greater than that of an analog cellular network. The number of users who can be serviced depends on the location of the users—how many of them are within a given cell and what signal-to-noise ratio the service provider deems acceptable. Spread spectrum allows for two compression ratios for digitized voice, and they vary according to the channel quality: 13Kbps, which is used to provide near-land-line voice qualities (e.g., in support of something like wireless local loop), and 8Kbps, which is used to maximize the use of the spectrum and extend battery life. It is important to realize that spread spectrum requires complex power control schemes, and power control is very important in spread spectrum.

Power Control Schemes in TDMA and Spread Spectrum

The classic example that instructors give their students when talking about wireless is the following: You walk into a TDMA cocktail party, and a group of people stands in a circle. Each person takes a turn at making a comment or answering a question. You can separate the conversations by the moment in time when each individual is speaking.

You walk into a spread spectrum party and you feel as though you've walked into the United Nations. There's German in the left-hand corner, Japanese in the right-hand corner, and English in the center. Somebody says a word in your language that you recognize, and you immediately focus your attention there. You're able to filter out the extraneous conversation as noise because you've tuned in on a code that's understandable to you. You can continue to filter out the extraneous conversation unless another 200 delegates walk in and add their conversations to the overall mix, making it impossible for you to distinguish between the conversations.

On spread spectrum networks, channels can be reused in adjacent cells without creating co-channel interference because different pseudorandom number (PN) codes are used in each cell site. Spread spectrum was developed by the military to be secure. The wide spreading of the signal makes if difficult to detect and jam.

As discussed in the following sections, there are three basic types of spread spectrum techniques: Frequency Hopping Spread Spectrum (FHSS), Direct Sequence Spread Spectrum (DSSS), and Orthogonal Frequency Division Multiplexing (OFDM).

FHSS   With FHSS, which is the oldest of the spread spectrum techniques, the frequency hopping varies in a known pattern, and separate error correction must be included. The concept involves a system that hops between frequencies in a random pattern, known only to the transmitter and receiver (see Figure 13.8). The transmitter sends on a channel for only a short period of time and then hops to a different channel. Slow frequency hopping is used to combat fading.

Along with providing resistance to jamming, an FHSS system also addresses the problem of frequency-selective fading. Because the transmitter does not stay on any one frequency for a long period of time, fading at a particular part of the frequency spectrum is minimized. The disadvantage of FHSS is that the more hopping channels needed, the greater the bandwidth required, although a set of hopping channels can be shared by a number of users.

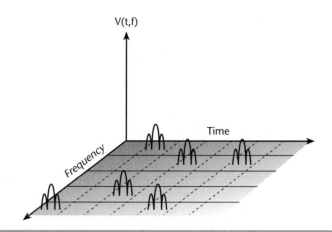

Figure 13.8 FHSS

FHSS is used by the original Bluetooth standard (IEEE 802.15.1) for PANs, which is discussed in detail in Chapter 15.

DSSS   DSSS is used in most contemporary systems, including 3G cellular networks, CDMA-based networks, and 802.11b WLANs. DSSS requires greater bandwidth than does FHSS, but that is exactly what makes its performance so good.

With DSSS, each transmitted bit is first converted into a series of narrower pulses, referred to as *chips*. DSSS multiplies the data bits by a very fast pseudorandom bit pattern (PN code) that spreads the data into a large coded stream that takes the full bandwidth of the channel. The chips are then transmitted through a digital modulator.

The *bandwidth expansion factor* refers to the number of bits in the spreading code. There are many types of spreading codes in use; for example, Barker Code is used in 802.11, Complementary Code Keying (CCK) is used in 802.11b, and 64-bit Walsh Code is used in CDMA cellular. Figure 13.9 shows an example of DSSS that uses Barker Code, which is an 11-bit chipping code. The 1 bits are encoded as a particular sequence of 1s and 0s, and the 0 bits are the inverse of that sequence. In the course of a transmission, if a bit is affected by noise and several chips get knocked out, the receiver can determine from the pattern of remaining bits whether a 1 or a 0 got knocked out and recover that information accurately. This is why DSSS provides such good performance and resistance to interference and noise. DSSS also provides great reliability because the DSSS operation generates more bits per second than it starts with, and the resulting signals spread over a wide range of frequencies when it is transmitted, minimizing the impact of interference and multipath fading.

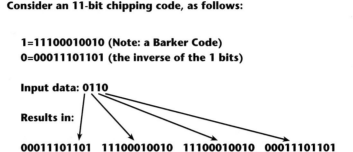

Figure 13.9 An example of DSSS

OFDM   OFDM is the newest spread spectrum technique, and its main purpose is to resolve the problems that result from multipath distortion. OFDM has some key advantages over CDMA, which is used in many of today's 3G cellular networks. First, it is more robust, which means it provides better performance in multipath situations. It also allows for simpler receivers. Perhaps most importantly, OFDM is more amenable to MIMO technologies than are the other spread spectrum techniques. A Nortel (www.nortel.com) trial conducted in early 2005 provides a good example: Nortel was able to demonstrate peak data rates of 37Mbps over a standard 5MHz PCS mobility band. Using OFDM and MIMO, wireless subscribers could download a 128MB file in approximately 30 seconds, 4 to 10 times faster than today's 3G networks can support (see www.nortel.com/corporate/news/newsreleases/2005a/03_09_05_mimo_ofdm.html). In another Nortel trial (see http://telephonyonline.com/wireless/technology/mimo_ofdm_091905/), using OFDM and MIMO enabled a mobile user to download a 264MB file at 37Mbps while simultaneously viewing two live streaming videos, over a standard 5MHz PCS band. The download took less than 1 minute in this trial; it would take 90 minutes with today's networks.

OFDM and MIMO are critical technologies associated with most of the advanced and emerging wireless systems, including Beyond 3G (B3G) or 3.5G and 4G. Many areas of wireless solutions employ OFDM. One is mobile wireless, which includes the IEEE 802.16e, IEEE 802.20, and Flash-OFDM standards. Another is fixed wireless broadband, encompassing IEEE 802.16a/Revision D, WLANs such as IEEE 802.11a and 802.11g, and the European HiperLan2. OFDM is also used in Ultra-Wideband (UWB) PANs. DTV and HDTV using the Digital Video Broadcasting-Terrestrial (DVB-T) and Digital Audio Broadcasting (DAB) standards also rely on OFDM. Military high-frequency modems also make use of OFDM. OFDM is also used in a variety of wired broadband alternatives, including ADSL (where it is known as Discrete Multitone [DMT]), cable modems, and powerline telecommunications (PLT).

OFDM is a combination of two key principles:

- **Multicarrier transmission**—Multicarrier transmission is a technique that divides the available spectrum into many subcarriers, with the transmission rate reduced on each subcarrier. OFDM is similar to FDM in that multiple-user access is achieved by subdividing the available bandwidth into multiple channels that are then allocated to users. However, OFDM uses the spectrum much more efficiently than FDM by spacing the channels much more closely together. This is achieved by making all the carriers orthogonal (i.e., at right angles to or independent of) to one another, preventing interference between the closely spaced carriers. Making the carriers for each channel orthogonal to one another allows them to be spaced very closely. For a good graphic representation of OFDM, see Telephony Online's article "Building Future Networks with MIMO and OFDM" at http://telephonyonline.com/wireless/technology/mimo_ofdm_091905/.

- **Adaptive modulation**—An adaptive modulation system supports a variety of modulation schemes. The quality of the radio path determines which modulation technique is most appropriate. Techniques supported include 16-QAM, 64-QAM, QPSK, and DPSK.

OFDM overcomes most of the problems with both FDMA and TDMA, including nonefficient use of spectrum and the requirement for clocking or synchronization with TDMA. OFDM splits the available bandwidth into many narrowband channels (typically 100 to 8,000), referred to as subcarriers.

OFDM offers improved resistance to noise and interference at particular frequencies as well as immunity to frequency-selective fading. Information can be reconstructed without receiving the entire transmission band. OFDM is almost always used in conjunction with channel coding or an error correction technique. One approach is referred to as Coded Orthogonal Frequency Division Multiplexing (COFDM). COFDM is widely used in Europe and other places where the DAB standard has been adopted for digital radio broadcasting and for terrestrial digital TV, as in the DVB-T standard. COFDM is also used in ADSL transmission. The major benefit of COFDM is that it makes broadcasts relatively immune to multipath distortion and signal fading due to atmospheric conditions or passing aircraft. It is a complex technique, but by combining OFDM with error-correcting codes, adaptive equalization, and reconfigurable modulation, COFDM provides many beneficial properties, including resistance to multipath, phase distortion, fading, and burst noise.

OFDM also offers improved bandwidth efficiency because it can support more users on the same transmission channel by using different spreading codes. OFDM makes it easy to filter out noise: If a particular range of frequencies suffers from interference, the carriers within that range can be disabled or made to run more slowly. Another feature of OFDM is that the speeds of the upstream and downstream channels can be varied by allocating either more or fewer carriers for each purpose. Some forms of Rate-Adaptive DSL (RADSL) use this feature in real-time so that bandwidth is allocated to whichever stream needs it most.

Orthogonal Frequency Division Multiple Access (OFDMA) is a proprietary enhancement to OFDM technology, introduced by Runcom Technologies (www.runcom.com) in 2000. Whereas OFDM involves 256 subcarriers, OFDMA defines either 2,048 or 4,096 subcarriers. In current OFDM systems, only a single user can transmit on all the subcarriers at any given time, and TDMA or FDMA is used to support multiple users. OFDMA, on the other hand, allows multiple users to transmit simultaneously on the different subcarriers per OFDM symbol. The end result is improved spectral efficiency. Because OFDMA enables more efficient duplexing techniques, including FDD and TDD, the created signal is immune to interference and is therefore capable of high data throughput. In addition, OFDMA improves the power gain per channel, providing better coverage and range availability, larger cell radius, and smaller power amplifiers and antennas, ultimately leading to lower investment in capital equipment.

OFDMA, also referred to as Multiuser-OFDM, is being considered as a modulation and multiple-access method for upcoming fourth-generation (4G) wireless networks, and it is being embraced by a number of current technologies, including DVB and WiMax. It is also a preferred technology driving the BWA market.

Improving Error Detection and Correction

Remember that in radio transmission systems, it is important to balance expanding capacity (i.e., increasing bandwidth efficiency) with maintaining quality (i.e., reducing the effects of noise and interference). Now that we've covered the various spectrum reuse techniques designed to achieve greater capacity in wireless networks, let's examine two techniques designed to improve the quality of wireless communications, or more specifically, the integrity of the data flow:

- **Forward error correction (FEC)**—FEC improves the reliability of digital radio systems by combining redundant information with the transmission. The receiver, using a probability technique, can detect and correct a certain percentage of errors. However, because this requires more bits to be transmitted, it affects bandwidth efficiency. There are a variety of FEC techniques that vary in the coding rate, or the amount of additional information that must be sent, which affects the receiver's ability to correct errors. FEC coding refers to the ratio of uncoded to coded bits. The improvement gained is generally expressed in improvements in signal-to-noise ratio or signal-to-interference ratio.

Different coding rates affect the FEC overhead. The coding rate is expressed as a fraction that represents the number of uncoded bits input to the FEC encoder and the number of coded bits output to the transmitter. For example, 3/4 means 3 uncoded bits are sent as 4 coded bits, resulting in 33% overhead; 1/2 means 1 uncoded bit is sent as 2 coded bits, resulting in 100% overhead.

In WLAN applications, OFDM transmission includes FEC coding that is spread across several subcarriers. If several of the subcarriers are lost, the receiver can reconstruct the information.

- **Convolutional coding**—This type of coding is used in 802.11a and 802.11g WLANs. This technique works by taking the transmitted bit sequence, selecting a group of the most recently occurring bits, distributing them into two or more sets, and performing a mathematical operation (convolution) to generate one coded bit from each set as the output. The receiver runs a comparison of the coded bit sequence and retains the best matches, which allows it to make a maximum likelihood estimate of the correct decoded bit sequence.

There are more complicated error correction techniques as well, including Trellis, Reed-Solomon, the Viterbi algorithm, Turbo coding, and the Walsh Code. A good source for more information on all these techniques is Wikipedia (www.wikipedia.org).

Duplexing Techniques

Another way in which the operations of wireless networks differ, and hence also the standards differ, is the *duplexing* technique—the procedure for separating the incoming and outgoing conversations. *Duplex transmission* refers to the ability to send information in both directions over a single channel. Two transmitters cannot use the same channel at the same time because they will interfere with one another, but there are two techniques for enabling full-duplex transmission: Frequency Division Duplex (FDD) and Time Division Duplex (TDD).

FDD

With FDD, two separate channels are assigned for transmission: the transmit channel and the receive channel. FDD requires more bandwidth than TDD. FDD is the legacy technique used for point-to-point links supporting voice, which is symmetric and defined by predictable traffic. Hence, FDD is the most widely used technique in cellular networks. Because there is much equipment based on legacy FDD point-to-point radio links, FDD is a top priority for some manufacturers.

TDD

In TDD, which is found in various standards across all the technology domains, including WWANs, WMANs, WLANs, and WPANs, the two ends take turns sending on the same channel. TDD can be designed as a contention system, where an access protocol (such as CSMA/CA) minimizes the chance of collision. TDD can also be designed for no contention, where time slots are defined, and each direction uses assigned time slots; this is referred to as a "ping-pong" technique. TDD makes practical the reallocation of spectral resources from uplink to downlink or vice versa. The ability to adapt the spectrum resources to the actual traffic pattern significantly improves frequency resource utilization. These characteristics make TDD an attractive alternative in support of triple play (i.e., a single carrier's offering of voice, data, and TV services).

TDD does have some drawbacks, including a requirement for burst demodulators and more difficult synchronization of uplink transmission due to the absence of frequency and clock references. However, due to its superior performance in supporting spectrum efficiency and flexibility, TDD is the preferred solution in broadband fixed wireless access (BFWA) networks. (BFWA systems are discussed in Chapter 15.)

Compression Techniques

After carving space into cells and applying multiple-access techniques within each cell to make better use of the bandwidth available, it is possible to apply compression to make greater use of the bandwidth within each given channel. Compression is very important because it improves the use of a precious resource: the communications channel.

Voice compression techniques use voice coders/decoders (vocoders), of which there are two general types:

- **High-bit-rate vocoders**—These vocoders are used by PCS, wireless local loops, and wireless office telecommunication systems applications. These vocoders carry voice by using 32Kbps Adaptive Differential Pulse Code Modulation (ADPCM). A bit rate this high emulates the quality achieved on the PSTN, and no additional error detection and correction is necessary.

- **Low-bit-rate vocoders**—These vocoders are used in cellular systems that deal with vehicular traffic, where large cells need to facilitate a large number of conversations, or anywhere bandwidth efficiency is critical, such as densely populated areas. These vocoders reduce the voice down to 8Kbps, using extensive channel coding techniques that help facilitate error correction, such as linear predictive coding (LPC), Quantized Code-Excited Linear Prediction (QCELP), or Vector Sum Excited Linear Prediction (VSLEP). GSM uses Regular Pulse Excitation Long Term Prediction (RPE LTP), which carries digitized voice at 13Kbps, achieving good voice quality (albeit not comparable to that achieved on good old-fashioned landlines).

Unfortunately, in the realm of data, there are no set standards for data compression; many techniques exist, and overall, data compression is underused.

Chapter 14

Wireless WANs

It is abundantly clear that wireless networks are a very important part of our future, promising to dramatically change the way society and industry function. Wireless networks fall into the same domains as wireline networks—wide area networks (WANs), metropolitan area networks (MANs), local area networks (LANs), and personal area networks (PANs)—and are applied in support of a growing number of applications, including mobile (such as cellular and PCS systems), fixed (as in wireless local loop), broadcast (television), and sensor-based (such as RFID) networks.

This chapter explores wireless wide area network (WWAN) standards and systems. WANs can be global, national, or regional in scope. Traditional WWAN solutions include cellular radio and PCS networks (including analog and digital cellular) as well as early wireless data networks (i.e., Cellular Digital Packet Data [CDPD] and packet radio). Newer generations are focused on supporting high-speed data as well as video and multimedia, with increased emphasis on mobile content delivery.

Given the basic human desire and need for freedom of movement, it is little surprise that the demand for wireless network solutions is enormous. With the introduction of cellular communications, we saw an increasing demand for wireless services. The growth was so rapid that by 2002, we witnessed a major shift in network usage: For the first time in the history of telecommunications, the number of mobile subscribers exceeded the number of fixed lines. And that trend continues. According to the ITU, at year-end 2004, the total number of mobile subscribers was

1.75 billion, while the total number of fixed lines worldwide was 1.2 billion. By September 2005, the number of mobile subscriber connections exceeded 2 billion. Although the history of cellular networks has been rather brief, it has already seen three generations, the fourth is emerging, and a fifth generation is on the drawing boards:

- **First generation (1G)**—The first generation, which initially debuted in Japan in 1979, is characterized by analog transmission systems. Key 1G standards included AMPS, TACS, JTACS, and NMT.

- **Second generation (2G)**—The second generation introduced digital transmission, and the first 2G networks were operational in 1992. GSM, UWC-136, cdmaOne, and PDC are the four major 2G cellular standards, along with the Personal Communications Services (PCS) standards GSM 1800, GSM 1900, and PDH. 2G networks are currently serving the vast majority of mobile subscribers.

- **Intermediate second generation (2.5G)**—An intermediate second generation called 2.5G offers enhancements to the data services on existing 2G digital platforms, achieving many of the same speeds offered by 3G networks but without requiring the operator to acquire new spectrum and put in an entirely new infrastructure. The key 2.5G standards include GPRS, HSCSD, and EDGE.

- **Third generation (3G)**—The third generation, which is now upon us, involves digital transmission but also permits per-user and terminal mobility, providing a single mobile communications service, adjusted for broadband applications (including voice, data, and multimedia streams) to be supported at higher data speeds, in the range of 144Kbps to 384Kbps, up to 2Mbps in some cases, and with visions of supporting 155Mbps. The major 3G standards include W-CDMA, UMTS, CMDA2000, CDMA450, TD-SCDMA, and FOMA. 3G standards deployment is occurring around the world, but universal deployment is still far from complete. The key advances in emerging technologies that greatly improve spectrum utilization and performance threaten 3G.

  An intermediate third generation, 3.5G, is introducing many enhancements designed for services running over an IP backbone, including high-speed data and video. Key 3.5G standards include HSDPA, HSUPA, and HSOPA.

- **Beyond 3G**—Also known as Long-Term Evolution (LTE), Super 3G, and Ultra 3G, Beyond 3G is an enhancement to 3G that involves today's 3G technologies but supports bandwidths greater than 5MHz and adds smarter and more efficient IP-based back-end infrastructure and additional one-way or two-way airlinks to provide further capabilities.

- **Fourth generation (4G)**—The fourth generation, which is under development, will bring with it new technologies that allow even better use of capacity and better performance. The introduction of 3G technology provides a huge expansion in mobile capacity and bandwidth, and 4G will do the same for broadband communications. 4G will support a wide range of data rates, promising a maximum of 50Mbps to 100Mbps while moving and an average of 20Mbps and up to 1Gbps while standing still. The two key technologies involved with 4G are OFDM and MIMO.

- **Fifth generation (5G)**—Beyond 2010, a new generation of network will emerge, rendering 3G and 4G obsolete. By the time 5G comes along, researchers predict a revolution that will enable fast downloads of large chunks of data across the Internet. The user could access a 5G network to download a movie or videogame and then store the data in a handset. More importantly, 5G will support the sorts of advanced multimedia applications discussed in the book's introduction, such as teleimmersion, virtual reality, and telerobotics.

1G: Analog Transmission

The first generation of cellular networks consisted of analog transmission systems for both voice and data. Although better—digital—systems are now available, it is important to understand the history of WWANs, so the following sections describe 1G systems for voice and data.

1G Analog Cellular Networks

Analog cellular systems have been largely replaced with 2G digital networks, but you're likely to still hear about 1G standards, including the following:

- **Advanced Mobile Phone System (AMPS)**—AMPS, also known as IS-54, is on the 800MHz band, involves some 832 channels per carrier, and originated in the United States.

- **Total Access Communication System (TACS)**—TACS operates in the 900MHz band, offers 1,000 channels, and originated in the United Kingdom.

- **Japanese Total Access Communication Systems (JTACS)**—JTACS works in the 800MHz to 900MHz band, and it comes from Japan.

■ **Nordic Mobile Telephone (NMT)**—The original variation of NMT was 450MHz, offering some 220 channels. NMT had a very large coverage area, thanks to its operation at 450MHz (you could probably travel through half of Scandinavia and still be within one cell), but the power levels are so intense that mobile sets were incredibly heavy. NMT originated in Denmark, Finland, Norway, and Sweden.

Other 1G standards used in Europe include Germany and Austria's C-Netz, Sweden's Comvik, NMT-F (France's version of NMT900), and France's Radiocom 2000 (RC2000).

The cellular radio system has three key components (see Figure 14.1): a transceiver station, a mobile telephone switching office (MTSO), and a mobile unit (i.e., the phone). Each cell needs a base transceiver station—a tower that transmits signals to and from the mobile unit. Each of these base transceiver stations connects to an MTSO. The MTSO then interfaces into the terrestrial local exchanges to complete calls over the PSTN. The connections from the base transceiver stations to the MTSO can be either microwave or wireline, and then typically from the MTSO to the local exchange there is a wireline facility, but it could also potentially be microwave. (Chapter 2, "Traditional Transmission Media," discusses the various media options in detail.)

When a mobile unit is on, it emits two numbers consistently: the electronic identification number and the actual phone number of the handset. These are

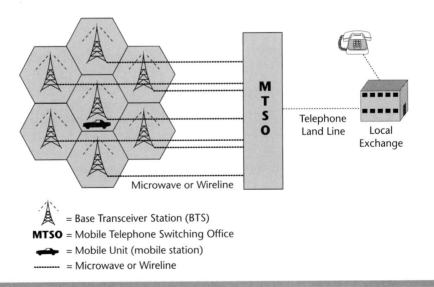

Figure 14.1 The analog cellular architecture

picked up by the base transceiver stations, and depending on the signal level, they can determine whether the unit is well within the cell or transitioning out of that cell. If the unit's power levels start to weaken and it appears that the unit is leaving the cell, an alert is raised that queries the surrounding base transceiver stations to see which one is picking up a strong signal coming in; as the unit crosses the cell perimeter, it is handed over to an adjacent frequency in that incoming cell. The mobile unit cannot stay on the same frequency in between adjacent cells because that would create co-channel interference (i.e., interference between cells).

1G Wireless Data Networks

Early wireless data networking methods included CDPD and packet radio. These technologies are not generally part of new deployments today because better solutions are now available. However, the following sections cover them briefly because you may encounter the language in your studies and should know what it means.

CDPD

CDPD is a packet data protocol designed to work over AMPS or as a protocol for TDMA. The initial concept of CDPD was publicly introduced in 1992. CDPD was envisioned as a wide area mobile data network that could be deployed as an overlay to existing analog systems, a common standard to take advantage of unused bandwidth in the cellular airlink (i.e., the wireless connection between the service provider and the mobile subscriber). (Unused bandwidth is a result of silence in conversations as well as the moments in time when a call is undergoing handover between cells. These periods of no activity can be used to carry data packets and therefore take advantage of the unused bandwidth.) That was the main objective, and it was backed mostly by large cellular network operators.

CDPD is defined as a connectionless, multiprotocol network service that provides peer network wireless extension to the Internet. CDPD's greatest advantage is that it was designed to operate as an extension of existing networks (i.e., IP networks); any application developed for CDPD can be adapted to run on any IP-based network. The complete network specification for CDPD—including architecture, airlink, network interfaces, encryption, authentication, network management, and security—is defined. Throughput is nominally 19.2Kbps, but 9.6Kbps is more common. CDPD looks like TCP/IP, which gives it some advantages, but it does require a specialized subscriber unit.

Figure 14.2 shows a CDPD network. A mobile user has a CDPD subscriber device, typically a proprietary modem provided by the network operator. Incorporated into the base station are elements such as a CDPD mobile data base station and a CDPD mobile data intermediate system (i.e., a router). The voice calls are

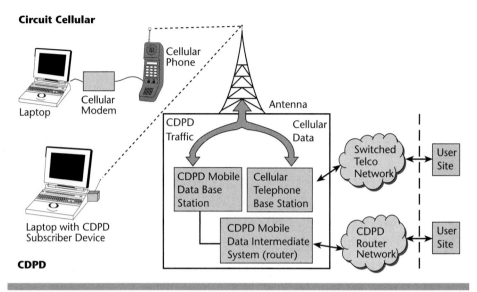

Figure 14.2   The CDPD network architecture

switched out over the telco network, and the data traffic is sent over the CDPD router network.

Packet Radio

Packet radio data networks are an offshoot of Specialized Mobile Radio (SMR). They use licensed bandwidth and are built specifically for two-way data, not for voice communications. The data rates supported by packet radio range up to 19.2Kbps, but the norm is 9600bps. The best applications for packet radio include sessions that are short, as in Short Messaging Service (SMS), transaction processing, and, in some cases, e-mail; packet radio is not a solution for bulk file transfers or client/server interactions. The key applications for packet radio include dispatching, order processing, airline reservations, financial services and banking, lottery, remote database access, messaging, point-of-sale, and telemetry.

In the packet radio data network configuration shown in Figure 14.3, the end user has a mobile unit, a laptop, and a proprietary packet modem that provides access to the private packet base station. A private packet network is the backbone, and it may interface into public data networks or be used on a private basis, for a company's own enterprise network.

Among the packet data options is Mobitex, a paging network developed by Ericsson (www.ericsson.com). It is an open standard for dedicated wireless data and emphasizes reliability and its use in safety-type applications. It is therefore mainly used by military, police, firefighters, and ambulance services. Around 150 such orga-

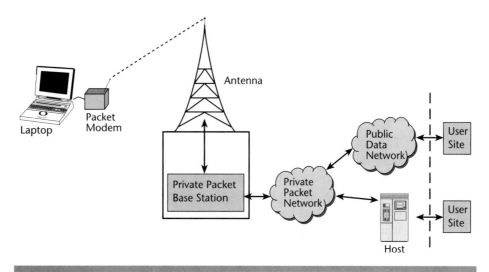

Figure 14.3 Packet radio data network architecture

nizations use Mobitex, which offers a highly reliable communications channel for data where communication must never fail. Mobitex is a trunked radio system based on X.25, originally operating at 8Kbps and now ranging up to 19.2Kbps, and it is built using a fault-tolerant architecture. It is a packet-switched, narrowband, data-only technology mainly for short-burst data. It is ideally suited for applications such as interactive messaging, e-mail, machine-to-machine, telematics/positioning, and forms-based applications. Mobitex channels are 12.5KHz wide. All Mobitex networks operate in one of five frequency families: 80MHz, 160MHz, 400MHz (generally between 415MHz and 430 MHz), 800MHz (generally between 820MHz and 870MHz), or 900MHz (generally between 895MHz and 910 MHz). Frequencies and channels are generally assigned by national government authorities.

Mobitex is offered on more than 30 networks on five continents, but by 2005 it was used primarily in the United States and Canada. European Mobitex networks withered in the face of the overwhelming success of GSM. However, now in its fifth major revision, Mobitex continues to be improved and enhanced for demanding professional use, and the Mobitex Association (www.mobitex.org) reported that its 2005 conference was a great success. The Mobitex system equipment, terminal equipment, and network architecture are continually being enhanced to meet and adapt to changing market needs. The detailed product roadmap extends five years into the future and includes a number of important hardware and software development projects that will result in improved performance, decreased investment, and cost-efficient operations for Mobitex operators. Mobitex is also being used in combination with GPRS, WLAN (802.11), satellite, and CDMA, and we are seeing

UWC

Universal Wireless Communications (UWC), also known as ANSI-136, was at one time the dominant technology in North America and Latin America. As of December 2005, the total number of TDMA subscribers worldwide was approximately 68 million. In comparison, GSM has established itself as the dominant technology on a global basis, with over 1.8 billion subscribers worldwide and a growing population of subscribers in both North America and Latin America.

UWC uses TDMA and Time Division Duplex (TDD) schemes, and it offers a total of six time slots. Because it employs TDD, one time slot is required for each end of the conversation, which means it can carry three conversations per channel. It operates in the 800MHz frequency band, uses AMPS for signaling to reserve resources, and transfers speech in digital form; therefore, it is a digital overlay that is interoperable with the analog AMPS infrastructure. TDMA can now support a 10-fold increase over AMPS capacity, using microcell and hierarchical cell engineering. In terms of data capabilities, the IS-136 standards that exist today include the following:

- IS-136 currently allows data rates up to 30Kbps.

- IS-136+ provides 43.2Kbps to 64Kbps.

- IS-136 HS (high-speed) ranges from 384Kbps to 2Mbps. It is looking toward the same sorts of data rates that 3G promises, it supports EDGE, and it uses the eight phase-shift keying (8-PSK) modulation scheme as well as GPRS (for packet data).

- UWC-136, an enhancement of IS-136, uses EDGE technology. It allows the U.S. TDMA community to migrate from 1G (IS-136) to 3G (UWC-136) systems. UWC-136 uses a wideband TDMA technique.

cdmaOne

cdmaOne is the CDMA Development Group's (CDG's; www.cdg.org) name for cellular carriers that use 2G CDMA technology (IS-95), and it offers a data rate range of 9.6Kbps to 14.4Kbps. cdmaOne describes a complete wireless system based on the TIA/EIA IS-95 CDMA standard, including the IS-95A, IS-95B, and IS-95 HDR revisions. It represents the end-to-end wireless system and all the necessary specifications that govern its operation. cdmaOne provides a family of related services, including cellular, PCS, and fixed wireless (i.e., wireless local loop).

The TIA/EIA IS-95 standard makes use of the spread spectrum technologies discussed in Chapter 13, "Wireless Communications Basics." It operates in the 800MHz and 1,900MHz frequency bands but can work on other frequency bands as well, depending on the country's standards; the appropriate radio frequency simply needs to be engineered on the front end. cdmaOne is full-duplex (i.e., FDD): 1.25MHz for the forward direction, and 1.25MHz for the reverse direction.

TIA/EIA IS-95 was first published in July 1993. The following are the key revisions to this standard:

- **IS-95A**—The IS-95A revision, published in May 1995, is the basis for many of the commercial 2G CDMA systems around the world. IS-95A describes the structure of the wideband 1.25MHz CDMA channels, power control, call processing, handoffs, and registration techniques for system operation. In addition to voice services, many IS-95A operators provide circuit-switched data connections at 14.4Kbps.

- **IS-95B**—The IS-95B revision combines IS-95A, ANSI-J-STD-008, and TSB-74 in a single document. The ANSI-J-STD-008 specification, published in 1995, defines a compatibility standard for 1.8GHz to 2.0GHz CDMA PCS systems. TSB-74 describes interaction between IS-95A and CDMA PCS systems that conform to ANSI-J-STD-008. IS-95B adds a data capability of up to 115Kbps; to achieve 115Kbps, up to eight CDMA traffic channels offering 14.4Kbps need to be aggregated. IS-95B also offers improvements in soft handoffs and interfrequency hard handoffs. Many operators that have commercialized IS-95B systems offer 64Kbps packet-switched data services in addition to voice services. Due to the data speeds IS-95B is capable of reaching, it is categorized as a 2.5G technology.

- **IS-95 HDR (High Data Rate)**—IS-95 HDR provides a spectrally efficient 2.4Mbps peak rate in a standard 1.25MHz channel bandwidth for fixed, portable, and mobile applications. Optimized for packet data services, IS-95 HDR incorporates a flexible architecture based on standard IP. IS-95 HDR is an evolution of CDMA technology with identical radio frequency characteristics to cdmaOne and CDMA2000 1X. IS-95 HDR supports e-mail, Web browsing, mobile e-commerce, telematics, and many other applications while offering end users continuous, untethered, always-on access to the Internet and next-generation data services. IS-95 HDR is categorized as a 3G technology.

cdmaOne offers numerous benefits to cellular operators and their subscribers, including capacity increases of 8 to 10 times that of an AMPS analog system and 4 to 5 times that of a GSM system; improved call quality, with better and more consistent sound compared to AMPS systems; simplified system planning through the use of the same frequency in every sector of every cell; enhanced privacy; improved coverage characteristics, allowing for the possibility of fewer cell sites; increased talk time for portables; and bandwidth-on-demand.

PDC

Personal Digital Cellular (PDC) is a 2G standard developed and used exclusively in Japan. It was originally defined in April 1991 by the standards body that is today known as the Association of Radio Industries and Businesses (ARIB). At its peak, PDC had more than 80 million subscribers, but with Japan's aggressive deployment of 3G mobile networks, as of December 2005, the number of PDC subscribers had dropped by nearly half, to 45.86 million.

PDC is based on TDMA and FDD schemes. It is the most spectrally efficient of the TDMA technologies, with six half-rate (or three full-rate) channels possible in a 25KHz frequency space, compared to three channels in a 30KHz space in IS-136 and eight channels in a 200KHz space for GSM. PDC can operate in two modes: full rate and half rate. Half-rate channels have reduced speech quality and data transmission rates but allow more channels to occupy the same bandwidth. Two voice codecs are supported, including a low-bit-rate 9.6Kbps codec for full-rate voice and a 5.6Kbps codec for half-rate voice. PDC is implemented in two frequency bands: the 800MHz band (specifically, 810MHz to 888MHz downlink and 893MHz to 958MHz uplink) and the 1,500MHz band (at 1,477MHz to 1,501MHz downlink and 1,429MHz to 1,453MHz uplink). The 1,500MHz band allows for the use of much smaller coverage areas, known as picocells, enabling indoor coverage in places such as subway and train stations, shopping malls, and offices. This is very important in Japan and serves as a key differentiator for PDC networks. This PCS version of PDC is also commonly known as Personal Handyphone System (PHS).

PDC offers services that are quite similar to those of GSM, including voice (full and half rate) and the usual supplementary services, such as call forwarding, call waiting, caller ID, three-way conferencing, voice mail, and text mail. It also supports Circuit-Switched Data (CSD) service at up to 9.6Kbps as well as PDC-P, a packet-switched wireless data service that offers data transfer rates of up to 28.8Kbps. Using intelligent network capabilities, PDC also supports prepaid calling, personal numbers, universal access numbers, advanced charging schemes, and wireless virtual private networks (VPNs).

As with all other 2G technologies, PDC is steadily losing ground to more robust and high-speed 3G networks, as well as various emerging broadband wireless technologies (which are covered in Chapter 15, "WMANs, WLANs, and WPANs").

■ 2.5G: Enhanced Data Services

2.5G is the realm of enhanced data services, and four primary techniques fall under this category: General Packet Radio Service (GPRS), High-Speed Circuit-Switched Data (HSCSD), Enhanced Data Rates for Global Evolution (EDGE), and the GSM

EDGE Radio Access Network (GERAN). These standards, as well as standards for messaging services, continue to evolve within the various working groups of the standards organizations.

HSCSD

HSCSD is an enhancement to GSM that uses existing circuit-switched equipment with software upgrades. The main difference between HSCSD and the original GSM data transmission mechanism lies in the ability to use different coding methods as well as multiple time slots for a single user in order to increase data throughput. By using time slot aggregation, HSCSD supports data rates from 9.6Kbps to 57.6Kbps; also performing channel aggregation enables up to 100Kbps. However, those are the theoretical possibilities. In general practice, the operational speed is closer to 28.8Kbps.

HSCSD also provides for several levels of error correction, which can be deployed according to the quality of the radio link. This means that with HSCSD, assuming the best of conditions, a time slot that would normally carry 9.6Kbps (in GSM's original CSD mechanism) can carry 14.4Kbps. By using multiple time slots at the same time, it is possible to achieve an increase in maximum transfer rates up to 57.6Kbps. The time slots being used for such higher-speed data transfer must be fully reserved for a single user. Because the GSM network is configured such that normal voice calls take precedence over additional time slots for HSCSD users, at some point during a call, it might not be possible to satisfy an HSCSD user's full request. In order to maintain the user connection, the user will be charged at a higher rate, sometimes multiplied by the number of time slots allocated and based on the amount of time the user has an active connection. This means that HSCSD can be relatively expensive; therefore, GPRS (discussed in the following section) is becoming the more common choice.

HSCSD is designed for applications that require continuous availability of bandwidth, such as large file transfers, remote access to corporate facilities where a user will be working on a remote server for some time, videoconferencing, and multimedia transmission. HSCSD is offered to subscribers using either voice terminals that support the feature or a special PC card with a built-in GSM phone that turns a notebook computer or other portable device into a complete high-speed mobile office, with the ability to make hands-free voice calls and engage in data transfer. All operators that support HSCSD have implemented national roaming agreements.

GPRS

GPRS, an enhancement to the GSM system, supports data packets. It is the world's most ubiquitous wireless data service, available now with almost every GSM network.

This IP-based connectivity supports a wide range of enterprise and consumer applications and provides users with throughput rates of up to 40Kbps, with the convenience of being able to connect from anywhere. GPRS customers enjoy advanced, feature-rich data services such as color Internet browsing, e-mail on the move, powerful visual communications such as video streaming, multimedia messages, and location-based services.

For operators, the adoption of GPRS is a fast and cost-effective strategy that not only supports the real first wave of mobile Internet services but also represents a big step toward 3GSM (i.e., W-CDMA) networks and services. GPRS has been integrated into GSM standards releases since Release 97. At the end of 2005, there were a total of 290 live GPRS networks.

GPRS is a packet-switched solution that works by overlaying a packet-based air interface on the eight time slots used for GSM transmissions. GPRS is an always-on service; it enables continuous flows of IP data packets over the system for applications such as Web browsing and file transfer. In theory, GPRS supports transmission speeds of up to 172.2Kbps. In practice, due to various interference issues that affect wireless communications, the experienced speeds are substantially lower than this.

Figure 14.5 shows the main elements of the GPRS network. Basically, two core modules are required: a gateway GPRS support node (GGSN) and a serving GPRS support node (SGSN). The GGSN acts as a gateway between the GPRS network and a public data network such as an IP network or perhaps even an X.25 network. The GGSN also connects to other GPRS networks to facilitate GPRS roaming. The SGSN provides packet routing to and from the SGSN service area for all users in that service area. It provides the packet-switched link to mobile stations. A few additional changes need to take place, including the addition of the packet control units, which, for the example shown in Figure 14.5, are hosted at the base station sub-

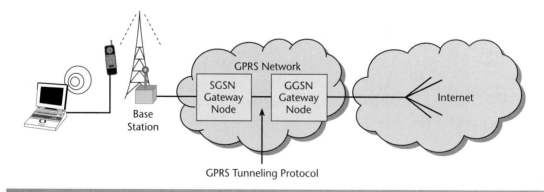

Figure 14.5 GPRS components

system. There is a requirement for some mobility management to locate the GPRS mobile station, as well as a new air interface for packet traffic (i.e., the GPRS handsets). Additional security features also need to be implemented, including firewalls and encryption. Finally, there is a requirement for GPRS-specific signaling.

All in all, GPRS is a migration strategy. It allows you to add packet-based data services to the existing network with minimal changes. It does not require new frequency allocations or licensing of new spectrum, and it does not require a whole new infrastructure to be put in place.

The key applications that GPRS supports include corporate e-mail, Internet e-mail, various information services, job dispatch, remote LAN access, file transfers, Web browsing, still image transfer, and, to some extent, moving images and video and audio. The data rates may be a bit low to support video and multimedia applications with the performance that users want to see, so GPRS is largely a tool for a variety of less complex data sessions.

The GSM Association (GSMA; www.gsmworld.com) has established a technical GPRS roaming platform that it calls *Roamfest*. Roamfest enables executives from GSMA member operators to meet, discuss, and reach bilateral agreements for GSM, GPRS, WLAN, and MMS interworking roaming. This program has been successful as a one-stop-shop to fast-track GSM roaming agreements.

EDGE

Of the 290 live GPRS networks at the end of 2005, nearly 60% had committed to the EDGE upgrade. EDGE builds on enhancements provided by GPRS and HSCSD technologies. By using EDGE, operators can handle three times more subscribers than with GPRS, triple their data rate per subscriber, or add extra capacity to their voice communications. EDGE uses the same TDMA frame structure, logic channel, and 200KHz carrier bandwidth as today's GSM networks, which allows it to be overlaid directly onto an existing GSM network. For many existing GSM/GPRS networks, EDGE is a simple software upgrade. EDGE allows the delivery of advanced mobile services such as the downloading of video and music clips, full multimedia messaging, high-speed color Internet access, and e-mail on the move. Due to the very small incremental cost of including EDGE capability in GSM network deployment, virtually all new GSM infrastructure deployments are also EDGE capable, and nearly all new mid- to high-level GSM devices also include EDGE radio technology.

EDGE basically enables a greater data transmission speed to be achieved in good conditions, especially near the base stations. It does so by implementing an 8-PSK modulation scheme instead of Gaussian Minimum-Shift Keying (GMSK). 8-PSK enables each pulse to carry 3 bits of information versus GMSK's 1 bit per pulse rate. Thus, EDGE has the potential to increase the data rate of existing GSM systems by a factor of three. For EDGE to be effective, it should be installed along with the packet-switching upgrades used for GPRS. Again, this entails the addition of the GGSN and the SGSN. In addition, an EDGE transceiver unit must be added to each cell, and the base stations must receive remote software upgrades. EDGE can coexist with GSM traffic, switching to EDGE mode automatically.

EDGE ultimately allows the combination of digital TDMA and GSM and provides an enhanced version of GPRS. It supports 48Kbps to 69.2Kbps per time slot, and by aggregating time slots, it can support up to 384Kbps. GSM's 200KHz channel spacing is also maintained in EDGE, allowing the use of existing spectrum bands. EDGE is also sometimes referred to as a 2.75G system.

At the end of 2005, there were 121 commercial EDGE networks in 70 countries, and there were 174 GSM/EDGE terminal devices available. There were also 57 mobile operators deploying combined EDGE/W-CDMA networks and 26 combined EDGE/W-CDMA networks already in service. EDGE has become a standard in most new data-enabled phones.

GERAN

GERAN is a second phase of EDGE that is planned to offer data rates of up to 1,920Kbps, to support packetized voice and real-time services. GERAN enables the common evolution of GSM and TDMA toward providing full 3G services. This includes introducing support for both generic real-time services and a spectrum-efficient service for packet-switched voice, as well as interfacing to an all-IP 3G core network common with UMTS.

GERAN is a common evolution path for GSM and TDMA that intends to provide a cost-efficient means to deliver 3G services within the existing frequency bands. The 3G Partnership Project (3GPP; www.3GPP.org), discussed later in this chapter, has completed a feasibility study to define the GERAN features to be standardized and incorporated into 3GPP Release 7.

Messaging Services Standards

Part of the GSM service spectrum involves messaging, and messaging services are evolving. The enormous success of SMS seems to indicate that person-to-person messaging will be the most likely driver of mobile data revenues for some time. Enhanced Messaging Service (EMS) and Multimedia Messaging Service (MMS), in combination with growth in the use of prepaid services, are likely to become critical drivers of the mobile Internet.

EMS

EMS is an extension of SMS that enables users to send a combination of simple melodies, images, sounds, animations, and formatted text as a message to another

EMS-compatible phone. EMS supports three image formats: small, which is 16×16 pixels; large, which is 32×32 pixels; and variable, which depends on the formats the phone manufacturer supports and how each individual phone model is designed. EMS also supports animated images in two formats: small, which is 8×8 pixels, and large, which is 16×16 pixels. EMS phones used predefined animations that represent various emotional states, such as sadness, skepticism, happiness, anger, and playfulness.

MMS

MMS is a further extension of both SMS and EMS designed to operate over both 2.5G and 3G networks. It makes use of newer and quicker mobile transmission methods, such as GPRS, HSCSD, EDGE, and UMTS. MMS involves attaching to messages multimedia extensions such as video and sound. MMS requires a new network infrastructure as well as MMS-enabled handsets. Unlike SMS and EMS, MMS is not limited to 160 characters per message. MMS will soon become a standard feature and the default messaging mode for mobile phones. At the end of 2005, 278 operators were offering MMS service. Although at this time MMS roaming and intercarrier exchange are not widely available, that will certainly improve as more networks are deployed and more subscribers choose MMS over SMS.

MMS supports standard image formats such as GIF and JPEG, video formats such as MPEG-4, and audio formats such as MP3, MIDI, and WAV. MMS standardization over GSM, GPRS, and W-CDMA is being managed through 3GPP. The dramatic shift toward the use of phones equipped with cameras, illustrating the growing importance of imaging from high-end smart phones down to basic midrange and even low-end mobile phones, is creating a growing market for MMS services.

■ 3G: Moving Toward Broadband Wireless

Data service is expected to rise sharply as a traffic stream on wireless networks. However, the allotted wireless spectrum and the compression techniques we have traditionally relied on will not allow us to make use of the existing wireless infrastructure as if it were a wireless Internet, let alone a platform for the delivery of multimedia content and TV programming. Visual traffic will play a very demanding role in the future of telecommunications networks, and the problems that traffic poses are magnified many times over with wireless media.

The future demands a new generation of infrastructure, and 3G is one step toward the broadband wireless realm. When you think about 3G, it is important to keep a number of things in mind. First, 3G is still under development. Although large-scale implementations were anticipated to occur beginning in 2001, 3G did not begin to flourish until several years after that. Aside from the fact that it requires licensing of new spectrum, as well as an entirely new infrastructure, 3G has been plagued by problems, including lack of 3G handsets, lack of interoperability between 2G and 3G networks, high costs for both operators and subscribers, and lower-than-promised performance. However, as of early 2006, there were around 245 million 3G subscribers worldwide, most of whom were serviced by CDMA2000 networks, with only a very small proportion subscribing to W-CDMA/UMTS.

Although we are not yet able to experience all the mobile broadband multimedia services and maximum data rates promised by 3G, we are seeing more deployments of 3G networks, and enhanced 3G service, referred to as 3.5G, is beginning to make an appearance. While we argue the lifetime of 3G, new generations, such as 4G and 5G, are already in development. At any point in time, new technologies are being developed and operating in labs that will emerge commercially within five to seven years. Between the time of the vision and the time of the implementation, enough changes will have occurred to render the solution somewhat outdated, yet the formalization of the new and improved version will still be too far off to be viable. (The visions of 4G and 5G are discussed later in this chapter.)

3G is designed for high-speed multimedia data and voice (see Figure 14.6). Its goals include high-quality audio and video and advanced global roaming, which means being able to go anywhere and automatically be handed off to any wireless system available. 3G is defined by the ITU under the International Mobile Telecommunications 2000 (IMT-2000) global framework. The main goals of IMT-2000 include achieving equivalency between wireline and wireless, support for messaging, Internet access, high-speed multimedia, improved throughput, QoS support, improved security, improved voice quality, and improved battery life. The IMT-2000 framework encompasses support for fixed applications and a broad range of mobility scenarios, from picocells serving in-building and local users to global coverage

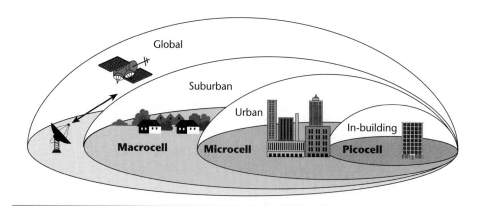

Figure 14.6 3G network coverage

via satellites. It calls for global deployment with seamless roaming, support for position-location services (including emergencies, navigation, and location-specific services), and support for technological evolution.

IMT-2000 was formerly known as the Future Public Land Mobile Telecommunications System (FPLMTS). In 1992, the World Administrative Radio Conference (WARC) allocated 1,885MHz to 2,025MHz and 2,110MHz to 2,200MHz for IMT-2000, including 1,980MHz to 2,010MHz and 2,170MHz to 2,200MHz for satellite. In 2000, WARC allocated additional spectrum in three frequency bands: below 1GHz, at 1.7GHz (where many 2G systems currently operate), and in the 2.5GHz range. WARC is now referred to as World Radiocommunications Conference, and information on the next conference is available at www.itu.int.

Terrestrial IMT-2000 services operate in the FDD mode in the bands 1,920MHz to 1,980MHz and 2,110MHz to 2,170MHz, with mobile stations transmitting in the lower subband and base stations transmitting in the upper subband. The bands 1,885MHz to 1,920MHz and 2,010MHz to 2,025MHz are unpaired for TDD operation. The GSMA feels that several additional frequency bands should be nonexclusively designated for the use of IMT-2000 to provide for up to an additional 160MHz of spectrum. These bands include 698MHz to 806MHz, 2,500MHz to 2,690MHz, and 2,700MHz to 2,900MHz.

3G also includes a satellite component, known as Mobile Satellite Service (MSS), which is the only IMT-2000 system that can be used worldwide. Intended to take over when a user is out of range of terrestrial base stations, MSS requires the participation and cooperation of companies and governments worldwide. The target data rate for MSS is 100Kbps, compared to 2Mbps for terrestrial systems. MSS operators hope to offer services similar to those of terrestrial 2.5G and 3G networks, including data at ISDN speeds, toll-quality voice, video, and multimedia messaging.

3G applications include traditional voice services, involving high-quality voice transmission, global roaming, 144Kbps to 2Mbps for packet and circuit data, always-on data availability, high-speed mobile Internet access, and high-capacity e-mail. More importantly, 3G involves support for a wide variety of broadband applications, such as videoconferencing, navigation/mapping systems, streaming video and TV, common billing/user profiles, multimedia messaging, mobile voice and video over IP, calling line image, mobile entertainment, m-commerce payment solutions, and location-based services.

3G Standards

The ITU started the process of defining the standard for 3G systems with IMT-2000. The European Telecommunications Standards Institute (ETSI; www.etsi.org) was responsible for the UMTS standardization process in Europe. The 3G Partnership Project (3GPP; www.3GPP.org) was formed in 1998, under the ETSI, to make a globally applicable 3G mobile phone system specification within the scope of the ITU's IMT-2000 project. 3GPP organizational members include ARIB (Japan), ATIS (United States), CCSA (China), ETSI (Europe), TTA (Korea), and TTC (Japan). 3GPP specifications are based on evolved GSM specifications—what is today commonly known as the UMTS system. 3GPP has five main UMTS standardization areas: radio access network, core network, terminals, services and system aspects, and GERAN. 3GPP standards are structured as releases, and discussions of 3GPP often refer to the functionality of the various releases. Current 3GPP releases include the following:

■ **Release 98**—This release specifies pre-3G GSM networks.

■ **Release 99**—This release specifies the first UMTS 3G networks, incorporating a CDMA air interface.

■ **Release 4**—Originally called Release 2000, this release adds features that include an all-IP core network.

■ **Release 5**—This release introduces IMS and HSDPA.

■ **Release 6**—This release integrates operation with WLAN networks and adds HSUPA.

■ **Release 7**—This release focuses on better integration with wired networks and examines advanced receivers. This release is still in the early stages of development.

The 3G Partnership Project 2 (3GPP2; www.3GPP2.org) was formed when ETSI refused to expand the scope of 3GPP to address CDMA2000. The American National Standards Institute (ANSI; www.ansi.org) then formed 3GPP2 to coordinate CDMA2000 developments. The 3GPP2 organizational members include ARIB (Japan), CCSA (China), TIA (United States), TTA (Korea), and TTC (Japan). More than 80 individual member companies are participating in 3GPP2. The work of producing 3GPP2's specifications resides in the project's four technical specification groups (TSGs), comprising representatives from the project's individual member companies. The TSGs include TSG-A, which covers access network interfaces; TSG-C, which covers CDMA2000 standards; TSG-S, which covers services and systems aspects; and TSG-X, which deals with core networks.

Despite the global efforts to define one standard for 3G, there remain different approaches. The IMT-2000 standard evolved with five possible radio interfaces based on three different access technologies: FDMA, TDMA, and CDMA. However, the majority of deployed 3G systems consist of the two main technologies: W-CDMA (known as UMTS in Europe) and CDMA2000. There are other important 3G variants, including Time Division Synchronous Code Division Multiple Access (TD-SCDMA), which is used primarily in China, and NTT DoCoMo's Freedom of Mobile Multimedia Access (FOMA), which is used in Japan. FOMA is based on W-CDMA and is compliant with IMT-2000. As shown in Table 14.1 and discussed in the following sections, there is a single W-CDMA standard with three modes.

UMTS/W-CDMA

Universal Mobile Telecommunications System (UMTS), the European implementation of the 3G wireless phone system, uses W-CDMA. Its development was driven by the need for a ubiquitous, very-high-speed, low-latency, packet-based platform to provide broadband and other packet services to users at home, at work, or on the road. UMTS defines both narrowband (2Mbps in the 2GHz band) and broadband (100Mbps and faster in the 60GHz band) services. Personal mobility is a major objective of UMTS. The UMTS Forum (www.umts-forum.org) estimates that over 60% of revenues from the UMTS networks will be derived from data communications in the long term. New approaches to content aggregation and delivery will be needed to drive the uptake of UMTS services, introducing new players, including content providers, ISPs, and virtual mobile network operators.

GSM-based operators in the United States and elsewhere favor a standard based on the UMTS Universal Terrestrial Radio Access (UTRA) standard, which is more typically referred to as W-CDMA. W-CDMA has two proposed implementations: UMTS, which is based on FDD, and UMTS TDD/TD-CDMA, which is based on TDD. UMTS/W-CDMA operates in the frequency bands 1,920MHz to 1,980MHz and 2,110MHz to 2,170MHz, using FDD transmission. The minimum frequency band required is two 5MHz channels. The frequency reuse is $N = 1$, which means that all the frequencies can be reused in each cell, including adjacent cells. UMTS/W-CDMA uses the modulation scheme QPSK and supports both circuit- and packet-based services. The maximum user data rate it supports is 1,920Kbps, but real-world experience at the moment is actually 384Kbps. The 3.5G enhancement

Table 14.1 3G Standards

Interface ITU Designation	Technology	Technique	Carrier
W-CDMA (UMTS, UTRA, FDD), IMT DS	W-CDMA	Direct-sequence FDD	Single 5MHz channel
CDMA2000 (1X and 3X RTT), IMT MC	W-CDMA	Multicarrier TDD	Multicarrier
TD-SCDMA and UMTS TDD, IMT TC	W-CDMA	DSSS (UMTS TDD), time code, TDD	1.6MHz or 5MHz channels
UWC-136/EDGE	TDMA	Single-carrier	Single-carrier

known as HSDPA (discussed later in this chapter) will offer data speeds up to 10Mbps, and with the addition of MIMO systems, 20Mbps may be possible.

At the end of 2005, 146 W-CDMA licenses had been awarded in 48 countries, and there were 100 commercial W-CDMA networks operating in 42 countries, plus 4 more W-CDMA operators in precommercial stages (see the Global Mobile Suppliers Association, at www.gsacom.com). Also at the end of 2005, the total number of W-CDMA subscribers was over 40 million, and some 2 million new subscribers were being added monthly. In addition, there were 272 W-CDMA device models available on the market from 37 device suppliers, with 14 models supporting HSDPA.

3.5G Standards: The 3G Evolution

The 3G evolution describes the seamless, compatible evolutionary path of enhancements to the existing GSM technology family. These enhancements will enable GSM operators to improve their ability to provide mobile broadband multimedia services by supporting higher data transfer speeds and greater system capacity. Because this is an evolutionary path, the generic benefits associated with the GSM family are maintained, including global roaming, seamless billing, network compatibility, and huge economies of scale.

The 3G evolutionary path consists of a series of well-defined technology enhancements, including High-Speed Downlink Packet Access (HSDPA), High-Speed Uplink Packet Access (HSUPA), and High-Speed OFDM Packet Access (HSOPA). The first of these to be realized, HSDPA, provides performance improvement in the downlink channel. The following sections describe each of these standards.

HSDPA HSDPA is part of the 3GPP/UTRAN (UMTS Terrestrial Radio Access Network) FDD Release 5 W-CDMA specifications. In 3GPP standards, HSDPA evolved from and is backward compatible with Release 99 W-CDMA systems. Release 4 specifications provide efficient IP support, enabling provision of services through an all-IP core network. Release 5 specifications focus on HSDPA to provide data rates from 8Mbps to 14Mbps (and 20Mbps for MIMO systems) over a 5MHz bandwidth in W-CDMA downlink to support packet-based multimedia services. HSDPA makes use of QPSK for noisy channels and 16-QAM modulation for clearer channels. As discussed in Chapter 5, "Data Communications Basics," QPSK is more robust and can tolerate higher levels of interference than 16-QAM but has a lower transmission bit rate. 16-QAM, on the other hand, offers twice the bit rate but is more prone to errors than QPSK due to interference and noise, and hence it requires stronger forward error correction (FEC).

Similar to the way EDGE enhances GSM/GPRS, HSDPA enhances W-CDMA. HSDPA doubles the air interface capacity and delivers a four- or five-fold increase in downlink data speeds. It also shortens the round-trip time between network and terminals and reduces variance in downlink transmission delay. The combination of faster data rates and increased spectral efficiency should result in lower cost per data bit transmitted. The theoretical peak rate is 14.4Mbps, but the realistic end-user experience is initially likely to be 1.8Mbps or possibly up to 3.6Mbps. The high download speeds offered by HSDPA will greatly enhance a wide range of mobile services, from Web browsing to video downloads.

HSDPA is a packet-based data service in the W-CDMA downlink channel. It was designed from the beginning to support IP and packet-based multimedia services. HSDPA offers many service-enhancing features, including Adaptive Modulation and Coding (AMC), which is a modulation technique that can be determined dynamically, depending on the conditions of the wireless channel at the time. Another key feature of HSDPA is the use of MIMO, which results in great improvements in capacity. (MIMO is discussed in Chapter 13.) MIMO antenna systems are the work item in the 3GPP Release 6 specifications, which support even higher data transmission rates (up to 20Mbps).

Another important enhancement to HSDPA is that error control is greatly improved through the use of hybrid automatic repeat request (HARQ). HARQ is a variation of the ARQ error control method that gives better performance than ordinary ARQ, particularly over wireless channels, albeit at the cost of increased implementation complexity. ARQ is an error control method for data transmission in which the receiver detects transmission errors in a message and automatically requests a retransmission from the transmitter. Generally, when the transmitter receives the ARQ, the transmitter retransmits the message until either it is correctly received or the error persists beyond a predetermined number of retransmissions. The simplest version of HARQ combines FEC (which is discussed in Chapter 13) and ARQ by encoding the data block plus error detection information with an error correction code prior to transmission. When the coded data block is received, the receiver first decodes the error correction code. If the channel quality is good enough, all transmission errors should be correctable, and the receiver can obtain the correct data block. If the channel quality is bad and not all transmission errors can be corrected, the receiver will detect this situation, using the error correction code, and then the received coded data block is discarded and a retransmission is requested by the receiver. Other features of HARQ include fast cell search and advanced receiver design.

As Figure 14.7 illustrates, because HSDPA is built on a distributed architecture and implements key processing at the base station, closer to the air interface, HSDPA achieves low delay link adaptation. By taking advantage of techniques including a fast Layer 1 retransmission scheme (HARQ) and link adaptation, HSDPA delivers significantly improved packet data throughput performance.

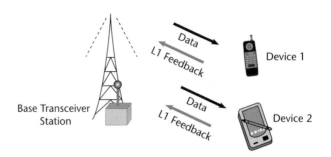

Figure 14.7 HSDPA

All operators are expected to evolve to HSDPA as the new baseline for mobile wireless broadband. HSDPA is widely embraced by the vendor community, and the majority of existing W-CDMA operators are expected to upgrade their 3GSM networks to support HSDPA technology. Many operators have confirmed interest in and are considering, planning, deploying, or trialing HSDPA.

HSDPA is expected to provide a user applications experience between 3 and 10 times faster than with traditional UMTS. HSDPA is often compared to WiMax (which is discussed in Chapter 15). Early HSDPA will focus on data, voice, and mobility from the handset perspective. WiMax will focus on broadband data, initially to underserved areas because of its distance capability. An advantage of HSDPA is that, unlike WiMax, it requires no new infrastructure, just the downloading of new software to the handset, using the existing cellular infrastructure.

HSUPA HSUPA is the sibling of HSDPA but has taken longer to reach consensus. Enhancements to the uplink data speed are being standardized in the 3GPP Release 6 specification. HSUPA is expected to use an uplink Enhanced Dedicated Channel (E-DCH) on which it will employ link adaptation methods similar to those employed by HSDPA: shorter transmission time interval (TTI), enabling faster link adaptation, and HARQ with incremental redundancy, making retransmission more effective. TTI is a parameter in many digital telecom networks related to encapsulation of data from higher layers into frames for transmission on the radio link layer. *Link adaptation*, a term used in wireless communications, describes the adaptation of various parameters, such as modulation, coding, signal, and protocol, to radio link conditions. The key is that the link adaptation process is dynamic and the parameters change as the radio link conditions change. In HSDPA, for example, this can take place every 2 milliseconds.

The HSUPA standard enables users to transmit data upstream at a speed of 5.8Mbps. As this standard appears commercially, mobile users will be able to exchange and access data and multimedia much more efficiently and enjoyably. HSUPA technology is expected to be introduced in 2007. Some consider HSUPA to be a 3.75G technology.

Jointly, downlink and uplink enhancements are referred to as High-Speed Packet Access (HSPA) services. Increased downlink and uplink speeds will further enhance user experiences and increase the use of applications and activities, especially where data is shared between users (e.g., with interactive multiplayer games).

HSOPA   HSDPA is just beginning to be deployed, and HSUPA isn't here yet, but vendors are already contemplating the next step beyond those technologies, HSOPA. Because it incorporates OFDM and MIMO, HSOPA promises to offer a 40Mbps download speed. Besides faster speeds, HSOPA is expected to dramatically reduce costs because OFDM allows more capacity with a given amount of spectrum. If HSOPA moves forward in the standards procedure, it is expected to make its commercial debut in late 2007 or early 2008.

UMTS TDD/TD-CDMA

TDD is specifically intended for high-data-rate services. Unlike W-CDMA, which uses FDD, UMTS TDD uses TDD and is designed to work in a single, unpaired frequency band. TDD uses a combined TDD and CDMA scheme. It was first defined by 3GPP in Release 99, and it has continued to evolve in the later releases.

UMTS TDD operates in the unpaired frequency bands 1,900MHz to 1,920MHz and 2,010MHz to 2,025MHz, using TDD transmission. To provide flexibility to service providers, UMTS TDD has also been rebanded to allow operation in other licensed spectrum bands, even up to 3.6GHz. UMTS TDD makes use of Direct Sequence Spread Spectrum (DSSS) and the QPSK modulation technique. It operates on a single 5MHz or 10MHz channel, and 20MHz channels are planned as well. The frequency reuse is $N = 1$, meaning the frequencies can be reused in all the cells. Peak download speeds of up to 12Mbps are promised.

One of the largest benefits of using TDD is that it supports variable asymmetry. This means than an operator can decide how much capacity is allocated to the downlink versus the uplink. Because data traffic patterns generally favor the downlink, the result is much better use of spectrum and higher efficiency. Another feature promoted by UMTS TDD proponents is mobility support, with claims that UMTS TDD allows subscribers to stay connected while traveling in excess of 75 mph (120 kph), as long as they remain within the network footprint. It also supports tower-to-tower handoff and network-to-network roaming. Finally, TD-CDMA devices consume significantly less power than other devices, resulting in improved talk times and standby times.

For more information, see the UMTS TDD Alliance Web site (www.umtstdd.org).

TD-SCDMA   TD-SCDMA was proposed by the China Communications Standards Association (CCSA; www.cwts.org/english/index.php) and approved by the ITU in 1999. The TD-SCDMA Forum (www.tdscdma-forum.org) includes eight member companies: China Mobile, China Telecom, China Unicom, Datang, Huawei, Motorola, Nortel, and Siemens. TD-SCDMA is primarily aimed at the mainland Chinese market, in support of voice services.

TD-SCDMA uses TDD, which significantly improves network performance by processing traffic in both the uplink and downlink directions. It transmits uplink traffic and downlink traffic in the same frame in different time slots. Uplink and downlink resources are assigned according to individual user needs. The S (for *Synchronous*) in its name signifies that TD-SCDMA can master both synchronous circuit-switched services (such as speech or video services) and asynchronous packet-switched services (such as Internet access). Data rates can range from 1.2Kbps to 2Mbps. In addition, TD-SCDMA improves performance by using the CDMA encoding transmission mode, supporting improved and highly efficient capacity and spectrum usage.

TD-SCDMA covers all application scenarios, being designed to address all cell sizes: metropolitan city centers, indoor and campus environments, hotspots, and rural areas. Because TD-SCDMA is based on TDD and uses unpaired frequency bands, it offers optimum efficiency for both symmetric and asymmetric data services. Due to its small bandwidth of 1.6MHz, this technology allows flexible spectrum allocation, depending on the type of information being transmitted. When asymmetrical data such as e-mail and Internet information are transmitted from the base station, more time slots are used for the downlink than for the uplink. A symmetrical split in the uplink and downlink takes place with symmetrical services such as telephony. Finally, seamless handoff between TD-SCDMA and GSM guarantees that no call is lost while the user is moving.

The main characteristics of TD-SCDMA are that it operates in the frequency band 2,010MHz to 2,025MHz in China (with wireless local loop applications in the 1,900MHz to 1,920MHz band) using the TDD mode. TD-SCDMA can operate in a minimum frequency band of 1.6MHz at 2Mbps or a 5MHz band at 6Mbps. The frequency reuse is $N = 1$ or $N = 3$, and TD-SCDMA supports the modulation schemes QPSK and 8-PSK.

Many believe that the TD-SCDMA air interface will be used by some of the operators Beijing is expected to license, though the time frame for awarding licenses has been delayed several times.

CDMA2000

With existing networks nearing saturation and demand for wireless services continuing to grow, operators have been looking at technologies that will deliver increased capacity at the lowest possible cost. In fact, one of the biggest drivers behind 3G is capacity improvement, and network capacity is one of the key criteria for 3G technology selection. In 2000, CDMA2000 was the first 3G technology to be commercially deployed as part of the ITU's IMT-2000 framework. CDMA2000, the common name for IMT-2000 CDMA Multi-Carrier (CDMA-MC), increases data transmission rates for existing CDMA (cdmaOne) network operators. Figure 14.8 shows the infrastructure of a CDMA2000 wireless network.

Key features of CDMA2000 devices include color displays, GPS, digital and video cameras, push-to-talk, support for streaming-type real-time video-on-demand (VOD)/audio-on-demand services, and voice recognition functions.

cdmaOne and CDMA2000 are the most spectrally efficient technologies and support at least twice the maximum number of voice calls as current non-CDMA 2G technologies. The CDMA industry is also deploying new solutions that will further enhance the capacity of existing networks. CDMA's capacity advantages are real, with operators experiencing these benefits today. cdmaOne delivers the most capacity in the 2G world, even considering the latest frequency-hopping techniques and adaptive multirate voice codecs in GSM networks. CDMA2000, which is now being deployed worldwide, doubles the capacity of cdmaOne networks.

IS-95 HDR is being used as the underlying technology for CDMA2000. IS-95 HDR is optimized for IP packets and Internet access, and it can be used to enhance data capabilities in existing cdmaOne networks or in standalone data networks. With existing CDMA networks, a number of channels are changed from voice to data. Using a combination of TDM and CDMA, IS-95 HDR shares each channel among several users, but on an as-needed basis rather than as fixed time slots, as in TDMA. CDMA2000 promises a 2.4Mbps peak data rate in a standard 1.25MHz CDMA voice channel. The IS-95 HDR data rate varies, depending on the distance between the mobile phone and the base station.

Some 94% of current 3G deployments use CDMA2000, but this represents only a fraction of all operators. As more GSM operators convert to 3G W-CDMA technology and implement HSDPA, HSDPA could dwarf CDMA2000.

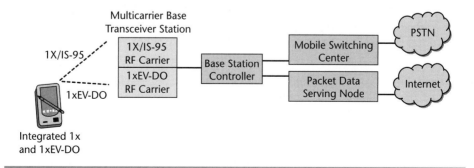

Figure 14.8 A CDMA2000 network

At the beginning of 2006, there were more than 300 million subscribers to CDMA networks, with an average growth rate of around 5 million subscribers per month, and CDMA2000 had surpassed 225 million subscribers as of March 2006 (see the CDMA Development Group Web site, at www.cdg.org).

CDMA2000 represents an entire family of technologies, including the following:

- **CDMA2000 1X RTT (Radio Transmission Technology)**—This technology can double the voice capacity of cdmaOne networks, delivering peak rate packet data speeds of 153Kbps downstream (Release 0) and 307Kbps downstream (Release 1) in mobile environments, using a single 1.25MHz carrier, in new or existing spectrum. Enabled services include entertainment (e.g., playing a videogame with a friend), e-mail and picture transfer (e.g., using a camera phone to send a photo postcard), and location/traffic/GPS service (e.g., navigating through rush hour or finding the nearest grocery store).

- **CDMA2000 1xEV-DO (Enhanced Version–Data Only)**—This 3G technology uses a separate 1.25MHz carrier for data, providing data-optimized channels. An asymmetrical implementation, it supports up to 2.4Mbps downstream and up to 153Kbps upstream. The average rate a user experiences is between 300Kbps and 600Kbps. 1xEV-DO Revision A supports IP packets, increases the downlink peak rate to 3.1Mbps, and substantially boosts the uplink rate to 1.2Mbps. The latest enhancement, CDMA2000 1xEV-DO Revision B, enables operators to aggregate up to 15 1.25MHz channels to deliver 73.5Mbps throughputs and greater network efficiencies. These enhanced data rates enable services including streaming video (e.g., downloading and viewing a movie trailer or mobile soap), broadcasts (e.g., watching live TV coverage of the Olympics or World Cup), videoconferencing (e.g., taking part on a videoconference call), streaming audio (e.g., MP3 music downloads), and location/traffic services (e.g., viewing real-time traffic and weather reports).

- **CDMA2000 1xEV-DV (Enhanced Version–Data and Voice)**—This technology integrates voice and data over the same 1.25MHz carrier as CDMA2000 1xEV-DO. It is asymmetrical, offering a peak data rate of up to 4.8Mbps downstream and up to 307Kbps upstream.

The next phase of CDMA2000, CDMA2000 3X, uses three 1.25MHz CDMA channels. It is part of the CDMA2000 specification for countries that require 5MHz of spectrum for 3G use. CDMA2000 3X is also known as 3X RTT, MC-3X, and IMT-CDMA Multi-Carrier 3X. CDMA2000 3X uses a pair of 3.75MHz channels (i.e., 3 × 1.25MHz) to reach higher data rates, with the promise to support integrated voice and data up to 3.09Mbps. CDMA2000 3X has not yet been deployed.

CDMA450

CDMA450 is a TIA/EIA-IS-CDMA2000 (CDMA-MC) system deployed at 450MHz. It includes the same family of technologies as CDMA2000. Currently, CDMA2000 1X and CDMA2000 1xEV-DO are commercially available for the 450MHz band, and CDMA2000 1xEV-DV is being developed.

The advantages of CDMA450 derive from the spectral efficiency and high-speed data capabilities of CDMA2000 and the expanded coverage afforded by a lower frequency band. CDMA450 provides a larger cell size compared to other bands, which translates to fewer cell sites and significantly lower capital and operating expenditures to service vast coverage areas. CDMA450 offers IMT-2000 services, such as high-quality voice and high-speed data access, and it represents an evolution path to advanced 3G services, allowing for a phased evolution. CDMA450 requires only a small amount of spectrum (1.25MHz), which is a significant consideration for NMT operators who have 4MHz to 5MHz allocated to them.

CDMA450 offers a solution for multiple markets. A number of operators in eastern and central European countries, Russia, and southeast Asia are using the 450MHz band to provide wireless services with first-generation analog equipment, based on the NMT standard. CDMA450 is the only technology commercially available to those operators that allows direct transition from a first-generation system to next-generation services. CDMA450 is also one of the few technologies that fits into 4MHz to 5MHz of spectrum (it requires 2 × 1.25MHz for a single channel and can fit three or four CDMA450 carriers, depending on the size of guard bands).

Providing access to communication services (voice and Internet access) is a key priority for governments and regulators around the world, especially in developing countries. Using lower-frequency bands offers a cost-effective solution for meeting these goals. Due to the favorable propagation characteristics of lower frequencies and their associated coverage benefits, there may be significant cost advantages associated with deploying a wireless system in the 450MHz band.

The 450MHz band can be used to provide broadband access for mobile or fixed data users. Many countries have indicated a need to provide their public safety communication markets with group communication, high-speed data access, push-to-talk, video streaming, and dispatch services. Some countries are also investigating the use of a high-speed data network to provide broadband access to schools, hospitals, and businesses. These networks could be seen as complementary to other cellular-based networks and could be employed in either a fixed, portable, or fully mobile setting, depending on the application.

3G Deployment Issues

A main barrier to 3G is that there is a lot of competition in this arena, with many different standards being advocated. Also, there is already an installed base of 2G and 2.5G networks, and companies want to protect their investment there. A number of important issues, including the following, have yet to be fully resolved:

■ **Problems providing seamless handoff between 2G and 3G networks**—Although there are dual-mode and triple-mode phones coming into the market, handoff troubles are still common. There are problems with handoffs from UMTS to GSM, with connections being dropped or handoffs being possible only in one direction (from UMTS to GSM), with the handset returning to UMTS mode only after the user hangs up, even if UMTS coverage returns. There is also the issue of initially poor coverage due to the time it takes to build a network.

■ **Service delivery problems**—There are large issues from a service delivery perspective. For example, in order to support true 3G VOD features, a base station needs to be set up every 1,000 yards to 1 mile (1 to 1.5 km). As you can imagine, although this may be economically feasible in urban areas, it is much more difficult to justify in less populated areas, such as suburbs or rural environments.

■ **The complexity of W-CDMA**—Not many knowledgeable engineers have substantial experience in W-CDMA. Because 3G standards are still evolving, 3G is a moving target to some extent. The fact that speeds are lower than promised creates concern and is one of the reasons that many have opted for 2.5G rather than moving forward with the brand-new infrastructure required by 3G.

■ **The availability and cost of 3G devices**—Large operators have an easier time ordering and receiving the limited number of available devices than do smaller operators, which affects their ability to market a diverse line of devices to go along with the new and more expensive service.

■ **Poor battery life and overweight devices**—When using the new 3G terminals for high-speed data communications or videoconferencing, a user can easily drain the battery after 15 minutes of a session. The size and weight of the devices is increased to accommodate a screen that has enough pixels to make an image worth looking at, and the need for more battery power to sustain high-speed data and videoconferencing adds to the weight. Of course, these devices generate more heat as well. As a result, there are also some additional health risks associated with 3G handsets: They emit even more power than their 2G counterparts. Dual-radio handsets—those that could cross between TDMA and CDMA—are not readily available, nor are handsets that can work across all the variations of CDMA.

- **The cost and ability of gaining new sites**—We've been building cellular networks since the 1980s, but finding a proper site and getting the agreement to place a base station may be limited in larger cities. The fact that carriers aren't spending as quickly as they used to is delaying rollouts as well.

Other barriers are differences in frequency allocations, proper assessment of the demand in terms of voice versus data versus video, and the cost and coverage associated with 3G versus what already exists and seems to be adequately accommodating medium-speed data. One of the biggest problems for 3G is a lack of significant consumer demand (which, in some cases, is a result of the reluctance of carriers, especially those in the United States, to envision services that people will pay for). In addition, Wi-Fi wireless LANs and WiMax wireless MANs, given what they can do for data, create some competition for 3G; Chapter 15 discusses these types of networks in detail.

■ Beyond 3G

While we are in the throes of finally seeing 3G networks deployed, there is already a buzz about its enhancement, going by names such as LTE, Beyond 3G, Super 3G (NTT DoCoMo's terminology; www.nttdocomo.com), and Ultra 3G (KDDI's term; www.kddi.com/english). In 2005 we saw the number of 3G networks deployed increase appreciably, with more networks also extending their coverage. At the same time, there was growth in the number of available 3G-capable devices, with reductions in their price. As the number of networks and customers grows, service providers are also extending their networks beyond the footprints initially planned. The bottom line is that 3G is making strides, despite its slow start.

With the pace of technology development speeding up each day, many industry players are working on enhancing the capabilities of 3G networks. Much of the research and development work is coming out of Japan, although efforts are occurring around the globe. The types of enhancements envisioned for Beyond 3G include IP technologies for the back end, faster data speeds, new business applications, and many other applications, including interactive games, video services, audio downloads, and location-based services. Given the range of advanced applications involved, higher-speed data services, QoS features, and new back-end systems that support the bridging between wireless and wired networks will be substantial components of the enhanced 3G networks. We are just beginning to see the range of services and content that can be delivered over 3G networks, and as discussed later in this chapter, there are also movements in the introduction of 4G networks, with 5G technologies already on the drawing boards.

The Beyond 3G vision involves today's 3G technologies, whether W-CDMA/UMTS or CDMA2000, but goes on to support bandwidths greater than 5MHz and adds smarter and more efficient IP-based back-end infrastructure and additional one-way or two-way airlinks to provide further capabilities. The intended result is to improve spectral efficiency, allowing for a great increase in system capacity, lower latency, increased data rates on both the downlink and uplink, full mobility, support for existing 3G networks, and reduced cost. Much of the vision is based on a new generation of handsets capable of handling a wide variety of technologies and communications links and providing all these services concurrently.

Both the NTT DoCoMo Super 3G and KDDI Ultra 3G plans assume that the 3G airlink will be the most widely used full mobility technology, although they also consider that Wi-Fi and other technologies will be integrated into these networks. The overall concept is to allow customers to use the best airlink available to them and to support voice and data services over the selected airlink.

Along with the NTT DoCoMo and KDDI efforts, 3GPP has formed a study group to determine the long-term evolution for W-CDMA/UMTS radio access networks and system architectures. The 3GPP standard is expected to be ready in mid-2007, with commercial products expected around 2009. 3G Long-Term Evolution (LTE) is the next version of the 3GPP-based radio standard. LTE will be based on many elements that will be included in Release 7 of the 3GPP standard, primarily OFDM and MIMO, although CDMA technology will be removed from Radio Layer 1 of LTE. The LTE and Super 3G visions are quite similar, and many industry observers view them as synonymous. One interesting industry observation is that 3G airlinks will continue to evolve, but, more importantly, so will the services, with one of the objectives being the ability to move away from having to select a communications medium to having the communications medium chosen for us, depending on what we wish to do and where we happen to be at that moment.

■ 4G: Wireless Broadband

Despite the fact that we have not yet fully implemented 3G and 3.5G technologies, 4G (which the IEEE officially calls "3G and Beyond") is already on its way, posing a major detriment for the future of 3G. In general, a *generation* is defined by the technology changes over a 10- to 15-year period, so 4G refers to whatever will be deployed in the 2010–2015 time frame.

The introduction of 3G technology provides a huge expansion in mobile capacity and bandwidth. 4G will do the same for the spectrum of broadband communications. By supporting mobility, and by being faster and cheaper to deploy, it is expected that 4G will disrupt today's wired broadband access alternatives, including DSL and cable modems. 4G is also expected to serve the next billion

Web users in developing countries. Generally speaking, 4G is an evolution not only to move beyond the limitations and problems associated with 3G but also to increase the bandwidth, enhance the quality of services, and reduce the cost of the resource. The main distinguishing characteristics between 3G and 4G will be increased data rates, enhanced multimedia services, new transmission techniques, new Internet access technology, greater compatibility in interfacing with wired backbone networks, and the addition of QoS and security mechanisms. 4G should also be able to provide smooth global roaming ubiquitously, at lower cost. At the very least, this means a new air interface supporting higher data rates and also a change in the way data transport is handled end to end. Unlike 3G networks, which are a mix of circuit-switched and packet-switched networks, 4G will be based solely on packet switching.

The major telecommunications players are already lining up behind their picks for success in the next generation. Intel (www.intel.com), working with startup Beceem Communications, Inc. (www.beceem.com), will begin putting WiMax silicon in notebooks starting in 2007, while Qualcomm (www.qualcomm.com) is expected to put the Flash-OFDM technology in handset chips. Sprint Nextel (www.sprint.com) is studying both technologies, as well as options on the CDMA and GSM roadmaps, as it plans to upgrade its CDMA cellular network in 2008 to 3Mbps in an attempt to compete with DSL and cable. Sprint Nextel conducted one successful trial of the Flash-OFDM technology in 2005 and plans additional trials of Flash-OFDM and WiMax in 2006. Sprint Nextel expects to offer 4G services to the top 100 U.S. markets by 2008.

Some countries have already begun cooperating on 4G standards. In late 2005, Japan and China signed a memorandum to work together on 4G. Japanese carrier NTT DoCoMo claims its 4G prototype phones can receive data at 100Mbps while moving and at 1Gbps while standing still; at these rates, an entire DVD could be downloaded within a minute. DoCoMo's current 3G phone network offers download speeds of 384Kbps and upload speeds of 129Kbps, and the company plans to have a 4G network in place by 2010. The technology behind NTT DoCoMo's high-speed phone network remains experimental, but the 4G tests used a method called Variable-Spreading-Factor Orthogonal Frequency Code Division Multiplexing (VSF-OFCDM), which increases downlink speeds by using multiple radio frequencies to send the same data stream. MIMO was also used to further increase data capacity (e.g., by sending data via various routes across a network); it can enable a mobile phone to receive data from more than one base station in range.

4G should support a wide range of data rates, including at least 100Mbps peak rates in full-mobility wide area coverage and 1Gbps in low-mobility local area coverage. The 4G vision includes asymmetrical and symmetrical services. It provides for QoS for real-time services, supports streaming audio and video, and provides an efficient transport of packet-oriented services, as well as a vision that supports broadcast and distribution services. It supports smart, adaptive antennas and uses an adaptive modulation or coding scheme. One of the main concerns about 4G is that the high frequency suggests that it will experience severe interference from multipath secondary signals reflecting off other objects. VSF-OFCDM is one of the proposed solutions to this problem.

As an IP-based network, 4G will be rolled out using IPv6, which is gradually making its way into telecommunications infrastructure now. In the 4G network, each node will be assigned a 4G-IP address (based on IPv6), which will be formed by a permanent "home" IP address and a dynamic "care-of" address that represents its actual location. For example, say that a device on the Internet, a computer, wants to communicate with a device on a wireless network, a mobile phone. The computer will send a packet to the 4G-IP address of the mobile phone, targeting its home address. A directory server on the mobile phone's home network will forward the packet to the mobile phone's care-of address through a tunnel, mobile IP. The directory server will then also inform the computer of the mobile phone's care-of address (the real location) so it can send subsequent packets directly to the mobile phone.

4G concerns involve cost and the compatibility of various applications, such as three-dimensional virtual reality and interactive video hologram images. 4G will increase interactions between corroborating technologies. For example, the smart card in your telephone will automatically pay for goods as you pass the linked payment kiosk, or the smart card will tell your car to warm up in the morning because your phone has noted you leaving the house or turning off your alarm clock.

Developments for 4G began in 2002, and there are many standards and technologies under consideration, many of which are still in the development stages. Therefore, no one can really say what the future 4G network will look like and what services it will offer. Keep in mind that today's pace of development is so rapid that often a given technology doesn't have a chance to become pervasive in the marketplace before its successor is already named. And that very well may be the case with 3G and 3.5G. Industry visions looking forward may be characterized as involving a horizontal communications model where different access technologies will be combined on a common platform to complement each other in an optimum way for different service requirements and radio environments, possibly including cellular mobile, broadband wireless access, wireless LANs, short-range connectivity, and wired systems.

■ 5G: Intelligent Technologies

Our view of future visions would not be complete without at least mentioning that 5G is also on the drawing boards. What we envision beyond 4G is a wireless world with incredible transmission speed and no limitation on access or zone sizes. 5G should comprise more intelligent technologies that interconnect the entire world without limits, creating a real wireless world—what is sometimes today referred to as the wireless World Wide Web (WWWW). For a truly wonderful example of the future of wireless and mobile communications, be sure to watch the NTT DoCoMo "Vision 2010" video at www.docomo-usa.com/vision2010/. It will open your eyes to a range of applications and usages you've not yet considered, and it will hopefully help you understand just how much new technology still needs to be introduced before we can truly call ourselves a mobile society.

15

WMANs, WLANs, and WPANs

Today's consumer appetite for wireless broadband and the high-bandwidth applications it supports—such as photos, games, and video—is enormous. However, the demands placed on a network to support these advanced applications create a technology dilemma for today's network equipment makers and wireless carriers. Among the issues is the question of how an already scarce spectrum can carry more bandwidth-intensive data and multimedia services and do so more economically and reliably. This chapter explores the developments, standards, and deployments in wireless metropolitan area networks (WMANs), wireless local area networks (WLANs), and wireless personal area networks (WPANs), which are all critical to enabling the wireless society the public is hungry for.

The next wave of personal productivity is all about mobility—being able to get access anywhere, anytime—which is driving the demand for wireless access. People use their laptops more when they have wireless access and are therefore more productive. It is easy to see why many industries will turn to wireless to boost productivity, and during the next 5 to 10 years, wireless MANs, LANs, and PANs will be instrumental to bringing wireless broadband not just to offices and homes but to users, wherever they may be.

Although in the past there were clear demarcations between what comprised a MAN, LAN, or PAN domain, today those boundaries are often blurred, particularly as the technologies complement one another. Therefore, the merging and working together of MANs, LANs, and PANs to create a seamless, always-on, and always-available network environment is a natural outcome. MANs, LANs, and PANs are each distinguishable today by definitions and parameters set in the standards, but

Table 15.1 U.S. and European Wireless Standards Comparison

Network Type	United States	Europe
WAN	IEEE 802.20x (Mobile-Fi)	EDGE (GSM), 3GPP (UMTS)
MAN	IEEE 802.16x (WiMax)	ETSI HiperMAN, HiperAccess
LAN	IEEE 802.11x (Wi-Fi)	ETSI HiperLAN
PAN	IEEE 802.15x (Bluetooth)	ETSI HiperLAN

as technologies advance, expand, and merge, we can expect that the application and implementation will define the domain rather than traditional physical parameters, such as range of coverage. In addition, domains will continue to evolve so that in the near future, we'll be discussing body area networks (BANs), fabric area networks (FANs), and, dare I say, even implant area networks. (Implant area networks do not exist as of yet, but given the rapid and vast progress in implants, from medical to financial to security to identity applications, it is only natural that we envision a network, perhaps relying on our own human physiology, that serves the communications needs of the multitude of life-enhancing implants lodged in the twenty-first-century definition of an intelligent being.)

As shown in Table 15.1, the IEEE (www.ieee.org) and ETSI (www.etsi.org) have both established hierarchies of wireless standards designed to complement each other. (As described later in this chapter, other areas of the world follow different standards; some follow the U.S. standards, some follow the European standards, and some create proprietary standards on top of those, such as WiBro in Korea, iBurst in Australia, and TD-SCDMA in China.) Each standard is designed for a distinct market and for different usage models. These standards and others used in WMANs, WLANs, and WPANs are discussed in this chapter.

■ WMANs

Recent years have seen a growing interest in employing wireless technologies for subscriber access. Many companies are becoming increasingly interested in deploying wireless connectivity, often referred to as *wireless local loop*, covering metropolitan areas, such as cities and rural areas, as an alternative to using copper- or fiber-based approaches.

As discussed earlier in this book, compared to other networking media, wireless is generally less expensive to install and support, and it can be deployed much more quickly. Until recently, the problem for wireless was a lack of standards-based solutions. For many years, the broadband wireless market was dominated by proprietary systems targeted at wireless backhaul and point-to-point microwave link applications. There was pressure in the industry for standardization in order to increase market growth and reduce costs. In order to provide a standardized approach to wireless local loop, the IEEE 802 committee set up the 802.16 working group in 1999 to develop broadband wireless standards. The first IEEE 802.16 standard, defining the WirelessMAN air interface for wireless MANs, was published in April 2002, creating standards for broadband wireless access in order to offer a high-speed, low-cost, scalable solution to extend fiber-optic backbones. Since the introduction of the 802.16 standards, the WMAN arena has begun to blossom.

The following sections discuss the most common WMAN standards:

- Broadband fixed wireless access (BFWA)
- IEEE 802.16 (WiMax)
- Wireless Broadband (WiBro)
- IEEE 802.20 (Mobile-Fi)
- HiperLan2, HiperAccess, and HiperMAN
- iBurst
- Flash-OFDM
- Digital Multimedia Broadcasting (DMB)
- Virtual fiber (VF)

BFWA

BFWA has awakened interest in the communications community because of the high capacity it offers. The ITU divides the world into three regions for the purposes of managing the global radio spectrum. The main reason for this division is that each region has its own set of frequency allocations. Region 1 includes Europe, Africa, the Middle East west of the Persian Gulf and including Iraq, and the former Soviet Union. Region 2 comprises the Americas. Region 3 contains non-former-Soviet-Union Asia east of and including Iran and Oceania. Table 15.2 shows the ITU BFWA frequency allocations.

There are two broad categories of BFWA standards:

- **High-frequency BFWA**—High-frequency BFWA includes cellular broadband two-way communication systems with fixed and nomadic access. It is focused on broadband services, including real-time video, streaming video, and video transfer. High-frequency BFWA operates in the frequency bands

Table 15.2 ITU BFWA Frequency Allocations

Region 1	Region 2	Region 3
	2,200MHz–2,690MHz (490MHz band)	
	3,400MHz–4,200MHz (800MHz band)	
	4,400MHz–5,000MHz (600MHz band)	
	5,800MHz–8,500MHz (2,650MHz band)	
10,000MHz–10,450MHz (450MHz band)		10,000MHz–10,450MHz (450MHz band)
	10,500MHz–10,680MHz (180MHz band)	
10,700MHz–12,500MHz (1,800MHz band)	10,700MHz–12,100MHz (1,400MHz band)	10,700MHz–12,750MHz (2,050MHz band)
14,300MHz–14,400MHz (100MHz band)		14,300MHz–14,400MHz (100MHz band)
	14,400MHz–15,350MHz (990MHz band)	
	17,700MHz–19,700MHz (2,000MHz band)	
	21,200MHz–23,600MHz (2,400MHz band)	
24,250MHz–25,250MHz (1,000MHz band)		24,250MHz–25,250MHz (1,000MHz band)
	22,250MHz–29,500MHz (3,750MHz band)	
	31,000MHz–31,300MHz (300MHz band)	
	31,800MHz–33,400MHz (1,600MHz band)	
	36,000MHz–43,500MHz (7,500MHz band)	

above 25GHz, which account for 75% of the available bandwidth for broadband radio. These very large and unused frequency bands serve as excellent candidates for broadband deployment. The most promising bands include 25GHz to 29.5GHz and 36GHz to 43.5GHz. In Europe, 3GHz of continuous bandwidth in the 40GHz to 43.5GHz band is reserved for Multimedia Wireless System (MWS).

High-frequency BFWA requires line of sight, and the range is greatly affected by atmospheric conditions. The air interface standards for high-frequency BFWA include IEEE 802.16, ETSI HiperAccess, and DVB–Return Channel for Local Multipoint Distribution Service (LMDS). Mass-market penetration is hindered by the high cost of equipment (both base stations and user radio terminals), but the technology is available, and costs can be reduced.

- **Low-frequency BFWA**—Low-frequency BFWA is used mainly for data communications. These systems operate on frequencies between 2GHz and 11GHz. Lower frequencies, specifically around 2.4GHz, 3.5GHz, 5GHz, and 5.8GHz, use both licensed and unlicensed spectrum. Standards for low-frequency BFWA have developed procedures to allocate spectrum in a more efficient manner, introducing Orthogonal Frequency Division Multiplexing (OFDM) under non-line-of-sight conditions. This allows for more simultaneous users, increased average throughput, security, and mobility. The main standards for low-frequency BFWA include IEEE 802.16a revised, IEEE 802.16e, WiBro, and ETSI HiperMAN.

BFWA systems are serious competitors for full-service broadband access technology. For an incumbent operator, high-frequency BFWA complements wired alternatives. For a new operator, it presents the opportunity to rapidly deploy an alternative broadband infrastructure. BFWA has numerous positive attributes. A radio multipoint network naturally supports broadcasting and multicasting services. It offers the flexibility of easy and rapid deployment, particularly with non-line-of-sight systems. BFWA requires low upfront investment because most of the cost lies in the user terminal. As traffic grows, the network can easily be expanded. BFWA can serve as a backup solution for purposes of disaster recovery or to support network diversity, and it even supports mobile services. In addition, in the developing world, BFWA can be deployed more quickly and cost-effectively than traditional wired broadband technologies.

IEEE 802.16 (WiMax)

The global IEEE 802.16 standard, known as the IEEE WirelessMAN air interface standard, was the first broadband wireless access standard from an accredited standards body. It is commonly referred to as WiMax (Worldwide Interoperability for Microwave Access). WiMax is designed from the ground up to provide wireless last-mile broadband access in MANs, and it represents an evolution to a standards-based, interoperable, carrier-class solution. Unlike Wi-Fi (discussed later in this chapter), which targets the end user, WiMax has been developed as the basis of a carrier service. The most exciting aspect of WiMax is the evolution to mobility.

The main advantages of WiMax include the ability to provision services quickly, the avoidance of costly installations, and the ability to overcome the physical limitations associated with wired infrastructures. By providing a standards-based, cost-effective, and flexible technology, WiMax can fill the existing gaps in broadband coverage and create new forms of wireless broadband services.

WiMax channel bandwidth is adjustable from 1.25MHz to 20MHz. The actual transmission rate of the channel is determined by the modulation technique used. Therefore, the bandwidth efficiency of a channel is determined by the bandwidth of the assigned channel and the modulation technique used. This is an important feature for carriers operating in licensed spectrum. The tradeoff is that the more efficiently the transmitter encodes a signal, the more impact noise and interference impairments have on the signal.

The WiMax standard defines six modulation techniques that result in varying levels of bandwidth efficiency: BPSK, QPSK, 16-QAM, 64-QAM, OFDM (256-subcarrier OFDM that also conforms to the ETSI HiperMAN standard), and OFDMA (2,048-subcarrier OFDM). The WiMax standard can also adjust the transmit power by incorporating adaptive burst profiles. In addition, the standard provides for forward error correction (FEC) coding. Therefore, WiMax can accommodate a wide variety of radio conditions.

WiMax provides for quality of service (QoS) through the use of a request/grant protocol. The base station controls access to the inbound channel. In order to transmit, users must first send requests on a contention-based access channel. The base station allocates the exclusive right to use the inbound traffic channel, using a system of transmission grants. Because only one station can be given permission to send at a time, there are no inbound collisions. WiMax supports four main types of QoS:

- **Unsolicited Grant Service–Real-Time**—In this isochronous service for real-time voice and video, stations are allocated inbound transmission capacity on a scheduled basis.

- **Real-Time Polling Service**—In this service for real-time voice and video, the base station polls each user device in turn.

- **Variable Bit Rate–Non-Real-Time**—This data service provides capacity guarantees and variable delay.

- **Variable Bit Rate–Best Effort**—This residential data service offers IP-like best effort.

Because WiMax is intended for public networks, encryption is a key component. The initial specification identifies the 168-bit Triple Data Encryption Standard (3DES) as mandatory. Future plans call for including Advanced Encryption Standard (AES) on an optional basis.

The WiMax standard incorporates Dynamic Frequency Selection, which means the radio automatically searches for an unused channel. WiMax can take advantage of multiple duplexing modes, including Time Division Duplex (TDD) dynamic asymmetry, allowing the uplink/downlink bandwidth to be allocated according to current traffic conditions. WiMax standards also define an optional mesh configuration.

802.16 Revisions

IEEE 802.16 first issued standards for the PHY (physical) and MAC (Media Access Control) layers of systems in the 10GHz to 66GHz bands, generally known as LMDS. LMDS is characterized by very high data rates and quite short range due to rain and foliage attenuation. The 802.16 standard requires line of sight to the base station. It accounts for high-frequency BFWA, where there is more available spectrum, along with larger frequency allocations. Operating at higher frequencies increases the cost of both base stations and customer premises equipment (CPE). In addition, user antennas require realignment whenever a new cell is added to the network.

Several revisions to the 802.16 standard have been released. The 802.16a standard, including 802.16a Revision d (REVd), supports operation in the 2GHz to 11GHz bands, using OFDM to mitigate the impairments fading and multipath. IEEE 802.16a aims to fill the gap between high-data-rate WLANs and high-mobility cellular WANs. The sub-11GHz frequency ranges specified in 802.16a make possible non-line-of-sight systems. Such systems are required for last-mile applications where obstacles such as trees or buildings exist and where base stations may need to be discreetly mounted on homes or buildings rather than on towers. A single 20MHz channel can simultaneously support up to 60 businesses with connectivity at the T-1/E-1 level and hundreds of residences with DSL-rate connectivity. The 802.16a REVd standard uses OFDM and supports fixed and nomadic access in line-of-sight and non-line-of-sight environments. Vendors are developing indoor and outdoor CPE and laptop PC cards.

The IEEE 802.16e standard, called Mobile WiMax, calls for operation on frequencies below 6GHz and does not require line of sight. It uses Scalable Orthogonal Frequency Division Multiple Access (SOFDMA), a multicarrier modulation technique that uses subchannelization, where channel bandwidths are selectable, ranging between 1.25MHz and 20MHz, with up to 16 logical subchannels. The key attribute of IEEE 802.16e is that it introduces mobility, including a handoff capability for users moving between cells. One of the goals is reduced power requirements for battery-powered mobile devices. IEEE 802.16e is planned to support

500Kbps, equivalent to CDMA2000 1xEV-DO services. However, IEEE 802.20 (Mobile-Fi) is a competing standard that Cisco (www.cisco.com) and Motorola (www.motorola.com) support. (Mobile-Fi is discussed later in this chapter.) Recently, IEEE 802.16 has requested changes to the scope of IEEE 802.16e to eliminate the requirement for backward compatibility with legacy fixed wireless systems. This additional freedom will enable significant improvements to IEEE 802. 16e and may cast doubt on the need for a separate standard.

Table 15.3 compares the features of 802.16, 802.16a/802.16a REVd, and 802.16e.

The Future of WiMax

The WiMax Forum (www.wimaxforum.org) offers an interoperability testing program whose goal is to ensure a broad choice of fairly priced equipment for carriers and other service providers. The "WiMax Forum Certified" designation guarantees that products have been independently verified to both conform to the standard and interoperate with other vendor equipment.

Table 15.3   Features of IEEE 802.16, 802.16a/802.16a REVd, and 802.16e

Feature	802.16	802.16a/802.16a REVd	802.16e
Standard published	April 2002	January 2003/July 2004	December 2005
Spectrum	10GHz–66GHz	2GHz–11GHz	<6GHz
Channel conditions	Line-of-sight only	Non-line-of-sight	Non-line-of-sight
Channel bandwidths	20MHz, 25MHz, and 28MHz	Selectable channel bandwidths between 1.25MHz and 20MHz, with up to 16 logical subchannels	Selectable channel bandwidths between 1.25MHz and 20MHz, with up to 16 logical subchannels
Bit rate	32Mbps–134Mbps (at 28MHz channelization)	Up to 75Mbps (at 20MHz channelization)	Up to 15Mbps (at 5MHz channelization)
Modulation	QPSK, 16-QAM, 64-QAM	OFDM, OFDMA, QPSK, 16-QAM, 64-QAM, BPSK	OFDM, OFDMA, QPSK, 16-QAM, 64-QAM, BPSK
Mobility	Fixed	Fixed and portable	Regional roaming
Typical cell radius	1–3 miles (1.5–5 km)	3–6 miles (5–10 km), max. range 30 miles (50 km)	1–3 miles (1.5–5 km)

Three major phases of development are associated with WiMax:

- **Phase 1: Fixed-location private-line and/or hotspot backhaul**—This phase involves dedicated facilities using outdoor antennas, supporting up to 100Mbps. Equipment providers are seeing an international market for such point-to-point systems, supporting basic voice services as well as cellular backhaul. With the continuing growth in hotspots, WiMax presents a solution to aggregating the traffic and backhauling it to a central, high-capacity Internet connection.

- **Phase 2: Broadband wireless access**—One of the first mass-market applications for WiMax is intended to be wireless DSL. The data rates supported will range from 512Kbps to 1Mbps. The WiMax Forum anticipates growth in this phase as large carriers begin deploying low-cost products.

- **Phase 3: Nomadic or mobile applications**—In this phase, new developments, such as Mobile WiMax, are expected to also support moving users, traveling at speeds up to 75 mph (120 kph). It will operate at lower frequencies, below 6GHz, and is planned to operate on a shared channel of 15Mbps and to support user data rates of 512Kbps.

In the 2006–2007 time frame, it is expected that WiMax will be incorporated into end-user devices such as notebook computers and PDAs along with Wi-Fi and Bluetooth. Also in the 2007 time frame, it is expected that WiMax will be integrated into 3G phones along with Wi-Fi. In the long-term future, it is expected that WiMax will become a last-mile access technology integrated in laptops and other end-user devices. In the near term, however, WiMax will probably have the most viability for backhauling the rapidly increasing volumes of traffic being generated by Wi-Fi hotspots.

The United States is looking to expand the spectrum to satisfy what could be enormous demand for WiMax technology. In 2006 and 2007, the U.S. government is expected to auction off the separate 1.71GHz and 2.11GHz frequency bands for WiMax applications. Also, the United States hopes to shift the TV market to digital by 2009, thereby freeing up more spectrum, possibly for WiMax. By early 2009, the U.S. Federal Communications Commission (FCC) will auction off the 700MHz band, which is currently occupied by analog TV.

Although WiMax has an edge because it is an open standard backed by multiple companies—notably Intel (www.intel.com)—it still faces plenty of challenges. Today, vendors must wade through many competing standards and proprietary technologies. There are also multiple WiMax spectrum bands to contend with, which makes it difficult to roam between networks. We are headed toward multiple WiMax systems, including 2.3GHz and 2.5GHz in the United States and Asia and 3.5GHz in Europe. Again, in the United States, WiMax vendors hope to get some of the 700MHz spectrum the U.S. government will reclaim from analog TV stations in early 2009. Although it is technically possible to have roaming across all these networks, stitching together a patchwork of global WiMax spectrum bands is another challenge. However, at this time, the industry consensus seems to be that 802.16e has the best shot at a mass market, although costs must come down first.

WiBro

Korea's ETRI (Electronics and Telecommunications Research Institute; www.etri.re. kr/www_05/e_etri/), along with Samsung (www.samsung.com), is the leading developer of the Wireless Broadband (WiBro) technology, which it calls the "portable Internet." Before WiBro, there was HPi (high-speed portable Internet), which was backed by SK Telecom and KT Corp. However, HPi was incompatible with the growing WiMax standard and was a barrier to non-Korean developers and manufacturers. This led to its replacement by the more compatible WiBro standard.

ETRI is focusing on both WiBro and a companion technology, DMB (which is described later in this chapter). According to Korea's Ministry of Information and Communication (MIC), WiBro is intended as an evolutionary technology. It will start slowly so as to not compete immediately with 3G systems. Several years after the arrival of WiBro, MIC projects 10 million WiBro subscribers. There are already several major chipsets available for it.

The use of licensed spectrum is one of the key differentiators between the U.S. WiMax technology and WiBro: In February 2002, the Korean government allocated 100MHz of spectrum in the 2.3GHz band, and in late 2004, WiBro Phase 1 was standardized by the Telecommunications Technology Association (TTA) of Korea. The advantage of using licensed spectrum is that it eliminates the problem of any potential interference from other sources using the same spectrum. On the other hand, WiBro's use of licensed spectrum that may not be available across the globe, along with its proprietary nature, may prevent it from becoming an international standard. These two characteristics of WiBro also lead to exacting requirements in terms of equipment design and spectrum use. On the other hand, WiMax leaves much of the equipment design up to the equipment provider, while providing enough detail to ensure interoperability between designs.

WiBro base stations will offer an aggregate data throughput of 30Mbps to 50Mbps and cover a radius of 0.5 to 3 miles (1 to 5 km). Portable Internet usage can be supported for a user who is within range of a base station. WiBro also provides for QoS, so it can reliably stream video content and other loss- and delay-sensitive data. WiBro is very similar to 802.16e (Mobile WiMax), and it allows users to access the Internet at initial speeds of 700Kbps from a vehicle moving at 60 mph (100 kph).

South Korea licensed three firms to launch commercial WiBro services in 2006: SK Telecom (www.sktelecom.com/eng), KT Corp. (www.kt.co.kr/kthome/eng/index.

jsp), and Hanaro Telecom (www.hanaro.com/eng). (However, Hanaro has dropped out of the race at this point.) WiBro functions in the 2.3GHz spectrum band. Because two of the companies licensed to launch commercial WiBro, SK Telecom and KT, also own 3G networks, it is likely that the eventual implementation of WiBro will coexist with 3G. WiBro will affect Korea's growing number of Wi-Fi hotspots (KT alone has more than 25,000) because WiBro can cover the same areas as Wi-Fi but has higher speeds, offers QoS, and works in licensed spectrum, with few interference problems.

WiMax and WiBro are both expected to conform to the final 802.16e (Mobile WiMax) standard. However, because even within a standard there can be mutually exclusive options, it remains uncertain how the two will eventually interoperate. There is currently a difference between the two in the PHY layer: While both Mobile WiMax and WiBro use SOFDMA, the channel bandwidths and the number of associated tones defined in the WiBro standard are not consistent with the WiMax Forum specifications.

There is now a serious competitor to WiBro, a 3.5G technology called High-Speed Downlink Packet Access (HSDPA) that uses W-CDMA. SK Telecom asked Samsung Electronics and LG Electronics to build facilities worth US$100 million to support W-CDMA. (HSDPA is discussed in detail in Chapter 14, "Wireless WANs.")

IEEE 802.20 (Mobile-Fi)

IEEE 802.20, also referred to as Mobile-Fi, is optimized for IP and roaming in high-speed mobile environments. This standard is poised to fully mobilize IP, opening up major new data markets beyond the more circuit-centric 2.5G and 3G cellular standards. The Mobile Broadband Wireless Access (MBWA) Working Group was established as IEEE 802.20 in December 2002. Its main mission is to develop the specification for an efficient packet-based air interface optimized for the transport of IP-based services. The goal is to enable global deployment of low-cost, ubiquitous, interoperable, and always-on multivendor mobile broadband wireless access networks. IEEE 802.20 has designed a new physical layer (Layer 1 protocol) and MAC/link layer (Layer 2 protocol) around IP packet Layer 3. It can operate in licensed bands below 3.5GHz, with cell ranges of 9 miles (15 km) or more. IEEE 802.20 can operate at speeds of up to 155 mph (250 kph).

While the data rate and range of Mobile-Fi are only half those of Mobile WiMax, Mobile-Fi is inherently more mobile. It has an astonishing latency of just 10 milliseconds (500 milliseconds is standard for 3G communications) and can maintain integrity at speeds as high as 155 mph (250 kph), compared to just 60 mph (100 kph) for WiMax. Because it uses more common spectrum—licensed bands up to 3.5GHz—it also offers global mobility, handoff, and roaming support.

Whereas Mobile WiMax is looking at the mobile user walking around with a PDA or laptop, Mobile-Fi addresses high-speed mobility issues. One key difference is the manner in which the two standards are deployed. One assumption is that the carriers are going to deploy Mobile WiMax in their existing (802.16a) footprint as opposed to deploying a more widespread footprint, like a cellular network. Because Mobile-Fi is aimed at more ubiquitous coverage, a larger footprint will be required.

Countries and companies often seek to control the market by developing standards they hope will dominate the global scene. The United States has led the way with IEEE standards, and the European Union's ETSI standards are their counterparts. The work of standards consensus is ongoing, uncertain, and difficult to predict. Mobile operators, who are generally friendly to Mobile WiMax, see Mobile-Fi as a competing standard that could make their 3G licenses worth rather less than they paid for them. The fact that Intel is behind WiMax is a strong force and will undoubtedly push the WiMax standards forward.

Mobile-Fi will have to overcome several hurdles. First among them is the fact that it can be used only in licensed bands below 3.5GHz. Another is that Mobile-Fi trails the Mobile WiMax standards process by a couple years. Another hurdle is whether there is indeed a large requirement for 155 mph (250 kph) handoff. In addition, we do not know what effect Mobile WiMax being nationalized in Korea will have. And, very importantly, cellular companies may not be willing to undercut their 3G service. Certainly, we can assume that the US$100 billion investment in 3G spectrum by the European mobile carriers alone might be weighed against a workable Mobile-Fi standard. With the possibility of proprietary systems (e.g., WiBro, Flash-OFDM) being in place a number of years before Mobile-Fi is standardized, the likelihood is that by then, Mobile WiMax will be backward compatible with WiMax fixed services. Licensed or unlicensed, Mobile-Fi will not be ubiquitous, and WiMax probably will.

Table 15.4 provides a quick summary of the key characteristics of the three major mobile data architectures: 802.16e, 802.20, and 3G.

ETSI BRAN

On the European front, in response to growing market pressure for low-cost, high-capacity radio links, ETSI established a standardization project for Broadband-Compliant Radio Access Networks (BRAN) in spring 1997. ETSI BRAN is the successor of the former Sub-Technical Committee RES10, which developed the HiperLan1 specifications. ETSI BRAN assists regulatory bodies with issues such as the needs for spectrum and the radio conformance specifications that will be required to implement the new broadband radio networks.

Table 15.4 Mobile Data Architectures

Technology	802.16e	802.20	3G
Function	IP 802.16a mobility (>1Mbps)	IP roaming and handoff (>1Mbps)	Circuit-switched cell data (<1Mbps)
Standard	Extensions to MAC and PHY from 802.16a; backward compatible with 802.16a	New MAC and PHY with IP and adaptive antennas; optimized for full mobility	W-CDMA and CDMA2000
Spectrum	2GHz–6GHz	Licensed bands below 3.5GHz	Licensed bands below 2.7GHz
Architecture	Packet architecture	Packet architecture	Circuit architecture
Latency	Low latency	Low latency	High latency

ETSI BRAN currently produces specifications for three major standards areas:

- **HiperLan2 (High-Performance Radio LAN 2)**—This is a mobile broadband short-range access network standard.
- **HiperAccess (High-Performance Radio Access)**—This is a fixed wireless broadband access network standard.
- **HiperMAN (High-Performance Radio MAN)**—This is a fixed wireless access network standard for operating below 11GHz.

To ensure harmonization with other similar efforts, ETSI coordinates with the MFA Forum (www.mfaforum.org), the HiperLan2 Global Forum, the IEEE Wireless LAN Committees 802.11a (http://grouper.ieee.org/groups/802/11/) and 802.16 (http://grouper.ieee.org/groups/802/16/), the IETF (www.ietf.org), the Multimedia Mobile Access Communication Systems Forum (MMAC-PC; www.arib.or.jp/mmac/e/), the ITU-R (www.itu.int/ITU-R), and a number of internal ETSI technical bodies.

HiperLan2

HiperLan2 will give consumers in corporate, public, and home environments wireless access to the Internet and future multimedia, as well as real-time video services at speeds of up to 54Mbps.

HiperAccess

The HiperAccess standards area creates standards for multimedia BFWA. It was developed to provide a truly broadband system with bit rates of up to approximately 100Mbps, although 25Mbps is expected to be the most widely deployed rate. HiperAccess is targeted at high frequency bands, especially the 40.5GHz to 43. 5GHz band. For these frequency bands, TDMA will be used to provide multiple access.

The first BRAN-compliant commercial product—a point-to-point derivative of HiperAccess—was rolled out in December 2004. Numerous operators are showing great interest in HiperAccess, and full HiperAccess-compliant products are becoming available.

HiperMAN

ETSI's HiperMAN is intended to be an interoperable BFWA system operating at radio frequencies between 2GHz and 11GHz. Designed for fixed wireless access provisioning to residences and small and medium-sized enterprises, the standard uses the basic MAC layer, data link layer, and connectionless service of the 802.16 standard. It has been developed in close cooperation with IEEE 802.16, so that the HiperMAN standard and a subset of the IEEE 802.16a standard will interoperate seamlessly. The IEEE 802.16 OFDM and ETSI HiperMAN standards share the same PHY and MAC specifications. For higher layers, these specifications are assumed to be available or to be developed by other bodies.

Although HiperMAN's main focus is IP traffic, it can also support ATM. It offers various service categories, full QoS, fast connection control management, strong security, fast adaptation of coding, and modulation; it is also capable of non-line-of-sight operation. HiperMAN enables both point-to-multipoint and mesh network configurations. HiperMAN also supports both FDD and TDD frequency allocations and H-FDD (Half-Duplex Frequency Division Duplex) terminals.

iBurst

iBurst is a niche broadband wireless technology that at first appears to compete for market share with Mobile WiMax and Mobile-Fi. In mid-2002, Australia's ArrayComm (www.arraycomm.com) developed what it called *personal broadband*. Working with chipset partner Taiwan Semiconductor Manufacturing Company (www.tsmc.com) and base station provider Kyocera (www.kyocera.com), ArrayComm began to deploy a trial iBurst network around Sydney. By the first quarter of 2004, the first commercial iBurst service was offered. Today, iBurst provides mobile wireless broadband Internet coverage throughout Sydney, Melbourne, Canberra, Brisbane, and the Gold Coast. Future plans include the enhancement of existing coverage areas as well as rollouts throughout Perth and Adelaide. When the network rollout has been completed, iBurst promises to provide coverage to over 75% of Australia's popula-

tion and to more than 90% of businesses. iBurst has also been licensed and is operating in the United States and South Africa, among other places.

iBurst technology has a number of important features:

- **High broadband data speeds**—iBurst supports speeds up to 1Mbps (downlink) per user, with protocol support for up to 16Mbps.

- **Wide area coverage**—iBurst's range is one of the best in the industry. It
offers always-on connectivity, and the network supports full handoff.

- **Low cost**—iBurst claims to have a market-leading cost structure.

- **Simplicity**—iBurst is easy to deploy, easy to install, and easy to use.

- **Commercialized**—iBurst is operationally proven and scalable.

- **Great capacity**—Each base station sector can deliver more than 30Mbps.

The iBurst technology is a pure IP, end-to-end system built on two primary
components: base stations deployed by a network operator, much as in today's cellular mobile services, and wireless modems or PC cards that a customer uses with
an existing Internet appliance, such as a notebook or desktop computer, to access
the service. iBurst relies on TDD to permit downlink and uplink paths to share
common spectrum. Most importantly, it uses ArrayComm's Intellicell smart antenna
spatial-processing system, which enhances the signal path between the base station
and customers.

iBurst employs end-to-end IP-over-PPP connectivity between service providers
and their customers. This means that providers already have the necessary infrastructure to support iBurst. Traffic from iBurst base stations is aggregated at a
packet services switch that sends the data to the appropriate service provider. The
base station is the boundary between wireless iBurst and the service provider's
backhaul network. Security is handled at all layers, using a combination of MPLS
and IPsec. In the end-user session, IPsec is combined with application security (e.g.,
HTTPS). Because iBurst supports IPv6, it can take advantage of the additional
security features not available in IPv4.

iBurst standardization at the wired layer conforms wholly to data networking
standards. ArrayComm is working to standardize the remaining components, especially the air interface, through the IEEE 802.20 Working Group. The air interface
combines smart antenna techniques with industry best practices for wireless data,
including adaptive modulation, fast ARQ, and a QoS-cognizant scheduler, to create
a high-performance, reliable, and high-capacity data delivery mechanism.

In most respects, iBurst appears to most closely align itself—with respect to
factors such as bandwidth, distance covered, and cost—with 3G+ technology.
However, it works on current 2.5G platforms, and it can extend the life of these
platforms, resulting in substantial cost savings.

Flash-OFDM

Flarion, which was acquired by Qualcomm (www.qualcomm.com), developed a variant of 802.20 called Flash-OFDM. Flash-OFDM (which stands for Fast Low-Latency Access with Seamless Handoff OFDM) uses a technique called *fast hopping*, a new signal-processing scheme that supports high data rates with very low packet and delay losses (i.e., latencies) over a distributed all-IP wireless network.

OFDM is nothing new; its core multiplexing principles have been applied to everything from satellite broadcast to ADSL. It has played a critical role in wireless, forming the basis of the IEEE 802.11a standard, and a crucial role in the WiMax Forum's multiplexing scheme. Lucent Technologies (www.lucent.com) modified OFDM by improving the signal-processing scheme and adding other improvements. To further this research and development and to commercialize the enhanced OFDM, Lucent formed Flarion Technologies in 2000. Because Flash-OFDM is not compatible with 2.5G or 3G technology, the business model requires carriers to move in a new direction. Flarion's argument is that conventional wireless systems, including 3G, have been designed primarily at the physical layer. But mobile users, demanding very high-speed applications, require new air interfaces at all protocol layers, including the MAC, data link, and network layers. The PHY layer, also known as the *pipe*, deals with the physical means of sending data over a communications medium. The MAC layer is responsible for efficiently controlling access to the pipe and efficiently sharing it among many users. The data link layer employs procedures and protocols to carry data across the link and ensures reliability by detecting and correcting transmission errors. The network layer is responsible for routing within the wireless network and for determining how data packets are transferred between modems. Flash-OFDM provides one such solution.

Flash-OFDM has a spectrally efficient, high-capacity PHY layer and uses a packet-switched air interface. It also has a contention-free, QoS-aware MAC layer. It provides support for interactive data applications, including voice, and efficient operation using all existing Internet protocols (such as TCP/IP). It also offers full vehicular mobility, and it offers low costs for subscribers.

The Flash-OFDM design, shown in Figure 15.1, produces a business model that might attract current and future users of 2.5G and 3G systems. For example, while most 3G services require at least 5MHz of bandwidth, Flash-OFDM's signals need only 1.25MHz, which translates into a lower cost per subscriber. From a PHY-layer perspective, Flash-OFDM is orthogonal and has comparatively fewer critical requirements for power control in the multiuser mobile environment. In addition, Flash-OFDM subscribers can be "active" (i.e., with always-on IP) without constantly communicating with base stations simply to maintain the communication link, which reduces both interference and power requirements. Flash-OFDM's MAC layer is extremely efficient in allocating bandwidth among subscribers, thereby increasing bandwidth utilization and providing built-in hooks for QoS

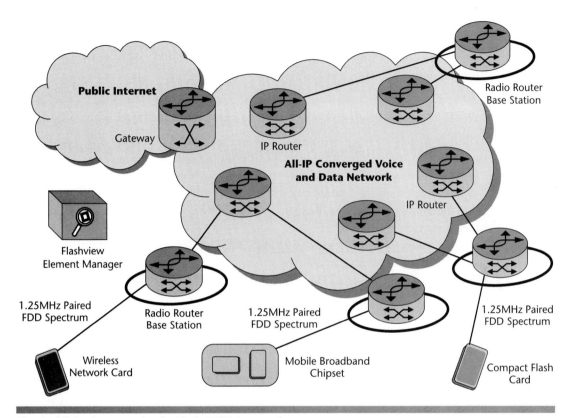

Figure 15.1 An example of a Flash-OFDM network

because both the forward link and the reverse link are fully scheduled. Flash-OFDM's link-layer fast retransmission mechanism reduces the required safety margin in transmission power, thereby improving capacity while supporting interactive data applications.

Flash-OFDM's highly reliable link quality makes upper-layer protocols (such as TCP/IP) perform efficiently, replicating the wired environment. Many other wireless technologies have a tendency to promote inefficient use of radio resources via Internet flow control protocols. The key is Flash-OFDM's use of the wideband spread spectrum technology fast-hopped OFDM, which uses multiple tones and fast hopping to spread signals over a given spectrum band. Fast hopping enables more users for a given spectrum, and orthogonality means less interference.

Flash-OFDM offers an enhancement to traditional OFDM, but it requires new equipment, including new base stations, which may offset the reduced cost per subscriber. The industry was watching closely as Flarion began trials with Nextel, and some of the preliminary data was encouraging in support of the claims of speed, reliability, QoS, and cost. However, the merger of Sprint and Nextel resulted in Nextel canceling the trials and any further work with Flash-OFDM. This is not surprising considering that Sprint is committed to CDMA, and Qualcomm is now looking to Europe and Asia for new business partners.

DMB

DMB is a new concept in multimedia mobile broadcasting service, converging broadcasting and telecommunications. It is a digital transmission system for sending data, radio, and TV to mobile devices such as mobile phones. Because DMB allows users to view content via mobile phones anytime, anywhere, even while moving at high speed, it is likely to change the way broadcast media is consumed, creating a new cultural trend.

The move to DMB started in Korea, where telecom companies were dealing with issues of limited spectrum resources. The first step toward the digitization of Korea's entire local broadcasting media actually came from first digitizing radio broadcasting through Terrestrial DMB (T-DMB), which operates over terrestrial facilities. T-DMB, an ETSI standard for mobile TV, has its roots in the European Eureka 147 Digital Audio Broadcasting (DAB) standard, which is used for digital radio worldwide. It so happens that the transmission and compression technologies used by DAB also work well in supporting video and data services. DMB is designed to broadcast TV and video to mobile devices, and in conjunction with existing DAB services, also both audio and data. DMB can be integrated wherever there is already a DAB infrastructure. The Korean T-DMB system's TV channels 7 through 13 use the 174MHz to 216MHz VHF band. Channel 12 has been allocated for DMB and is divided into three frequency blocks. Each of these blocks is allocated 1.54MHz of bandwidth and is capable of receiving one channel of video and three channels of audio or data, for a total of three video channels and nine audio or data channels.

The Korean domestic Satellite DMB (S-DMB) system, which operates via satellite facilities, is an ITU-T standard. With S-DMB, signals transmitted by a satellite directly can be received by subscribers on most areas on the ground. Where there are areas that can't be reached by the satellite signal, gap fillers (e.g., base stations) can be used to extend the signal and coverage. Several frequency bands are used in S-DMB, as illustrated in Figure 15.2:

- Ku-band (13.824GHz to 13.883GHz) is used between the signal transmission center and the satellite.
- S-band (2.605GHz to 2.655GHz) is used between the satellite or gap fillers and the terminals.
- Ku-band (12.214GHz to 12.239GHz) is used between the satellite and gap fillers.

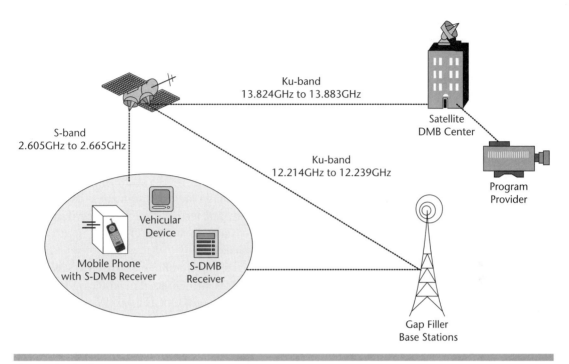

Figure 15.2 S-DMB

S-DMB service, as offered by SK Telecom, can provide for a total of 39 channels: 11 video channels, 25 audio channels, and 3 data channels. Being satellite based, S-DMB offers the advantage of having a much larger coverage area (e.g., the entire Korean peninsula), whereas T-DMB is today limited to a coverage area the size of the Seoul metropolitan area.

One important distinction between T-DMB and S-DMB is that T-DMB is a free service, with the business profit model being advertising revenue, while S-DMB is a paid service. The main competitor of DMB is the DVB-H standard for mobile TV. (DVB-H is discussed in Chapter 10, "Next-Generation Networks.")

The DMB initiative is part of the larger effort Broadband Convergence Network (BcN), much of which is being developed through ETRI, a nonprofit Korean government–funded research organization that has been at the forefront of technological excellence for more than 25 years. Korea has established a world-class infrastructure that provides high-speed access to businesses and homes and is recognized globally for its technological leadership. Key to this continued leadership is strong national growth-engine technologies, and DMB has been identified as one of them.

The DMB industry is focusing on core technologies that are essential for next-generation broadcasting, such as intelligent broadcasting, telecom, and broadcasting convergent services and interactive DMB services, and it is seeking standardization of related technologies both in domestic and global markets. DMB will not only provide high-definition services but also intelligent, personalized, realistic, and paid services in addition to those converged with telecommunications. DMB is discussed in more detail in Chapter 16, "Emerging Wireless Applications."

VF

Virtual fiber (VF), also referred to as *wireless fiber* (WiFiber), is a solution to the "first-mile" problem of delivering high-speed access to the end user. The first-mile problem is especially severe in rural and large metropolitan areas where it is impractical or cost-prohibitive to install fiber. The term *virtual fiber* is used in a wide variety of contexts and has no specific technical definition. The most recent use of the term refers to very-high-frequency radio waves.

The use of VF as a last-mile solution is based on millimeter wave (MMW) technology to deliver line-of-sight broadband. MMW is often used in wireless local loops, and it usually covers the range between 10GHz and 300GHz. MMW produces very narrow beams, called *pencil beams* (less than one degree), but at the ultra-high frequencies, wide channel bandwidths can be used to provide high data rates.

MMW grew out of the Free Space Optics (FSO) technology of the mid-1990s. FSO allowed transmission of digital data across the air using lasers, at the same speeds as could be achieved in fiber-optic cables. VF is an improvement on MMW for higher bandwidths and lower environmental losses. It is still a point-to-point line-of-sight technology, but it operates in the frequency range 70GHz to 90GHz. In February 2003, the FCC authorized commercial licensing rules for this very-high-frequency spectrum. In February 2005, the FCC approved the use of the 71GHz to 76GHz, 81GHz to 86GHz, and 92GHz to 95GHz frequency bands, offering 13GHz of bandwidth for wireless fiber-speed point-to-point communications. This is more than 50 times the amount of all cellular spectrum combined!

High-speed wireless communications require a large amount of spectrum with the lowest possible potential for atmospheric resistance (particularly in terrestrial environments)—characteristics uniquely provided by the spectrum bands authorized by the FCC. Other frequency bands that support Gbps speeds cannot provide fiber-like reliability for the entire last mile. The 60GHz frequency band is impeded by high oxygen absorption, while the FSO (light wave) frequencies are severely affected by fog. Unlike FSO and 60GHz wireless, VF systems are very insensitive to common weather effects; they are affected only by heavy rain. At 0.5 mile (1 km), roughly 4 inches (100 mm) per hour of rain would be needed to cause interruption of a VF link. Based on statistical weather patterns, at least in the United States, VF systems can offer 99.9% weather availability at approximately 1.75 miles (3 km).

In comparison, FSO, which is very sensitive to fog, dust, snow, and small occlusions, is 99.9% available to only about 1,000 feet (300 m); 60GHz wireless is very sensitive to oxygen in the air and, based on statistical weather information, is effective to only about 0.5 mile (800 m) with 99.9% availability. As is the case for microwave links, the range-versus-weather availability performance of MMW links is calculated based on rain rate statistics for different regions.

MMW systems have several other problems. First, free space loss increases with the square of the frequency, and losses are much higher in the MMW range. Second, multipath losses can be quite high. Finally, security is an important consideration. The best practice for security when using MMW is to prevent sniffing between the links. In other words, line-of-sight links should be positioned so no one can tap into the beam. In addition, some vendors offer multiple encryption levels. Because VF is not currently standards based, it is important to evaluate claims of interoperability carefully.

VF technology deployed as point-to-point links and using ultra-high radio frequencies supports multi-Gbps transmission of data, voice, and video, as well as streaming HDTV, enabling it to support implementation of triple-play and quadruple-play services. In addition to support of high-bandwidth applications, VF promises to make it easy for IT managers to interconnect LANs among buildings because the transceivers can be set up in a day. There are also many additional applications of VF, including fiber (backbone) POP access, network diversity (providing redundant access), enterprise campus connectivity, LAN extension, local loop, MANs, WAN access, local exchange bypass, storage access (including storage area networks [SANs] and network attached storage [NAS]), wireless backhaul (3G, 4G, WiMax, and Wi-Fi), and high-definition video.

The two principal companies producing VF products, GigaBeam (www.gigabeam.com) and Loea (www.loeacom.com), support duplex rates of at least 1.5Gbps, with promised future enhancements reaching 10Gbps. Distances offering 99.999% reliability are short, roughly 1 to 1.25 miles (1.5 to 2 km), which means many pairs of radios are needed even for moderate distances. Effective reach can be extended to 3 miles (5 km), pending availability requirements; reliability at the longer distance is only 99.9%.

VF technology is based on arrays of low-noise amplifiers developed to let military aircraft see through fog. These amplifiers receive very subtle signals created by the electromagnetic radiation coming off objects. At the center of a VF network are transceivers that resemble satellite TV dishes (see Figure 15.3). The transceivers must have line of sight, but they work through windows, so they can be placed inside buildings. The system offers 99.999% weather reliability, which translates to only 5 minutes of downtime annually. Laser-based communications (such as FSO), on the other hand, historically have 99.9% weather availability over 750 feet (230 m).

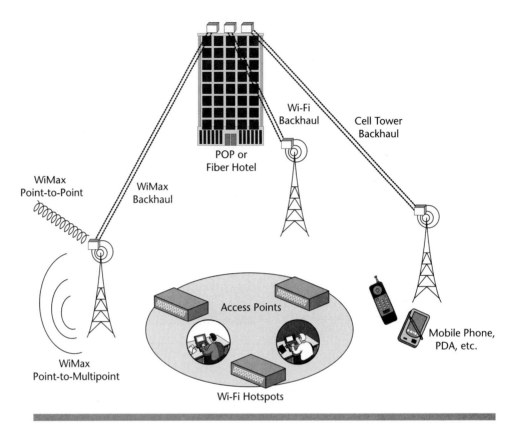

Figure 15.3 An example of a VF network

The key benefits associated with VF include reduced costs (by lowering or eliminating fiber deployment and access charges), reduced risk (by increasing network resiliency through diverse access paths), and reduced time-to-market (by reducing network backlog and deployment time).

■ WLANs

The world of WLANs is truly an exciting area, with major activity worldwide, challenging traditional service providers and business models. Initially, WLANs were meant to be an augmentation, not a replacement, of wired LANs and premises telephone systems. WLANs were deployed in enterprise or corporate locations where there might be a number of factors that limited or prevented wired systems from being installed. Today, we see much greater utility for WLANs, as evidenced by the emergence of thousands of hotspots around the world. In some cases, it is cheaper to deploy wireless in an office than to replace a crumbling old token-ring cable plant with shiny new Ethernet. In general, WLANs operate over short ranges, anywhere from 10 to 500 feet (3 to 150 m), so their coverage areas are microcells or picocells.

Like many other telecom technologies, WLANs have gone through various generations, and the data rates supported reflect that evolution. The early products were quite limited, operating at only 1Mbps to 11Mbps, with the actual throughput being 50% or less of the maximum rate quoted. But the newer standards support data rates of up to 54Mbps, with the actual throughput being up to 32Mbps, and emerging standards promise 100Mbps to 200Mbps.

From the standpoint of an enterprise user, the primary applications for early WLANs were to reduce the costs associated with moves, adds, and changes; simplify installation procedures; and enable mobility within the building or campus environment. In the realm of the public domain today, the primary application for WANs is simply mobility—to accommodate the rapidly growing number of road warriors as well as consumers who want to communicate, work, and play anytime, anywhere.

WLANs typically operate on unlicensed frequency bands, either the 2.4GHz or 5GHz bands. They do not require line-of-sight conditions, which is a very desirable feature. The key element of a WLAN is a wireless access point (WAP), or base station. WAPs are connected to an Ethernet hub or server and transmit a radio frequency over an area of several hundred feet, which can penetrate walls and other nonmetal barriers. The total coverage area can be extended by connecting numerous WAPs. Roaming users are accommodated by handoffs between the WAPs. Figure 15.4 shows an example of a WLAN.

The applications for WLANs include low-cost installation, mobility, and support for temporary arrangements. For example, retailers often reconfigure their displays within a store and reassign where the cash registers need to be, and the only rapid deployment solution is wireless. As another example, if a natural disaster such as a flood or an earthquake disables the existing wireline facilities, the only quick road to disaster recovery is wireless. Other applications include scenarios where there may be environmental hazards such as asbestos in the building, or where there is a desire or requirement to preserve a historic building containing marble walls or oak paneling where it would be a shame to destroy such richness with intrusive installation procedures. In each of these cases, wireless presents an elegant, fast, and low-cost solution to getting service in and running.

The following sections describe a number of facets of WLANs:

- Wireless Fidelity (Wi-Fi)
- IEEE 802.11x standards
- WLAN security

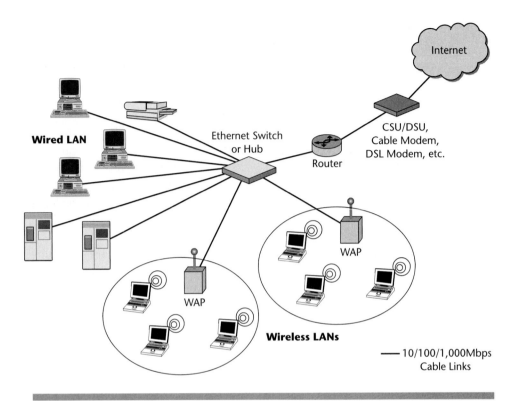

Figure 15.4 An example of a WLAN

- Voice over WLAN (VoWLAN)
- The integration of WLANs and cellular networks
- Mesh networks

Wi-Fi

The concept of readily available WLANs is being globally embraced. Many WLANs are being set up by grassroots groups that want to get on the Internet by sharing local connections. This opportunity is putting the grassroots networks on a collision course with cable companies and telecom carriers because it provides an opportunity for even an individual citizen to become a "telecom provider" to his or her neighbors. These new community wireless networks are based on Wi-Fi technology.

Wi-Fi allows users to plug a single high-speed Internet connection such as a cable modem into a US$100 to US$175 WAP and share it with scores of people in a building, park, or small neighborhood. Anyone can snap a US$50 antenna into a laptop and tap into many of these unsecured mini-networks for free, without permission. Those with clever entrepreneurial tendencies might charge their neighbors anywhere from US$5 to US$75 per month and become the neighborhood high-speed data access provider, and it's all legal (at least at the moment and in the United States).

Wi-Fi is popping up at thousands of hotspots, in locations including hotels, airports, shopping centers, restaurants/cafes, and educational environments; basically, wherever people congregate, there is an application for a hotspot. Hotspots are much less expensive to build than 3G systems, and they offer similar data capabilities, although voice service is not yet a reliable application on WLANs. Therefore, WLANs and cellular are uniting to provide road warriors with a complete toolkit.

Wi-Fi is a trade term promulgated by the Wi-Fi Alliance (www.wirelessethernet. org). Products that the Wi-Fi Alliance certifies are interoperable with each other, even if they are from different manufacturers. A user with a Wi-Fi product can use any brand of WAP with any other brand of client hardware built to the Wi-Fi standard.

Even though Wi-Fi is extremely cost-effective to deploy and is extremely popular today, some issues need to be recognized:

- **Limited range of service**—Today's Wi-Fi implementations are limited to coverage areas of 150 to 300 feet (50 to 100 m). Whenever there is a problem to be addressed, clever minds find a solution, and in the case of limited range, techniques such as mesh networking can extend the coverage area substantially; in fact, individual hotspots can be interconnected to blanket a large area, such as an entire metropolitan area.

- **Lack of QoS**—Wi-Fi is not inherently suitable for voice and video because it lacks the ability to control bandwidth allocation, delays, and losses. New standards such as 802.11e are specifically designed to introduce these capabilities.

- **Lack of security**—WLANs, by their very nature, pose a higher security threat than their wired network counterparts. The original Wi-Fi specifications are infamous for their lax security mechanisms, but 802.11i improves the situation substantially.

WLANs are being set up by all sorts of groups, from grassroots organizations to powerful retailers, hospitality organizations, and transportation enterprises—all focused on the benefits of allowing their constituents the opportunity to get on the Internet by sharing local connections. What is the motivation for them to implement and market WLAN services? For small entrepreneurs and technology lovers, doing so supports the dream of doing something positive in the development and deployment of communications technology required by the average citizen. For large business enterprises, doing so creates an opportunity to grow customer loyalty, an all-important objective today, and also provides a venue for generating new revenues—not just from the subscription to the network service or usage fees, but also because clients are likely to spend more time in the establishment working on e-mails and Web surfing and thus likely to buy more of the core product, whether it is another cup of coffee or another order of fries.

IEEE 802.11*x* Standards

WLANs encompass a number of different standards, but the most important are those from the IEEE 802.11 Working Group. The 802.11 Working Group comprises many individual task groups charged with developing various aspects of WLAN standards, referenced as 802.11*x*, with *x* denoting the specific task group and its objective. (The *x* does not, in this case, indicate the name of a specific protocol.)

This section focuses primarily on the standards that are essential to your knowledge of WLANs, but you should have a general feel for what each specification addresses, so Table 15.5 gives a quick summary of the whole 802.11 family.

The 802.11 specifications were initially introduced in 1997 for operation in the unlicensed 2.4GHz band, and they included two spread spectrum methods for transmission: 1Mbps Frequency Hopping Spread Spectrum (FHSS) and 1Mbps and 2Mbps Direct Sequence Spread Spectrum (DSSS). An infrared method was also specified. Ultimately, the Wi-Fi Alliance dropped both FHSS and infrared, but the 1Mbps DSSS method is still used by WAPs to advertise themselves (in a process known as *beaconing*). Now 802.11 is sometimes called 802.11 legacy.

WLAN Speeds

Despite the maximum speeds quoted in the specifications, the actual data throughput is generally quite a bit lower. This is because 802.11 uses a collision *avoidance* access technique (Carrier Sense Multiple Access/Collision Avoidance [CSMA/CA]) rather than the collision *detection* method (Carrier Sense Multiple Access/Collision Detection [CSMA/CD]) used in wired Ethernet LANs. Unlike wired LANS, wireless systems cannot detect collisions. The CSMA/CA method waits for an acknowledgment from the other end to determine whether the packet was transmitted properly, thus reducing the throughput.

In addition, the speed of a WLAN depends on the distance. The farther away the remote device is from the WAP, the lower the speed, or bit rate. Depending on the distance involved, different modulation techniques are used, including BPSK, QPSK, 4-QAM, 16-QAM, and 64-QAM.

The bottom line is that you should assume that the actual transmission speed of a WLAN is going to be 50% or less of the rated speed.

Table 15.5 The IEEE 802.11x Standards

Standard	Description
802.11	The original 1Mbps and 2Mbps, 2.4GHz radio frequency and infrared standard (1999)
802.11a	A 54Mbps, 5GHz standard (1999; products began shipping in 2001)
802.11b	Enhancements to 802.11 to support 5.5Mbps and 11Mbps (1999)
802.11c	Bridge operation procedures; included in the 802.1D standard (2001)
802.11d	International (country-to-country) roaming extensions (2001)
802.11e	Enhancements for QoS, including packet bursting (2005)
802.11F	Inter-Access Point Protocol (2003)
802.11g	A 54Mbps, 2.4GHz standard (backward compatible with 802.11b) (2003)
802.11h	Spectrum-managed 802.11a (5GHz) for European compatibility (2004)
802.11i	Enhanced security (2004)
802.11j	Extensions for Japan (2004)
802.11k	Radio resource measurement enhancements
802.11l	Reserved; typologically unsound (can be confused with other 802 standards)
802.11m	Maintenance of the standard; odds and ends
802.11n	Higher-throughput improvements
802.11o	Reserved; typologically unsound (can be confused with other 802 standards)
802.11p	Wireless Access for the Vehicular Environment (WAVE), such as ambulances and passenger cars
802.11q	Reserved; typologically unsound (can be confused with 802.1Q VLAN trunking)
802.11r	Fast roaming
802.11s	Extended Service Set (ESS) mesh networking
802.11T	Wireless Performance Prediction (WPP) test methods and metrics
802.11u	Interworking with non-802 networks (e.g., cellular)
802.11v	Wireless network management
802.11w	Protected management frames

Commonly Used 802.11 Standards: 802.11b, 802.11a, and 802.11g

The standards 802.11b, 802.11a, and 802.11g are the most commonly used today; their specifications are shown in Table 15.6.

IEEE 802.11b, published in 1999, was the first widely accepted wireless networking standard. The main objective of this standard was to boost the original 802.11 data rate (1Mbps to 2Mbps) to 11Mbps. However, due to the CSMA/CA access technique and distance variables, the actual throughput is likely to be more on the order of 5Mbps or less. IEEE 802.11b operates in the unlicensed 2.4GHz band, over a range of approximately 300 feet (100 m). It relies on DSSS transmission technology. This standard makes use of a variety of different phase-shift keying (PSK) modulation schemes, depending on the data rate required. At the basic rate of 1Mbps, it uses DBPSK (Differential Binary PSK). To provide the extended rate of 2Mbps, it uses DQPSK (Differential Quadrature PSK). In reaching 5.5Mbps and the full rate of 11Mbps, 802.11b uses QPSK, coupled with an error control technique called Complementary Code Keying (CCK).

IEEE 802.11a, also published in 1999, makes use of OFDM transmission, increasing the speeds to a theoretical rate of 54Mbps, but with a real throughput experience of 27Mbps or less. This standard operates in the 5GHz range over a smaller coverage range of 150 feet (50 m). (Remember that the higher the frequency, the faster the signal loses power, which means the coverage area must be smaller.) IEEE 802.11a is not backward compatible with 802.11b.

Published in 2003, IEEE 802.11g uses OFDM and operates in the 2.4GHz band, with a range of up to 300 feet (100 m). Because 802.11g transmits in the same band as 802.11b, the standards are compatible. However, if 802.11b and 802.11g devices are communicating with each other, they perform at the lowest common denominator, so they operate at the slower 802.11b speed. IEEE 802.11g supports 54Mbps in theory, but it offers an actual throughput of 27Mbps under ideal conditions and

Table 15.6 IEEE 802.11b, 802.11a, and 802.11g Standards

Standard	Capacity per Channel (Theoretical)	Capacity per Channel (Actual)	Band Used/ Range	Technology	Number of Channels (U.S.)	Number of Channels (Asia)	Number of Channels (Europe)
802.11b	11Mbps	5Mbps	2.4GHz/100 m	DSSS	3	3	4
802.11a	54Mbps	27Mbps	5GHz/50 m	OFDM	12	4	15
802.11g	54Mbps	27Mbps	2.4GHz/100 m	OFDM	3	3	4

less when the distance between the transmitter and receiver is longer. In addition, in networks where the WAPs support a mix of 802.11b and 802.11g, the throughput drops to 18Mbps, and when multiple clients are transmitting, the throughput is further reduced to approximately 6Mbps to 9Mbps.

Crowded Bands

The 2.4GHz band is getting increasingly crowded, so 802.11b and 802.11g networks share spectrum with the likes of household microwave ovens, cordless telephones, and many industrial, scientific, and medical systems, not to mention a growing number of WMAN and WPAN technologies designed to operate in the unlicensed frequency bands. These competing devices can cause interference for one another.

Standards 802.11a and 802.11g have eight data rates: 6Mbps, 9Mbps, 12Mbps, 18Mbps, 24Mbps, 36Mbps, 48Mbps, and 54Mbps. The 6Mbps and 9Mbps modes use the BPSK modulation technique. The 12Mbps and 18Mbps modes use QPSK. The 24Mbps and 36Mbps modes use 16-QAM, and 48Mbps and 54Mbps use 64-QAM.

The 802.11 systems divide the spectrum into channels, enabling multiple WAPs to operate close to each other without interference because each one can be set to a different channel. However, 802.11b and 802.11g use overlapping channels. This means that in the United States and Asia, only 3 channels can be used, effectively allowing only 3 WAPs to operate without interference. In Europe, 4 channels are available. With 802.11a, the channels do not overlap, so in the United States, 12 channels are available, allowing 12 WAPs to operate in the same vicinity. In Asia, 4 channels can be used, and in Europe, 15 channels are available.

Two modes of operation are specified in 802.11: infrastructure and ad hoc. In the infrastructure mode, the laptops or other wireless devices transmit to a base station, the WAP, which then connects to a wired LAN. Each WAP with its wireless devices is known as a basic service set (BSS). When there are two or more BSSs in the same subnet, it is called an extended service set (ESS). In the ad hoc mode, also called *peer-to-peer mode*, laptops and other wireless devices communicate directly with one another in a peer-to-peer fashion; no WAP is used. This is called an independent BSS (IBSS).

Emerging 802.11 Standards: 802.11e, 802.11i, and 802.11n

Three emerging standards—802.11e, 802.11i, and 802.11n—show promise in terms of addressing the deficiencies of current WLANs.

The objective of IEEE 802.11e is to provide for QoS extensions to the 802.11 protocol in support of LAN applications that have QoS requirements. The 802.11e standard allows for real-time audio and video streams to be given a higher priority over regular data. Examples of applications include transport of audio and video over 802.11 wireless networks, videoconferencing, media stream distribution, enhanced security applications, and mobile and nomadic access applications. The operation of the 802.11e standard is discussed further later in this chapter, in the section "VoWLAN."

IEEE 802.11i, ratified in 2004, is a critical standard because it specifies enhanced security mechanisms for Wi-Fi. The initial security mechanism for 802.11 networks, called Wired Equivalent Privacy (WEP), was shown to have severe security weaknesses—enough to discourage many people from deploying wireless. In response, the Wi-Fi Alliance introduced Wi-Fi Protected Access (WPA), a subset of 802.11i, as an intermediate solution to WEP insecurities. The Wi-Fi Alliance refers to its approved, interoperable implementation of the full 802.11i as WPA2. The next section, "WLAN Security," examines the specifics of 802.11i and WPA2.

Perhaps the most eagerly awaited 802.11 standard is IEEE 802.11n, which is expected by 2007. A major enhancement to the 802.11 standard, its objective is to increase transmission speeds to 100Mbps and beyond. In fact, the real data throughput is estimated to reach a theoretical 54Mbps. IEEE 802.11n makes use of multiple-input multiple-output (MIMO) technology, which significantly improves performance and boosts the data rate. At the moment, two competing technologies are both MIMO based:

- **WorldWide Spectrum Efficiency (WWiSE)**—WWiSE is backed by Broadcom (www.broadcom.com) and other companies. The WWiSE group (www.wwise.org) wants to stay in the 2.4GHz band and use the same 20MHz channels as 802.11b and 802.11g for compatibility.

- **TGn Sync**—This technology is backed by Intel (www.intel.com) and Philips (www.philips.com). IEEE 802.11 Task Group n (TGn; www.tgnsync.org) wants to increase the channel width to 40MHz to increase the data rate and use the 5GHz band like 802.11a.

In order to speed the 802.11n development process and promote a technology specification for interoperability of next-generation WLAN products, the Enhanced Wireless Consortium (EWC; www.enhancedwirelessconsortium.org) was formed. The 802.11n Working Group approved the EWC's specification as the draft approval of 802.11n in January 2006.

WLAN Security

The flaws in Wi-Fi security have given rise to *war drivers*—individuals who drive through an area, scan for wireless networks (using programs such as NetStumbler), and publish their findings on the Web. The term is derived from *war dialing*, a method hackers use to locate nonsecure computers by dialing through phone numbers.

The original 802.11b security mechanism is static WEP. Static WEP uses a 40- or 104-bit encryption key, which is manually entered and applied and then is not typically changed. WEP has been shown to be easily compromised and is generally not considered secure. Programs such as AirSnort can obtain encryption keys. Most wireless networks fail to make use of even WEP.

The good news is that WEP is not the only available WLAN security mechanism. The continuum of IEEE wireless security standards also includes static WEP with initialization vector (IV), dynamic WEP, WPA, and WPA2.

Static WEP with IV

Static WEP is today often enhanced with IV, a 24-bit "starting point" value appended to basic WEP. Adding 24 bits to a WEP key results in 64- or 128-bit composite key values. Static WEP with IV is supported by all current VoWLAN handsets.

Dynamic WEP

Dynamic WEP, which has generally replaced static WEP, is an incremental security improvement over basic static WEP. It involves mutual authentication using 802.1X and generation of unique encryption keys for each associated client.

WPA

WPA is the current state-of-the-art in standards-based WLAN security. It is an enhanced wireless security environment that replaces dynamic WEP. WPA includes three main elements:

- **Temporal Key Integrity Protocol (TKIP)**—TKIP, based on RC4 encryption, uses a 304-bit key (a 128-bit base key plus a 128-bit IV plus the 48-bit MAC address) and generates new encryption keys after various configurable intervals (a time period, a bit quantity, or even every frame), which makes it much more difficult to break.

- **Message Integrity Code (MIC)**—MIC introduces a kind of digital signature to each frame to ensure that messages are not tampered with or captured and replayed. It helps to thwart the introduction of unauthorized WAPs.

- **802.1X authentication framework**—802.1X is a popular IEEE standard for port-based access control that is included in the latest wireless security specifications. This standard defines how to authenticate the identity of wireless (and wired) clients, such as via an external Remote Authentication Dial-in User Services (RADIUS) server or by using other authentication methods, such as Extensible Authentication Protocol (EAP). RADIUS is an authentication, authorization, and accounting (AAA) protocol for applications such as IP mobility and network access. It works in both local and roaming environments. EAP, specified under IETF RFC 3748, is a protocol that allows incorporation of various external authentication methods— digital certificates, usernames and passwords, secure tokens, and so on— into wireless security environments. As used in 802.11i, 802.1X provides a framework for robust user and device authentication, a feature that was missing from the original 802.11 standard.

Like dynamic WEP, WPA generates unique keys for each associated client computer and takes care of distributing them securely.

WPA2

WPA2 is embodied in the IEEE 802.11i specification, and it is the most long-term solution of the current WLAN security standards. It is the latest-generation wireless security environment, meant to enhance and supplant WPA. WPA2 differs from WPA in that it uses AES rather than RC4 and doesn't need a MIC because the same AES key is used for both encryption and integrity. WPA2 still relies on 802.1X for authentication. AES supports encryption keys of 128, 196, and 256 bits. All Wi-Fi hardware manufactured after August 2004 includes support for WPA2.

VoWLAN

Two hot networking technologies, VoIP and WLANs, have come together to provide a local voice solution, VoWLAN, that marries the convenience of mobility with the cost-effectiveness of an IP PBX.

VoWLAN Support Concerns

There are three primary concerns regarding support of VoWLAN: security, handoff capability, and capacity and QoS. The following sections discuss these concerns.

VoWLAN Security   The major struggle with WLANs has been to start with a technology created for residential and consumer applications and to strengthen it to the point where it can support enterprise requirements. The most critical issue has been the ongoing security problems created by 802.11's weak WEP encryption and authentication systems. As discussed in the preceding sections, however, there is plenty of good news regarding recent developments in WLAN security. Most security concerns should be addressed by the WPA standard, along with IEEE's 802.1X authentication framework, and ultimately the 802.11i encryption standard.

VoWLAN Handoffs   Another potential problem with VoWLAN has to do with handoffs. Voice users' requirements for mobility will be greater than those of data users, so voice handoffs are more likely. A call handoff must occur quickly, and the authentication and encryption must remain intact. Handoffs can be several seconds long. The problem is that most traditional data-oriented authentication systems require that the device be reauthenticated when moving to a new WAP. The IEEE is looking for a 20-millisecond handoff capability for voice calls. Vendors today have introduced proprietary solutions to address the handoff concern, but eventually a standards-based solution will emerge. Meanwhile, a user must weigh the functionality that can be delivered immediately against the potential risk of being locked in by a vendor's proprietary solution.

The VoWLAN solution is typically implemented as an adjunct to an existing circuit-switched or IP-based PBX. In either case, there are three main elements in a VoWLAN solution: VoWLAN telephone sets, WLANs, and gateways. VoWLAN telephone sets include digital telephones and other voice-capable devices that support an 802.11 WLAN interface. One issue regarding VoWLAN phones is the codec or voice-encoding rate. The main choices include G.711, the public network standard that requires 64Kbps per voice channel, and G.729a, a more bandwidth-efficient low-bit-rate option, which calls for 8Kbps per voice channel. The main tradeoff between the two standards is a 15- to 30-millisecond increase in delay due to compression when using G.729a.

VoWLAN Capacity and QoS   Capacity and QoS are discussed together here because the issues of providing adequate capacity while minimizing delay and jitter can be addressed by increasing the overall network capacity by offering higher bandwidth or by ensuring that voice packets are recognized and given priority over data packets—in other words, through managed bandwidth.

Remember that WLANs were designed first and foremost for the requirements of data devices. They incorporate no inherent mechanisms for controlling latency or jitter. WLANs are half-duplex (only one part can send at a time), they share media (all users in an area share one radio channel), and the transmission rate depends on the distance from the end station to the WAP and on the effects of any impairments in the environment. The CSMA/CA process used in the 802.11 MAC protocol uses a system of backoff timers to help avoid collisions. All successful transmissions must be acknowledged, and if no acknowledgment is received, the transmitter sets a backoff counter with a random value. That backoff value is increased with every unsuccessful attempt. Because of these processes, the effective throughput of a WLAN is only some 50% to 55% of the raw transmission rate. These factors—channel contention, waiting intervals, acknowledgments, and retransmissions—make it virtually impossible to provide a service that has consistent delay. To work around this, as with other packet voice systems, a time stamp is placed in the Real-Time Transport Protocol (RTP) header of each voice packet, and a buffer at the receiving end is used to mask the jitter effect.

The long-term solution to the problem of capacity and QoS in VoWLANs is an enhanced MAC-layer protocol called Hybrid Coordination Function (HCF) that is developed in the IEEE 802.11e specification. The 802.11e HCF protocol is a very important development in VoWLAN systems. In order to improve service for voice, the standard includes two operating modes, either of which can be used: Enhanced Digital Control Access (EDCA) and Polled Access.

EDCA   EDCA, which is mandatory, is an enhanced version of the Distributed Control Function (DCF) defined in the original 802.11 MAC protocol. EDCA defines eight levels of access priority to the shared wireless channel. EDCA access is a contention-based protocol (as is DCF) and relies on a set of waiting intervals and backoff timers designed to avoid collisions. However, there is a difference between DCF and EDCA. In DCF, all the stations use the same values and therefore have the same priority for transmitting on the channel. In the case of EDCA, each of the different access priorities uses a different range of waiting intervals and back-off counters; therefore, stations with higher-access priority are assigned shorter intervals. The standard also includes a packet-bursting mode that allows a WAP or a mobile station to reserve a channel and send three to five packets in sequence. EDCA can ensure that voice transmissions wait less than data transmissions, but it lacks a mechanism to deliver truly consistent delay.

Polled Access   Delivering true consistent delay is the role of the optional operating mode Polled Access. Polled Access periodically broadcasts a control message that forces all stations to treat the channel as busy and not attempt to transmit. During that period, the WAP polls each station that is defined for time-sensitive service. The Polled Access function requires that devices request a traffic profile regarding bandwidth, latency, and jitter. If the WAP lacks resources to meet the traffic profile, the WAP returns a busy signal. Polled Access is optional because WAPs that do not support the feature must be able to return a "service not available" response to stations' profile requests.

VoWLAN Support Solutions

Although 802.11e will provide a more predictable WLAN environment, voice can still be carried over WLANs with the existing tools and techniques. In addition, the IEEE is beginning work on higher-capacity channels. It is developing the 802.11n radio link, with the goal of delivering throughput of 100Mbps. By employing MIMO, 802.11n will offer up to eight times the coverage and up to six times the speed of current 802.11g networks. In January 2006, the task group working on this faster standard for Wi-Fi settled on a draft proposal that was to be refined into a final specification. A few wireless networking manufacturers have released "pre-N" hardware in anticipation of an eventual standard, and products built according to the draft specification are expected to become available in 2006. Broadcom has announced the availability of a family of chipsets that it claims are the first products designed to comply with the draft. The chipsets, called Intensi-fi, can be used in routers, laptops, and add-in PC cards. There are also proprietary solutions that boost transmission rates to 100Mbps by using MIMO antenna systems. (MIMO is discussed in Chapter 13, "Wireless Communications Basics.")

The major vendors of VoWLAN address different classes of user applications, although all focus on several key vertical markets: the mobile workforce, health care, warehousing and distribution, education, and hospitality. The general enterprise market is considered to be the main market, where the VoWLAN phone could become an adjunct or a replacement for PBX and key system stations. However, general office users are just beginning to embrace WLANs for data, so voice is likely to be a future phase of those projects. Given the evolving nature of VoWLAN, for the next several years, the primary users are likely to be in specialized applications with a great need for mobility or where wired devices are simply impractical.

The Integration of WLANs and Cellular Networks

The wireless industry saw a major development in 2004: Avaya (www.avaya.com), Motorola (www.motorola.com), and Proxim (www.proxim.com) announced the first workable solution that allows voice calls to be handed off between WLANs and cellular networks. A similar capability was also developed by Nortel Networks (www.nortel.com), in partnership with Airespace (now part of Cisco [www.cisco.com]) and SpectraLink (www.spectralink.com). In the recent past, some specialized configurations have integrated wired PBX systems and cellular, but these were the first arrangements to permit voice calls to be handed off from the cellular network to the WLAN and vice versa. The handoff is virtually unnoticeable to the user because it takes less than 100 milliseconds. However, these initial offerings have shortcomings. For instance, there are different sets of features on WLAN and cellular calls. Also, not all cellular calls are automatically transferred to the WLAN when the user gets within range. These shortcomings are to be addressed in future releases.

Meanwhile, two major questions have been at issue in the integration of WLANs and cellular: Can WLANs support voice effectively? Do cellular carriers have any real desire, or incentive, to support VoWLAN? The following sections discuss these issues.

Technology Issues for Integrating WLANs and Cellular Networks

The main concerns in using a WLAN to support voice include network capacity and traffic prioritization, battery life, security, handoffs, and feature integration. The recently announced systems address these concerns by implementing WPA, proprietary architectures, and proprietary approaches to feature access.

The issues of network capacity and traffic prioritization present a rather difficult problem, due to the limitations of using a shared-media LAN. These concerns are being addressed by providing handsets that support the three major radio link standards, 802.11a, 802.11b, and 802.11g. IEEE 802.11b and g, operating over the 2.4GHz band, provide only 3 noninterfering channels, leaving them open to interference from cordless phones, microwave ovens, baby monitors, and neighbors' WLANs. IEEE 802.11a, operating in the 5GHz band, provides 12 channels, 8 dedicated to indoor and 4 dedicated to point-to-point. However, given the higher-frequency band, 5GHz, more WAPs are required to cover an area. By using G.729 compression, vendors currently claim that they can handle 8 voice calls on an 802.11b WLAN channel and 20 on an 802.11a or 802.11g channel, while using some 50% of a WLAN's capacity. However, because there are few large-scale voice installations in place, it is difficult to verify these claims.

Battery life is a critical element in all mobile devices. Wi-Fi consumes far more power than cellular. The Wi-Fi standards define a power-saving mode, but using it is not an optimum solution because it requires that the handset wake up to receive beacon messages from the WAP several times per second to see if any traffic is awaiting delivery. Vendors are developing more efficient power-saving schemes and are proposing them to standards bodies.

Security continues to be one of the major issues affecting the use of WLANs, particularly in commercial organizations. The fact that radio signals propagate through free space, combined with the very limited security features associated with 802.11b, creates a major security concern for large enterprises as well as small offices and home businesses. Fortunately, there have been several important enhancements to WLAN security standards, such as WPA2 and 802.11i (as discussed earlier in this chapter).

Another important area of functionality has to do with seamless handoffs—that is, the ability to hand off a call from the cellular network to a WLAN, or vice versa. This is particularly vital to voice calls, where handoffs are much more likely to be required because the user's mobility is greater. Handoffs are so important that the emerging standard IEEE 802.21 addresses them. This standard is designed to enable seamless handoffs between networks of the same type as well as handoffs between different network types, such as cellular, GSM, GPRS, 802.11 networks, and Bluetooth. Another emerging area that addresses the need to move between networks is cognitive radio (discussed in Chapter 16), which is a smart wireless technology that will serve the user by first locating and then connecting with any nearby open radio frequency.

Finally, feature integration is a highly desirable part of dual-network (i.e., WLAN and cellular) functionality. The goal of integrating 802.11 technology within the enterprise with cellular telephony outside the enterprise is to simplify business communications and support contiguous communications across networks. This integration means that IP-PBX features can be available to mobile workers on the road. In addition, productivity can be greatly enhanced by having only one device, one phone number, and one voicemail account to manage, while enabling access to enterprise data from many locations. With such feature integration, the mobile worker has the same level of functionality, accessibility, and productivity on the road as in the office.

Cellular Carrier Cooperation with VoWLAN

Aside from technology issues, the real issue that will determine the success of WLAN/cellular integration is whether the cellular carriers will cooperate. The handset Motorola has developed is GSM compatible, but it is unclear how many carriers will actually offer VoWLAN services. The "free" model associated with WLANs is not the traditional philosophy pursued by carriers. In addition, Wi-Fi roaming threatens to take minutes off the cellular carriers' networks. Another potential stumbling block is that many of the emerging handsets, such as the one from Motorola, require Generic Access Network (GAN). GAN technology provides access to GSM and GPRS mobile services over unlicensed spectrum technologies, including Bluetooth and 802.11. By deploying GAN technology, service providers can enable subscribers to roam and hand over between cellular networks and public and private unlicensed wireless networks using dual-mode mobile handsets.

Because WLAN implementation is transparent to carriers, they may not be able to do much about it. In a typical operation, when a call is transferred from a cellular network to a WLAN, all the carrier knows is that the subscriber hung up. It has no way of knowing that the call was actually continued on the WLAN. Similarly, when a call is transferred to a cellular network, the carrier simply sees a new call origination. It has no idea that a WLAN handoff has occurred. Although calls can always be transferred from a WLAN to a cellular network, the reverse is not true. For cellular calls to be transferred into a WLAN, the PBX has to be in control of the call—that is, a call to the user's PBX number must be transferred to the user's cellular device. If the user has received a cellular call directly from the cellular network and enters the WLAN coverage area, the PBX has no idea that the call exists and has no way to effect the transfer. Instead, the call is "dragged into" the facility—it simply continues on the cellular network, and cellular usage charges apply.

Leading VoWLAN suppliers plan to use Signaling System 7 (SS7) connections between the WLAN and cellular networks, transferring calls between the two wireless networks in the same manner as calls are transferred between different PSTN carriers. Such SS7 connections can be leased from third-party aggregators rather than from carriers directly, putting even this high-level functionality beyond the carriers' control. Cooperation is yet to be tested between cellular carriers and WLAN suppliers, not to mention between the voice and data camps within the enterprise.

Mesh Networks

A quickly maturing alternative to wireless broadband metro and campus area networks is mesh networking, which is of special interest to those who just can't wait for WiMax. Mesh networking represents an innovative do-it-yourself approach to easily building wireless broadband data networks. It specifically caters to mobile nodes, instant growth, and unpredictable variations in reception and coverage.

Mesh networks essentially route voice, data, and instructions between nodes, creating a resilient network in which connections are continuous, reconfiguring around blocked paths by hopping from node to node until a connection is established. Both wireless and wired networks can benefit from mesh network topologies.

Using intelligence embedded in each component, meshing joins the components into a self-organizing structure, overcoming the limitations of traditional centralized models of wireless networking. Mesh networks turn WAPs into router nodes with peer radio devices that can automatically self-configure and communicate with each other. Mesh networks can also self-learn changes in the network: Transmission paths can be adjusted according to changes for optimal throughput.

Mesh networking extends the potential of wireless networking. There are two types of mesh networks: full and partial. Full mesh networks connect all WAPs to each other and dynamically self-organize with themselves and clients. In partial mesh networks, nodes are connected to only some, not all, of the other nodes. Each WAP finds routes through the mesh, adjusting for hardware failure, delay, and so on. Does this sound familiar? It should: The Internet is the ultimate mesh network. Figure 15.5 illustrates possible mesh topologies in support of both low- and high-traffic networks.

In a mesh network, only one WAP needs to be connected directly to the wired network, with the rest sharing a connection over the air. This simplifies installation and design because mesh WAPs can be taken out of the box, plugged in, and discovered by the network. WAPs that are moved are automatically rediscovered. It is expected that the IEEE 802.11s standard for mesh networks will see final approval by mid-2008.

Other standards in development that will affect mesh networks are IEEE 802.11v, which addresses interoperability of radios, and the IETF effort Control and Provi-

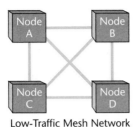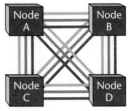

Low-Traffic Mesh Network   High-Traffic Mesh Network

Figure 15.5 Mesh networks

sioning of Wireless Access Points (CAPWAP), which addresses different vendors' WAPs working together. Results from these two camps are expected sometime in 2006 or 2007.

Mesh Network Protocols and Implementations

A number of protocols and implementations are associated with mesh and ad hoc networking, each with different goals and design criteria:

- **Ad Hoc, On Demand, Distance Vector (AODV)**—AODV is recognized as the leading standard for wireless mesh networking. Published by the National Institute of Standards and Technology (NIST; www.nist.gov), AODV is designed with mobile wireless devices in mind. It is in the public domain and is therefore subject to no copyright protection.

- **Mobile Mesh**—This implementation involves three separate types of protocols, each addressing a specific function: link discovery protocol, routing protocol, and border discovery protocol. Mobile Mesh is covered in the GNU General Public License version 2.

- **Topology Broadcast Based on Reverse-Path Forwarding (TBRPF)**—TBRPF is a proactive link-state routing protocol designed for mobile ad hoc networks. It provides hop-by-hop routing along minimum-hop paths to each destination. It is now patent protected but may become an IETF standard.

- **Open Shortest Path First (OSPF)**—OSPF is a link-state routing protocol designed to be run internal to a single autonomous system. (Autonomous systems are discussed in Chapter 8, "The Internet and IP Infrastructures.")

- **GNU Zebra**—This free software manages TCP/IP-based routing protocols. It is distributed under the GNU General Public License. It supports BGP-4, RIPv1, RIPv2, and OSPFv2.

- **LocustWorld**—This is a free bootable CD solution based on AODV. Locust-World (www.locustworld.com) also sells a complete ready-to-deploy Mesh-Box product that runs its software.

- **4G MeshCube**—This product was developed by the German company 4G Mobile Systems (www.4g-systems.com). It runs Debian Linux on a MIPS processor, using MITRE Mobile Mesh routing software. It is a ready-to-deploy gateway with both wireless and wired interfaces. It features low power consumption of 4 watts or lower.

Of course, there are many more protocols and implementations under development, so stay tuned.

Benefits of and Considerations for Mesh Networks

The key attributes of mesh networks include the following:

- **Cost-effective**—Mesh networks have affordable components, installation, and ongoing maintenance.

- **Rapid, easy, and simple deployment**—The setup of mesh networks is extremely easy, involving a box that is preinstalled with wireless mesh software and uses standard wireless protocols such 802.11b and 802.11g.

- **Self-organizing**—Each node of a mesh network works out the routing for itself.

- **Dynamic routing**—A mesh network does real-time reconfiguration in response to additions, failures, or load changes.

- **Resilient**—A mesh network automatically reroutes around blockages in real-time, offering greater stability in the face of changing conditions or failure at single nodes.

- **Wide range of operation**—Multihop networks extend the wireless range around obstacles and over greater distances.

- **Wide range of applications**—A mesh network supports a wide variety of meshes, from macromeshes suitable for metro area deployments to the micromeshes that dominate in the realm of sensor-based, telemetry, and control applications.

- **Scalable deployment**—The routing configuration in a mesh network is automatic; there is no exponential rise in complexity as the number of network nodes grows.

- **Organization and business models**—The decentralized nature of mesh networks lends itself well to decentralized ownership models, where each participant in the network owns and maintains its own hardware.

- **Low power consumption**—Substrate nodes can be deployed as completely autonomous units with solar power, wind power, or hydropower.

In addition to these benefits of mesh networking, there are also a number of considerations, including the following:

- **Unpredictable throughput**—Throughput is dependent on the number of hops and is not predictable.
- **WAP dependency**—The further you get from the WAP, the lower the data rate.
- **Scalability**—A wireless mesh network's scalability depends on the number of radios in the WAP.
- **Uncertain reliability**—Reliability is uncertain in less than a full mesh.
- **QoS**—QoS remains a critical problem to resolve.
- **Proprietary technology**—Many prestandard vendors continue to emerge in Wi-Fi and WiMax. Wireless mesh solutions involve some proprietary technology, so it is not always possible to mix WAPs from different vendors.
- **Radio interference**—Radio interference is a potentially significant issue when working with unlicensed spectrum, as in building a large Wi-Fi grid. Unlicensed spectrum is good for campuses, but carriers prefer to use licensed spectrum, which they have control over.
- **Load balancing**—Mesh WAPs may need to practice load balancing to keep interference to a minimum, using 802.11a as the backhaul frequency while using 802.11b and 802.11g for client traffic. It is in the area of backhaul spectrum that WiMax is initially expected to be most important, as the backhaul link from the mesh network to the PSTN. (WiMax is discussed in detail earlier in this chapter, in the section "IEEE 802.16 (WiMax).") However, finalized WiMax standards and widespread availability of antennas and base stations at a reduced cost are not expected until 2007 at the earliest.

When to Use Mesh Networks

Enterprise users are likely to consider mesh networks when the cost and time to install are barriers to a wireless network, when site surveys cannot be done, when WAPs need to be moved frequently, and when client roaming is required (especially if the application involves VoWLAN). Self-configuration, scalability, and self-healing are drivers in the enterprise user's selection of a network.

As far as service providers go, mesh networks are indicated when Wi-Fi operators are seeking to extend the range of the Wi-Fi grid. With mesh networks, there is no need to provide individual backhaul connections for each and every WAP, as is generally required by regular Wi-Fi WAPs. Service providers also look to mesh networks when a few nodes can be connected to the PSTN, allowing the others to provide their own backhaul links to each other. In addition, mesh deployments are particularly useful in remote locations. Finally, service providers stand to play a major role in operating and managing networks built by city governments and municipalities. Municipalities across North America, Taiwan, and Australia already have mesh networks deployed, sometimes over well-financed objections by the local incumbent telcos. Hong Kong, Singapore, Korea, and Japan have also displayed interest in mesh networks, and wireless mesh networking is predicted to grow as the first networks deployed demonstrate real-world benefits.

Mesh networks are also of great interest to local communities and nonprofits in the developing world, particularly those interested in planning, deploying, and maintaining a local, sustainable network infrastructure to enable voice and data communications, both locally and on the Internet. University and enterprise campuses seeking to extend their WLANs outdoors are also good candidates. National Taiwan University and Edith Cowan University in Western Australia are early examples. By using a wireless mesh network, Edith Cowan University offers voice services to students, who can use Wi-Fi/cellular handsets to make intranetwork Wi-Fi calls on campus and roam to cellular for off-campus calls.

Wireless Micromesh Networks

One of the most important applications of mesh networks is their ability to dynamically support and make possible large-scale sensor networks (e.g., those that use RFID, telemetry, and control applications) that collect real-time data. Wireless micromeshes eliminate the need to wire every node and thus provide the greatest degree of flexibility possible in sensor/control networks. A micromesh network is designed for short range (i.e., up to 300 feet [100 m] between any two nodes). This class of mesh network is characterized by long battery life, relatively low data rates, and good tolerance for latency.

Core applications of micromeshes include the following, among many other industrial, commercial, and residential applications:

- **Physical security**—Micromeshes enable access control, monitoring, alarms, and other forms of physical security.
- **Environmental sensing**—Micromeshes can sense shock, vibration, thermal, optical, chemical, biological, and other environmental factors.
- **Building automation**—Micromeshes can be used in a building to automate HVAC, security, energy management, and so on.

- **Agriculture**—Micromeshes can be used for soil monitoring, water management, chemical deployment, and other uses in agriculture.

- **Applications requiring mobility**—Micromeshes can be used in situations in which it is frequently necessary to move the entire network, such as in military, intelligence, and national security environments.

For example, imagine a horse ranch with sensors, each the size of a quarter, dispersed over the land, measuring environmental variables such as temperature and humidity. If each sensor were connected to a base station, the cost would be prohibitive, but in a micromesh network, they are all connected to each other and then to the base station. They synchronize with each other, collect data, and sleep until the next iteration.

As illustrated in Figure 15.6, a sensor mesh network must bridge to processing elements that deal with the data collected by sensor nodes. It must also provide monitoring and command and control of the mesh in response to changing conditions. This functionality is best implemented in a gateway. As the size of a micromesh network grows, there is increasing need for a gateway-based systems-level architecture. It is predicted that gateways will become a core element of sensor-mesh networks in the coming years.

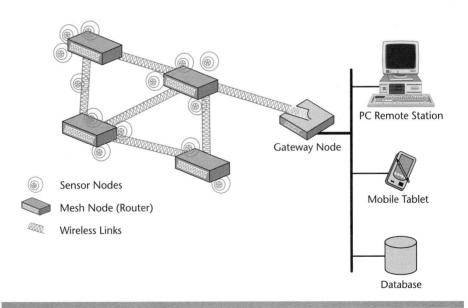

Figure 15.6 A sensor mesh network

■ WPANs

A WPAN is a network that serves a single person or small workgroup and is characterized by limited distance, limited throughput, and low volume. PANs have traditionally been used to transfer data between a laptop or PDA and a desktop machine or server and a printer. In this case, there is usually support for virtual docking stations, peripheral sharing, and ad hoc infrared links. Another application of WPANs is in support of building automation and control. An increasing number of machine-to-machine (m2m) applications are emerging, as are future applications involving wearables, all of which require PANs to realize their key benefits.

As with many of the other technologies discussed so far in this book, there are a variety of PAN standards, some of which are from the IEEE, and some of which are more recent and specifically geared toward m2m communications and sensor-based networks.

The IEEE 802.15 WPAN Working Group effort focuses on the development of consensus standards for WPANs. These standards address wireless networking of portable and mobile computing devices—such as PCs, PDAs, peripherals, mobile phones, pagers, and consumer electronics—allowing these devices to communicate and interoperate with one another. One of the main goals of the working group is to publish standards, recommended practices, and guidelines that have broad market applicability and deal effectively with the issues of coexistence and interoperability with other wired and wireless networking solutions. Four major 802.15 task groups are addressing WPAN standards:

- **Task Group 1 (802.15.1: WPAN/Bluetooth)**—This group deals with Bluetooth. It produced the 802.15.1 standard, published in 2002, which includes MAC- and PHY-layer specifications derived from the Bluetooth v1.1 foundation specifications published by the Bluetooth Special Interest Group (Bluetooth SIG; www.bluetooth.org).

- **Task Group 2 (802.15.2: WPAN Coexistence)**—This group developed recommended practices to facilitate coexistence of WPANs (802.15) and WLANs (802.11). It developed a coexistence model to quantify the mutual interference of a WLAN and a WPAN. The task group also developed a set of coexistence mechanisms to facilitate coexistence of WLAN and WPAN devices. This task group is now in hibernation until further notice.

- **Task Group 3 (802.15.3: WPAN High Rate and WPAN Alternate High Rate)**—This group currently has two subgroups: 802.15.3 is referred to as WPAN High Rate (WPAN-HR), and 802.15.3a is referred to as WPAN

Alternate High Rate (WPAN-AHR). Both of them deal with high-data-rate WPANs (i.e., WPANs that operate at 20Mbps or more).

■ **Task Group 4 (802.15.4: WPAN Low Rate)**—This group is focused on low-data-rate WPANs with very long battery life (months or years). The 802.15.4 standard, known as ZigBee, was produced by this group. The first edition of the standard was released in 2003. The 802.15.4 task group is now in hibernation. The 802.15.4a standard aims to provide a PHY-layer wireless communication protocol with ranging capabilities for low-power applications such as sensor networks. A new task group, 802.15.4b, is also working on enhancing the original standard.

The following sections cover these task groups and the main WPAN standards in use today:

■ IEEE 802.15.1 (Bluetooth)

■ IEEE 802.15.3 (WPAN-HR and WPAN-AHR)

■ Ultra-Wideband (UWB)

■ IEEE 802.15.4 (ZigBee)

■ Radio frequency identification (RFID)

■ Near Field Communication (NFC)

IEEE 802.15.1 (Bluetooth)

IEEE 802.15.1, known as Bluetooth, is an industry specification for short-range RF-based connectivity for portable personal devices. This specification was originally developed by Ericsson (www.ericsson.com) and was ultimately formalized by the Bluetooth SIG (www.bluetooth.org), which includes more than 3,000 members, including Sony, Ericsson, IBM, Intel, Toshiba, and Nokia.

The IEEE licensed wireless technology from the Bluetooth SIG to adapt and copy a portion of the Bluetooth specification as base material for IEEE 802.15.1-2002. The approved IEEE 802.15.1 standard, which defines the lower transport layers of the Bluetooth wireless technology, is fully compatible with the Bluetooth v1.1 specification. Bluetooth technology defines specifications for small-form-factor, low-cost wireless radio communications among notebook computers, PDAs, mobile phones, and other portable, handheld devices and for connectivity to the Internet.

The primary focus of Bluetooth technology is to provide a standard designed for low power consumption, operating over a short range, and including a low-cost transceiver microchip in each device. Bluetooth devices can talk to each other

Where Bluetooth Got Its Name

In the tenth century, there was a king in Denmark named Harald Blatand, which translates to *Harold Bluetooth* in English. King Blatand was instrumental in uniting warring factions in parts of what is now Norway, Sweden, and Denmark. He was renowned for his ability to help people communicate.

Fast-forward to the twentieth century: During the formative stage of the IEEE 802.15.1 trade association, the effort required a code name. One evening, as the members were discussing European history and the future of wireless technology, they came upon the notion of naming the technology after King Blatand: Just as he had united warring factions, Bluetooth technology is designed to allow collaboration between differing industries, such as the computing, mobile phone, and automotive markets. The code name stuck, and the technology today lives up to its name.

Even the Bluetooth logo has an interesting origin. To read about it, visit http://bluetooth.com/Bluetooth/SIG/Who/History/.

whenever they come within range, with the actual distance allowed depending on the power class of the devices. There are three power classes:

- **Class 1**—Class 1 devices consume 100 milliwatts of power and support the longest range, up to 300 feet (100 m). This class of device is readily available.

- **Class 2**—Class 2 devices consume 2.5 milliwatts of power and allow transmission over a distance of up to 30 feet (10 m). It is the most common class of device.

- **Class 3**—Class 3 devices consume 1 milliwatt of power and supports transmission over a range from 4 inches to 3 feet (10 cm to 1 m). This class of device is the least common.

The initial focus of Bluetooth was ad hoc interoperability between mobile phones, headsets, and PDAs, but today it is also seeing application in sensor-based networks. Most Bluetooth devices are recharged regularly. Bluetooth uses FHSS (discussed in Chapter 13) and splits the 2.4GHz ISM band into 79 1MHz channels. Bluetooth devices hop among the 79 channels 1,600 times per second in a pseudo-random pattern. Connected Bluetooth devices are grouped into networks called *piconets*; each piconet contains one master and up to seven active slaves. The channel-hopping sequence of each piconet is derived from the master's clock. All the slave devices must remain synchronized with that clock. FEC is used on all packet headers, by transmitting each bit in the header three times. The Hamming Code is also used for FEC of the data payload of some packet types. The Hamming Code introduces a 50% overhead on each data packet but is able to correct all single-bit errors and detect all double-bit errors in each 15-bit codeword (each 15-bit codeword contains 10 bits of information).

Bluetooth wireless technology is set to revolutionize the personal connectivity market by providing freedom from wired connections for portable handheld devices. The Bluetooth SIG is driving development of the technology and bringing it to market. The IEEE Bluetooth standard gives the Bluetooth SIG's specification greater validity and support in the market and is an additional resource for those who implement Bluetooth devices. This collaboration is a good example of how a standards development organization and a special interest group can work together to improve an industry specification and also create a standard.

As of May 2005, 5 million Bluetooth units were shipping per week, demonstrating the wide acceptance of Bluetooth technology in a multitude of applications, such as mobile phones, cars, portable computers, MP3 players, mouse devices, and keyboards. New applications are routinely introduced. For example, one new application involves the digital music kiosks found in thousands of retail locations. These kiosks are beginning to appear with Bluetooth wireless technology, allowing songs to be transferred directly to music-capable mobile phones.

Bluetooth wireless technology is the leading short-range wireless technology on the market today. It is now available in its fourth version of the core specification and continues to develop, building on its inherent strengths—small-form-factor radio, low power, low cost, built-in security, robustness, ease-of-use, and ad hoc networking abilities. Alas, some North American carriers view Bluetooth as a competitive threat. In an attempt to maximize income, these carriers disable file transfer functionality on the Bluetooth-enabled phones they sell, thus requiring users to incur airtime charges associated with e-mailing files to their computers.

The Bluetooth SIG has identified several key markets for Bluetooth technology, including automotive, consumer, core technology, computing, and telephony. In addition, Bluetooth wireless technology is beginning to play a major role in wireless seismology and telemetry, adding high-data-rate wireless capability to a sensor market that is estimated at some 1 trillion sensors currently deployed. The growing new generation of wireless sensors will take on many roles, including functions such as monitoring ice on roadways, measuring structural fatigue on bridges, and monitoring beachfronts for pollution and littering.

Recently, in keeping with its namesake, Bluetooth came to very positive terms in working with UWB technology (discussed later in this chapter). Demonstrating the next step in the ongoing evolution of WPAN functionality, in January 2006, Alereon (www.alereon.com) hosted the industry's first public demonstration of Bluetooth+WiMedia UWB operating smoothly together under an existing Bluetooth software stack. When it comes to large files and multimedia applications, Bluetooth version 2.0 devices operate at data rates that are frustratingly slow. Bluetooth's maximum data rate of 3Mbps is simply too slow for today's media-centric applications. Combining Bluetooth with WiMedia UWB brings major improvements. The combination of a WiMedia UWB solution from Alereon and Bluetooth software from Open Interface (www.oi-us.com) enables Bluetooth applications that run 500 times the speed of regular Bluetooth and use less than 2% of the battery energy of Bluetooth. Consumers can use this type of solution to share images, phone books, videos, and other Bluetooth content at up to 480Mbps, allowing devices such as megapixel camera phones to download in seconds, rather than minutes.

IEEE 802.15.3 (WPAN-HR and WPAN-AHR)

The IEEE 802.15.3 (WPAN-HR) Task Group for WPANs was chartered to draft and publish a standard for high-rate (20Mbps or greater) WPANs. Besides a high data rate, the new standard provides for low-power, low-cost solutions that address the needs of portable consumer digital imaging and multimedia applications. IEEE 803.15.3 defines the PHY and MAC specifications for high-data-rate wireless connectivity with fixed, portable, and moving devices within or entering a personal operating space. One goal of the WPAN-HR Task Group is to achieve a level of interoperability or coexistence with other 802.15 task groups.

The IEEE 802.15.3 standard has been developed to meet the demanding requirements of portable consumer imaging and multimedia applications, offering QoS to address such environments. It is based on a centralized and connection-oriented ad hoc peer-to-peer networking topology. IEEE 802.15.3 is optimized for low-cost, small-form-factor, and low-power consumer devices, enabling multimedia applications that are not optimized by existing wireless standards.

The current technology operates in the unlicensed 2.4GHz band and supports five selectable data rates—11Mbps, 22Mbps, 33Mbps, 44Mbps, and 55Mbps—and three to four nonoverlapping channels. The range is 3 to 150 feet (1 to 50 m), with most usage anticipated in the 15- to 60-foot (5- to 20-m) range. The standard is also secure because it implements privacy, data integrity, mutual-entity authentication, and data-origin authentication for consumer applications.

The IEEE 802.15.3a (WPAN-AHR) Task Group is working to define a project to provide a higher-speed PHY enhancement to 802.15.3, addressing imaging and multimedia applications. This task group is working on an alternative physical layer for piconets with a 30-foot (10-m) range and for a minimum data rate of 110Mbps. The higher data rates being considered by the 802.15.3a Task Group will enable a host of new applications, including the likes of wireless digital TV, high-definition MPEG-2 motion picture transfer, DVD playback, and digital video camcorders. This 802.15.3a PHY work is currently under consideration.

The 802.15.3b Task Group is working on an amendment to 802.15.3 to improve implementation and interoperability of the MAC layer, including minor optimizations, while preserving backward compatibility. The intention is for this amendment to correct errors, clarify ambiguities, and add editorial clarifications.

Another interest group (802.15.4IGa) is gathering companies to create a study group to look at support for low-data-rate applications.

UWB

The term *ultra-wideband* is often used to refer to anything associated with very large bandwidth, and indeed, one of the reasons UWB is called *Ultra-Wideband* is that it spreads its signal over a very wide band of frequencies. Depending on the application, the actual frequency band used ranges from 960MHz to 10.6GHz. On a more specific basis, in relationship to radio communications, *UWB* refers to a technique based on transmitting very short-duration pulses, where the occupied bandwidth is very large, allowing for very high data rates.

UWB has a spectrum that occupies a bandwidth greater than 20% of the center frequency, or a bandwidth of at least 500MHz. UWB also uses only a small amount of power and operates in the same bands as existing communications without producing significant interference. Furthermore, UWB is not limited to wireless communications; it can use twisted-pair and coax cables as well, with the potential to transmit data at rates of 1Gbps or faster. Very importantly, UWB complements other longer-range radio technologies, such as Wi-Fi, WiMax, and cellular WANs. It is used to relay data from a host device to other devices in the immediate area (up to 30 feet [10 m]).

UWB is like a twenty-first-century version of Marconi's spark-gap transmitter, which was based on short electromagnetic pulses, transmitting a whopping total of 10bps. However, UWB can send more than 100Mbps, with the potential of up to 1Gbps. The basic concept is to develop, transmit, and receive an extremely short-duration burst of radio frequency energy, typically a few tens of picoseconds (trillionths of a second) to a few nanoseconds (billionths of a second) in duration. UWB can not only carry huge amounts of data over a short distance at very low power but also has the ability to carry signals through doors and other obstacles that tend to reflect signals at more limited bandwidths and higher power.

Familiar forms of radio communications use what is called a *carrier wave*. Data messages are impressed on the underlying carrier signal through modulation of the amplitude, frequency, or phase of the wave in some way and then are extracted upon reception. UWB does not employ a carrier wave; instead, emissions are composed of a series of intermittent pulses. By varying the pulses' amplitude, polarity, timing, or other characteristics, information is coded into the data stream. This is similar to the technique used in radar applications.

UWB operates at a very low power level, 0.2 milliwatts, thus restricting its range to distances of 300 feet (100 m) or, more typically, as little as 30 feet (10 m).

Because the energy levels of the pulses are simply too low to cause problems, interference from UWB transmitters is generally not an issue. A UWB transmitter radiates only 1/3,000 of the average energy emitted by a conventional 600-milliwatt mobile phone, which means it reduces many of the health concerns being expressed and studied in relationship to cellular and PCS networks.

Advantages and Disadvantages of UWB

UWB offers a number of advantages, including the fact that there is growing demand for greater wireless data capacity, and the crowding of regulated radio frequency spectrum favors systems that offer not only high bit rates but also high bit rates concentrated in smaller physical areas. Given the latest trends toward the use of wireless and mobile communications, a new metric called *spatial capacity* has evolved. Spatial capacity is a measure of the number of bits per second per square meter that can be supported. Table 15.7 compares the spatial capacities of several commonly used short-range networking technologies.

There are three key factors of interest in selecting a short-range technology: the range over which the technology can operate, how much power it consumes, and the spatial capacity. As you can see in Table 15.7, while 802.11b can operate over a larger coverage area, up to 300 feet (100 m), it can support only 1Kbps per square meter. In a well-attended cafe or hotel lobby, that is not going to provide hotspot users with the capacity needed to work in a multimedia environment. On the other hand, while UWB has a very short range, only 30 feet (10 m), it can support 1,000Kbps per square meter, and it also consumes very little power as an added bonus. Spatial capacity, which is a gauge of data intensity, will be critical to servicing growing number of users in crowded spaces such as airports, hotels, convention centers, and workplaces.

UWB is expected to achieve a data rate of 100Mbps to 500Mbps across distances of 15 to 30 feet (5 to 10 m), and it is anticipated that these high bit rates will give birth to applications that are not possible today. It is also expected that UWB units will be cheaper, smaller, and less power-hungry than today's devices.

Table 15.7 Comparison of Short-Range Spatial Capacities

Technology	Power	Range	Spatial Capacity
IEEE 802.11b	50 mW	100 m	1Kbps/m^2
Bluetooth	1 mW	10 m	30Kbps/m^2
IEEE 802.11a	200 mW	50 m	55Kbps/m^2
UWB	0.2 mW	10 m	$1{,}000\text{Kbps/m}^2$

Short-range technology is an ideal way to handle networks of portable (battery-powered) electronic devices, including PDAs, digital cameras, camcorders, audio/video players, mobile phones, laptop computers, and other mobile devices. The growing presence of wired connections to the Internet is another driver of short-distance wireless technology. Many in the developed world already spend most of the day within 30 feet (10 m) of some kind of wired link to the Internet.

UWB's precision pulses give it the ability to discern buried objects or movement behind walls. It can also be used to determine the position of emitters indoors. UWB provides a location-finding feature, much like a local version of GPS. UWB capabilities are therefore crucial to rescue and law-enforcement missions.

One drawback of UWB is that it is susceptible to interference from other emitters. The ability of a UWB receiver to overcome this problem is sometimes called *jamming resistance*. This is a key characteristic of good receiver design. Multipath interference is also an issue, and one that also needs to be addressed in the receiver design.

UWB Applications

Key UWB applications include communications, imaging, telematics, location tracking, and various military and government applications. UWB also has the key attributes necessary to add significant value for consumers of wireless home entertainment and mobile multimedia products. Smart phones, media servers, set-top boxes, flat-panel screens, digital camcorders, and other multimedia applications need a high-data-rate and high-QoS wireless connection to help ensure wire-like performance.

UWB applications cover a wide range of scenarios, including the following:

- Monitoring large numbers of sensors dispersed over an area for nuclear, biological, or chemical threats
- Conducting geospatial registration for warfighter visualization
- Supporting survey and construction needs
- Keeping track of mines, armaments, equipment, vehicles, and so on
- Keeping track of personal items, such as one's children, pets, car, purse, luggage, and so on
- Controlling inventory in stores, warehouses, shipyards, railyards, and so on
- Arbitrating rules in a sporting event, providing playback for coaching, or viewing the re-creation of an event
- Automating the home environment, such as keyless locks and rooms that adjust light, temperature, and music sound levels
- Automatically adjusting camera focus and motion-tracking for matching digital effects in motion pictures

- Creating automotive collision detection systems and suspension systems that respond to road conditions

- Performing medical imaging, similar to x-ray and CAT scans

- Performing through-wall imaging for detecting people or objects in law-enforcement or rescue applications

The Future of UWB

Proponents of UWB see a future in which UWB technology will reach ubiquity in LANs and PANs. In addition, UWB has the potential to penetrate WAN markets by using ad hoc or managed mesh networks and to eventually make competing technologies such as W-CDMA and GPRS obsolete. UWB could become the dominant technology in WPANs, WLANs, and WWANs. However, a limiting factor to UWB's dominance in the worldwide WAN is unification of global wireless spectrum allocation standards. The greatest challenges UWB faces are regulatory issues and deadlocked UWB standards disputes in the IEEE.

Some have raised doubts about the future of UWB. Some industry observers suggest that regulations in Europe will be substantially more restrictive than those applied by the FCC. Japan is likely to be even more conservative. Stiff regulations would limit UWB to a smaller slice of spectrum and reduce its speed and range. It would then have more trouble competing against faster versions of Wi-Fi. In addition, IEEE 802.11n is expected to be established by 2007, offering a theoretical limit of 110Mbps to 200Mbps. Accounting for overhead, the resulting throughput will be some 45Mbps. Although UWB can support 480Mbps at short ranges, it would drop off with distance—particularly if the regulations limit the spectrum it can use. By the time it goes across a room, the data rate of UWB could be more like that of 802.11n.

However, UWB vendors claim that if the lower frequencies are cut out, they can move higher in the spectrum and offer speeds well beyond the currently proposed 480Mbps. Only UWB can promise enough speed to stream HDTV. However, at higher frequencies, there is more absorption, so the effective range—and the throughput at a given range—is reduced. Some suggest that that its alliance with Bluetooth may help UWB get regulatory approval.

As mentioned earlier in this chapter, the Bluetooth SIG has been working with the developers of UWB to combine the strengths of Bluetooth and UWB. This alliance allows Bluetooth technology to extend its long-term roadmap to meet the high-speed demands of synchronizing and transferring large amounts of data as well as enabling high-quality video applications for portable devices, while UWB benefits from Bluetooth technology's manifested maturity, qualification program, brand equity, and comprehensive application layer.

WiMedia

In September 2002, nine leading technology companies announced the formation of the WiMedia Alliance (www.wimedia.org). Initial WiMedia Alliance activity was based on the IEEE 802.15.3a (WPAN-AHR) standard, with amendments and enhancements planned for future wireless systems such as UWB. Today, the WiMedia Alliance is a not-for-profit open industry association that promotes and enables the rapid adoption, regulation, standardization, and multivendor interoperability of UWB worldwide. It is dedicated to collaboratively developing and administering specs from the physical layer up, enabling connectivity and interoperability for multiple industry-based protocols. Alliance board members include Alereon (www.alereon.com), Hewlett-Packard (www.hp.com), Intel (www.intel.com), Kodak (www.kodak.com), Microsoft (www.microsoft.com), Nokia (www.nokia.com), Philips (www.philips.com), Samsung Electronics (www.samsung.com), Sony (www.sony.com), STMicroelectronics (www.st.com), Staccato Communications (www.staccatocommunications.com), Texas Instruments (www.ti.com), and Wisair (www.wisair.com).

In June 2003, the Multiband OFDM Alliance SIG (MBOA-SIG) was formed to support the development of the best possible technical solution for the emerging UWB (IEEE 802.15.3a) PHY specification for a diverse set of wireless applications. Today, the WiMedia Alliance represents a combination of the original WiMedia Alliance and the MBOA-SIG, the two leading organizations creating UWB industry specifications and certification programs for PC, consumer electronic, mobile, and automotive applications. The combined WiMedia Alliance is an open industry association that defines the WiMedia/MBOA technology. Alliance members consist of industry leaders based in Asia, Europe, and North America.

WiMedia defines a UWB common radio platform that enables high speeds (480Mbps and beyond), low power consumption, and multimedia data transfers in a WPAN. It is optimized for several key market segments, including PC, consumer electronic, mobile, and automotive applications. The platform incorporates MAC-layer and PHY-layer specifications based on Multiband OFDM (MB-OFDM). ECMA-368 and ECMA-369 are international ISO-based specifications for the WiMedia UWB common radio platform (see www.ecma-international.org).

WiMedia now includes the MBOA UWB technologies that will permit the long battery life that is key for mobile applications. The Wireless USB Promoter Group (www.usb.org/developers/wusb) has endorsed WiMedia as a common platform for its next-generation wireless implementations. The 1394 Trade Association (TA) Wireless Working Group (www.1394ta.org) has approved WiMedia's MAC Convergence Architecture (WiMCA) as a platform for a high-speed wireless IEEE 1394 (FireWire) protocol adaptation layer (PAL) development. The 1394 TA also said it will collaborate with the WiMedia Alliance to develop interoperability test specifications and certification programs for wireless IEEE 1394. WiMedia also plans to develop universal IP addressing protocols in alignment with organizations such as the UPnP Forum (www.upnp.org) and the Digital Living Network Alliance (DLNA; www.dlna.org). In addition, as mentioned earlier, January 2006 saw the successful demonstration of Bluetooth+WiMedia UWB operating smoothly together under an existing Bluetooth software stack.

UWB technology has the inherent capability to optimize wireless connectivity between multimedia devices within a WPAN. The WiMedia UWB common radio platform is unique in that no other existing wireless standard can fulfill the market's stringent requirements, such as low cost, low power consumption, small form factor, high bandwidth, and multimedia QoS support.

IEEE 802.15.4 (ZigBee)

At the end of the 1990s, many engineers began to see that Bluetooth and Wi-Fi, while excellent short-range solutions, were not the best solutions for some applications, particularly self-organizing ad hoc networks of various industrial controls, building and home automation devices, security and smoke alarms, and medical devices. With inspiration from the simple one-chip design of Bluetooth radios, a community of like-minded engineers began the development of ZigBee, a wireless communication protocol designed for small building devices. The IEEE 802.15.4 standard, completed in May 2003, defines the technical specifications of the PHY and MAC layers for ZigBee. The IEEE 802.15.4 specification is mainly designed for command and control, for which a 200Kbps data rate is more than adequate.

The IEEE 802.15 Task Group 4 (TG4; www.ieee802.org/15/pub/TG4.html) was chartered to investigate a solution with several key characteristics: a low data rate with a very long battery life (months to even years) and very low complexity. ZigBee operates, internationally, in the unlicensed frequency bands. Potential applications for ZigBee include sensors, interactive toys, smart badges, remote controls, and home and building automation tools. The ZigBee 1.0 specifications were ratified in December 2004, and version 1.1 is now in the works.

As with many of the other WPAN technologies, there are relationships between the formal IEEE task group and the representative industry alliance—in this case between 802.15 TG4 and the ZigBee Alliance (www.zigbee.org). The ZigBee Alliance, formed in October 2002, is a nonprofit industry consortium of companies working together to enable reliable, cost-effective, low-power, wirelessly networked monitoring and control products based on an open global standard. The member companies are working together to develop standardized application software on top of the IEEE 802.15.4 standard. The goal of the ZigBee Alliance is to give consumers the most flexible building systems available by introducing the ZigBee wireless technology into a number of building devices. As of mid-December

2005, the ZigBee Alliance membership had surpassed 200 member companies from 24 countries spanning six continents, with OEMs and end product manufacturers representing over 30% of the global membership. The ZigBee Alliance focuses on four main areas: defining the network, security, and application software layers of the protocol; providing interoperability and conformance testing for ZigBee devices; promoting the ZigBee brand globally; and managing the evolution of the technology.

ZigBee Devices and Networks

ZigBee was created to support wireless communications between devices without the expense of having to run wires between them. ZigBee's benefits include flexibility and scalability, reduction in design and installation time, interoperability, longer battery life, and low cost. It is made for two-way communication among devices and can be used to build a general-purpose, inexpensive, self-organizing network of devices. This protocol opens the door to the flexibility and benefits of interoperability. Because ZigBee uses open standards, it reduces the costs and risks associated with building the technology into devices. ZigBee is a short-range, low-power protocol specifically designed for small building devices such as thermostats, lighting controls, ballasts, environmental sensors, and medical devices. It is meant to offer short-distance, low-speed transmissions that require little power. As a result, the battery life of ZigBee devices can range from six months to two years or longer, using only a single alkaline battery.

There are three types of ZigBee devices:

- **Reduced-function device (RFD)**—The simplest ZigBee device is the *RFD*, also referred to as the *end device*. It is smart enough to talk to the network but has no routing abilities; in other words, it cannot relay data from other devices. End devices are often battery powered. Typical end devices function as thermostats, humidistats, light switches, smoke detectors, and various other sensors. These devices are often built as peel-and-stick products, where installation is intended to be simple and product placement is either aesthetic, functional, or according to some governmental requirement. These end devices do not form a mesh by themselves; instead, they are usually asleep in order to conserve their batteries.

- **Full-function device (FFD)**—The next level up the network from the RFD is called the *FFD*, or *router*. It is fully mesh capable and mains powered (i.e., powered from some other permanent source). FFDs can establish multiple peer-to-peer links with other routing nodes, and they accept connections from RFD devices, performing the role of intermediate routers, passing data from other devices. An FFD may also serve as a gateway to the Internet or other networks. Packets generated by RFD devices may pass through multiple FFDs to travel from the source to a destination, which is generally a load-controlling function (e.g., HVAC motor, lighting load control, damper actuator, siren). However, the destination may also be a data-collecting device (e.g., a computer or security console) or even a gateway to the Internet or other non-ZigBee network.

▪ **ZigBee coordinator**—The mains-powered coordinator assumes the most important role in a ZigBee network, acting as the root of the network tree and bridging to other networks. It has the authority to establish networks and perform any network management that might be required. The coordinator also has routing capability and may serve as a gateway to the Internet or to other networks, and it can store information about the network. Because it contains the most memory, it is the most expensive of the three devices in a ZigBee network.

A ZigBee network is capable of supporting up to 254 FFDs, 1 coordinator, and potentially thousands of RFDs. Most importantly, because the ZigBee protocol expects most messages to receive acknowledgments in order to verify successful reception, all devices are transceivers (i.e., they transmit and receive). Figure 15.7 shows an example of a ZigBee home network.

ZigBee devices operate in unlicensed spectrum worldwide and are based on DSSS technology. They operate at the maximum data rates shown in Table 15.8, and their transmission range is 30 to 250 feet (10 to 75 m).

The ZigBee standard is designed to provide reliable data transmission of modest amounts of data up to 250 feet (75 m) while consuming very little power. It also

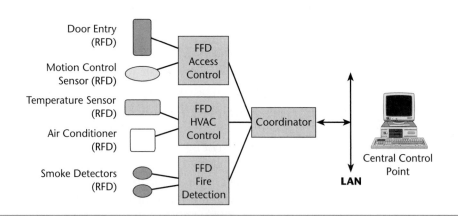

Figure 15.7 An example of a ZigBee home network

Table 15.8 ZigBee Maximum Data Rates

Location	Data Rate	Bandwidth	Number of Channels Supported
Worldwide	250Kbps	2.4GHz	16
The Americas	40Kbps	915MHz	10
Europe	20Kbps	868MHz	1

offers support for critical-latency devices, such as joysticks. ZigBee offers lower power consumption, lower cost, higher density of nodes per network, and simplicity of protocols compared with other wireless connectivity schemes. Because ZigBee's topology allows as many as 254 nodes per network, it is ideal for industrial applications. ZigBee is the only standards-based technology designed to address the unique needs of low-cost, low-power, wireless sensor networks for remote monitoring, home control, and building automation network applications in the industrial and consumer markets.

ZigBee supports three network topologies:

- **Star**—This topology can provide for very long-life operation and is the most common topology.

- **Mesh**—This topology enables high levels of reliability and scalability while providing more than one communications path through the network wireless link.

- **Cluster tree**—This topology uses a hybrid star/mesh topology that combines the benefits of both for high levels of reliability and support for battery-powered nodes.

The Future of ZigBee

Future applications of the ZigBee protocol include its use in tracking and asset management systems, generators, elevators, and so on, gathering data that can be transformed into viable information and enabling users to run their businesses more efficiently.

The IEEE 802.15.4 group says that one day it might be common to find 50 ZigBee radio chips in a house. Those chips could serve duty in a home's 10 to 15 light switches, several fire and smoke detectors, thermostats, 5 or 6 toys and interactive game machines, and other human input devices. Radio-frequency-based ZigBee will eventually replace all the infrared (IR) links at home. ZigBee is not designed for video or CD-quality audio, but it could be used to send text or voice messages. No QoS provision is built into ZigBee.

In January 2006, the ZigBee Alliance announced its ZigBee Certification program, which ensures that products are fully interoperable out of the box and can easily participate in a ZigBee network. Member companies can now test the growing number of ZigBee-ready products already on the consumer market so they can be fully branded as ZigBee Certified for home, industrial, or commercial use. Independent test service providers will oversee and conduct the ZigBee Alliance's certification testing to ensure that products are interoperable in a variety of environments and end-user applications.

RFID

RFID is a method of remotely storing and retrieving data by using devices called *RFID tags*. An RFID tag is a small object that can be attached to or incorporated into a product, an animal, or a person and then read by an RFID reader. The origins of RFID technology take us back to the early 1920s, when MIT developed a similar technology as a way for robots to talk to one another. The first known device that has been recognized as a predecessor to RFID technology was a passive covert listening device invented in 1945 by Leon Theremin to be used as an espionage tool for the Soviet government. A similar technology, called Indentification Friend or Foe (IFF), was invented by the British in 1939 and used extensively by the Allies during World War II to identify and authenticate allied planes and other vehicles. RFID is being used today for the same purposes. However, it is now also recognized that an investment in RFID technology can improve the efficiency of many enterprise operations, reduce errors, and improve on operating costs.

With RFID, any movable item or asset can be identified and tracked better and more efficiently. The first RFID systems deployed for tracking and access applications entered the marketplace during the 1980s. As the technology matures, it is clear that we can expect more pervasive and most likely more invasive applications for RFID. Industry analysts predict explosive growth for RFID over the next several years, forecasting that by 2010, there will be some 33 billion tags produced, compared to just 1.3 billion in 2005. Retail, automotive, and pharmaceutical companies are expected to lead in the adoption of RFID.

Several organizations are involved in drafting standards for RFID technology. Both the ISO (www.iso.org) and EPCglobal (www.epcglobalinc.org) have had many initiatives related to RFID standards. EPCglobal is an important organization to the RFID movement: It is leading the development of industry-driven standards for the electronic product code (EPC) to support the use of RFID in today's fast-moving, information-rich trading networks. It is a subscriber-driven organization comprising industry leaders and organizations, focused on creating global standards for the EPCglobal network.

Currently, the purpose of an RFID system is to allow a tag to transmit data to an RFID reader, which then processes the data according to the application requirements. The information transmitted can provide identification or location data and can also include more specific information, such as date of purchase, price, color, size, and so on.

RFID tags are envisioned as a replacement for universal product code (UPC) barcodes because they have a number of important advantages over the older barcode technology. RFID codes are long enough that every RFID tag may have a unique code, whereas UPC codes are limited to a single code for all instances of a particular product. The uniqueness of RFID tags means that a product may be individually tracked as it moves from location to location, finally ending up in the consumer's hands. This may help to combat theft and other forms of product loss. It has also been proposed to use RFID for point-of-sale store checkout to replace the cashier with an automatic system, with the option of erasing all RFID tags at checkout and paying by credit card or inserting money into a payment machine. Other innovative uses have also been proposed, such as allowing a refrigerator to track the expiration dates of the food it contains.

How an RFID System Works

RFID systems are composed of several components: tags, readers, edge servers, middleware, and application software. The key element of RFID technology is an RFID transponder, usually called a *tag*. An RFID tag is a small object, such as an adhesive sticker, that can be attached to or incorporated into an object (anything from a pallet of laundry detergent to a racecar tire to a pet's neck). An RFID tag is a tiny microchip composed of a processor, memory, and a radio transmitter that is mounted onto a substrate or an enclosure. The amount of memory varies from just a few characters to kilobytes. An RFID tag's antenna enables it to receive and respond to radio frequency queries from an RFID reader, also known as a *transceiver* or an *interrogator*, which has its own antenna.

Here's how an RFID system works (see Figure 15.8):

1. An RFID reader, which can interface through wired or wireless media to a main computer, transfers energy to RFID tags by emitting electromagnetic waves through the air.

2. RFID tag antennas collect the RF energy from the reader antenna and use it to power up the microchip.

3. Tags listen for a radio signal sent by an RFID reader.

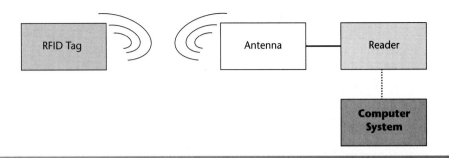

Figure 15.8 An example of an RFID system

4. When an RFID tag receives a query, it responds by transmitting its unique ID code and other data back to the reader. The data transmitted from the tags can provide identification or location information about the object or specifics such as date of purchase or price.

5. The reader receives the tag responses and processes them accordingly, sending the information to a host computer or external devices through its control lines.

No contact or even line of sight is needed to read data from a product that contains an RFID tag. RFID technology works in rain, snow, and other environments where barcode or optical scanning technology is useless.

RFID Tags
Different types of RFID tags address different applications requirements:

■ **Read-only**—A read-only tag is preprogrammed with a unique identification.

■ **Read/write**—A read/write tag is used for applications that require data to be stored in the tag so the information can be dynamically updated.

■ **Write once, read many times (WORM)**—WORM tags allow for an ID number to be written to the tag once, and it can't be changed, but the information can be read many times.

In addition, RFID tags can be either active or passive. Active RFID tags must have a power source but have longer ranges of operation and larger memories than passive tags, providing the ability to store additional information sent by the reader. Active tags, about the size of a dime and designed for communications up to 100 feet (30 m) from the RFID reader, are powered by a battery and are always on. They are larger and more expensive than passive RFID tags but can hold more data about the tagged object and are commonly used for high-value asset tracking. Active RFID tags can be read/write. Many active tags have practical ranges of tens of meters and a battery life of up to 10 years. One of the most common applications for active tags is in the transportation sector (e.g., for highway tolls).

Passive RFID tags do not have their own power supplies or batteries. Instead, the minute electrical current induced in the antenna by the incoming RF scan from the reader provides enough power for the tag to send a response. The received signal charges an internal capacitor on the tag, which in turn supplies the power required to communicate with the reader. Because passive tags do not contain power supplies, they can be much smaller than active tags and have an unlimited life span. As of 2006, the smallest commercially available passive tags measured just 0.3 mm across and were thinner than a sheet of paper, making them just about invisible. Due to its power and cost, the response of a passive RFID tag is generally brief, typically just an ID number. Passive RFID tags can be read from a distance of about 20 feet (6 m). A semipassive RFID tag contains a small battery that boosts the range. Passive tags are generally read-only, so the data they contain cannot be altered or written over. Some of the most common uses of passive RFID include animal identification, waste management, security and access control, work-in-process, asset tracking, and electronic commerce. The Chek Lap Kok airport in Hong Kong uses passive RFID tags to track the movement of every piece of luggage that passes through the baggage-handling system.

Because passive tags are cheaper to manufacture than active tags, the majority of RFID tags in existence today are the passive type. As of 2006, passive tags, when bought in high volumes, cost an average of US$0.24 each. With volumes of 10 million units or more, the cost can drop to around US$0.07 per tag. The goal is to produce tags for less than US$0.05 to make widespread RFID tagging commercially viable.

The main benefits of RFID include the fact that tags can be read from a distance and from any orientation, so they do not require line-of-sight conditions in order to be read. Read/write tags offer the additional benefit of allowing data to be changed dynamically at any time. Another benefit of RFID is that multiple tags can be read at the same time and in bulk very quickly. Finally, the tags can be easily embedded into any nonmetallic object, enabling the tags to work in harsh environments and providing permanent identification for the life of the object. However, the environment into which RFID will be implemented must be carefully considered because factors such as the presence of metal, electrical noise, extreme temperatures, liquids, and physical stress may affect performance.

RFID Readers

RFID readers are used to query RFID tags in order to obtain identification, location, and other information about the object the tag is embedded in. In addition, the reader antenna sends RF energy to the RFID tag antennas, which use that energy to power up the microchip.

There are two types of RFID readers:

■ **Read-only**—These readers can only query or read information from a nearby RFID tag; they cannot write information to tags. They are found in fixed, stationary applications as well as portable, handheld varieties.

■ **Read/write**—These readers, also known as *encoders*, read and also write information in RFID tags. RFID encoders can be used to program information into a blank RFID tag. A common application is to combine this type of RFID reader with a barcode printer to print smart labels. A smart label contains a UPC barcode on the front and an RFID tag embedded on the back.

RFID Frequencies

Even though no global body currently governs RFID frequencies (each country can set its own rules), there are four main frequency bands for RFID tags, as shown in Table 15.9.

Table 15.9 RFID Frequency Bands

Frequency Type	Frequency Band	Typical Range	Tag Cost	Description	Applications
Low (LF)	125KHz–134.2KHz and 140 KHz–148.5KHz	3 ft. (1 m)	US$1+	Short reading ranges, slow read speeds, and lower cost	Pet and ranch animal identification, car key locks
High (HF)	13.56MHz	3 ft. (1 m)	US$0.50	Longer read ranges and fast reading speeds	Library book identification, clothing identification, smart cards
Ultrahigh (UHF)	433MHz and 868MHz–956MHz	25 ft. (8 m)	US$0.50	Even longer read ranges; high data throughput, which facilitates higher read rates	Supply-chain tracking: boxes, pallets, containers, trailers
Microwave	2.45GHz and 5.8GHz	100 ft. (30 m)	US$25+	Very long range and access control applications	Highway toll collection, vehicle fleet identification

LF and HF can be used globally without a license. UHF cannot be used globally because there is no single global standard. Despite the availability of various bands in which RFID can operate, there is not just one that can address all applications. Each band has specific attributes that make it suitable for different applications.

LF RFID   The reading range of LF RFID can vary from a few centimeters to a couple meters, depending on the size of the tags and the reader being used. One of the key features of LF RFID is that it is not as affected by surrounding metals as other types of RFID, making it ideal for identifying metal items such as vehicles, equipment, tools, and metal containers. The largest user for LF RFID is the automotive industry. A car key has an LF tag embedded in it that works with a reader mounted in the ignition. Other automotive applications include vehicle identification for highway and parking lot access. LF RFID penetrates most other materials, such as water and body tissue, which makes it ideal for animal identification (for endangered species and for pets and livestock) and beer keg tracking.

The limitations of LF RFID are that if used in industrial environments, electric motors may interfere with the LF system. Due to the size of the antenna required, LF tags are typically more expensive than HF tags, which limits LF to applications where the tags can be reused. However, LF is used worldwide, and there are no restrictions on its use.

HF RFID   Passive HF, at 13.56MHz, is a globally accepted frequency, which means any system operating at HF can be used globally. However, there are some differences between the regulations in the different regions of the world, related primarily to power and bandwidth. In North America, the FCC limits the reader antenna power to 3 watts, while European regulations allow for 4 watts. HF is also the basis of numerous standards, such as ISO 14443, 15693, and 18000-3.

With HF, the signal travels well through most materials, including liquid and body tissue. However, it is more affected by surrounding metals than LF. In comparison to LF, the benefits of HF are lower tag costs, better communication speed, and the ability to read multiple tags at once. The higher the frequency, the higher the data throughput and the faster the communications between the tags and the reader, and at HF, a reader can read up to 50 tags per second. The increase in speed also allows for the reader to communicate with multiple tags at the same time.

HF RFID tags are used in book tracking for libraries and bookstores, pallet tracking, building access control, airline baggage tracking, apparel item tracking, and identification badges.

UHF RFID   Whereas HF and LF work fairly well in the presence of liquids, today's UHF systems do not work in such environments. Metal poses a serious challenge for any RFID implementation, but especially in the UHF range. More-over, the longer read distance of UHF is a disadvantage in applications such as banking and access control. However, its high data throughput facilitates higher read rates, with 800 reads per second possible in theory, although 200 reads per second is closer to reality. UHF RFID tags are commonly used commercially to track pallets and containers as well as trucks and trailers in shipping yards, and UHF vendors are targeting the supply-chain market, where longer read distances are required.

UHF tags can be used globally when they are specially tailored according to regional regulations because there are no globally unified regulations for radio frequencies in this ISM band range. However, one of the biggest challenges that has impeded the widespread implementation of UHF RFID is lack of globally accepted standards and regulations. Different frequency designations and power and safety regulations are in place in different regions of the world. In North America, UHF operates at 902MHz to 928MHz; in Europe, it works in the 860MHz to 868MHz range; and in Japan, it operates at 950MHz to 956MHz.

EPCglobal (www.epcglobalinc.org) worked through 2004 to pave the way for ratification of the UHF Generation 2 Air Interface Protocol (commonly referred to as the Gen2 standard) by driving regulatory agencies—from the ETSI to Japan's Ministry Post and Telecom—to open bandwidth in the UHF spectrum so RFID could operate seamlessly through supply chains across continents. Gen2, which was ratified as an EPCglobal standard in December 2004, has been accepted by the ISO. Some of the requirements for this standard include convergence to one global, interoperable standard; increased speed and ease of global adoption; increased functionality and performance; and increased production and competition.

Gen2 is heralded as the first UHF RFID open architecture designed by a committee. Many supply-chain benefits depend on Gen2: global interoperability, international vendor support, multiple read and write capabilities that could potentially change the economic climate by delivering a quicker return on investment, and increased data communication speeds more than double those of the tags available today. The read rate for Gen2 tags in the United States under a simulated environment is 1,500 per second, versus roughly 100 tags per second for tags available today. (The read rate for Gen2 tags in Europe, however, is only 500 to 600 tags per second because U.S. regulations allow for wider frequency bandwidth.) As the industry switches to Gen2, many companies will face huge conversion costs. On the other hand, because Gen2 establishes interoperability and bandwidth technologies, it is anticipated that Gen2 will boost adoption of RFID.

Microwave RFID Microwave RFID tags are used in long-range access control for vehicles, such as GM's OnStar system. Additional microwave RFID applications

include electronic highway toll collection; reading of seismic activity, greatly simplifying remote data collection; and vehicle tire tracking.

RFID Privacy

There are some major privacy concerns regarding RFID use, including the following:

- The purchaser of an item will not necessarily be aware of the presence of
  the tag or be able to remove it.

- The tag can be read at a distance without the knowledge of the individual.

- If a tagged item is paid for by credit card or in conjunction with use of a
  loyalty card, it would be possible to tie the unique ID of that item to the
  identity of the purchaser.

- Tags create, or are proposed to create, globally unique serial numbers for all
  products, even though that would create privacy problems and is unneces-
  sary for most applications.

- The ability to continue to enjoy a lifestyle that offers relative anonymity
  today is undermined by the presence of tags and readers.

- Governments could obtain information gathered by RFID readers for the
  surveillance or monitoring of citizens' activities. Equally frightening, such
  information could be misused by hackers and criminals.

- Even our most intimate activities could be monitored if tags were implemented in everyday objects such as floor tiles, shelf paper, cabinets, appliances, exercise equipment, medications, medical implants, and all sorts of
  packaged products and consumer goods.

Most concerns revolve around the fact that RFID tags affixed to products remain
functional even after the products have been purchased and taken home and thus
can be used for surveillance and other nefarious purposes unrelated to their supply-
chain inventory functions. Although RFID tags are only officially intended for short-
distance use, they can be interrogated from greater distances by anyone who has a
high-gain antenna, potentially allowing the contents of a house to be scanned at a
distance. Even short-range scanning is a concern if all the items detected are logged
in a database every time a person passes a reader, or if it is done for nefarious reasons,
such as a mugger using a handheld scanner to obtain an instant assessment of the
wealth of potential victims. With permanent RFID serial numbers, an item leaks
unexpected information about a person even after disposal—for example, items
being resold or given away enable mapping of a person's social network.

Another privacy issue has to do with RFID's support for a singulation (i.e.,
anticollision) protocol. This is the means by which a reader enumerates all the tags

responding to it without them mutually interfering. The structure of the most common version of this protocol is such that all but the last bit of each tag's serial number can be deduced by passively eavesdropping on just the reader's part of the protocol. Because of this, whenever RFID tags are near readers, the distance at which a tag's signal can be eavesdropped is irrelevant; what counts is the distance at which the much more powerful reader can be received. Just how far this is depends on the type of the reader, but in the extreme case, some readers have a maximum power output of 4 watts, which could be received from tens of kilometers away.

Rarely is information encrypted between a tag and the reader. This creates opportunities for malicious people to eavesdrop on communications and reuse them in nefarious ways—for instance, quickly and easily duplicating a passport. Similarly, there is no standard authentication protocol between a tag and the reader. Again, considering the passport as an example, it is currently possible to conduct a man-in-the-middle attack between a tag-equipped passport and the reader on the desk of the passport control officer. An attacker could substitute information on-the-fly, possibly circumventing detention in one case while making life very difficult for some other innocent citizen standing in line. Fortunately, governments are starting to realize the risks associated with electronic passports and are examining security controls to mitigate such risks.

EPCglobal's Gen2 standard includes privacy-related guidelines for the use of RFID-based EPCs. The Guidelines on EPC Usage for Consumer Products were adopted as a basic framework for responsible use and deployment of EPC (see www. epcglobalinc.org/public_policy/public_policy_guidelines.html). These guidelines include the requirement to give consumers clear notice of the presence of EPCs and to inform them of the choice they have to discard, disable, or remove EPC tags.

It is crucial that we ensure that RFID technology is used to improve our lives and our business practices without intruding on privacy. To this end, governments, the private sector, and other agencies must safeguard principles of informed consent, data confidentiality, and security; courts and governments around the world are now in the process of determining related legal issues. The Electronic Privacy Information Center (EPIC) has a great deal of additional information about RFID privacy as well as interesting projects on its Web site (www.epic.org/privacy/rfid).

The Future of RFID

It appears that RFID is well on its way to becoming a large part of our lives. More than 1.3 billion RFID tags were produced in 2005, and that figure is expected to soar to 33 billion by 2010 (In-Stat, "RFID Tags and Chips: Opportunities in the Second Generation," www.instat.com, January 18, 2006). Production will vary widely by industry segment for several years. For example, RFID has been used in automotive keys since 1991, with 150 million units now in use. This quantity greatly exceeded other segments until recently. By far the biggest RFID segment in coming years will be supply-chain management. Wal-Mart, the world's largest retailer, has spurred this projected growth by mandating that its top 100 (and then its top 300) suppliers use RFID at the pallet/case level.

The spread and use of RFID in most sectors will be largely determined by cost, and the costs of RFID tags and labels are dropping quickly. Pharmaceutical companies are investigating using RFID tags to reduce counterfeiting and black-market sales. Other market segments expected to incorporate the use of RFID include live-stock, domestic pets, humans, cartons/supply-chain uses, large freight containers, package tracking, consumer products, and security/banking/purchasing/access control. But will RFID replace UPC barcode technology? Most likely not, and certainly not in the near term. RFID tags still cost more than UPC labels, and different data capture and tracking technologies offer different capabilities. Many businesses will likely combine RFID with existing technologies such as barcode readers or digital cameras to achieve expanded data capture and tracking capabilities that meet their specific business needs.

NFC

In the midst of the various WPAN technologies discussed so far in this chapter, a new technology is quietly taking shape that could alter the use of consumer electronics and change the way users shop, travel, and send data. Near Field Communication (NFC) evolved from a combination of RFID, interconnection (i.e., information exchange via network technology), and contactless identification technologies. (With *contactless identification*, a smart card has an antenna embedded inside it, enabling communication with a card reader without physical contact. The chip on the smart card stores data and programs that are protected by advanced security features. Contactless smart cards are passed near an antenna, or reader, to carry out a transaction.) With NFC-enabled mobile phones, transactions can be conducted by simply touching a point-of-sales device or ticket gate. Contactless cards are the ideal solution for transactions that must be processed very quickly, as in physical access control, mass transit, or vending services. NFC provides high-bandwidth content acquisition and transfer, contactless payment capability, and smart object interaction. One of the key attributes of NFC is that it introduces convenience to increasingly connected digital consumers, allowing new genres of interactions with interactive advertising posters and kiosks, instant ticketing, and the transmission of audio, pictures, and video.

NFC technology is showing tremendous promise for transforming consumer commerce, connectivity, and content consumption, enhancing end-user experiences while redefining communications, content, and payment business models. NFC is expected to be deployed beginning in 2007, first in wireless handsets and then in other kinds of consumer electronics, from PCs to cameras, printers, set-top boxes, and the growing range of smart devices.

The success of NFC depends on open, interoperable, standards-based NFC environments. To help in this quest, the NFC Forum (www.nfc-forum.org) is adding fuel to the technology's expansion. The NFC Forum was founded by Nokia (www.nokia.com), Philips (www.philips.com), and Sony (www.sony.com) in 2004, and since then, dozens of companies have signed up for the industry group. The NFC Forum now boasts more than 60 collaborating members, including wireless carriers, handset OEMs, application developers, payment processors, infrastructure providers, content owners, card issuers, and banks and merchants. NFC is standardized in a number of ISO, Ecma International, and ETSI standards, providing for maximum flexibility as the technology seeks compatibility with existing devices, especially smart cards.

NFC, a short-range, contactless communications protocol, enables easy-to-use, secure connectivity between devices. It can also be used to configure and initiate other wireless network connections, including Bluetooth and Wi-Fi. It is a wireless technology that operates in the globally available and unregulated 13.56MHz frequency band, over a typical distance of a few centimeters, but with a maximum working distance of 5 to 6.5 feet (1.5 to 2 m). It supports three data transfer rates: 106Kbps, 212Kbps, and 424Kbps. By using magnetic field induction, NFC allows two devices embedded with chips to exchange information by being in close proximity. There are no intermediate devices, which means NFC acts as a peer-to-peer transmission. NFC enables a handset or mobile device to act as a contactless transfer medium.

NFC chips will be embedded in a variety of devices, allowing the exchange of information within a very short distance. This makes for a very intuitive pairing of devices with a minimal authentication process. There are three modes of operation:

- **Passive communication mode**—In this one-way mode, the initiator device provides a carrier field, the target device responds by modulating that field, and the target device draws power from the initiator's electromagnetic field.

- **Active communication mode**—In this bidirectional mode, both devices need power supplies, and the initiator and target devices generate their own fields to communicate.

- **Transponder**—This bidirectional mode allows tags without access to electric grids or batteries to communicate with an NFC device within range by drawing power from that NFC device.

Nokia and Motorola have both introduced devices supporting the technology, and they are designed in part to serve as payment devices. Nokia has an NFC-enabled phone available, the 3220. With the Nokia NFC shell, this handset allows consumers access to browsing and text message services simply by touching tags that contain service shortcuts. The NFC-enabled phone can be used as a loyalty card, credit card, or train or bus ticket. Purchases normally made with a credit card can be made with the phone because the phone is, in fact, a credit card. NFC will find uses in areas such as e-ticketing, where the customer holds his or her mobile phone close to the ticket kiosk to start the transaction. The customer interacts with the service and then completes the purchase by confirming the transaction on the NFC-enabled mobile phone. Arriving at the concert hall, the customer then holds his or her mobile phone close to a reader fitted to the entrance turnstile, which allows access after the reader checks the validity of the ticket.

Each NFC device has the potential to replace a wallet full of credit cards, which is a liability if it falls into the wrong hands. NFC proponents are quick to note that a lost or stolen mobile phone can be disabled with a single call to the service provider, but canceling a wallet full of credit and bank cards requires at least an hour. One of the most important things to be aware of is that NFC security is a matter of accepting or not accepting a message from another device. Users must therefore constantly be aware of the status of their devices, and know, for example, whether they are configured to automatically connect with nearby NFC devices. There are also some threats unique to NFC, as well as opportunities for clever thieves. For example, as RFID chips and readers become more pervasive, we can imagine a new technique emerging, something being referred to as *billboard phishing*, where the impersonator could possibly paste posters, with embedded phony RFID chips, over kiosks, posters, or turnstiles. In this case, how is the user to know whether what they are touching is fake or legitimate? As with RFID technology, security professionals need to help shape the security policies and protocols that might affect device authentication and other issues. To this end, the NFC Forum has formed a security workgroup to develop industry standards.

NFC technology is currently being used extensively in Asia and the Pacific, and it is being used less in Europe and even less in the United States. However, we can expect to see NFC expand rapidly, especially in payment transaction scenarios and public transportation.

Chapter 16

Emerging Wireless Applications

Realizing the utopian visions of the wireless world requires continued innovation, and indeed, the innovation occurring in the wireless arena today is nothing short of amazing. Throughout the long history of radio, wireless has been largely concerned with long range and limited throughput. Today's focus is on broadband: offering higher data rates, capable of carrying many simultaneous interactions, increasingly in support of voice, data, video, and converged applications. We are now closer than ever before to achieving wireless broadband capabilities, and the future looks bright indeed. While the wireless industry is reaching a level of maturity to be celebrated, it is also vital to recognize that in many ways, we are just beginning to explore a new era of computing and communications, and more innovations will be required to realize the full potential. It is also worth noting that while data is overtaking voice in many parts of the world, in developing countries, voice remains the primary revenue stream for operators, and most of this comes not from the purchase of new handsets but from sales of reconditioned ones.

As discussed in Chapter 13, "Wireless Communications Basics," we still face substantial challenges, largely due to the fact that wireless is constrained by the inverse relationship between distance and throughput. In addition, the interactions of the radio signals with their surrounding environment result in a variety of impairments and degradations due to path loss, multipath, adverse weather, obstacles, interference, and so on. For wireless to compete effectively with its wired counterparts, innovations must continue. Fortunately, new solutions that are vital to realizing broadband wireless are emerging, including access to more radio spectrum, or bandwidth, improved modulation schemes and related elements, and advances in wireless network protocols. However, even with these improvements, the basic relationship between distance and throughout must always remain a fore-most consideration.

The wireless landscape is very much colored by range, moving from shorter- to longer-reach technologies, culminating in a future where multiple radio systems will be integrated into a single device. The idea of having one universal radio is very compelling. It is therefore likely that the future holds a combination of both WLAN and WWAN technologies as the preferred solution for most enterprise users. The following sections describe some of the key emerging applications in wireless telecommunications: the handset revolution, Mobile IP, the IP Multimedia Subsystem (IMS), mobile gaming, mobile video, mobile TV, and mobile content.

■ The Handset Revolution

There is little question that mobile handsets have progressed far beyond being sim-ple voice communications devices, and the advances are continuing at a bewilder-ing pace. Many of us grew up awed by the unbelievable gadgets James Bond had at his disposal. Those are no longer the product of Hollywood fantasy; in the near future, many such gadgets will be readily available from your local shop for just a few dollars. Tomorrow's mobile services and devices may sound like the stuff of dreams, but what we can only imagine is in fact already on the drawing boards. As mentioned in Chapter 14, "Wireless WANs," Japanese carrier NTT DoCoMo has produced a wonderful video, "Vision 2010," that illustrates what you can expect to experience in the near term and that will help you appreciate just how major the developments are (www.docomo-usa.com/vision2010/).

From a business standpoint, the mobile handsets industry is enormous—and continuing to grow. Some 2 million devices are sold per day, resulting in a global device market worth more than US$100 billion. Needless to say, the handset and application trends we are about to discuss have a major impact on all the players in the mobile and wireless industry, signaling the emergence of new business models.

The fact that 3G networks have finally taken off in Europe and North America, following the lead taken by Japan and South Korea, has caused the mobile market to develop substantially since 2005. The migration to 3G signals dramatic changes in the industry value chain, with the mobile handset community increasingly shift-ing its focus to data rather than voice services. This, of course, means we can expect the industry landscape to change as well, with leading players needing to differentiate their products, resulting in new standards, alliances, partnerships, and investment opportunities.

Vendors are finding that an increasing proportion of their sales are occurring in emerging markets, and these are not the markets for the James Bond gadgets.

Instead, they represent a new category of consumer, often at poverty level, with very low expenditure potential. However, they do represent a pool of more than a billion users, so low-end, entry-level products for these regions will also play a key role in generating revenues.

From Mobile Phones to Multimedia Handsets

What is occurring in the world of handsets can be simply described as a transition from mobile phones to multimedia handsets; the new generation of devices can handle functions that include not just voice services but also text, graphics, images, animation, audio, and video. The handset industry has been undergoing a steady evolution, as mobile phones are transformed into high-capacity multimedia devices running intuitive user interfaces.

We have already gone through four phases in the development of mobile multimedia devices, and we are now embarking on the fifth stage. It all began, in 2001–2002, with the introduction of chord ringtones, replacing what were boring monophonic tones with chords and tunes more pleasing to the human psyche. Much demand and competition were seen in this arena, ultimately producing a downloadable ringtone market with great revenue potential. The second upgrade occurred in 2002–2003, with the introduction of color screens and easy-to-use graphic interfaces. The third major development, taking place in 2003–2005, integrated the camera on the handset. In fact, an increasing number of today's devices boast more bells and whistles than most manual cameras, including features such as autofocus, red-eye reduction, digital zoom, and flash. Camera technology will continue to see many advances, with up to 5-megapixel models emerging in 2006. A recent InfoTrends/CAP Ventures study projects that more than 860 million camera phones will be shipped worldwide by 2009, accounting for 89% of all mobile phone handsets shipped (www.capv.com/home/Multiclient/MobileImaging.html). However, there may be a backlash against these devices in some cases. For instance, many establishments ban camera phones because they fear the owners will use them inappropriately or illegally. The fourth major development involves the addition of music-playing capabilities to the handset. Starting in 2005, MP3 players embedded in the handset started the trend toward entertainment being a key function of a mobile device. It also led to competition in terms of storage capacity and battery lifespan. Handsets equipped with MP3 players, FM/AM radio tuners, and voice recorders are now increasingly common, and online music services enable users to play tracks over mobile phones. Apple's iTunes has made a dramatic impact with its model for marketing and delivering digital music. It is believed that mobile music will form a key battleground for handset manufacturers, but the winners and losers may surprise many. The emerging fifth phase is the phase of video functions and applications, heralding handsets capable of DV, MP4, streaming media, and TV. Multimedia will no longer be the exclusive function of high-end handsets; it will quickly become the standard configuration for mainstream handsets as the costs to add the multimedia functions continue to drop. Just as chord ringtones, color screens, and cameras have become standard features, music and video are following.

Mobile Music

There is little doubt that mobile music is high on the list of mobile applications users desire and are willing to pay for. There is particularly high interest among 3G users, and it will come as no surprise that both music and gaming are ranked highest among young users. Support from the music industry is expected to make mobile music the most popular mobile consumer application.

Large music publishers, such as EMI and Warner Music, are moving into the mobile music markets due to the closed nature of cellular networks, which presents a more secure environment for intellectual entertainment property. One of the reasons the mobile music market began to develop is that music publishers became aware that they could convert songs into ringtones, which could be used on mobile phones to alert customers to incoming calls or messages. Combined with falling prices of handsets, new music applications and highly visible cobranded devices will create even more opportunities for mobile content services and drive this market to grow.

Warner Mobile Music Streaming Jukebox (a demo is available at http://wireless.wmg-is.com/javadotcom/index.html) is an innovative service that gives you access to ringtones, lets you view and download artist images, provides updated information about the artists, and has exclusive offers. It also allows you to stream actual music clips to your mobile device. Tools like the java.com Ringtone ReMixer (www.java.com) allow you to create custom mixes of your favorite hits on your PC browser and then send them to your mobile handset, so you can compose your own ringtones and caller IDs.

Motorola has introduced its iRadio service, a service that allows users to access Internet radio and music files through mobile phones in their cars, computers, or home audio systems. iRadio will use two-way Bluetooth technology and a mobile phone to offer listeners continuous entertainment. A user will be able to start playing a song in his or her car, pause it, and continue listening on a home audio system.

According to the Jupiter Research (www.jupiterresearch.com) study, "Mobile Music: Ringtones, Ring-backs & Full-tracks (second edition)," mobile music revenues are expected to exceed US$9.3 billion by 2009 due to the increased popularity of full-track downloads and ringtones. Ringtones alone are expected to be worth US$2.7 billion worldwide by 2010. Europe is expected to lead in revenue growth in the short term but to be overtaken by Asia-Pacific by 2007. From an application standpoint, there were 60 million ringback tone subscribers worldwide in 2005, and that number is forecast to grow to more than 300 million in 2009. Finally, the annual number of full-track downloads is projected to reach 1 billion in 2008.

Over the coming years, intelligence embedded into handsets will become increasingly dense, equipping handsets with features familier in the PC world and converting the traditional mobile phone into an advanced audiovisual device requiring fast, high-capacity wireless networks. In the future, the successful use of new mobile multimedia device services will demand more and more capacity from the network. (Chapters 14, "Wireless WANS," and 15, "WMANs, WLANs, and WPANs," discuss the developments under way to provide such networks.)

The future will also bring what are called *multiradio terminals* that can deploy different network technologies, allowing the user to flexibly shift from one network to another while moving about between home, workplace, and hobbies. The user will automatically be connected to any number of network alternatives, such as GSM, GPRS, 3G, WLANs, WMANs, and WPANs, without interruptions. (Multiradio technology is discussed in the following sections.)

In the near term, we can expect an increasing number of devices embedded with utility and entertainment applications for both enterprise and consumer use. Road warriors and travellers will see a service portfolio that offers maps, time, currency, and weather applications, all downloadable onto the handsets over the network. Whether it's games, ringtones, pictures, entertainment, sports, or lifestyle, there will be something for everyone.

Software-Defined Radio

One forthcoming application of multiradio technology is software-defined radio (SDR), a collection of hardware and software technologies that enable reconfigurable system architectures for wireless networks and user terminals. SDR-enabled devices and equipment can be dynamically programmed in software to reconfigure the characteristics of equipment. In other words, a single piece of hardware can perform different functions at different times, depending on the software programming. A radio device can become a cellular phone, a GPS receiver, an amateur packet radio, or any other sort of radio transmitting or receiving device. SDR provides an efficient and comparatively inexpensive solution to the problem of building multimode, multiband, multifunctional wireless devices that can be enhanced using software upgrades.

SDR architecture is based on a high-level generic model with specific functional blocks connected via open interface standards recommendations. The SDR architecture supports three specific domains: handheld, mobile, and base station (or fixed site). The software is implemented by controlling the characteristics of equipment/device subsystems through hierarchical and peer-level modules that support scalability and flexible extensions of applications.

The military has successfully demonstrated SDR's abilities and will continue to push this technology to its limits. Commercial wireless products, as well, have slowly evolved toward SDR architectures. The SDR Forum (www.sdrforum.org) has been working closely with global standards bodies and other industry groups, such as Global Radio Standardization Collaboration (GRSC, previously known as RAST; www.rast.etsi.org), the 3G Partnership Project (3GPP; www.3gpp.org), and ANSI (www.ansi.org) to develop standards for bringing SDR to full commercial viability.

Cognitive Radio

What would be the ultimate handset? To many, it would be a device that could seamlessly switch call and transmission modes to whatever makes the most sense, given the location at a given time—sometimes cellular, other times Wi-Fi, and yet other times Voice over IP (VoIP). The March 2006 edition of *Scientific American* magazine describes how such technology, called *cognitive radio (CR)*, will work (www.sciam.com/article.cfm?chanID=sa006&articleID=000C7B72-2374-13F6-A37483414B7F0000&pageNumber=1&catID=2).

CR is the next step in the evolution of SDR. It starts with SDR's ability to adapt to changing communications protocols and frequency bands and adds the ability to perceive the world around it and learn from experience. The term *cognitive radio* describes a smart system in which a radio device and its antenna can adapt their spectrum use in response to their operating environment, including the radio frequency spectrum, user behavior, and network state. CR detects temporarily unused spectrum segments, such as amateur radio and paging frequencies, and jumps into and out of them without interfering with the transmissions of the authorized users of those segments.

There are several types of CR:

- **Full CR (also known as Mitola radio)**—With this type of CR, every possible parameter is taken into account, including radio frequency spectrum, network state, and user behavior.

- **Spectrum-sensing CR**—This type of CR considers only the radio frequency parameter.

- **Licensed band CR**—This type of CR is capable of using unlicensed bands as well as bands assigned to licensed users.

- **Unlicensed band CR**—This type of CR can use only the unlicensed parts of the radio frequency spectrum.

The majority of research is currently focused on spectrum-sensing CR, particularly on the utilization of TV bands for communication.

CR introduces a unique design problem: interference temperature. A CR device must know its location and sense the interference it may cause to nearby radios, and it must also know exactly which air interfaces are available for it to use at any given moment, regardless of the band. Debate continues on how to best resolve the problem of interference temperature.

Most of the interest in CR to date has come from the military and public-sector emergency services, but the commercial sector recently became interested as well, when the FCC published a report concluding that CR architectures can make efficient and intelligent use of the radio spectrum and encouraging the use and development of CR. The FCC is considering using unused television frequencies (between 54MHz and 862MHz) for CR. The FCC proposes to open up 300MHz of this UHF/ VHF spectrum as its first major test of CR. It would permit fixed-access systems transmitting up to 1 watt in power and portable devices up to 100 milliwatts.

CR standards work is taking place as IEEE 802.22, the Working Group on WRANs (www.ieee802.org/22), which is working on the construction of wireless regional area networks (WRANs) using free TV bands. Its goal is to specify a cognitive air interface for fixed, point-to-multipoint WRANs that operate on the unused channels in the UHF/VHF TV bands that the FCC is opening up for experimentation. There is ongoing contention between the WiMax community and the IEEE 802.22 group over who should have access to unused TV spectrum. (WiMax is discussed in more detail in Chapter 15.) The IEEE 802.18 group, Radio Regulatory Technical Advisory Group, has a difficult task ahead in trying to coordinate the various international bodies and existing and emerging standards surrounding radio and radio regulation.

Mobile IP

Trains, planes, and automobiles were once simply ways to transport people between locations, but they now offer yet another opportunity to stay connected to the Internet. While this was not easily accomplished in the past, today we have Mobile IP, an open standard defined by the IETF in RFC 3344. With the advent of packet-based mobile data applications and the increase of wireless computing, there is a corresponding need for seamless communication between mobile node devices and packet data networks, such as the Internet.

Mobile IP allows a user with a mobile device whose IP address is associated with one network to stay connected when moving to a network that has a different IP address. In other words, a user can keep the same IP address, stay connected, and maintain ongoing applications while roaming between IP networks. When a user leaves the network with which his or her device is associated (i.e., the home network) and enters the domain of a foreign network, the foreign network uses the Mobile IP protocol to inform the home network of a care-of address to which all packets for the user's device should be sent. The way it works can be illustrated through a post office analogy. Let's say I move from San Francisco to Hong Kong. When I get to Hong Kong, I drop off a note at the Hong Kong post office with my new Hong Kong address. The Hong Kong post office then notifies the San Francisco office of my new address. When the San Francisco post office receives mail for me, it knows to forward it to my Hong Kong address. Mobile IP is highly desirable in wireless WAN environments where users need to carry their mobile devices across multiple LANs that have different IP addresses.

Mobile IP is the underlying technology for support of various mobile data and wireless networking applications. Mobile IP technology is embedded in the functionality of packet equipment for 2.5G and 3G networks. For example, General Packet Radio Service (GPRS) depends on Mobile IP to enable the relay of messages to a GPRS phone via the serving GPRS support node (SGSN) from the gateway GPRS support node (GGSN) without the sender needing to know the serving node IP address. (GPRS is discussed in Chapter 14.) In addition, Mobile IP enables advanced applications such as unified messaging.

As shown in Figure 16.1, there are several key elements to Mobile IP:

- **Mobile node**—A mobile node is a device capable of performing network roaming.

- **Home agent**—A home agent is a router on the home network that serves as the point for communications with the mobile node.

- **Foreign agent**—A foreign agent is a router that functions as the mobile node's point of attachment when it travels to the foreign network.

- **Care-of address**—The care-of address is the termination point of the tunnel toward the mobile node when it is not in the home network.

- **Correspondent node**—The correspondent node is the device that the mobile node is communicating with, such as a Web server.

To accomplish seamless communication between a mobile node device and a packet network, such as the Internet, Mobile IP establishes the visited network as a foreign node and the home network as the home node. Mobile IP uses a tunneling protocol to allow messages from the packet network to be directed to the mobile node's IP address. This is accomplished by way of routing messages to the foreign node for delivery via tunneling the original IP address inside a packet destined for the temporary IP address assigned to the mobile node by the foreign node. The home agent and foreign agent continuously advertise their services on the network through an agent discovery process, enabling the home agent to recognize when a new foreign agent is acquired and allowing the mobile node to register a new care-of address. This method allows for seamless communications between the mobile

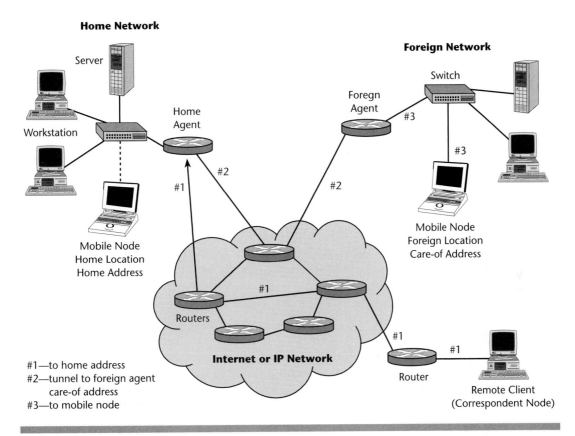

Figure 16.1   Elements of a Mobile IP network

node and applications residing on the packet network, providing seamless, always-on connectivity for mobile data applications and wireless computing.

The many applications for Mobile IP include support of VoIP, streaming video and audio, VPN clients (who can stay connected to the office without having to reauthenticate themselves when they switch networks), access to all database applications using remote connections (e.g., in customer relationship management and similar applications), any kind of peer-to-peer applications on the Internet, chat sessions, true mobility in hardware devices, and new cross-network services for operators and wireless service providers.

Enhancements to the Mobile IP technique are being developed to improve mobile communications in certain circumstances by making the processes more secure and more efficient. These enhancements include Mobile IPv6 and Hierarchical Mobile IPv6 (HMIPv6).

■ The IP Multimedia Subsystem

The IP Multimedia Subsystem (IMS) is the most recent refinement of an enhanced services architecture. It is an architectural framework for introducing a wide variety of IP-based services to the wireless realm, and it is designed to ease convergence via its various specifications. Whereas 3G wireless technology addresses the issue of growing bandwidth requirements, the purpose of IMS is to address the critical signaling and session controls issues associated with multimedia services. Advanced radio technology alone is not sufficient to provide true multimedia services. Other enabling technologies are crucial components of IMS, such as session management protocols, confidentiality and integrity protection schemes, end-to-end quality of service (QoS), traffic management, service control platforms, and billing. IMS, which establishes IP connections between various client devices, was developed with two main goals: to support access convergence with 2G, 3G, 4G, Wi-Fi, and WiMax networks and to support multimedia convergence of voice, video, messaging, and data.

IMS was created by 3GPP, which, as discussed in Chapter 14, develops technical specifications for IMT-2000, the ITU framework for 3G standards. The group represents a global effort, involving six of the world's major standards bodies from China, Europe, Japan, Korea, and the United States. As a note of historical reference, enhanced services have traditionally been deployed as a collection of single solutions, delivered using a vertically integrated approach. The 3GPP architects recognized that this traditional vertical approach was not efficient and, based on this understanding, began to pursue a horizontally layered architecture. The main objectives of this horizontal approach were to support the universal delivery of enhanced services, regardless of the access technology used by the subscriber, while minimizing the costs for the service provider.

The base IMS functionality was first defined in the 3GPP Release 5 (R5) standards, with a focus on 3G mobile telecommunications systems. R5 was optimized for use by GSM UMTS wireless networks. 3GPP Release 6 (R6) standards add a specification for fixed-wireless and wireline networks, as well as interworking with WLANs. 3GPP Release 7 (R7), working together with Telecoms and Internet Converged Services & Protocols for Advanced Networks (TISPAN; www.etsi.org/tispan) R1, adds support for fixed networks. TISPAN is a standardization body of the European Telecommunication Standards Institute (ETSI; www.etsi.org) that specializes in fixed network and Internet convergence. The TISPAN architecture is based on the concept of cooperating subsystems sharing common components.

IMS is such an important development that even wireline carriers are looking toward IMS as the basis for achieving a single enhanced services architecture for delivering any service, using any media, to reach any customer, regardless of how the person connects to the network. (Chapter 10, "Next-Generation Networks," discusses the details of IMS. This section focuses on the relevance of IMS to wireless networks.)

IMS is key to IP for 3G networks because its purpose is to create a telephony-oriented signaling network that overlays an underlying IP network. IMS is designed to support IP-based multimedia services, and as you know, multimedia is the main application driving the requirement for broadband infrastructures in both the wired and wireless realms. The 3GPP IMS and the 3GPP2 (www.3gpp2.org) version, Multimedia Domain (MMD), provide the technological basis for the provision of mobile multimedia services in next-generation networks.

IMS is a service infrastructure that relies on Session Initiation Protocol (SIP) to establish and maintain call control. IMS is an internationally recognized standard that defines a generic architecture that will offer VoIP and other multimedia services in wireline and wireless applications. Because voice is still the primary application for wireless telephony today, by adopting SIP as the signaling protocol, wireless service providers have a standard that works well for both voice and data. In fact, VoIP has now become the foundation of almost every service provider's next-generation network architecture, including wireless, wireline, and cable/MSP operators. As we examine the role of VoIP in these providers' networks, it is clear that it constitutes a vital part of their strategies for differentiation, reduced costs, and increased competitiveness.

The IMS architecture is divided into three layers: transport (or access), control, and service (or application) (refer to Figure 10.2 in Chapter 10). IMS assumes that each user is associated with a home network, and it supports the concept of roaming across other wired or wireless networks. IMS also includes a policy engine and an authentication, authorization, and accounting (AAA) server for operator control and security. Rather than the vertically integrated service stacks of today, as Figure 16.2 shows, IMS calls for a single support structure for all services: one billing system, one set of operational support system (OSS) elements, and one subscriber database, accessed by applications that are created and delivered on-the-fly to any number of endpoints, as defined by the user. It is a vision of seamless, contextual personal communications that means not only new revenue-generating services for carriers but also a radical reduction in operational complexity.

The IMS architecture is composed of many components, operating at various layers, as illustrated for next-generation wireline networks in Figure 10.3 in Chapter 10. While Figure 10.3 covers the full set of IMS components, Figure 16.2 is a simplified illustration that incorporates components specific to wireless networks, showing the connectivity between radio access networks (RANs) and the IMS layers.

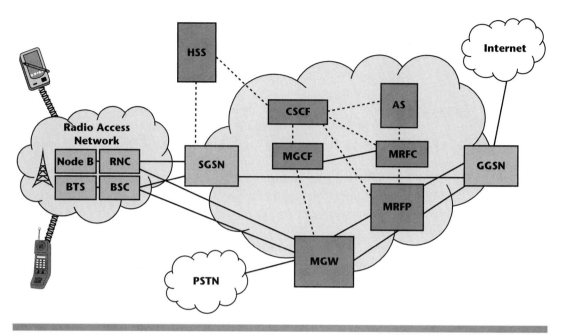

Figure 16.2   Moving up the value chain: the wireless IMS architecture

As shown in Figure 16.2, the wireless IMS architecture includes the following key components:

■ Service- or application-layer components:

- **Application servers (AS)**—The main responsibilities of an application server are to execute service-specific logic and deliver to IMS value-added services, such as push-to-talk, ringback tone, prepaid calling card, multimedia messaging, and multimedia conferencing service logic.

■ Control-layer components:

- **Call session controller function (CSCF)**—This element is the central brain of IMS, interacting with the various service platforms. It maintains session state, while interacting with the gateways, service platform elements, and charging functions for the overall orchestration of service delivery.

- **Home subscriber servers (HSSs)**—An HSS has the role of the main data storage for all subscriber and service-related data.

- **Multimedia resource function controller (MRFC)**—The MRFC acts as a media resource broker between the application server and MRFP resources, and it can be implemented as part of an application server or as a separate network element.

- **Multimedia gateway controller function (MGCF)**—The MGCF, also known as a softswitch or call agent, communicates with the CSCF and controls the connections for media channels in an IMS media gateway.

■ Transport- or access-layer components:

- **Multimedia resource function processor (MRFP)**—Also known as the IP media server, the MRFP supports media processing for the application layer, such as audio mixing, DTMF digit collection, content recording and playback, and codec transcoding. However, unlike traditional approaches, where resources are dedicated to a single application, the MRFP provides media processing as a shared resource to a number of different applications.

- **Media gateway (MGW)**—The MGW provides interworking with the PSTN and the Internet. Whereas earlier-generation wireless networks make use of the MGW, newer networks are served by the GGSN for connectivity with the Internet.

- **Serving GPRS support node (SGSN)**—The SGSN provides packet routing to and from the SGSN service area for all users in that service area. The SGSN provides the packet-switched link to mobile stations.

- **Gateway GPRS support node (GGSN)**—The GGSN acts as a gateway between the GPRS network and public data networks such as IP and X.25 networks. GGSNs also connect to other GPRS networks to facilitate GPRS roaming.

- **RAN components**—The transport layer is also home to the RAN components, including the following:

  - **Base transceiver station (BTS)**—The BTS handles the radio interface to the mobile station. It is the radio equipment (transceivers and antennas) needed to service each cell in the network.

  - **Base station controller (BSC)**—The BSC controls a group of BTSs and provides all the control functions and physical links between the mobile switching center and BTS. Its functions include handover operations, cell configuration data, frequency administration between BTSs and mobile stations, and control of radio frequency power levels in BTSs.

  - **Node B**—In 3G UMTS networks, the base transceiver station is called Node B. It is differentiated from the base stations in 2G GSM networks by the fact that is uses W-CDMA as the air transport technology.

– **Radio network controller (RNC)**—In 3G UMTS networks, the RNC is in charge of controlling Node Bs. In traditional implementations, Node B has minimum functionality, but with the advent of HSDPA (described in Chapter 14), some logic (such as retransmission) is handled on Node B in order to reduce response times.

IMS service delivery platforms enable the enhanced service components to communicate using industry-standard and open interfaces such as SIP. This then allows the service providers to mix and match the best of application servers with the best of MRFP/media servers. IMS applications include voice telephony, video telephony, multimedia streaming, HTTP/TCP/IP browsing, instant messaging, file sharing, gaming, push-to-talk/push-to-media, and presence-based services.

Two of the first applications making use of IMS are expected to be push-to-talk and presence-based services, which are discussed in the following sections.

Push-to-Talk

Thanks to its revenue potential, push-to-talk is one of the most talked-about mobile applications. Push-to-talk, which turns a mobile phone into a walkie-talkie by giving it trunked radio functionality, ended up being one of Nextel's (www.nextel. com) key market differentiators, causing the cellular industry to see it as the next killer application for mobile networks after voice and Short Messaging Service (SMS). Push-to-talk gives end users the ability to quickly find one another and engage in brief, burst-oriented communication. Rather than being a replacement of long, interactive communication, push-to-talk is best suited for quick communication among end users. Due to the fact that it is provided in half-duplex mode (i.e., transmission occurs in both directions, but not at the same time—each party must wait to speak), the users are unable to interrupt each other.

Because push-to-talk is by definition a group activity, and not everyone in a group may subscribe to the same mobile network or own the same handset model, push-to-talk absolutely depends on standardization and interoperability. Push-to-Talk over Cellular (PoC) is the official standard that defines how push-to-talk can be deployed over a cellular operator's packet data network using VoIP. The key to PoC is IMS. Although the IMS standard has been completed by the 3GPP in its Release 5 specification, it has yet to pass the trial stage even in existing 3G networks. The PoC standard was submitted to the 3GPP in September 2003, and in June 2005 the Open Mobile Alliance (OMA; www.openmobilealliance.org) announced the availability of the OMA Push-to-Talk over Cellular 1.0 Candidate Enabler (OMA PoC 1.0). After announcing its PoC 1.0 specifications, OMA held the first interoperability TestFest for OMA PoC 1.0, where six servers and eight clients deploying OMA PoC 1.0 were tested. Any PoC offerings prior to OMA PoC 1.0 are prestandard.

At this time, at least 35 operators are deploying push-to-talk services or trialing them. Not all operators deploying push-to-talk are relying on the PoC standard. At least 14 operators are using technology from Kodiak Networks (www. kodiaknetworks.com) that enables push-to-talk via the 2G circuit-switched voice network. A number of handset suppliers are supporting the Kodiak technology. Many in the industry, particularly those who support PoC, feel that the Kodiak technology is threatening the potential market for push-to-talk.

QoS is a top priority, particularly as voice, or "talk," is only the first application in the family of push-to-*x* services. Push-to-talk is destined to be combined with other applications, including presence, picture sharing, and video clips (push-to-view, or streaming video during a PoC session). Although PoC is anticipated to have a strong future, it will not be here for some time.

Presence-Based Services

Presence-based services are beginning to evolve in the mobile space, although mobile carriers have been slow to offer presence-based services, largely due to constraints associated with usability and user awareness. The most basic impact of presence services is to allow mobile users to view the availability and communication means of other users. Presence can be a key enabler to stimulate use of services such as voice, Multimedia Messaging Service (MMS), SMS, instant messaging (IM), push-to-talk, and multiple-player gaming. One of the key advantages of deploying IM is to build on the success of SMS by offering new, more sophisticated messaging services.

Presence is expected to get a boost from PoC, as well as from an increasing penetration of mobile phones equipped with Instant Messaging and Presence Service (IMPS). IMPS has four features:

- **Instant messaging**—Instant messaging is a type of electronic communication service that involves instant communication between two or more people over a network such as the Internet.

- **Presence**—OMA's definition of *presence* includes client device availability (my phone is on/off or on a call), user status (available, unavailable, in a meeting), location, client device capabilities (voice, text, GPRS, multimedia), and searchable personal status, such as mood and hobbies.

- **Groups or chat**—IMPS enables both wireless operators and end users to create and manage groups and group discussions.

■ **Shared content**—IMPS allows users and operators to set up their own storage areas where they can post pictures, music, and other multimedia content. That content can then be shared with other individuals or groups of users in either an IM or chat session.

The IMPS standard was originally proposed by Nokia (www.nokia.com), Ericsson (www.ericsson.com), and Motorola (www.motorola.com). The IMPS specification, which is managed by the industry consortium OMA, defines how the system should interface with existing wireless network infrastructures. IMPS also provides an open interface to existing IM communities such as AOL (www.aol.com), Yahoo (www.yahoo.com), and MSN (www.msn.com). In order to engage in IM on a mobile with IMPS, the user needs a phone with an IM client as well as IMPS to connect to. The OMA IMPS Enabler release is designed for exchanging instant messages and presence information not only between mobile devices but also between mobile and fixed devices. IMPS 1.2 was approved and released in January 2005. IMPS 1.3 Enabler, a candidate for the next upgrade, is a significant enhancement of IMPS 1.2 Enabler, although it is not designed to be backward compatible with previous IMPS versions.

There are many obstacles to bringing mobile presence and IM services to market, from technical and business issues to user awareness. The biggest challenge is the lack of interoperability between services and between handsets. Other major issues include concerns about privacy and ease of use. Finally, business issues also present problems, including usage cases, appropriate applications and content, negotiation of deals with IM providers, cannibalization of voice and SMS services revenues, and the cost of installing a presence server. Analysts suggest that the main application for mobile presence services will be in the peer-to-peer consumer segments rather than the enterprise market. Until there is widespread adoption of mobile IM/presence by users, it is unlikely that it will be used with any significance as a medium for business-to-consumer communication.

■ Mobile Gaming

Mobile gaming is definitely more than a fad. In recent times, mobile games have grown increasingly popular as a means of providing personal entertainment on the go. According to a 2006 eMarketer report (www.emarketer.com/Report.aspx?mobile_gaming_feb06), worldwide revenues for mobile gaming reached US$2.5 billion in 2005 and are projected to top US$11 billion by 2010. eMarketer also cites recent IDC (www.idc.com) numbers that show U.S. revenues from mobile games rising to US$1.5 billion in 2008, from US$600 million in 2005. The study further finds that nearly half of all free mobile game downloads are for puzzle and card games, producing over 25% of all mobile gaming revenues. Part of the reason for the popularity of these simple games comes from the impact of the limited screen size and navigation options of the mobile handsets, but as the devices become more sophisticated, so will the type of games users engage in.

With the number of mobile gamers around the world growing, with some estimates predicting 220 million global users by 2009, the mobile gaming business is projected to expand and be a bigger portion of the profit pie for the cellular carriers and handset makers. However, aside from the value of the revenues earned from games sales, there is additional potential: Users who engage in mobile gaming spend more money on wireless phone services in general; they can be high sources of revenue because of their propensity to remain online for extended periods. Also, advertisers and marketers find that mobile games provide a strategically important tool via the branding power of games and in-game ads. Mobile gaming also plays a pivotal role in generating revenues and numerous opportunities for game publishers, game developers, and associated professionals.

Two factors have elevated mobile gaming to a new high. First, with mobile penetration in developed countries reaching saturation, service providers have had to consider and plan on new nonvoice services. Second, the emergence of downloadable technologies and enabled handsets has offered a simple and billable platform for the delivery of games. The following sections discuss the various mobile game categories and platforms.

Mobile Game Categories

There are several techniques for playing games on a mobile phone, with each platform affecting the game-playing experience. There are three main categories of mobile games:

- **Embedded games**—This was the first approach, with the games being hardcoded into the mobile handset's system and shipped with the device. These games are likely to soon be considered outdated and obsolete and are often deleted by those who enjoy hacking handsets.
- **SMS games**—This category involves games that are played by sending text messages and generally are in the form of live contests and polls. The popularity of this approach is decreasing as the cost of playing the game increases each time an SMS is sent to the game server. Most importantly, these games are void of the exciting sensory aspects that multimedia introduces; they are not colorful, graphical, or highly interactive.

■ **Downloadable, or browser, games**—Using a mobile device's built-in micro-browser (an Internet browser specifically designed for mobile devices), games can be played in both online and offline modes. These games are played through either the service provider's or a third-party game provider's Web site. For offline gaming, the games can be downloaded. This category encompasses the widest range of games, including individual and multi-player games, network games, offline games, and arcade games.

Of the three categories, downloadable games are the most popular approach today, largely due to the creative and rich multimedia content, appealing presentation, and lower cost compared with SMS games. Very importantly, these games play like conventional handheld games.

Downloadable games are very attractive in their format, permitting animation and the ability to be played offline. They can also be played similar to the traditional retail model: The user pays once and can play offline as long as he or she likes. But in order to support downloadable games, new technologies are required that allow a game program to be transmitted over a wireless network and to be understood and run on a mobile device. In addition, the devices need to be able to handle a greater range of features, such as graphics, sound, larger screen sizes, improved user interfaces, security, and, of course, digital rights management (i.e., content security).

Mobile Game Platforms

Various technologies are now available to develop downloadable games, including Java ME (formerly Java 2 Micro Edition [J2ME]), BREW (Binary Runtime for Wireless), ExEn (Execution Environment), and Mophun. The most widely adopted technology is Java ME, which is used worldwide. However, competing technologies are increasingly being used, with varying degrees of market penetration. BREW is used in the United States, China, Taiwan, and Korea; ExEn is found in France and Germany; and Mophun is popular in parts of Scandinavia.

Java ME

Sun's (www.sun.com) Java ME runs on top of a virtual machine, an extra layer of software that serves as a barrier of protection from malicious or erroneous software. A key advantage is that the virtual machine allows the Java software to operate between a wide variety of different types of mobile phones and other devices without modification, even though the devices may contain very different electronic components. However, although it provides added flexibity, the virtual machine decreases the potential speed of the game and reduces the ability to use the full functionality of a mobile phone (due to the fact that Java software can only do what this middle layer will support). On the other hand, due to the extra security and increased compatibility, the process of writing and distributing Java mobile applications (including games) to a wide variety of mobile devices is greatly simplified. This results in free and easy tools that are made available by Sun, including the Java Development Kit (JDK) used to create the Java software, the Java Wireless Toolkit (Java ME tools) required for packaging and testing the mobile software, and room on a Web server to host the application.

The main advantages of Java ME are that is has such widespread adoption worldwide, free and easy access to tools, and a fast-growing handset base. The disadvantages include the fact that it runs slowly and has technical drawbacks associated with the Java ME MIDP1 (Mobile Information Device Profile version 1) specification, including the fact that it cannot query key status, has no active rendering APIs, has no support for audio, requires only HTTP support, and has a lack of clarity in the specifications that often leads to differences in implementations.

BREW

Qualcomm's (www.qualcomm.com) BREW is perhaps the most powerful mobile gaming technology because it provides complete access to its functionality and control of the mobile device. However, for this reason, Qualcomm and a handful of mobile content providers are the only ones allowed to issue the necessary tools to build BREW applications. Although the BREW software development kit (SDK) is free, BREW applications require a digital signature that can be generated only by Qualcomm and its sanctioned associates. In addition, the game will work only on test-enabled devices, meaning that Qualcomm must give its approval after it checks and tests the software. The main advantages of BREW include its robustness, its acknowledged success in the United States, and its favorable terms for developers. Its disadvantages are the tight control that Qualcomm exerts and the fact that it runs only on CDMA phones.

ExEn

IN-FUSIO's (www.infusio.com) ExEn is best known for its business model, which supports a variety of revenue models, including pay-per-level and SMS high scores. Its disadvantages lie in the fact that it is a single-vendor system and has been deployed in only a small number of networks.

Mophun

In the Synergenix Interactive Mophun (www.mophun.com) development environment, games are developed in C/C++, using an open and free SDK that is available upon request from Mophun. A complier is used to make the translation to a system-independent application. Because the application is required to be certified to run on a mobile phone, there are no freeware Mophun games. Mophun's main advantage is its technical performance, and its key disadvantage is that it can be preinstalled only on Sony-Ericsson devices.

■ Mobile Video

Video telephony is 3G's chief differentiator, its signature service. Delivering high-quality video is crucial and is generally not done in many 3G networks when they launch. The number-one complaint operators receive has to do with video quality. Commonly referenced problems with mobile video include jerky video, sync problems between video and audio, poor lip synchronization, inability to deal with fast-moving images, blank picture transmission, long times required to establish video calls, unavailability in some places, and enormous battery consumption. QoS is difficult to guarantee, and there is not enough bandwidth. These problems are compounded by the fact that 3G video quality has to compete with benchmarks set by streaming video on the Internet. 3G video telephony today is a circuit-switched application using 3G-324M, a protocol based on H.324 that was adopted because the UMTS packet network wasn't ready to handle real-time full-duplex video.

Live video requires intensive use of capacity. Many 3G operators allocate 64Kbps channels for video telephony and often find that this is not enough. However, going up to 128Kbps affects overall network capacity. In addition, reducing the number of users supported in a cell increases the price of providing video telephony. Another problem that results in degraded video telephony quality is poor radio performance. Unfortunately, there is no easy fix for this: It is a matter of weighing the parameter tradeoffs for different services in each cell. A good example of maintaining balance is in the area of power control. High-quality video requires almost perfect power control, but you cannot demand too much power from the handset without significantly reducing the battery life.

Another current shortcoming of mobile video is that cellular companies have little or no experience running live video over a network, which requires serious network management. Monitoring video service is a major issue for 3G operators. Today, video management is limited to fault monitoring, but there are few, if any, mechanisms for evaluating services. Part of the problem has been lack of proper test-and-measurement equipment. The test-and-measurement community is responding with new or upgraded tools to analyze 3G video quality. New products are also addressing the network engineering part of the equation, referred to as *performance engineering*. Actix (www.actix.com) claims to allow engineers to squeeze more capability out of the existing network and to more accurately pinpoint trouble spots in the network.

The complexity of mobile video is going to increase when video calls go from the circuit-switched 3G-324M approach to SIP-based video calls. 3GPP adopted

H.324 with a few modifications and called the new specification 3G-324M. The modifications were made mainly in codec requirements, the network interface, and call control. Among other things, interoperability will be required to enable customers with new SIP phones to call customers using the older 3G-324M handsets. The migration to SIP is now inevitable, thanks to the introduction of three new ingredients for packet-based high-quality mobile live video:

- **IMS**—As discussed earlier in this chapter, IMS will provide a more efficient IP backbone to support real-time and multimedia applications, including video over IP.

- **High-Speed Downlink Packet Access (HSDPA)**—As discussed in Chapter 14, HSDPA vastly improves the access link.

- **Mobile phone chipsets**—Mobile phone chipsets capable of processing video at 30fps make the video-viewing experience akin to what we are used to with movies and television.

However, there remains the major issue of latency in the IP network itself. The key factor for live video is the round-trip time (RTT), which ideally should be less than 80 milliseconds. Currently, average response times range from 100 to 500 milliseconds (depending on the world region), which means that during busy times, latencies can easily be over 1,000 milliseconds. The Internet Traffic Report Web site (www.internettrafficreport.com/main.htm) contains reports on the current performance of major Internet routes around the world and includes statistics on latencies and packet loss.

The future of mobile video goes far beyond video telephony. Live video is expected to become the basis for a wide range of potential 3G revenue producers, including security camera feeds, video chat, video-enabled call centers, video sharing, and music videos. In support of these advanced services, operators need to measure not just QoS but the quality of the experience.

■ Mobile TV

Many analysts see a strong market for mobile TV, provided that it is packaged and priced correctly, but others offer a much more conservative viewpoint. Mobile TV broadcasts have started in South Korea, Japan, and the United States, with a number of other trials taking place around the world. For example, in the United States, Verizon Wireless (www.verizonwireless.com) has launched V-Cast, offering dozens of channels with 60-second "mobisodes" for US$15 per month, and Cingular (www.cingular.com) and Sprint Nextel (www.sprint.com) both offer

MobiTV for US$10 per month. Many other countries are also beginning to offer mobile TV as well.

A number of vendors are preparing for mobile digital TV solutions. It is already becoming a standards war. As discussed in the next sections, the following standards are being promoted in different places around the world:

- Digital Multimedia Broadcasting (DMB)
- Digital Video Broadcasting–Handhelds (DVB-H)
- Integrated Services Digital Broadcasting (ISDB)
- MediaFLO

Which of these standards lives to dominate remains to be seen. After all, we have never created a global standard for analog TV, but then again, normal TVs aren't mobile and therefore don't require a global standard. Other issues need to be addressed, including potential regulatory problems, spectrum planning, network and access capacity, the reality of figuring out how to actually make money (monthly subscription fees? pay-per-view? pay-per-minute?), the fact that such offerings stand to cannibalize other 3G data services, the usability factor (will people actually want to watch TV on a 2-inch screen?), and, most importantly, content issues.

TV plays a significant role in the lives of people worldwide. In addition, mobile subscriber penetration has reached, if not surpassed, what is statistically a very high level of saturation in many markets. Finally, there is little doubt about the inevitable convergence of the broadcast and mobile industries because it is already happening. Therefore, broadcast mobile TV definitely has potential, and interactive TV and the extension of advertising are at the forefront of that success.

DMB

DMB was the first mobile TV standard to market, being put into use in a number of countries. It is currently operating in South Korea, where S-DMB (satellite DMB) and T-DMB (terrestrial DMB) services are in use. There are also some T-DMB trials currently occurring and planned around Europe. Germany is launching T-DMB for the 2006 World Cup. France is currently conducting a trial in Paris. Switzerland, Italy, and the United Kingdom are also preparing for trials during 2006.

The DMB standard is derived from the Digital Audio Broadcasting (DAB) standard that enjoys wide use in Europe for radio broadcasts. The acronym DAB is used both to identify the generic technology of digital audio broadcasting and specific technical standards, particularly the Eureka 147 (EU147) standard. DAB is based on Orthogonal Frequency Division Modulation (OFDM) for transmitting digital data over a lossy radio channel. DAB broadcasts use the MP2 audio coding technique, a close relative of the popular MP3 format, which was also created as part of the EU147 project.

S-DMB is a new concept in multimedia mobile broadcasting service that converges telecommunications and broadcasting. S-DMB delivers high-quality content for both stationary and mobile clients. It uses the same Code Division Multiplexing (CDM) technology as the mobile phone service. Initially, there are 3 video channels among the 9 offered; the other 6 are audio channels. Eventually there will be a total of 39 channels: 11 for video, 25 for audio, and 3 for data. As a satellite-based service, one of S-DMB's problems may be reception within buildings. SK Telecom (www.sktelecom.com), for instance, plans to overcome this problem by extending the signal receiving areas by installing "gap fillers," although not all areas will get filled. Another drawback is the lack of available handsets.

Whereas S-DMB was developed mostly by the private sector, T-DMB was part of South Korea's national initiative to digitize radio broadcasting. T-DMB has reason to be encouraged. In March 2005 the Korean Broadcasting Commission (www.kbc.go.kr/english), which regulates South Korea's airwaves, selected three broadcasting companies and three consortia comprising dozens of companies each to provide terrestrial-based multimedia services. A big plus for T-DMB is that terrestrial broadcasts will be free because the government forbids charging for what are considered public broadcasts. Although DMB is proprietary and designed for the Korean market, because DMB can send content to numerous consumers on the same frequency band, the technology scales gracefully and profitably. In fact, as the number of users increases, operational costs decrease. As a result, Korea is interested in having DMB adopted globally as a standard. Both LG (www.lg.co.kr/english) and Samsung (www.samsung.com) have major investments in DMB and hope that it will be adopted throughput Europe as a standard. South Korea's ministry of communications has created a special task force to lobby for European use of the DMB standard, and Korean companies have performed several demonstrations.

DVB-H

The ETSI chose DVB-H as a standard in November 2004. ETSI recommendations for a standard are voluntary, not compulsory, but DVB-H has already generated significant industry activity, including technical and commercial trials and a range of product launches. Based on DVB-T, DVB-H is fully backward compatible. It offers additional features to support handheld portable and mobile reception. The specification calls for 15Mbps in an 8MHz channel. Key advantages of DVB-H include the fact that it saves batteries and offers mobility with high data rates, single-antenna reception, impulse noise tolerance, increased general robustness, and seamless handoffs.

DVB-H is meant for IP-based services. It can share DVB-T "multiplex" (i.e., the bandwidth of a DTV channel subdivided into multiple subchannels) with MPEG-2 services. For a TV-like experience on a handheld device with a smaller screen, the next-generation MPEG standard (MPEG-4-AVC) will be needed. Although DVB-H will deliver a TV broadcast signal to a mobile TV device, any two-way interaction would be handled by mobile networks such as GPRS, EDGE, or 3G.

Technical trials of DVB-H services are currently under way in Europe, the United States, and Australia, and major events such as the International Broadcasting Convention (IBC; www.ibc.org), the 3GSM World Congress (www.3gsmworldcongress.com), CeBIT (www.cebit.de), and DVB World (www.iab.ch/dvbworld2006_prog.htm) have featured full end-to-end demonstrations. Commercial launches of DVB-H services are occurring in 2006 in Italy and the United States. Most major U.S. markets are expected to have DVB-H infrastructure ready for use by 2007.

ISDB

ISDB encompasses several core standards, including ISDB-S (satellite TV), ISDB-T (terrestrial digital TV), ISDB-C (digital cable TV), and ISDB-Tsb (terrestrial digital sound broadcasting in the 2.6GHz band). The TV standards are all based on MPEG-2 video and audio coding and can deliver high-definition TV (HDTV). ISDB-T and ISDB-Tsb are for mobile reception in TV bands.

The ISDB standards vary in the modulation schemes used due to the particular requirements of the different frequency bands. ISDB-S uses PSK modulation; ISDB-T and ISDB-Tbs use QPSK, DQPSK, 16-QAM, or 64-QAM; and ISDB-C uses 64-QAM.

Japan adopted ISDB-T in commercial transmissions in December 2003, and it had a total market of about 100 million TV receivers in early 2006. (ISDB standards are discussed in more detail in Chapter 10.)

MediaFLO

MediaFLO, a wireless innovation from Qualcomm (www.qualcomm.com), is a comprehensive end-to-end solution that simultaneously and cost-effectively delivers very high volumes of high-quality, streaming, or clipped audio and video multimedia to wireless subscribers. Based on Qualcomm's proprietary Forward Link Only (FLO) technology, it is an air interface with multicast delivery capabilities designed to increase capacity and reduce content delivery costs to mobile handsets. It is designed from the ground up for superior mobility. FLO is based on OFDM outbound high-speed technology.

MediaFLO works on the 700MHz spectrum and is being embraced in the United States. However, global movements are also involved, largely through the FLO Forum (www.floforum.org). The purpose of the FLO Forum is to assemble wireless industry stakeholders around the central mission of establishing FLO as an internationally supported technology standard. Its position is that FLO technology is poised to significantly change the way multimedia is delivered to mobile devices. As these changes take hold, possibilities for the entire wireless industry stand to increase dramatically.

MediaFLO is designed to be a one-way, high-speed wireless system to deliver content, including audio and video, to mobile devices. The concept is to make the channels (multiple) CDMA and W-CDMA operators. Mobile virtual network operators (MVNOs) and resellers of the service and/or content are expected to make use of the network. (MVNOs are companies that do not own licensed spectrum of their own but instead make use of another mobile operator's network, while reselling the wireless services under their own brand names.) But wireless operators are not the only potential customers of MediaFLO; the technology is seen as an ideal way for broadcast stations to include an entire new group of viewers—mobile users. MediaFLO will be made available to both CDMA and W-CDMA network operators and TV, cable, and satellite operators. The major innovation is that MediaFLO will allow content that is usually available only for fixed viewing to now be available to mobile devices, whether they are laptops or mobile phones equipped with color screens and enough storage to buffer the content. This obviously suggests that mobile devices will need to accommodate mass storage and the ability to cache content for later viewing, allowing customers who experience any problems in live reception to view the program later. And, of course, the system must ensure full security.

Whereas TV stations can broadcast a single program in the 6MHz or 8 MHz of bandwidth allocated to broadcast TV, MediaFLO can deliver between 50 and 100 nationwide and local content channels, including up to 15 live streaming channels and numerous clip-case and audio channels. Wireless service providers can send audio, video, and large data files to the customer while also maintaining their own data channels for other two-way applications. Using Quarter Video Graphics Array (QVGA) resolution, 30fps video, and high-quality stereo audio, the content on MediaFLO channels promises to be delivered in a familiar and easy-to-use format.

With MediaFLO, each wireless device requires a receiver and circuitry capable of receiving the 700MHz band in addition to traditional transceivers on the 850MHz and 1,900MHz bands (in the United States). Of course, we anticipate that such devices will be available shortly. Being based on the 700MHz band, MediaFLO has better coverage than the 850MHz or 1,900MHz bands. The fact that it is an outbound-only system means that it requires fewer 700MHz transmitters to cover the United States than do standard wireless two-way systems. According to Qualcomm's estimates, MediaFLO will be able to provide nationwide coverage with 30 to 50 times fewer transmitter sites, which represents a huge savings in building the system.

Designed as an end-to-end solution, MediaFLO has given consideration to everything needed to make the system work, including the MediaFLO content distribution system, program guides that will be available to customers, a billing system, and the 700MHz channels over which the content will be delivered. MediaFLO is scheduled to go live in the United States in 2006. Qualcomm says that it will require about $800 million to build the system, some of which may come from third parties. It is likely that the system will be built on a city-by-city basis. MediaFLO could be deployed today in some areas of the country where UHF-TV channels 54, 55, and 56 are not in use. As the UHF-TV stations on these channels are turned off or moved in other cities, MediaFLO can be brought online.

■ Mobile Content

While voice revenues still dominate in all markets, operators worldwide are placing increased emphasis on content and data services as the drivers of their future growth. Traditional media companies see mobile as an attractive source of revenue and are also looking to extend their audience base to mobile subscribers. As a result, cellular companies and content providers are learning to work together. Major music labels, movie studios, and TV broadcasters in Europe, the United States, and Asia have set up mobile development arms. Most major game manufacturers have also developed mobile versions of their leading titles.

As discussed earlier in this chapter, the simple mobile phone is morphing into a futuristic entertainment system and the most exciting new technology platform since the Internet. As of March 2006, there were more than 1 billion mobile subscribers worldwide, which means there were at least that many mobile devices in use, compared to 690 million PCs and laptops. Entertainment giants and newly inspired entrepreneurs are rushing to develop songs, graphics, games, and videos to populate millions of tiny screens on the new "superphones."

Mobile is the fourth screen, after movies, TV, and the PC. Whereas production costs for a big-budget film run about US$1 million per minute, production costs for the mobile world range from US$2,000 to US$8,000 per minute. Some call the mobile phone the most exciting software platform in history. After all, mobile has become an essential part of daily life around the world. There is content for everyone—commuters, cooks, children, adults, sports enthusiasts, navigators, mothers, gamblers, poets, gardeners, musicians, game players, romantics, and so on; the list is as endless as imagination.

Currently the major drivers for mobile content come from the entertainment industry. The following are some examples:

■ MTV (www.mtv.com) is working with operators and content aggregators to deliver SMS- and MMS-based applications to consumers. Applications include VJ recorded messages; exclusive MTV content such as ringtones, logos, news and updates, and picture downloads; and, in the future, streaming video of artist sessions.

- Time Warner's Turner (www.turner.com) is enabling its millions of NASCAR fans to follow each of NASCAR's 36 races per season live on mobile devices.

- Disney (www.disney.com), which sells 6,000 items through 48 carriers in 27 countries, sees the mobile phone as a marketing tool, a new form of advertising. With releases of new movies, Disney offers downloadable ringtones, images, and games.

- Match.com (www.match.com) and MyCupid (www.ideas.singtel.com/dating/i_wap.jsp) let you flirt anytime, anywhere.

- Vindigo (www.vindingo.com) provides movie reviews and lets you buy tickets and book restaurants. It also offers a bathroom finder service that ranks the nearest public toilets by cleanliness.

- Picsel Technologies (www.picsel.com) lets you download PowerPoint files and other attachments to your phone. You plug the mobile into a projector via a USB port and let the show go on.

- "Adult" content is anticipated to produce gigantic revenues on mobile devices, even as it does currently on the Internet.

The rapid growth in mobile communications is having an enormous impact on both national economies and societies. Penetration levels are high around the world—and rising. As new mobile data services are introduced, we are seeing a paradigm shift. Some of the key challenges to deal with include the following:

- **Interoperability**—There is an urgent need for the industry to improve the interoperability of mobile broadband services.

- **Value-added content**—The creation of high-value content is mandatory, and there needs to be a regulatory framework for intellectual property rights.

- **E-payments**—As the volume of mobile payments begins to grow, rules governing the use of "e-money" are required.

- **Base stations and masts**—Each country must address any regulatory barriers and take action to ensure the growth of wireless broadband services.

- **Spectrum policy**—Efforts need to be coordinated across regions and ultimately globally to ensure availability and flexible usage.

The many challenges ahead need to be addressed by supporting targeted R&D, supplementing basic research, and accelerating technical innovation.

Glossary

Numerals

1G (first-generation) wireless The first generation of wireless communication, which is characterized by analog transmission systems. Key 1G standards included AMPS, TACS, JTACS, and NMT.

10BASE2 Thin coax Ethernet cable.

10BASE5 Thick coax Ethernet cable.

10BASE-FL Two strands of multimode optical fiber Ethernet cable.

10BASE-T 2-pair UTP Ethernet cable.

10GigE (10 Gigabit Ethernet) An Ethernet standard that supports a data rate of 10Gbps. Sometimes referred to as 10Gbps Ethernet.

100BASE-FX Two strands of multimode optical fiber Fast Ethernet cable.

100BASE-T2 2-pair Cat 3 UTP Fast Ethernet cable.

100BASE-T4 4-pair Cat 3 UTP Fast Ethernet cable.

100BASE-TX 2-pair Cat 5 UTP Fast Ethernet cable.

1000BASE-CX Coax patch cable/Gigabit Ethernet cable.

1000BASE-LX Long-wavelength single-mode optical fiber Gigabit Ethernet cable.

1000BASE-SX Short-wavelength multimode optical fiber Gigabit Ethernet cable.

1000BASE-T 4-pair Cat 5 or Cat 5e UTP Gigabit Ethernet cable.

1000BASE-TX 2-pair Cat 6 (currently a TIA draft proposal) Gigabit Ethernet cable.

2B1Q (2 Binary 1 Quaternary) A single-carrier modulation scheme that provides for 2 bits/Hz and is used in ISDN, HDSL, and IDSL.

2G (second-generation) wireless The second generation of wireless communication, which introduced digital transmission and includes digital cellular and PCS systems, such as TDMA (ANSI-136), GSM, and IS-95.

2.5G (2.5-generation) wireless The generation of wireless communication between 2G and 3G, which offers enhancements to the data services on existing second-generation digital platforms. 2.5G can support faster data rates, ranging from 64Kbps to 384Kbps, depending on the standard and the technology.

23B+D The North American and Japanese infrastructure for PRI, which provides 23 64Kbps B-channels for information and 1 64Kbps D-channel for signaling and additional packet data.

3DES (Triple DES) A 168-bit encryption technique that uses three 56-bit keys. 3DES applies the DES algorithm to a plaintext block three times.

3G (third-generation) wireless The third generation of wireless communication, which includes digital transmission; it also permits per-user and terminal mobility by providing a single mobile communication service, adjusted for broadband applications (including voice, data, and multimedia streams), that will support higher data speeds, 2Mbps, with the objective of ultimately supporting up to 155Mbps.

3.5G (3.5-generation) wireless An intermediate third generation of wireless technology after 3G, which is introducing enhancements designed for services running over an IP backbone, including high-speed data and video. Key 3.5G standards include HSDPA, HSUPA, and HSOPA. 3.5G will offer data speeds up to 10Mbps and possibly up to 20Mbps.

3GPP (3G Partnership Project) A group formed in 1998, under the ETSI, to make a globally applicable 3G mobile phone system specification within the scope of the ITU's IMT-2000 project.

3GPP2 (3G Partnership Project 2) A group formed when ETSI refused to expand the scope of 3GPP to address CDMA2000. ANSI formed 3GPP2 to coordinate CDMA2000 developments.

30B+D The ITU infrastructure for PRI, which provides 30 64Kbps B-channels and 1 64Kbps D-channel.

4G (fourth-generation) wireless The fourth generation of wireless communication, which will support a wide range of data rates, promising a maximum of 50Mbps to 100Mbps while moving and an average of 20Mbps and up to 1Gbps while standing still. The two key technologies involved with 4G are OFDM and MIMO.

5G (fifth-generation) wireless The fifth generation of wireless communication, which will enable fast downloads of large chunks of data across the Internet and will support advanced multimedia applications, such as teleimmersion, virtual reality, and telerobotics.

6bone An experimental network used as an environment for IPv6 research. More than 1,173 networks in some 60 countries were connected to the 6bone IPv6 network. 6bone ceased to operate in 2006, and IANA reclaimed all 6bone prefixes.

6to4   A technique for enabling IPv4-to-IPv6 interworking and coexistence that interconnects IPv6 networks over IPv4 networks without explicitly defined tunnels.

8-PSK (eight phase-shift keying)   A PSK modulation scheme in which 3 bits at a time are encoded.

A

A (access) link   A link that interconnects an STP with either an SSP or an SCP. The SSP and SCP, collectively, are referred to as the signaling endpoints. A message sent to and from the SSPs or SCPs first goes to its home STP, which in turn processes or routes the message.

AAA (authentication, authorization, and accounting)   A network server used for access control. Authentication identifies the user, authorization implements policies that determine which resources and services a valid user may access, and accounting keeps track of time and data resources used for billing and analysis.

AAL (ATM adaptation layer)   The ATM layer that is responsible for the adaptation of the information of the higher layer to the ATM cells. It is composed of two layers, the Segmentation and Reassembly sublayer and the Convergence sublayer. ATM adaptation layer 1 supports CBR voice and video network services. ATM adaptation layer 2 supports VBR voice and video network services. ATM adaptation layer 3 supports VBR connection-oriented data services. ATM adaptation layer 4 supports VBR connectionless data services. ATM adaptation layer 5 supports connectionless VBR data (e.g., IP or signaling) over ATM. The native stream (whether it's real-time, analog, voice, MPEG-2 compressed video, or TCP/IP) goes through the AAL, where it is segmented into 48-byte cells.

ABR (available bit rate)   One of the ATM service classes. ABR supports VBR data traffic with average and peak traffic parameters (e.g., LAN interconnection and internetworking services, LAN emulation, critical data transfer that requires service guarantees). Remote procedure calls, distributed file services, and computer process swapping and paging are examples of applications that would be appropriate for ABR.

access charge   A cost assessed to interexchange carriers for access to the local exchange network.

access concentrator   A device that can be used to concentrate local subscriber lines and multiplex them over high-speed transport to another point in the network, creating a virtual POP.

access line   A connection from the customer to the local telephone company for access to the PSTN, also known as the local loop; can also refer to the connection between the serving toll exchange and the serving office of the interexchange carrier used to access PSTN transport services.

ACK (acknowledge character)   A transmission control character transmitted by a station as an affirmative response to the station with which a connection has been set up. An acknowledge character may also be used as an accuracy control character.

adaptive equalization   Line equalization, sometimes known as impedance equalization, used for optimizing signal transmission to adapt to changing line characteristics.

adaptive routing   Routing that automatically adjusts to network changes such as traffic pattern changes or failures.

address   (1) A coded representation of the destination of data, as well as of its source. Multiple terminals on one communications line, for example, must each have a unique address. (2) A group of digits that makes up a telephone number. Also known as the called number. (3) In software, a location that can be specifically referred to in a program. (4) A name, label, or number that identifies a location in storage, a device in a network, or any other data source.

address signals   Signals that carry information that has to do with the number dialed, which essentially consists of country codes, city codes, area codes, prefixes, and the subscriber number.

ADM (add/drop multiplexer)   A device that facilitates easy dropping and adding of payload by converting one or more lower-level signals, such as T-1 or E-1 signals, to and from one of the optical carrier levels.

administrative domain   A collection of hosts, routers, and networks governed by a single administrative authority.

ADPCM (Adaptive Differential Pulse Code Modulation)   An encoding technique, standardized by the ITU-T, that allows analog voice signals to be carried on a 32Kbps digital channel. The voice input is samples at 8KHz with 4 bits used to describe the difference between adjacent samples.

ADSL (Asymmetrical Digital Subscriber Line)   A technology for supporting high bandwidth over conventional twisted-pair local loop lines that enables subscribers to access multimedia-based applications such as video-on-demand. ADSL supports a downstream channel of up to 7Mbps, with an upstream channel of up to 800Kbps.

ADSL2   A technology standardized under ITU G.992.1 that supports a downstream channel of up to 12Mbps and an upstream channel of up to 1Mbps.

ADSL2+   A technology standardized under ITU G.992.5 that supports a downstream channel of up to 24Mbps and an upstream channel of up to 1Mbps.

ADSL2-RE   A reach-extended version of the ADSL2 specification that is standardized under ITU G.992.3. ADSL2-RE allows DSL systems to reach up to 3.75 miles (6 km). While it can support up to 8Mbps downstream and 1Mbps upstream, when taking advantage of its main feature, ADSL2-RE extends a 768Kbps downstream service by approximately 0.5 mile (1 km), to 3.5 miles (5.5 km).

AES (Advanced Encryption Standard)   An encryption algorithm for securing sensitive material, both unclassified and classified, by U.S. government agencies; replaces the previously sanctioned standard, DES. It may eventually become the de facto encryption standard for commercial transactions in the private sector. AES uses the Rijndael algorithm to specify three key lengths—128 bits, 192 bits, and 256 bits.

agent   Software that processes queries and sends responses on behalf of an application.

agnostic device   A device that supports multiple data protocols (e.g., IP, Frame Relay, ATM, MPLS) and supports multiple traffic types, such as voice, data, and video.

AIN (advanced intelligent network)   The second generation of intelligent networks, pioneered by Bellcore (which is now Telcordia). An AIN is a service-independent network architecture that enables carriers to create and uniformly support telecom services and features via a common architectural platform, with the objective of allowing for rapid creation of customizable telecommunication services.

AIP (application infrastructure provider)   A provider that manages the data center servers, databases, switches, and other gears on which applications run.

air interface   A term used in mobile communications to refer to the radio frequency portion of the circuit between the mobile station and the base station.

A-law encoding   Encoding, according to ITU-T Recommendation G.711, that is used with European 30-channel PCM systems that comply with ITU-T Recommendation G.732. It employs nonuniform quantization to obtain the desired compression characteristic.

alerting signals   The ringing tones, busy tones, and any specific busy alerts used to indicate network congestion or unavailability.

alternate routing   Routing of a call or message over a substitute route when an established route has failed, is busy, or is otherwise unavailable for immediate use.

AM (amplitude modulation)   Varying of a carrier signal's strength (amplitude) depending on whether the information being transmitted is a 1 bit or a 0 bit.

ambient noise   Communications interference that is present in a signal path at all times.

AMC (Adaptive Modulation and Coding)   A technique used in HSDPA that allows the modulation and coding schemes to be determined dynamically, depending on the conditions of the wireless channel at that time.

AMI (alternate mark inversion)   An encoding method used with Dataphone Digital Service, the oldest data service still in use, which uses 64Kbps channels. AMI requires the use of 8Kbps of the 64Kbps of each channel to maintain synchronization, which means that in reality only 56Kbps is available for data transmission. The signal carrying the binary value alternates between positive and negative polarities; 0 and 1 values are represented by the signal amplitude at either polarity; no-value "spaces" are at 0 amplitude. Also called bipolar.

amplifier   A device that boosts an attenuated signal back up to its original power level so that it can continue to make its way across the network.

amplitude   A measure of the height of a wave, which indicates the strength of the signal.

AMPS (Advanced Mobile Phone System)   A standard for analog telephony that is deployed widely in the United States.

analog   A signal that varies continuously (e.g., sound waves), along two parameters: amplitude (strength) and frequency (tone). The unit of measurement is the Hertz (Hz), or cycle per second.

analog loopback   A technique for testing transmission equipment and devices that isolates faults to the analog signal receiving or transmitting circuitry, and a device, such as a modem, echoes back a received (test) signal that is then compared with the original signal.

ANI (automatic number identification)   A feature, often associated with SS7, that passes a caller's telephone number over the network to the receiver so that the caller can be identified. Also referred to as caller ID.

ANSI (American National Standards Institute)   A standards-forming body affiliated with the ISO that develops U.S. standards for transmission codes, protocols, media, and high-level languages, among other things.

ANSI X12   A U.S. standard for electronic data interchange.

answer signal   A supervisory signal (usually in the form of a closed loop) from the called telephone to the exchange and back to the calling telephone (usually in the form of a reverse battery) when the called number answers.

anycast   In IP routing, the point-to-point flow of packets between a single client and the nearest destination server identified by an anycast address. Anycast involves a one-to-many association in which each destination address identifies a group of receivers; at any given time, only one of them is chosen to receive information from any given sender.

AODV (Ad Hoc, On Demand, Distance Vector)   The leading protocol for routing data across wireless mesh networks. It is designed with mobile wireless devices in mind. It is in the public domain and is therefore subject to no copyright protection.

API (application programming interface)   A set of routines that an application program uses to request and carry out low-level services performed by the operating system.

AppleTalk   Apple Computer's set of specifications for connecting computers and other devices to share information over LANs. It describes network hardware, software, and protocols and lets an assortment of Mac and non-Mac devices communicate over a variety of transceivers and communications media.

application   (1) Software with which the user interacts. (2) The use to which a system is put (e.g., e-mail, videoconferencing, high-speed data access, network management).

application layer   Layer 7 of the OSI model, which enables users to transfer files, send e-mail, and perform other functions that involve interaction with network components and services.

application-layer multicasting   A technique that ensures that just one stream goes across the backbone whenever possible.

application program   A software program that contains no I/O coding (except in the form of macro instructions that transfer control to the supervisory programs) and is usually unique to one type of application.

architecture   The physical interrelationship between the components of a computer or a network.

area code   A three-digit code designating a toll center that is not in the NPA of the calling party.

area code restriction   The capability of switching equipment to selectively identify three-digit area codes and to either permit or deny passage of long-distance calls to those specific area codes.

ARP (Address Resolution Protocol)   A protocol that determines the physical address of a node, given that node's IP address. ARP is the mapping link between IP addresses and the MAC address.

ARQ (automatic repeat request)　　An error control technique that requires retransmission of a data block that contains detected errors. A special form, called "go-back-n," allows multiple blocks to be acknowledged with a single response. "Stop and wait" requires an acknowledgment after each block.

artificial intelligence　　The capability of a computer to perform functions associated with human logic such as reasoning, learning, and self-improvement.

ASCII (American Standard Code for Information Interchange)　　The code developed by ANSI for information interchange among data-processing systems, data communications systems, and associated equipment. The ASCII character set consists of 7-bit coded characters (8 bits, including the parity bit), providing 128 possible characters. The ASCII character set consists of 34 control codes and 94 text characters, including the letters of the alphabet in both upper- and lowercase, the 10 digits, and a number of special characters.

ASIC (application-specific integrated circuit)　　An integrated circuit that is customized for a particular use (e.g., to run a mobile phone), rather than intended for general-purpose use.

ASON (Automatic Switched Optical Network)　　ANSI specification ITU G.8080, which describes a network based on a technology that enables the automatic delivery of transport services. ASON describes the set of control-plane components used to manipulate transport network resources in order to provide the functionality of setting up, maintaining, and releasing connections.

ASP (application service provider)　　A supplier that makes applications available on a subscription basis.

aspect ratio　　The horizontal:vertical size ratio used for television. Traditional television has an aspect ratio of 4:3, and DTV has a 16:9 aspect ratio, which more closely resembles human vision.

ASTN (Automatic Switched Transport Network)　　ANSI specification ITU G.807, which describes a network that allows traffic paths to be set up automatically through a switched network. ASTN allows the user to specify the start point, endpoint, and bandwidth required.

asynchronous　　(1) Occurring without a regular or predictable time relationship to a specified event. (2) In data communications, a method of transmission in which the bits representing a character are preceded by a start bit and followed by a stop bit, which are used to separate the characters and to synchronize the receiving with the transmitting station. It does not use a regular time relationship between the sending and receiving devices.

asynchronous transmission　　A transmission in which each information character, or sometimes each word or small block, is individually synchronized, usually by the use of start and stop elements. Also called start–stop transmission.

ATM (Asynchronous Transfer Mode)　　An international packet-switching standard that uses a cell-based approach in which each packet of information features a uniform cell size of 53 bytes. ATM is a high-bandwidth, fast packet-switching and multiplexing technique that allows the seamless end-to-end transmission of voice, data, image, and video traffic. It is a high-capacity, low-latency switching fabric that is adaptable for multiservice and multirate connections and offers an architected approach to QoS.

ATM layer   A layer that performs four main functions: multiplexing and demultiplexing of cells of different connections, translation at ATM switches and cross-connects, cell header extraction or addition before or after a cell is delivered to or from the adaptation layer, and flow control.

ATM physical layer   A layer that is composed of two sublayers: Physical Medium, which supports pure medium-dependent functions, and Transmission Convergence, which converts the ATM cell stream into bits to be transported over the physical medium.

ATM reassembly   Restructuring of data units from information contained in cells.

ATM segmentation   Parsing of the information units of the higher layers into ATM cells.

ATSC (Advanced Television Systems Committee)   An organization that establishes voluntary technical standards for advanced television systems, including DTV.

attenuation   A decrease in the power of a received signal due to loss through lines, equipment, or other transmission devices. It is usually measured in decibels.

audible ringing tone   A tone received by the calling telephone indicating that the called telephone is being rung (formerly called ringback tone).

audio frequencies   Frequencies that correspond to those that can be heard by the human ear (usually 30Hz to 20,000Hz).

AUI (attachment unit interface)   The connector used to attach a device to an Ethernet transceiver.

authentication   A technique that enables the receiver to automatically identify and reject messages that have been altered deliberately or by channel errors. Authentication also can be used to provide positive identification of the sender of a message.

autonomous system   A collection of TCP/IP gateways and networks that fall under one administrative entity and cooperate closely to propagate network reachability (and routing) information among themselves, using an interior gateway protocol. Sometimes abbreviated AS.

B

B8ZS (bipolar 8-zero substitution)   An encoding method used on T-1 circuits (in the United States and Japan) that inserts two successive ones of the same voltage into a signal whenever eight consecutive zeros are transmitted. B8ZS is not compatible with older AMI equipment. In Europe, E-1 uses the encoding scheme HDB3 instead of B8ZS. Also called binary 8-zero substitution, clear channel, and clear 64.

B (bidirectional) frame   The part of the MPEG video compression process in which both past and future pictures/frames are used as references. B frames typically result in the most compression.

B/D link (bridge/diagonal link)   A link that interconnects two mated pairs of STP. It carries signaling messages beyond the initial point of entry to the signaling network, toward the intended destination.

backbone   A central network that connects several other, usually lower-bandwidth, networks so that those networks can pass data to each other. The backbone network is usually composed of a high-capacity communications medium, such as fiber optics or microwave.

backhaul   The practice of routing telecommunications traffic beyond its intended destination and then back to the intended destination, usually to take advantage of tariffs or prices that are lower than those afforded by direct routing. In telecommunications, the term has evolved into a more generic meaning used to define a way to get data to a point from which it can be distributed over a network. In satellite technology, *backhaul* means to transmit data to a point from which it can be uplinked to a satellite. In the context of broadcast TV, *backhaul* refers to program content that is transmitted to a TV station or receiving entity, where it will be integrated into a finished show.

backplane   The board that contains a bus.

backup   The provision of facilities, logical or physical, to speed the process of restart and recovery following failure.

backup copy   A copy of information, usually on a floppy disk, zip disk, or CD-ROM, that is kept and can be used if the original information is lost or destroyed.

bandpass filter   A circuit that is designed to allow a single band of frequencies to pass, neither of the cutoff frequencies being zero or infinity.

bandwidth   The transmission capacity of a telecommunications pathway, electronic or optical. Bandwidth refers to the range of frequencies, expressed in Hertz (Hz), that comprise a given transmission channel; in other words, it is the difference between the lowest and highest frequencies carried on the channel. The bandwidth determines the rate at which information can be transmitted through a circuit. The greater the bandwidth, the more data that can be carried, and in digital facilities, bandwidth is expressed in bits per second.

bandwidth efficiency   The efficiency with which a radio signal can be encoded and, therefore, how many bits per second can be carried on one cycle of radio bandwidth.

bandwidth exchange   An organization or a facility that functions as an exchange where bandwidth is the commodity. Some exchanges bring together buyers and sellers of bandwidth and facilitate contract negotiations and transactions; other exchanges actually switch traffic in real-time based on changes in bandwidth prices throughout the course of the day.

bandwidth-on-demand   A concept in wide area networking in which the user can access additional WAN bandwidth as the application warrants. It enables users to pay for only the bandwidth they use, when they use it.

Barker Code   An 11-bit chipping code. The 1 bits are encoded as a particular sequence of 1s and 0s, and the 0 bits are the inverse of that sequence.

base station controller   An intermediate device in the cellular system that controls a group of base-station transceivers.

baseband signaling   Transmission of a digital signal without any additional modulation, or conversion. The term is typically used to refer to the pure digital side of a circuit when the other side is broadband, or frequency based, which means that the signal is modulated.

batch processing   A processing method in which a program or programs process data with little or no operator interaction.

baud   The signaling rate of a transmission line, which refers to the number of transitions (voltage or frequency changes) made per second. The term is often confused with the number of bits per second that can be supported. At very low speeds and with modulation schemes, there is 1 bit per baud, so the number of baud can equal the number of bits per second. However, modern devices, using more efficient modulation schemes, carry multiple bits per signal; for example, with 64-QAM, there are 6 bits per baud, resulting in higher-speed transmissions.

Baudot code   A data code that uses a 5-bit structure and was used on vintage teleprinters (e.g., Telex).

BcN (Broadband Convergence Network)   An ETRI initiative designed to provide Internet access at speeds of 50Mbps to 100Mbps, about 50 times faster than current conventional services, with nationwide Korean coverage.

beacon frame   A frame sent by a token-ring adapter indicating that it has detected a serious problem. An adapter sending such frames is said to be *beaconing*.

BECN (backward explicit congestion notification)   A bit field in a Frame Relay header that the network uses to inform the transmitter of network congestion and the need to initiate a congestion avoidance procedure.

BER (bit error rate)   In data communications testing, the ratio between the total number of bits transmitted in a given message and the number of bits in that message received in error. The BER is a measure of the quality of a data transmission, usually expressed as number as a power of 10 (e.g., 1 bit error in 10^5 bits transmitted, or 1 in 100,000).

best-effort QoS   QoS that is not guaranteed but is as good as possible under the circumstances.

beta test   The stage at which a new product is tested under actual usage conditions.

Beyond 3G   An enhancement to 3G that involves today's 3G technologies but supports bandwidths greater than 5MHz and adds smarter and more efficient IP-based back-end infrastructure and additional one-way or two-way airlinks to provide further capabilities. Also referred to as Super 3G and Ultra 3G.

BFWA (broadband fixed wireless access)   A wireless broadband technology that offers high capacity. There are two categories of BFWA standards: high-frequency BFWA (which is focused on broadband services, including real-time video, streaming video, and video transfer and operates on frequencies above 25GHz) and low-frequency BFWA (which is used mainly for data communications and operates on frequencies between 2GHz and 11GHz).

BGP (Border Gateway Protocol)   A gateway protocol that allows routers to communicate with each other. BGP is an exterior routing protocol used between autonomous systems and is of concern to service providers and other large or complex organizations. BGP4, the latest version of BGP, provides mechanisms for supporting (CIDR) and allowing aggregation of routes, including aggregation of autonomous system paths.

BGP MPLS VPN   As described in RFC 2547, a VPN in which BGP is used to distribute VPN routing information across the provider's backbone and MPLS is used to forward VPN traffic from one VPN site to another.

binary   A base-two system of numbers; the binary digits are 0 and 1.

bipolar   The predominant signaling method used for digital transmission services, such as DDS and T-1, in which the signal carrying the binary values successfully alternates between positive and negative polarities. The 1 values are represented by the signal amplitude at either polarity, and no-value "spaces" are at 0 amplitude.

bipolar violation   An encoding method used on T-1 circuits that inserts two successive 1s of the same voltage. The device receiving the signal interprets the bipolar violation as a timing mark, which keeps the transmitting and receiving devices synchronized.

B-ISDN (Broadband ISDN)   A standard that was envisioned for use with advanced applications. SDH/SONET and ATM were both born out of the B-ISDN standard and a desire to deliver advanced applications.

bit   The smallest unit of information in a digital device. In binary notation, a bit is either the character 0 or the character 1.

bit duration   The time it takes an encoded bit to pass a point on the transmission medium. In serial communications, a relative unit of time measurement used for comparison of delay times, where the data rate of a transmission channel can vary.

bit errors   Missing video elements, synchronization problems, or complete loss of picture.

bitmap   A pixel-by-pixel description of an image in which each pixel is a separate element.

bit-oriented protocol   A communications protocol or transmission procedure in which control information in encoded in fields of one or more bits.

bit rate   The speed at which bits are transmitted, usually expressed in bits per second (bps).

blocking   A network in which there are connection sets that prevent some additional desired connections from being set up between unused ports, even with rearrangement of existing connections.

Blowfish   A 64-bit block code that has key lengths of 32 to 448 bits. Blowfish is used in more than 100 products, and it is viewed as one of the best available encryption algorithms.

Bluetooth   A WPAN technology that is an open standard for short-range transmission of digital voice and data that supports point-to-point and multipoint applications, providing up to 720Kbps data transfer with a range of 33 feet (10 m) and up to 330 feet (100 m) with a power boost. A Bluetooth chip is a very low-cost chip that gives a device short-range wireless capability. PDAs, laptops, mobile phones, and other intelligent appliances embedded with Bluetooth chips can communicate and link with each other wirelessly.

BNC connector   A commonly used plug and socket that provides a tight connection for audio, video, and networking applications. Thinnet uses BNC connectors.

board   A circuit card on which integrated circuits are mounted.

BPL (broadband over powerlines)   Another term for PLT.

bps (bits per second)   A measure of the data transfer rate possible on a digital communications line. For example, a 10Gbps backbone can support 10 billion bits per second. Bytes are used as a measure of storage, so a 10GB hard drive is not the same thing as a 10Gbps communications link. The abbreviation Kbps is used for thousands of bits per second; Mbps is used for millions of bits per second; Gbps is used for billions of bits per second; Tbps is used for trillions of bits per second; Pbps is used for 1,000Tbps; and Ebps is used for 1 billion Gbps.

BPSK (Binary Phase-Shift Keying)   The simplest and most robust form of PSK. BPSK uses a 180-degree phase shift and is a good solution under noisy conditions.

BRAN (Broadband-Compliant Radio Access Networks)   An ETSI technical committee for broadband radio access networks. BRAN is responsible for all aspects of standardization for present and future broadband radio access networks, using both existing and emerging technologies. BRAN's three main standards areas are HiperLAN, HiperAccess, and HiperMAN.

BRI (Basic Rate Interface)   In ISDN, the interface to the basic rate, which is 2B+D: two 64Kbps information-carrying channels plus one 16Kbps signaling channel. Also called Basic Rate Access (BRA).

bridge   An attaching device that connects two LAN segments to allow the transfer of information from one LAN segment to the other. Bridges operate by filtering packets according to their destination addresses. Most bridges automatically learn where these addresses are located and, thus, are called *learning bridges*. A bridge works at OSI Layer 2 and is transparent to upper-layer devices and protocols.

broadband   A method of transmitting data, voice, and video by using FDM, as with cable TV. Modems are required to modulate digital data streams onto the channel. Broadband in this context is used in contrast with *baseband*, which is all-digital transmission and uses TDM. In simple terms, broadband refers to a multichannel, high-bandwidth transmission line. According to the ITU-T, broadband means any transmission rate over 2Mbps. The most common use of the term today is to refer to a channel capable of high-speed transmission. The term is often used to refer to Internet access via cable modems, DSL, fiber options, and wireless alternatives, all of which are much faster than dialup.

broadcast   A transmission to multiple receiving locations simultaneously. A broadcast can be made, for example, over a multipoint line to all terminals that share the line or over a radio or television channel to all receivers tuned to that channel.

broadcast storm   A pathological network condition in which an increasing and insupportable number of broadcast packets are generated.

brouter   A device that can transparently bridge protocols as well as route them. It is a hybrid of a bridge and a router.

brownout operation   An operation in response to heavy demand, in which main system voltages are lowered and power is reduced but not lost. Although conventional networking equipment is relatively immune to brownouts, the computer controlling the system is very sensitive to voltage variations and could fail under these conditions. Most equipment today has the capability to cope with these reductions, or a heavy-duty power supply or UPS can be furnished.

BSC (Binary Synchronous Communications)   A half-duplex, character-oriented data communications protocol originated by IBM in 1964. It includes control characters and procedures for controlling the establishment of a valid connection and the transfer of data. Also called bisync.

buffer   A storage device used to compensate for a difference in rate of data flow, or time of occurrence events, when transmitting data from one device to another.

buffered network   A real-time store-and-forward message-switching network, with computers at the switching points that act as buffers for the packets.

buffered repeater   A hybrid device of a repeater and a bridge. Entire packets are received and retransmitted (as with a bridge), but no address filtering is implemented (as with a repeater).

bundled   A pricing strategy in which a service provider or manufacturer includes all products—hardware, software, services, training, and the like—in a single price.

burst   In data communications, a sequence of signals counted as one unit in accordance with some specific criterion or measure.

burst switching   A switching method for switching digitized voice and data characters in an integrated fashion.

bus   (1) A physical transmission path or channel. A bus is typically an electric connection, with one or more conductors, wherein all attached devices receive all transmissions at the same time. (2) A LAN topology, such as that used in Ethernet and token bus, in which all network nodes listen to all transmissions and select certain ones based on address identification. A bus involves some type of contention control mechanism for accessing the bus transmission medium.

bus topology   A network architecture in which all the nodes are connected to a shared cable.

bypass   To establish a communications link without using the facilities of the local exchange carrier (e.g., the telephone company).

byte   The amount of storage required to represent one alphanumeric character, or 8 bits. Bytes are used as a measure of storage, as in a 2GB hard drive. This is different from the measurement for transmission capacity, which is expressed in bits per second (e.g., a 10Gbps backbone).

C

C7 (Common Channel Signaling 7)   A signaling protocol specified by the ITU-T and used in high-speed digital networks to provide communication between intelligent network nodes. C7 is the European equivalent of SS7. Also sometimes called CCS7, for Common Channel Signaling System 7.

C (cross) link   A link that interconnects mated STPs.

CA (certificate authority)   A trusted third-party organization that issues digital certificates used to create digital signatures and public–private key pairs. The CA guarantees that the individual granted the unique certificate is, in fact, who he or she claims to be.

cable modem   A device designed to operate over cable TV networks to provide high-speed access to the Internet.

CableHome   A CableLabs HAN standard. The CableHome 1.1 specification includes gateway security features; standardized prioritized QoS for HANs; support for home servers, teleworkers, and home offices; simple parental control; and LAN management messaging and LAN IP statistics monitoring.

CableLabs   A nonprofit research and development consortium that is dedicated to helping its cable operator members integrate new cable telecommunications technologies into their business objectives. CableLabs has developed industry specifications such as DOCSIS, OpenCable, PacketCable, VOD Metadata, and CableHome.

call processing   A sequence of operations performed by a switching system from the acceptance of an incoming call through the final disposition of the call.

campus network   A network that connects LANs from multiple departments in a single building or campus. Campus networks are LANs; although they may span several miles, they do not include WAN services.

CAP (Carrierless Amplitude Phase Modulation)   A single-carrier modulation scheme used in early deployments of ADSL.

carrier frequency   The frequency of the carrier wave that is modulated to transmit signals.

carrier system   A means of obtaining a number of channels over a single path by modulating each channel on a different carrier frequency and demodulating at the receiving point to restore the signals to their original frequency.

Cat 1 (Category 1) UTP   An EIA/TIA 568 standard for commercial building telecommunications wiring. This old-style UTP telephone cable is unsuitable for data transmission.

Cat 2 (Category 2) UTP   An EIA/TIA 568 standard of cable that can be used for data rates up to 4Mbps.

Cat 3 (Category 3) UTP   An EIA/TIA 568 standard of cable that can be used for data rates up to 10Mbps. This is the minimum cable requirement for 10BASE-T.

Cat 4 (Category 4) UTP   An EIA/TIA 568 standard of cable that can be used as the lowest-grade UTP, acceptable for data rates up to 16Mbps (token ring).

Cat 5 (Category 5) UTP   An EIA/TIA 568 standard of cable that can be used for data rates up to 100Mbps.

Cat 5e (Category 5e) UTP   An EIA/TIA 568 standard of cable that provides performance of up to 125MHz and is frequently used for 1000BASE-T Gigabit Ethernet.

Cat 6 (Category 6) UTP   An EIA/TIA 568 standard of cable that provides performance of up to 400MHz, more than double that of Category 5 and 5e, and is used for 10BASE-T/100BASE-TX and 1000BASE-T (Gigabit Ethernet) connections.

Cat 7 (Category 7) UTP   An emerging category of cable that is expected to operate up to 600MHz and will use STP or ScTP.

CATV (community antenna television)   Signals that can be received at a selected site by sensitive, directional antennas and then transmitted to subscribers via a cable network. Additional channels, not normally available in that area, can also be transmitted. Traditional analog CATV is based on RF transmission, generally using 75-ohm coaxial cable as the transmission medium. CATV offers multiple frequency-divided channels, allowing mixed transmissions to be carried simultaneously.

C-band   A portion of the electromagnetic spectrum, approximately 4GHz to 6GHz, that is used primarily for satellite and microwave transmission.

CBQ (Class-Based Queuing)   A fully open, nonproprietary technology that brings bandwidth-controlled CoS to IP network infrastructures. It allows traffic to be prioritized according to IP application type, IP address, protocol type, and other variables. It allocates unused bandwidth more effectively than other QoS mechanisms do, and it uses priority tables to give critical applications the most immediate access to unused bandwidth.

CBR (constant bit rate)   The highest ATM service class. CBR provides a constant, guaranteed rate to real-time applications such as streaming video, providing continuous bandwidth. It emulates a circuit-switched approach and is associated with minimum latencies and losses.

CCITT (Comité Consultatif International de Téléphonie et de Télégraphie)   An advisory committee to the ITU whose recommendations covering telecommunications have international influence among engineers, manufacturers, and administrators. It is now known as the ITU-T.

CCK (Complementary Code Keying)   A modulation scheme used with 802.11b WLANs. CCK was adopted to replace the Barker Code in wireless digital networks.

CCS (common-channel signaling)   An electronic means of signaling between two switching systems, independent of the voice path. The use of CCS makes possible new customer services, versatile network features, more flexible call routing, and faster connections.

CDDI (Copper-Distributed Data Interface)   A version of FDDI that runs on UTP cable rather than on fiber-optic cable.

CDM (Code Division Multiplexing)   A form of multiplexing that encodes data with a special code associated with each channel and uses the constructive interference properties of the special codes to perform the multiplexing.

CDMA (Code Division Multiple Access)   A digital cellular technology that uses spread spectrum techniques. With CDMA, every channel uses the full available spectrum, and individual conversations are encoded with a pseudorandom digital sequence or frequency-hopping schedule.

CDMA2000   A family of 3G mobile standards that use CDMA to send voice, data, and signaling data between mobile phones and cell sites. CDMA2000 devices include color displays, GPS, digital and video cameras, push-to-talk, support for streaming-type real-time VOD/audio-on-demand services, and voice recognition functions. Also known as IMT-2000 CDMA Multi-Carrier (CDMA-MC).

CDMA450   A TIA/EIA-IS-CDMA2000 (CDMA-MC) system deployed at 450MHz. CDMA450 provides a larger cell size compared to other bands, which translates to fewer cell sites and significantly lower capital and operating expenditures to service vast coverage areas.

cdmaOne   A 2G CDMA technology (IS-95) that offers data rates of 9.6Kbps to 14.4Kbps. cdmaOne describes a complete wireless system based on the TIA/EIA IS-95 CDMA standard and represents the end-to-end wireless system and all the necessary specifications that govern its operation. cdmaOne provides a family of related services, including cellular, PCS, and wireless local loop.

CDPD (Cellular Digital Packet Data)   A North American standard for transferring packet data over cellular phone channels.

CD-ROM (compact disc–read only memory)   A storage device that is used in computer systems and typically contains multimedia information.

cell   A fixed-length packet.

cell relay   A form of packet transmission used by ATM networks. Cell relay transmits 53 octet fixed-length packets over a packet-switched network. Because the cells are tiny and of fixed length, they can be processed and switched at very high speeds. ATM makes it possible to use a single transmission scheme for voice, data, and video traffic on LANs and WANs.

cellular   A communication service in which voice or data is transmitted by radio frequencies. The service area is divided into cells, each served by a transmitter. The cells are connected to a mobile switching exchange, which is connected to the worldwide telephone network.

CELP (Code-Excited Linear Prediction)   A vector-quantization-based compression scheme for speech. CELP can compress speech down to 4.8Kbps. There is also a low-end variant called LPC.

centrex   A local exchange carrier service in which switching occurs at a local exchange rather than at customer-owned PBXs. The telephone company owns and manages all the communications equipment.

CEPT (Conférence Européenne des Administrations des Postes et des Télecommunications [European Conference of Postal and Telecommunications Administrations])   An organization formed by the European PTTs for the discussion of operational and tariff matters. CEPT-0 (or E-0) is the basic increment, and it operates at 64Kbps. CEPT-1 is a 2.048Mbps 32-channel circuit; CEPT-2 is an 8.488Mbps 128-channel circuit; CEPT-3 is a 34.368Mbps 512-channel circuit; CEPT-4 is a 139.246Mbps 2,048-channel circuit; CEPT-5 is a 565.148Mbps 8,192-channel circuit.

CERN (Conseil Européen pour la Recherche Nucléaire [European Organization for Nuclear Research])   The world's largest particle physics laboratory and the birthplace of the World Wide Web.

channel   A logical conversation path. A channel is the frequency band, time slot, or wavelength (also referred to as lambda) over which a given conversation flows.

channel bank   Equipment typically used in a telephone exchange that performs multiplexing of lower-speed, digital channels into a higher-speed composite channel. The channel bank also detects and transmits signaling information for each channel and transmits framing information so that time slots allocated to each channel can be identified by the receiver.

channel capacity   The maximum data traffic that a channel can handle.

CHAP (Challenge Handshake Authentication Protocol)   A protocol that uses a three-way handshake to periodically verify the identity of the peer throughout the life of the connection. The server sends to the remote workstation a random token that is encrypted with the user's password and sent back to the server. The server performs a lookup to see if it recognizes the password. If the values match, the authentication is acknowledged; if not, the connection is terminated. A different token is provided each time a remote user dials in, which provides additional robustness.

chirped-pulse WDM   A Bell Labs system in which a specialized mode-locked laser rapidly emits very wide pulses of light. Because each part of a fiber interacts differently with varying frequencies of light, the result of chirped-pulse WDM is unequal dispersion. The pulse is stretched out when it enters the fiber, and data can be put on the discrete frequencies that emerge.

CIDR (Classless Interdomain Routing)   An IP addressing scheme that replaces the older system based on Classes A, B, and C. With CIDR, a single IP address can be used to designate many unique IP addresses. The CIDR addressing scheme is hierarchical. Large national and regional service providers are allocated large blocks of contiguous Internet addresses, which they then allocate to other smaller ISPs or directly to organizations. Networks can be divided into subnetworks, and networks can be combined into supernetworks, as long as they share a common network prefix.

CIR (committed information rate)   The amount of bandwidth that a user can expect from a Frame Relay carrier on a particular virtual circuit.

circuit   The physical path that runs between two or more points that can be used for two-way communication or to perform another specific function.

circuit grade   The data-carrying capability of a circuit. The grades of circuit are broadband, voice, subvoice, and telegraph.

circuit switching   The temporary direct connection of two or more channels between two or more points in order to provide the user with exclusive use of an open channel with which to exchange information. A discrete circuit path is set up between the incoming and outgoing lines, in contrast to message switching and packet switching, in which no such physical path is established.

cladding   In fiber-optic cable, a low-refractive-index material that surrounds the core and provides optical insulation and protection to the core.

clear-forward/clear-back signal   A signal transmitted from one end of a subscriber line or trunk, in the forward/backward direction, to indicate at the other end that the established connection should be disconnected. Also called a disconnect signal.

CLEC (competitive local exchange carrier)   A telephone company that competes with an ILEC. CLECs in the United States today focus mainly on delivering dial tone to business customers.

client   A computer that requests network or application services from a server. A client has only one user; a server is shared by many users.

client/server model   The model of interaction in a distributed system in which a program at one site sends a request to a program at another site and awaits a response. The requesting program is called a client; the program satisfying the request is called the server.

CLNP (Connectionless Network Protocol)   The OSI protocol for OSI connectionless network service. CLNP is the OSI equivalent to IP.

clocking   The use of clock pulses to control synchronization of data and control characters.

closed user group   A group of users in a network who are permitted to communicate with each other but not with users outside the group.

cluster   Two or more terminals connected to a single point or node.

cluster controller   A device that handles the remote communications processing for multiple (usually dumb) terminals or workstations.

CMIP (Common Management Information Protocol)   The OSI management information protocol for network management. CMIP is an alternative to SNMP and is not widely implemented.

CMIS (Common Management Information Services) A service interface created and standardized by the ISO for managing heterogeneous networks.

CMTS (cable modem termination system) A device on which coax trunks terminate. CMTSs are linked by a common Ethernet hub, which, in turn, feeds into the IP router, which then develops the optimum path to take over an optical backbone onto the ISP.

CO (central office) The physical location where local service providers terminate subscriber lines and locate the switching equipment that interconnects those lines. CO is used as a term in North America; elsewhere in the world, it is also referred to as a local exchange or Class 5 office.

coax (coaxial cable) A transmission medium that consists of one (sometimes more) central wire conductor, surrounded by a dielectric insulator and encased in either a wire mesh or extruded metal sheathing. There are many varieties of coax, depending on the degree of EMI shielding afforded, voltages, and frequencies accommodated.

code The conventions that specify how data may be presented in a particular system.

code character A set of conventional elements established by code to enable the transmission of a written character (letter, figure, punctuation sign, arithmetical sign, and so on) or the control of a particular function (spacing, shift, line-feed, carriage return, phase corrections, and so on).

codec (coder-decoder) A device used to convert analog signals, such as speech, music, or television, to digital form for transmission over a digital medium and back again to the original analog form. One codec is required at each end of a channel.

coding scheme A pattern of bits used to represent the characters in a character set, as well as carriage returns and other keyboard functions. Examples of coding schemes are ASCII, EBCDIC, and Unicode.

COFDM (Coded Orthogonal Frequency Division Multiplexing) A complex technique that combines OFDM with error-correcting codes, adaptive equalization, and reconfigurable modulation to provide many beneficial properties, including resistance to multipath, phase distortion, fading, and burst noise. COFDM is used in Europe and other places where the DAB standard has been adopted for digital radio broadcasting and for terrestrial DTV. It is also used in ADSL transmission.

collision Overlapping transmissions that interfere with one another. A collision occurs when two or more devices attempt to transmit at or about the same instant.

collision domain A small cluster in a LAN where collisions occur. Collision domains are used to reduce collisions throughout a network.

command A signal or group of signals that cause a computer to execute an operation or series of operations.

command-driven Programs requiring that the task to be performed be described in a special language with strict adherence to syntax.

common-battery signaling A method by which supervisory and telephone address information is sent to an exchange by depressing and releasing the switch on the cradle of the handset.

common carrier An organization in the business of providing regulated telephone, telegraph, Telex, and data communications services.

common control   An automatic switching arrangement in which the control equipment necessary for the establishment of connections is shared and is associated with a given call only during the period required to accomplish the control function.

communication adapter   A hardware feature that permits telecommunication lines to be attached to the processor.

communication line   A link (e.g., wire, telephone circuit, microwave, satellite) used to transmit data between computers and/or remote devices.

communications controller   (1) A hardware device for attaching either communication lines, ASCII devices, or a LAN to the processing unit. (2) A dedicated device with special processing capabilities for organizing and checking data and handling information traffic to and from many remote terminals or computers, including functions such as message switching. Also called a communications processor.

communications satellite   A satellite designed to act as a telecommunications radio relay and usually positioned in geosynchronous orbit 23,000 miles (35,800 km) above the equator so that it appears from earth to be stationary.

compander   A compressor at one point in a communications path for reducing the volume range of signals, followed by an expander at another point for restoring the original volume range. A compander is designed to improve the ratio of the signal to the interference entering in the path between the compressor and expander.

compression   The application of any of several techniques to reduce the number of bits required to represent information in data transmission or storage, thereby conserving bandwidth and/or memory.

compressor   An electronic device that compresses the volume range of a signal.

concatenation   (1) The linking of transmission channels (e.g., phone lines, coaxial cable, optical fiber) end to end. (2) The linking of SONET STS-1 frames in order to carry a broadband information stream.

concentrator   A device that connects a number of circuits that are not all used at once to a smaller group of circuits for economical transmission. A telephone concentrator achieves the reduction with a circuit-switching mechanism. In data communications, a multiport repeater or hub brings together the connections from multiple network nodes. Concentrators have moved past their origins as wire concentration centers and often include bridging, routing, and management devices.

conditioning   A procedure for making transmission impairments of a circuit lie within certain specified limits, typically used on telephone lines leased for data transmission to improve the possible transmission speed. Two types are used: C conditioning and D conditioning. Also called line conditioning.

configuration   The devices and programs that make up a system, subsystem, or network. The term *configuration* may refer to a hardware configuration or a software configuration.

configure   To describe to the system the devices and optional features installed on the system and describe their utilization.

connect time   The amount of time that a circuit, typically in a circuit-switched environment, is in use.

connectionless network   A network that treats each packet or datagram as a separate entity that contains the source and destination address. Connectionless services can drop packets or deliver them out of sequence, based on encountering various network conditions, such as congestion or outages.

connection-oriented network   A network in which the connection setup is performed before information transfer occurs. The path is conceived at the outset, and after the path is determined, all the subsequent information follows the same path to the destination. In a connection-oriented network, there can be some delay up front, while the connection is being set up, but because the path is predetermined, there is no delay at intermediate nodes after the connection is set up.

connectivity   A term used to describe the physical interconnections of multiple devices/ computers/networks employing similar or different technology and/or architecture together to accomplish effective communication between and among connected members involving data exchange and/or resource sharing.

contactless identification   A technology in which a smart card has an antenna embedded inside it, enabling communication with a card reader without physical contact. The chip on the smart card stores data and programs that are protected by advanced security features. Contactless smart cards are passed near an antenna, or reader, to carry out a transaction.

content delivery network   A network with delivery services that are structured specifically for a client and are focused on streaming audio, video, and media, as well as the supporting e-commerce applications.

contention   A method of line control in which the terminals request permission to transmit. If the channel in question is free, transmission proceeds; if it is not free, the terminal has to wait until it becomes free. A computer can build up a queue of contention requests; this queue can be organized in a prearranged sequence or in the sequence in which requests are made.

control character   A character inserted into a data stream for signaling the receiving station to perform a function to identify the structure of the message. Newer protocols use bit-oriented control procedures.

control network   A type of HAN network for home automation and control that is typically a low-speed powerline network. Control networks have relatively low cost and simple implementation, but they are not designed to support real-time, high-bandwidth, or mobility requirements.

control plane   An operational part of a network, including infrastructure and distributed intelligence, that executes various signaling, routing, and other control protocols (e.g., OSPF, RIP, RSVP). The control plane protocols exchange data with their peers and generate control information such as routing tables that is needed to forward data packets. Additional functions include managing user interfaces and monitoring system status and health.

control station   The station in a point-to-point or multipoint network that controls the sending and receiving of data. This station can poll or address tributary stations.

control unit   Circuitry or a device used to coordinate and control the operation of one or more I/O or storage devices and to synchronize the operation of such devices with the operation of the computer system as a whole.

controlled access unit   A managed MAU or a managed multiport siring hub for token-ring networks.

convergence   The trend for multiple network technologies and products to come together to form one network with the advantages of all the technologies and products, reducing costs and simplifying operations, administration, and management. In telecommunications, convergence can refer to network infrastructure convergence, device convergence, and applications convergence.

conversion   The process of changing from one method to another. It may refer to changing processing methods, data, or systems.

COPS (Common Open Policy Service)   An IETF query/response-based client/server protocol for supporting policy control. It addresses how servers and clients on a network exchange policy information, and it transmits information between a policy server and its clients, which are policy-aware devices such as switches.

core   The central part of a network.

CoS (class of service)   A categorization of subscribers or traffic according to priority levels. Network resources are allocated based on the CoS.

CPE (customer premises equipment)   Equipment that is located at the customer premises and is owned and managed by the customer.

CR (cognitive radio)   A forthcoming device that can seamlessly switch call and transmission modes to whatever makes the most sense, given the location at a given time, whether cellular, Wi-Fi, or VoIP. CR is a smart system in which a radio device and its antenna can adapt their spectrum use in response to their operating environment, including the radio frequency spectrum, user behavior, and network state.

CRC (cyclic redundancy check)   A powerful error-detecting technique. By using a polynomial, a series of two 8-bit block-check characters are generated that represent the entire block of data. The block-check characters are incorporated into the transmission frame and then checked at the receiving end.

CR-LDP (Constraint-Based Routed Label Distribution Protocol)   A protocol in the MPLS architecture that can set up paths to meet traffic-engineering requirements.

crossbar switch   A switch that has a crosspoint for each input/output pair, and only one contact pair needs to be closed to establish an input to output connection.

crosstalk   Interference or an unwanted signal from one transmission circuit detected on another, usually parallel, circuit.

CRTP (Compressed Real-Time Transport Protocol)   RTP compression that affects IP/UDP/RTP headers.

CSD (Circuit-Switched Data)   The original form of data transmission developed for TDMA-based mobile phone systems such as GSM.

CSMA (Carrier Sense Multiple Access)   A LAN access technique in which multiple stations connected to the same channel can sense transmission activity on that channel and defer the initiation of transmission while the channel is active. CSMA is similar to contention access.

CSMA/CA (Carrier Sense Multiple Access/Collision Avoidance)   A scheme for controlling network traffic that enables any of multiple nodes to send information over a shared network cable if the cable is free. It avoids collisions by having all nodes signal their intention to transmit before transmitting. If two nodes send intentions to transmit messages at the same time, both nodes wait for random amounts of time before trying again.

CSMA/CD (Carrier Sense Multiple Access/Collision Detection)   A LAN protocol that is a refinement of CSMA in which stations can detect the interference caused by simultaneous transmissions by two or more stations (collisions) and retransmit colliding messages in an orderly manner.

CSU (channel service unit)   A component of CPE used to terminate a digital circuit, such as a leased line or T-1/E-1 facility, at the customer site. A CSU performs certain line-conditioning functions and responds to loopback commands from the local exchange. It also ensures proper 1s density in a transmitted bitstream and performs bipolar violation correction.

CTS (clear to send)   A control circuit that indicates to the DTE that data can or cannot be transmitted.

customization   The process of designing or configuring a device, installation, or network to meet the requirements of particular users.

cutover   The physical changing of lines from one system to another, usually at the time of a new system installation.

CVSD (Continuous Variable Slope Delta Modulation)   A speech encoding and digitizing technique that uses 1 bit to describe the change in the slope of the curve between two samples rather than the absolute change between the samples.

CWDM (Coarse Wavelength Division Multiplexing)   A WDM system that was specifically developed for metro area applications. CWDM is based on the same principle as DWDM of accommodating multiple wavelengths on a single fiber, but it uses less expensive lasers, making it cost-effective for metro deployments, cable TV, and enterprise networks. The tradeoff is that greater spacing is required between wavelengths, reducing the total number of wavelengths that can be supported.

CXR (carrier)   A signal of known characteristics (e.g., frequency) that is altered (i.e., modulated) to transmit information.

cycle   One complete repetition of a regularly repeating electronic function. The number of cycles per second, measured in Hertz (Hz), is called the *frequency*.

D

DAB (Digital Audio Broadcasting)   A standard that enjoys wide use in Europe for radio broadcasts.

DAMA (demand assigned multiple access)   A system for allocation of communication satellite time to earth stations as the need arises.

dark fiber   Fiber-optic cable that has been installed but is not lit (i.e., that has no active light sources).

data center   The computer-equipped, central location within an organization. The data center processes and converts information to a desired form such as reports or other types of management information records.

data circuit   A communications facility that enables transmission of information in digital form.

data communication   The transmission and reception of data between computers and/or remote devices according to appropriate protocols.

data compression and coding   Techniques used to reduce bandwidth requirements for transmission of information over a particular communications link. These techniques may also be used in noncommunications applications, such as data storage and retrieval.

data exchange   The use of data by more than one program or system.

data line privacy   The evolving relationship between technology and the legal right to, or public expectation of, privacy in the collection and sharing of data.

data link   (1) The equipment and rules (protocol) used for sending and receiving data. (2) Any serial data communications transmission path, generally between two adjacent nodes or devices and without any intermediate switching nodes.

data link layer   OSI Layer 2, which defines how data is packetized and transmitted to and from each network device. It is divided into two sublayers: Media Access Control (MAC) and Logical Link Control (LLC). The MAC layer controls access to a communications link and shares it among many users, while the data link layer uses procedures and protocols to carry data across the link. The data link layer also detects and corrects transmission errors.

data management   Provision of access to data, monitoring or storage of data, and control of input/output devices.

data PBX   A switch that enables a user on an attached circuit to select from other circuits, usually one at a time and on a contention basis, for the purpose of establishing a through connection. A data PBX is distinguished from a PBX in that it supports data transmission and not voice.

data rate   The speed at which a channel carries data, measured in bits per second (bps).

data service   A digital service offered for data communications at subscriber locations.

data set   An infrequently used term for a modem.

data-switching exchange   The equipment installed at a single location to provide switching functions, such as circuit switching, message switching, and packet switching.

data system   A system for the storage and retrieval of data, its transmission to terminals, and controls to provide adequate protection and ensure proper usage.

data transmission   The movement of information from one location to another by means of some form of communication media.

datagram   A message of fixed maximum length, sent without network-provided facilities for assuring its accuracy, delivery, or correct sequencing with respect to related messages, that carries the full destination address used for routing.

dB (decibel)   A unit for measuring the relative strength of a signal parameter such as power or voltage. The number of decibels is 10 times the logarithm (base 10) of the ratio of the power of two signals, or the ratio of the power of one signal to a reference level.

DBPSK (Differential Binary PSK)   A form of phase-shift keying used for digital transmission in which the phase of the carrier is discretely varied in relation to the phase of the immediately preceding signal element and in accordance with the data being transmitted. The demodulator determines the changes in the phase of the received signal rather than the phase itself. DBPSK is used in low-speed 802.11 WLANs (operating at 1Mbps).

DBS (Direct Broadcast Satellite)   A satellite system that can transmit DTV signals directly to individual homes.

DCCP (Datagram Congestion Control Protocol)   A protocol in the TCP/IP protocol suite that provides congestion control for unreliable data flows. DCCP adds end host congestion control behavior to high-rate UDP streams such as streaming media.

DCE (data communications [or channel or circuit-terminating] equipment)   Equipment that provides an interface between the DTE and the transmission channel (i.e., between the carrier's networks). It establishes, maintains, and terminates a connection between the DTE and the transmission channel and is responsible for ensuring that the signal that comes out of the DTE is compatible with the requirements of the transmission channel.

DCLEC (data competitive local exchange carrier)   A company that is specifically focused on supporting data services in the local loop (e.g., providers that offer DSL services to end users).

DCS (Digital Cellular System)   A global system for mobile communications-based PCS networks used outside the United States.

DCS (digital cross-connect system)   A device that enables the reconfiguration of a digital network in response to congestion or failure in the network, as well as on-demand reconfiguration. DCSs add, drop, and/or switch payload as necessary across multiple links.

DDS (digital data service)   A digital transmission service that supports speeds up to 56Kbps/64Kbps.

DECnet   A proprietary suite of network protocols created by Digital Equipment Corporation to connect two minicomputers. It evolved into one of the first peer-to-peer network architectures.

dedicated line   An end-to-end communications line used exclusively by an organization. Also called a dedicated circuit.

delay distortion   The change in a signal from the transmitting end to the receiving end that results from the tendency of some frequency components within a channel to take longer to be propagated than others.

delta modulation   A method of representing a speech waveform (or another analog signal) in which successive bits represent increments of the waveform. The increment size is not necessarily constant. It produces digitized voice at 56Kbps.

demodulation   The process of recovering data from a modulated carrier wave. It is the reverse of modulation.

DEN (Directory Enabled Networking)   An industry group formed by Microsoft and Cisco to create a common data format for storing information about users, devices, servers, and applications in a common repository. DEN describes mechanisms that enable equipment, such as switches and routers, to access and use directory information to implement policy-based networking.

DES (Data Encryption Standard)   A cryptographic algorithm that enciphers and deciphers data using a 56-bit key. As a secret-key, symmetric system, it requires the exchange of secret encryption keys between users.

diagnostics   Software routines or microcode used to check equipment malfunctions or to pinpoint faulty components.

dial tone   A signal, generated by a service circuit within the local exchange or PBX, that is sent to an operator or a user as an audible indication that the switch is ready to receive dialing digits.

dialup   The process of, or the equipment or facilities involved in, establishing a temporary connection via the PSTN.

dialup line   A circuit that is established by a switched-circuit connection. The term generally refers to the PSTN.

DIAMETER   An AAA protocol for applications such as network access and IP mobility. DIAMETER provides a base protocol that can be extended in order to provide AAA services to new access technologies.

DID (direct inward dialing)   A system in which incoming calls from the exchange network can be completed to specific station lines without attendant assistance. Also called direct dialing in (DDI).

Diffie-Hellman   A public key algorithm used mostly for exchanging keys. Its security rests on the difficulty of computing discrete algorithms in a finite field, generated by a large prime number.

DiffServ (Differentiated Services)   An approach to providing QoS in networks that use a small, well-defined set of building blocks from which a variety of services can be built. DiffServ evolved from IETF's IntServ. It is a prioritization model with preferential allocation of resources based on traffic classification.

digital   Communications procedures, techniques, and equipment whereby information is encoded as either binary 1 or 0; the representation of information in discrete binary form, discontinuous in time, as opposed to the analog representation of information in variable, but continuous, waveforms.

digital certificate   A method for registering user identities with a third party, a CA. A digital certificate binds a user to an electronic signature that can be trusted like a written signature and includes authentication, access rights, and verification information.

digital loopback   A technique for testing the digital processing circuitry of a communications device. It can be installed locally or remotely via a telecommunications circuit. The device being tested echoes back a received test message, after first decoding and then reencoding it, the results of which are compared with the original message.

digital network   A network that incorporates both digital switching and digital transmission.

digital signal   A discrete or discontinuous signal, one whose various states are identified with discrete levels or values.

digital switching   The process of establishing and maintaining a connection, under stored program control, where binary-encoded information is routed between an input port and an output port. Generally, a virtual circuit is derived from a series of time slots (TDM), which is more efficient than requiring dedicated physical circuits for the period of time for which connections are set up.

Dijkstra algorithm   An algorithm that determines routes based on path length. It is used in OSPF.

directory service   A service that provides a white pages–like directory of the users and resources located on an enterprise network. Instead of having to know a device's or user's specific network address, a directory service provides an English-like listing for a user. The directory is being standardized collaboratively by the ITU (X.500 standards) and ISO.

distance-vector routing   Routing in which a router is aware only of routers directly connected to it. Each router sends its routing table to each of its neighbors; they in turn merge this routing table with their own.

distortion   The modification of the waveform or shape of a signal caused by an outside interference or by imperfections of the transmission system. Most forms of distortion are the result of the varying responses of the transmission system to the different frequency components of the transmission signal.

distributed computing environment   An architecture in which portions of the applications and the data are broken up and distributed among the server and client computers.

distributed data processing   Data processing in which some or all of the processing, storage, and control functions, in addition to I/O functions, are situated in different places and connected by transmission facilities.

distributed database   An application in which there are many clients as well as many servers. All databases at remote and local sites are treated as if they were one database. The data dictionary is crucial in mapping where all the data resides.

distributed system   A corporate system that can function independently from the host to provide local processing capabilities that meet end-user requirements yet can connect into the host network for file transfer, access to other applications, and host-specific functions.

distribution frame   A structure (typically wall-mounted) for terminating telephone wiring, usually the permanent wires from or at the telephone exchange, where cross-connections are readily made to extensions. Also called a connector block, a distribution block, an MDF, or an IDF.

DLC (digital loop carrier)   A type of concentrator, also called a remote concentrator or remote terminal. Traditional DLCs are not interoperable with some of the DSL offerings, including ADSL and SDSL.

DLCI (data link connection identifier)   An identifier in a Frame Relay header that specifies the Layer 2 virtual circuit.

DLI (data-line interface)   The point at which a data line is connected to a telephone system.

DMB (Digital Multimedia Broadcasting)   The first mobile TV standard to market, derived from the DAB standard. S-DMB (Satellite DMB) and T-DMB (Terrestrial DMB) are currently available in Korea, and other countries are considering adopting DMB as well.

DMB-T (Digital Multimedia Broadcasting-Terrestrial)   A new major broadcast standard that provides the best reception quality for the power required. DMB-T and DAB are the preferred Chinese standards.

DMT (Discrete Multitone)   A multicarrier modulation scheme used in ADSL.

DNS (Domain Name System)   A set of protocols and databases that translates between Web site names and physical IP addresses in the Internet or in any other TCP/IP-based internet.

DOCSIS (Data Over Cable Service Interface Specification)   An international standard developed by CableLabs that defines the communications and operation support interface requirements to permit the addition of high-speed data transfer to an existing cable TV system. There are several generations of DOCSIS standards: DOCSIS 1.0, 1.1, 2.0, and 3.0. The ITU has adopted DOCSIS 1.1 and 2.0 as international standards.

DOD (direct outward dialing)   A system in which trunks are used specifically for outgoing calls (e.g., when you dial an access code such as the number 9 or the number 8 to get an outside-line dial tone before you can dial the actual number that you want to reach).

downlink   The portion of a satellite circuit that extends from the satellite to the earth station.

download   To receive data from a remote system.

downstream   The direction of transmission flow from the source toward the user.

downtime   The total time a system is out of service due to equipment failure.

DPNSS (Digital Private Network Signaling System)   The European standard for common channel signaling between PBXs.

DPSK (Differential Phase-Shift Keying)   A form of phase-shift keying used for digital transmission in which the phase of the carrier is discretely varied in relation to the phase of the immediately preceding signal element and in accordance with the data being transmitted.

DQDB (distributed queue dual bus)   The media access method of the IEEE 802.6 standard for MANs.

DQPSK (Differential Quadrature PSK)   A digital modulation scheme used with extended-rate 2Mbps 802.11 WLANs.

drop   A connection point between a communicating device and a communications network.

DRR (Deficit Round Robin)   A queuing mechanism in which a maximum packet size number is subtracted from the packet length, and packets that exceed that number are held back until the next visit of the scheduler.

DS (Digital Signal) level   The increments of the PDH hierarchy (North American standard). DS-0 is a single channel with a capacity of 64Kbps; DS-1 is 24 DS-0 channels multiplexed into one 1.544Mbps T-1 digital trunk; DS-1C is a 3.152Mbps digital signal carried on a T-1 C facility; DS-2 is a 6.312Mbps digital signal carried over 96 DS-0 channels on a T-3 facility; DS-3 is a 44.736Mbps digital signal carried over 672 DS-0 channels on a T-3 facility; and DS-4 is a 274.176Mbps digital signal carried over 4,032 DS-0 channels on a T-4 facility.

DSCP (DiffServ Code Point)   A field in the packets transported over DiffServ networks that classifies the packets according to priority. DiffServ uses a DSCP to select the per-hop behavior of the packet at each DiffServ-capable node.

DSG (DOCSIS Set-top Gateway)   An extension to the DOCSIS standards that gives operators a standard method to deliver out-of-band data, such as channel lineups and program guides, and more advanced streaming applications via a DOCSIS channel to the digital cable set-top box.

DSI (digital speech interpolation)   A system of digitized speech in which the speech can be cut into slices such that no bits are transmitted when a person is silent. As soon as speech begins, bits flow again.

DSL (Digital Subscriber Line)   A family of broadband technologies that use sophisticated modulation schemes to pack data onto copper wires. They are sometimes referred to as last-mile technologies because they are used only for connections from a telephone switching station to a home or office, not between switching stations. The family of technologies is often referred to as xDSL.

DSL bonding   The process of linking several DSL lines to configure bandwidth between the T-1/T-3 and E-1/E-3 rates.

DSLAM (DSL access multiplexer)   A device at a phone company's central location that links many customer DSL connections to a single high-speed ATM line.

DSP (digital signal processing)   The study of signals in a digital representation and the processing methods for these signals.

DSSS (Direct Sequence Spread Spectrum)   A spread spectrum technique in which each data bit is converted to a series of 10 to 144 transmitted bits or chips.

DSU (data service unit)   A synchronous serial data interface that buffers and controls the flow of data between a digital terminal and the CSU attached to a digital communications facility, converting between incompatible digital formats. DSUs can be considered modem replacements in digital networks.

DTE (data terminal equipment)   Equipment (including any type of computer terminal, such as a PC, as well as printers, hosts, front-end processors, multiplexers, and LAN interconnection devices such as routers) that transmits data between two points without error. Its main responsibilities are to transmit and receive information and to perform error control. The DTE generally supports the end-user applications program, data files, and databases.

DTH (direct to home)   A satellite system that can transmit DTV signals directly to individual homes.

DTMF (dual-tone multifrequency) signaling   The basis for operation of pushbutton telephone sets. DTMF is a method of signaling in which a matrix combination of two frequencies, each from a group of four, is used to transmit numerical address information. The two groups of four frequencies are (a) 697Hz, 770Hz, 852Hz, and 941Hz, and (b) 1,209Hz, 1,336Hz, 1,477Hz, and 1,633Hz.

DTT (digital terrestrial television)   An implementation of digital technology to provide a greater number of channels and/or better quality of picture (via HDTV) and sound through a conventional antenna instead of a satellite dish or cable connection.

DTV (digital TV)   Television sent over a digital network. DTV is nearly immune to interference and degradation, and it can display a much better range of colors than can analog television.

Dual Stack   A technique for enabling IPv4-to-IPv6 interworking and coexistence that allows IPv4 and IPv6 to exist in the same host.

duplex   Communications in which data can be transmitted between two stations in both directions at the same time, with the use of a four-wire circuit. It is the same as full-duplex.

duplex circuit   A four-wire circuit used for transmission in both directions at the same time. It can be called *full-duplex* to distinguish it from *half-duplex*.

duplex signaling   A signaling system that occupies the same cable pair as the voice path yet does not require filters.

duplex transmission   Simultaneous, two-way, independent transmission. Also called full-duplex transmission.

duplexing technique   A procedure for separating incoming and outgoing conversations.

DVB (Digital Video Broadcasting)   A suite of internationally accepted, open standards for DTV.

DVB (Digital Video Broadcasting) Project   A European organization that has authored many specifications for satellite and cable broadcasting of digital signals.

DVB-C (DVB-Cable)   An open standard for digital video transmission over cable.

DVB-H (DVB-Handheld)   A mobile TV standard promoted by ETSI that saves batteries and offers mobility with high data rates, single-antenna reception, impulse noise tolerance, increased general robustness, and seamless handoffs.

DVB-MHP (DVB–Multimedia Home Platform)   The DVB Project's open middleware system for DTV that enables the reception and execution of interactive, Java-based applications on a TV set.

DVB-S (DVB-Satellite)   An open standard for digital video broadcast over satellites. DVB-S supports only MPEG-2 encoded video streams.

DVB-S2 (DVB-Satellite 2)   An open standard for digital video broadcast over satellites that has improved quality over DVB-S.

DVB-T (DVB-Terrestrial)   A European consortium standard for the broadcast transmission of digital terrestrial television.

DWDM (Dense Wavelength Division Multiplexing)   An optical technology used to increase bandwidth over existing fiber-optic backbones. DWDM works by combining and transmitting multiple signals simultaneously at different wavelengths on the same fiber. In effect, one fiber is transformed into multiple virtual fibers.

dynamic routing   Routing that automatically adjusts to network topology or traffic changes.

E

E.164   The ITU-T's international public telecommunication numbering plan for the PSTN.

E (extended) link   A link that provides enhanced reliability by providing a set of links from the SSP to a second STP pair.

E&M signaling   A signaling arrangement that uses separate paths for signaling and voice signals. The M lead (derived from "mouth") transmits ground or battery to the distant end of the circuit, while incoming signals are received as either a grounded or open condition on the E (derived from "ear") lead.

EAP (Extensible Authentication Protocol)   A protocol that enables various external authentication methods—digital certificates, usernames and passwords, secure tokens, and so on—to be incorporated into wireless security environments.

earth station   An assemblage of communications equipment, including signal generator, transmitter, receiver, and antenna, that receives (and usually transmits) signals to/from a communications satellite. Also called a ground station.

EBCDIC (Extended Binary Coded Decimal Interchange Code)   A character set that consists of 8-bit code characters and is widely used for exchanging data between computer systems. It has 256 possible combinations: 17 are used for control purposes; 96 are used for text characters; and the remaining code combinations are unassigned.

eBIP (e-business infrastructure provider)   A provider that saves small businesses time and money with Web-based solutions for human resources, accounting, marketing, group collaboration, and other services.

Ebps (exabits per second)   1 billion Gbps, or 1 billion billion bps.

E-carrier   A time-division-multiplexed, digital transmission facility that operates at an aggregate data rate of 2.048Mbps and above. E-carrier is a PCM system that uses 64Kbps for a voice channel. E-0 is the basic increment of the PDH hierarchy; it is a single channel with a capacity of 64Kbps. In E-1, 32 channels are multiplexed into one 2.048Mbps E-1 digital channel, also referred to as G.703; 30 channels are used for information, and 2 channels are reserved for signaling and control. Other E-carrier levels are E-2 (8.488Mbps over 128 channels), E-3 (34.368Mbps over 512 channels), E-4 (139.246Mbps over 2,048 channels), and E-5 (565.148Mbps over 8,192 channels).

echo   A wave that has been reflected or otherwise returned with sufficient magnitude and delay for it to be perceived as a wave distinct from that directly transmitted.

echo cancellation   A process that allows full-duplex transmission to occur over a single electrical path. It relies on frequency splitting to derive separate voice and data channels from one wire. This feature is necessary for voice transmission but often interferes with data transmission.

Ecma International (formerly European Computer Manufacturers Association)   A European standards organization that creates ICT and consumer electronics standards.

e-commerce (electronic commerce)   The secure exchange of funds, executed over a network, for goods and services exchanged between parties.

EDFA (erbium-doped fiber amplifier)   An optical amplifier. Erbium is injected into fiber, and as a light pulse passes through the erbium, it is amplified; thus, it does not have to be stopped and processed as an electrical signal. The introduction of EDFAs opened up the opportunity to make use of fiber-optic systems operating at 10Gbps.

edge   The network boundary between a customer and the core or central network.

EDGE (Enhanced Data Rates for Global Evolution)   An enhanced version of GPRS that combines digital TDMA and GSM to provide 48Kbps to 69.2Kbps per time slot on an aggregated basis, up to 384Kbps.

edge caching   A system in which Web content is duplicated on a machine close to the end user the first time the user requests the content. Subsequent requests for this content are satisfied from the nearby machine. This improves the speed and reliability of access because it avoids the Internet backbone and its peering points.

edge device   A device that can pass packets between a legacy type of network such as an Ethernet network and an ATM network, using data link layer and network layer information. An edge device does not have responsibility for gathering network routing information but simply uses the routing information it finds in the network layer using the route distribution protocol.

EDI (electronic data interchange)   The asynchronous exchange from computer to computer of intercompany business documents (e.g., purchase orders, bills of lading, invoices) and information. EDI can be accomplished through OSI standards or through proprietary products.

EDTV (enhanced-definition TV)   Video with picture quality beyond what can be broadcast in NTSC or PAL but not sharp enough to be considered HDTV.

EFM (Ethernet First Mile)   IEEE 802.3ah, a standard that uses Ethernet to provide connectivity from the customer to the carrier.

EGP (Exterior Gateway Protocol)   A routing protocol used to exchange network reachability information among organizational networks. EGP indicates whether a network is reachable; it does not weight that decision. EGP has largely been replaced by BGP4.

EIA (Electronic Industries Association)   A U.S. organization that develops standards in the areas of electrical and electronic products and components.

EIA interface   A standardized set of signal characteristics (i.e., time duration, voltage, and current) specified by the EIA.

EIGRP (Enhanced Interior Gateway Routing Protocol)   A Cisco proprietary routing protocol based on IGRP. EIGRP has optimizations to minimize the routing instability incurred after topology changes and the use of bandwidth and processing power in the router.

EIR (excess information rate)   The maximum amount of uncommitted data (in bits) in excess of committed burst size that a Frame Relay network can attempt to deliver.

elastic application   A traditional Internet application that can work without guarantees of timely delivery. Because it can stretch in the face of greater delay, it can still perform adequately when the network faces increased congestion and degradation in performance.

ELEC (Ethernet local exchange carrier)   A competitive provider that specializes in providing Ethernet solutions in the local loop and metro area.

electromagnetic spectrum   The electromagnetic waves that can propagate through free space and are created when electrons move. It ranges from extremely low-frequency radio waves of 30Hz—with a wavelength of nearly the earth's diameter—to high-frequency cosmic rays of more than 10 million trillion Hz—with wavelengths smaller than the nucleus of an atom. The electromagnetic spectrum is depicted as a logarithmic progression: The scale increases by multiples of 10, so that the higher regions encompass a greater span of frequencies than the lower regions. The greater the span of frequencies, the greater the bandwidth of the media operating over that portion of the electromagnetic spectrum.

electronic tandem networking The operation of two or more switching systems in parallel.

e-mail (electronic mail) An application that enables users to send and receive messages and files over their computer networks.

EMI (electromagnetic interference) Noise on data transmission lines that reduces data integrity. Motors, machines, and other generators of electromagnetic radiation cause EMI, but shielding can reduce EMI.

EMS (Enhanced Messaging Service) An extension of SMS that enables the sending of a combination of simple melodies, images, sounds, animations, and formatted text as a message to another EMS-compatible phone.

emulate To imitate one system with another so that the imitating system accepts the same data, executes the same computer programs, and achieves the same result as the imitated system.

encapsulation The process of encasing one protocol in another protocol's format. Also called tunneling.

encryption The process of coding data so that a specific code or key is required to restore the original data. Encryption is typically applied for secure data transmission or to prevent unauthorized reception of broadcast material. Sometimes referred to as scrambling.

end office The first point of access to the PSTN, or the point at which the subscriber loop terminates. Also referred to as a Class 5 office, local exchange, central office, or serving office.

end-to-end optical architecture A network in which the optical signal never needs to be converted to an electronic signal.

enterprise network A network that connects the computer resources throughout a company and supports a wide variety of the company's applications.

enterprise wiring hub A hub that connects the PCs on a LAN and also provides the flexibility to perform a number of network functions that can benefit network administrators and network users in general.

ENUM (Electronic Number Mapping Standard) A protocol that is the result of work of the IETF's Telephone Number Mapping working group, whose charter was to define a DNS-based architecture and protocols for mapping a telephone number to a uniform resource identifier (URI), which can be used to contact a resource associated with that number.

ephemeral port A TCP or UDP port number that is automatically allocated from a pre-defined range by the TCP/IP stack software, typically to provide the port for the client end of a client/server communication.

equalization The introduction of components to an analog circuit by a modem to compensate for signal attenuation and delay distortion. Generally, the higher the transmission rate, the greater the need for equalization.

ERL (echo return loss) Attenuation of echo currents in one direction caused by telephone circuits operating in the other direction.

error In data communications, any unwanted change in the original contents of a transmission.

error burst   A concentration of errors within a short period of time as compared with the average incidence of errors. Retransmission is the normal correction procedure in the event of an error burst.

error control   A process of handling errors that includes the detection and correction of errors.

error correction code   A code that incorporates sufficient additional signal elements to enable the nature of some or all of the errors to be indicated and corrected entirely at the receiving end.

error rate   The ratio of the amount of data incorrectly received to the total amount of data transmitted.

ESCON (Enterprise Systems Connection)   A proprietary optical networking system.

ESP (Encapsulated Security Payload)   A security system in which IP datagram data is encrypted.

ESS (electronic switching system)   A system that uses computer-like operations to switch telephone calls.

Ethernet   A baseband LAN specification that operates at 10/100/1,000Mbps by using CSMA/CD running over thick or thin coaxial, twisted-pair, or fiber-optic cable. Standards have been developed for Gigabit Ethernet and 10Gbps Ethernet, and they are being developed for 100Gbps Ethernet as well. Ethernet is defined in IEEE 802.3.

ETRI (Electronics and Telecommunications Research Institute)   A nonprofit Korean government–funded research organization that has been at the forefront of technological excellence for more than 25 years.

ETSI (European Telecommunication Standards Institute)   A telecommunications standardization organization.

Euro-DOCSIS   The European version of the U.S. DOCSIS standard. The goal of Euro-DOCSIS is to ensure correct and optimal performance of Euro-DOCSIS modems and CMTSs in European networks as well as being fully compliant with the European DVB standard in the downstream.

even parity check   A test of whether the number of digits in a group of binary digits is even.

exchange   The assembly of equipment in a communications system that controls the connection of incoming and outgoing lines and includes the necessary signaling and supervisory functions. Different exchanges, or switches, can be colocated to perform different functions (e.g., local exchange/central office, tandem exchange, toll/trunk/transit exchange).

extranet   A network between partnering organizations.

extranet VPN   A VPN that allows an external organization to have defined access into an enterprise's internal networks and resources.

F

F (fully associated) link   A link that directly connects to signaling endpoints, generally SSPs.

facility   (1) Any or all of the physical elements of a plan used to provide communications services. (2) A component of an operating system. (3) A transmission path between two or more points, provided by a common carrier.

fading   The reduction in intensity of the power of a received signal. In this phenomenon, which generally affects microwave or radio transmission, atmospheric, electromagnetic, or gravitational influences cause a signal to be deflected or diverted away from the target receiver.

Fast Ethernet   A standard for high-speed Ethernet that has a rate of 100Mbps.

fast hopping   A signal-processing scheme that supports high data rates with very low packet and delay losses (i.e., latencies) over a distributed all-IP wireless network.

fast packet switching   A packet-processing technology that has streamlined protocol handling, including Frame Relay and ATM.

fault   A condition that causes any physical component of a system to fail to perform in acceptable fashion.

fault tolerance   The capability of a program or system to operate properly even if a failure occurs.

FCC (Federal Communications Commission)   A regulatory agency established by the Communications Act of 1934 that is charged with regulating all electrical and radio communications in the United States.

FDD (Frequency Division Duplex)   A full-duplex technique used when there is a significant contiguous spectrum allocated and when synchronization between the base stations is not possible. Each direction (incoming and outgoing) occupies a different portion of the frequency band, and a rather large portion of the spectrum is consumed.

FDDI (Fiber Distributed Data Interface)   A 100Mbps, fiber-based token-passing ANSI standard. FDDI consists of dual fiber-optic counter-rotating rings, each capable of supporting 100Mbps data rates. FDDI is defined for fiber-optic cable, but it has a twisted-pair alternative called CDDI. FDDI II is an enhanced version of FDDI that supports isochronous transmission (for voice and video) as well as the packet-oriented (both asynchronous and synchronous) traffic handling of FDDI.

FDM (Frequency Division Multiplexing)   A technique of dividing the bandwidth of a communications line into multiple smaller units of bandwidth, each of which supports an independent information stream.

FDMA (Frequency Division Multiple Access)   A multiple-access technique used in analog cellular systems, in which each user is assigned to a different frequency.

FEC (forward error correction)   An error control system for data transmission that differs from standard error detection and correction in that the technique is specifically designed to allow the receiver to correct some errors without having to request a retransmission of data.

FEC (Forwarding Equivalence Class)   In MPLS, a term used to describe a set of packets with similar or identical characteristics that may be forwarded the same way.

FECN (forward explicit congestion notification)   A bit in the Frame Relay header by which the network can inform the receiver of network congestion. DTE receiving frames with the FECN bit set can request that higher-level protocols take flow control action, as appropriate.

femtosecond   0.000000000000001 (i.e., 10^{-15}) second.

FEP (front-end processor)   A dedicated communications system that intercepts and handles activity for the host. It may perform line control, message handling, code conversion, and error control, as well as such application functions as control and operation of special-purpose terminals.

FHSS (Frequency Hopping Spread Spectrum)   A spread spectrum technique in which the frequency hopping varies in a known pattern, and separate error correction must be included.

fiber-optic waveguides   Thin filaments of glass through which a light beam can be transmitted for long distances by means of multiple internal reflections. Occasionally, other transparent materials, such as plastic, are used.

fiber optics   A technology that uses light as a digital information carrier. Fiber-optic cables (light guides) are a direct replacement for coaxial cables and twisted-wire pairs. The glass-based transmission facilities occupy far less physical volume yet provide a tremendous amount of transmission capacity, which is a major advantage in crowded underground ducts. The fibers are immune to electrical interference, which is another advantage. Also called lightwave communications, photonics, or, simply, fiber.

Fibre Channel   A high-speed interface, standardized by ANSI, that supports up to 800Mbps over 6.2 miles (10 km) of fiber.

FIFO (first in, first out)   A queuing technique in which the next item to be retrieved is the item that has been in the queue for the longest time. This ensures that cells remain in the correct sequence.

file server   In local networks, a station dedicated to providing file and mass data storage services to the other stations on the network.

filter   To selectively forward data, based on criteria specified by the network manager.

firewall   A system designed to prevent unauthorized access to or from a private network. Firewalls can be implemented in both hardware and software, or a combination of both.

five-nines reliability   A desired level of network or system reliability that equates to 99.999% uptime (i.e., about 5 minutes of downtime per year).

fixed wireless local loop   A stationary installation that dramatically cuts down on the cost of installing and maintaining the local loop. It uses a fixed antenna location, so it is relatively easy to engineer.

Flash-OFDM (Fast Low-Latency Access with Seamless Handoff OFDM)   A WMAN standard that is a variant of 802.20. Flash-OFDM uses a technique called *fast hopping*, a signal-processing scheme that supports high data rates with very low packet and delay losses (i.e., latencies) over a distributed all-IP wireless network. Flash-OFDM is not compatible with 2.5G or 3G technology.

flat network   A network that is constructed by using bridges or Layer 2 LAN switches. This type of network is easy to configure, and it promises better performance than hierarchical networks; it offers higher throughput and therefore also lower latencies. However, the scalability of a flat network is limited, and a flat network is subject to broadcast storms.

flat rate   A fixed cost for service. Additional charges may be applied for additional services or usage if so specified.

flow control   A system that uses buffering and other mechanisms, such as controls that turn a device on and off, to prevent data loss during transmission.

FM (frequency modulation)   One of three ways to modify a sine wave signal to carry digital bits. The sine wave, or carrier, has its frequency modified in accordance with the information to be transmitted. The frequency function of the modulated wave may be continuous or discontinuous.

FMC (fixed-mobile convergence)   The vision of being able to use one phone with one number, address book, and voicemail bank while enjoying the benefits of low-cost, high-speed connectivity in the office or fixed-line residential environment, while still enjoying the freedom of mobility in the WAN. FMC features seamless handoff between fixed and mobile networks.

FOMA (Freedom of Mobile Multimedia Access)   The proprietary 3G standard used by Japanese mobile phone operator NTT DoCoMo.

forward channel   The communications path that carries voice or data from the call initiator to the network.

four-wire circuit   A circuit that contains two pairs of wire (or their logical equivalent) for simultaneous (i.e., full-duplex) two-way transmission. Two pairs of conductors, one for the inbound channel and one for the outbound channel, are connected to the station equipment.

FQ (Fair Queuing)   A queuing mechanism whose objectives are to provide fair access to bandwidth, resources, and routers and to ensure that no one flow receives more than its fair share.

FQDN (fully qualified domain name)   An unambiguous domain name that specifies a node's position in the DNS tree hierarchy absolutely.

fractional T-1/E-1   T-1/E-1 lines that have apportioned bandwidth for separate transmission channels (DS-0/64Kbps subchannels), generally in increments of four channels.

fragmentation   The process of splitting a packet into pieces when it is larger than the MTU it must transmit.

frame   (1) In data transmission, the sequence of contiguous bits bracketed by and including beginning and ending flag sequences. (2) In a TDM system, a repetitive group of signals resulting from a signal sampling of all channels, including any additional signals for synchronizing and other required system information.

frame bandwidth allocation   The sum of the committed information rates associated with all the PVCs for a specific customer.

Frame Relay   A packet-switching technology that is simpler and more powerful than the X.25 standard. Frame Relay provides a multiplexed channel between a router and a T-1/E-1 nodal processor. It increases bandwidth utilization while reducing overall equipment costs. The Frame Relay standard addresses data communications speeds up to 45Mbps.

framing   A control procedure used with multiplexed digital channels, such as T-1 carriers, in which bits are inserted so that the receiver can identify the time slots allocated to such subchannels. Framing bits may also carry alarm signals indicating specific alarm conditions.

frequency   An expression of how frequently a periodic (repetitious) waveform or signal regenerates itself at a given amplitude. Frequency can be expressed in Hertz (Hz), kilohertz (KHz), megahertz (MHz), and so on.

frequency-selective fading   A type of fading based on multipath time delay spread in which the bandwidth of the signal is greater than the coherence bandwidth of the channel or the delay spread is greater than the symbol period.

FSK (frequency-shift keying)   A modulation method that uses two different frequencies to distinguish between a mark (digital 1) and a space (digital 0) when transmitting on an analog line. FSK is used in modems that operate at 1,200bps or slower.

FSO (Free Space Optics)   An optical wireless networking option that uses low-powered infrared lasers. There are two options in FSO: point-to-point products, used to provide high-speed connection between two buildings, and multiple high-speed connections through the air that operate over much shorter distances, either in a point-to-multipoint or meshed architecture.

FTAM (File Transfer Access and Management)   An ISO standard that describes how to create, delete, read, and change file attributes as well as transfer and access (at the file or record level) files stored at remote sites. It is an application-layer protocol.

FTP (File Transfer Protocol)   A protocol that enables a TCP/IP user on any computer to get files from another computer or to send files to another computer. Usually implemented as application-level programs, FTP uses the Telnet and TCP protocols. The server side requires a client to supply a login identifier and password before it will honor requests.

FTTC (fiber-to-the-curb)   A system in which fiber cable extends from a switching office to a curb.

FTTH/FTTP (fiber-to-the-home/fiber-to-the-premises)   A system in which fiber cable extends from a switching office to the subscriber's house/premises.

FTTN (fiber-to-the-node)   A system in which fiber cable extends from a switching office to a point near the premises, such as a curb.

FTTx (fiber-to-the-x)   A system in which fiber cable extends from a switching office to the *x* (where *x* means premises, curb, building, or home).

full-duplex   A communication system or equipment that is capable of transmission simultaneously in both directions.

full-motion video   Moving images that the human eye perceives as being fully realistic. While there are no defined standards, full-motion video is frequently referred to as VHS-quality. Frame rates range from 24 frames per second (fps) in motion pictures, 25fps in the PAL system, and 30fps in the NTSC system.

FX (foreign exchange) line   A line that makes a toll call appear to be a local call.

G

GAN (Generic Access Network)   A telecommunication system that allows seamless roaming and handoffs between LANs and WANs, using the same dual-mode mobile phone. Formerly known as Unlicensed Mobile Access (UMA), it was adopted by the 3GPP in 2005.

gateway   A device or program (i.e., hardware or software) that connects two different networks that use different protocols and translates between these protocols, allowing devices on the two networks to communicate with each other.

gateway daemon   A program that runs under BSD UNIX on a gateway to allow the gateway to collect information from within one autonomous system using RIP, HELLO, or other IGPs, and to advertise routes to another autonomous system using the EGP.

Gateway-to-Gateway Protocol   The original IGP used by Internet core gateways (i.e., by routers).

GB (gigabyte)   1 billion bytes, or 1,000MB.

Gen2 standard (UHF Generation 2 Air Interface Protocol)   An EPCglobal standard that forms the backbone of RFID tag standards.

GEO (geosynchronous orbit)   A circular orbit with a 24-hour orbital period approximately 22,300 miles (36,000 km) above the earth's equator. Because satellites in this orbit appear stationary relative to the earth's surface, GEO is especially useful for communications satellites that transmit to fixed earth stations.

GERAN (GSM EDGE Radio Access Network)   A second phase of EDGE that is planned to offer data rates of up to 1,920Kbps, to support packetized voice and real-time services. GERAN is a common evolution path for GSM and TDMA that intends to provide a cost-efficient means to deliver 3G services within the existing frequency bands

GFP (Generic Framing Procedure)   A protocol that allows mapping of variable-length, higher-layer client signals over transport networks such as SDH/SONET and OTN networks.

GGSN (gateway GPRS support node)   A device that acts as a gateway between the GPRS network and public data networks such as IP and X.25 networks. GGSNs also connect to other GPRS networks to facilitate GPRS roaming.

GHz (gigahertz)   1 billion cycles per second.

GigE (Gigabit Ethernet)   An Ethernet standard that supports 1Gbps. Sometimes referred to as 1Gbps Ethernet.

global information infrastructure   A vision of individual national information infrastructures joined together to form an international network.

GMPLS (Generalized Multiprotocol Label Switching)   An enhancement to MPLS technology that allows service providers to dynamically provision resources and provide the necessary redundancy for implementing various protection and restoration techniques for optical networks.

GMSK (Gaussian Minimum-Shift Keying)   A kind of continuous-phase frequency-shift keying modulation that produces one bit per symbol time. GSM uses GMSK.

GPRS (General Packet Radio Service)   An always-on nonvoice value-added service that enables information to be sent and received across a mobile telephone network via GSM phones.

GPS (global positioning system)   A navigation system in which satellites broadcast precise timing signals by radio to GPS receivers, allowing them to accurately determine their location in any weather, at any time of day, anywhere on earth.

GRE (Generic Routing Encapsulation)   A simple stateless protocol that allows for the tunneling of IP in IP. GRE tunnels can be used to form VPNs, connecting remote sites by using private IP addresses via a public network.

grooming   The process of selectively removing channels from a digital facility for routing to a designated remote location via another digital facility. Grooming basically enables the flexible dropping and adding of payload.

ground circuit   (1) A circuit in which energy is carried one way over a metallic path and returned through the earth. (2) A circuit connected to the earth at one or more points.

ground start   A signaling method whereby one station detects that a circuit is grounded at the other end.

Group 3 fax   An ITU-T standard for encoding an image and transmitting it over dialup lines.

Group 4 fax   An ITU-T standard for encoding an image and transmitting it over ISDN or other wideband digitized services.

G.SHDSL (Symmetric High-Speed DSL)   A member of the DSL family that offers symmetrical service with options to operate over one pair or two pairs of copper wires, and also has rate-adaptive capability. G.SHDSL supports data rates of up to 5.6Mbps in each direction over a distance of up to 2 miles (3 km). G.SHDSL was the first international standard for DSL. Also referred to as SHDSL.

GSM (Global System for Mobile Communications)   A European standard for 2G wireless digital communications that is globally implemented and supports both voice and data communications. GSM operates in several frequency bands: GSM 850 (850MHz), GSM 900 (900MHz), DCS 1800 (1.8GHz), and PCS 1900 (1.9GHz). New GSM data standards include HSCSD, GPRS, and EDGE and are referred to as 2.5G.

GTP (GPRS Tunneling Protocol)   An IP-based protocol used within GSM and UMTS networks.

H

H.323   An ITU standard that defines how audiovisual conferencing data is transmitted across networks. In theory, H.323 should enable users to participate in the same conference even though they are using different videoconferencing equipment.

half-duplex   Communications in which data can be transmitted between two stations in both directions but in only one direction at a time.

Hamming Code   A linear error-correcting code that can detect single- and double-bit errors.

HAN (home area network)   A broadband network in a smart house that connects the various smart devices.

handoff   The transfer of duplex signaling as a mobile terminal passes to an adjacent cell in a cellular radio network.

handshake   The exchange of predetermined signals for control when a connection is established between two modems or other devices.

haptic interface   An interface that enables virtual touch.

hard wired   (1) Referring to a communications link, whether remote phone line or local cable, that permanently connects two nodes, stations, or devices. (2) Descriptive of electronic circuitry that performs fixed logical operations by virtue of an unalterable circuit layout, rather than under computer or stored-program control.

hardware   The physical equipment, as opposed to programs or procedures, of a computer system.

harmonic distortion   A waveform distortion that is usually caused by the nonlinear frequency response of a transmission.

HARQ (hybrid automatic repeat request)   A variation of the ARQ error control method that gives better performance than ordinary ARQ, particularly over wireless channels, albeit at the cost of increased implementation complexity.

hash function   The process of producing hash values for accessing data or for security. A hash value (or simply hash) is a number generated from a string of text. The hash is substantially smaller than the text itself and is generated by a formula in such a way that it is extremely unlikely that some other text will produce the same hash value.

HCF (Hybrid Coordination Function)   An IEEE MAC-layer protocol that is an important development in VoWLAN systems. In order to improve service for voice, the standard includes two operating modes: Enhanced Digital Control Access (EDCA) and Polled Access.

H-channel   A class of high-speed ISDN channels. H-0 is 384Kbps, H-11 is 1.536Mbps, and H-12 is 1.920Mbps.

HCSD (high-speed circuit-switched data)   A standard for transferring high-speed data over aggregated GSM channels. HCSD provides data rates up to 64Kbps.

HDB3 (high-density bipolar 3)   A line interface standard for E-1 that is similar to B8ZS. HDB3 eliminates data streams with eight or more consecutive 0s, allows for 64Kbps clear channel capacity, and still assures the minimum 1s density required by E-1 lines.

HDLC (High-Level Data Link Control)   A form of communications line control that uses a specified series of bits rather than control characters to control data transmission over a communication line. HDLC is a bit-oriented protocol developed by the ISO.

HDSL (High-Bit-Rate DSL)   A symmetrical service that can be deployed over a distance of about 2.2 miles (3.6 km). HDSL is deployed over two twisted-pair cables, and it affords equal bandwidth in both directions. HDSL2 provides symmetrical capacities of up to 1.5Mbps or 2Mbps over a single twisted-pair cable.

HDTV (high-definition television)   A television format for which several competing standards exist but which normally requires a screen aspect ratio of 16:9 (versus 4:3 with analog TVs) and which is capable of reproducing at least four times more detail than in the analog broadcasting system.

headend   The control center of a cable TV network.

header   The initial portion of a message or file, which contains statistical and control information.

HELLO   The protocol used by a group of cooperative, trusting packet switches to allow them to discover minimal delay routes.

heuristic   An exploratory method of problem solving in which solutions are discovered through an interactive, self-learning method.

hexadecimal   A system of numbers in base 16. Hexadecimal digits range from 0 through 9 and A (10) through F (15). Each hexadecimal digit is represented by 4 binary bits.

HFC (hybrid fiber coax)   A networking arrangement that supports a wide range of services, including traditional telephony, broadcast video, and interactive broadband services. It involves the use of fiber in the backbone and in the access network. The fiber terminates at a neighborhood node, and from that neighborhood node, coax (normally 750MHz or 1,000MHz) is run to the home, in a two-way subsplit system.

hierarchical routing   Routing that is based on a hierarchical addressing scheme. Most TCP/IP routing is based on a two-level hierarchy in which an IP address is divided into a network portion and a host portion. Routers use only the network portion until the datagram reaches a router that can deliver it directly. Subnetting introduces additional levels of hierarchical routing.

high frequency   The portion of electromagnetic spectrum that is typically used in shortwave radio applications. High frequencies are approximately in the 3MHz to 30MHz range.

HiperAccess (High-Performance Radio Access)   A fixed wireless broadband access network standard that gives broadband access to both the home and small- and medium-sized enterprises, as well as providing backhaul for mobile systems. HiperAccess was developed to provide a truly broadband system, with bit rates of up to approximately 100Mbps, although 25Mbps is expected to be the most widely deployed rate. HiperAccess is targeted at high frequency bands, especially the 40.5GHz to 43.5GHz band.

HiperLAN (High-Performance Radio LAN)   A mobile broadband short-range access network standard. This WLAN standard is defined by the BRAN project of ETSI and is a European alternative for the IEEE 802.11 standards. The first version of HiperLAN, called HiperLan1, was designed to provide faster data rates than the IEEE 802.11 standards. The second version of the standard, HiperLan2, will give consumers wireless access to the Internet and future multimedia, as well as real-time video services, at speeds of up to 54Mbps.

HiperMAN (High-Performance Radio MAN)   A fixed wireless access network standard for operating between 2GHz to 11GHz that is aimed at providing a broadband wireless solution for metropolitan area networks.

HIPPI (High-Performance Parallel Interface)   A gigabit-per-second OSI Layer 1 and 2 interface standardized by ANSI. HIPPI supports 800Mbps up to 82 feet (25 m) using a 32-bit parallel copper connector and can be extended up to several miles/kilometers by using fiber-optic technology. A higher-speed option uses 64 parallel lines to support operation at up to 1.6Gbps.

HMIPv6 (Hierarchical Mobile IPv6)   An enhancement to the Mobile IP technique that is being developed to improve mobile communications in certain circumstances by making the processes more secure and more efficient.

holding time   The length of time a communications channel is in use for each transmission. The holding time includes both message tone and operating time. Also called connect time.

HomeRF   An open standard for short-range transmission of digital voice and data between mobile devices.

hop   A unit of network distance. The number of hops between a source and a destination is the number of nodes between them (e.g., number of routers between hosts on the Internet).

hop-by-hop retransmission   A system in which an intermediate device retransmits so that the retransmission travels a shorter path over a fewer number of hops and is therefore less delayed.

horizontal distribution frame   A hub for terminating cables run on a floor.

host   An end-user computer system that connects to a network. Hosts range in size from PCs to supercomputers.

host interface   The link between a communications processor or network and a host computer.

host system   (1) The computing system to which a network is connected and with which other devices can communicate. (2) The primary or controlling computer in a network.

hotspot   A location that enables Internet access from mobile devices (such as laptops and PDAs) without connection cables to networked services, usually through Wi-Fi. Hotspots are often found in restaurants, train stations, airports, cafes, libraries, and other public places.

howler tone   The tone that alerts a subscriber when a telephone is off the hook.

HSCSD (High-Speed Circuit-Switched Data)   A high-speed transmission technology that enables users to send and retrieve data over GSM networks at transmission speeds between 28.8Kbps and 43.2Kbps by enabling the concurrent usage of up to four traffic channels of a GSM network.

HSDPA (High-Speed Downlink Packet Access)   A key 3.5G standard that provides data rates from 8Mbps to 14Mbps over a 5MHz bandwidth in W-CDMA downlink to support packet-based multimedia services. HSDPA enhances W-CDMA similarly to the way EDGE enhances GSM/GPRS.

HSOPA (High-Speed OFDM Packet Access)   A key 3.5G standard that incorporates OFDM and MIMO, promising to offer a 40Mbps download speed.

HSPA (High-Speed Packet Access)   The combination of HSDPA and HSUPA services.

HSSI (high-speed serial interface)   A physical-layer interface between a DTE, such as a high-speed router or similar device, and a DCE, such as a DS-3 (45Mbps) or SDH/SONET OC-1 DSU.

HSUPA (High-Speed Uplink Packet Access)   A key 3.5G standard that enables users to transmit data upstream at a speed of 5.8Mbps.

HTML (Hypertext Markup Language)   A document standard that defines a simple logical structure including titles, headings, paragraphs, lists, forms, tables, and mathematical equations, as well as a language to specify hypertext links.

HTTP (Hypertext Transfer Protocol)   The standard mechanism used on the World Wide Web for the transfer of documents between server and client systems.

HTTPS (HTTP over SSL)   A Web protocol that encrypts and decrypts user page requests as well as the pages that are returned by the Web server.

hub   A device that extends the maximum physical length of a network by cleaning and retransmitting signals among network segments. A hub provides the central connecting point in a star network topology. Also called a multiport repeater.

Huffman encoding   A statistical encoding technique for lossless compression. Statistical encoding is an entropy-encoding method. The Huffman algorithm calculates the frequency of occurrence of each octet for a given portion of the data stream. It then determines the minimum number of bits to allocate to each character and assigns an optimal code accordingly. The codes are stored in a codebook. This technique is used in sound, still, and moving image compression.

hybrid circuit   A circuit that has four sets of terminals arranged in two pairs designed so that there is high loss between the two sets of terminals of a pair when the terminals of the other pair are suitably terminated. Hybrid circuits are commonly used to couple four-wire circuits to two-wire circuits.

hybrid network   A network composed of both public and private facilities.

Hz (Hertz)   A unit of electromagnetic frequency that is equal to one cycle per second.

I

IAD (integrated access device)   A device that consolidates voice, data, Internet, and video services using DSL, ATM, TDM, or MGCP over T-1/E-1 lines. The IAD, installed on the end-user's site, is a form of CPE.

IANA (Internet Assigned Numbers Authority)   An organization that oversees IP addresses and top-level domain name allocations.

iBurst   An Australian WMAN technology that provides mobile wireless broadband Internet access. iBurst is a pure IP, end-to-end system.

ICANN (Internet Corporation for Assigned Names and Numbers)   A nonprofit corporation that manages the domain name and root server systems.

ICMP (Internet Control Message Protocol)   An integral part of IP that handles error and control messages. Routers and hosts use ICMP to send reports of problems about datagrams back to the original sources that sent the datagrams. ICMP also includes an echo request/reply that is used to test whether a destination is reachable and responding.

ICP (Internet content provider)   A service provider that specializes in providing content rather than infrastructure.

ICT (information and communications technologies)   A broad field concerned with technology and other aspects of managing and processing information.

IDEA (International Data Encryption Algorithm)   An algorithm developed by ETH Zurich that is free of charge for noncommercial use. Viewed as a good algorithm, it is used in PGP and in Speak Freely, a program that allows encrypted digitized voice to be sent over the Internet.

IDF (intermediate distribution frame)   A frame that has distributing blocks on both sides, permitting the interconnection of telephone circuitry.

IDSL (ISDN DSL) A transmission medium that has a maximum loop length of 3.4 miles (5.5 km) and is deployed as a single twisted-pair cable that offers 128Kbps in each direction. IDSL is not used much anymore.

IEC (International Electrotechnical Commission) An international standards organization that deals with electrical, electronic, and related technologies. Some of its standards are developed jointly with the ISO.

IEEE (Institute of Electrical and Electronics Engineers) A scientific, engineering, and educational society that develops and publishes standards in a variety of electrical engineering and computer-related areas. IEEE membership is open to any dues-paying individual. The IEEE is responsible for 802 LAN standards.

IETF (Internet Engineering Task Force) A nonprofit organization that produces the standards used in TCP/IP and the Internet.

I-frame (intracoded frame) A frame that is not reconstructed from another frame. An I-frame is also a reference frame; it serves as a reference to construct other frames.

IFRB (International Frequency Registration Board) A board within the ITU that is responsible for the maintenance of an international list of radio frequency usage and the allocation of new frequencies.

IGMP (Internet Group Management Protocol) A protocol that allows Internet hosts to participate in multicasting. It describes the basics of multicasting IP traffic, including the format of multicast IP addresses, multicast Ethernet encapsulation, and the concept of a host group (i.e., a set of hosts interested in traffic for a particular multicast address).

IGP (interior gateway protocol) Any protocol used to propagate network reachability and routing information within an autonomous system. RIP and IGRP are examples of IGPs.

IGRP (Interior Gateway Routing Protocol) A proprietary network protocol developed by Cisco Systems that is designed to work on autonomous systems. IGRP is a distance-vector routing protocol.

IKE (Internet Key Exchange) The key exchange protocol used by IPsec. IKE supports pre-shared keys, which is a simplified form of key exchange. It does not require digital certificates.

ILEC (incumbent local exchange carrier) A telephone company that was providing local service in the United States when the Telecommunications Act of 1996 was enacted. For most residents in the United States, this would be one of the four "baby Bells"—Qwest, SBC, BellSouth, and Verizon.

IMA (Inverse Multiplexing over ATM) A specification that provides a way to combine an ATM cell stream over two or more circuits, thus allowing an organization to lease just the bandwidth it needs (e.g., more than T-1 and less than T-3).

immersion In virtual reality, the user's subjective sensation of being inside the virtual world and not observing it from an outside perspective.

i-mode A proprietary protocol for transforming Internet information so that it can be displayed on the small screen of a mobile telephone or other portable device. i-mode is used in Japan and is also called DoCoMo (which means "anywhere").

impairment   A radio signal quality problem caused by degradations due to path loss, multipath, adverse weather, obstacles, interference, or other obstacles.

IMPS (Instant Messaging and Presence Service)   A mobile phone standard that enables instant messaging, presence, groups or chat, and shared content.

IMS (IP Multimedia Subsystem)   A standard that defines a generic architecture that offers VoIP and other multimedia services within wireline and wireless infrastructures. The aim of IMS is to provide all the services, current and future, that the Internet provides. IMS creates a telephony-oriented signaling network that overlays an underlying IP network. Using the IP protocol as its foundation, IMS supports data, video, SIP-based VoIP, and non-SIP packetized voice, such as H.323 and MGCP. IMS was designed to integrate with the PSTN and provide traditional telephony services such as 800 numbers, caller ID, and local number portability.

IMT-2000 (International Mobile Telecommunications 2000)   An evolving standard for 3G mobile communications that enables personal mobility and converging mobile and fixed networks.

IMUN (International Mobile User Number)   A number used to dial a subscriber in 3G mobile networks.

IN (intelligent network)   An architecture for providing advanced services in telecommunications networks.

in-band management   A system in which management information is communicated across the network.

induction coil   An apparatus for obtaining intermittent high voltage consisting of a primary coil through which the direct current flows, an interrupter, and a secondary coil with a larger number of turns in which the high voltage is induced.

information infrastructure   High-speed communications networks capable of carrying voice, data, text, image, and video (multimedia) information in an interactive mode serving an enterprise computing architecture.

information path   The functional route by which information is routed.

information signals   Signals associated with activating and delivering various enhanced features, such as call waiting.

information systems network   A network of multiple operating-level systems and one management-oriented system (centered around planning, control, and measurement processes). The network retrieves data from databases and synthesizes the data into meaningful information to support the organization.

infrared   The frequency range in the electromagnetic spectrum that is higher than radio frequencies but below the range of visible light.

infrastructure   The underlying structure or framework of the telecommunications system (e.g., switching, multiplexing, and transmission systems) that allows for the transmission of voice, video, and data.

InP (indium phosphide)   A semiconductor composed of indium and phosphorus that is used for making electronic and optoelectronic devices. InP is useful for optoelectronics devices such as laser diodes.

input queue   A holding area for packets that come to the input port more quickly than the router can process them.

Integrated IS-IS   A routing protocol that combines routing for TCP/IP and OSI protocols. It is a superset of IS-IS, the OSI routing technology that combines the functionality of both OSPF and IS-IS.

integrated photonic circuit   The optical equivalent of an integrated circuit. The goal of integrated photonic circuits is to consolidate large numbers of separate optical devices into a single chip, customizing them for different applications to improve performance.

interactive   A term that describes the mode of transaction for a particular information service. An interactive service allows for both input and output. It is sometimes referred to as a two-way, as opposed to a one-way, service.

interactive processing   A processing method in which each operator action causes a response from the program or system.

interconnected systems   Systems that are linked together in local and/or remote networks. The exchange of data between systems in a network is through standard channels or through communications lines. Communication between interconnected systems normally occurs without manual intervention; it is provided by combined hardware and software that support the interconnection.

interconnection   The interworking of two separate wireline and/or wireless networks. *Interconnection* is used to refer both to the technical interface and to the commercial arrangements between two network operators providing service.

interface   A boundary between two pieces of equipment across which all signals that pass are carefully defined. The definition includes the connector signal levels, impedance, timing, sequence of operation, and meaning of signals.

interior routing   Routing that occurs within an autonomous system.

international business service   A satellite-based service at up to 8Mbps. Services include data, fax, digital voice, and video- and audioconferencing.

international gateway   A device that connects calls between different countries.

international number   Digits that have to be dialed after the international prefix to call a subscriber in another country; that is, the country code followed by the subscriber's national number.

internet   A collection of packet-switching networks interconnected by routers along with protocols that allow them to function logically as a single, large, virtual network.

Internet   The worldwide Internet consisting of large national and regional backbone networks, local Internet service providers, and IP networks.

Internet 2   A network that replaces what the original Internet was for—the academic network. Internet 2 acts as a testbed for many of the latest and greatest technologies. Universities stress-test Internet 2 to determine how applications perform and which technologies suit which applications or management purposes best.

Internet-based VPN   A VPN composed of multiple ISPs that provide local access services in defined geographical regions. Because it requires an enterprise to receive end-to-end services from multiple suppliers, performance is difficult to control and guarantee.

interoffice channels   A portion of a leased circuit between IXC exchanges.

interoffice trunk   A direct trunk between local exchanges (Class 5 offices) or between tandem, toll, or international exchanges. Also called interexchange trunk.

interoperability   The ability to exchange information in a network that contains computers and additional devices that have dissimilar operating systems or protocols.

intranet   A network based on TCP/IP protocols (i.e., an internet) that belongs to an organization and is accessible only by the organization's members, employees, or others with authorization.

intranet VPN   A site-to-site connection whose key objective is to replace or reduce the use of leased-line networks, traditional routers, and Frame Relay services.

IntServ (Integrated Services)   The IETF's scheme to introduce QoS support over IP networks. IntServ provides extensions to the best-effort service model to allow control over end-to-end packet delays. IntServ is a per-flow resource reservation model that requires RSVP. Its key building blocks include resource reservation and admission control.

Inverse ARP   An extension to ARP that permits a station to request a protocol address (e.g., an IP address) given a hardware address (e.g., a Frame Relay DLCI).

inverse multiplexer   A device that spreads a high-bandwidth information stream over multiple lower-speed transmission channels (e.g., a 1.5Mbps signal transmitted over 24 64Kbps channels of a T-1).

I/O (input/output)   (1) A device or channel that may be involved in an input process, and, at a different time, in an output process. (2) A device whose parts can be performing an input process and an output process at the same time. (3) Pertains to either input or output, or both.

IP (Internet Protocol)   The protocol that specifies the exact format of all data as it travels through a TCP/IP network. In addition, IP performs the routing functions and selects the transmission path on which data will be sent. As part of these two functions, IP also provides a mechanism for dealing with unreliable data, specifying the manner in which network nodes will process data, how and when to generate error messages, and when to discard unreliable data.

IP address   The 32-bit address assigned to a host that wants to participate in a TCP/IP internet. IP addresses are the abstraction of physical hardware addresses just as an internet is an abstraction of physical networks. Actually assigned to the interconnection of a host to a physical network, an IP address consists of a network portion and a host portion.

IP backbone   A packet-switching network interconnected by routers along with protocols that allow them to function logically as a single, large, virtual network. IP backbones are operated by individual service providers, unlike the Internet, which is composed of more than 10,000 service providers.

IP Cablecom   The name by which the international community knows PacketCable. *See also* PacketCable.

IP datagram   The basic unit of information passed across a TCP/IP internet. An IP datagram is to an internet as a hardware packet is to a physical network. It contains a source and destination address along with data.

IP forwarding   The process of forwarding internet packets from one network to another.

IP fragmentation   A multibridge feature that handles packet size mismatch problems between FDDI and Ethernet endpoints. The maximum FDDI packet size is 4,500 bytes. The maximum Ethernet packet size is 1,548 bytes. Messages that are longer than 1,548 bytes must be fragmented into smaller packets to allow them to enter the Ethernet network.

IP long-distance wholesaler   A VoIP service provider that offers IP services to domestic and international carriers, corporations, and service providers to carry their traffic, particularly international transit.

IP Multicast   A protocol for transmitting IP datagrams from one source to many destinations in a LAN or WAN.

IP over DWDM   The use of IP on an intermediate architecture that runs on a DWDM network. Today's networks operate largely with IP running over ATM running over SDH/SONET running over DWDM.

IP PBX   A new-generation PBX that uses packet-switching technology and offers an attractive platform for the integration of voice and data in the enterprise.

IP switch   A switch that replaces slower, more processing-intensive routers. An IP switch is a router that provides connection-oriented services in the IP layer.

IP voice   The routing of voice conversations over an IP-based network such as the Internet. Voice traffic has a low bandwidth requirement but requires very high QoS.

IPDC (Internet Protocol Device Control)   A specification that creates flexible management of media gateway devices.

IPN (Interplanetary Internet)   A network project that defines the architecture and protocols necessary to permit interoperation of the Internet resident on earth with other remotely located internets resident on other planets or spacecraft in transit.

IPS7 (IP Signaling System 7)   A signaling protocol that works with SS7.

IPsec (IP Security)   A set of protocols developed by the IETF to support secure exchange of packets at the IP layer. IPsec has been deployed widely to implement VPNs.

IPT (IP telephony)   The use of the Internet or a private IP network for telephony.

IPTV (IP television)   A system in which DTV is delivered to subscribers using Internet Protocol over a broadband connection. IPTV is often provided in conjunction with VOD and Internet services such as Web access and VoIP.

IPv4 (Internet Protocol version 4)   The original generation of IP, in which an IP address has two parts: The first is the network ID and the second is the host ID. Under IPv4, there are five classes (Class A through Class E), which differ in how many networks and hosts are supported.

IPv6 (Internet Protocol version 6)   An IP addressing scheme that uses a 128-bit address, which allows a total of 340 billion billion billion billion unique addresses. IPv6 offers many benefits, but it requires a major reconfiguration of routers. Also called IPng (IP Next Generation).

IPX (Internetwork Packet Exchange)   The Novell equivalent of IP. IPX is used to route NetWare packets between LANs. IPX does not guarantee the delivery of messages; NetWare's SPX protocol handles that task.

IrDA (Infrared Data Association)   A short-range wireless technology that allows connection between devices using infrared links instead of wired cabling.

IRP (Interdomain Routing Protocol)   A protocol that provides routing for OSI-defined network environments and is similar to BGP in the TCP/IP network. In an OSI network, there are end systems, intermediate systems, areas, and domains. IRP is designed to provide routing among domains.

IS-54   TIA's Interim Specification 54, also called NADC and Digital AMPS, and updated by IS-136. It is a TDMA-based wireless network that operates at 800MHz.

IS-95   TIA's Interim Specification 95. It is a spread spectrum wireless network that operates in the 800MHz range, using a CDMA/FDD scheme.

IS-136   TIA's Interim Specification 136. It is an updated TDMA-based standard that updates IS-54. Provides 3x spectral efficiency over analog AMPS systems.

ISC (international switching center)   An exchange used to switch traffic between different countries over international circuits.

ISDB (Integrated Services Digital Broadcasting)   A Japanese DTV and DAB format created to allow radio and TV stations to convert to digital. ISDB can be used for both fixed and mobile reception, and it encompasses several core standards: ISDB-S (satellite TV), ISDB-T (terrestrial digital TV), ISDB-C (digital cable TV), and ISDB-Tsb (terrestrial digital sound broadcasting in the 2.6GHz band).

ISDN (Integrated Services Digital Network)   A circuit-switched digital subscriber line service; an access technology. ISDN is part of the physical layer of the OSI reference model. ITU-T I.430 defines a 144Kbps Basic Rate Interface (BRI), and ITU-T I.431 defines a Primary Rate Interface (PRI) of 1.544Mbps in North America and Japan and 2.048Mbps in Europe.

IS-IS (Intermediate System to Intermediate System)   A protocol that uses a link-state algorithm to provide routing services for TCP/IP and OSI. It determines the best path for TCP/IP and OSI packets through the network and keeps routers informed of the status of the network and the systems available.

ISM (Industrial, Scientific, and Medical)   Unlicensed radio bands that operate at 900MHz, 2.4GHz, and 5.8GHz.

ISO (International Organization for Standardization)   An organization established to promote the development of standards to facilitate the international exchange of goods and services and to develop mutual cooperation in areas of intellectual, scientific, technological, and economic activity.

ISO Ethernet   An isochronous Ethernet standard designed to provide an efficient way to share normal Ethernet and isochronous traffic on a single twisted-pair cable in a local area environment.

ISOC (Internet Society)   A nongovernmental, nonprofit organization dedicated to maintaining and enhancing the Internet. Through its committees, such as the Internet Advisory Board and the IETF, ISOC is responsible for developing and approving new Internet standards and protocols.

isochronous   A descriptor that signifies enabling network characteristics, including the ability to simultaneously transport disparate data types (voice, video, and data) across the same circuit. It also includes the capability to dynamically allocate bandwidth as the application warrants.

isochronous data stream   A nonpacketized data transmission. An isochronous data stream is a circuit-switched, fixed-rate, continuous data stream, such as voice, video, or real-time sensor data.

ISP (Internet service provider)   A company that gives users access to the Internet and related services.

ISV (independent software vendor)   A vendor that develops the applications that ASPs then put up for sale or for rent.

IT (information technology)   A broad term that describes the computer hardware, software, and networking industry, including telecommunications and audiovisual equipment.

ITU (International Telecommunication Union)   A telecommunications agency of the United Nations that was established to provide standardized communications procedures and practices, including frequency allocation and radio regulations, on a worldwide basis. It is the parent group of the ITU-T (telecommunications), ITU-R (radio), and ITU-D (developing nations).

IV (initialization vector)   In cryptography, a block of bits that is required to allow a stream cipher or a block cipher executed in any of several streaming modes to produce a unique stream independent from other streams produced by the same encryption key, without having to go through a rekeying process.

IXC (interexchange carrier)   A long-distance telephone company that offers circuit-switched, leased-line, or packet-switched service.

IXP (Internet exchange point)   A physical infrastructure that allows different ISPs to exchange Internet traffic between their networks by means of mutual peering agreements, which allow traffic to be exchanged without cost.

J

jack   A device used generally for terminating the permanent wiring of a circuit, access to which is obtained by the insertion of a plug.

J-carrier   The Japanese standard of the PDH, a TDM digital transmission system. J-carrier is a PCM system that uses 64Kbps per channel as the basis of the hierarchy. Higher levels reflect aggregation of the 64Kbps channels. J-1 is a 1.544Mbps 24-channel communications circuit; J-2 is a 6.312Mbps 96-channel communications circuit; J-3 is a 32.064Mbps 480-channel communications circuit; J-4 is a 97.728Mbps 1,440-channel communications circuit; and J-5 is a 565.148Mbps 8,192-channel communications circuit.

jitter   The slight movement of a transmission signal in time or phase that can introduce errors and loss of synchronization for high-speed synchronous communications.

JPEG (Joint Pictures Expert Group)   An international standard used primarily for still image compression.

JTACS (Japanese Total Access Communication Systems)   A Japanese wireless system that operates in the 800MHz to 900MHz band.

JTAPI (Java TAPI)   An extensible object-oriented API that supports telephony call control.

jumper   A patch cable or wire used to establish a circuit, often temporarily, for testing or diagnostics.

K

Ka-band   The portion of the electromagnetic spectrum allotted for satellite transmission. Its frequencies are approximately in the 20GHz to 30GHz range.

Kbps (kilobits per second)   1,000 bits per second.

KHz (kilohertz)   1,000 cycles per second.

Ku-band   The portion of the electromagnetic spectrum that is being used increasingly for satellite communications. Frequencies are approximately in the 12GHz to 14GHz range.

L

L2TP (Layer 2 Tunneling Protocol)   A Layer 2 protocol that can work in a non-IP enterprise environment. L2TP is used primarily by service providers to encapsulate and carry VPN traffic through their backbones.

LAN (local area network)   (1) A system for linking terminals, programs, storage, and graphic devices at multiple workstations over relatively small geographic areas. (2) A network that is limited to a small area, such as the premises of an office building or plant.

LANE (LAN Emulation)   An ATM Forum standard for emulating a LAN across an ATM network.

LAPB (Link Access Protocol Balanced)   A modified form of HDLC that the ITU-T chose as the link-level protocol for X.25 networks. LAPB provides for the reliable transfer of a packet from a host to an X.25 packet switch, which then forwards the packet to its destination.

LAPD (Link Access Protocol on the D Channel)   An ISDN data link layer protocol for the D channel. LAPD was derived from the LAPB protocol, designed primarily to satisfy the signaling requirements of ISDN basic access.

laser (light amplification by simulated emission of radiation)   A device that converts electrical energy into radiant energy in the visible or infrared parts of the spectrum, emitting light with a small spectral bandwidth. Lasers are widely used in fiber-optic communications, particularly as sources for long-haul links.

LATA (Local Access and Transport Area)   Geographic regions within the United States that define areas within which the RBOCs can offer exchange and exchange access services (local calling, private lines, and so on).

latency   The delay associated with the time it takes a packet to travel from entry point to exit point.

layer   In the OSI reference model, a collection of related network-processing functions that comprise one level of a hierarchy of functions.

Layer 1   The physical layer of the seven-layer OSI reference model, which deals with the physical means of sending data over a communications medium, defining physical characteristics such as media type, physical interfaces, electrical and optical coding schemes, and data transfer rates.

Layer 2   The data link layer of the seven-layer OSI reference model, which responds to service requests from the network layer and issues service requests to the physical layer. Layer 2 is sometimes split into two sublayers: the Logical Link Control (LLC) layer and the Media Access Control (MAC) layer. The MAC layer controls access to communications links and shares it among many users, and the LLC layer uses procedures and protocols to carry data across the link (and also detects and corrects transmission errors). Examples of Layer 2 protocols in a LAN environment include Ethernet, Token Ring, and FDDI. Examples of Layer 2 protocols in a WAN environment include Frame Relay and ATM. Examples of Layer 2 protocols in the PSTN are SS7 and MTP2.

Layer 3   The networking layer of the seven-layer OSI reference model, which identifies computers on a network and determines how to direct information transfer over that network. The key responsibility of Layer 3 is to add the addressing information and the control functions needed to move the data through the network and its intermediate nodes. It is involved in establishing, maintaining, and terminating connections, including packet switching, routing, data congestion, reassembly of data, and translation of logical addresses to physical addresses. Examples of Layer 3 protocols are X.25, IP, IPX, and MTP3.

Layer 4   The transport layer of the seven-layer OSI reference model, which corrects transmission errors and ensures that the information is delivered reliably. Layer 4 provides end-to-end error recovery and flow control capability. It deals with packet handling, repackaging of messages, division of messages into smaller packets, and error handling. Examples of Layer 4 protocols include TCP, UDP, and SPX.

Layer 5   The session layer of the seven-layer OSI reference model, which supports connections between sessions and handles administrative tasks and security. Layer 5 establishes and monitors connections between computers, and it provides the control structure for communication between applications. Examples of Layer 5 protocols include NetBIOS and LDAP.

Layer 6   The presentation layer of the seven-layer OSI reference model, which formats information so that a software application can read it. It performs transformations on the data to provide a standardized application interface and common communication services. Layer 6 offers services such as encryption, compression, and reformatting. It adds a field in each packet that tells how the information within the packet is encoded. It also indicates whether any compression has been performed and, if so, indicates what type of compression so that the receiver can decompress it properly. It also indicates whether there has been any encryption, and if there has, it indicates what type so that the receiver can properly decrypt it. Layer 6 ensures that the transmitter and receiver are seeing information in the same format.

Layer 7   The application layer of the seven-layer OSI reference model, which is responsible for exchanging information between the programs running on a computer and other services on a network. Layer 7 supports application and end-user processes. It acts as a window for applications to access network services. It handles general network access, flow control, error recovery, and file transfer. Examples of Layer 7 protocols include FTP, Telnet, SMTP, and HTTP.

L-band   The portion of the electromagnetic spectrum commonly used in satellite and microwave applications. L-band operates in the 390MHz to 1,550MHz range, and it supports various mobile and fixed applications.

LCD (liquid crystal display)   A graphic display on a terminal screen using an electroluminescent technology to form symbols or shapes.

LDAP (Lightweight Directory Access Protocol)   The standard directory server technology for the Internet. LDAP allows retrieval of information from multivendor directories.

LDP (Label Distribution Protocol)   An MPLS signaling protocol.

leased line   A communications channel contracted for exclusive use from a common carrier, frequently referred to as a private line.

LEC (local exchange carrier)   The incumbent local telephone company. There was originally no competition among LECs, but as soon as competition in the local loop picked up, LECs were segmented into ILECs, CLECs, and DCLECs.

LED (light-emitting diode)   A semiconductor junction diode that emits radiant energy and is used as a light source for fiber-optic communications, particularly for short-haul links. LEDs are also used in alphanumeric displays in electronic telephones, calculators, and other devices.

LEO (low-earth-orbit) satellite   A satellite that orbits at about 400 to 1,000 miles (640 to 1,600 km) above the earth.

lightwave communications   A term sometimes used in place of *optical communications* to avoid confusion with visual information and image transmission, such as facsimile or television.

limited-distance modem   A device that translates digital signals into analog signals (and vice versa) for transfers over limited distances. Some limited-distance modems operate at higher speeds than modems that are designed for use over analog telephone facilities.

line   (1) The communications path between two or more points, including a satellite or microwave channel, also referred to as the transmission line. (2) In data communications, a circuit that connects two or more devices. (3) The transmission path from a nonswitching subscriber terminal to a switching system.

line hit   Electrical interference that causes the introduction of undesirable signals on a circuit.

line of sight   (1) A characteristic of some open-air transmission technologies (e.g., microwave, infrared, open-air laser-type transmissions) in which the path between a transmitter and a receiver must be clear and unobstructed. (2) A clear, open-air, direct transmission path that is free of obstructions such as buildings but may in some cases be impeded by adverse weather or environmental conditions.

line speed   The maximum data rate that can be reliably transmitted over a line.

link   (1) A physical circuit between two points. (2) A conceptual (or virtual) circuit between two users of a packet-switched (or other) network that allows them to communicate even when different paths are used.

link redundancy level   The ratio of the actual number of paths to the minimum number of paths required to connect all nodes of a network.

link state   A state in which each router is aware of the topology of the entire network. Each router sends out information about the links that the router has to all other routers on the network. The final routing table is based on the shortest path to each destination. Most new routing protocols are based on this algorithm.

link-state protocol   A generic class of routing protocols in which information about the status of the entire network is propagated to every node and used in routing decisions. OSPF, IS-IS, and NLSP are link-state routing protocols.

LLC (Logical Link Control)   A protocol developed by the IEEE 802, common to all of its local network standards, for data link–level transmission control. It is the upper sublayer of the OSI Layer 2 protocol that complements the MAC protocol (IEEE 802.2). LLC 1 is a minimal-function LLC that supports connectionless link layer service. LLC 2 supports connection-oriented data link service.

LMDS (Local Multipoint Distribution Service)   A technique for supplying broadband access via a point-to-point microwave digital system. Referred to as Multipoint Video Distribution service in Europe, it operates over a very large frequency allocation, a 1.3GHz band that is generally located in the range of 28GHz to 45GHz, depending on the country. LMDS is a popular technique for deploying wireless local loop.

LMI (local management interface)   A Frame Relay specification for the method of exchanging status information between the user (e.g., bridge, router) and the network.

LMP (Link Management Protocol)   A protocol used in GMPLS networks that accommodates neighbor identification and link verification, as well as shared-risk groups, fault isolation, and topology-aware networks.

load balancing   A technique used to spread work between many processes, computers, disks, or other resources. Load balancing is a scalability problem for networks.

loading   Adding loading coils to a transmission line to minimize amplitude distortion.

loading coil   An induction device used in local loops, generally those exceeding 3.4 miles (5.5 km) in length, that compensates for the wire capacitance and boosts voice-grade frequencies. Loading coils are often removed for new-generation, high-speed, local loop data services because they can distort data signals at higher frequencies than those used for voice.

local   Pertains to a device that is connected directly to a computer without using a WAN communication line.

local exchange   The switching center in which subscribers' lines terminate. The local exchange has access to the other exchanges and to national trunk networks. Also called a central office, end office, serving office, or Class 5 office.

local exchange trunk   A trunk between the CPE and the local exchange. Also referred to as a central office trunk.

local loop   A line that connects a customer's telephone equipment with the local telephone company exchange. Often referred to as a subscriber line, an access line, or the last mile.

local number portability   A service that enables a person to keep his or her own telephone number when moving to a new location.

local service area   The area within which the telephone operating company uses local rates for calling charges.

LocalTalk   Apple Computer's proprietary 230.4Kbps baseband CSMA/CA network protocol.

location-based online services   Services provided over a wireless infrastructure that are based on the location of the user. The location of the user can be determined through GPSs or by cellular networks. Radio signals emitted from cellular phones can be tracked from cellular towers and triangulated, yielding locations nearly as accurate as those from a GPS receiver.

logical address   An address used to identify a communications program by name to the protocol stack. No matter where the program is put in the network, an individual's logical address will remain the same, even though the person's physical address may change.

long-haul   Long-distance, describing (primarily) telephone circuits that cross out of the local exchange.

loop   (1) A local circuit between an exchange and subscriber CPE, either residential (single-line telephone) or business (PBX). Also called a subscriber loop, local line, or local loop. (2) In programming, a sequence of computer instructions that repeats itself until a predetermined count or other test is satisfied.

loop circuit   A circuit that connects a subscriber's equipment with the local exchange switch. Also called a metallic circuit or local loop.

loop signaling systems   Any of the three methods of transmitting signaling information over the metallic loop formed by the trunk conductors and the terminating equipment bridges. Transmission of the loop signals can be accomplished by opening and closing the DC path around the loop, reversing the voltage polarity, or varying the value of the equipment resistance.

loop start   The most commonly used method of signaling an off-hook condition between an analog phone set and a switch, whereby picking up the receiver closes a wire loop, allowing DC current to flow, which is detected by a PBX or local exchange and interpreted as a request for service.

loopback   A diagnostic procedure used for transmission devices. In a loopback, a test message is sent to a device being tested, which then sends the message back to the originator for comparison with the original transmission. Loopback testing may be performed within a locally attached device or conducted remotely over a communications circuit.

loss   A decrease in signal power in transmission along the circuit as a result of the resistance of impedance of the circuit or equipment.

lossless compression   In data compression, the process by which information is recovered without any alteration after the decompression stage. This technique is used for computer-based data or programs. It may also be required in certain multimedia applications where the accuracy of the information is essential, such as in medical imaging. Lossless compression is also called bit-preserving or reversible compression. Examples of lossless compression include run-length encoding and Huffman encoding.

lossy compression   In data compression, a situation in which the decompressed information is different from the original uncompressed information. This mode is suitable for most continuous media, such as sound and motion video, as well as for many images. That the decompressed information is different from the original in lossy compression does not imply that the perceptual response of an observer is different. Also called irreversible compression.

low frequency   Generally, frequencies between 30KHz and 300KHz.

low-level language   A programming language in which instructions have a one-to-one relationship with machine code.

LPC (linear predictive coding)   A vector-quantization-based compression scheme for speech. LPC can compress speech down to 2.4Kbps.

LSP (label-switched path)   A path through an MPLS network that is set up by a signaling protocol based on criteria in the forwarding equivalence class (FEC).

LSR (label-switching router)   An MPLS-enabled router and/or MPLS-enabled ATM switch. As each packet enters the network, an ingress LSR assigns it a label, based on its destination, VPN membership, ToS bits, and other considerations. At each hop, an LSR uses the label to index a forwarding table.

M

m2m (machine-to-machine)   A term that refers to the concept of communications between a device holding some amount of data that is of interest to another and another device that desires the use of that data. Telemetry is the most common implementation of m2m. Also sometimes stands for man-to-machine.

MAC (Media Access Control)   The part of OSI Layer 2 that describes how devices share access to the network. Token Ring, Ethernet, and FDDI are MAC-layer specifications. Wiring hubs primarily deal with MAC-layer equipment.

macrocell   A cell architecture in the cellular system that covered up to 8 miles (12.8 km) and used a lot of power, from 0.6 to 3 watts. This type of network was for fast-moving users, traveling distances of miles on their end-to-end journey. A macrocell could support up to about 60 users.

MAE (metropolitan area exchange)   An interconnection and exchange point where public Internet backbones meet and exchange traffic. Also called a NAP.

mains powered   Being powered by a permanent source such as an AC electrical power supply.

MAN (metropolitan area network)   A network that spans a geographical distance of up to a 62-mile (100-km) diameter; a citywide network.

managed object   A data-processing or data communications resource that can be managed through the use of an OSI management protocol. The resource itself need not be an OSI resource. A managed object may be a physical item of equipment, a software component, some abstract collection of information, or any combination of the three.

MAPI (Messaging Application Programming Interface)   A messaging API from Microsoft that consists of two components: Simple MAPI and Extended MAPI. Simple MAPI provides hooks to various messaging systems, so developers can create message-enabled applications by writing those applications to Simple MAPI rather than developing those hooks themselves. Extended MAPI is platform specific to Windows.

mapping   In network operations, the logical association of one set of values, such as addresses on one network, with quantities or values of another set, such as devices on a second network (e.g., name–address mapping, internet work-route mapping).

mark   The signal (communications channel state) that corresponds to a binary 1.

marker   A wired-logic control circuit that, among other functions, tests, selects, and establishes paths through a switching state(s) in response to external signals.

matrix   (1) An arrangement of elements (numbers, characters, dots, diodes, wires, and so on) in perpendicular rows. (2) In switch technology, the portion of a switch architecture where input leads and output leads meet, any pair of which can be connected to establish a through circuit. Also called a switching matrix.

MAU (media attachment unit)   A transceiver that connects to the AUI port of an Ethernet interface card and provides attachments to some type of data communications medium.

MB (megabyte)   1,048,576 bytes; usually referred to as 1 million bytes.

MB-OFDM (Multiband OFDM)   A UWB standard that transmits data simultaneously over multiple, accurately spaced carrier frequencies and features high spectral flexibility as well as resilience to RFI and multipath.

mbone (multicast backbone)   A virtual network on top of the Internet that supports routing of IP multicast packets, intended for multipoint multimedia transmission. With mbone, a single packet can have multiple destinations and is replicated only at the closest node before the final receiver. This means that it can pass through several routers before it needs to be replicated to reach its final destinations. This leads to much more efficient transmission and also ensures that packets reach multiple destinations at roughly the same time.

Mbps (megabits per second)   1,048,576 bits per second; usually referred to as 1 million bits per second.

MBS (mobile broadband services)   Very high-bit-rate services (over 100Mbps) over wireless channels.

MCML (Multi-Class Multi-Link) PPP   A protocol that makes it possible to have multiple classes of latency-sensitive traffic carried over a single multilink bundle with bulk traffic.

m-commerce (mobile commerce)   Financial transactions that occur on mobile devices.

MCU (multipoint control unit)   A device that supports multiparty videoconferencing between several individual-circuit videoconferencing systems. The MCU acts as a videoconference hub.

MD5 (Message Digest-5)   An algorithm used to create digital signatures. MD5 is intended for use with 32-bit machines. It is a one-way hash function, which means it converts a message into a fixed string of digits called a message digest.

MDF (main distribution frame)   A structure that contains all the necessary power and test equipment to support terminal strip connections and wiring arrangements that connect outside and inside telephone exchange circuitry.

measured rate   A message rate structure that includes payment for a specified number of calls within a defined area, plus a charge for additional calls.

mechatronics   A system that uses mechanics, electronics, and computing to generate simpler, more economical, reliable, and versatile systems. Automotive applications of mechatronics, for example, include obstacle detection, door control, and climate control, as well as support for telematics and multimedia.

media filter A filter used in token-ring lobe wiring to convert STP-only adapter cards to UTP wiring.

media gateway A device that provides seamless interoperability between circuit-switched, or PSTN, networking domains and those of the packet-switched realm (i.e., IP, ATM, and Frame Relay networks). A media gateway interconnects with the SS7 network and enables the handling of IP services.

MediaFLO A mobile TV standard from Qualcomm. MediaFLO is a comprehensive end-to-end solution that simultaneously and cost-effectively delivers very high volumes of high-quality, streaming, or clipped audio and video multimedia to wireless subscribers.

medium (1) The material on which data is recorded (e.g., magnetic tape, CD-R). (2) Any material substance that is or can be used for the propagation of signals, usually in the form of modulated radio, light, or acoustic waves, from one point to another (e.g., optical fiber, cable, wire, water, air, free space).

medium frequency Frequencies in the range between 300KHz and 3MHz.

mega 1 million.

Megaco (Media Gateway Control) An ITU standard that describes how the media gateway should behave and function. It is standardized under ITU-T H.248.

memory An area of a computer system that accepts, holds, and provides access to information.

MEMS (microelectromechanical system) switch An optical switch that uses an array of microscopic mirrors to reflect light from an input port to an output port.

menu A displayed list of items from which a user can make a selection.

menu-driven Programs that are run by instructions presented as a list of commands and available options. Unlike in a command-driven program, the user only has to select the desired option.

MEO (middle-earth-orbit) satellite A satellite that orbits at an elevation of about 6,200 to 9,400 miles (9,900 to 15,000 km) above the earth.

mesh A topology in which nodes are connected in an unconstrained way and may contain loops. A fully connected mesh has every pair of nodes directly connected.

message An arbitrary amount of information whose beginning and end are defined. In data communications, a message consists of a header, a body, and a trailer.

message authentication Authentication that verifies the integrity of an electronic message and also verifies that an electronic message was sent by a particular entity.

message format Rules for the placement of such portions of a message as message heading, address, text, end-of-message indication, and error-detecting bits.

message numbering Identification of each message within a communications system by the assignment of sequential numbers.

message switching   A technique that transfers messages between points that are not directly connected. The switching facility receives messages, stores them in queues for each destination point, and retransmits them when a facility becomes available. Synonymous with store-and-forward.

message unit   A unit of measure for charging local calls that details the length of call, distance called, and time of day.

metric   Information that a routing algorithm uses to determine the best path to the destination. Some examples of metrics include path length, destination, next-hop associations, reliability, delay, bandwidth, load, and communication cost.

metro access product   A MAN product that brings fiber closer to the customer, to reduce deployment costs.

metro core product   A MAN product used in building citywide rings.

MGCP (Media Gateway Control Protocol)   A combination of the SGCP and IPDC specifications. In this protocol, softswitches provide the external control and management, making MGCP a good way to connect an IAD to a gateway.

MHz (megahertz)   A unit of frequency equal to 1 million cycles per second.

MIB (Management Information Base)   The specification for how data is stored, monitored, and managed in an SNMP device. MIB I and MIB II are revisions of the database used on TCP/IP networks.

micro   One-millionth.

microbrowser   An Internet browser specifically designed for mobile devices.

microcell   A small cell architecture in the cellular system that covers about 1 mile (1.5 km) and uses only about 100 milliwatts of power. Microcells allow greater frequency reuse than cells, increasing the overall network capacity and therefore the number of subscribers that can be served.

microsecond   One-millionth of a second.

microwave   (1) The portion of the electromagnetic spectrum between 1GHz and 100GHz. (2) High-frequency transmission signals and equipment that employ microwave frequencies, including line-of-sight open-air microwave transmission and satellite communications.

MIDI (Musical Instrument Digital Interface)   A standard for defining how to code all the elements of musical scores, such as sequences of notes, timing conditions, and the instrument that is to play each note.

milli   One-thousandth.

millisecond   One-thousandth of a second.

MIME (Multipurpose Internet Mail Extensions)   An Internet standard that enables a message to contain textual, binary, or arbitrarily formatted data. An advantage of MIME is that it encodes the data into an SMTP-compatible format.

MIMO (multiple-input multiple-output) antenna   An advanced antenna technology that can carry several times more data traffic than today's most advanced 3.5G networks. MIMO enables a network to quickly deliver multimedia content. Multiple antennas are used at both the transmitter and receiver and are combined at each end to minimize errors and optimize data speed.

MIPS (million instructions per second)   A measure of a computer's processor speed.

MMD (Multimedia Domain)   The 3GPP2 name for IMS, which provides the technological basis for the provision of mobile multimedia services in next-generation networks.

MMDS (Multichannel Multipoint Distribution Service)   A technique for supplying broadband access via a point-to-point microwave digital system. It operates in the 2GHz to 3GHz band and can cover a fairly large area (approximately 30 miles [48 km]). It provides great capacity in that it enables 150 channels. Also called wireless cable.

MMS (Multimedia Messaging Service)   A presence-based technology for transmitting text messages and also multimedia content, such as images, audio, and video clips, over wireless networks, using WAP.

MMW (millimeter wave)   A technology that is often used in wireless local loops. MMW produces very narrow beams, called *pencil beams*. MMW usually covers the range between 10GHz and 300GHz.

mobile earth station   A radio transmitter and/or receiver situated on a ship, on a vehicle, on an aircraft, or in a briefcase that is used for satellite communications.

Mobile IP   An IETF standard that allows users to roam between IP networks without their mobile devices losing connections.

Mobile IPv6   An enhancement to the Mobile IP technique that is being developed to improve mobile communications in certain circumstances by making the processes more secure and more efficient.

Mobile Mesh   A wireless network implementation that uses all the nodes in the network to support communication. Because each node acts like a repeater, the greater the number of nodes, the greater the bandwidth and the better the signal that reaches the access point.

mobile TV   Television delivered over mobile devices. A number of standards are being promoted for mobile TV, including DMB, DVB-H, ISDB, and MediaFLO.

mobile wireless local loop   A last-mile solution that uses cellular telephone or cordless technology, along with satellites. This approach enables subscriber mobility, so it could replace a fixed line when in a home and could also be used to move outside those boundaries as a mobile line.

Mobile-Fi   A standard that is optimized for IP and roaming in high-speed mobile environments. Also known as IEEE 802.20.

mobility network   A wireless network that allows a user to roam within the range of his or her home and the outdoor area surrounding it.

modal dispersion   The tendency of light to travel in a wavelike motion rather than a straight line. The greater the level of wave fluctuations, the greater the dispersion of the signal and the associated degradation of performance.

modem (modulator-demodulator)   A conversion device installed at each end of an analog communications line. The modem at the transmitting end modulates digital signals locally from a computer or terminal; the modem at the receiving end demodulates the incoming signal, converting it back to its original (i.e., digital) format and passing it to the destination business machine.

modular   A design technique that permits a design or system to be assembled from interchangeable components. A modular system or device can be expanded or modified simply by adding another module.

modulation   The process of converting voice or data signals for transmission over a network. Also called line coding.

modulation division multiplexing   A multiplexing method in which the signals that modulate the optical carriers are multiplexed.

modulator   A device that converts a signal (voice or other) into a form that can be transmitted.

module   A hardware or software component that is discrete and identifiable.

monitor   (1) A software tool used to supervise, control, or verify the operations of a system. (2) A device used to display computer-generated information.

Moonv6   The largest permanently deployed multivendor IPv6 network in the world. Moonv6 is a global effort.

MP2 (MPEG-1 Audio Layer 2)   An audio codec that has largely been replaced by MP3 for PC and Internet applications but remains a dominant standard for audio broadcasting as part of the DAB and DVB standards.

MP3 (MPEG Audio Layer 3)   (1) A popular digital audio encoding and lossy compression format that was designed to greatly reduce the amount of data required to represent audio yet still sound like a faithful reproduction of the original uncompressed audio to most listeners. (2) Files of sound or music recordings stored in the MP3 format on computers or other devices.

MP4 (MPEG-4 Part 14)   A multimedia container format standard that is most commonly used to store digital audio and digital video streams, but also used to store other data, such as subtitles and still images. MP4 allows streaming over the Internet.

MP-BGP (Multiprotocol Border Gateway Protocol)   An IPv6-enabled routing protocol used to announce IPv6 routes across MPLS tunnels.

MPEG (Moving Picture Experts Group)   The ISO standards body responsible for the MPEG international video compression standards. MPEG-1 addresses VHS-quality images with a 1.5Mbps data rate. MPEG-1 can play back from a single-speed CD-ROM player at 352 × 240 (i.e., quarter-screen) at 30 frames per second (fps). MPEG-2, which today is the compression scheme of choice, addresses DTV—or computer-quality—images with a 6Mbps data rate. MPEG-2 offers resolutions of 720 × 480 and 1,280 × 720 at 30fps, with full CD-quality audio. MPEG-3 will address HDTV-quality images, at data rates up to 60Mbps. MPEG-4, an evolution of MPEG-2, features audio, video, and systems layers and offers VBR encoding for both narrowband and broadband delivery in a single file. It also uses an object-based compression method, rather than MPEG-2's frame-based compression. MPEG-4 allows objects—such as two-dimensional or three-dimensional video objects, text, graphics, and sound—to be manipulated and made interactive through Web-like hyperlinks and/or multimedia triggers. MPEG-4 Advanced Video Compression (AVC) is a digital video codec standard noted for achieving very high data compression. MPEG-7 is a multimedia content description standard for information searching. MPEG-21 is a framework for the all-electronic creation, production, delivery, and trade of content.

MPLS (Multiprotocol Label Switching)   An IETF initiative that integrates Layer 2 information about network links (e.g., bandwidth, latency, utilization) into Layer 3 (IP) within a particular autonomous system in order to simplify and improve IP packet exchange. MPLS gives network operators a great deal of flexibility to divert and route traffic around link failures, congestion, and bottlenecks.

MPλS (Multiprotocol Lambda Switching)   A variation of MPLS in which specific wavelengths serve in place of labels as unique identifiers. The specified wavelengths, like the labels, make it possible for routers and switches to perform necessary functions automatically, without having to extract instructions regarding those functions from IP addresses or other packet information.

MP-MLQ (Multipulse Maximum Likelihood Quantization)   An ITU compression standard that reduces voice to 4.8Kbps and can permit up to 10 voice channels on a single 64Kbps connection.

MPOA (Multiprotocol over ATM)   An ATM Forum standard for linking a number of local networks across an ATM backbone that caters to many different network protocols.

mrouter (multicast router)   A router that enfolds IP packets in special multicast packets and forwards them toward a destination mrouter.

MSAU (multistation access unit)   A device that enables workstations on a LAN to be cabled in a star configuration. Also known as a token-ring hub.

MSO (multiple-system operator)   A cable TV operator of multiple cable systems.

MSP (management service provider)   A provider that takes over the actual management and monitoring of a network.

MSPP (multiservice provisioning platform)   A product designed to deliver convergence, revenue generation, and cost reductions on a single edge device. The multiservice edge is an emerging market segment of edge devices optimized for converging Layer 2/Layer 3 services over IP/MPLS. An MSPP can handle all the popular data protocols and interfaces on the access side, and it can interface to high-speed optical links on the transport side of the network.

MSS (Mobile Satellite Service)   A satellite network that is an IMT-2000 system that can be used worldwide. MSS is intended to take over when a user is out of range of terrestrial base stations. MSS is expected to offer services similar to those of terrestrial cellular networks, including data at ISDN speeds, toll-quality voice, video, and multimedia messaging. However, given the level of multinational cooperation required to achieve global availability, MSS is not likely to be realized as a solution anytime soon.

MSU (modem sharing unit)   A device that permits two or more terminals to share a single modem.

MTBF (mean time between failures)   The average length of time for which a system, or a component of a system, works without fault.

MTP (Message Transfer Part)   Part of SS7 used for communication in the PSTN. MTP is responsible for the correct and reliable end-to-end data transport of SS7 messages between communication partners. MTP Level 2 (MTP2) corresponds to OSI Layer 2, and MTP Level 3 (MTP3) corresponds to OSI Layer 3.

MTS (mobile telephone service) A telephone service provided between mobile stations and the PSTN in which radio transmission provides the equivalent of a local loop.

MTSO (mobile telephone switching office) A component in the cellular radio system that links the base transceiver stations with the terrestrial local exchanges to complete calls over the PSTN.

MTTR (mean time to repair) The average time required to perform corrective maintenance on a failed device.

MTU (maximum transmission unit) The maximum packet size that can be transmitted over a LAN or an internet.

mu-law encoding Encoding according to ITU-T recommendation G.711 that is used with 24-channel PCM systems in the United States and Japan. It is similar to A-law encoding, but the two differ in the size of the quantizing intervals.

multicarrier modulation A modulation scheme that uses and aggregates a certain amount of bandwidth and then subdivides it into subbands. Each subband is encoded by using a single-carrier technique, and bitstreams from the subbands are bonded together at the receiver.

multicasting Simultaneous distribution of data to a defined subset of all receive points in a network. The subset may be redefined for each transmission and range from one to all receive points.

multichannel Pertaining to broadcasting media capable of carrying multiple different television and radio channels.

multidrop A communications arrangement in which multiple devices share a common transmission channel, although only one may transmit at a time.

multimedia The presentation of more than one medium—typically images, sound, and text—in an interactive environment.

multimode fiber A fiber-optic cable with a core diameter large enough to allow light to travel on different paths, supporting propagation to multiple nodes.

multipath A propagation phenomenon that results in radio signals' reaching the receiving antenna by two or more paths. Multipath affects the quality of communication because it can create secondary and tertiary signals that compete or interfere with the primary signal.

multiple-access technique A method that enables sharing of spectrum by multiple users. FDMA, TDMA, and CDMA are examples of multiple-access techniques.

multiple trunk groups Groups that indicate that the switching system is capable of being equipped for more than one group of trunk circuits.

multiplex To interleave or simultaneously transmit two or more messages on a single channel.

multiplexer A device that enables more than one signal to be sent simultaneously over one physical channel. A multiplexer, sometimes called a mux, combines inputs from two or more terminals, computer ports, or other muxes and transmits the combined data stream over a single high-speed channel. At the receiving end, the high-speed channel is demultiplexed, either by another mux or by software.

multipoint   Pertaining or referring to a communications line to which three or more stations are connected. Multipoint implies that the line physically extends from one station to another until all are connected.

multipoint network   In data communications, a configuration in which more than two terminal installations are connected to a single port.

multiprocessing   The simultaneous execution of two or more computer programs.

mux   *See* multiplexer.

MVNO (mobile virtual network operator)   Companies that do not own licensed spectrum of their own but instead make use of another mobile operator's network, while reselling the wireless services under their own brand names.

MWS (Multimedia Wireless System)   A European term for high-frequency BFWA that is focused on broadband services, including real-time video, streaming video, and video transfer.

N

NACK or NAK (negative acknowledgment)   A message that indicates an error in transmission and says the previous block needs to be resent before anything else can happen.

NADC (North American Digital Cellular)   A TIA standard that uses TDMA and TDD schemes and offers a total of three time slots. NADC operates on the 800MHz frequency band, uses AMPS for signaling to reserve resources, and transfers speech in digital form; therefore, it is a digital overlay that is interoperable with analog AMPS infrastructure.

nailed-up connection   A slang term for a permanent, dedicated path through a switch. A nailed-up connection is often used for lengthy, regular data transmission going through a PBX.

name resolution   The process of mapping a name to a corresponding address. DNS provides a mechanism for naming computers in which programs use remote name servers to resolve machine names into IP addresses for those machines.

nanosecond   One-billionth of a second.

NAP (network access point)   The point at which backbones interconnect to exchange traffic between providers. Bottlenecks at NAPs greatly affect the ability to roll out new time-sensitive, loss-sensitive applications, such as Internet telephony, VoIP, VPNs, streaming media, and TV over Internet.

narrowband   A service occupying low bandwidth (64Kbps or below).

narrowcast   Transmission of specific programming to predetermined users of a telecommunications network. With narrowcast, only some users of the network are receiving the same information.

NAS (network attached storage)   Storage devices that can be accessed over a computer network rather than being directly connected to the computer. This enables multiple computers to share the same storage space, which minimizes overhead.

NAT (Network Address Translation)   An Internet standard that enables a LAN to use one set of IP addresses for internal traffic and a second set of addresses for external traffic. A NAT box located where the LAN meets the Internet makes all necessary IP address translations.

NCP (network control program) Software that represents a centralized database that stores a subscriber's unique VPN information. The NCP screens every call and applies call processing according to customer-defined requirements.

near-end crosstalk Unwanted energy transferred from one circuit usually to an adjoining circuit. It occurs at the end of the transmission link where the signal source is located, with the absorbed energy usually propagated in the opposite direction of the absorbing channel's normal current flow. Near-end crosstalk is usually caused by high-frequency or unbalanced signals and insufficient shielding.

NetBIOS (Network Basic Input/Output System) A session-layer interface that is widely used in PC networks.

NetBIOS extended user interface A transport-layer protocol designed to support NetBIOS over 802.2 LANs.

network (1) A collection of devices connected by communication lines for data processing or information interchange. (2) A series of points connected by communications channels. (3) A collection of telephone lines normally used for dialed telephone calls. (4) A group of computers and peripherals that are interconnected so that they can communicate with each other.

network architecture The philosophy and organizational concept for enabling communications between data-processing equipment at multiple locations. The network architecture specifies the processors and terminals and defines the protocols and software that must be used to accomplish accurate data communications.

network control In a network, the establishment, authorization, and maintenance of logical and physical connections between stations and applications, plus the synchronization, routing, integrity, and recovery of data transmitted during the established connections.

network layer In the OSI model, the logical network entity that services the transport layer. The network layer is responsible for ensuring that data passed to it from the transport layer is routed and delivered through the network.

network node A point on a network where communications lines interface. Thus, a network node might be a PBX, a local exchange, a multiplexer, a modem, a host computer, or one of several other devices.

network redundancy Including in a communication pathway additional links in order to connect all nodes.

network topology The physical and logical relationship of nodes in a network; the schematic arrangement of the links and nodes of a network, typically either a star, ring, tree, or bus topology, or some hybrid combination thereof.

networking Communication between stations in a network.

next-generation gateway switch A switch designed to support a wide variety of traffic—data, voice, fax, multimedia, and other emerging sensory forms—over a data backbone. It provides seamless interoperability between the circuits that network the PSTN and packet-switching networks.

next-generation network A high-speed packet-based network that is capable of transporting and routing a multitude of services, including voice, data, video, and multimedia. A next-generation network is a common platform for applications and services that the customer can access across the entire network as well as outside the network. Next-generation networks offer unrestricted access by users to different service providers and support generalized mobility, which will allow consistent and ubiquitous provision of services to users.

NFC (Near Field Communication) A technology standard for very-short-range (typically 1 to 2 inches) wireless connectivity that enables quick, secure, two-way interactions among electronic devices. NFC technology, which operates in the 13.56MHz range, typically takes the form of a small chip embedded in a phone or a plastic card (such as a credit card). With NFC-enabled mobile phones, transactions can be conducted by simply touching a point-of-sales device, entry point, or ticket gate.

NGI (Next-Generation Internet) A U.S. government project that is intended to drastically increase the speed of the Internet. Note that there is a distinct difference between NGI and NGi; the former is a U.S. government initiative, and the latter is a generic movement.

NGi (Next-Generation internet) A generic movement toward the future Internet, which will be so pervasive, reliable, and transparent that it will be a seamless part of life—like electricity or plumbing. NGi projects that are under way include Internet 2, Abilene, HOPI, NLR, MAN LAN, GÉANT2, and TEIN2.

NIC (network interface card) A component that connects a station to a network (e.g., LAN). Also called a network adapter card.

NIOD (Network Inward/Outward Dialing) A system that provides the capability for dialing both ways between a toll network and a local network.

N-ISDN (Narrowband ISDN) A network architecture and set of standards for an all-digital network. N-ISDN was intended to provide end-to-end digital service using the public telephone networks worldwide and, therefore, to provide high-quality, error-free transmission.

NIST (National Institute of Standards and Technology) A nonregulatory agency that promotes U.S. innovation and industrial competitiveness by advancing measurement science, standards, and technology.

NLSP (NetWare Link Services Protocol) A link-state protocol that offers low network overhead and fast convergence.

NMC (network management center) A center used for control of a network. An NMC may provide traffic analysis, call detail recording, configuration control, fault detection and diagnostics, and maintenance.

NMT (Nordic Mobile Telephone) A Scandinavian wireless system that originally operated at 450MHz, offered around 220 channels, and had a very large coverage area.

node (1) A device on a network that can independently send or receive information and that has a network address. (2) The point at which a device is linked to a network.

noise Unwanted electrical signals, introduced by circuit components or natural disturbances, that tend to degrade the performance of a communications channel.

nonblocking   A switch that has a through-traffic path for each attached station. A nonblocking switch or switching environment is designed to never experience a busy condition due to traffic volume.

nonswitched line   In data communications, a permanent connection between computers or devices that does not have to be established by dialing.

nonvolatile storage   A storage medium whose contents are not lost when the power is removed.

NPA (numbering plan area)   A geographic subdivision of the territory covered by a national or integrated numbering plan. An NPA is identified by a distinctive area code.

NRZ (nonreturn to zero)   A digital signaling technique in which the signal is at a constant level for a duration of time.

NSIS (Next Steps in Signaling)   A network architecture that addresses the introduction of QoS on an end-to-end basis. The design goals of NSIS include applicability across different QoS technologies, such as DiffServ and MPLS, as well as resource availability upon request prior to a reservation request.

NSP (network service provider)   A very large, global backbone carrier that owns its own infrastructures (e.g., AT&T, Sprint, Verizon).

NTSC (National Television Standards Committee)   A television broadcasting system that uses 525 picture lines and a 60Hz field frequency. It is used primarily in the United States, Canada, Mexico, and Japan. *See also* PAL and SECAM.

NTU (network termination unit)   A device that connects the PSTN with CPE. An NTU marks the final interconnect between the public network and a customer's private equipment. It is owned by the service provider and typically has communication standards, such as voltages and protocols, that allow specific types of equipment to communicate with the PSTN.

null attached   The operation of an FDDI concentrator without being attached to the backbone network. This configuration establishes a small, autonomous, single-ring FDDI network consisting of a limited number of directly connected single-attached stations.

NXX   The current exchange numbering plan, in which N is any digit from 2 to 9 and X is any digit from 0 to 9.

O

OADM (optical add/drop multiplexer)   An optical multiplexing device that uses special filters to extract the wavelengths that need to be dropped off at a given location. It eliminates the costly electronics used to convert between light and electricity in a nonoptical multiplexer.

OC-1 to OC-768 (Optical Carrier-1 to Optical Carrier-768)   Optical carrier levels used for the categories of bandwidth in a SONET fiber-optic network. OC-1 is the base optical carrier transmission speed of 51.840Mbps. To calculate OC-2 to OC-768 speeds, simply multiply the OC-1 base by the desired magnitude. Common OC levels include OC-1 (51Mbps), OC-3 (155Mbps), OC-12 (622Mbps), OC-48 (2.5Gbps), OC-192 (10Gbps), and OC-768 (40Gbps).

OCAP (OpenCable Applications Platform)   The OpenCable software specification, which creates a common platform on which interactive services can be deployed. OCAP is intended to enable the developers of interactive TV services and applications to design such products so that they will run successfully on any cable TV system in North America, regardless of the set-top or television receiver, hardware, or operating system software choices.

octet   8 bits. An octet is equivalent to a byte, as long as the byte is also 8 bits. Whereas bytes can range from 4 to 10 bits, octets are always 8 bits.

odd parity check   A test of whether the number of digits in a group of binary digits is odd.

OFDM (Orthogonal Frequency Division Multiplexing)   A multicarrier modulation scheme that broadcasts on many frequencies, reducing interference from collisions with walls and objects.

OFDMA (Orthogonal Frequency Division Multiple Access)   A multiple-access scheme for OFDM systems that defines either 2,048 or 4,096 subcarriers. In current OFDM systems, only a single user can transmit on all the subcarriers at any given time. OFDMA allows multiple users to transmit simultaneously on the different subcarriers per OFDM symbol.

off-hook   A state in which a telephone set is in use (i.e., the handset is removed from its cradle).

offline   (1) Pertaining to equipment or devices not under direct control of the central processing unit. (2) Used to describe terminal equipment that is not connected to a transmission line. (3) Not controlled directly by or communicating with a computer.

offload   To move data or programs out of storage.

OGT (outgoing trunk)   A one-way trunk that carries only outgoing traffic.

OLT (optical line termination)   A switch that sends traffic downstream to subscribers and that also handles the upstream traffic.

ones density rule   A scheme that allows a CSU/DSU to recover the data clock reliably. The CSU/DSU derives the data clock from the data that passes through it. In order to recover the clock, the CSU/DSU hardware must receive at least one 1-bit value for every 8 bits of data that pass through it. Also called pulse density.

one-way trunk   A trunk between a switch (e.g., a PBX) and an exchange or between exchanges, where traffic originates from only one end.

on-hook   A state in which a telephone set is not in use (i.e., the handset is resting in the cradle).

online   (1) Being controlled directly by or directly communicating with a computer. (2) Connected to a computer so that data can pass to or from the computer without human intervention. (3) Directly in the line loop.

online services   Computer functions offered to end users who do not own host computers. Online services include time sharing, archival storage, and prepared software programs.

ONP (Open Network Provision)   A pan-European standard that ensures the provision of the network infrastructure by European telecommunications administrations to users and competitive service providers on terms equal to those for the administrations themselves.

ONU (optical network unit)   A device in which optical-to-electrical conversions take place.

open system   A system that facilitates multivendor, multitechnology integration based on publicly available standards for subsystem interaction. Three characteristics of an open system are portability, scalability, and interoperability.

OpenCable   A CableLabs initiative to publish specifications that define digital cable network interfaces and the nature of next-generation cable set-top boxes. The goal of OpenCable is to help the cable industry deploy interactive services over cable, create a common standard for digital cable TV within the United States, and promote competition among licensed device manufacturers.

optical carrier   Specifications that define line speeds and transmission encoding and multiplexing methods for the SDH/SONET fiber-optic backbone network.

optical fiber   Any filament, or fiber, made of dielectric materials that is used to transmit laser- or LED-generated light signals, usually for digital communications. An optical fiber consists of a core, which carries the signal, and cladding, a substance with a slightly higher refractive index than the core, which surrounds the core and reflects the light signal back into it. Also called lightguide or fiber-optic.

optical switch   A device that resides at a junction point in an optical backbone and enables signals in optical fibers or integrated optical circuits to be selectively switched from one circuit to another. An optical switch links any of several incoming lines to any of several outgoing lines and automatically reroutes traffic when a network path fails.

OPX (off-premises extension)   A telephone extension located other than where the main switch is.

OSI (Open Systems Interconnection) model   A seven-layer logical network architecture used to define network protocol standards to enable an OSI-compatible computer or device to communicate with any other OSI-compliant computer or device for a meaningful exchange of information. Layer 7, the application layer, is responsible for exchanging information between the programs running on a computer and other services on a network. Layer 6, the presentation layer, formats information so that a software application can read it. Layer 5, the session layer, supports connections between sessions and handles administrative tasks and security. Layer 4, the transport layer, corrects transmission errors and ensures that the information is delivered reliably. Layer 3, the network layer, identifies computers on a network and determines how to direct information transfer over that network. Layer 2, the data link layer, groups data into containers to prepare that data for transfer over a network. Layer 1, the physical layer, defines how a transmission medium connects to a computer, as well as how electrical or optical information is transferred on the transmission medium.

OSP (online service provider)   A provider that organizes online content and provides intuitive user navigation.

OSPF (Open Shortest Path First)   A routing protocol used on TCP/IP networks in which routers maintain an internal map of the network and exchange information about the current state of each network link. OSPF's features include least-cost routing, multipath routing, and load balancing.

OSS (operational support system)   A set of programs that help a communications service provider monitor, control, analyze, and manage problems with a telephone or computer network.

OTDR (optical time domain reflectometer)   A device that can be used in fiber networks to detect potential leaks that could be the result of unwanted intrusion.

OTN (Optical Transport Network)   A network that is composed of a set of optical network elements connected by optical fiber links and is able to provide functionality of transport, multiplexing, routing, management, supervision, and survivability of optical channels carrying client signals, according to the requirements given in ITU-T Recommendation G.872.

out-of-band management   A system in which management data is communicated through a link, outside the network, typically through a modem or some other serial connection.

out-of-band signaling   Signaling in which the conversation and the signaling take place over different paths. A separate digital channel (called a signaling link) is created, where messages are exchanged between network elements at 56Kbps or 64Kbps. Out-of-band signals run no danger of interference from speech or data, which allows signaling to take place during the conversation. However, the out-of-band signal needs extra bandwidth and extra electronics to handle the signaling band.

output   Data that has been processed.

overflow   Excess traffic, on a particular route, that is offered to another (alternate) route.

overlay network   A high-performance digital network that interconnects with the main public network but has its own lines, exchanges, and, often, a separate international gateway.

overnet   A PNAP.

override   To seize a circuit even though the circuit is already occupied.

P

PABX (private automatic branch exchange)   *See* PBX.

packet   A group of binary digits, including data and call control signals, that is switched as a composite whole. The data, call control signals, and error control information are arranged in a specific format. Also called block, frame, cell, or datagram.

packet loss   A problem that occurs when there is congestion at the packet switches or routers. Packet loss can considerably degrade real-time applications.

packet overhead   A measure of the ratio of the total packet bits occupied by control information to the number of bits of data, usually expressed as a percentage.

packet radio   A data network that uses licensed bandwidth and is specifically built for two-way data, not for voice communications.

packet switching   A method of transmitting messages through a communication network in which long messages are subdivided into short packets. Each packet contains the data and a destination address and is passed from source to destination through intermediate nodes. At each node, the packet is received, stored briefly, and then passed to the next node. The packets are then reassembled into the original message at the receiving end.

PacketCable   A CableLabs initiative that defines standards for the cable TV industry. It develops interoperable interface specifications for two-way cable networks in order to deliver advanced real-time multimedia services. PacketCable interconnects three networks: the HFC access network, the PSTN, and IP networks. Known internationally as IP Cablecom.

packet-switched network   A network that consists of a series of interconnected switches that route individual packets of data over one of several redundant routes. Packet-switched networks include X.25, Frame Relay, IP, ATM, and MPLS.

PAD (packet assembler/disassembler)   A protocol conversion device that accepts characters in a serial data stream and converts them into packets to send across a packet-switched network, such as an IP network.

PAL (Phase Alternating Line)   The color television broadcasting system developed in West Germany and the United Kingdom that uses 625 picture lines and a 50Hz field frequency. *See also* NTSC and SECAM.

PAM (pulse amplitude modulation)   A form of modulation in which the amplitude of the pulse carrier is varied in accordance with successive samples of the modulating signal.

PAN (personal area network)   A network that surrounds an individual and provides networking between badge-based computers and other input/output devices.

PAP (Password Authentication Protocol)   A protocol that uses a two-way handshake for the peer to establish its identity upon link establishment. The peer repeatedly sends the password to the authenticator until verification is acknowledged or the connection is terminated.

parallel transmission   The simultaneous transmission of all the bits making up a character or byte, either over separate channels or on different carrier frequencies on the same channel.

parity   The state of being even numbered or odd numbered. A parity bit is a binary digit appended to a group of binary digits to make the sum of the digits either all odd (odd parity) or all even (even parity).

parity check   A procedure in which noninformation bits are added to data to make the number of 1s in a grouping of bits either always even or always odd. This procedure allows detection of bit groupings that contain single errors. It can be applied to characters, blocks, or any specific bit grouping. Also called vertical redundancy check (VRC).

passive optical splitter   A device used in a PON that splits the power of the optical signal and distributes it to multiple customers and in the reverse direction combines multiple light streams onto a single fiber. Passive optical splitters don't need any power, hence the term *passive*; they work like a prism, splitting light into the colors of the rainbow. This means that a passive optical splitter is not sensitive to temperature or other elements that would be problematic for electrical components. Optical splitters can be located in a telco building, outside plant, or any other building along the fiber route.

password   A word or set of characters that must be given to satisfy security needs.

patch panel   A passive wiring device that facilitates manual patching of end-user machines onto ports on one or more network hubs.

path   (1) In a network, any route between any two nodes. (2) The route traversed by the information exchanged between two attaching devices in a network.

Pbps (petabits per second)   1,000Tbps.

PBX (private branch exchange)   A telephone switch located on a customer's premises that primarily establishes voice-grade circuits between individual users (extensions) and the switched telephone network. Typically, the PBX also provides switching within a customer's premises and usually offers numerous other enhanced features, such as least-cost routing and call-detail recording. Also called a PABX.

PCM (Pulse Code Modulation)   A scheme used to convert an analog voice signal into a digital bitstream for transmission. PCM is a digital transmission technique that involves sampling of an analog information signal at regular time intervals and coding of the measured amplitude into a series of binary values, which are transmitted by modulation of a pulsed, or intermittent, carrier. PCM is a common method of speech digitizing by using 8-bit codewords, or samples, and a sampling rate of 8,000 times per second.

PCS (Personal Communication Services)   A digital service that operates in the 1.8GHz to 2GHz band and uses both microcell and picocell architectures.

PDC (Personal Digital Cellular)   Also known as Japanese Digital Cellular (JDC), a 2G standard for digital wireless communications deployed widely in Japan.

PDH (Plesiochronous Digital Hierarchy)   The first generation of digital hierarchy, which defines the available digital transmission rates and number of channels. PDH is used by telecommunications operators and implemented according to three standards: T-carrier in North America, E-carrier in ITU-T countries, and J-carrier in Japan. PDH is defined by the ITU-T in its G.703 standard.

PDN (public data network)   A generic term for the collection of packet-switching networks that provide public data services. Well-known examples are the Internet and X.25.

PDU (protocol [or packet] data unit)   A message of a given protocol, comprising payload and protocol-specific control information, typically contained in a header. PDUs pass over the protocol interfaces that exist between the layers of protocols (per the OSI model).

peering agreement   An arrangement in which operators agree to exchange with one another the same amount of traffic over high-speed lines between their routers so that users on one network can reach addresses on the other.

peer-to-peer   The interaction by which computers and other network devices communicate with each other as equals and on their own initiative (as opposed to a client/server environment).

performance   A major factor on which the total productivity of a system depends. Performance is largely determined by a combination of several other factors: throughput, latencies, response time, and availability.

pervasive computing   An environment in which computers are taken out of standalone boxes to which people are tied and put into ordinary things, in everyday objects. Also called ubiquitous computing.

P-frame (predicted frame)   In MPEG terminology, a frame that is only reconstructed from preceding reference frames. It can also be a reference frame because it reconstructs other frames in some instances.

PGP (Pretty Good Privacy)   A technique for encrypting messages. Using PGP is one of the most common ways to protect messages on the Internet because it is effective, easy to use, and free. PGP is based on the public key method, which uses two keys: a public key disseminated to individuals who should receive a message and a private key used to decrypt messages that are received.

phantom circuit   A third voice circuit that is superimposed on two 2-wire voice circuits.

phase   The angle of a waveform at a given moment.

phase jitter   A random distortion of signal lengths caused by the rapid fluctuation of the frequency of the transmitted signal. Phase jitter interferes with interpretation of information by changing the timing.

phased-array antenna   A small, flat antenna that is steered electronically. It is actually a group of antennas in which the relative phases of the respective signals feeding the antennas are varied in such a way that the effective radiation pattern of the array is reinforced in a desired direction and suppressed in undesired directions. It provides great agility and fast tracking, as well as the ability to form multiple antenna beams simultaneously. It allows for very fast and precise steering of the communications beam, which is very important for high-bandwidth communication because the data rate is inversely proportional to the angular offset.

PHS (Personal Handyphone System)   A Japanese standard for 2G PCS wireless networks.

PHY (physical layer)   Layer 1 of the OSI model. It defines the electrical, optical, mechanical, and procedural characteristics of the interface.

physical address   The address of a physical communications device in a system.

physical interface   The definition of the number of pins in a connector, the number of wires in a cable, and what signal is being carried over which of the pins and over which of the wires, to ensure that the information is being viewed compatibly.

picocell   A tiny cell architecture in the cellular system that covers about 150 feet (46 m). Compared to the microcell design, the picocell design offers even better frequency reuse, even lower power, even smaller subscriber units, and even better, longer battery life.

piconet   An ad hoc computer network of devices that use Bluetooth protocols to allow a master device to interconnect with slave devices.

ping (packet Internet groper)   The name of a program used with TCP/IP internets to test reachability of destinations by sending them an ICMP echo request and waiting for a reply.

pixel (picture element)   In computer graphics, the smallest element of a display space that can be independently assigned color and intensity.

PKE (public key encryption)   A message authentication mechanism that is part of most Web browsers.

PKI (public key infrastructure)   A process that secures e-business applications such as private e-mail, purchase orders, and workflow automation. It uses digital certificates and digital signatures to authenticate and encrypt messages and a CA to handle the verification process.

plant   The physical equipment of a telephone network that provides communications services.

plotter   A device that converts computer output into drawings on paper or displays the output on display-type terminals instead of printing a listing.

PLP (Packet Layer Protocol)   A standard in the network layer of X.25.

PLT (powerline telecommunications)   A wireline technology that provides the transmission of data to users over the same lines that bring electric power to homes and businesses. PLT could allow electrical utilities to provide high-speed Internet, voice, data, and video services to customers of all classes via power transmission and distribution lines. Current technologies offer speeds ranging from 1Mbps to 45Mbps. Also known as powerline communications (PLC) and broadband over powerlines (BPL).

PM (phase modulation)   A way to modify a sine wave signal to make it carry information. The sine wave, or carrier, has its phase changed in accordance with the information to be transmitted.

PNAP (private network access point)   A private point of access to the Internet, also called a peering point, that bypasses public NAPs.

PoC (Push-to-Talk over Cellular)   An open standard for push-to-talk (i.e., walkie-talkie) technology that defines how push-to-talk can be deployed over a cellular operator's packet data network using VoIP. PoC uses VoIP technology to stream voice over data networks such as GPRS. The key to PoC is IMS.

point-to-point line   A circuit that connects two points directly, where there are generally no intermediate processing nodes, although there could be switching facilities. Synonymous with two-point and always-on.

policy-based management   A system in which information about individual users, groups, organizational units, and entire organizations, as well as events (e.g., the beginning of the accounting department's month-end closing), can be associated with various network services or classes of service.

polling   A host-system-controlled method for determining whether each of the stations on a communication line has data to send.

PON (passive optical network)   A network in which one access line is shared among multiple buildings. Optical splitters and couplers are used at each fiber connection in the network.

POP (point of presence)   The physical access location into a network.

POP (Post Office Protocol)   An application-layer protocol that e-mail clients use to retrieve e-mail from a remote server over a TCP/IP connection.

port   (1) A point of access into a communications switch, a computer, a network, or another electronic device. (2) The physical or electrical interface through which a person gains access to a computer, a network, or another electronic device. (3) The interface between a process and a communications or transmission facility.

port number   A number in the range 1 to 65,535 that identifies a port. The port number does not represent a physical port, such as the serial port to which a modem or a mouse might be attached; instead, it is like a regional memory address.

port speed   The maximum signaling rate on a digital access line.

PoS (Packet over SDH/SONET)   A communications protocol for transmitting packets over the circuit-switched protocols SDH and SONET. Much of the traffic on the Internet is carried over PoS links.

POTS (plain old telephone service)   The standard analog telephone service that most homes have traditionally used.

powerline   Broadband data transmission over electrical powerlines.

PPP (Point-to-Point Protocol)   A protocol that provides router-to-router and host-to-network connections over synchronous and asynchronous circuits. PPP is a successor to SLIP.

PPTP (Point-to-Point Tunneling Protocol)   A Layer 2 protocol that can work in a non-IP enterprise environment, which is one of its strengths for customers who use multiple protocols rather than using only IP. PPTP provides low packet overhead and good compression, but it has security weaknesses.

presence-based services   The ability to see in real-time where someone is, how that person prefers to be reached, and even what the person is doing. Presence-based services involve the ability, willingness, desire, and capability of a user to communicate across media end devices and even time and space.

presentation layer   Layer 6 in the OSI model, which provides services to the application layer, enabling it to interpret the data exchanged, as well as to structure data messages to be transmitted in a specific display and control format.

preventive maintenance   The routine checking of components to keep a system functioning.

PRI (Primary Rate Interface)   A bundle of ISDN circuits, primarily a PBX interface. The United States and Japan use 23B+D, and the ITU uses 30B+D. Also called Primary Rate Access (PRA).

primary station   On a point-to-point communication line, the station that gains control of the line first. On a multipoint line, the station that controls communications.

private key   The decryption (reception) or encryption (signature) component of an asymmetrical key set.

private line   The channel equipment furnished to a customer as a unit for exclusive use, generally with no access to or from the PSTN. Also called a leased line.

private network   A network based on leased lines or other facilities that provides telecommunication services within an organization or within a closed user group, as a complement to or a substitute for the public network.

proprietary   Hardware or software that is privately owned.

protocol   A set of rules that govern network communications. Low-level protocols define transmission rates, data encoding schemes, physical interfaces, network addressing schemes, and the method by which nodes contend for the chance to transmit data over a network. High-level protocols define functions such as printing and file sharing.

protocol header   Information in a packet that the protocol needs in order to do its work.

protocol stack (or protocol suite)   A collection of protocols that computers use to exchange information.

provisioned VPN   A packet-switched VPN that runs across the service provider's backbone, generally using Frame Relay or ATM.

proxy ARP (proxy Address Resolution Protocol)   A technique in which one machine, usually a router, answers ARP requests intended for another by supplying its own physical address. By pretending to be another machine, the router accepts responsibility for routing packets to it. The purpose of proxy ARP is to allow a site to use a single IP network address with multiple physical networks.

proxy server   A server that provides firewall functionality, acting as an intermediary for user requests and establishing a connection to the requested resource either at the application layer or at the session or transport layer.

PSK (phase-shift keying)   A modulation technique for transforming digital information to analog whereby that information is conveyed as varying phases of a carrier signal.

PSTN (public switched telephone network)   The complete traditional public telephone system, including telephones, local and interexchange trunks, transport equipment, and exchanges.

PTO (public telecommunications operator)   An incumbent carrier. This term is used in countries other than the United States.

PTT (post, telegraph, and telephone) organization   Usually a governmental department that acts as its nation's common carrier. Also called PT&T.

public key   A device used by algorithms that encrypt and decrypt using asymmetric yet mathematically linked keys. Each security module is assigned a pair of keys: The encryption key is public and does not require distribution by secure means. The decryption, or private, key cannot be discovered through knowledge of the public key or its underlying algorithm. Public key algorithms can apply to one or more of the following: key distribution, encryption, authentication, or digital signature.

pulse   A momentary, sharp alteration in the current or voltage produced in a circuit to operate a switch or relay that can be detected by a logic circuit. A pulse is a sharp rise and fall of finite duration.

punchdown block   A common termination point in the wiring closet for wires going out to the individual offices and wall sockets.

push technology   A program that updates news, weather, or other selected information on a computer user's desktop interface through periodic and generally unobtrusive transmission over the World Wide Web.

push-to-talk   A mobile application that turns a mobile phone into a walkie-talkie by giving it trunked radio functionality. Sometimes abbreviated PTT.

push-to-*x*   A mobile application that is based on push-to-talk and combined with other applications, including presence, picture sharing, and video clips.

PVC (permanent virtual circuit)   A defined path that provides essentially a dedicated private line between users in a packet-switching network. The network is aware of a fixed association between two stations, permanent logical channel numbers are assigned exclusively to the permanent circuit, and devices do not require permission to transmit to each other.

PWM (pulse width modulation)   The process of encoding information based on variations of the duration of carrier pulses. Also known as pulse duration modulation (PDM).

Px64   The ITU-T H.320 standard for interoperability in videoconferencing over ISDN.

Q

QAM (Quadrature Amplitude Modulation)   A single-carrier scheme that modulates both the amplitude and phase to yield higher spectral efficiency. Various levels of QAM exist, and they are referred to as *nn*-QAM, where *nn* indicates the number of states per Hertz (Hz). The number of bits per symbol time is k, where $2^k = nn$. So, 4 bits/Hz is equivalent to 16-QAM, 6 bits/Hz is equivalent to 64-QAM, and 8 bits/Hz is equivalent to 256-QAM.

QoS (quality of service)   In networking, a concept by which applications can indicate their specific requirements to the network before they actually start transmitting information data. *Implicit QoS* means that the application chooses the required levels of QoS. With *explicit QoS*, the network manager controls that decision.

QPSK (Quadrature Phase-Shift Keying)   A single-carrier modulation scheme that supports 2 bits per symbol time.

Q.Sig   The Ecma International standard for common-channel signaling between PBXs.

quadruple-play services   A service provider's bundle of voice, data, video/TV, and wireless/mobile services, delivered over the same infrastructure.

quantization noise   Signal errors caused by the process of digitizing a continuously variable slope.

query   A request for information that is entered while a computer system is processing.

queue   An ordered accumulation of data or transactions stored for later processing.

queuing   A process in which communications calls, processing requests, processes, and so on are stacked or held so that they can be worked with in sequence.

QVGA (Quarter Video Graphics Array)   A computer display with 320×240 resolution, such as on a mobile phone, PDA, or handheld gaming console.

R

radio channel   The frequency band allocated to a service provider or transmitter.

radio wave   An electromagnetic wave of frequencies between approximately 20KHz and 3GHz.

RADIUS (Remote Authentication Dial-in User Services)   An authentication and access control server used to determine whether a user is allowed access to corporate resources.

RADSL (Rate-Adaptive DSL)   A symmetrical or asymmetrical transmission medium that has a maximum loop length of 18,000 feet (5.5 km) and is deployed as a single twisted-pair cable. RADSL adapts the data rate dynamically, based on any changes that may be occurring in the line conditions and based on the loop length. With RADSL, the rates can vary widely, from 600Kbps to 7Mbps downstream and from 128Kbps to 1Mbps upstream.

RAM (random-access memory)   A type of computer memory that can be accessed randomly (i.e., any byte of memory can be accessed without touching the preceding bytes).

Raman amplifier   An optical amplifier that uses a powerful laser source to boost the signal power in standard optical fiber. In this type of amplifier, the amplification effect is achieved by a nonlinear interaction between the signal and a pump laser within an optical fiber.

RAN (radio access network)   Part of a mobile telecommunication system that sits between the mobile phone and the core network. It is possible for a single handset to be simultaneously connected to multiple RANs (e.g., both GSM and UMTS RANs).

RARP (Reverse Address Resolution Protocol)   The TCP/IP protocol that a diskless machine uses at startup to find its address. The machine broadcasts a request that contains its physical hardware address, and a server responds by sending the machine its IP address.

RBOC (regional Bell operating company)   One of several independent telephone companies created from the breakup of AT&T.

RBS (Robbed Bit Signaling)   A type of channel-associated signaling used in North America on T-1 trunks in which one of the bits of digital voice is stolen and replaced with the proper signaling bit.

RC4 (Rivest Cipher 4)   A streaming cipher technique. A stream cipher adds the output of a pseudorandom number generator bit by bit to the sequential bits of the digitized plain text.

RED (random early detection)   A queue management algorithm and a congestion avoidence algorithm that monitors the average queue size and drops packets based on statistical probabilities.

redundancy   (1) The portion of the total information contained in a message that can be eliminated without loss in essential information. (2) The provision of duplicate, backup equipment to immediately take over the function of equipment that fails. (3) In a database, the storage of the same data item or group of items in two or more files.

redundancy check   An automatic or a programmed check based on the systematic insertion of components or characters used especially for checking purposes.

regenerative repeater   (1) A repeater used in telegraph applications to retime and retransmit the received signal impulses and restore them to their original strength. These repeaters are speed and code sensitive and are intended for use with standard speeds and codes. (2) A repeater used in PCM or digital circuits that detects, retimes, and reconstructs the bits transmitted. (3) A LAN interconnect relay device that copies electrical signals from one LAN to another. Also called a regenerator.

register   The first unit in the assembly of common control equipment in an automatic exchange. The register receives address information in the form of dial pulses or DTMF signals and stores it for possible conversion or translation.

reliability   The measure of a network's availability. Reliability is often measured in terms of the number of nines; for example, five-nines reliability means that the network is available 99.999% of the time.

remote   Pertains to a computer or device that is connected to another computer or device over a communication line.

remote access   Communication between a computer or PBX in one location and a device that is physically removed from the location of the computer or PBX.

remote access server   A server that provides network access to remote users, generally via analog POTS lines, or perhaps ISDN connections, including dialup protocols and access control for authentication.

remote access software   Sometimes called remote control software, a program that is a superset of the asynchronous communications software market. It allows a PC to have complete control over another PC at a different site.

remote data concentration   A communications processor used for multiplexing data from low-speed lines or terminals onto one or more high-speed lines.

remote maintenance   A feature or service in which a service technician can dial into a system and be connected to the system and the system processor to run diagnostics and perform system administration.

remote monitoring MIB (remote monitoring Management Information Base)
The MIB that enables any SNMP management console to extract information from a protocol analyzer running remote monitoring.

repeater   (1) In analog transmission, equipment that receives a pulse train, amplifies it, and retimes it for retransmission. (2) In digital transmission, equipment that receives a pulse train, reconstructs it, retimes it, and then amplifies the signal for retransmission. (3) In fiber optics, a device that decodes a low-power light signal, converts it to electrical energy, and then retransmits it via an LED or a laser-generating light source, often including some form of signal amplification.

resale carrier   A company that redistributes the services of another common carrier and retails the services to the public.

Resilient Packet Ring   A standard for the optimized transport of data traffic over fiber rings. Its main goal is to increase the efficiency of IP services and Ethernet.

reverse channel   A simultaneous data path in the reverse direction over a half-duplex facility. Normally the reverse channel is used for positive/negative acknowledgments of previously received data blocks.

RF (radio frequency)   A frequency that is much higher than the audio frequencies but below the infrared frequencies. RF is usually above 20KHz.

RFI (radio frequency interference)   EMI that causes unwanted signals (interference or noise) in radio communications.

RFID (radio frequency identification)   At a simple level, a technology that involves tags that emit radio signals and devices called readers that pick up the signal. RFID is a method of remotely storing and retrieving data by using RFID tags and readers. RFID can be used to identify and track any movable item or asset. RFID is an alternative to bar coding. Its advantages include data capacity, read/write capability, and a lack of line-of-sight requirements.

RFID encoder   A read/write RFID reader. RFID encoders can be used to read information from an RFID tag and to program information into a blank RFID tag.

RFID reader   A device that processes the data from RFID tags according to the application requirements. RFID readers are used to query RFID tags in order to obtain identification, location, and other information about the object the tag is embedded in.

RFID tag   A small object that can be attached to or incorporated into a product, an animal, or a person and then read by an RFID reader. An RFID tag is a tiny microchip composed of a processor, memory, and a radio transmitter that is mounted onto a substrate or an enclosure. Also referred to as an RFID transponder.

Rijndael algorithm   The algorithm used for AES. The algorithm was designed by two Belgian cryptologists, Vincent Rijmen and Joan Daemen.

ring   (1) A ring-shaped contact of a plug, usually positioned between but insulated from the tip and sleeve. (2) An audible alerting signal on a telephone line. (3) A network topology in which stations are connected to one another in a closed logical circle, with access to the medium passing sequentially from one station to the next by means of polling from a master station or by passing an access token from one station to another. Also called a loop.

ring in/ring out   A connection on a token-ring MAU that is used to tie multiple MAUs into a larger ring.

ringing signal   Any AC or DC signal transmitted over a line or trunk for the purpose of alerting a party at the distant end of an incoming call. The signal can operate a visual- or sound-producing device.

RIP (Routing Information Protocol)   A routing protocol used on TCP/IP networks that distributes the addresses of reachable networks and metrics reflecting the degree of difficulty involved in reaching particular networks form particular locations.

RJ-11   A standard four-wire modular connector used with telephones.

RJ-45   An eight-wire modular connector used with UTP.

RO (receive only)   (1) A printer terminal without a keyboard for data entry. (2) A satellite earth station that can receive but not transmit signals.

ROADM (reconfigurable optical add/drop multiplexer)   An add/drop mux that is software based and adds the capability to switch between different networks. ROADMs can switch traffic at both the SDH/SONET and wavelength layers.

robot   An easily reprogrammable, computer-controlled device that can physically manipulate its surroundings.

rotary dial calling   A system that accepts dialing from conventional rotary dial sets that generate pulses.

router   A device that connects two LAN segments that use similar or different architectures at the OSI network layer (Layer 3). A router determines the most efficient route for passing data through an internet. Packets that contain a network address different from the originating PC's address are forwarded to an adjoining network. Multiprotocol routers can handle this job for two or more protocols simultaneously.

routing algorithm   A formula that uses metrics (e.g., path length, destination, next-hop associations, reliability, delay, bandwidth, load, communication cost) to determine the best path to the destination.

routing protocol   A protocol that enables routers to communicate with each other. Routing protocols include RIP, IGP, OSPF, EGP, and BGP.

routing table   A database that tells a router how to send packets to various destinations.

RPC (remote procedure call)   A system that enables an application programmer to distribute programs between computer systems interconnected by a network. RPC development tools eliminate the need for in-depth knowledge of diverse network protocols and computing platforms, enabling a programmer to concentrate on developing the application itself.

RS-232-C   A technical specification published by the EIA that establishes mechanical and electrical interface requirements between DTE and DCE, employing serial binary data interchange and operating at speeds up to 19.2Kbps.

RS-366-A   An EIA standard for interfaces between DTE and automatic calling equipment for data communication.

RS-422-A   An EIA specification for electrical characteristics of balanced-voltage digital interface circuits.

RS-423-A   An EIA specification for electrical characteristics of unbalanced-voltage digital interface circuits.

RS-449   An EIA specification for general-purpose, 37-position and 9-position interfaces for DTE and DCE, employing serial binary data interchange and operating at speeds up to 2Mbps.

RSA (Rivest, Shamir, and Adelman)   A public key algorithm whose security derives from the difficulty of factoring large prime integers.

RSVP (Resource Reservation Protocol)   A protocol that enables an internet to support specified levels of QoS. By using RSVP, an application can reserve resources along a route from source to destination. RSVP-enabled routers then schedule and prioritize packets to fulfill the QoS.

RSVP-TE (Resource Reservation Protocol–Traffic Engineering)   A router-based RSVP modification for MPLS traffic engineering that supports the instantiation of explicitly routed label-switched paths with or without resource reservations. It also supports smooth rerouting of label-switched paths, preemption, and loop detection.

RTCP (Real-Time Transport Control Protocol)   An ITU protocol that provides status feedback from senders to receivers.

RTCP XR (RTCP Reporting Extension)   An emerging media transport standard that allows information hidden by SRTP to be extracted directly from the digital signal processor software and IP phones and gateways and reported directly in the RTCP XR message.

RTMP (Routing Table Maintenance Protocol)   A communication protocol used by AppleTalk to ensure that all routers on the network have consistent routing information.

RTP (Real-Time Transport Protocol)   An Internet protocol for transmitting real-time data such as audio and video. RTP itself does not guarantee real-time delivery of data, but it does provide mechanisms for the sending and receiving applications to support streaming data.

RTSP (Real-Time Streaming Protocol)   A protocol that runs on top of IP multicasting, UDP, RTP, and RTCP.

S

sampling   A statistical procedure whereby generalizations are drawn from a relatively small number of observations.

SAN (storage area network)   A network designed to attach computer storage devices such as disk array controllers and tape libraries to servers. SANs are common in enterprise storage.

satellite communications   The use of orbiting satellites to relay transmissions from one earth station to another or to multiple earth stations.

scattering   A cause of lightwave signal loss in optical fiber transmission. Diffusion of a light beam is caused by microscopic variations in the material density of the transmission medium.

SCP (service control point)   A centralized node that contains service logic for the management of a call.

scrambler   A coding device that is applied to a digital channel to produce an apparently random bit sequence. A corresponding device is used to decode the channel (i.e., the coding is reversible).

ScTP (screened twisted-pair)   STP cabling with metal shielding also covering the group of shielded copper pairs. This type of cabling offers improved protection from interference from external sources.

SCTP (Stream Control Transmission Protocol)   A transport protocol that supports multistreaming and multihoming.

SDH (Synchronous Digital Hierarchy)   An ITU-T standard for digital broadband communications.

SDLC (Synchronous Data Link Control)   An IBM data link–layer protocol associated with SNA. In contrast to BSC, SDLC provides for full-duplex transmission and is more efficient.

SDP (Session Description Protocol)   A protocol used to describe and encode the capabilities of multimedia session participants. This description is then used to negotiate the characteristics of the session so that all the devices can participate.

SDR (software-defined radio)   A forthcoming application of multiradio technology that is a collection of hardware and software technologies that enable reconfigurable system architectures for wireless networks and user terminals. An SDR device can become a cellular phone, a GPS receiver, an amateur packet radio, or any other sort of radio transmitting or receiving device.

SDSL (Symmetrical [or Single-Line] DSL)   A symmetrical service that has a maximum loop length of 18,000 feet (5.5 km) and is deployed as a single twisted-pair cable. It can be deployed in various capacities, in multiples of 64Kbps, up to a maximum of 2Mbps in each direction.

SDTV (standard-definition television)   A DTV format that provides a picture quality similar to that of DVD.

SECAM (Systeme Electronique Couleur Avec Memoire [Sequential Color with Memory])   A TV system used in France and the former French colonies, as well as in parts of the Middle East. Russia and the former Soviet-allied countries use a modified form of SECAM. There are two versions of SECAM: SECAM vertical and SECAM horizontal. *See also* PAL and NTSC.

secondary channel   A low-speed channel established on a four-wire circuit over which diagnostics or control information is passed. User data is passed on the primary, high-speed channels of the circuit.

security   Protection of information against unauthorized access or use.

Segmentation and Reassembly sublayer   A sublayer of the AAL that supports mapping between variable-length data units and ATM cells.

selective ringing   A system that has the capability of ringing only the desired subscriber's telephone on a multiparty line. Ringers tuned to one of five possible frequencies are used to achieve this effect.

Semantic Web   Tim Berners-Lee's latest project, which is focused on creating a universal medium for information exchange using refined indexing and searching—in other words, providing meaning (semantics) to the content of documents in a manner that is understandable to machines.

sensor mesh network   A type of wireless micromesh network that uses many connected sensors to monitor a variety of factors. The sensors are all connected to each other and then to a base station. The sensors synchronize with each other, collect data, and sleep until the next iteration.

server   A processor that provides a specific service to the network. A routing server connects nodes and networks of like architectures, a gateway server connects nodes and networks of different architectures, and so on.

server-based network   A network in which one computer is the repository (i.e., the *server*) and the other computers request information from and store information on the server.

session   A period of time in which an end user engages in dialog with an interactive computer system.

session layer   Layer 5 of the OSI model. It manages a logical connection between two communication points.

set-top box   A locally powered piece of cable equipment that resides in the subscriber's home and provides tuning, descrambling, and pay-per-view capabilities.

SGSN (serving GPRS support node)   A device that provides the packet-switched link to mobile stations in the mobile IMS architecture. The SGSN provides packet routing to and from the SGSN service area for all users in that service area.

SHA-1 (Secure Hash Algorithm-1)   A message authentication mechanism that hashes a file of arbitrary length into a 160-bit value. It is more processor intensive than other mechanisms (such as MD5) but renders greater security.

SHDSL (Symmetric High-Speed DSL)   *See* G.SHDSL.

SHF (superhigh frequency)   Frequencies from 3GHz to 30GHz.

shielded cable   A cable in which the signal-carrying wire is enclosed by an outer sheath to reduce the effects of EMI on the signals. The shielding also reduces the effect of these signals on nearby electrical components and helps to prevent electronic eavesdropping.

ships-in-the-night routing   An approach to routing multiple protocols by which each protocol is routed based on a separate routing mechanism. For example, IP routed via OSPF and Connectionless Network Protocol (CLNP) routed via IS-IS might be used to handle the routing for both IP and CLNP.

sideband   The frequency band on either the upper or lower side of the carrier frequency band within which the frequencies produced by the process of modulation fall. Various modulation techniques make use of one or both of the sidebands, and some of them also suppress the carrier frequency.

signal   A physical, time-dependent energy value used for conveying information through a transmission line.

signaling   The process by which a caller or equipment on the transmitting end of a line informs a particular party or equipment at the receiving end that a message is to be communicated.

SIM (subscriber identity module) card   A smart card that defines the accounting and personal details of a service and can be used in any GSM handset to activate service.

SIMPLE (SIP for Instant Messaging and Presence Leveraging Extensions)   A set of SIP extensions for IM and presence capabilities.

simplex   Pertaining to the capability to transmit in one direction only.

simplex circuit   A circuit that permits the transmission of signals in one specified direction only.

single-attached station   A station connected to an FDDI network over a single fiber pair using a concentrator as the dual-attached station. Single-attached stations can be attached to only one ring. These stations are less expensive than dual-attached stations but are less reliable because the optics, electronics, and physical link must all be operational for the single-attached station to connect to the network.

single-carrier modulation   A modulation scheme in which a single channel occupies the entire bandwidth.

SIP (Session Initiation Protocol)   An application-layer control or signaling protocol for creating, modifying, and terminating sessions with one or more participants. SIP can establish sessions for features such as audio- or videoconferencing, interactive gaming, and call forwarding to be deployed over IP networks, thus enabling service providers to integrate basic IP telephony services with Web, e-mail, and chat services.

SIP telephony   Voice telecommunications that occur over a data network, using the SIP protocol. SIP telephony enables capabilities such as presence management across both voice and instant messaging, instant messaging archiving, click-to-talk voice functionality, speech-to-text functionality, personal mobility, and time-of-day routing.

skin effect   An occurrence in which as electricity migrates to the medium's skin, resistance increases because less of the wire is used.

SLA (service-level agreement)   A contract between an ASP and an end user that stipulates and commits the ASP to a required level of service. An SLA should contain a specified level of service, support options, enforcement or penalty provisions for services not provided, a guaranteed level of system performance as related to downtime or uptime, a specified level of customer support, and what software or hardware will be provided and for what fee.

sleeve   The third contacting part of a telephone plug, preceded in the location by the tip and ring.

SLIP (Serial Line Internet Protocol)   A minimal character-oriented protocol that provides basic IP encapsulation over dedicated or dialup asynchronous lines. It has largely been replaced by PPP.

smart card   A credit-card-sized device with embedded processors that provide a means of secure electronic storage. A smart card can be programmed to decrypt messages, to verify messages and digital signatures, and to create digital signatures for outgoing messages.

smart house   A home in which broadband services connect various intelligent devices, such as smart appliances.

SMDS (Switched Multimegabit Data Service)   A high-speed, packet-switched, datagram-based WAN networking technology that is offered by some telephone companies. It operates from 1.544Mbps to 44.736Mbps.

SMP (Simple Management Protocol)   An SNMP extension that includes security features, bulk retrieval, manager-to-manager communication, better definition of managed objects, improved error handling, and configurable exception reporting while running over protocols other than UDP, and requiring less memory for implementation.

SMR (Specialized Mobile Radio)   Any two-way radio system in which two or more mobile/portable wireless transceivers are linked by a single repeater. The repeater is elevated above average terrain to maximize the area of coverage. An SMR system is similar to but simpler than a cellular telephone network.

SMS (service management system)   A system that is used to build and maintain a PSTN-based VPN database and that allows customers to program specific functions to accommodate their particular business applications.

SMS (Short Messaging Service)   A system that enables text messages up to 160 alphanumeric characters in length to be sent to and from a GSM phone and to an external system such as e-mail, paging, and voicemail systems.

SMTP (Simple Mail Transfer Protocol)   The message transport protocol used by TCP/IP networks, such as Internet and other UNIX-based network systems, for the exchange of electronic messages.

SNA (Systems Network Architecture)   (1) IBM's standardized relationship between its Virtual Telecommunications Access Method (VTAM) and the NCP. (2) An architecture that specifies how products connect and communicate with one another in a network. SNA is a design for a total data communications system, encompassing every part of the communication network, from the user's application program at the central site to the terminal at a remote location.

SNMP (Simple Network Management Protocol)   A standard low-level protocol used to monitor and manage nodes on a network. SNMP consists of agent software, which runs on the managed device, and manager software, which resides on a central system that polls the agents. SNMP is an alternative to CMIP.

SNMPv2 (Simple Network Management Protocol version 2)   A revision of SNMP that includes additional security features, the ability to transfer a large chunk of data at once, and the ability to communicate between SNMP management stations.

SNR (signal-to-noise ratio)   The relative power of a signal compared to the power of noise on a line, expressed in decibels. As the ratio decreases, it becomes more difficult to distinguish between information and interference.

SOA (semiconductor optical amplifier)   An optical amplifier that is built on a single chip. SOAs can be integrated into multifunction optical chips and can be less expensive than EDFAs. The disadvantage of SOAs is a higher signal-to-noise ratio.

socket   An interface to the transport layer of the OSI model that consists of a group of functions that can be called from a program written in C. The calls that make up sockets are system calls (i.e., they are direct calls to an operating system). Sockets permit an application program to access the services provided by TCP and UDP.

SOFDMA (Scalable Orthogonal Frequency Division Multiple Access)   A multicarrier modulation technique in which the number of tones, or subcarriers, used to transport the data and signaling traffic scales with the channel bandwidth. Mobile WiMax uses SOFDMA.

softswitch   A device that implements service logic to control external trunking gateways, access gateways, and remote access servers. Softswitches run on commercial computers and operating systems, and they provide open applications programming interfaces. Also called a call agent or a media gateway controller.

software   Computer instructions that perform a common function for all users as well as specific applications for particular user needs.

solid-state device   Electronic pathways made of solid materials (e.g., chips, bubble memories).

SONET (Synchronous Optical Network)   An ANSI standard, incorporated into the SDH standard, that defines a line rate hierarchy and frame formats for use with high-speed optical fiber transmission systems (50.84Mbps to 2.488Gbps).

source route bridging   A bridging protocol supported by the 802.5 Token Ring standard. With source routing, the sending station is responsible for providing routing information for messages that cross multiple network segments. The sending station acquires routing information by first issuing a command to find the location of a particular destination. When the message is sent, the source station specifies the route to use by using the routing information field of the frame.

source routing transparent   The combination of source routing and transparent bridging in the same device.

SP (service provider)   A generic term for providers of different types of services.

space division   The carving up of a cellular service area into smaller coverage areas.

Space Division Multiplexing   The use of multiple antennas to simultaneously transmit data to the receivers in small pieces. The receivers then process the data flows and put them back together. This process proportionally boosts the data transmission speed by a factor equal to the number of transmitting antennas (i.e., using four antennas increases the data rate by a factor of four). In addition, because all data is transmitted both in the same frequency band and with separate spatial signatures, Space Division Multiplexing uses spectrum very efficiently. Also referred to as spatial multiplexing.

space division switching   A method for switching circuits in which each connection through the switch takes a physically separate path.

spanning tree   A loop-free subset of a network's topology.

spatial capacity   A measure of the number of bits per second per square meter that can be supported over a given technology. UWB has a much greater spatial capacity than the 802.11a and 802.11b standards and than Bluetooth.

S-PCS (Satellite Personal Communications System)   A system that uses satellites to provide ubiquitous mobile communications.

SPE (synchronous payload envelope)   The payload portion of an STS or STM frame.

spectral compatibility   The capability of two DSL systems to operate inside a single cable bundle. The spectral compatibility of the DSL systems depends on the effect of crosstalk that one DSL system has on the other inside the cable bundle.

spectral efficiency   A measure of the number of digital bits that can be encoded in a single cycle of a waveform.

spectrum utilization   The efficient use of the available bandwidth by many competing devices. Spectrum utilization techniques include space division, multiple-access techniques, spread spectrum, duplexing, and compression techniques.

splitter   A filter used at each end of a copper pair to split the frequency bands.

spooling   Temporarily storing input and output data streams on disk or tape files until the processor is ready.

spread spectrum technique   A technique by which a signal is transmitted in a bandwidth considerably greater than the frequency content of the original information. FHSS, DSSS, CDMA, and OFDM are examples of spread spectrum techniques.

SPX (Sequenced Packet Exchange)   The NetWare communications protocol used for interprocess communications. SPX guarantees that an entire message arrives intact and uses the NetWare IPX protocols as its delivery mechanism.

SRTP (Secure Real-Time Transport Protocol)   A security profile for RTP that adds confidentiality, message authentication, and replay protection to RTP. It provides a framework for encryption and message authentication of RTP and RTCP streams.

S/S (Start/Stop) signaling   A form of asynchronous communication line control that uses start elements and stop elements to control the transfer of data over a communication line. Each group of signals representing a character is preceded by a start signal and followed by a stop element.

SS7 (Signaling System 7)   A group of telephony signaling protocols used in the PSTN to set up calls and provide services. SS7 is characterized by high-speed circuit switching and out-of-band signaling using SS7 nodes. The SS7 network sets up and tears down a call, handles all the routing decisions, and supports all telephony services, such as 800 numbers, call forwarding, caller ID, and local number portability. Because the signaling network is separate, a voice circuit is not tied up until a connection is made between two parties.

SS7 gateway   A device that allows an interface between circuit-switched networks (with their powerful SS7 infrastructure) and packet-switched networks for support of traditional telephony applications.

SSL (Secure Sockets Layer)   A commonly used protocol for managing the security of a message transmission on the Internet.

SSP (service-switching point)   A switch that originates or terminates a call.

ST connector   A type of connector used on optical fiber cable, using a twist and lock coupling similar to the BNC connector that is used with thinnet.

star   A network topology in which nodes are connected to a single central hub rather than to each other, forming a star-shaped configuration. If the hub is an intelligent device that controls the nodes' access to the network, the star topology is called active; when the hub is only a wiring connector, it is called passive.

static routing   Routing in which the routes are manually entered into the routing table.

station   A computer or device that can send and receive data over a communication line.

statistical multiplexer   A multiplexer that uses the idle time of connected devices to carry data traffic from active devices.

STDM (Statistical Time Division Multiplexing)   A method of TDM in which time slots on a shared medium are allocated on demand.

STM (Synchronous Transport Module)   The basic building block of SDH. STM-1 consists of 9 rows of 270 bytes each. The first 9 columns contain the section and line overhead for all STS-3s. The remaining 261 columns contain the combined envelope capacity of the component STS-1s. Common STM levels include STM-0, STM-1, STM-4, STM-16, STM-64, and STM-256.

stop bit   In asynchronous transmission, the quiescent state following the transmission of a character; usually required to be at least 1-, 1.5-, or 2-bit times long.

stop element   The last bit of a character in asynchronous serial transmission, used to ensure recognition of the next start element.

store-and-forward   A technique that involves accepting a message or packet on a communications pathway, retaining it in memory, and retransmitting it to the next station. Synonymous with message switching.

STP (shielded twisted-pair)   Two insulated wires in a cable that is wrapped with metallic braid or foil to prevent interference and to provide noise-free transmission.

STP (signal transfer point)   A switch that is responsible for translating SS7 messages and then routing those messages between the appropriate network nodes and databases.

STP (Spanning Tree Protocol)　　A protocol for complex bridge configurations defined by IEEE 802.1D. This protocol ensures that a complex bridge configuration has no loops (i.e., there is one and only one possible path from any particular endpoint to any other).

streaming media　　Data that is transferred so that it can be processed as a steady and continuous stream. Streaming technologies are increasingly important with the growth of the Internet because many users do not have fast enough access to download large multimedia files quickly. With streaming media, the client browser or plug-in can start displaying the data before the entire file has been transmitted.

STS (Synchronous Transport Signal)　　The basic building block of SONET. The basic building block signaling rate for a SONET transmission medium is STS-1, which is 51.8Mbps. The signal is composed of 8,000fps, with 810 8-bit bytes per frame (8 bits/byte × 810 bytes/frame × 8,000fps = 51.840Mbps). A SONET STS-1 frame contains more than 30 times the data of a T-1 frame. Other STS rates are STS-3, STS-12, STS-48, STS-192, and STS-768.

subnet mask　　A configuration feature of a router that is used to select the portion of a 32-bit TCP/IP node address that refers to the LAN and to select the portion that refers to the node on the LAN.

subnetting　　A technique used to impose a hierarchy on IP addresses that supports a form of area routing.

subrate　　Transmission speeds below DS-0/64Kbps.

subsplit　　To split the frequencies in a cable so that the lower frequencies are used for one purpose and the higher for another. Subsplitting is used when two cables are not used but there is a need to simulate a dual-cable system.

subsystem　　A part of a system that performs defined functions.

subvoice grade channel　　A channel with bandwidth narrower than that of voice-grade channels. Such channels are usually subchannels of a voice-grade line.

superphone　　A feature-rich new-generation mobile phone that offers applications such as music, graphics, games, and videos.

supervision　　The process of detecting a change of state between idle and busy conditions on a circuit.

supervisory signal　　A signal that handles the on-hook/off-hook condition.

SVC (switched virtual circuit)　　A virtual connection that is set up on a call-by-call basis.

switched digital access　　A dialup option in which facilities are allocated based on demand rather than being associated with a specific customer all the time.

switched line　　A temporary connection between computers or devices that is established by dialing.

switching　　Establishing a transmission path from a particular inlet to a particular outlet of a group of such inlets and outlets.

switching center　　A location that terminates multiple circuits and can interconnect circuits or transfer traffic between circuits.

switching system   A device that connects two transmission lines together.

switchook   A switch on a telephone set that is associated with the structure supporting the receiver or handset and is often used to signal the switching equipment or an attendant during a call.

switchover   A switch to an alternative component that happens when a failure occurs in the equipment.

symmetric encryption   Encryption in which the sender and the receiver use the same key or machine setup.

synchronization   The process of adjusting a receiving terminal's clock to match the clock of the transmitting terminal.

synchronous   (1) Having a constant time interval between successive bits, characters, or events. Synchronous transmission uses no extra information (such as the start and stop bits in asynchronous transmission) to identify the beginning and end of characters and thus is faster and more efficient than asynchronous transmission. The timing is achieved by transmitting sync characters prior to data. Usually, synchronization can be achieved in two- or three-character times. (2) Occurring with a regular or predictable time relationship. In data transmission, the time of occurrence of each signal representing a bit is related to a fixed time frame.

synchronous communications   High-speed transmission of contiguous groups of characters in which the stream of monitored and read bits uses a clock rate to transfer the characters over a communication line.

synchronous network   A network in which all the communications links are synchronized to a common clock.

Synchronous TDM (Synchronous Time Division Multiplexing)   A method of TDM in which time slots on a shared transmission line are assigned on a fixed, predetermined basis.

synchronous transmission   In data communications, a method of transmission in which the sending and receiving of characters is controlled by timing signals. The sending and receiving terminals operate continuously in step with each other.

system   A computer and its associated devices and programs.

system test   A complete simulation of an actual running configuration for purposes of ensuring the adequacy of the configuration.

T

TA (terminal adapter)   A protocol converter that connects a non-ISDN device to the ISDN network.

TACS (Total Access Communication System)   A standard for analog telephony that was deployed widely in Europe before GSM became the most popular approach.

tandem   (1) The connection of networks or circuits in series (i.e., the connection of the output of one circuit to the input of another). (2) An intermediate switch used in a tandem network, which connects only to other switches instead of to customers.

tandem data circuit   A data circuit that contains two or more pieces of DCE in series.

tandem switch   A switch used to connect local exchanges throughout the metropolitan area. Also called a junction exchange or a tandem office.

tap   An open point on a cable bundle that is left so that technicians can easily splice off a pair to bring new or additional service to a home.

TAPI (Telephony Applications Programming Interface)   An API that enables PCs to use telephone services. TAPI is a call-processing protocol that resides between the signaling and application layers.

tariff   (1) The published rate for the use of a specific unit of equipment, facility, or type of service provided by a communications common carrier. (2) The vehicle by which regulating agencies approve or disapprove such facilities or services.

TASI (Time-Assignment Speech Interpolation)   Specialized switching equipment that connects a party to an idle circuit while speech is taking place and disconnects the party when speech stops so that a different party can use the same circuit. During the periods of heavy traffic, TASI can improve line efficiency by 45% to 80%.

Tbps (terabits per second)   Trillions of bits per second.

TBRPF (Topology Broadcast Based on Reverse-Path Forwarding)   A proactive link-state routing protocol designed for mobile ad hoc networks. It provides hop-by-hop routing along minimum-hop paths to each destination.

TCAP (Transaction Capabilities Applications Part)   A system that supports intelligent network service by enabling the exchange of non-circuit-related information between different signaling points (i.e., network nodes).

T-carrier   The North American standard of the PDH, a TDM digital transmission system. T-carrier is a PCM system that uses 64Kbps per channel as the basis of the hierarchy. Higher levels reflect aggregation of the 64Kbps channels. T-1 is a 1.544Mbps 24-channel communications circuit; T-2 is a 6.312Mbps 96-channel communications circuit; T-3 is a 44.736Mbps 672-channel communications circuit; and T-4 is a 274.176Mbps 4,032-channel communications circuit.

TCP (Transmission Control Protocol)   One of the core protocols of the Internet Protocol suite. Using TCP, applications on networked hosts can create connections to one another, over which they can exchange data. TCP supports many of the Internet's most popular application protocols and applications.

TCP stack   A suite of multiple protocols used to exchange information between computers. The Internet and most commercial networks run on the TCP stack.

TCP/IP (Transmission Control Protocol/Internet Protocol)   The most widely used internetworking protocol. It ensures that packets of data are delivered to their destinations in the sequence in which they were transmitted. TCP roughly corresponds to Layer 4 (the transport layer) of the OSI model. It provides reliable transmission of data. IP corresponds to Layer 3 (the network layer) of the OSI model and provides connectionless datagram service.

TD-CDMA (Time Division Code Division Multiple Access)   A 3G combined time division and CDMA scheme used by UMTS TDD. TD-CDMA mobile devices consume significantly less power than other devices, resulting in improved talk times and standby times.

TDD (Time Division Duplex)   A half-duplex technique in which each end of the conversation makes use of the same frequency.

TDM (Time Division Multiplexing)   A means of obtaining a number of channels over a single path by dividing the path into a number of time slots and assigning each channel its own intermittently repeated time slot. At the receiving end, each time-separated channel is reassembled.

TDMA (Time Division Multiple Access)   A multiple-access technique that first divides the available or allocated frequency spectrum into a number of channels. Then, within each channel, TDM is applied to carry multiple users interleaved in time.

TD-SCDMA (Time Division Synchronous Code Division Multiple Access)   A 3G mobile telecommunications standard used primarily in China. It is based on spread spectrum CDMA technology.

telco   A telephone company.

telecommunication lines   Telephone and other communication pathways used to transmit information from one location to another.

telecommunications   Any process that permits the passage of information from a sender to one or more receivers in any usable form (e.g., printed copy, fixed or moving pictures, visible or audible signals) by means of any electromagnetic system (e.g., electrical transmission by wire, radio, optical transmission, waveguides).

teledensity   The number of main telephone lines per 100 inhabitants.

teleimmersion   A technology that combines virtual reality and videoconferencing in order to enable people who are geographically separated from one another to collaborate in real-time in a shared, simulated environment, with access to the same media, computer applications, images, audio, and simulation.

telephone channel   A transmission path designed for the transmission of human speech or other telephone communication (e.g., fax) requiring the same bandwidth. The bandwidth of an analog telephone channel is 4,000Hz.

telephony   A generic term for voice telecommunications.

Telnet   The TCP/IP site protocol that supports a remote login capability.

tera   One trillion.

terabit switch router   A class of backbone platform that supports Tbps capacity. This type of router is agnostic, and it involves short and predictable delay, robust QoS features, multicast support, and carrier-class availability.

terminal   (1) A point at which information can enter or leave a communication network. (2) Any device capable of sending and/or receiving information over a communications channel. (3) A workstation.

terminal multiplexer   A device that permits two or more terminals to share one cable as a data transmission path.

terminal server   A device that connects terminals to a network that is typically running Ethernet.

thicknet (thick Ethernet cable)   Coaxial cable with electrical characteristics that meet the 10BASE5 specification for Ethernet networks. Thicknet enables a signal to be carried as far as 1,640 feet (500 m) before requiring a repeater. Also called 10BASE5 cable.

thinnet (thin Ethernet cable)   Coaxial cable with electrical characteristics that meet the 10BASE2 specification for Ethernet networks. Thinnet enables a signal to be carried as far as 607 feet (185 m) before requiring a repeater. Also called 10BASE2 cable or cheapernet.

throughput   The useful information processed or communicated during a specific time period, expressed in bits per second or packets per second.

TIA (Telecommunications Industry Association)   An organization that recommends standards for telecommunications.

time division switching   A switching method for a TDM channel that requires the shifting of data from one slot to another in the TDM frame. The slot in question can carry a bit, a byte, or, in principle, any other unit of data.

timeout   A set time period for waiting before a terminal system performs some action. Typical uses include a poll release (when a terminal is disconnected if the time-out period elapses before keying resumes) and an access timeout (when a terminal on a LAN using a CSMA/CD access method is prevented from transmitting for a specified time after a collision occurs).

time-slot interchange   The interchange of time slots within a TDM frame.

Time to Live   A field in an IP datagram that is decremented by each router in order to guarantee that datagrams do not circulate on the Internet forever.

time transparency   The absence of delay and delay jitter through an ATM network, thus allowing high-speed transportation of real-time services.

tip   The contacting part at the end of a telephone plug or the top spring of a jack; the conductors associated with these contacts. The other contact is called a ring.

TMN (Telecommunications Management Network)   A protocol model defined by the ITU-T for managing open systems in a communications network. TMN can be used in the management of ISDN, B-ISDN ATM, and GSM networks. It is not as commonly used for purely packet-switched data networks.

token   An 8-bit word that is circulated in a unidirectional fashion among the devices on a network.

token passing   A network access method that uses a special bit pattern called a token that gives permission to nodes to transmit data, one node at a time. Each node is allowed to transmit a message only when it has the token. If a node has no messages to transmit when it receives the token, it passes the token to the next node.

token ring   A networked ring of devices that passes a special bit pattern called a token from node to node to determine which device can transmit data on the network. Token ring operates at either 4Mbps or 16Mbps.

toll center   The exchange that is responsible for establishing and completing national, long-distance communications. Also called the Class 4 office, transit switch, toll office, or trunk exchange.

tone signaling   Transmission of supervisory, address, and alerting signals over a telephone circuit by means of tones.

tone-to-dial-pulse conversion   A system of converting DTMF signals to dial pulse signals when the trunks associated with outgoing trunk calls are not equipped to receive tone signals. Auxiliary dial pulse conversion equipment is not necessary.

topology   The connectivity among a group of nodes. Physical topology relates to how devices are cabled. Logical topology refers to how nodes actually interact.

trace packet   In packet switching, a packet that functions as a normal packet but causes a report of each stage of its process to be sent to the network control center.

traffic   (1) Messages sent and received over a communications channel. (2) A quantitative measurement of the total messages and their length, expressed in 100 call seconds or other units.

traffic flow   A measure of the density of traffic.

transaction   An item of business (e.g., the handling of customer orders and billing).

transaction processing   (1) In batch or remote batch processing, the processing of a job or job step. (2) In interactive processing, an exchange between a terminal and another device that does a particular action (e.g., entering a customer's deposit and updating the customer's balance).

transceiver   A device that connects a host interface to a LAN.

transducer   A device for converting signals from one form to another, such as a microphone or a receiver.

transfer rate   The speed at which information can be sent across a bus or communications link.

translational bridge   A bridge that may connect two different MAC layers (e.g., 802.3 and FDDI).

transmission   Information that is sent in the form of electrical signals over electric wires, waveguides, or radio.

transmission line   A connection over which communications devices communicate. There are five main types of transmission lines: circuits, channels, lines, trunks, and virtual circuits.

transmission medium   A physical pathway that connects computers, other devices, and people on a network. Transmission media can be either wireline (e.g., twisted-pair, fiber, coax) or wireless (e.g., microwave, satellite, infrared).

transmission speed   The rate at which information is passed through communications lines, generally measured in bits per second.

transmit   To send information from one location to another.

transparent bridging   A system in which a bridge functions as a node on each of the connected networks, and its presence in the communications path between nodes is transparent. Communication proceeds as if the nodes were on the same network.

transponder   The receiver, transmitter, and antenna equipment that forms a single repeater channel on a satellite.

transport layer   Layer 4 of the OSI model, which provides reliable, transparent transfer of data between endpoints.

tree   A type of bus network topology in which the medium branches at certain points along its length to connect stations or clusters of stations; also called a branching bus.

triple-play services   A service provider's bundle of voice, data, and video/TV services, delivered over the same infrastructure.

troubleshooting   Monitoring and testing the performance of a network to detect and fix problems.

trunk   A circuit that is configured to support the calling loads generated by a group of users; the transmission facility that ties together switching systems.

TTC (Telecommunications Technology Committee)   A body that creates telecommunications standards that are followed in Japan.

tunneling   The encapsulation of one protocol within another. Tunneling is often used to transport a LAN protocol across a backbone network that does not support the LAN protocol.

turnkey system   A complete communications system, including hardware and software, that is assembled and installed by a vendor and sold as a total package.

twisted-pair cable   A cable that consists of two insulated wires twisted around each other (and sometimes wrapped in additional insulation to help shield the signals from electromagnetic noise). Twisted-pair cable is often used in telephone wires; it also serves as the transmission medium in some LANs.

Twofish   A very strong encryption algorithm that was one of the five initial candidates for AES.

two-wire circuit   A circuit formed by two insulated electrical conductors. One wire is used for the transmission of information, and the other wire acts as a return to complete the circuit.

type approval   An administrative procedure of technical tests and vetting that is applied to items of telecommunication equipment before they can be sold or interconnected with the public network. Also known as *homologation*.

U

UBR (unspecified bit rate)   An ATM service class that provides best-effort service. UBR offers no service guarantee, so it is used for text data, image transfer, messaging, and distribution of information that is noncritical, where it is not necessary to have a set response time or service guarantee.

UDP (User Datagram Protocol)   A minimal-functionality transport-layer protocol in the TCP/IP protocol suite.

UHDV (Ultra High Definition Video)   A digital video format proposed by NHK of Japan. UHDV provides a resolution that is 16 times greater than that of HDTV.

UHF (ultrahigh frequency)   The portion of the electromagnetic spectrum that ranges from about 300MHz to about 3GHz and includes television and cellular radio frequencies.

UMTS (Universal Mobile Telecommunications System) An evolving European standard for 3G mobile communications. UMTS represents the convergence of mobile and fixed networks as well as terrestrial wireless and satellite-based networks.

UMTS TDD A 3G mobile standard that uses TDD and is designed to work in a single, unpaired frequency band. UMTS TDD uses the TD-CDMA scheme.

UNI (User-to-Network Interface) A type of network interface that defines how customers can access their providers' networks. It shields the client from network complexities.

unicasting Sending streams from a single origination point directly to a single destination point.

Unicode A coding scheme that assigns 16 bits per character (i.e., 2^{16}), which translates to more than 65,000 possible characters.

uniform-spectrum random noise Noise distributed over the spectrum in such a way that the power-per-unit bandwidth is constant. Also called white noise.

UNII (Unlicensed National Information Infrastructure) Unlicensed radio bands that operate at 5.2GHz.

Universal Service Fund A U.S. government program that provides subsidies for telephone service in areas that might otherwise have difficulties obtaining economical telephone service, particularly low-income areas and rural areas.

UNIX A multiuser, open operating system developed by Bell Laboratories.

unlicensed bands Radio bands that can be used to provide broadband access, without the need for obtaining a license. Networks that use unlicensed bands have a range of about 35 miles (55 km) and offer throughput from 128Kbps to 10Mbps over shared media.

unshielded cable A cable in which the signal-carrying wire or circuit is not shielded to keep out electromagnetic noise that can potentially damage the data stream.

upload To send data from a local system to a remote system.

UPS (uninterruptible power supply) A device that usually includes an inverter, drawing its power from batteries, which generates an extremely well-behaved AC power signal for a PBX or other equipment. If a particularly heavy demand is anticipated, the system can be coupled with an auxiliary generator that is started when commercial power is interrupted.

upstream The direction of transmission flow away from a user.

UPT (Universal Personal Telephony) An ITU-R standard for the provision of personal mobility across many different kinds of fixed and mobile networks.

UTP (unshielded twisted-pair) A twisted-pair cable in which the two insulated wires that twist around each other are not surrounded by additional insulation.

UWB (Ultra-Wideband) A technique based on transmitting very-short-duration pulses, where the occupied bandwidth is very large, allowing for very high data rates. UWB is used in both wired and wireless PANs to relay data from a host device to other devices up to 30 feet (10 m) away.

UWC (Universal Wireless Communications) Also called ANSI-136, a wireless standard that uses TDMA and TDD schemes.

V

V.11   An ITU-T standard that describes electrical characteristics for balanced double-current interchange circuits for general use with integrated circuit equipment.

V.21   An ITU-T standard that describes 300bps modems for use in the PSTN.

V.24   An ITU-T definition for interchange circuits between data terminal equipment and data circuit-terminating equipment.

V.25   An ITU-T standard that describes automatic calling and/or answering equipment on the general switched network.

V.29   An ITU-T standard that describes 9,600bps modems for use in the PSTN.

V.35   An ITU-T standard that describes data transmission at 56Kbps that uses balanced transmission methods through a 34-pin physical interface.

VAD (voice activity detection)   A technique that reduces the amount of information needed to re-create voice at the destination end by removing silent periods and redundant information found in human speech. VAD also helps with compression.

validation   An attempt to find errors by executing a program in a given environment.

value-added carrier   A company that sells services of a value-added network. It can be a PTT, a subsidiary, or an independent company.

VAN (value-added network) services   Telecommunication services provided over public or private networks that, in some way, add value to the basic carriage, usually through the application of computerized intelligence (e.g., reservation systems, bulletin boards, information services).

VAR (value-added reseller)   A provider that deals with distribution and sales.

VAS (value-added service)   A communications facility that uses communications common carrier networks for transmission and that provides enhanced extra data features with separate equipment. Such extra features, including store-and-forward message switching, terminal interfacing, and host interfacing, are common.

VBR (variable bit rate)   An ATM service class for network traffic that is typically from bursty data transfer applications, such as client/server and LAN-to-LAN interconnection. VBR offers guaranteed service delivery. VBR-RT (real-time) is designed for real-time voice and videoconferencing applications, and VBR-NRT (non-real-time) is for mission-critical data applications.

VC (virtual circuit)   A series of logical, rather than physical, connections between sending and receiving devices. With a virtual circuit, two hosts can communicate as though they have a dedicated connection, although the packets may be taking very different routes to arrive at their destination.

VC (virtual container)   A data structure designed for the transport and switching of sub-STM-0 network services such as CEPT-1. All network services below E-3 are mapped into VCs, and VCs are multiplexed into the SPE of an STM-1.

VCI (virtual channel identifier)   In ATM, the part of a cell header that identifies the channel associated with the cell.

VDSL (Very-High-Bit-Rate DSL)   A transmission medium that provides a maximum span of about 5,000 feet (1,500 m) over a single twisted-pair cable. Over this distance, VDSL can provide a rate of up to 13Mbps downstream, and with a shorter distance of 1,000 feet (300 m), it can provide up to 52Mbps downstream, which is enough capacity to facilitate DTV. VDSL provides 1.5Mbps to 2.3Mbps upstream.

VDSL2 (VDSL version 2)   A broadband wireline medium whose key applications are the next generation of TV—VOD, DTV, HDTV, and forms of interactive multimedia Internet access. VDSL2 has two bandwidth options: LR-VDSL2–12MHz (the "long reach" alternative) and SR-VDSL2–30MHz (the "short reach" alternative).

VDT (video dial tone)   A U.S. term that defines the capability of a network access provider to offer video access and carriage directly to or from subscribers.

vertical blanking interval   Unused lines in each field of a TV signal. Some of these lines may be used for captions and specialized signal and cable service.

VF (virtual fiber)   A wireless solution to the "first-mile" problem of delivering high-speed access to the end user. The use of VF as a last-mile solution is based on MMW technology to deliver line-of-sight broadband. Also referred to as wireless fiber (WiFiber).

VF (voice frequency)   Any frequency within the part of the audio frequency range that is essential for the transmission of speech of commercial quality (i.e., 250Hz to 3,400Hz). Also called telephone frequency.

VHF (very high frequency)   The portion of the electromagnetic spectrum with frequencies between about 30MHz and 300MHz. VHF is the operating band for radio and television channels.

video signal   A signal in the frequencies normally required to transmit moving image information.

videoconferencing   A two-way communication between two or more parties that involves the exchange of images as well as voice. The images may or may not be in full motion.

videotelephony   Interactive communication between two parties involving the transmission and reception of images as well as voice. The degree to which the images are in full motion depends on the level of data compression used and on the available bandwidth.

videotext   A public or private telecommunications service that offers interactive browsing of a menu of textual and graphical information. The most widely used public videotext service is France Telecom's service, offered via Minitel terminals.

virtual channel   In ATM, the specific conversation path over which the cells from a given conversation flow from one ATM switch to another.

virtual router   An abstract representation that has the same mechanisms as a physical router and, therefore, can inherit all existing mechanisms and tools for configuration, deployment, operation, troubleshooting, monitoring, and accounting. Multiple virtual routers can exist in a single physical device, and virtual routers can be deployed in various VPN configurations.

VISP (virtual Internet service provider)   A provider that offers outsourced Internet service, running as a branded ISP. It is a turnkey ISP product aimed at affinity groups and mass marketers that want to add Internet access to their other products and services.

VLAN (virtual local area network)   A network of computers that behave as if they are connected to the same wire even though they may actually be physically located on different segments of a LAN. VLANs are configured through software rather than hardware, which makes them extremely flexible. A big advantage of VLANs is that when a computer is physically moved to another location, it can stay on the same VLAN without any hardware reconfiguration.

VLF (very low frequency)   Frequencies below 30KHz.

VoATM (Voice over ATM)   A technology for transporting integrated digital voice, video, and data over ATM networks.

vocoders (voice coder/decoder)   A device used for compression of voice traffic. High-bit-rate vocoders are used by PCS, wireless local loops, and wireless office telecommunication systems applications. Low-bit-rate vocoders are used in cellular systems that deal with vehicular traffic, where there are large cells and a need to facilitate a large number of conversations.

VOD (video-on-demand)   A service whereby a subscriber can order and almost immediately view films and other entertainment from a television set. In true VOD, the film can be paused, rewound, and fast-forwarded. In "near" VOD, these functions are not possible.

VOD Metadata   A project established by CableLabs that is pertinent to the future of interactive services. The initial efforts of VOD Metadata are focused on creating specifications for VOD and subscription VOD (SVOD) applications.

VoDSL (Voice over DSL)   A technology for delivering voice transmissions over DSL lines. VoDSL enables service providers to deliver high-speed data access and up to 16 telephone lines over 1 DSL line.

VoFR (Voice over Frame Relay)   A technology for transporting integrated digital voice, video, and data over Frame Relay networks.

voice digitization   Conversion of an analog voice into digital symbols for storage or transmission.

voice grade   A telecommunications link with a bandwidth (about 4KHz) appropriate to an audio telephone line.

voice-grade channel   A channel with a frequency range of 4KHz. Also referred to as a telephone channel.

Voice over Cable   A technology for delivering cable-based IP telephony.

voice-over-packet   A technology for transporting real-time voice traffic over packet networks. VoIP and VoFR are examples of voice-over-packet solutions.

voice recognition   A technology that allows spoken words in the form of human voice to provide input to a computer.

voice synthesis   Computer-generated sounds that simulate the human voice.

VoIP (Voice over IP)   A technology for transporting integrated digital voice, video, and data over IP networks.

VoIP gateway   A device that bridges the traditional circuit-switched PSTN and the packet-switched Internet.

volatile storage   Memory that loses its contents when electrical power is removed.

VoWLAN (Voice over Wireless Local Area Network)   A local voice solution that uses VoIP and WLANs to marry the convenience of mobility with the cost-effectiveness of an IP PBX.

VP (virtual path)   A generic term for a collection of virtual channels that have the same endpoint.

VPDN (virtual private dial network)   A type of network that was developed for telecommuters and road warriors who needed secure and convenient access to their enterprise servers. VPDNs have included the use of PPTP, L2TP, or IPsec.

VPI (virtual path identifier)   In ATM, the portion of a cell header that identifies the virtual path to which the cell belongs. Virtual paths are defined to permit groups of virtual channels to be manipulated as if they were a single channel.

VPLS (Virtual Private LAN Services)   A VPN technology that provides Ethernet-based multipoint-to-multipoint communication over IP-only networks. VPLS allows geographically dispersed sites to share an Ethernet broadcast domain by connecting sites through pseudo-wires.

VPN (virtual private network)   A software-defined network offered by telephone carriers for voice and data communications among multiple sites. A VPN provides the appearance of a private-line network, except that it makes use of the PSTN rather than physically dedicated leased lines. In *customer-based VPNs*, carriers install gateways, routers, and other VPN equipment on the customer premises. This is preferred when customers want to have control over all aspects of security. In *network-based VPNs*, the carrier houses all the necessary equipment at a POP near the customer's location. Customers that want to take advantage of the carrier's VPN economies of scale prefer this type of VPN.

VPN gateway   A device that enables VPNs to set up and maintain secure tunnels through the Internet.

VPWS (virtual private wire service)   A type of VPN that emulates a point-to-point link and provides a single service that is perceived by its user as an unshared link or circuit of the chosen service. VPWS provides a mesh of point-to-point customer edge–to–customer edge Layer 2 connections over a packet-switched network.

VR (virtual reality)   A computer-based application that provides a human–computer interface such that the computer and its devices create a sensory environment called a virtual world. The sensory environment is dynamically controlled by actions of the individual so that the environment appears real.

VRC (vertical redundancy check)   *See* parity check.

VSAT (very-small-aperture terminal)   An earth station with a small antenna, usually 2 feet (0.6 m) or less.

VSF-OFCDM (Variable-Spreading-Factor Orthogonal Frequency Code Division Multiplexing)   A form of multiplexing used in 4G wireless. It increases downlink speeds by using multiple radio frequencies to send the same data stream.

VT (virtual tributary)   A data structure designed for the transport and switching of sub-STS-1 network services such as DS-1, DS-1C, and DS-2. All network services below DS-3 are mapped into VTs, and VTs are multiplexed into the SPE of an STS-1.

W

Walsh Code   An algorithm that generates statistically unique sets of numbers for use in encryption and cellular communications. It is an orthogonal code used to uniquely define individual communications channels. Walsh Code is used in DSSS systems such as CDMA as well as in FHSS systems.

WAN (wide area network)   A group of computer networks connected over long distances, often by telephone lines and satellite transmission.

WAP (wireless access point)   A device that connects wireless communication devices to form a wireless network. A WAP usually connects to a wired network and can relay data between wireless devices and wired devices.

WAP (Wireless Application Protocol)   A protocol for transforming Internet information so that it can be displayed on the small screen of a mobile telephone or other portable device.

war dialing   A method hackers use to locate nonsecure computers by dialing through phone numbers.

war driver   An individual who drives through an area, scanning for wireless networks (using programs such as NetStumbler), and publishing his or her findings on the Web.

WARC (World Radiocommunications Conference)   A regular meeting of global authorities to decide on spectrum allocation. Originally called the World Administrative Radio Conference.

waveform   A curve that shows the shape of a wave at any given time.

waveguide   A transmission path in which a system of boundaries guides electromagnetic energy. The most common of these are hollow metallic conducting tubes (microwave communications) or rods of dielectric material.

wavelength   The distance between two consecutive maxima or minima of a waveform.

wavelength changer   A device that converts an optical signal to an electronic signal and then sends the signal to a laser that produces an optical signal at a different wavelength than the original.

wavelength division switching   Switching in which input information is used to modulate a light source that has a unique wavelength for each input. All the optical energy is combined and then split, so it can be distributed to all the output channels.

W-CDMA (Wideband CDMA)   A multiple-access technique that operates over allocations of either 5MHz, 10MHz, or 15MHz. W-CDMA can support higher data rates than first-generation CDMA.

WDM (Wavelength Division Multiplexing)   The multiplexing of signals by transmitting them at different wavelengths through the same fiber.

wearables   Smart devices that can be networked and are small enough to be worn on the human body.

WEP (Wired Equivalent Privacy)   An encryption standard used to secure wireless networks. WEP has some serious weaknesses and has therefore been superseded by other standards, such as WPA and WPA2.

WFQ (Weighted Fair Queuing)   A packet-scheduling technique that allows guaranteed bandwidth services and lets several sessions share the same link.

WiBro (Wireless Broadband)   A Korean WMAN standard for wireless broadband Internet access that operates in licensed bands.

wideband   Refers to the range of speeds between narrowband and broadband, typically ranging between $n \times 64$Kbps up to 45Mbps.

wideband channel   A channel that is wider in bandwidth than a voice-grade channel.

Wi-Fi (Wireless Fidelity)   A WLAN technology that allows users to plug a single high-speed Internet connection such as a cable modem into an inexpensive WAP and share it with scores of people in a building, park, or small neighborhood. Wi-Fi is used to create hotspots in locations such as hotels, airports, shopping centers, restaurants/cafes, and educational environments.

WiMax (Worldwide Interoperability for Microwave Access)   The global IEEE 802.16 standard, also known as the IEEE WirelessMAN air interface standard, which was designed to provide wireless last-mile broadband access in MANs. WiMax represents an evolution to a standards-based, interoperable, carrier-class solution.

WiMedia   A UWB common radio platform that enables high speeds (480Mbps and beyond), low power consumption, and multimedia data transfers in a WPAN. WiMedia is optimized for several key market segments: PC, consumer electronic, mobile, and automotive applications.

wireless   A generic term for mobile communications services such as cellular, radiopaging, or PCS that do not use wireline networks for direct access to the subscriber.

wireless local loop   A technology that uses low-power radio transmission, cellular radio, and/or cordless telephony as an alternative to local loops for accessing the PSTN.

wireless mesh network   A wireless LAN that routes voice, data, and instructions between nodes, creating a resilient network in which connections are continuous, reconfiguring around blocked paths by hopping from node to node until a connection is established.

wireless micromesh network   A wireless network that is designed for short ranges, up to 300 feet (100 m) between any two nodes. It is characterized by long battery life, relatively low data rates, and good tolerance for latency. Wireless micromeshes eliminate the need to wire every node and thus provide the greatest degree of flexibility possible in sensor/control networks.

wiring closet   A location in a building where the building's wiring terminates and where equipment (e.g., hub electronics) is placed.

WISP (wireless ISP)   A company that gives users wireless access to the Internet and related services.

WLAN (wireless local area network)   A network that covers a single room to an entire campus and uses wireless media. The last link with the users is wireless, and the backbone network usually uses cables, with one or more WAPs connecting the wireless users to the wired network. WLANs typically operate on unlicensed frequency bands, and they do not require line of sight.

WLL (wireless local loop)   The use of a wireless communications link as the last-mile connection for delivering POTS and broadband Internet to customers. Also referred to as radio in the loop, fixed-radio access, or fixed-wireless access.

WMAN (wireless metropolitan area network)   A network that provides broadband wireless network access over a metro area. The WMAN standards most commonly used today are BFWA, IEEE 802.16 (WiMax), WiBro, IEEE 802.20 (Mobile-Fi), HiperAccess, iBurst, Flash-OFDM, DMB, and VF.

WML (Wireless Markup Language)   A markup language used in the WAP environment.

workstation   A device (e.g., display station, printer) that can transmit information to or receive information from a computer, or both, as needed to perform a job.

world numbering plan   An ITU-T numbering plan, E.164, that divides the world into nine zones. Each zone is allocated a number that forms the first digit of the country code for every country in that zone. The zones are as follows: (1) North America (including Hawaii and Caribbean islands, except Cuba), (2) Africa, (3 and 4) Europe, (5) South America and Cuba, (6) South Pacific (Australasia), (7) Russia, (8) North Pacific (Eastern Asia), and (9) Asia and the Middle East. A spare code (0) is available for future use.

WPA (Wi-Fi Protected Access)   A wireless encryption standard that the Wi-Fi Alliance created in response to serious weaknesses in WEP. A second version of WPA is called WPA2.

WPAN (wireless personal area network)   A wireless network that serves a single person or small workgroup and is characterized by limited distance, limited throughput, and low volume. The WPAN standards in use today include IEEE 802.15.1 (Bluetooth), IEEE 802.15.3 (WPAN-HR and WPAN-AHR), UWB, IEEE 802.15.4 (ZigBee), RFID, and NFC.

WRAN (wireless regional area network)   A regional wireless network being created by the IEEE 802.22 working group that is to use the UHF/VHF TV bands that the FCC is opening up for experimentation.

WRR (Weighted Round Robin)   A queuing mechanism that assigns a weight to each queue and then services each nonempty queue in proportion to its weight, in round-robin fashion. WRR is optimal when using uniform packet sizes, a small number of flows, and long connections.

WWAN (wireless wide area network)   A network that is global, national, or regional in scope and that operates without wires. Traditional WWAN solutions include cellular radio and PCS networks as well as early wireless data networks. Newer generations are focused on supporting high-speed data as well as video and multimedia, with increased emphasis on mobile content delivery.

WWDM (Wide WDM)   CWDM operating at 1310 nm, compared to traditional CWDM, which operates at 850 nm.

WWW (World Wide Web)   An Internet application that uses hypertext links between remote network servers for accessing and displaying multimedia information.

X

X.3   An ITU-T standard that defines the basic functionality of an asynchronous PAD, usually used in conjunction with ITU-T standards X.28 and X.29.

X.21   An ITU-T recommendation that defines a general-purpose physical interface between a DTE and DCE for full-duplex synchronous operation on circuit-switched or packet-switched data networks.

X.25   A standard that defines the interface between a DTE and DCE for equipment operating in the packet mode on public data networks. It also defines a link control protocol.

X.75   A standard for connecting X.25 networks, developed by the ITU-T

X.121   The ITU-T standard for the addressing plan used with X.25 PDNs.

X.400   An ITU-T standard for electronic mail exchange.

X.500   The family of protocols that define the operation of the ITU-T/ISO directory service.

X.509   The ITU-T/OSI recommendation for a directory authentication framework.

xDSL (Digital Subscriber Line)   The DSL family of broadband technologies that use sophisticated modulation schemes to pack data onto copper wires. They include ADSL, HDSL, and VDSL.

XMPP (Extensible Messaging and Presence Protocol)   An XML-based extensible open-source protocol that drives the Jabber IM client.

Z

ZigBee   The IEEE 802.15.4 standard, a wireless communication protocol designed for WPANs. ZigBee operates, internationally, in the unlicensed frequency bands, and it supports a low data rate, a very long battery life (months to even years), and very low complexity.

Index

LIDO Telecommunications Essentials® e-Learning

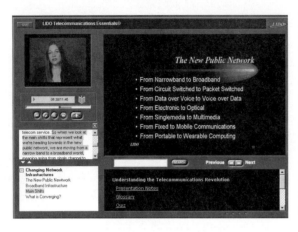

Part I—Communications Fundamentals

Part II—Data Networking and the Internet

Part III—Next-Generation Networks

Part IV—Wireless Communications

Lillian Goleniewski's innovative new e-Learning series includes

- Thirty hours of dynamic multimedia lectures
- Simultaneous word-for-word transcripts
- Synchronized slide presentations
- Dynamic search capabilities
- Comprehensive notes and diagrams
- Clickable links to related resources
- An online learning center

Previous customers have said:

"This is an excellent 'starter course' for new people in the industry and an outstanding 'refresher course' for those already in the industry."
—*Keith Holdt, Senior Consultant, IBM*

"Excellent content, knowledge of the issues, and ability to communicate key areas."
—*Justin Forsell, Head of Legal Affairs, BT Japan*

"Covered many technical areas while still being clear and engaging."
—*Alexandra Rehak, Manager Asia Pacific, Motorola*

*For more information, or to order, please visit www.telecomessentials.com,
or send an email to lili@lidoorg.com.*

THIS BOOK IS SAFARI ENABLED

INCLUDES FREE 45-DAY ACCESS TO THE ONLINE EDITION

The Safari® Enabled icon on the cover of your favorite technology book means the book is available through Safari Bookshelf. When you buy this book, you get free access to the online edition for 45 days.

Safari Bookshelf is an electronic reference library that lets you easily search thousands of technical books, find code samples, download chapters, and access technical information whenever and wherever you need it.

TO GAIN 45-DAY SAFARI ENABLED ACCESS TO THIS BOOK:

- Go to **http://www.awprofessional.com/safarienabled**
- Complete the brief registration form
- Enter the coupon code found in the front of this book on the "Copyright" page

If you have difficulty registering on Safari Bookshelf or accessing the online edition, please e-mail customer-service@safaribooksonline.com.

Addison
Wesley

Register
Your Book

at www.awprofessional.com/register

You may be eligible to receive:
- Advance notice of forthcoming editions of the book
- Related book recommendations
- Chapter excerpts and supplements of forthcoming titles
- Information about special contests and promotions throughout the year
- Notices and reminders about author appearances, tradeshows, and online chats with special guests

Contact us

If you are interested in writing a book or reviewing manuscripts prior to publication, please write to us at:

Editorial Department
Addison-Wesley Professional
75 Arlington Street, Suite 300
Boston, MA 02116 USA
Email: AWPro@aw.com

Visit us on the Web: http://www.awprofessional.com